WOTAKOI:
LOVE IS HARD FOR OTAKU

FUJITA

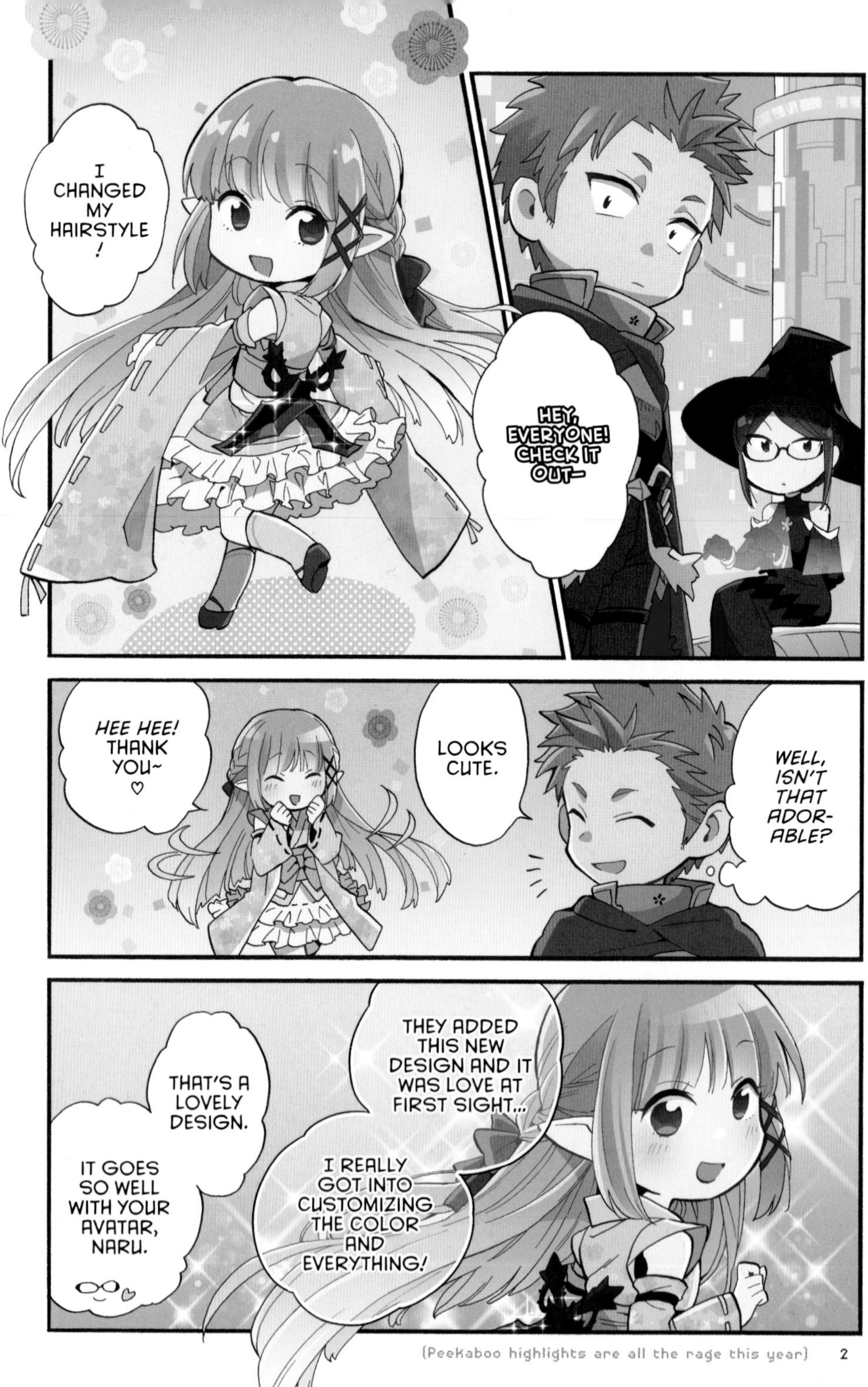
HEY, EVERYONE! CHECK IT OUT~
I CHANGED MY HAIRSTYLE!
WELL, ISN'T THAT ADORABLE?
LOOKS CUTE.
HEE HEE! THANK YOU~ ♡
THEY ADDED THIS NEW DESIGN AND IT WAS LOVE AT FIRST SIGHT...
THAT'S A LOVELY DESIGN.
I REALLY GOT INTO CUSTOMIZING THE COLOR AND EVERYTHING!
IT GOES SO WELL WITH YOUR AVATAR, NARU.

(Peekaboo highlights are all the rage this year)

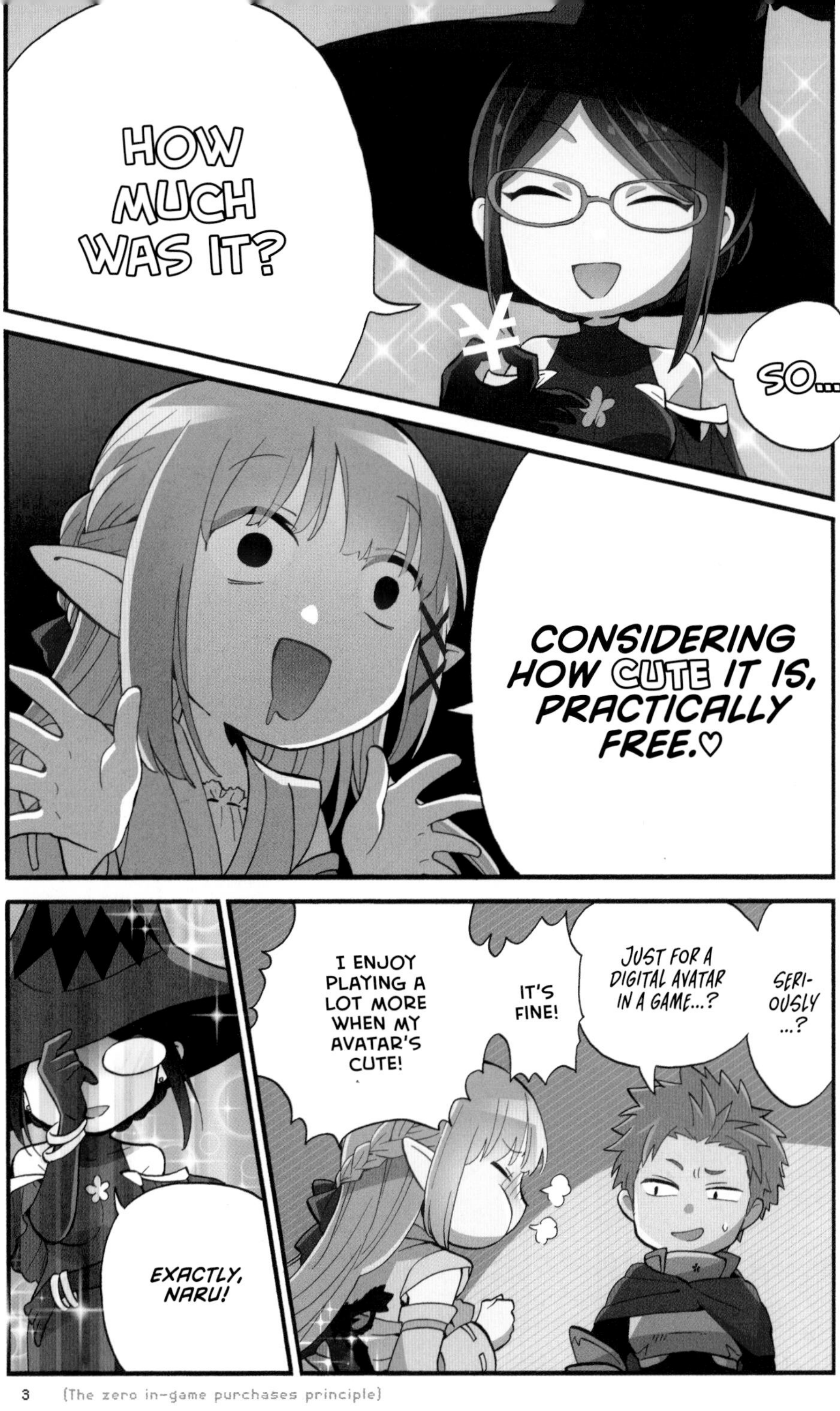
SO...
HOW MUCH WAS IT?
CONSIDERING HOW CUTE IT IS, PRACTICALLY FREE.♡
SERI-OUSLY ...?
JUST FOR A DIGITAL AVATAR IN A GAME...?
IT'S FINE!
I ENJOY PLAYING A LOT MORE WHEN MY AVATAR'S CUTE!
EXACTLY, NARU!

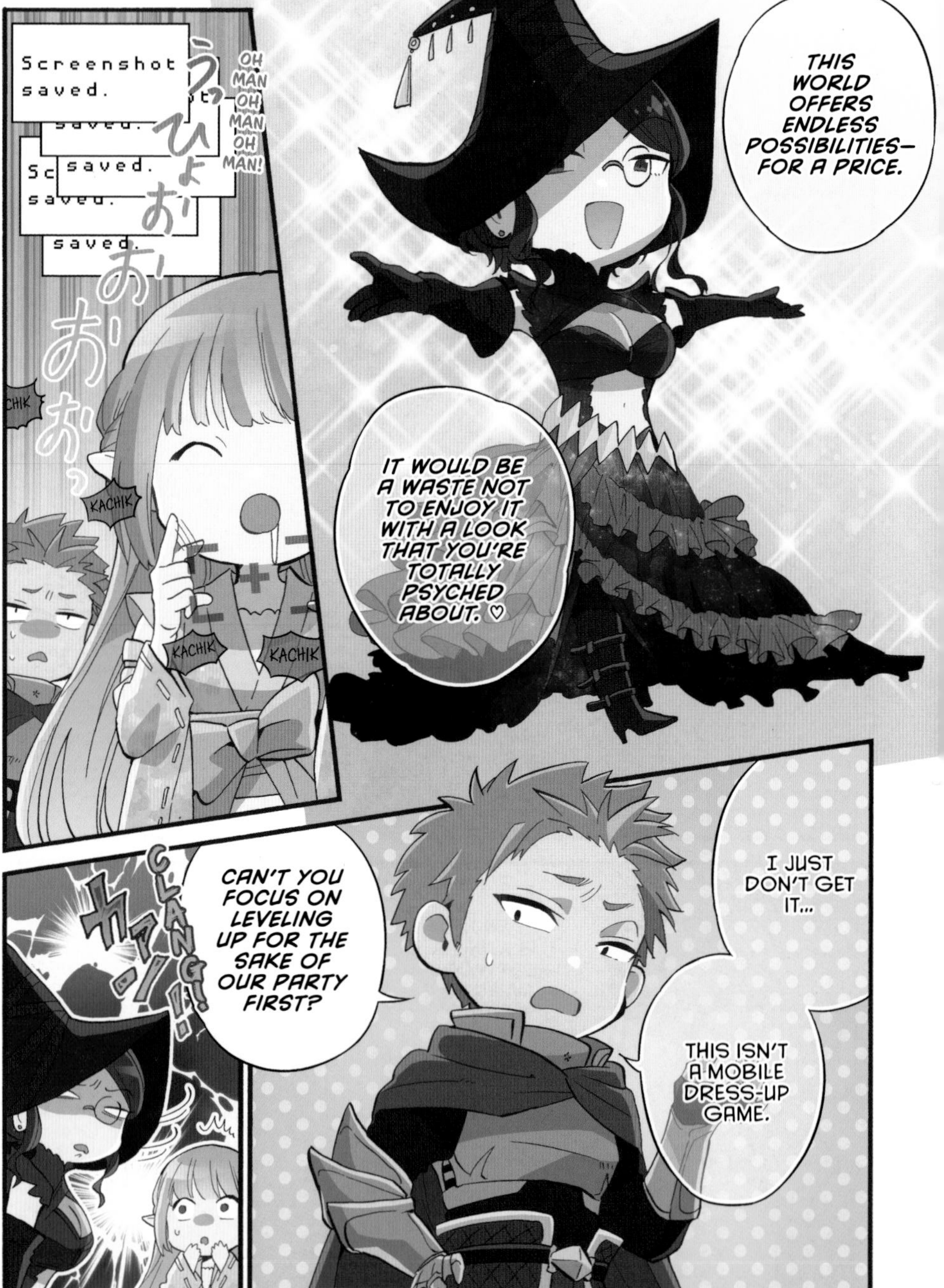
THIS WORLD OFFERS ENDLESS POSSIBILITIES—FOR A PRICE.
IT WOULD BE A WASTE NOT TO ENJOY IT WITH A LOOK THAT YOU'RE TOTALLY PSYCHED ABOUT. ♡
Screenshot saved.
saved.
saved.
saved.
saved.
うっひょおおおおおっ
OH MAN OH MAN OH MAN!
KACHIK
KACHIK
KACHIK
KACHIK
I JUST DON'T GET IT...
THIS ISN'T A MOBILE DRESS-UP GAME.
CAN'T YOU FOCUS ON LEVELING UP FOR THE SAKE OF OUR PARTY FIRST?
CLANG!!
カッ!!

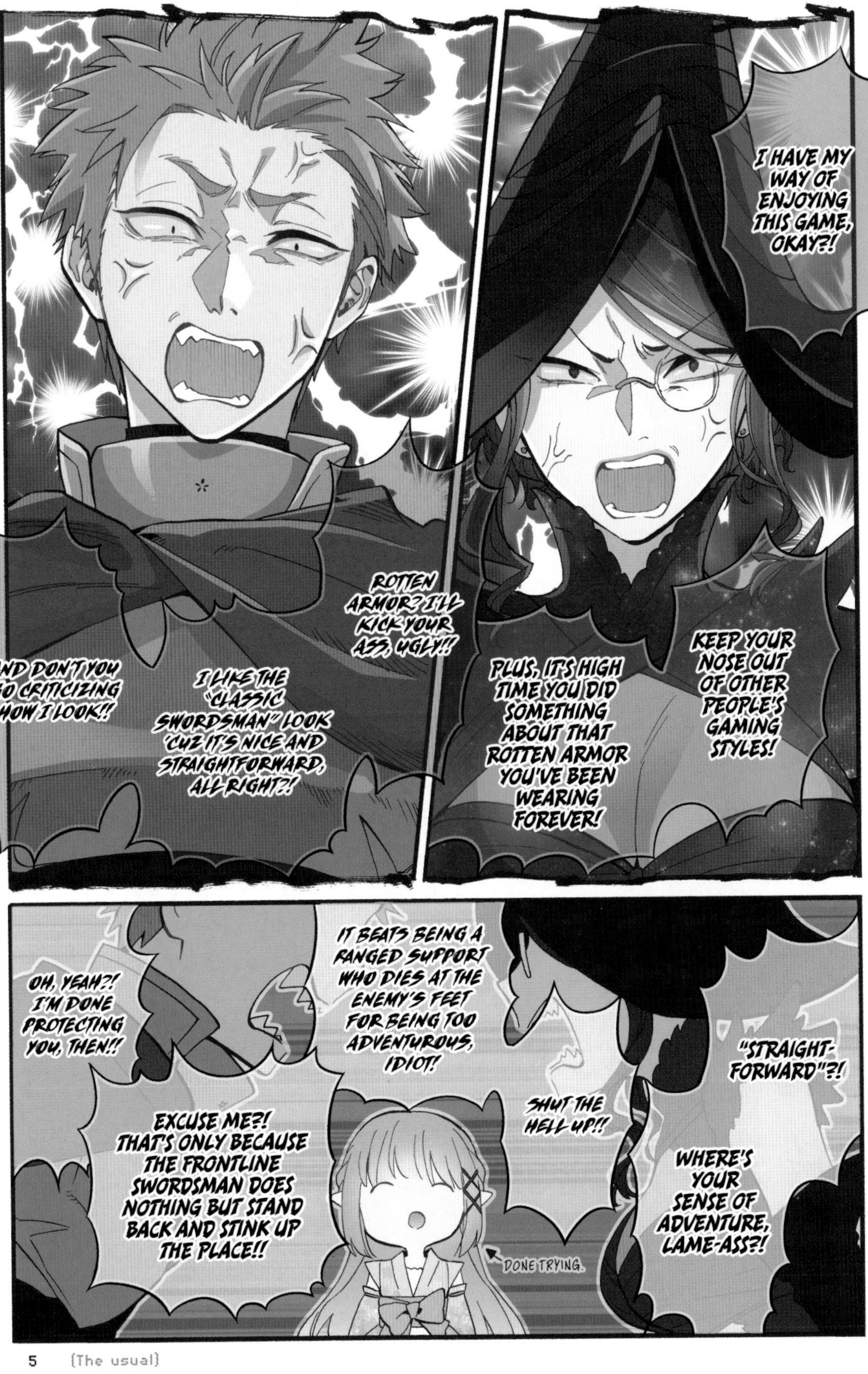
I HAVE MY WAY OF ENJOYING THIS GAME, OKAY?!
KEEP YOUR NOSE OUT OF OTHER PEOPLE'S GAMING STYLES!
PLUS, IT'S HIGH TIME YOU DID SOMETHING ABOUT THAT ROTTEN ARMOR YOU'VE BEEN WEARING FOREVER!
ROTTEN ARMOR? I'LL KICK YOUR ASS, UGLY!!
I LIKE THE "CLASSIC SWORDSMAN" LOOK 'CUZ IT'S NICE AND STRAIGHTFORWARD, ALL RIGHT?!
AND DON'T YOU GO CRITICIZING HOW I LOOK!!
"STRAIGHT-FORWARD"?!
WHERE'S YOUR SENSE OF ADVENTURE, LAME-ASS?!
IT BEATS BEING A RANGED SUPPORT WHO DIES AT THE ENEMY'S FEET FOR BEING TOO ADVENTUROUS, IDIOT!
SHUT THE HELL UP!!
DONE TRYING.
OH, YEAH?! I'M DONE PROTECTING YOU, THEN!!
EXCUSE ME?! THAT'S ONLY BECAUSE THE FRONTLINE SWORDSMAN DOES NOTHING BUT STAND BACK AND STINK UP THE PLACE!!

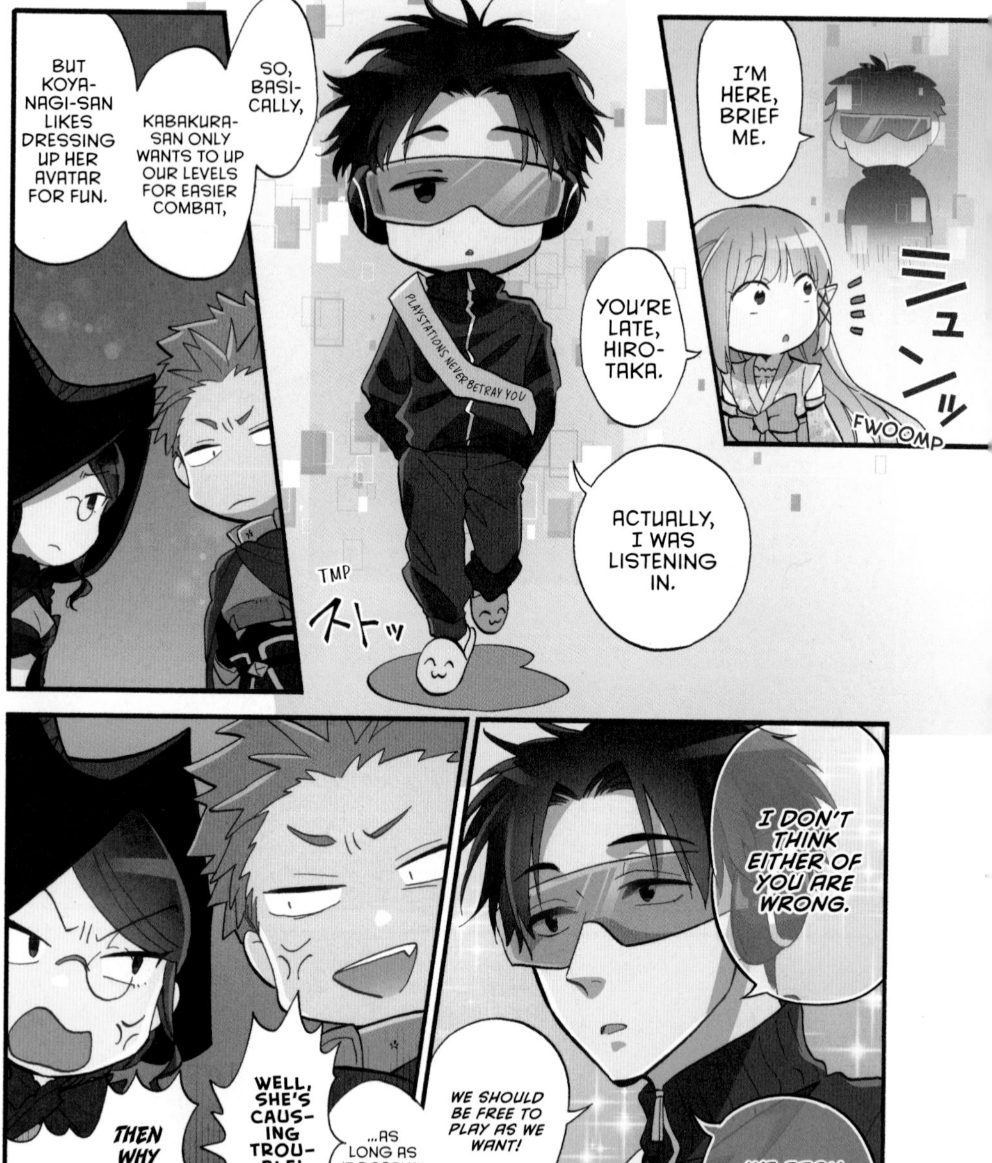
I'M HERE, BRIEF ME.
YOU'RE LATE, HIRO-TAKA.
シュンッ
FWOOMP
ACTUALLY, I WAS LISTENING IN.
PLAYSTATIONS NEVER BETRAY YOU
TMP
ストッ
SO, BASI-CALLY,
KABAKURA-SAN ONLY WANTS TO UP OUR LEVELS FOR EASIER COMBAT,
BUT KOYA-NAGI-SAN LIKES DRESSING UP HER AVATAR FOR FUN.
I DON'T THINK EITHER OF YOU ARE WRONG.
WE EACH HAVE OUR OWN WAY OF ENJOYING GAMES.
WE SHOULD BE FREE TO PLAY AS WE WANT!
...AS LONG AS IT DOESN'T CAUSE ANYONE TROUBLE, OF COURSE.
WOW...
WELL, SHE'S CAUSING TROUBLE!
WE CAN'T GO ON ANY HIGHER-RANK QUESTS WHEN SHE'S WITH US 'CUZ OF LEVEL REQUIREMENTS!
THEN WHY DON'T YOU GO ALONE?
LET'S SEE IF YOU COME BACK ALIVE!
URK.

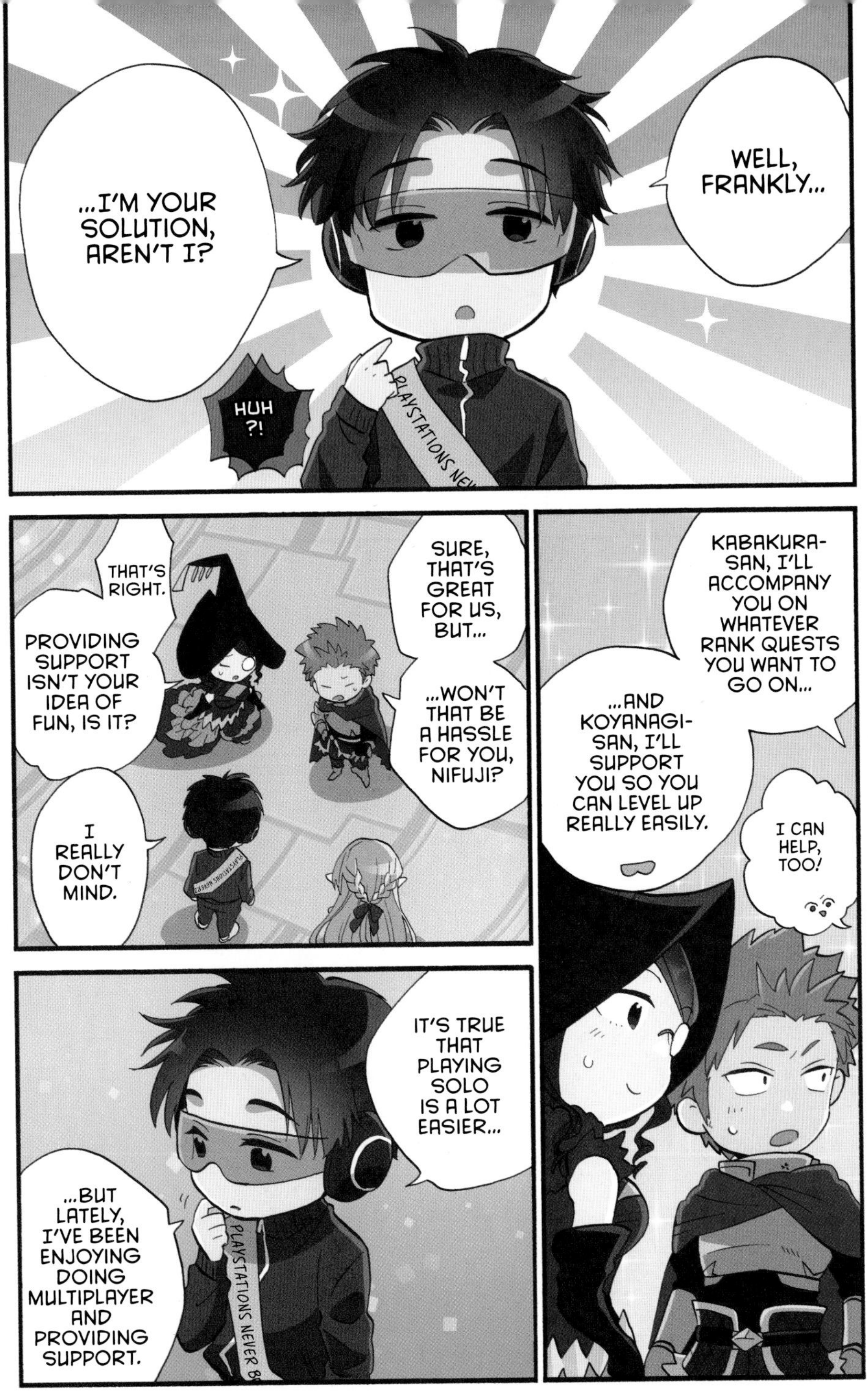
WELL, FRANKLY...
...I'M YOUR SOLUTION, AREN'T I?
HUH ?!
KABAKURA-SAN, I'LL ACCOMPANY YOU ON WHATEVER RANK QUESTS YOU WANT TO GO ON...
...AND KOYANAGI-SAN, I'LL SUPPORT YOU SO YOU CAN LEVEL UP REALLY EASILY.
I CAN HELP, TOO!
SURE, THAT'S GREAT FOR US, BUT...
...WON'T THAT BE A HASSLE FOR YOU, NIFUJI?
THAT'S RIGHT.
PROVIDING SUPPORT ISN'T YOUR IDEA OF FUN, IS IT?
I REALLY DON'T MIND.
IT'S TRUE THAT PLAYING SOLO IS A LOT EASIER...
...BUT LATELY, I'VE BEEN ENJOYING DOING MULTIPLAYER AND PROVIDING SUPPORT.

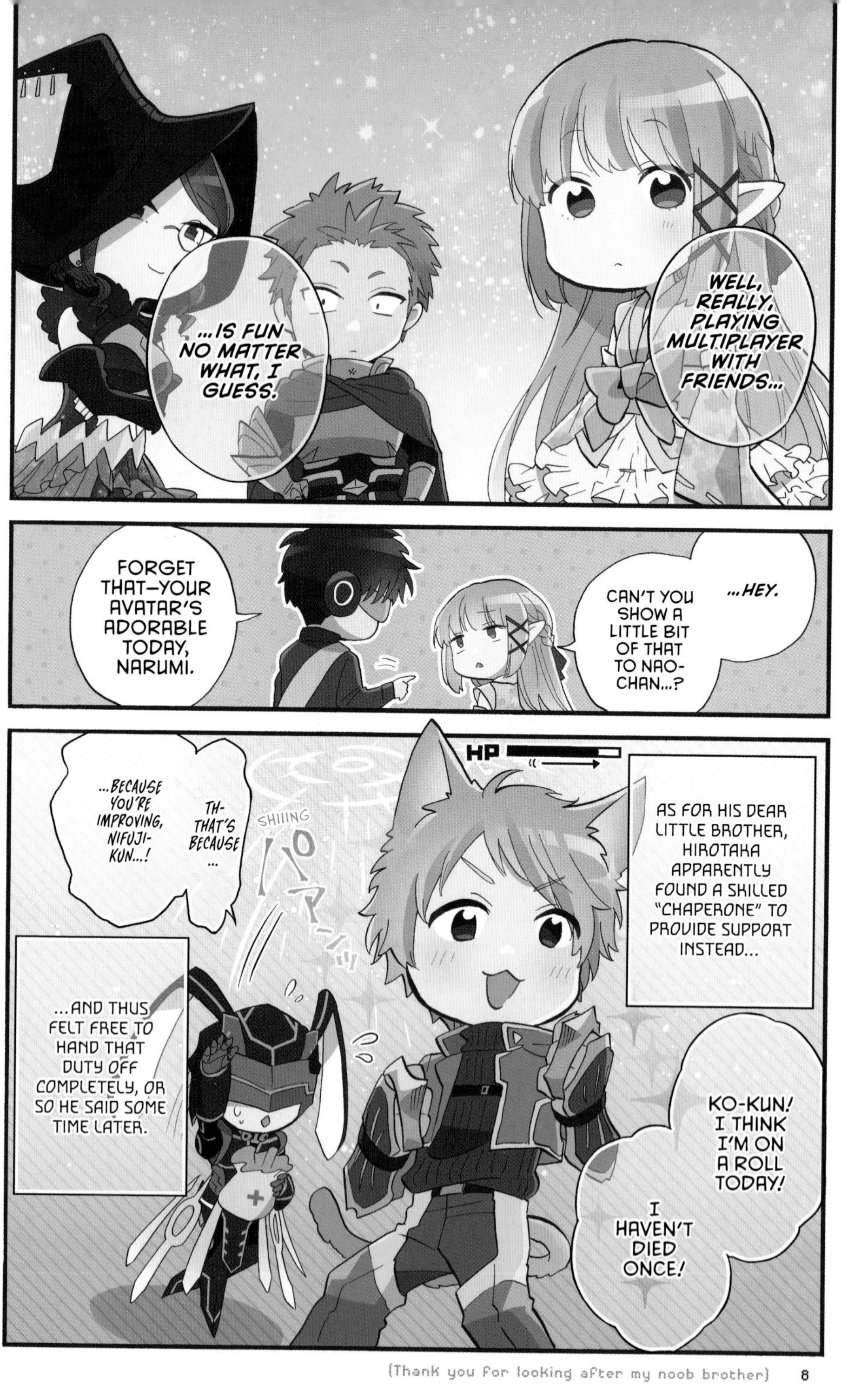

WELL, REALLY, PLAYING MULTIPLAYER WITH FRIENDS...
...IS FUN NO MATTER WHAT, I GUESS.
...HEY.
CAN'T YOU SHOW A LITTLE BIT OF THAT TO NAO-CHAN...?
FORGET THAT—YOUR AVATAR'S ADORABLE TODAY, NARUMI.
HP
AS FOR HIS DEAR LITTLE BROTHER, HIROTAKA APPARENTLY FOUND A SKILLED "CHAPERONE" TO PROVIDE SUPPORT INSTEAD...
TH-THAT'S BECAUSE...
...BECAUSE YOU'RE IMPROVING, NIFUJI-KUN...!
SHIIING
KO-KUN! I THINK I'M ON A ROLL TODAY!
I HAVEN'T DIED ONCE!
...AND THUS FELT FREE TO HAND THAT DUTY OFF COMPLETELY, OR SO HE SAID SOME TIME LATER.

Episode....47

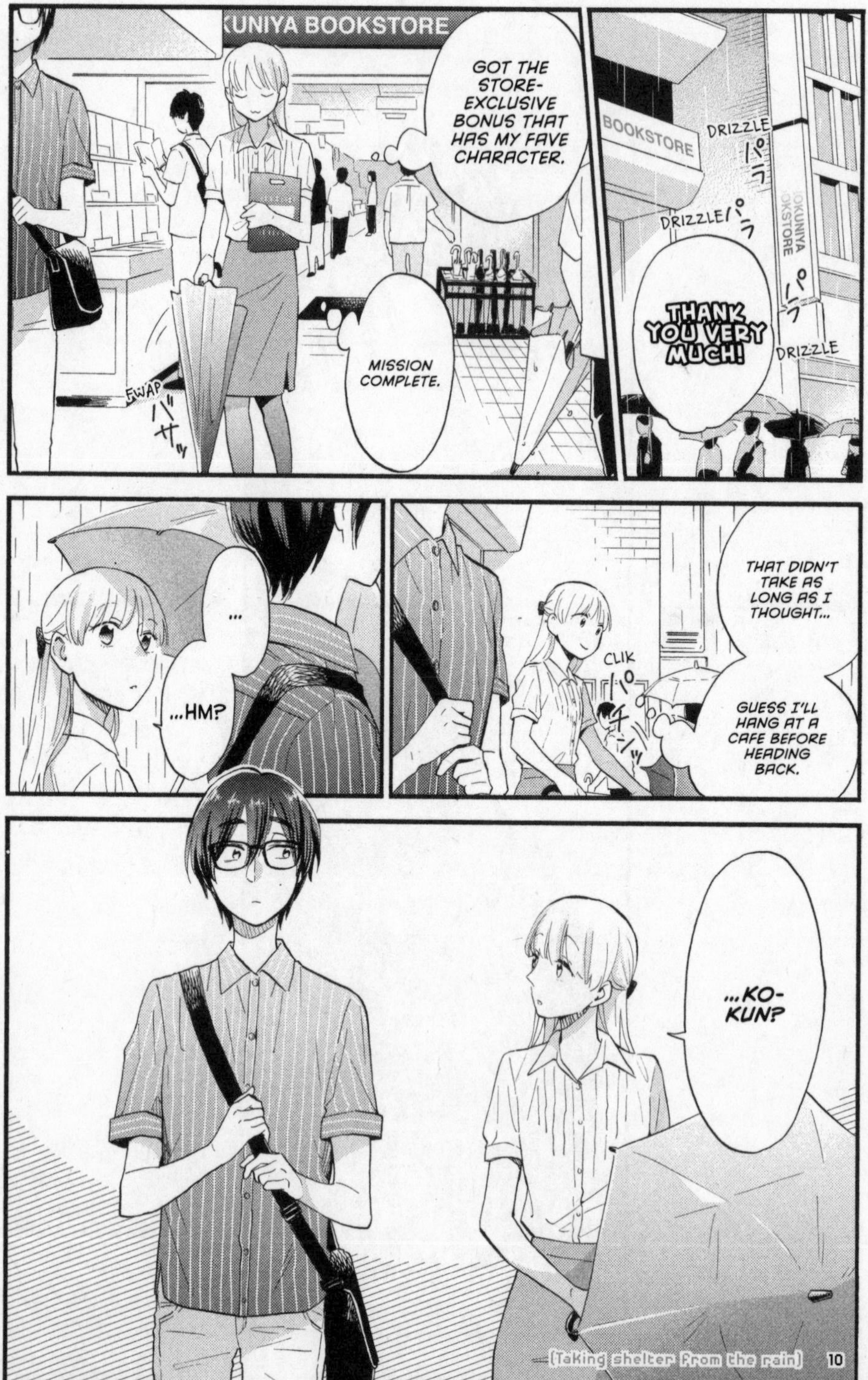
BOOKSTORE
OKUNIYA BOOKSTORE
DRIZZLE
DRIZZLE
THANK YOU VERY MUCH!
DRIZZLE
KUNIYA BOOKSTORE
GOT THE STORE-EXCLUSIVE BONUS THAT HAS MY FAVE CHARACTER.
MISSION COMPLETE.
FWAP
THAT DIDN'T TAKE AS LONG AS I THOUGHT...
GUESS I'LL HANG AT A CAFE BEFORE HEADING BACK.
CLIK
...
...HM?
...KO-KUN?

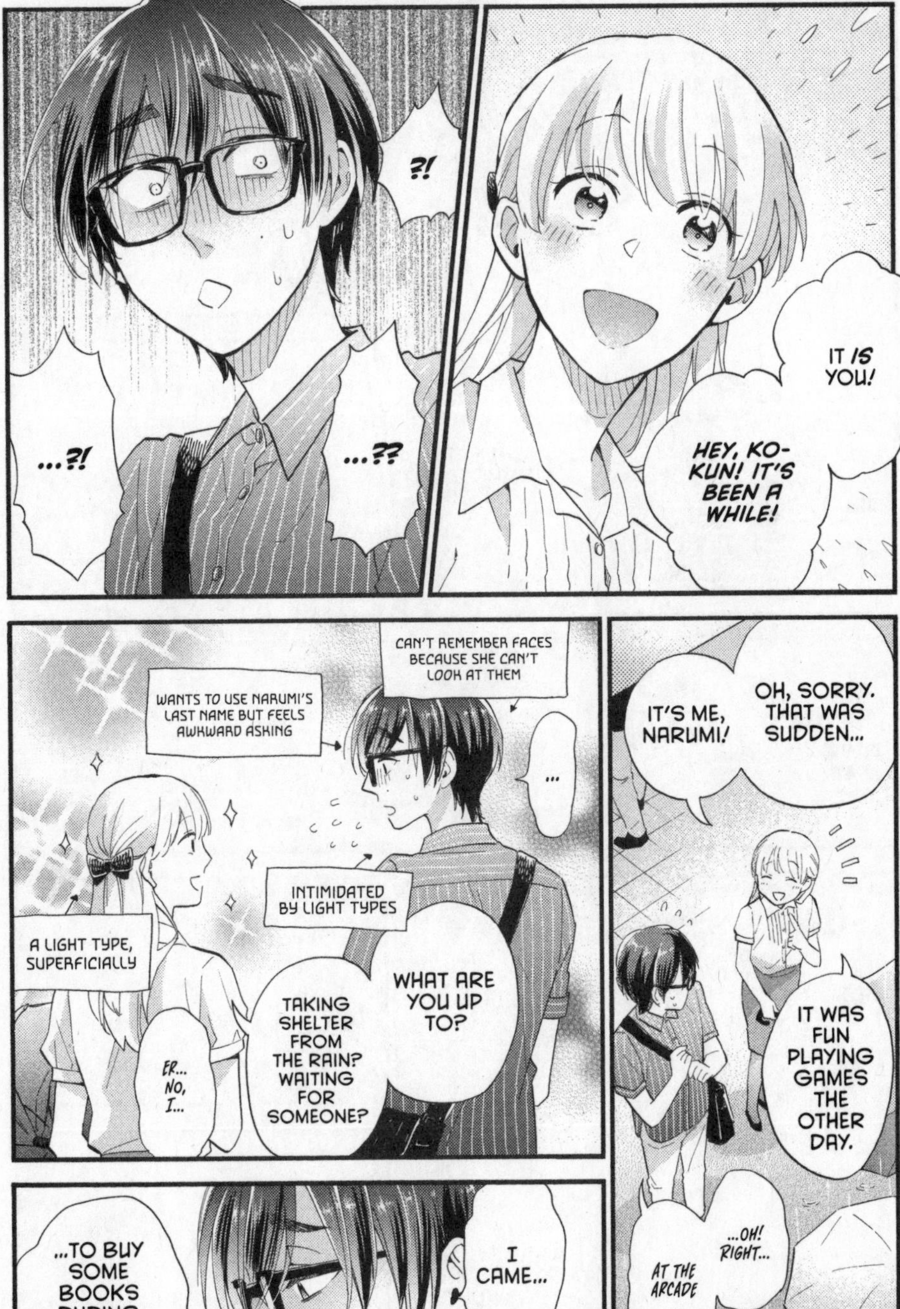
IT IS YOU!
HEY, KO-KUN! IT'S BEEN A WHILE!
?!
...??
...?!
OH, SORRY. THAT WAS SUDDEN...
IT'S ME, NARUMI!
IT WAS FUN PLAYING GAMES THE OTHER DAY.
...OH! RIGHT...
AT THE ARCADE ...
CAN'T REMEMBER FACES BECAUSE SHE CAN'T LOOK AT THEM
WANTS TO USE NARUMI'S LAST NAME BUT FEELS AWKWARD ASKING
...
INTIMIDATED BY LIGHT TYPES
A LIGHT TYPE, SUPERFICIALLY
WHAT ARE YOU UP TO?
TAKING SHELTER FROM THE RAIN? WAITING FOR SOMEONE?
ER... NO, I...
I CAME...
...TO BUY SOME BOOKS DURING LUNCH TIME...

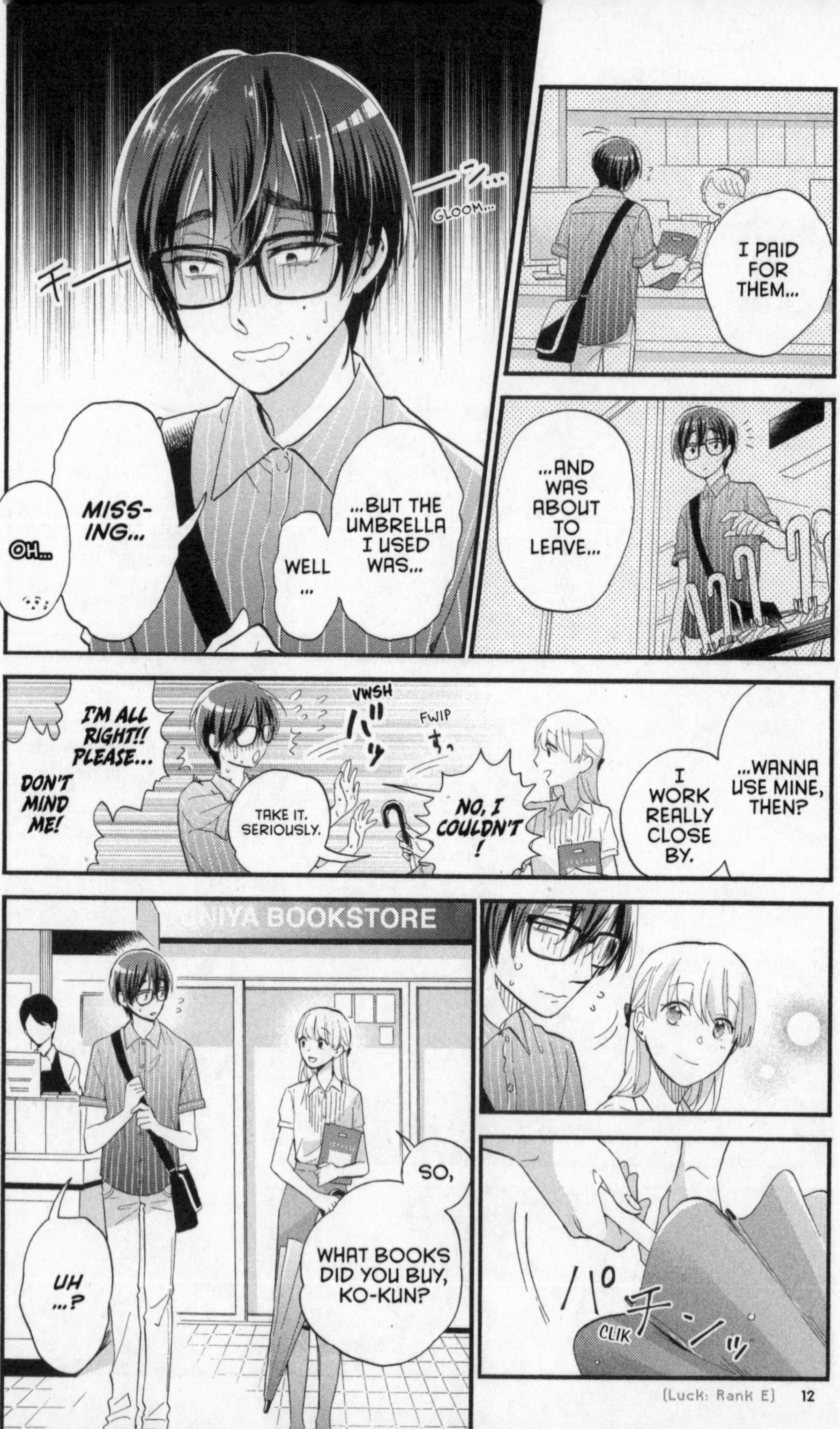

I PAID FOR THEM...
...AND WAS ABOUT TO LEAVE...
GLOOM...
...BUT THE UMBRELLA I USED WAS...
WELL ...
MISS-ING...
OH...
...WANNA USE MINE, THEN?
I WORK REALLY CLOSE BY.
NO, I COULDN'T!
FWIP
VWSH
TAKE IT. SERIOUSLY.
I'M ALL RIGHT!! PLEASE...
DON'T MIND ME!
CLIK
NIYA BOOKSTORE
SO,
WHAT BOOKS DID YOU BUY, KO-KUN?
UH ...?

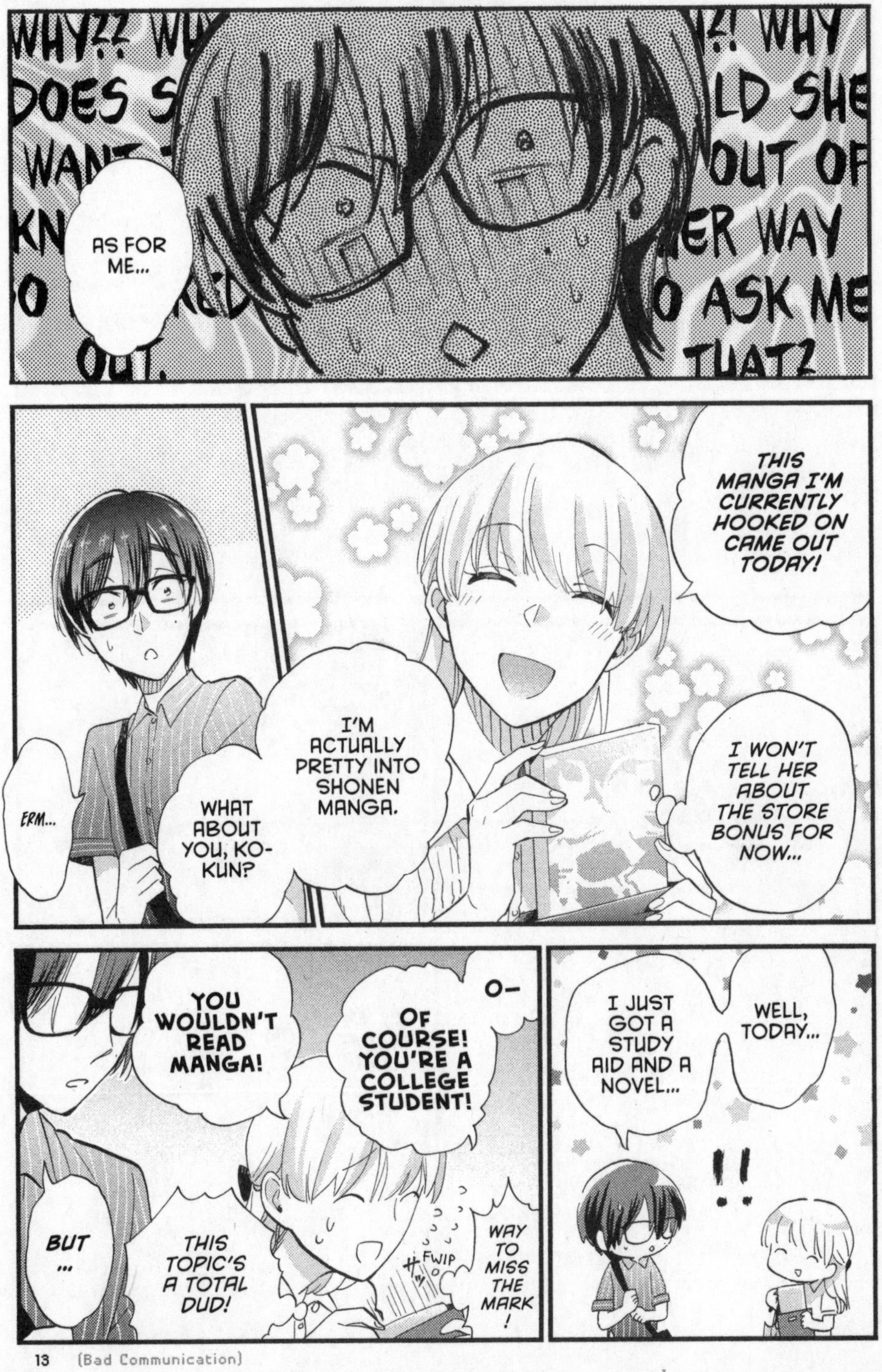
AS FOR ME...
THIS MANGA I'M CURRENTLY HOOKED ON CAME OUT TODAY!
I WON'T TELL HER ABOUT THE STORE BONUS FOR NOW...
I'M ACTUALLY PRETTY INTO SHONEN MANGA.
WHAT ABOUT YOU, KO-KUN?
ERM...
WELL, TODAY...
I JUST GOT A STUDY AID AND A NOVEL...
!!
O-
OF COURSE! YOU'RE A COLLEGE STUDENT!
YOU WOULDN'T READ MANGA!
WAY TO MISS THE MARK!
FWIP
THIS TOPIC'S A TOTAL DUD!
BUT ...

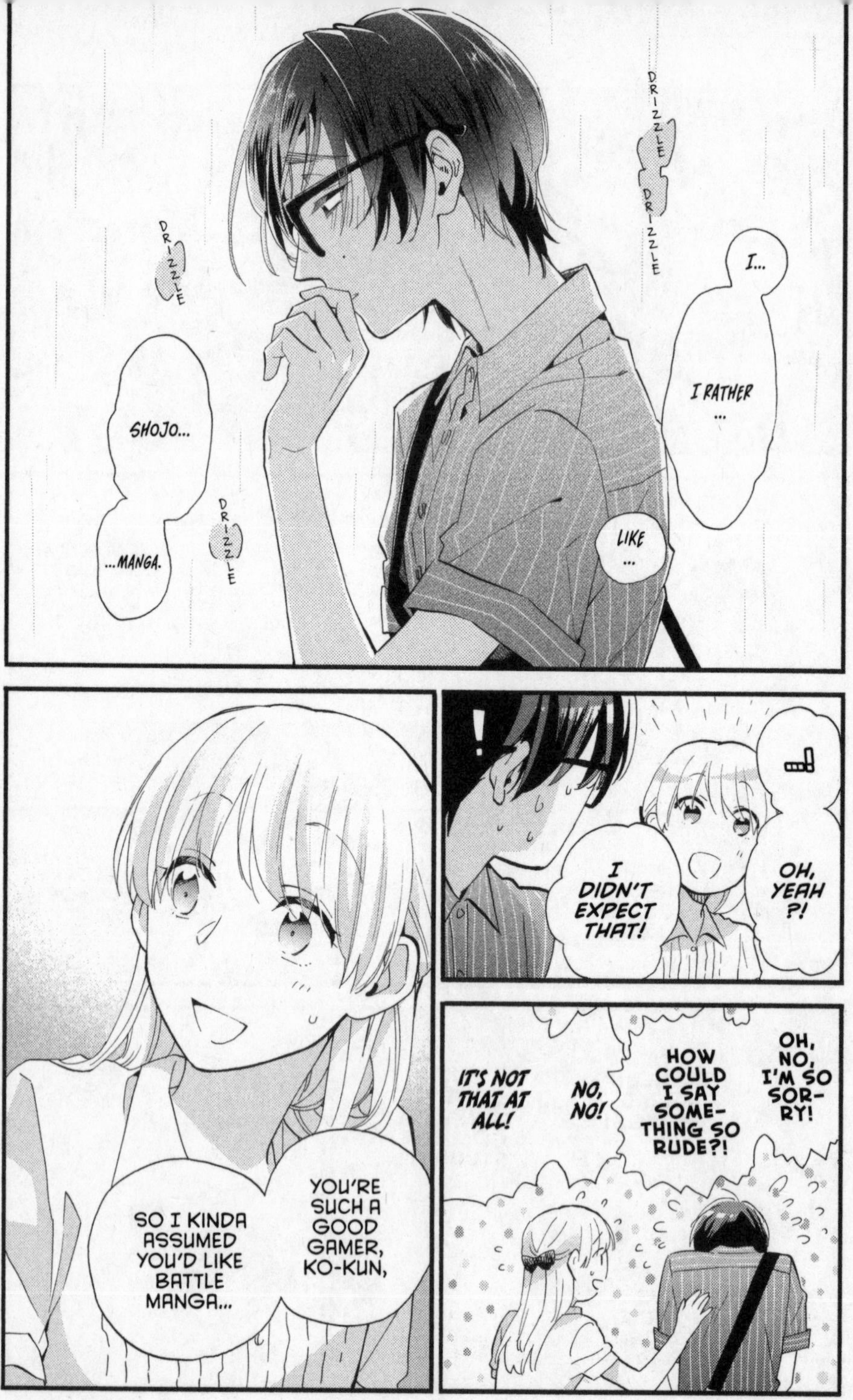
DRIZZLE DRIZZLE
I...
I RATHER ...
LIKE ...
DRIZZLE
SHOJO...
...MANGA.
DRIZZLE
!
..!
OH, YEAH?!
I DIDN'T EXPECT THAT!
OH, NO, I'M SO SORRY!
HOW COULD I SAY SOMETHING SO RUDE?!
NO, NO!
IT'S NOT THAT AT ALL!
YOU'RE SUCH A GOOD GAMER, KO-KUN,
SO I KINDA ASSUMED YOU'D LIKE BATTLE MANGA...

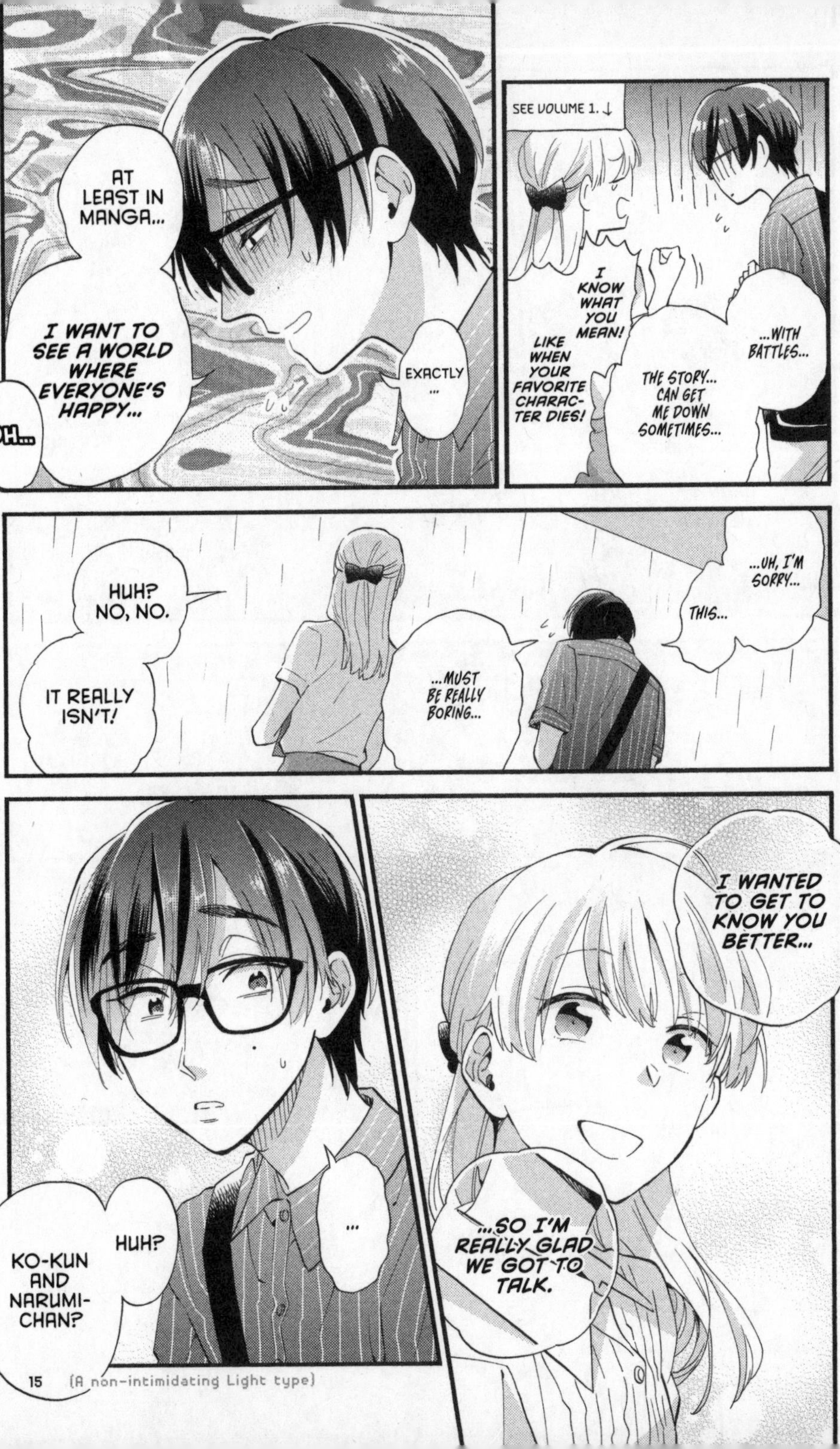
SEE VOLUME 1. ↓
...WITH BATTLES...
THE STORY... CAN GET ME DOWN SOMETIMES...
I KNOW WHAT YOU MEAN!
LIKE WHEN YOUR FAVORITE CHARAC-TER DIES!
EXACTLY ...
AT LEAST IN MANGA...
I WANT TO SEE A WORLD WHERE EVERYONE'S HAPPY...
OH...
...UH, I'M SORRY...
THIS...
...MUST BE REALLY BORING...
HUH? NO, NO.
IT REALLY ISN'T!
I WANTED TO GET TO KNOW YOU BETTER...
...SO I'M REALLY GLAD WE GOT TO TALK.
...
HUH?
KO-KUN AND NARUMI-CHAN?

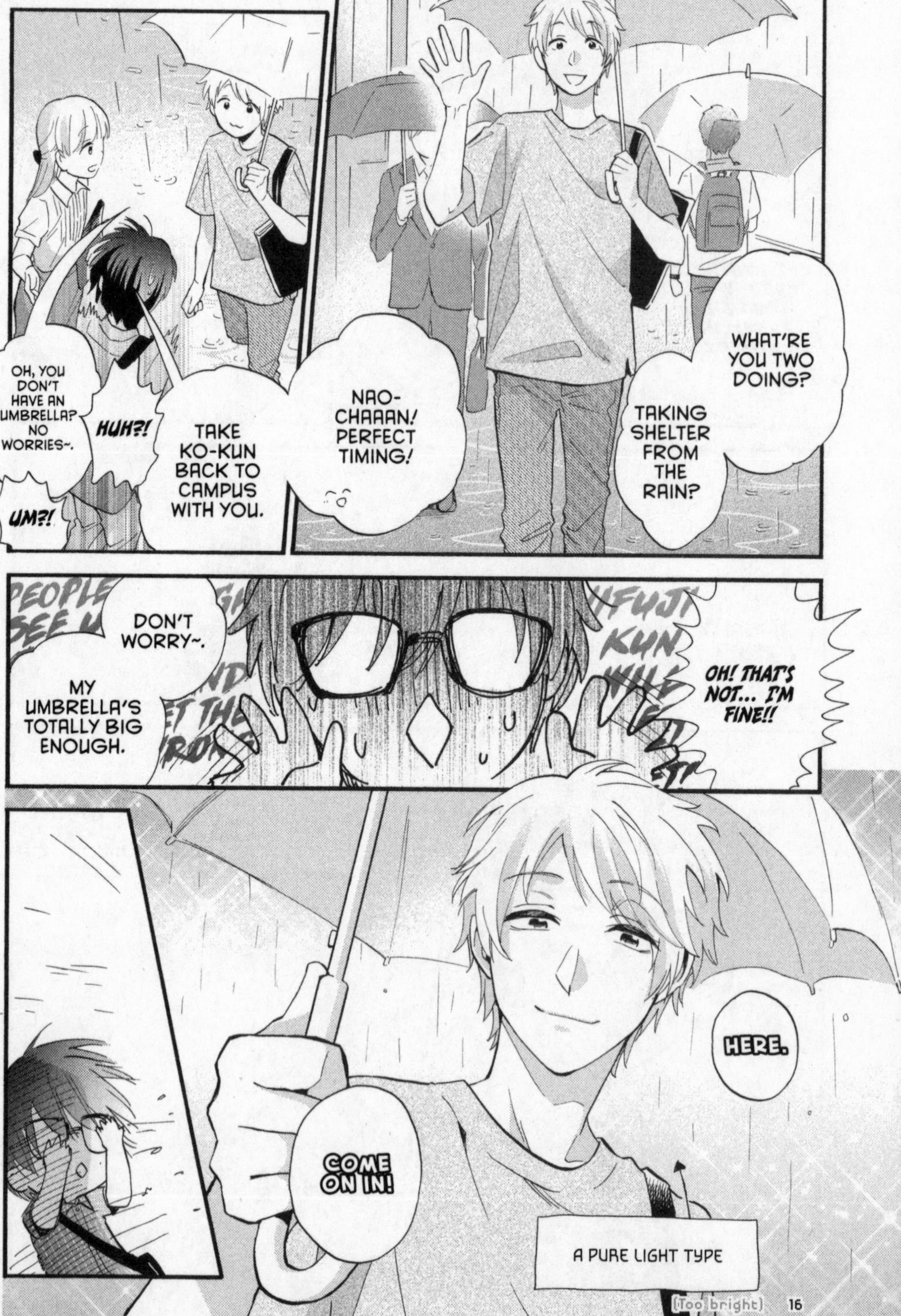
WHAT'RE YOU TWO DOING?
TAKING SHELTER FROM THE RAIN?
NAO-CHAAAN! PERFECT TIMING!
TAKE KO-KUN BACK TO CAMPUS WITH YOU.
HUH?!
OH, YOU DON'T HAVE AN UMBRELLA? NO WORRIES~.
UM?!
OH! THAT'S NOT... I'M FINE!!
DON'T WORRY~.
MY UMBRELLA'S TOTALLY BIG ENOUGH.
HERE.
COME ON IN!
A PURE LIGHT TYPE
[Too bright]

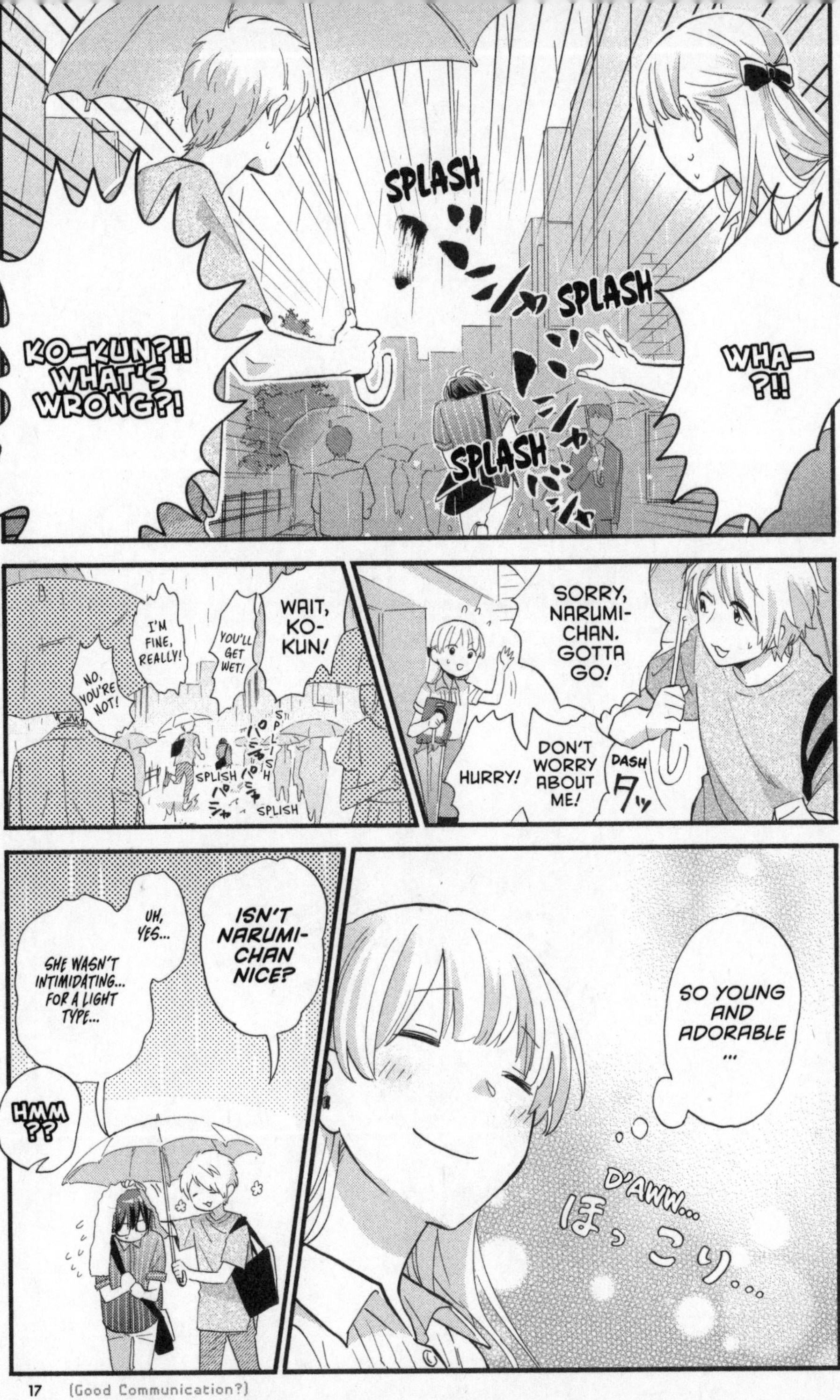
SPLASH
WHA-?!!
SPLASH
SPLASH
KO-KUN?!! WHAT'S WRONG?!
SORRY, NARUMI-CHAN. GOTTA GO!
DASH
DON'T WORRY ABOUT ME!
HURRY!
WAIT, KO-KUN!
YOU'LL GET WET!
I'M FINE, REALLY!
NO, YOU'RE NOT!
SPLISH
SPLISH
SPLISH
SO YOUNG AND ADORABLE...
D'AWW...
ほっこり。。。
ISN'T NARUMI-CHAN NICE?
UH, YES...
SHE WASN'T INTIMIDATING... FOR A LIGHT TYPE...
HMM??

CHARACTERS
MENU

桃瀬 成海

Narumi Momose

LOVES CUTE SWEETS!

HAS A SECOND STOMACH THAT ALWAYS HAS A SHOCKING AMOUNT OF ROOM FOR DESSERT.

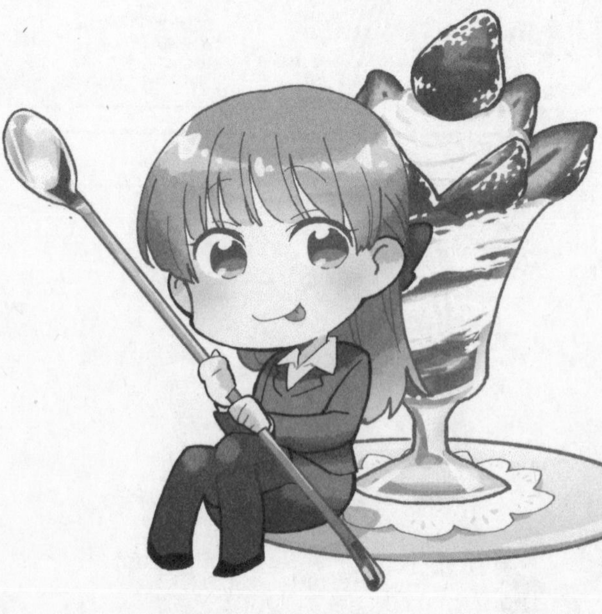

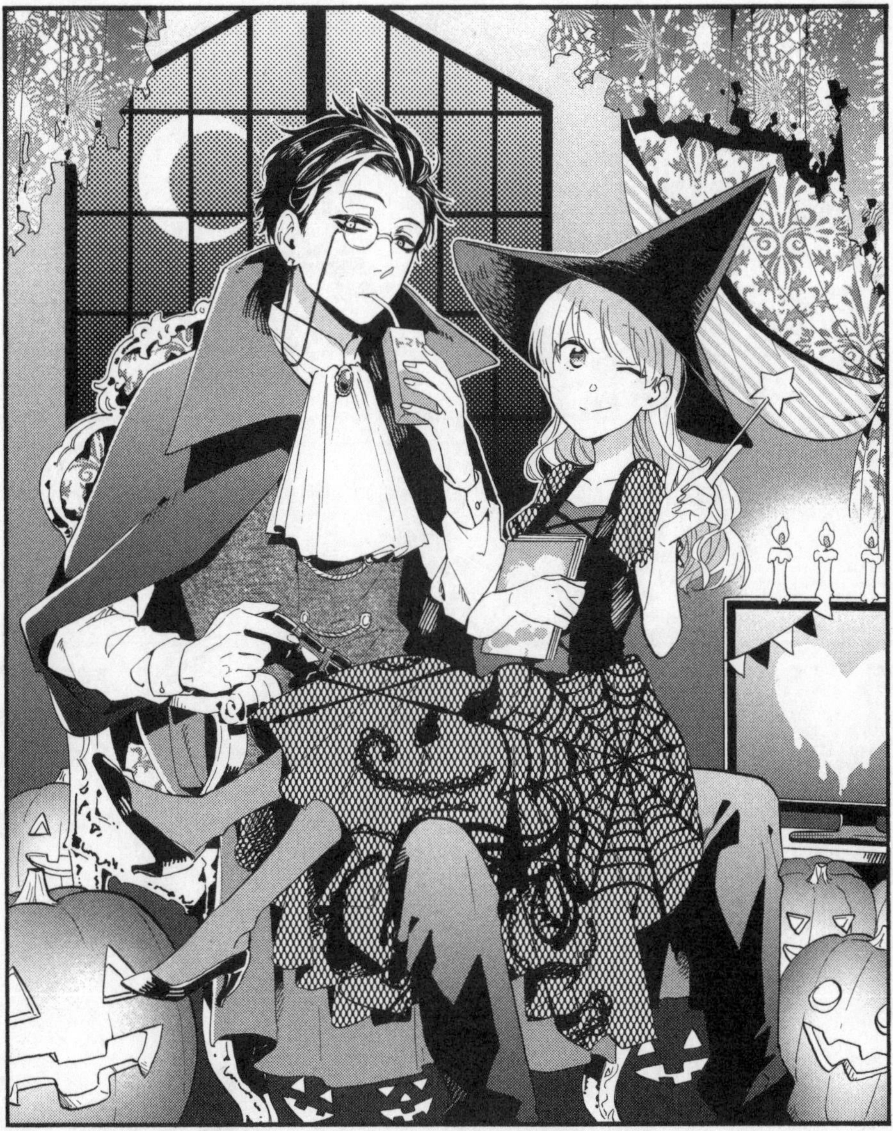

Episode.... 48

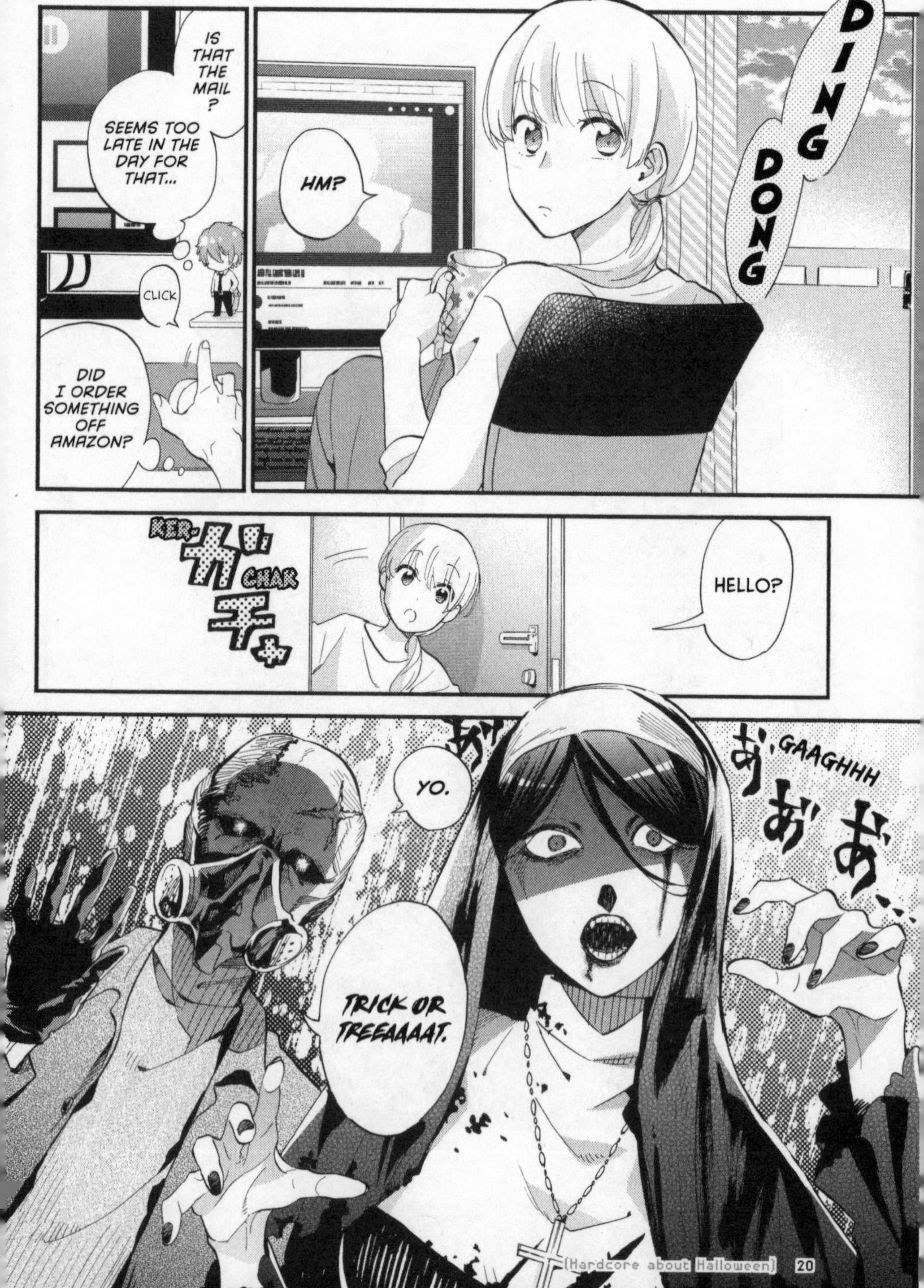
DING DONG
HM?
IS THAT THE MAIL?
SEEMS TOO LATE IN THE DAY FOR THAT...
CLICK
DID I ORDER SOMETHING OFF AMAZON?
HELLO?
KER-CHAK
GAAGHHH
YO.
TRICK OR TREEAAAAT.

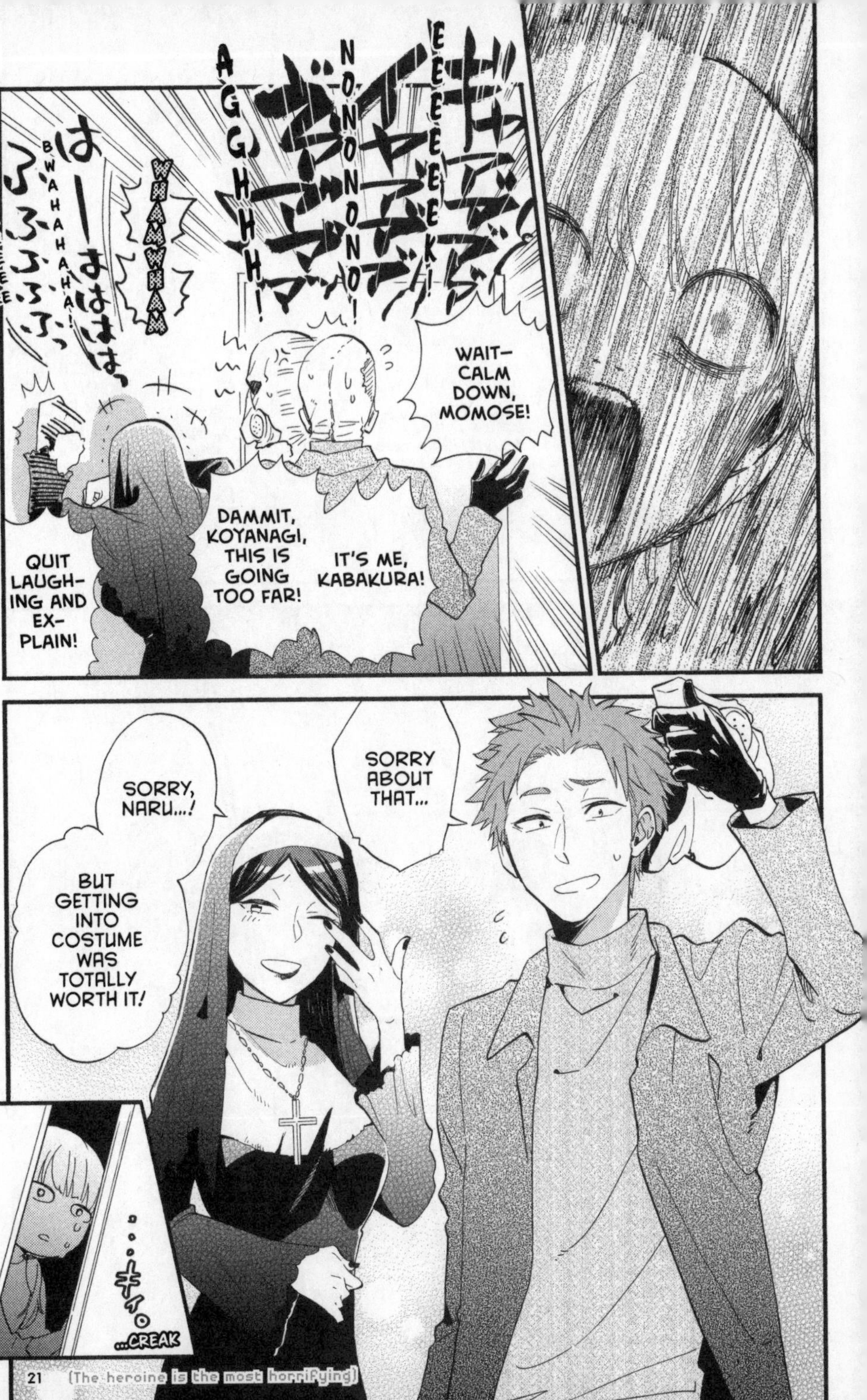
EEEEEEK!
NONONONO!
AGGHHH!
WAIT—CALM DOWN, MOMOSE!
IT'S ME, KABAKURA!
DAMMIT, KOYANAGI, THIS IS GOING TOO FAR!
QUIT LAUGH-ING AND EX-PLAIN!
はーははは、
BWAHAHAHA!
ふふふふっ
HEE HEE HEE HEE HEE
SORRY ABOUT THAT...
SORRY, NARU...!
BUT GETTING INTO COSTUME WAS TOTALLY WORTH IT!
...CREAK

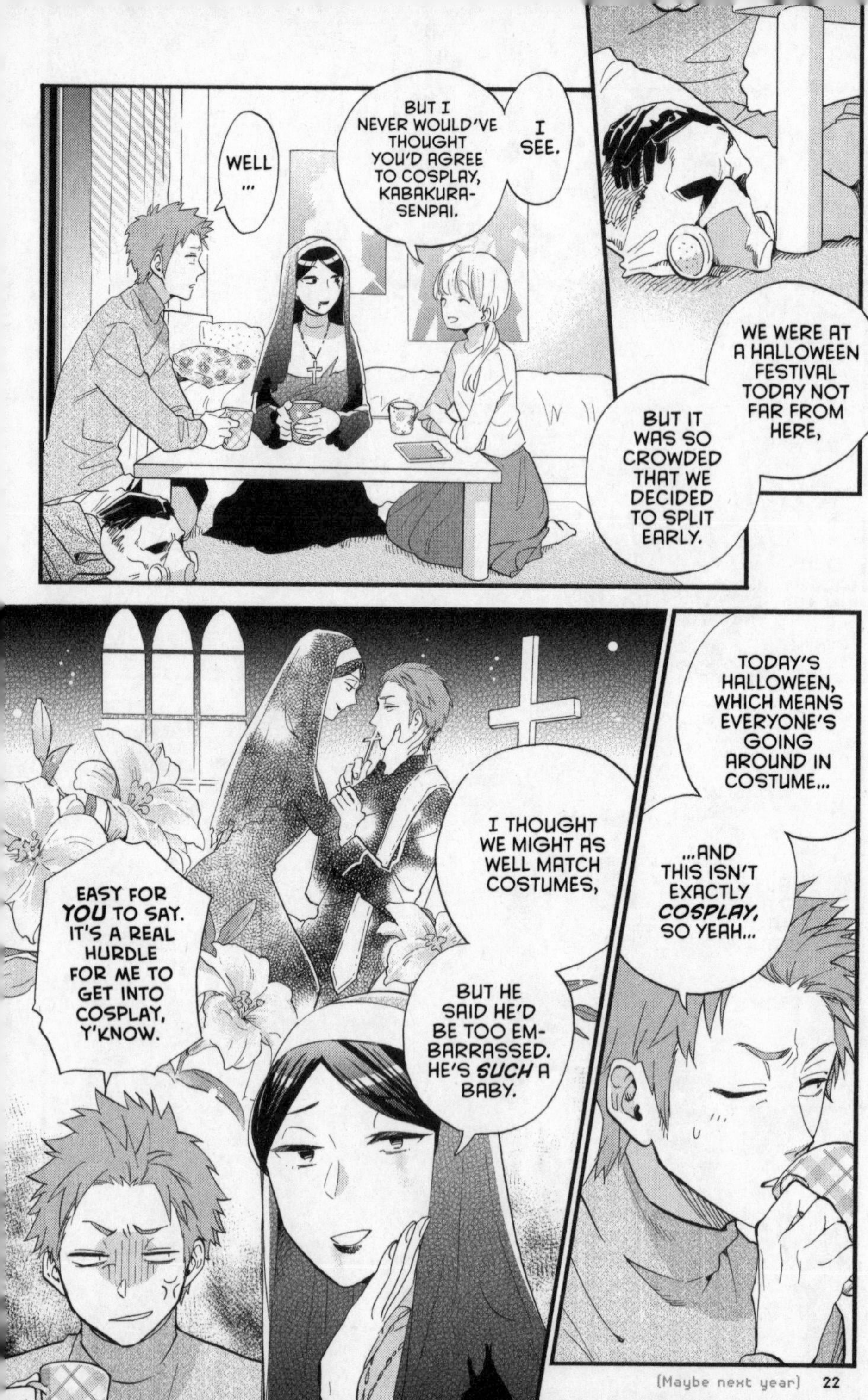
WE WERE AT A HALLOWEEN FESTIVAL TODAY NOT FAR FROM HERE,
BUT IT WAS SO CROWDED THAT WE DECIDED TO SPLIT EARLY.
I SEE.
BUT I NEVER WOULD'VE THOUGHT YOU'D AGREE TO COSPLAY, KABAKURA-SENPAI.
WELL ...
TODAY'S HALLOWEEN, WHICH MEANS EVERYONE'S GOING AROUND IN COSTUME...
...AND THIS ISN'T EXACTLY *COSPLAY,* SO YEAH...
I THOUGHT WE MIGHT AS WELL MATCH COSTUMES,
BUT HE SAID HE'D BE TOO EMBARRASSED. HE'S *SUCH* A BABY.
EASY FOR *YOU* TO SAY. IT'S A REAL HURDLE FOR ME TO GET INTO COSPLAY, Y'KNOW.

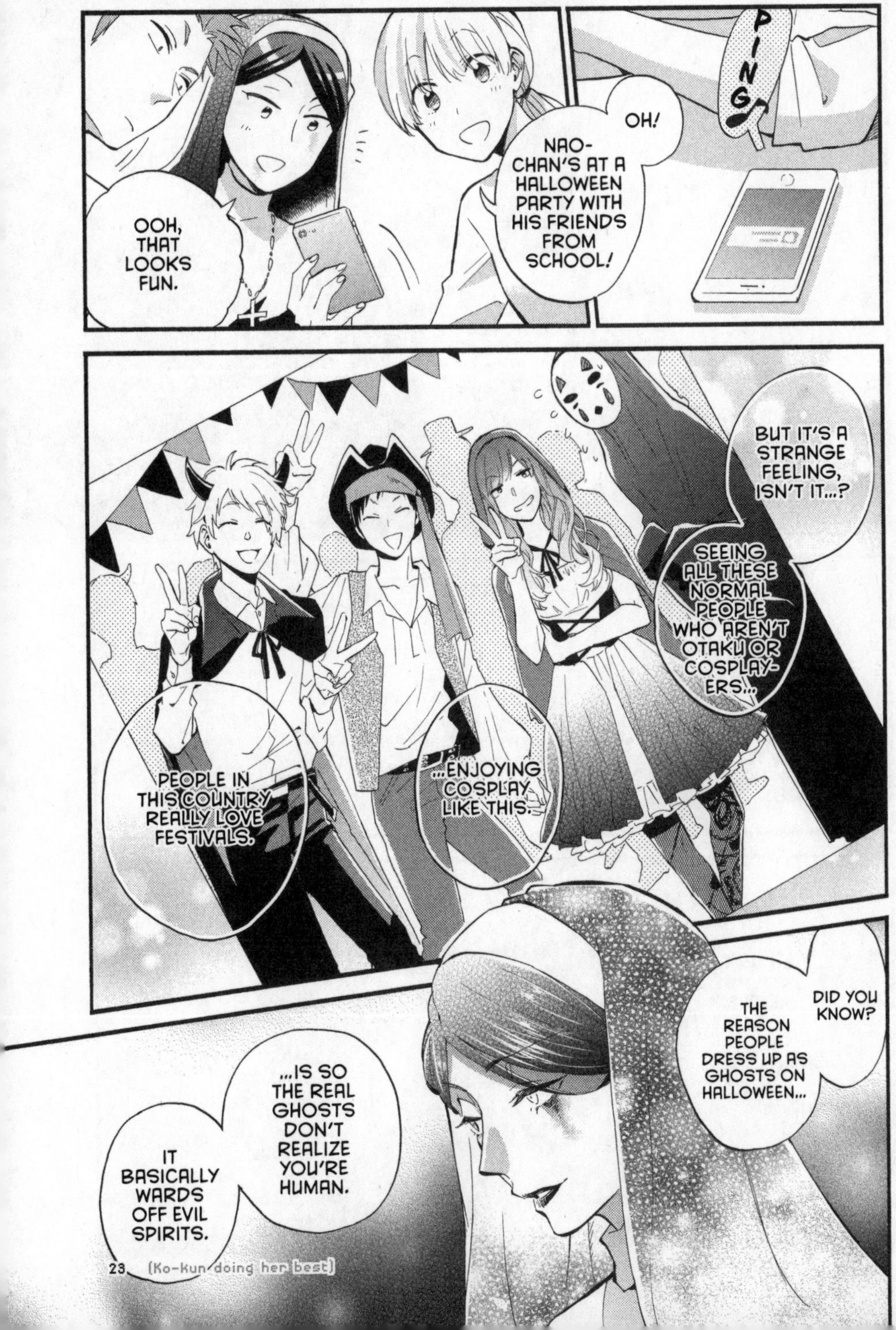
PING
OH!
NAO-CHAN'S AT A HALLOWEEN PARTY WITH HIS FRIENDS FROM SCHOOL!
OOH, THAT LOOKS FUN.
BUT IT'S A STRANGE FEELING, ISN'T IT...?
SEEING ALL THESE NORMAL PEOPLE WHO AREN'T OTAKU OR COSPLAYERS...
...ENJOYING COSPLAY LIKE THIS.
PEOPLE IN THIS COUNTRY REALLY LOVE FESTIVALS.
DID YOU KNOW?
THE REASON PEOPLE DRESS UP AS GHOSTS ON HALLOWEEN...
...IS SO THE REAL GHOSTS DON'T REALIZE YOU'RE HUMAN.
IT BASICALLY WARDS OFF EVIL SPIRITS.

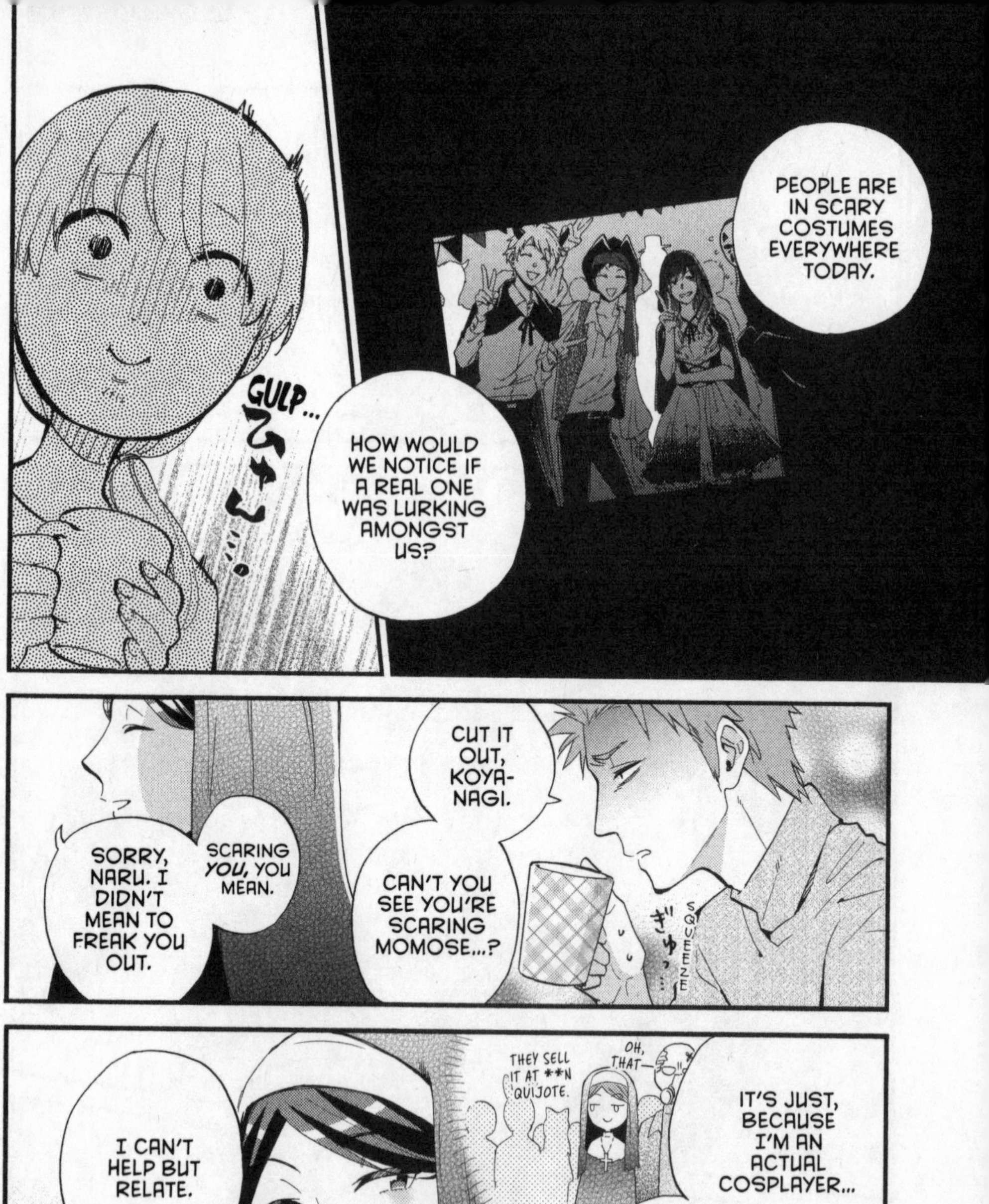
PEOPLE ARE IN SCARY COSTUMES EVERYWHERE TODAY.
HOW WOULD WE NOTICE IF A REAL ONE WAS LURKING AMONGST US?
GULP...
ひゃん…
CUT IT OUT, KOYA-NAGI.
CAN'T YOU SEE YOU'RE SCARING MOMOSE...?
SQUEEZE
ぎゅっ…
SCARING *YOU,* YOU MEAN.
SORRY, NARU. I DIDN'T MEAN TO FREAK YOU OUT.
IT'S JUST, BECAUSE I'M AN ACTUAL COSPLAYER...
...MINGLED IN AMONG NORMAL PEOPLE IN COSTUME TODAY...
OH, THAT—
THEY SELL IT AT **N QUIJOTE.
I CAN'T HELP BUT RELATE.
HUH?
TO THE GHOSTS?

(Wrong one)

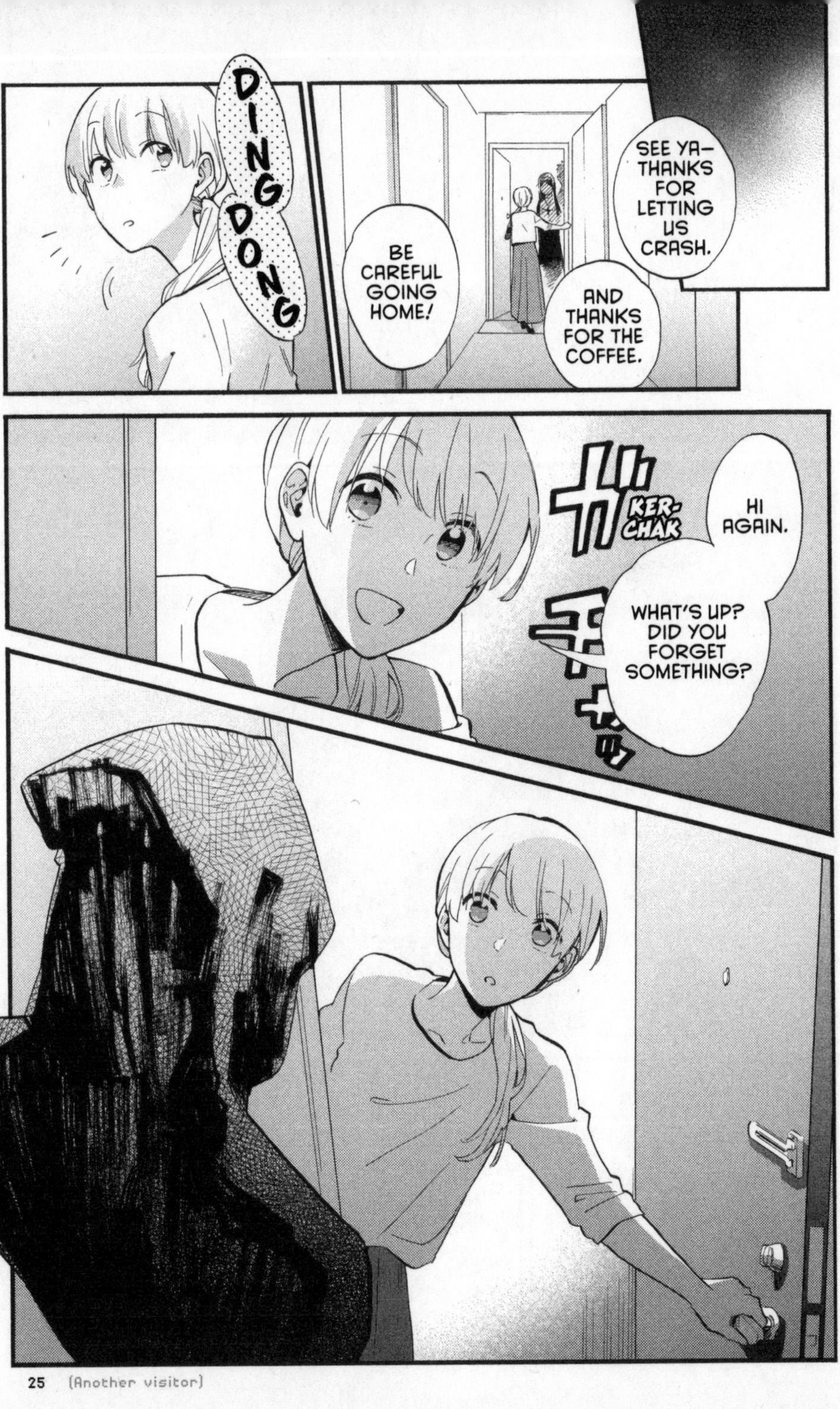

SEE YA— THANKS FOR LETTING US CRASH.
AND THANKS FOR THE COFFEE.
BE CAREFUL GOING HOME!
DING DONG
KER-CHAK
HI AGAIN.
WHAT'S UP? DID YOU FORGET SOMETHING?

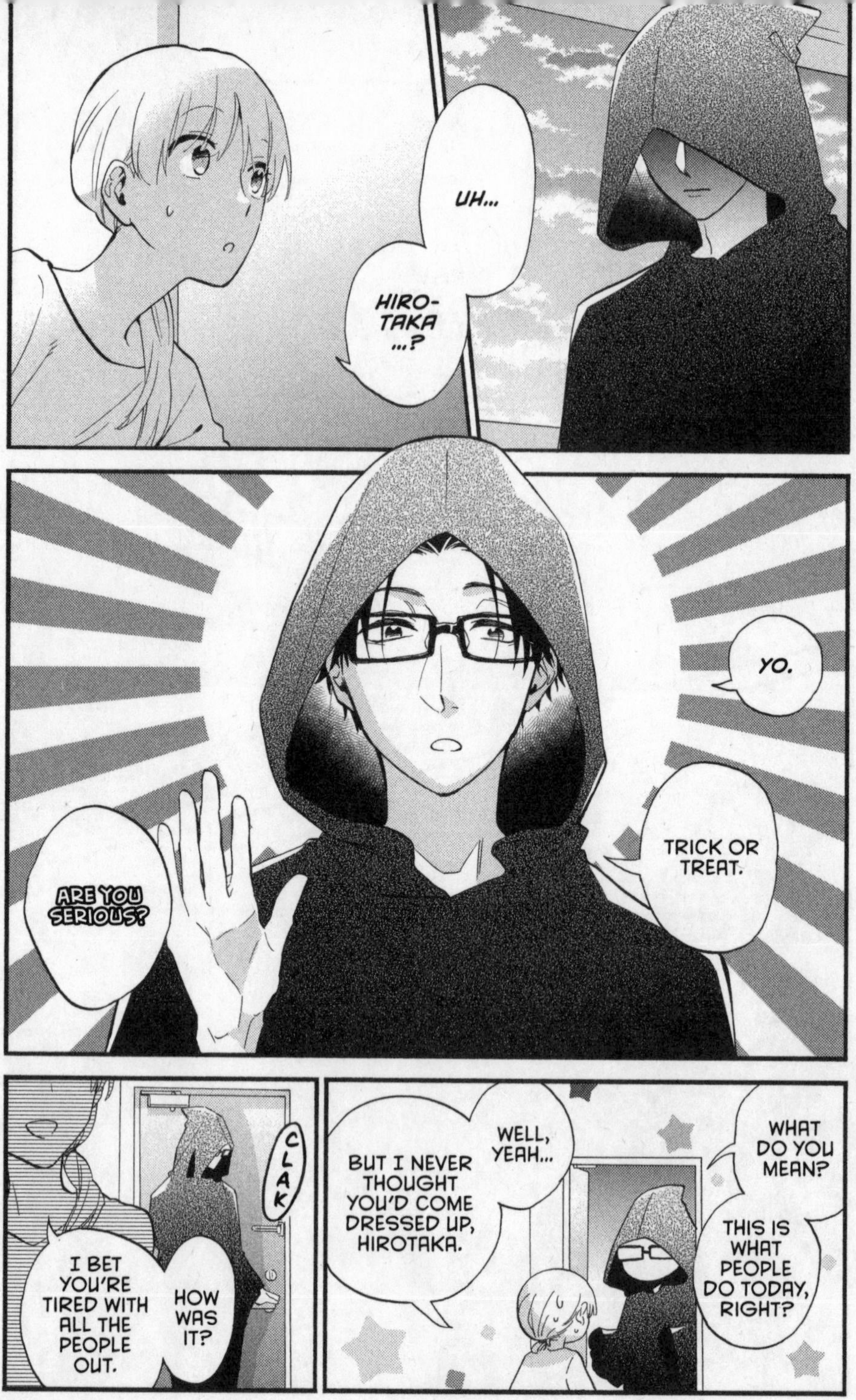
UH...
HIRO-TAKA...?
YO.
TRICK OR TREAT.
ARE YOU SERIOUS?
WHAT DO YOU MEAN?
THIS IS WHAT PEOPLE DO TODAY, RIGHT?
WELL, YEAH...
BUT I NEVER THOUGHT YOU'D COME DRESSED UP, HIROTAKA.
CLAK
HOW WAS IT?
I BET YOU'RE TIRED WITH ALL THE PEOPLE OUT.

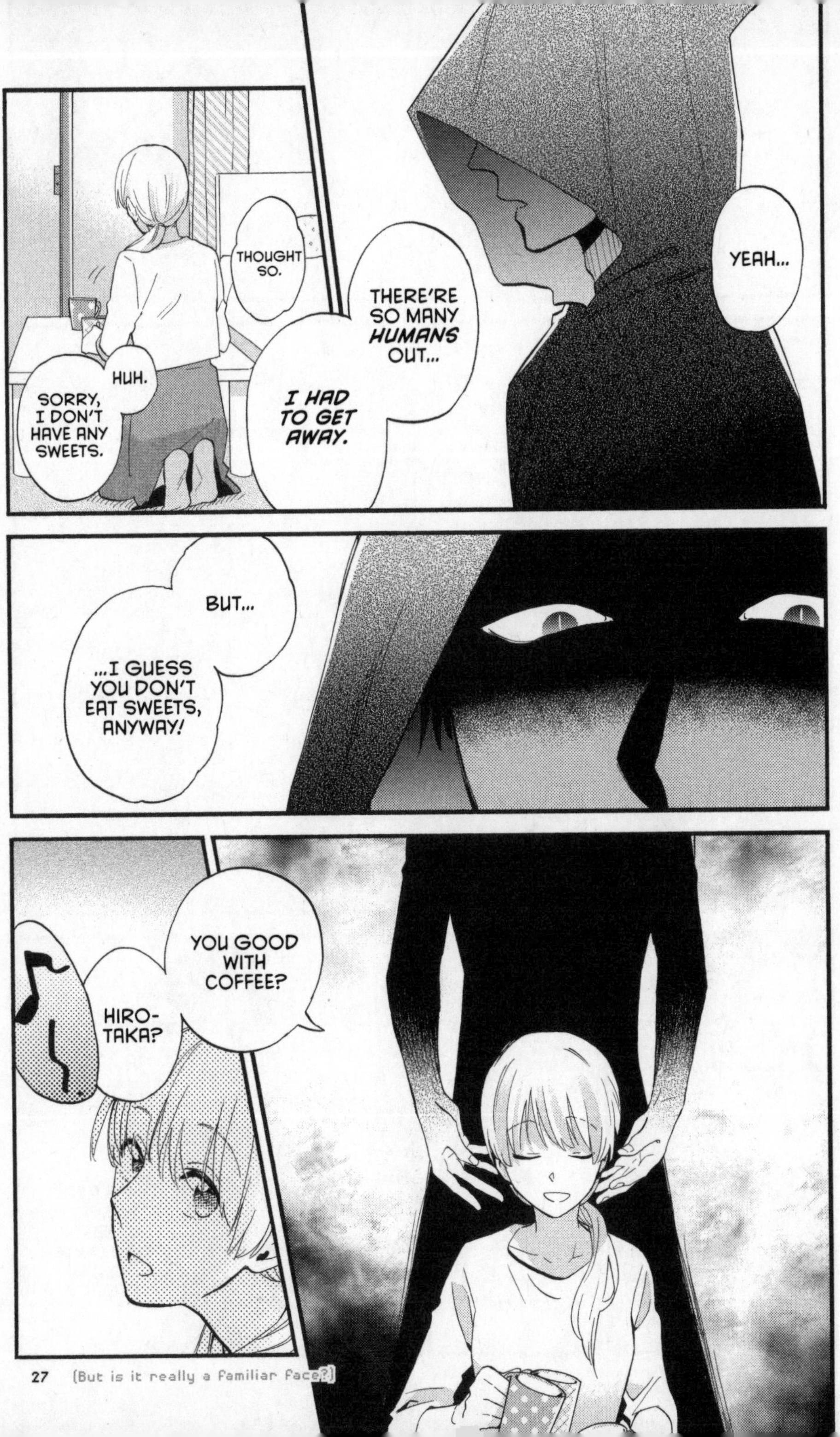
YEAH...
THERE'RE SO MANY *HUMANS* OUT...
I HAD TO GET AWAY.
THOUGHT SO.
HUH.
SORRY, I DON'T HAVE ANY SWEETS.
BUT...
...I GUESS YOU DON'T EAT SWEETS, ANYWAY!
YOU GOOD WITH COFFEE?
HIRO-TAKA?

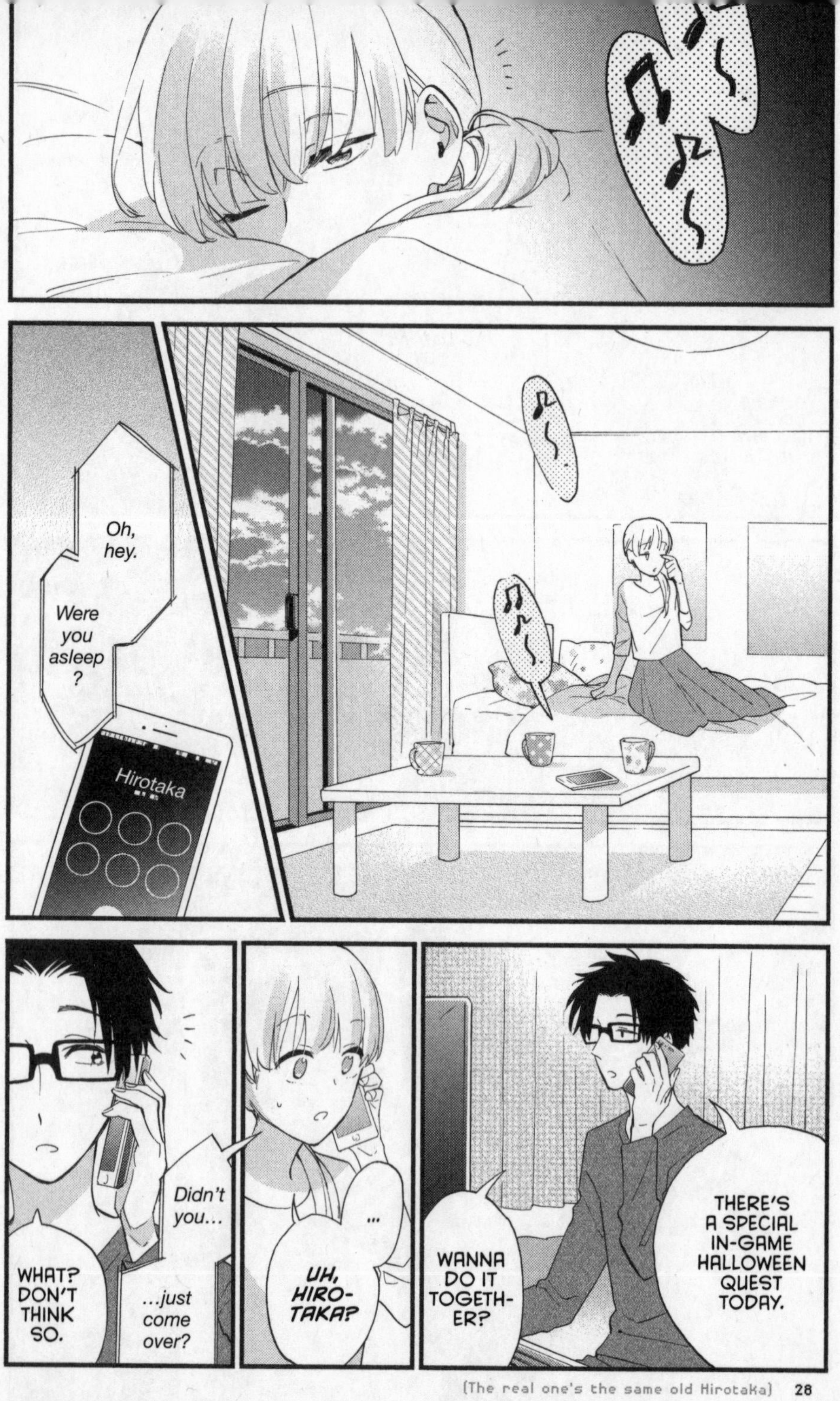
Hirotaka
Oh, hey.
Were you asleep?
THERE'S A SPECIAL IN-GAME HALLOWEEN QUEST TODAY.
WANNA DO IT TOGETH-ER?
...
UH, HIRO-TAKA?
Didn't you…
…just come over?
WHAT? DON'T THINK SO.

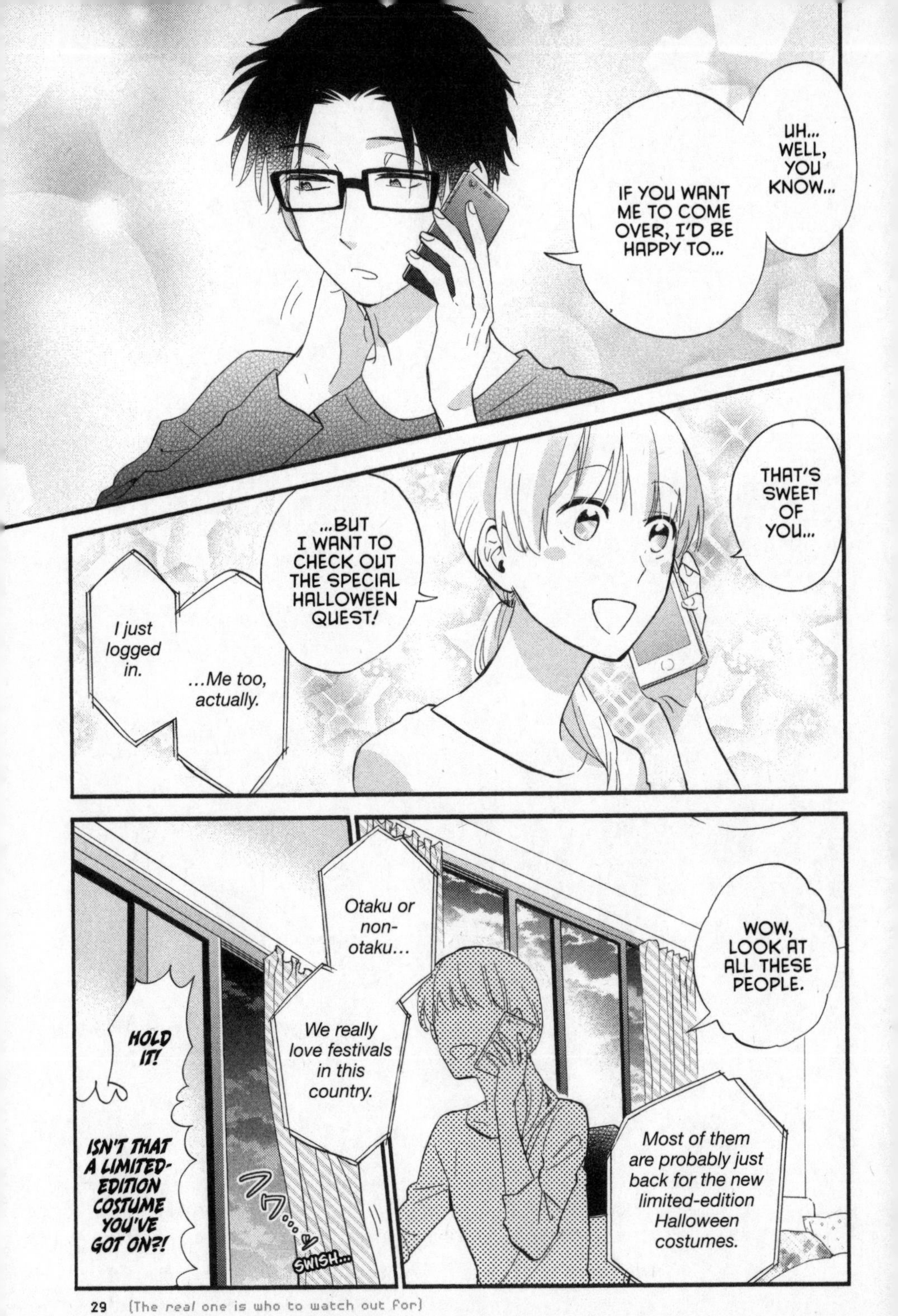
UH... WELL, YOU KNOW...
IF YOU WANT ME TO COME OVER, I'D BE HAPPY TO...
THAT'S SWEET OF YOU...
...BUT I WANT TO CHECK OUT THE SPECIAL HALLOWEEN QUEST!
I just logged in.
...Me too, actually.
WOW, LOOK AT ALL THESE PEOPLE.
Most of them are probably just back for the new limited-edition Halloween costumes.
Otaku or non-otaku...
We really love festivals in this country.
SWISH...
HOLD IT!
ISN'T THAT A LIMITED-EDITION COSTUME YOU'VE GOT ON?!

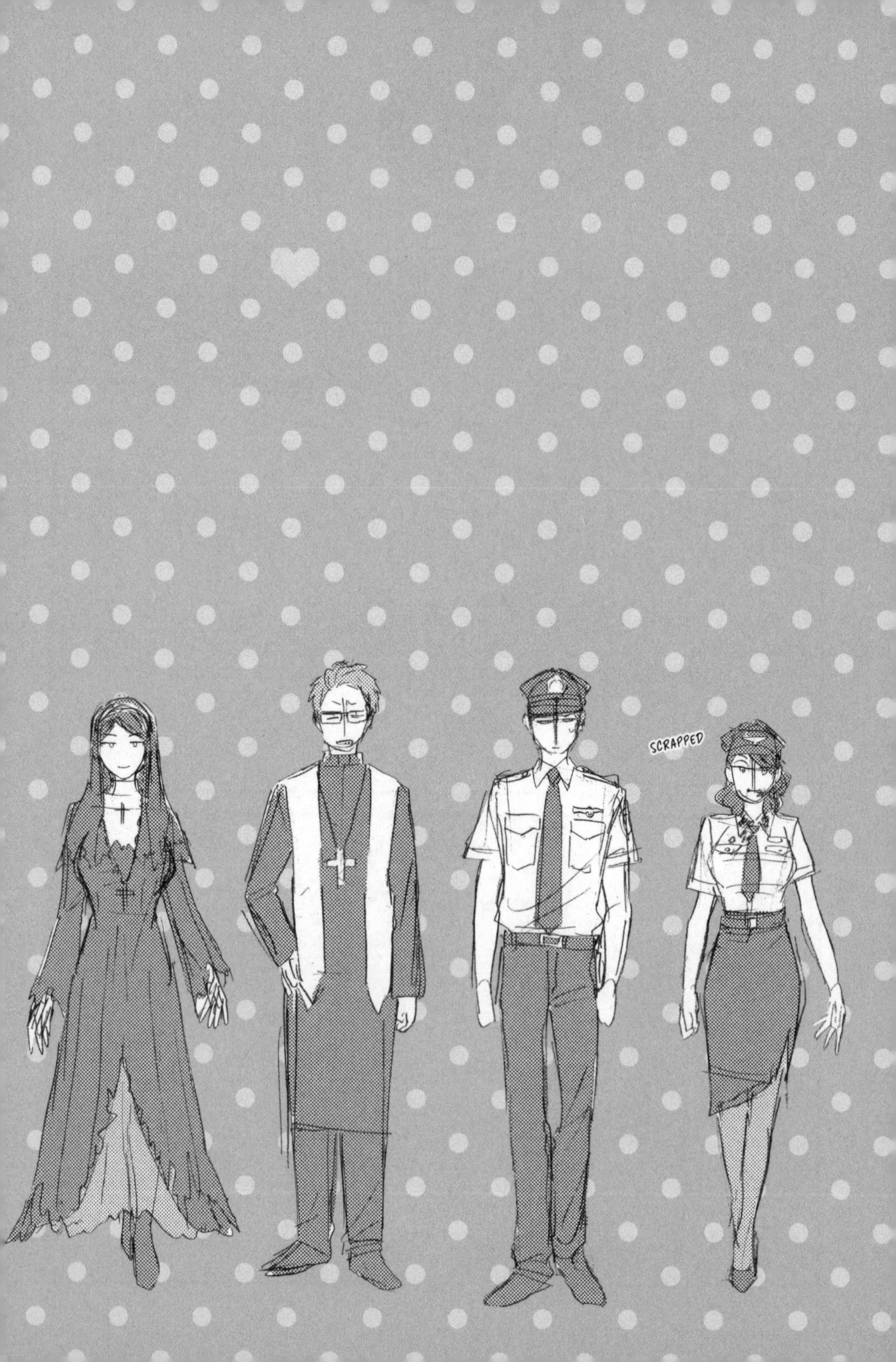
SCRAPPED

CHARACTERS
MENU

二藤 宏嵩

Hirotaka Nifuji

ISN'T FOND
OF SWEET THINGS.

HE FEARS THAT ONE DAY
NARUMI WILL INVITE HIM
TO THE DESSERT BUFFET
AT SWEETS PARADISE*.

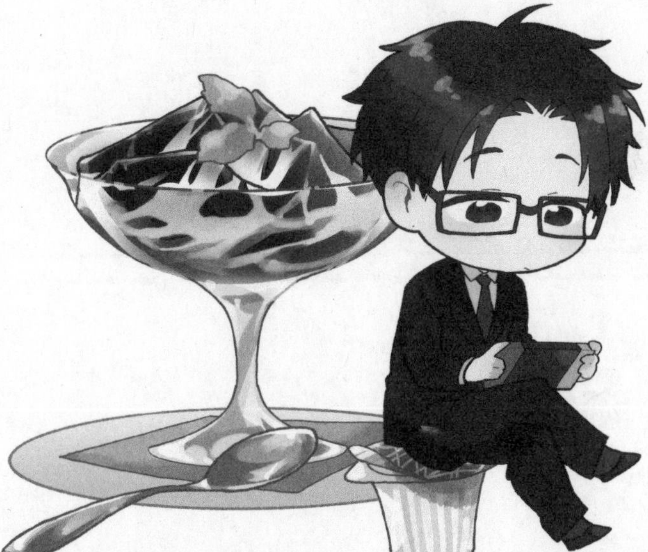

*A famous chain restaurant featuring all-you-can-eat sweets.

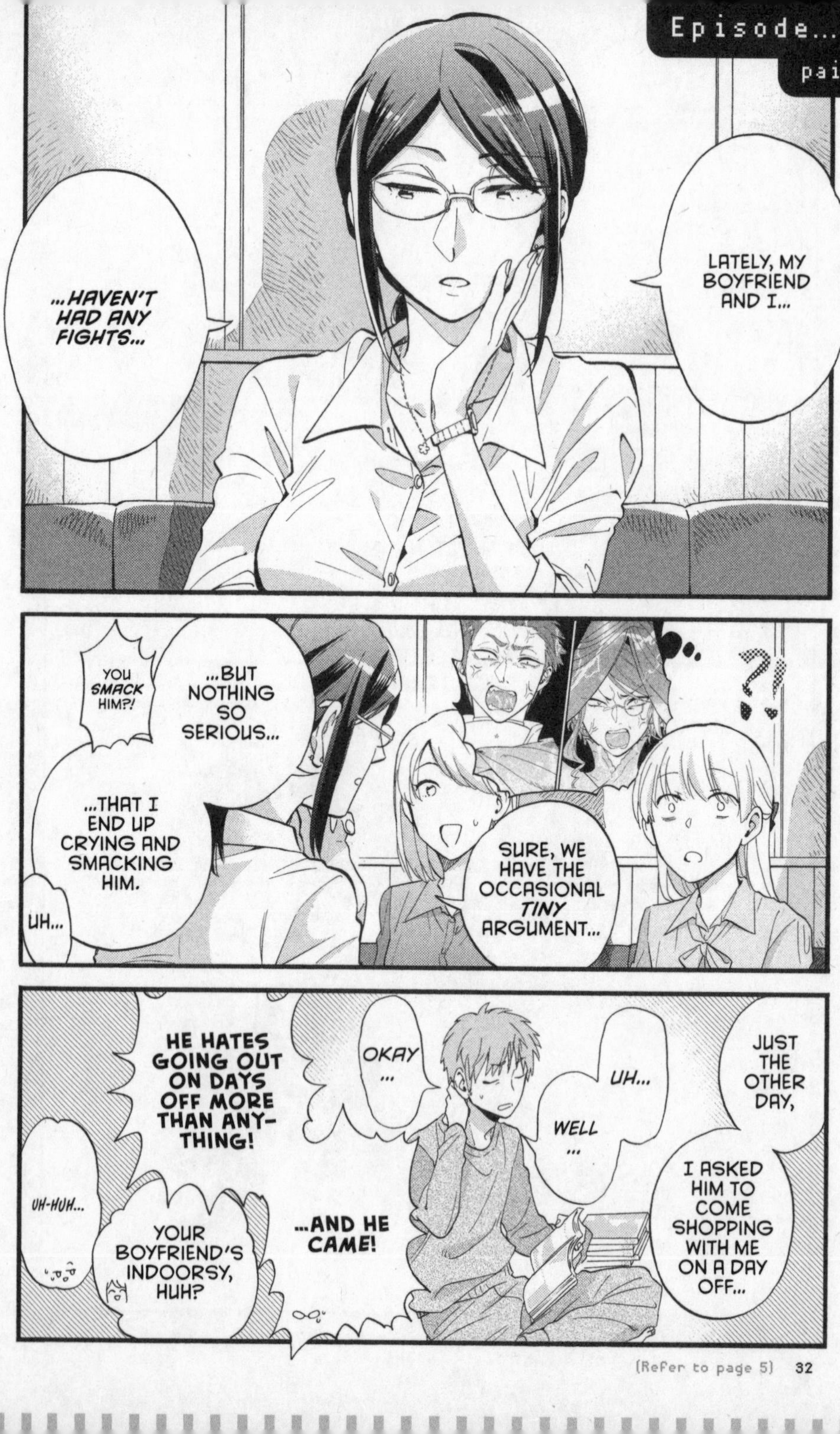
LATELY, MY BOYFRIEND AND I...
...HAVEN'T HAD ANY FIGHTS...
SURE, WE HAVE THE OCCASIONAL TINY ARGUMENT...
...BUT NOTHING SO SERIOUS...
...THAT I END UP CRYING AND SMACKING HIM.
YOU SMACK HIM?!
UH...
JUST THE OTHER DAY,
I ASKED HIM TO COME SHOPPING WITH ME ON A DAY OFF...
UH...
WELL...
OKAY...
HE HATES GOING OUT ON DAYS OFF MORE THAN ANYTHING!
...AND HE CAME!
YOUR BOYFRIEND'S INDOORSY, HUH?
UH-HUH...

(Refer to page 5)

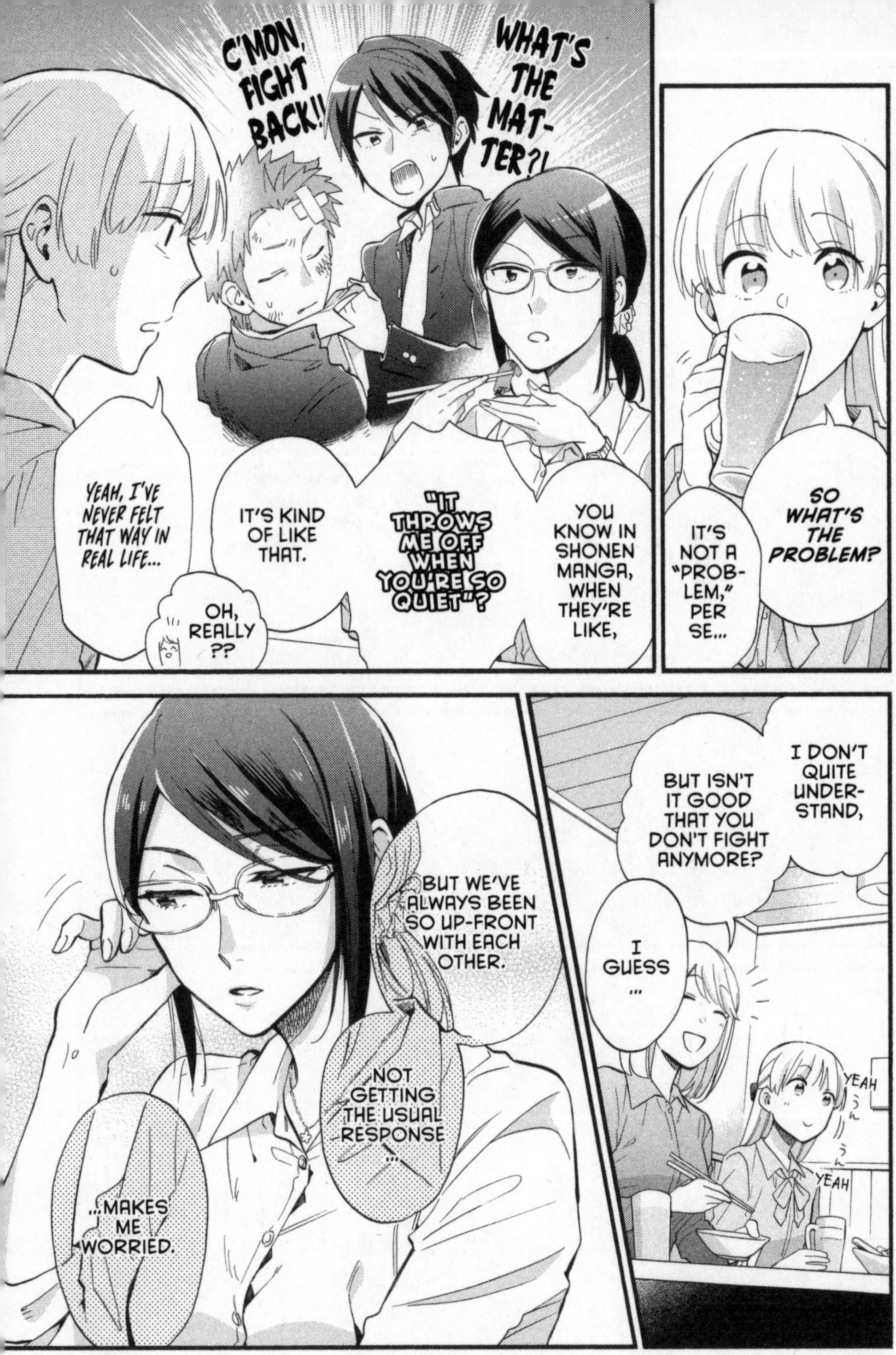
SO WHAT'S THE PROBLEM?
IT'S NOT A "PROBLEM," PER SE...
WHAT'S THE MATTER?!
C'MON, FIGHT BACK!!
YOU KNOW IN SHONEN MANGA, WHEN THEY'RE LIKE,
"IT THROWS ME OFF WHEN YOU'RE SO QUIET"?
IT'S KIND OF LIKE THAT.
YEAH, I'VE NEVER FELT THAT WAY IN REAL LIFE...
OH, REALLY??
I DON'T QUITE UNDERSTAND,
BUT ISN'T IT GOOD THAT YOU DON'T FIGHT ANYMORE?
I GUESS...
YEAH
YEAH
BUT WE'VE ALWAYS BEEN SO UP-FRONT WITH EACH OTHER.
NOT GETTING THE USUAL RESPONSE...
...MAKES ME WORRIED.

 (Isn't that more of a rival than a boyfriend...?)

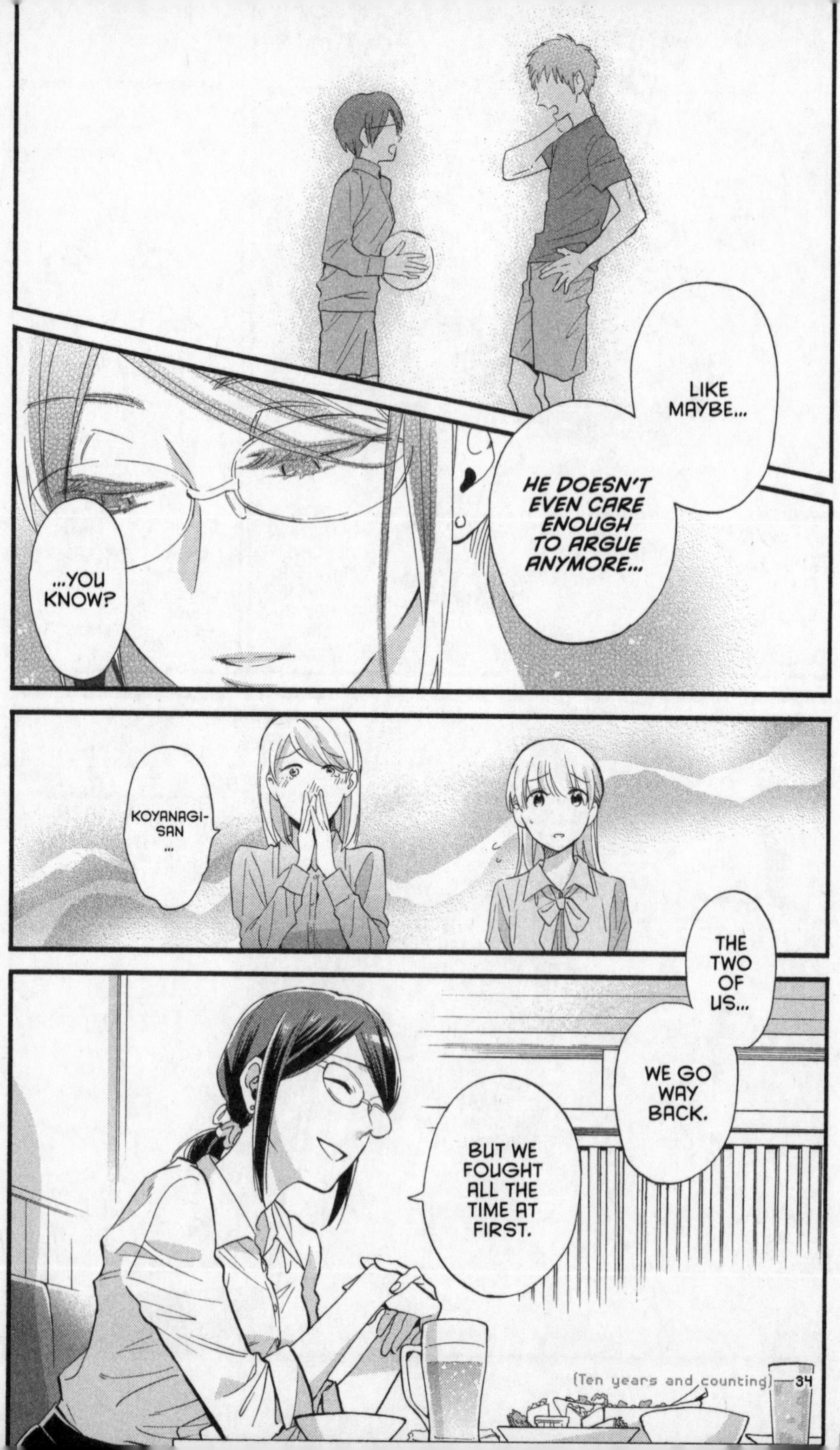
LIKE MAYBE...
HE DOESN'T EVEN CARE ENOUGH TO ARGUE ANYMORE...
...YOU KNOW?
KOYANAGI-SAN ...
THE TWO OF US...
WE GO WAY BACK.
BUT WE FOUGHT ALL THE TIME AT FIRST.

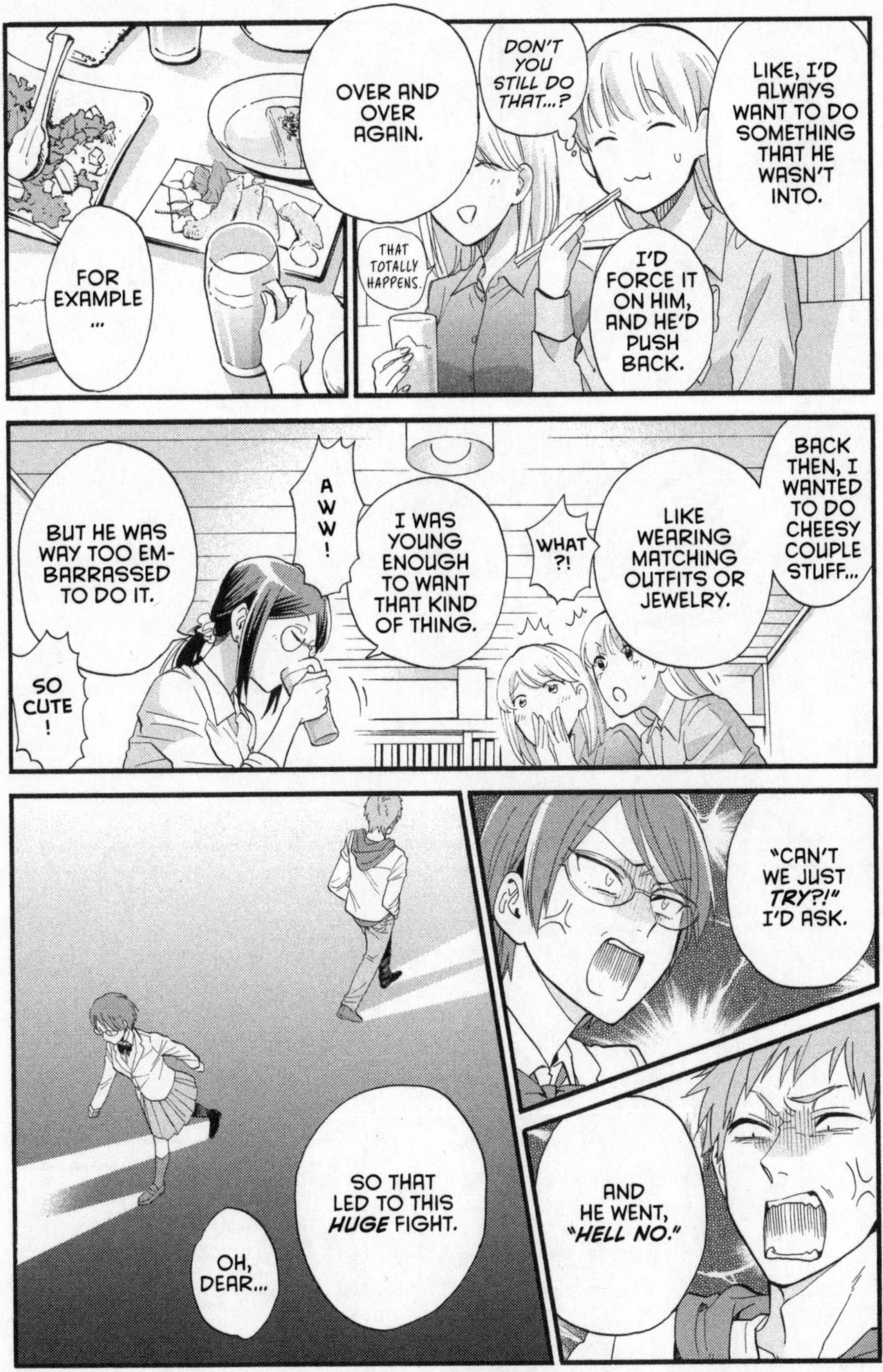
LIKE, I'D ALWAYS WANT TO DO SOMETHING THAT HE WASN'T INTO.
DON'T YOU STILL DO THAT...?
I'D FORCE IT ON HIM, AND HE'D PUSH BACK.
THAT TOTALLY HAPPENS.
OVER AND OVER AGAIN.
FOR EXAMPLE ...
BACK THEN, I WANTED TO DO CHEESY COUPLE STUFF...
LIKE WEARING MATCHING OUTFITS OR JEWELRY.
WHAT?!
I WAS YOUNG ENOUGH TO WANT THAT KIND OF THING.
AWW!
BUT HE WAS WAY TOO EM-BARRASSED TO DO IT.
SO CUTE!
"CAN'T WE JUST *TRY?!*" I'D ASK.
AND HE WENT, ***"HELL NO."***
SO THAT LED TO THIS ***HUGE*** FIGHT.
OH, DEAR...

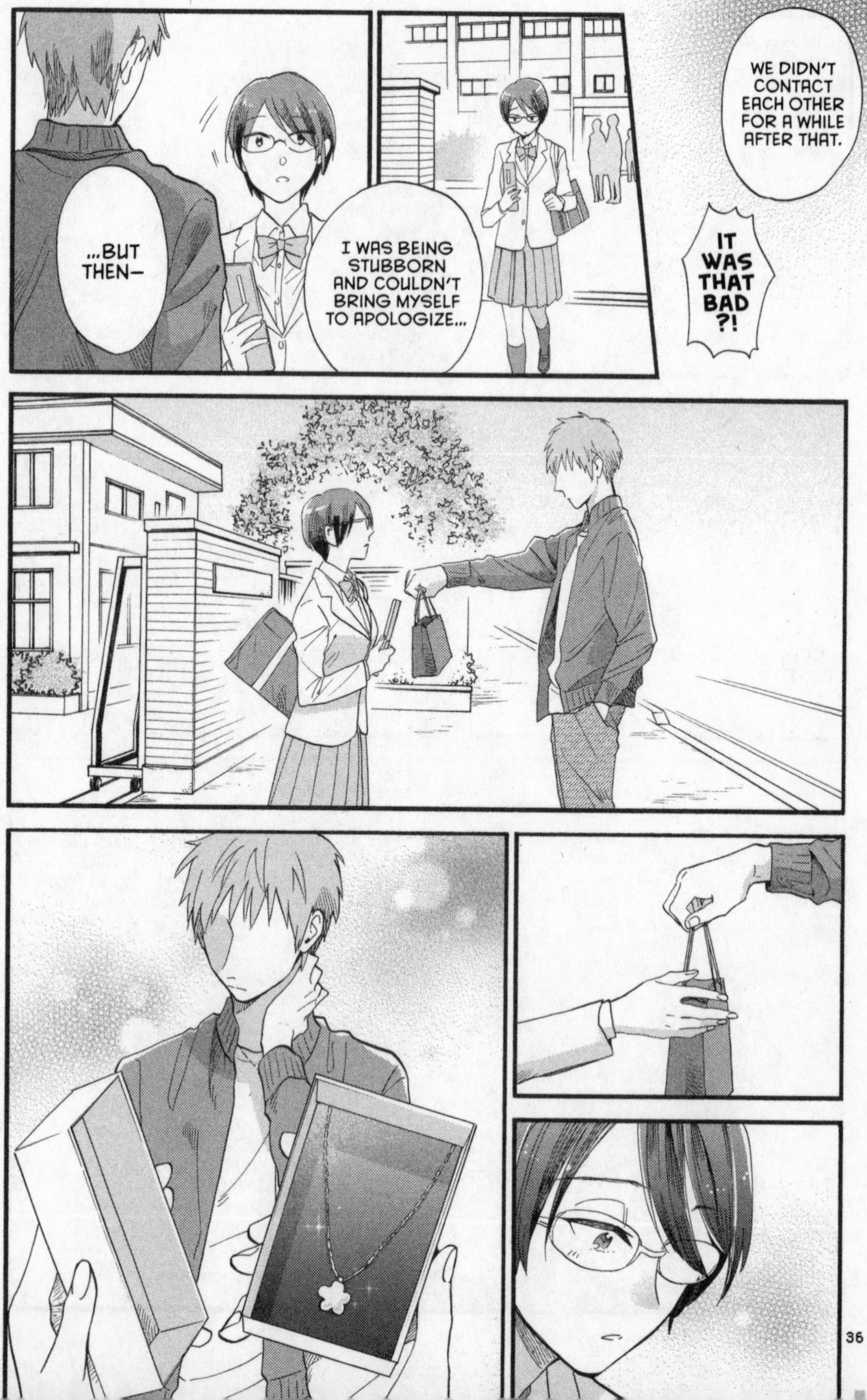
WE DIDN'T CONTACT EACH OTHER FOR A WHILE AFTER THAT.
IT WAS THAT BAD?!
I WAS BEING STUBBORN AND COULDN'T BRING MYSELF TO APOLOGIZE...
...BUT THEN—

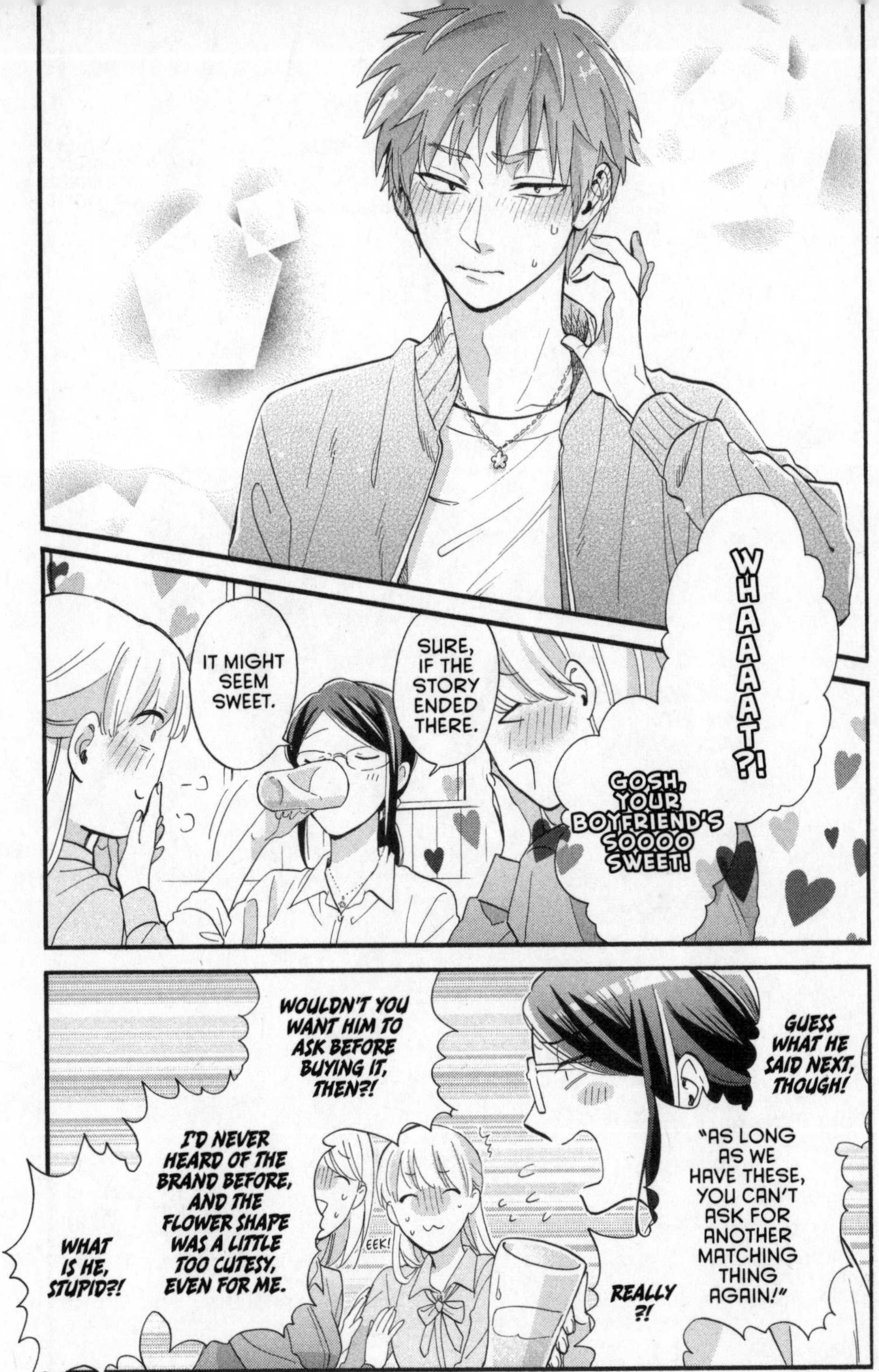
WHAAAAAT?!
GOSH, YOUR BOYFRIEND'S SOOOO SWEET!
SURE, IF THE STORY ENDED THERE.
IT MIGHT SEEM SWEET.
GUESS WHAT HE SAID NEXT, THOUGH!
"AS LONG AS WE HAVE THESE, YOU CAN'T ASK FOR ANOTHER MATCHING THING AGAIN!"
REALLY?!
WOULDN'T YOU WANT HIM TO ASK BEFORE BUYING IT, THEN?!
I'D NEVER HEARD OF THE BRAND BEFORE, AND THE FLOWER SHAPE WAS A LITTLE TOO CUTESY, EVEN FOR ME.
EEK!
WHAT IS HE, STUPID?!

 (The things you do when you're young!)

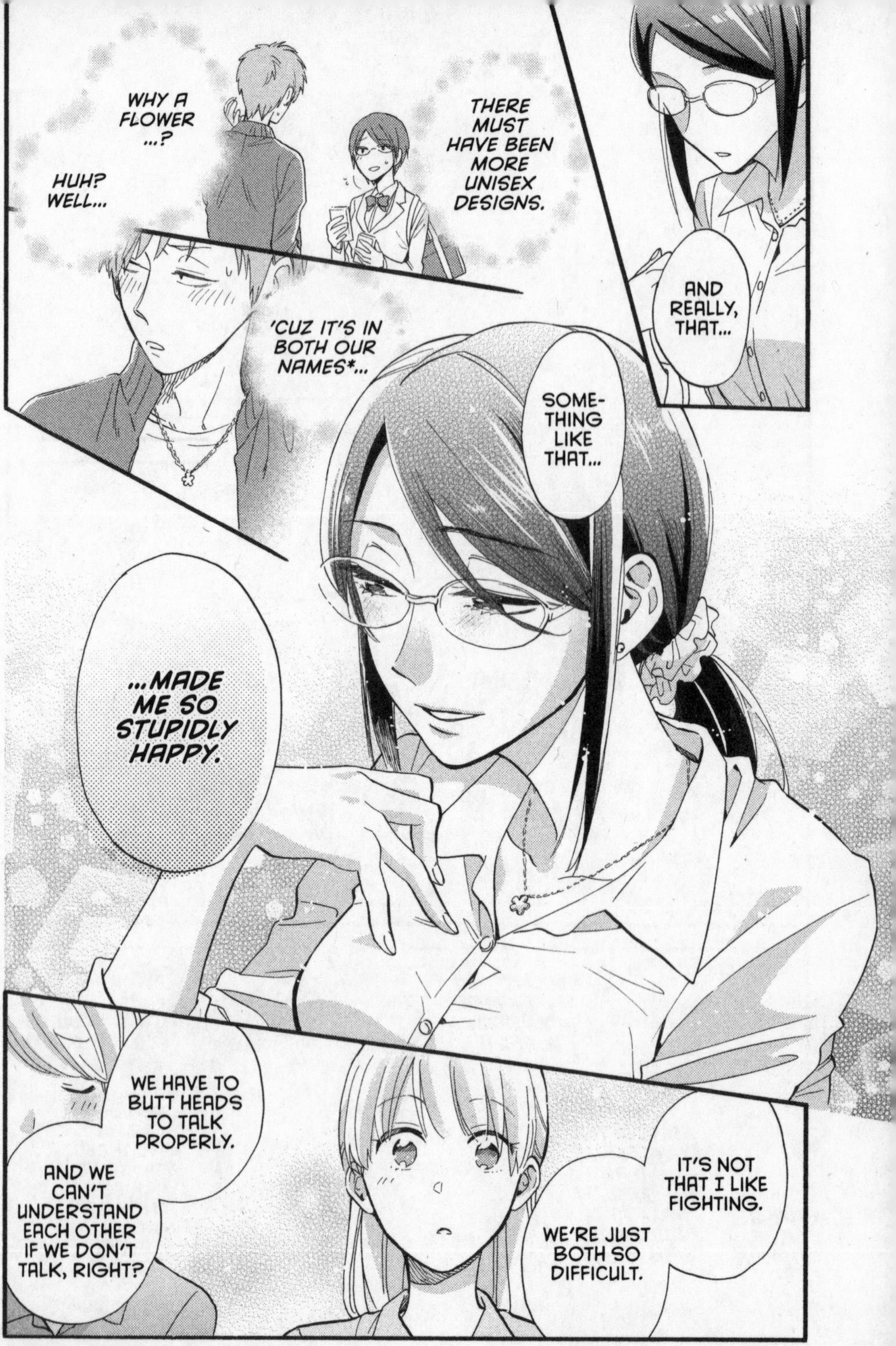
AND REALLY, THAT...
THERE MUST HAVE BEEN MORE UNISEX DESIGNS.
WHY A FLOWER ...?
HUH? WELL...
'CUZ IT'S IN BOTH OUR NAMES*...
SOME-THING LIKE THAT...
...MADE ME SO STUPIDLY HAPPY.
IT'S NOT THAT I LIKE FIGHTING.
WE'RE JUST BOTH SO DIFFICULT.
WE HAVE TO BUTT HEADS TO TALK PROPERLY.
AND WE CAN'T UNDERSTAND EACH OTHER IF WE DON'T TALK, RIGHT?

*The "Kaba" in Kabakura is written with the characters for "tree" and "flower," while the "Hana" in Hanako uses another character for "flower."

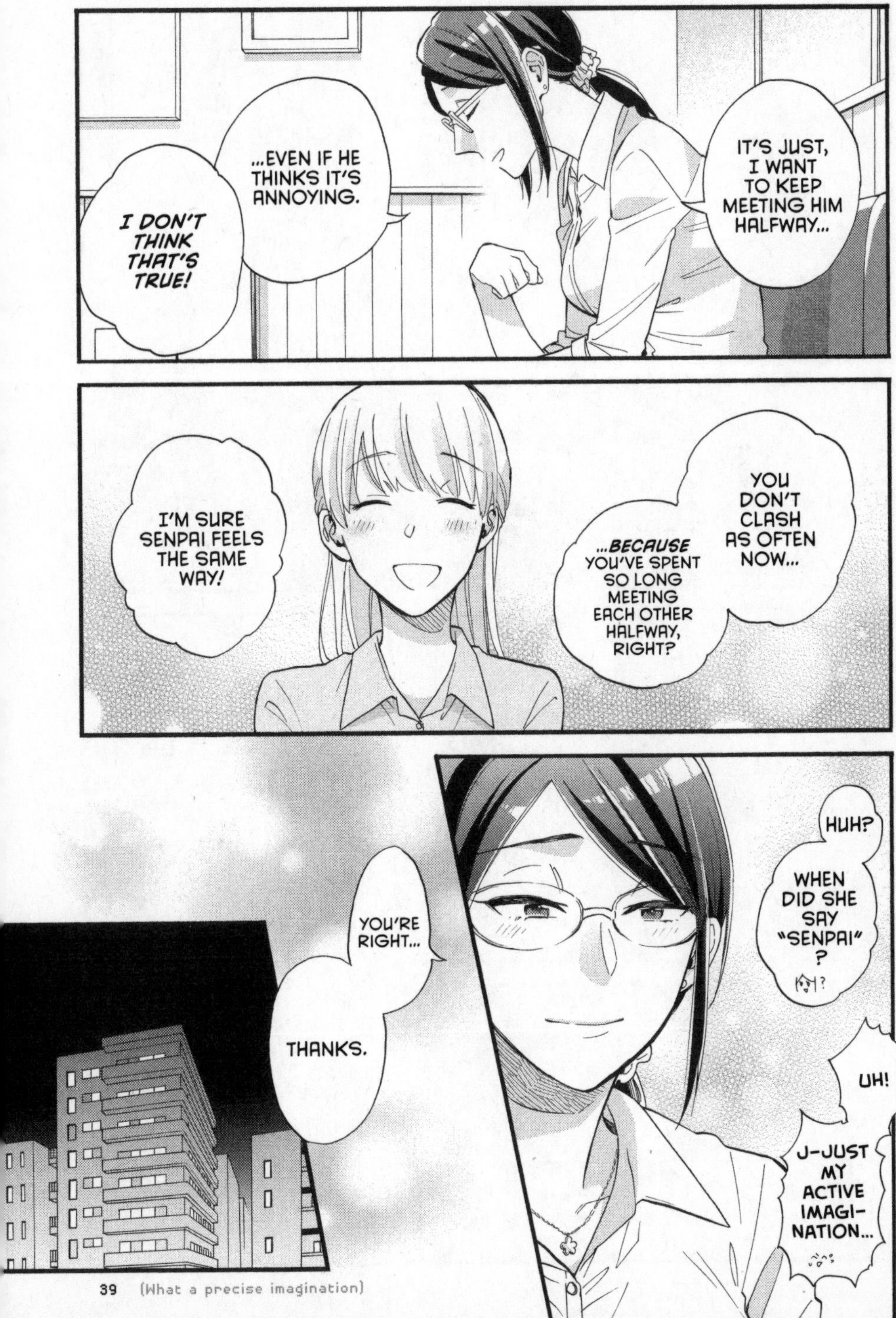
IT'S JUST, I WANT TO KEEP MEETING HIM HALFWAY...
...EVEN IF HE THINKS IT'S ANNOYING.
I DON'T THINK THAT'S TRUE!
YOU DON'T CLASH AS OFTEN NOW...
...*BECAUSE* YOU'VE SPENT SO LONG MEETING EACH OTHER HALFWAY, RIGHT?
I'M SURE SENPAI FEELS THE SAME WAY!
HUH?
WHEN DID SHE SAY "SENPAI" ?
YOU'RE RIGHT...
THANKS.
UH!
J-JUST MY ACTIVE IMAGI-NATION...

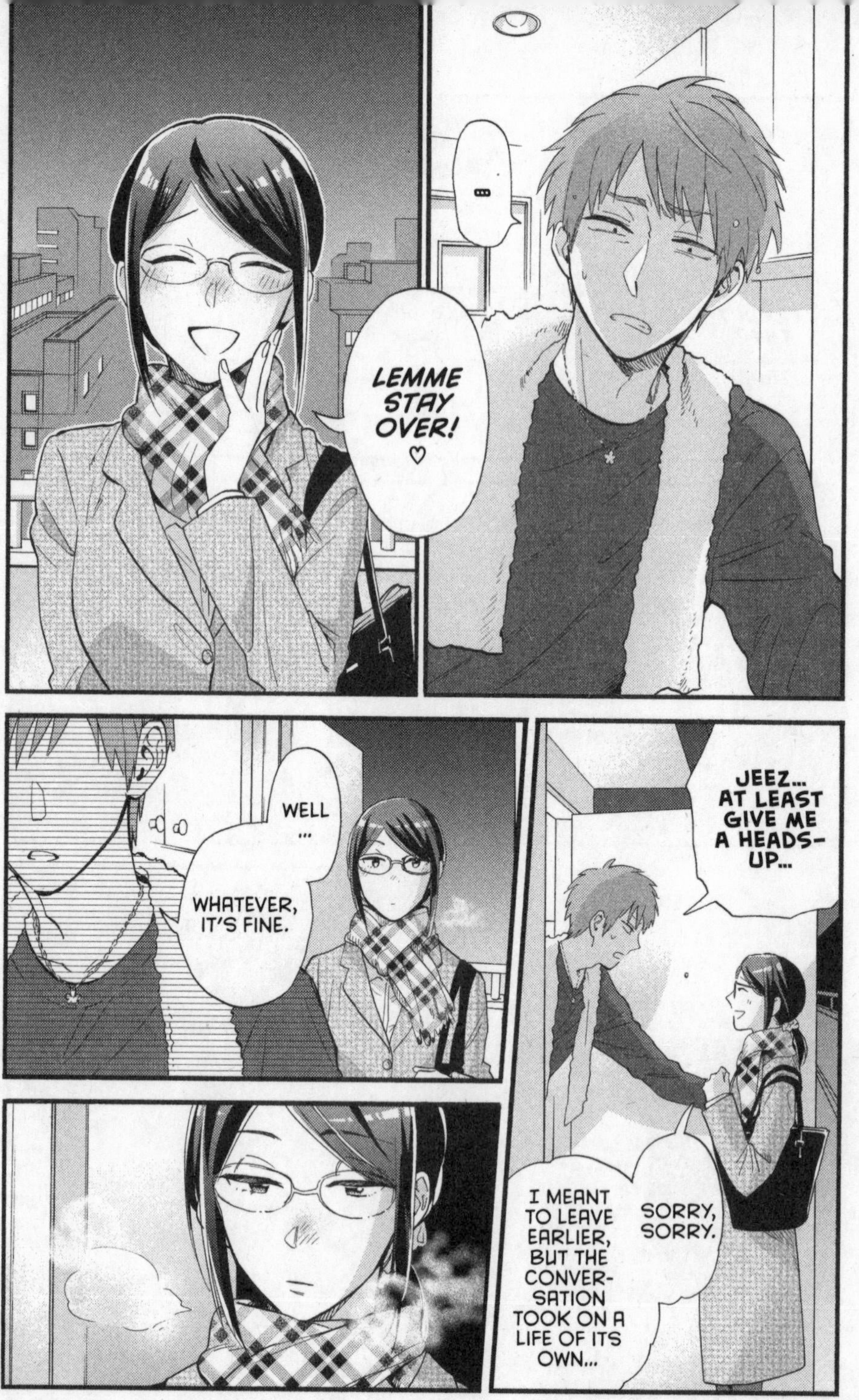
...
LEMME STAY OVER! ♡
JEEZ... AT LEAST GIVE ME A HEADS-UP...
SORRY, SORRY.
I MEANT TO LEAVE EARLIER, BUT THE CONVERSATION TOOK ON A LIFE OF ITS OWN...
WELL...
WHATEVER, IT'S FINE.

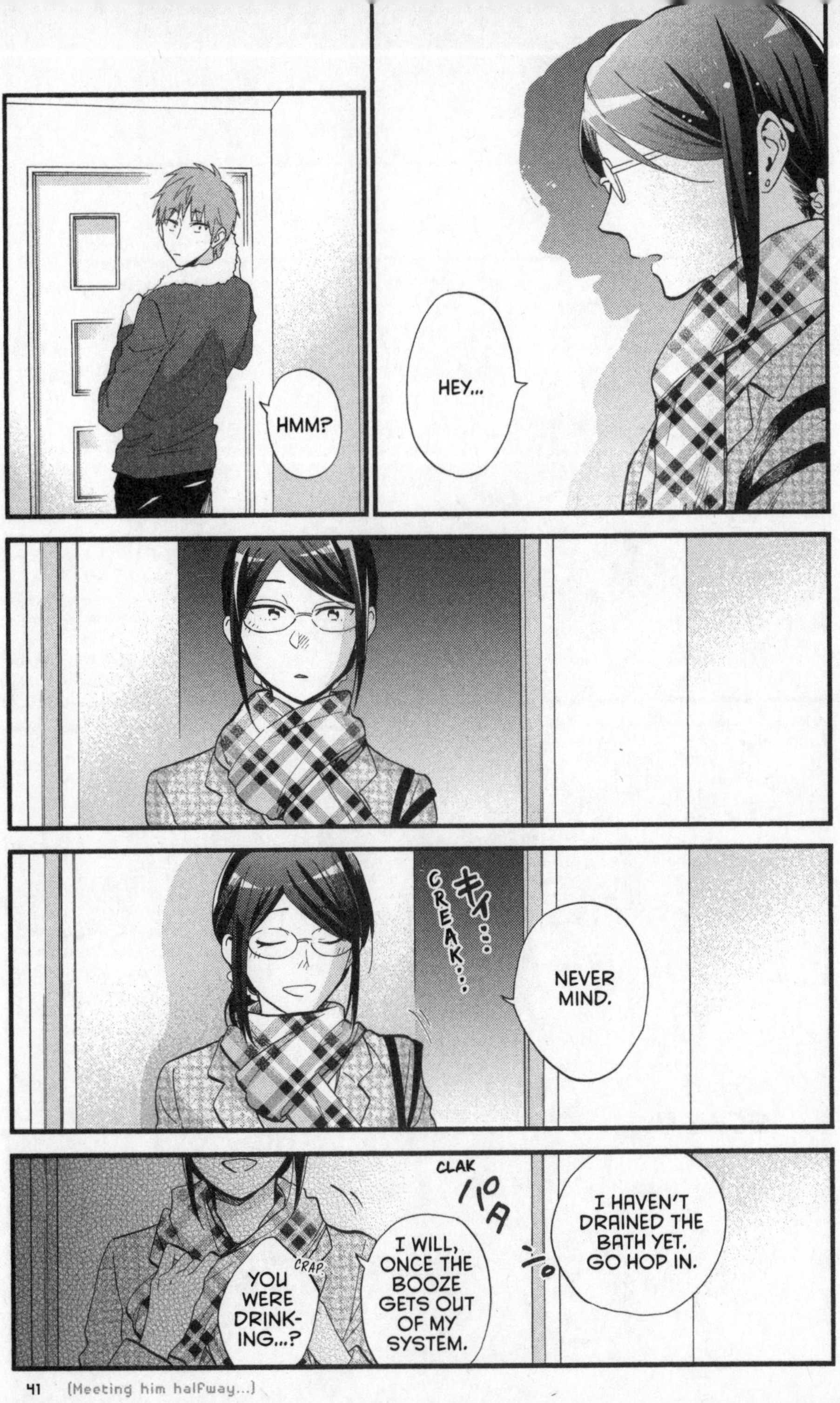
HEY...
HMM?
NEVER MIND.
キィ...
CREAK...
CLAK
パタ
I HAVEN'T DRAINED THE BATH YET. GO HOP IN.
I WILL, ONCE THE BOOZE GETS OUT OF MY SYSTEM.
CRAP.
YOU WERE DRINKING...?

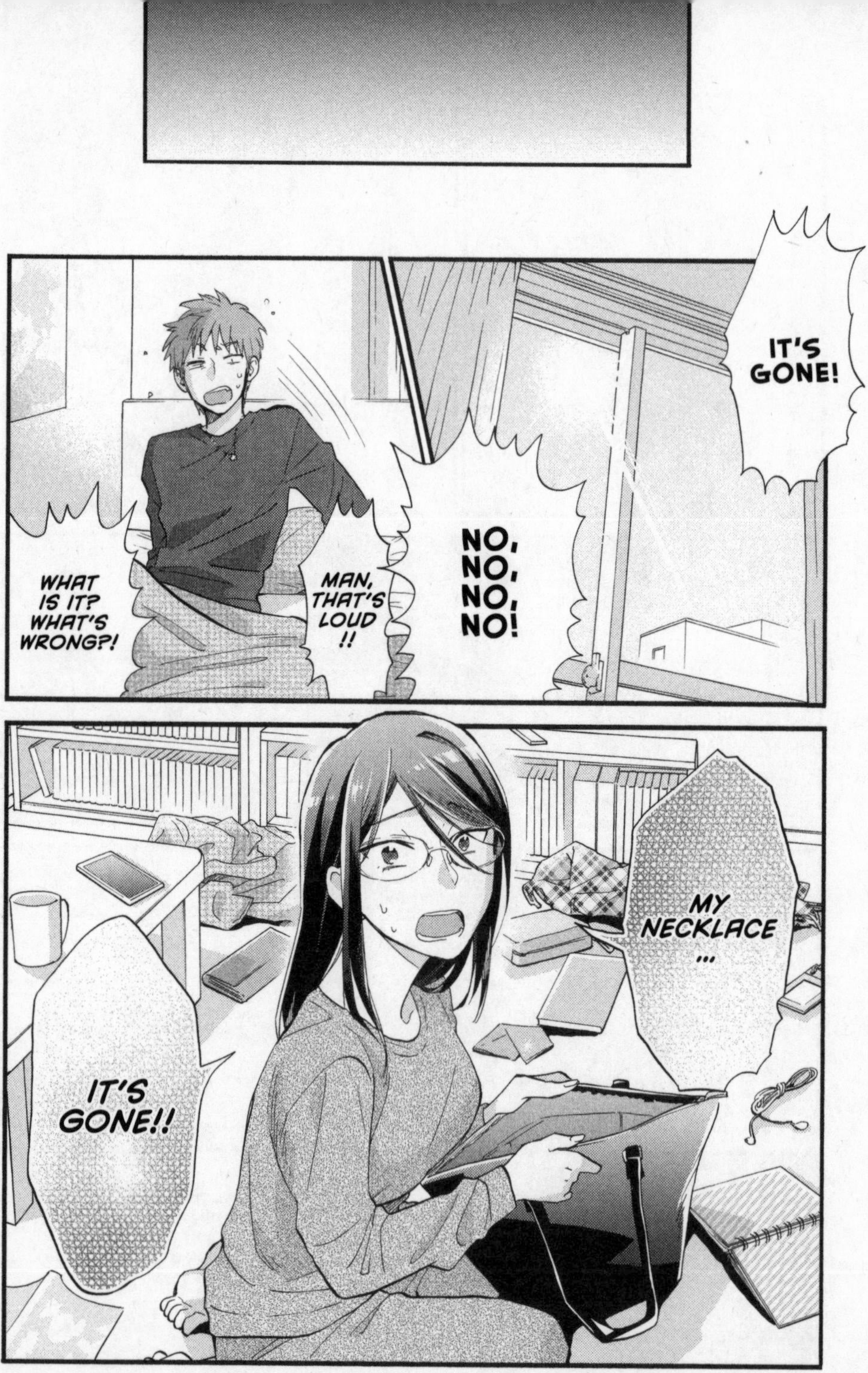
IT'S GONE!
NO, NO, NO, NO!
MAN, THAT'S LOUD !!
WHAT IS IT? WHAT'S WRONG?!
MY NECKLACE ...
IT'S GONE!!

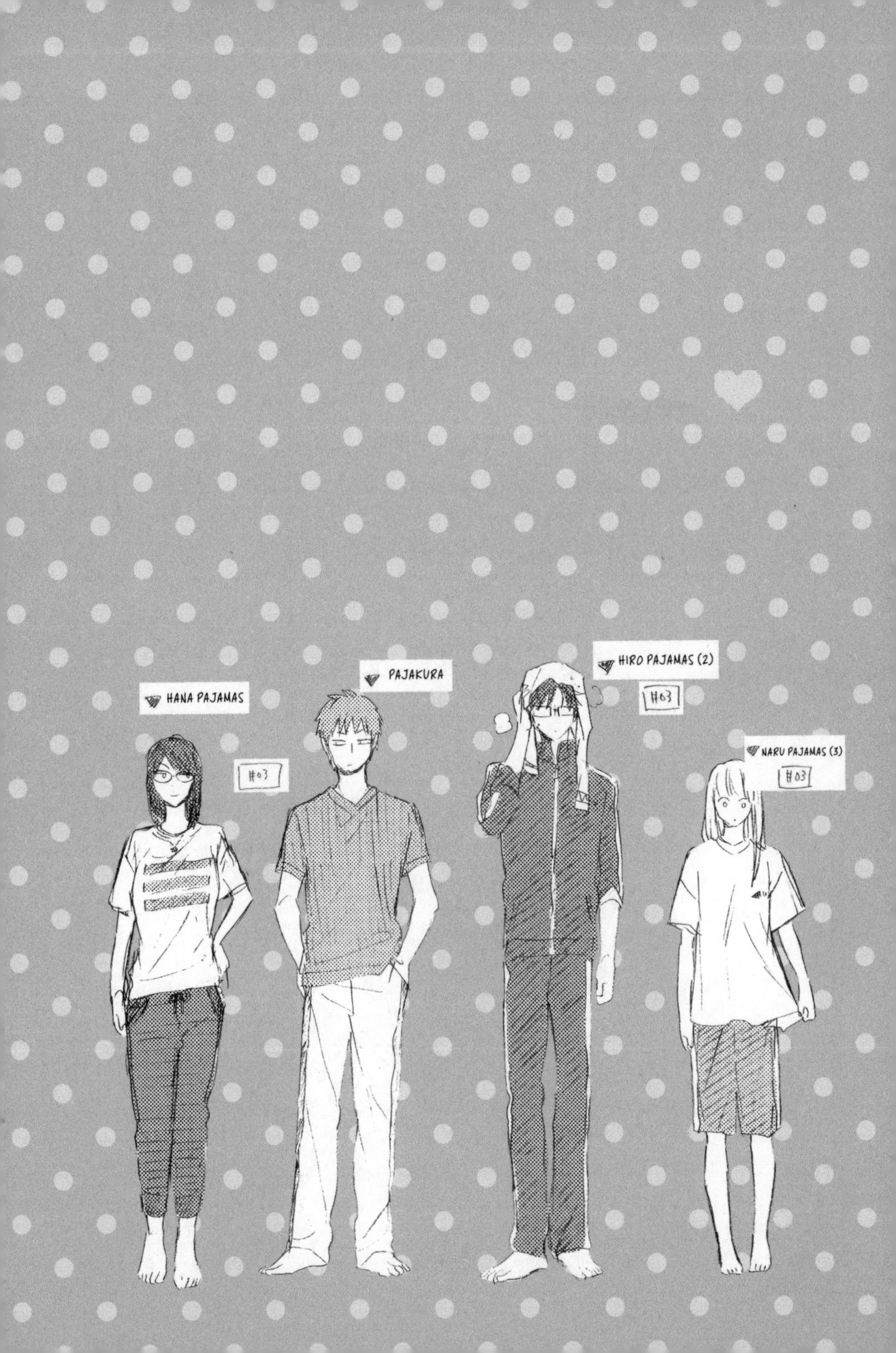
HANA PAJAMAS
#03
PAJAKURA
HIRO PAJAMAS (2)
#03
NARU PAJAMAS (3)
#03

CHARACTERS
MENU

小柳 花子

Hanako Koyanagi

DOESN'T EAT
SWEET THINGS OFTEN,
BUT LIKES BITTER CHOCOLATE.

SHE'S FINE EATING
DESSERTS, BUT DOESN'T
HAVE A PARTICULAR
THING FOR THEM, EITHER.
IT'S A HEALTHY
RELATIONSHIP.

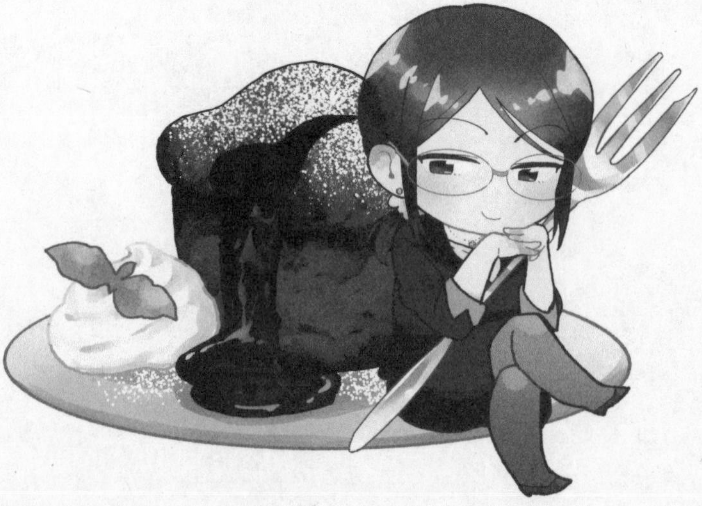

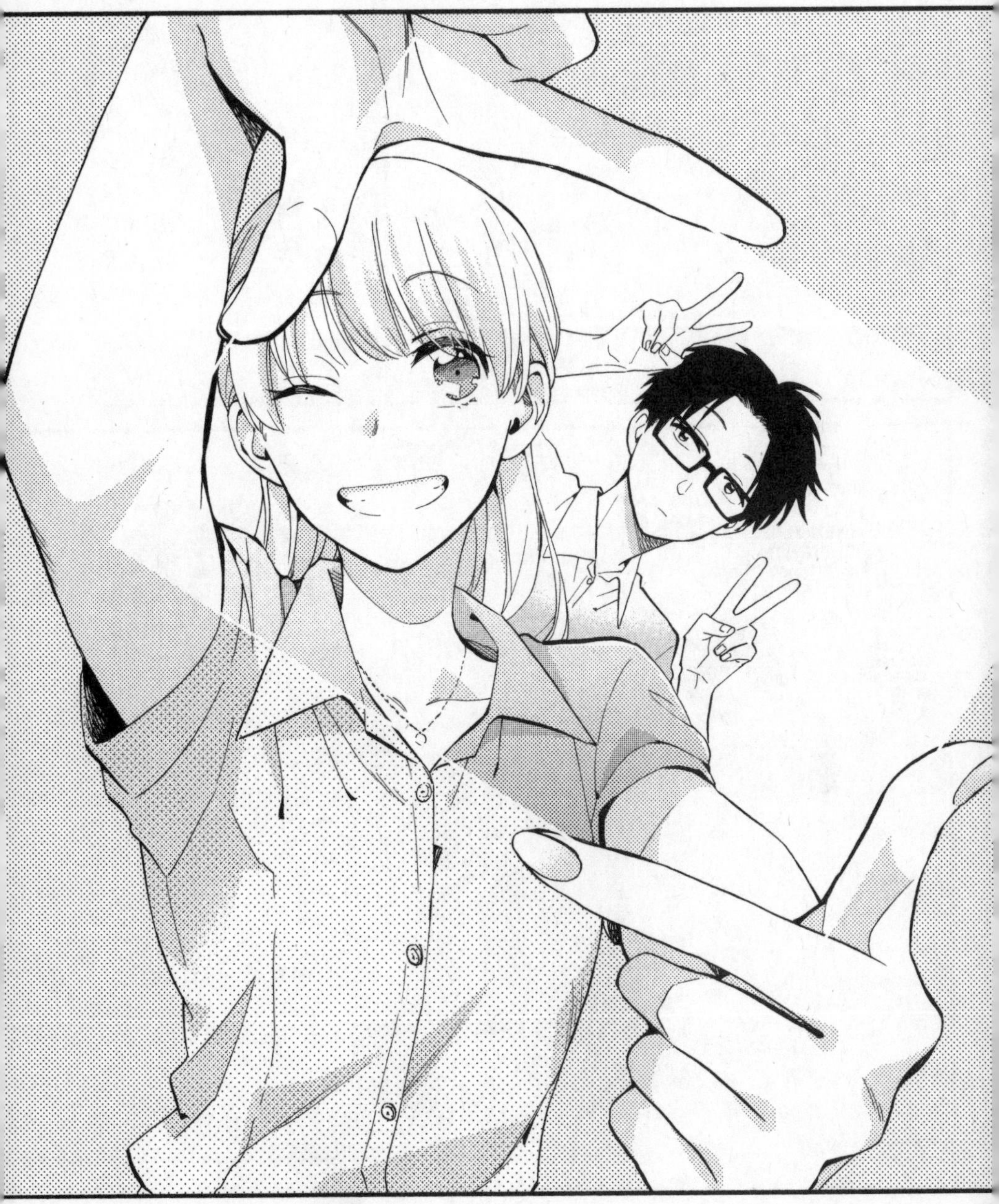

Episode....50

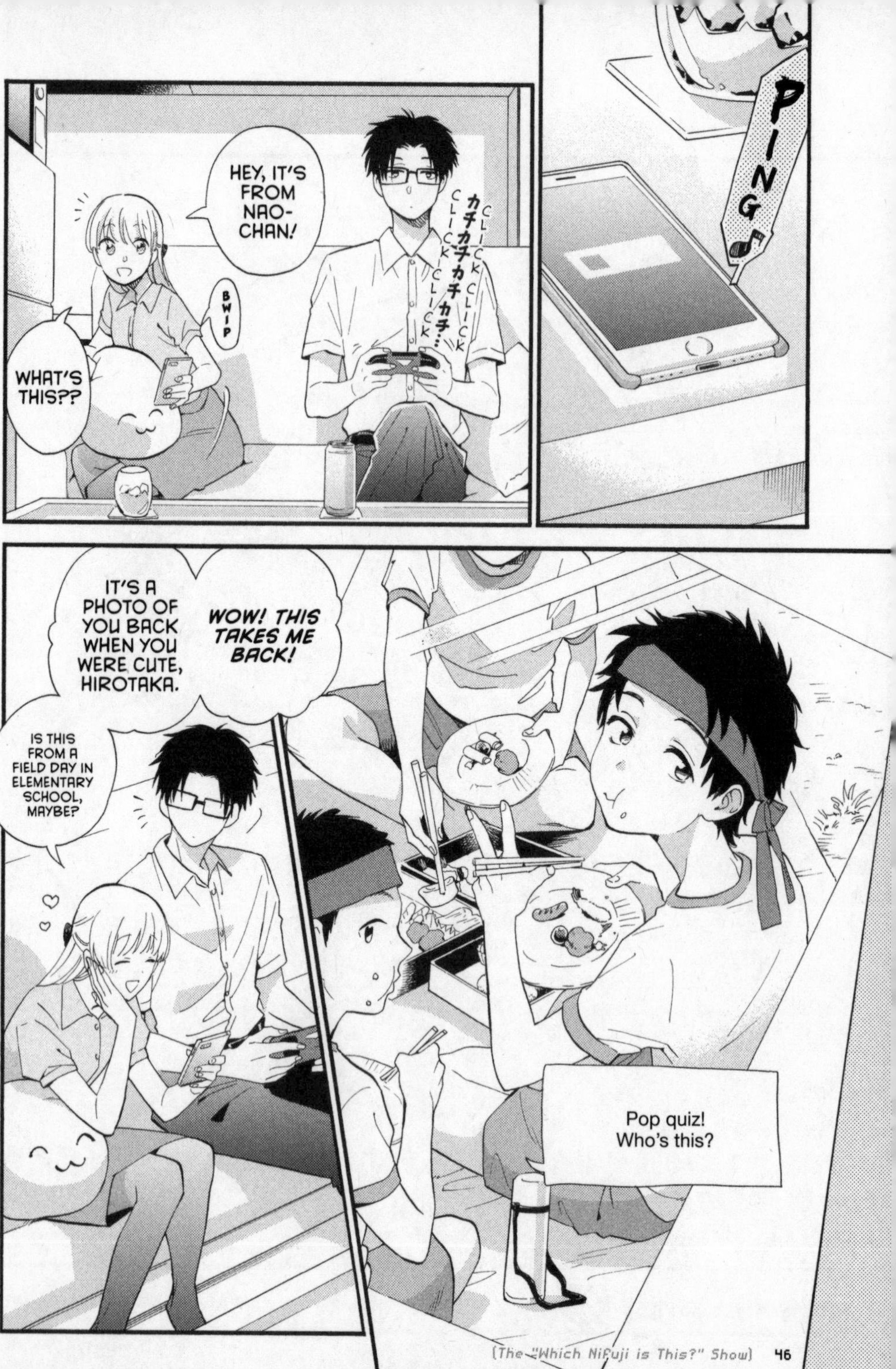
PING
HEY, IT'S FROM NAO-CHAN!
カチカチカチカチ…
CLICK CLICK CLICK CLICK
BWIP
WHAT'S THIS??
Pop quiz! Who's this?
WOW! THIS TAKES ME BACK!
IT'S A PHOTO OF YOU BACK WHEN YOU WERE CUTE, HIROTAKA.
IS THIS FROM A FIELD DAY IN ELEMENTARY SCHOOL, MAYBE?

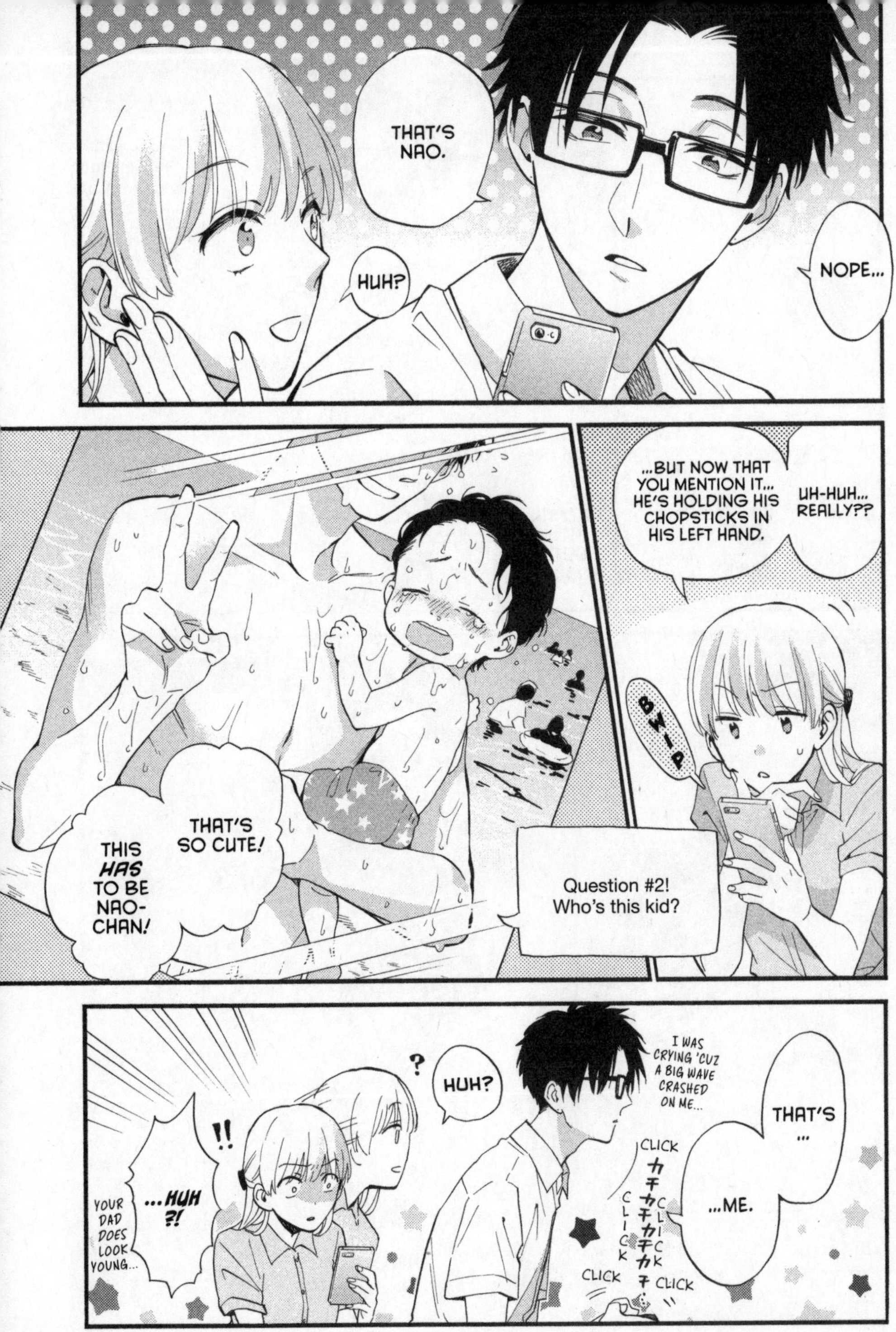
NOPE...
THAT'S NAO.
HUH?
UH-HUH... REALLY??
...BUT NOW THAT YOU MENTION IT... HE'S HOLDING HIS CHOPSTICKS IN HIS LEFT HAND.
BWIP
Question #2! Who's this kid?
THAT'S SO CUTE!
THIS *HAS* TO BE NAO-CHAN!
THAT'S ...
...ME.
I WAS CRYING 'CUZ A BIG WAVE CRASHED ON ME...
CLICK
CLICK
CLICK
CLICK
CLICK
HUH?
?
!!
...HUH?!
YOUR DAD DOES LOOK YOUNG...

I found an album while cleaning the house…
…so I'm sharing a trip down memory lane!
HIROTAKA, I GUESS YOU AND NAO-CHAN…
…REALLY *ARE* BLOOD-RELATED, HUH?
WHAT DID YOU THINK WE WERE BEFORE?
AND TELL NAO TO CUT IT OUT.
WHOA!
I'M IN THIS ONE… YIKES!
SHOW ME.
WOW, THIS TAKES ME BACK…
RIGHT?!
YOU HAVEN'T CHANGED AT ALL, HIROTAKA!
YOU'RE ALWAYS GAMING!
THE NARUMI IN THIS PHOTO…
…WASN'T ROTTEN* YET—
SHUT IT.

*Fujoshi literally means "rotten girl."

OH, THIS ONE...
IT MUST BE FROM THE CLASS TRIP IN MIDDLE SCHOOL.
WASN'T THAT FUN?
DO YOU REMEMBER WHO WAS IN YOUR GROUP?
SORRY.
THAT'S RIGHT, HE'S ALWAYS BEEN OBLIVIOUS ABOUT THE PEOPLE AROUND HIM...
IT'S JUST HOW HE IS...
NO.
WAIT...
I MIGHT REMEMBER...!
I THINK ...

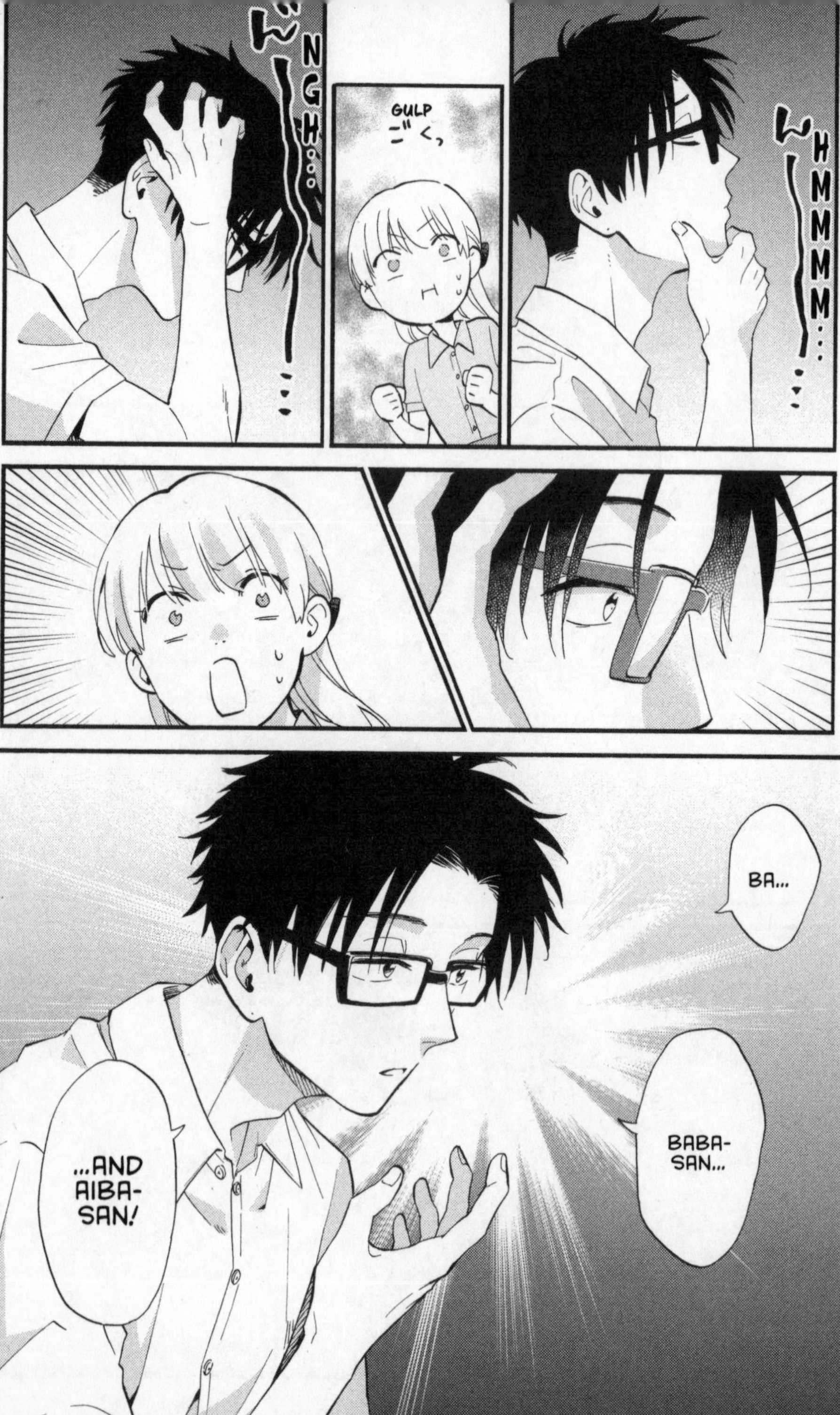
HMMMM...
GULP
ごくっ
NGH...
BA...
BABA-SAN...
...AND AIBA-SAN!

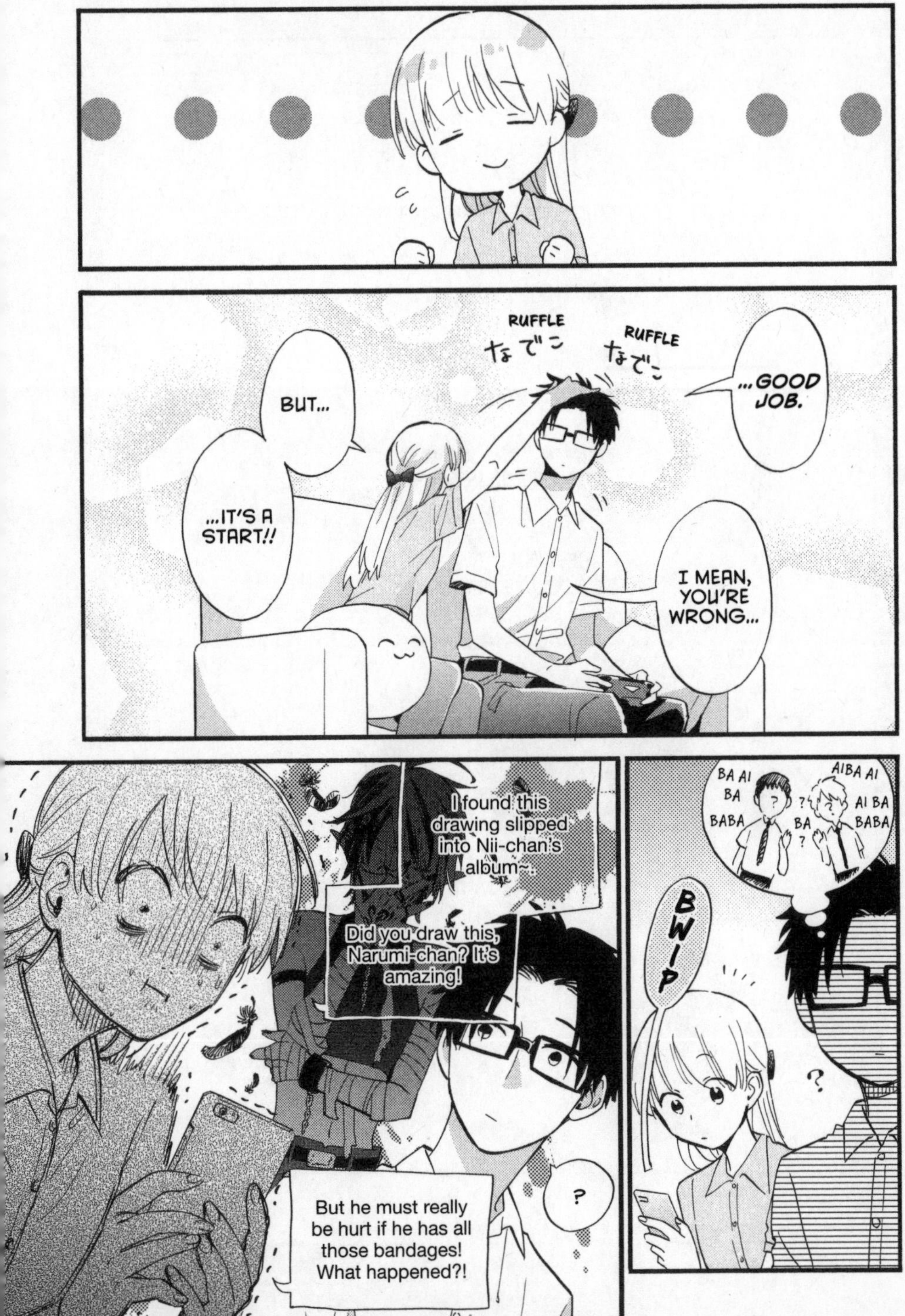
...GOOD JOB.
RUFFLE
なでこ
RUFFLE
なでこ
I MEAN, YOU'RE WRONG...
BUT...
...IT'S A START!!
BA AI BA BABA
?
BA ?
AIBA AI
?
AI BA BABA
BWIP
?
I found this drawing slipped into Nii-chan's album~.
Did you draw this, Narumi-chan? It's amazing!
?
But he must really be hurt if he has all those bandages! What happened?!

CHARACTERS

MENU

樺倉太郎

Taro Kabakura

HE MAY NOT LOOK IT, BUT HE LOVES SWEET THINGS.

HE WOULD TOTALLY GO TO SWEETS PARADISE IF ASKED. BUT KOYANAGI NEVER ASKS.

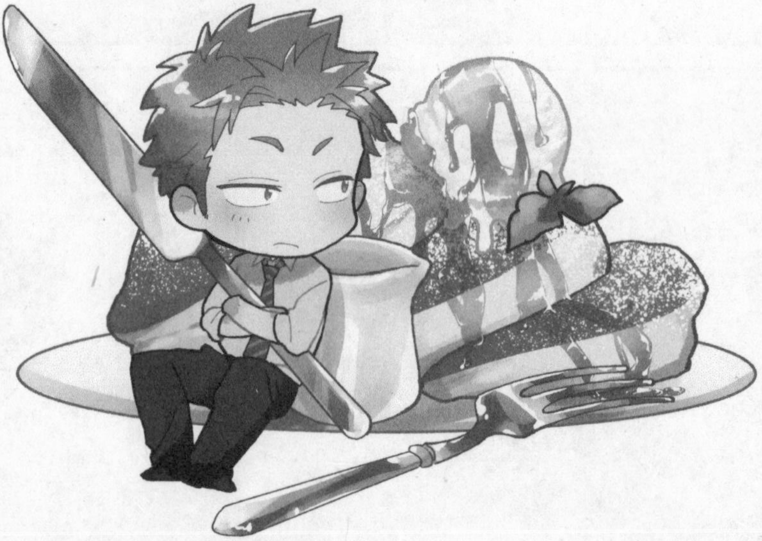

Episode... 51

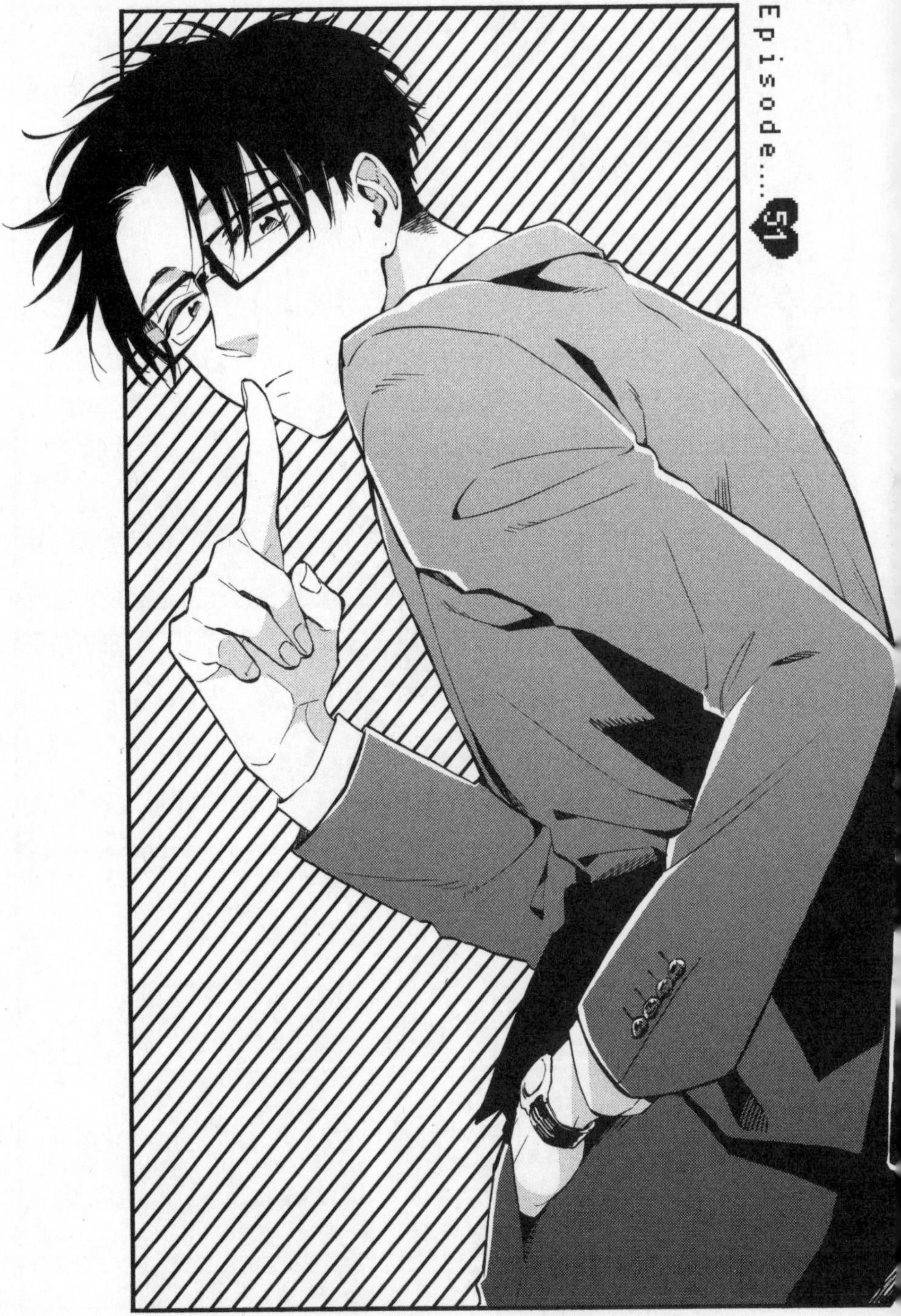

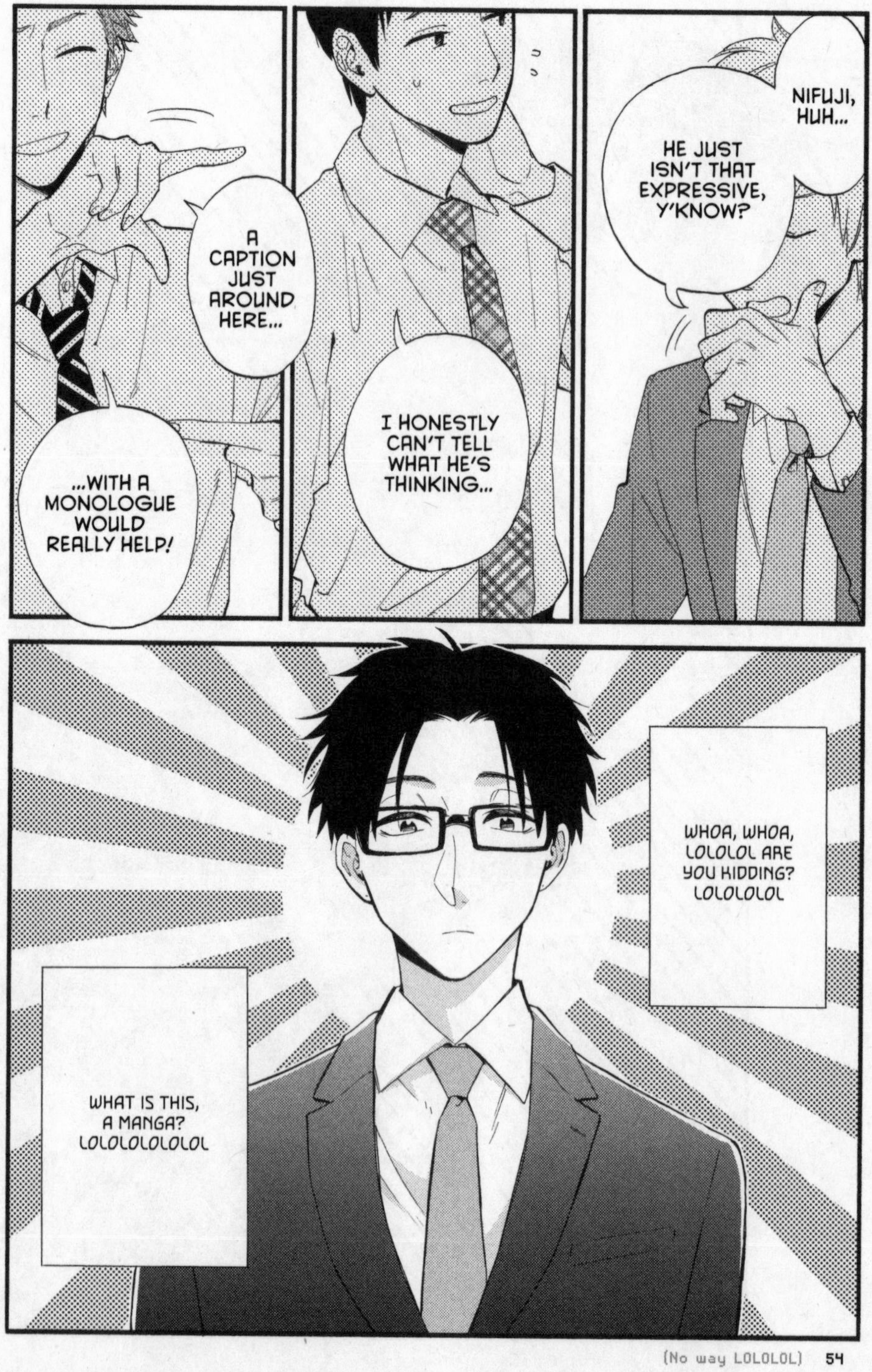
NIFUJI, HUH...
HE JUST ISN'T THAT EXPRESSIVE, Y'KNOW?
I HONESTLY CAN'T TELL WHAT HE'S THINKING...
A CAPTION JUST AROUND HERE...
...WITH A MONOLOGUE WOULD REALLY HELP!
WHOA, WHOA, LOLOLOL ARE YOU KIDDING? LOLOLOLOL
WHAT IS THIS, A MANGA? LOLOLOLOLOLOL

(No way LOLOLOL)

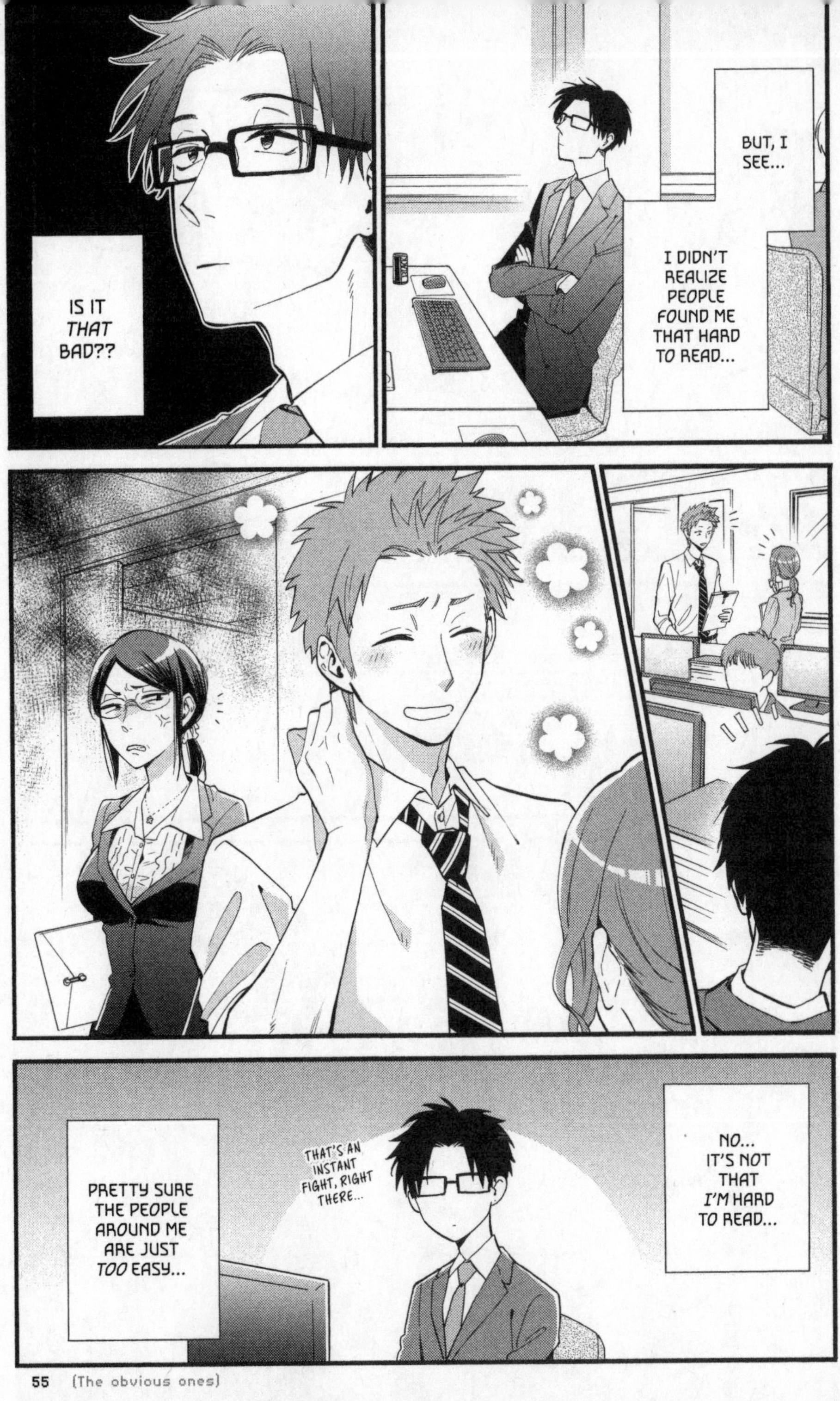
BUT, I SEE...
I DIDN'T REALIZE PEOPLE FOUND ME THAT HARD TO READ...
IS IT *THAT* BAD??
NO... IT'S NOT THAT *I'M* HARD TO READ...
THAT'S AN INSTANT FIGHT, RIGHT THERE...
PRETTY SURE THE PEOPLE AROUND ME ARE JUST *TOO* EASY...

 (The obvious ones)

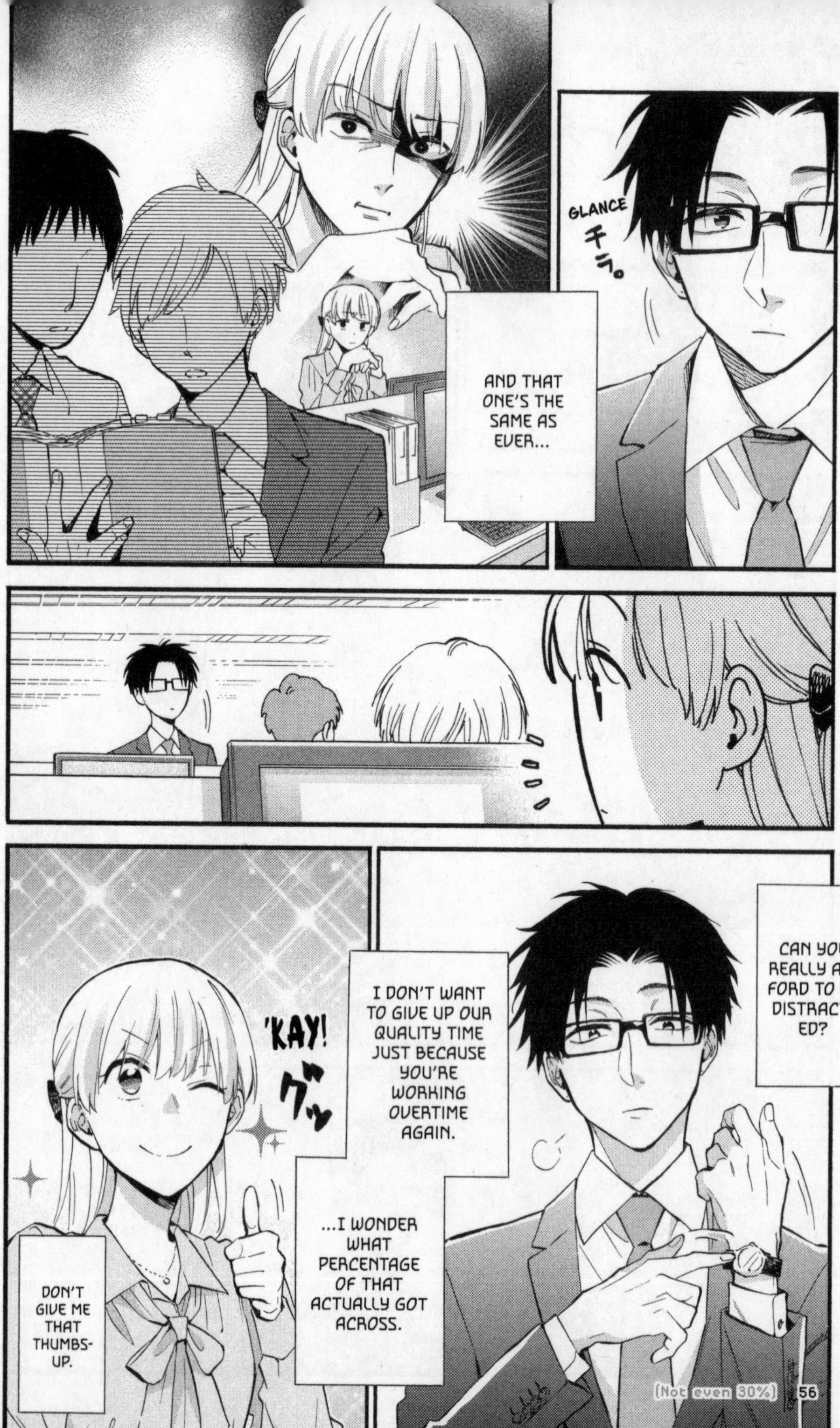
GLANCE
チラ。
AND THAT ONE'S THE SAME AS EVER...
CAN YOU REALLY AF-FORD TO BE DISTRACT-ED?
I DON'T WANT TO GIVE UP OUR QUALITY TIME JUST BECAUSE YOU'RE WORKING OVERTIME AGAIN.
'KAY!
グッ
...I WONDER WHAT PERCENTAGE OF THAT ACTUALLY GOT ACROSS.
DON'T GIVE ME THAT THUMBS-UP.
[Not even 30%]

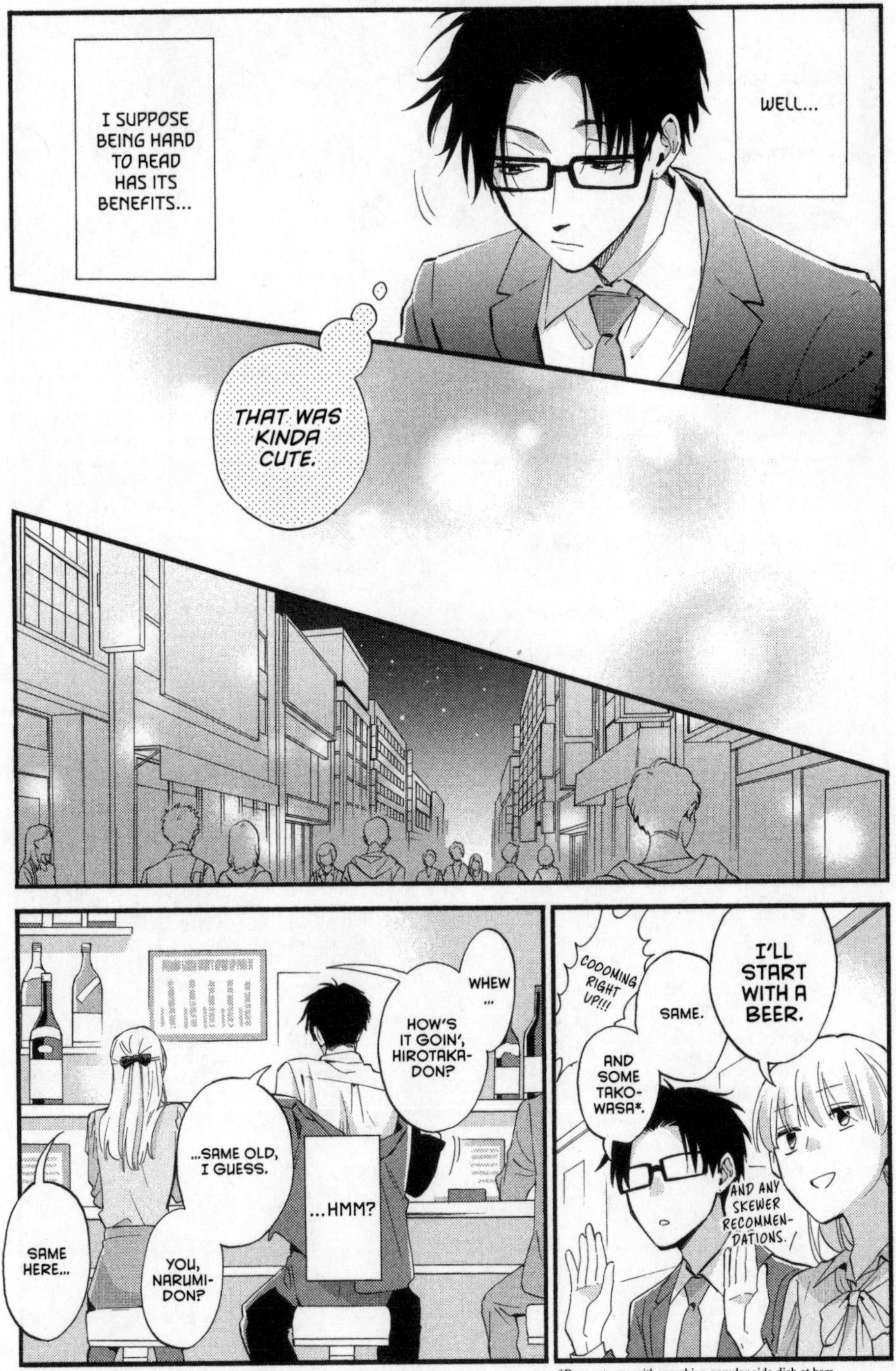
WELL...
I SUPPOSE BEING HARD TO READ HAS ITS BENEFITS...
THAT WAS KINDA CUTE.
I'LL START WITH A BEER.
SAME.
AND SOME TAKO-WASA*.
AND ANY SKEWER RECOMMENDATIONS.
COOOMING RIGHT UP!!!
WHEW...
HOW'S IT GOIN', HIROTAKA-DON?
...SAME OLD, I GUESS.
...HMM?
YOU, NARUMI-DON?
SAME HERE...

*Raw octopus with wasabi; a popular side dish at bars.

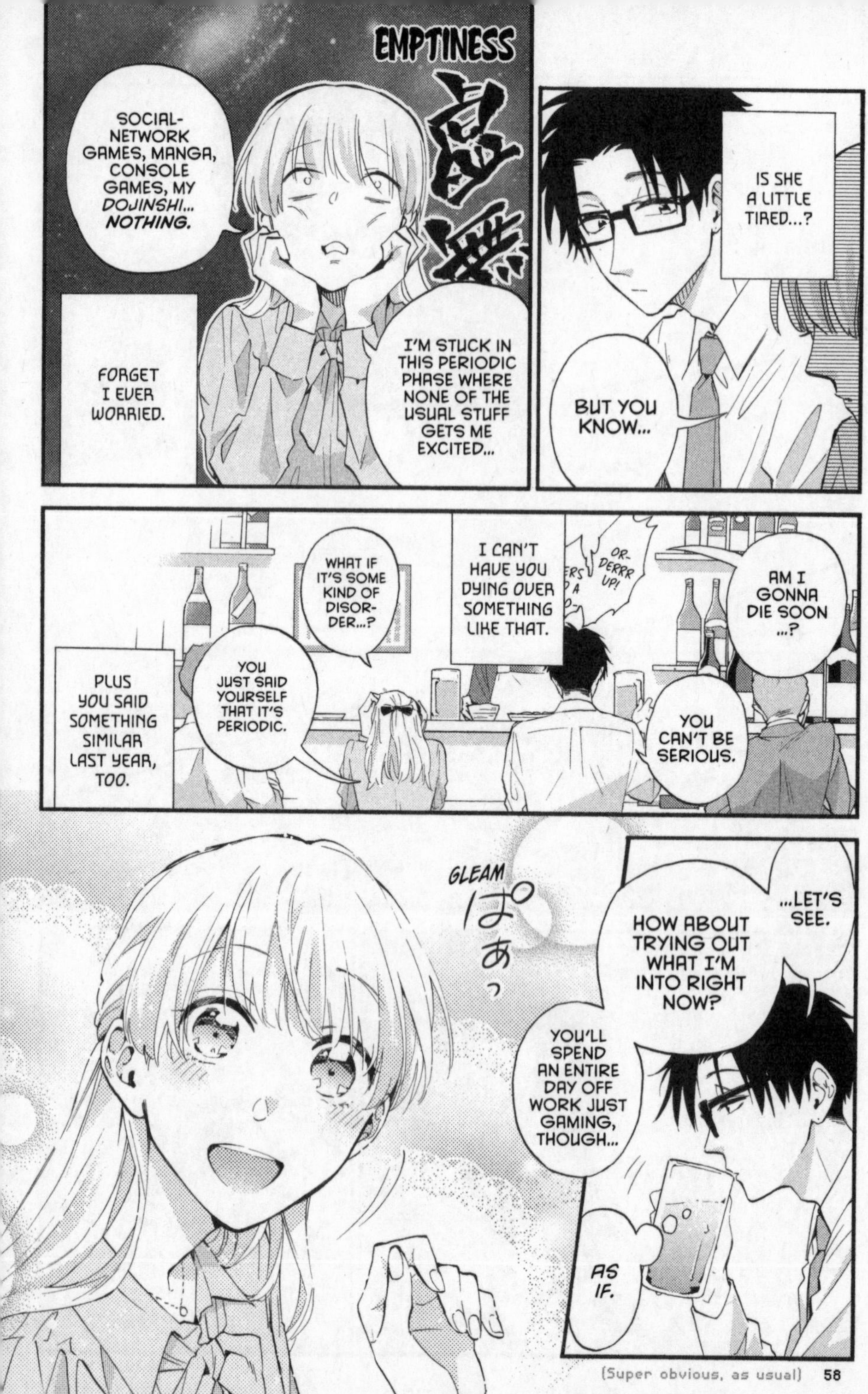
IS SHE A LITTLE TIRED...?
BUT YOU KNOW...
EMPTINESS
SOCIAL-NETWORK GAMES, MANGA, CONSOLE GAMES, MY *DOJINSHI*... ***NOTHING.***
I'M STUCK IN THIS PERIODIC PHASE WHERE NONE OF THE USUAL STUFF GETS ME EXCITED...
FORGET I EVER WORRIED.
AM I GONNA DIE SOON ...?
YOU CAN'T BE SERIOUS.
OR-DERRR UP!
I CAN'T HAVE YOU DYING OVER SOMETHING LIKE THAT.
WHAT IF IT'S SOME KIND OF DISOR-DER...?
YOU JUST SAID YOURSELF THAT IT'S PERIODIC.
PLUS YOU SAID SOMETHING SIMILAR LAST YEAR, TOO.
...LET'S SEE.
HOW ABOUT TRYING OUT WHAT I'M INTO RIGHT NOW?
YOU'LL SPEND AN ENTIRE DAY OFF WORK JUST GAMING, THOUGH...
AS IF.
GLEAM
ぱあっ

(Super obvious, as usual)

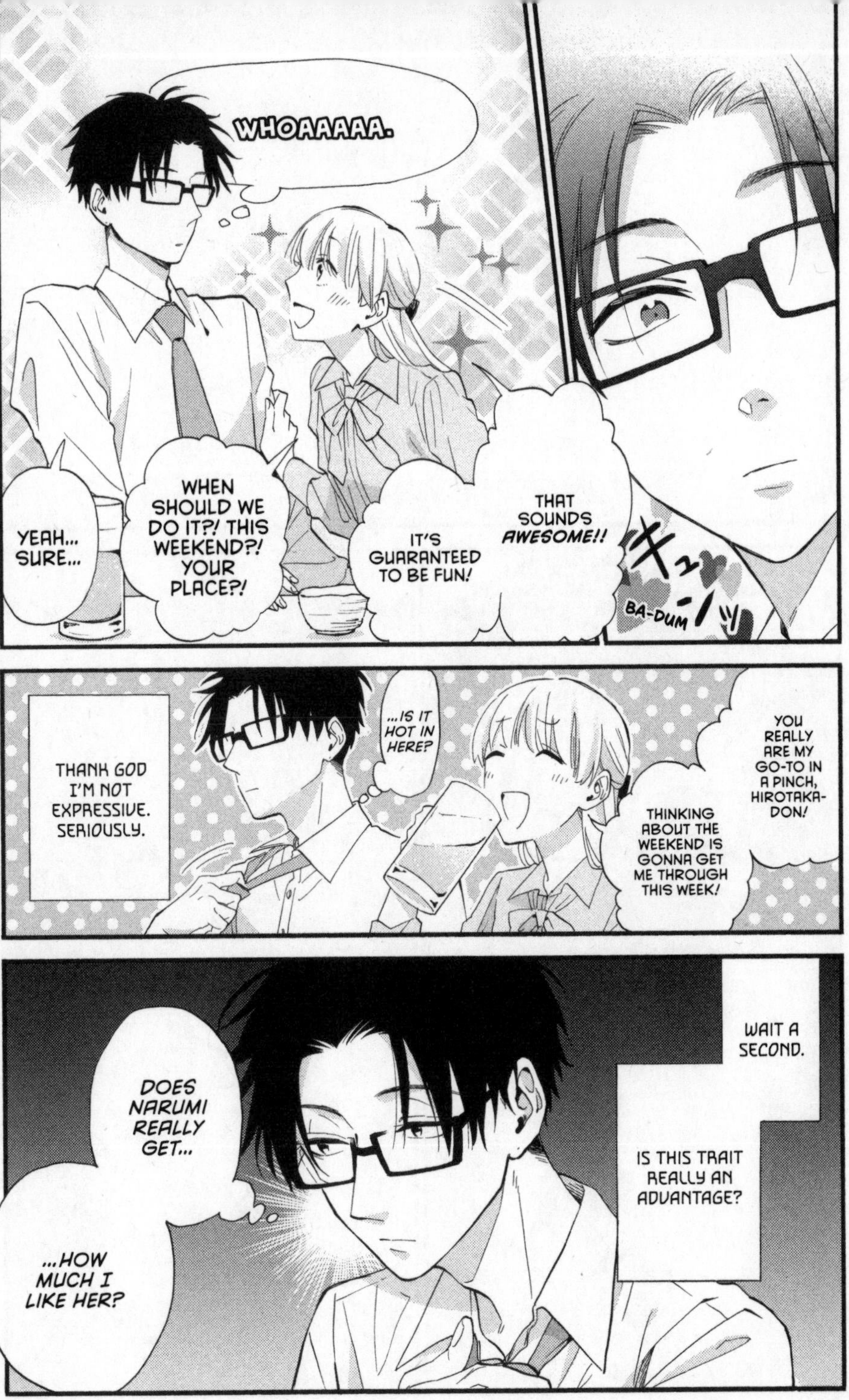
THAT SOUNDS AWESOME!!
BA-DUM
WHOAAAAA.
IT'S GUARANTEED TO BE FUN!
WHEN SHOULD WE DO IT?! THIS WEEKEND?! YOUR PLACE?!
YEAH... SURE...
YOU REALLY ARE MY GO-TO IN A PINCH, HIROTAKA-DON!
THINKING ABOUT THE WEEKEND IS GONNA GET ME THROUGH THIS WEEK!
...IS IT HOT IN HERE?
THANK GOD I'M NOT EXPRESSIVE. SERIOUSLY.
WAIT A SECOND.
IS THIS TRAIT REALLY AN ADVANTAGE?
DOES NARUMI REALLY GET...
...HOW MUCH I LIKE HER?

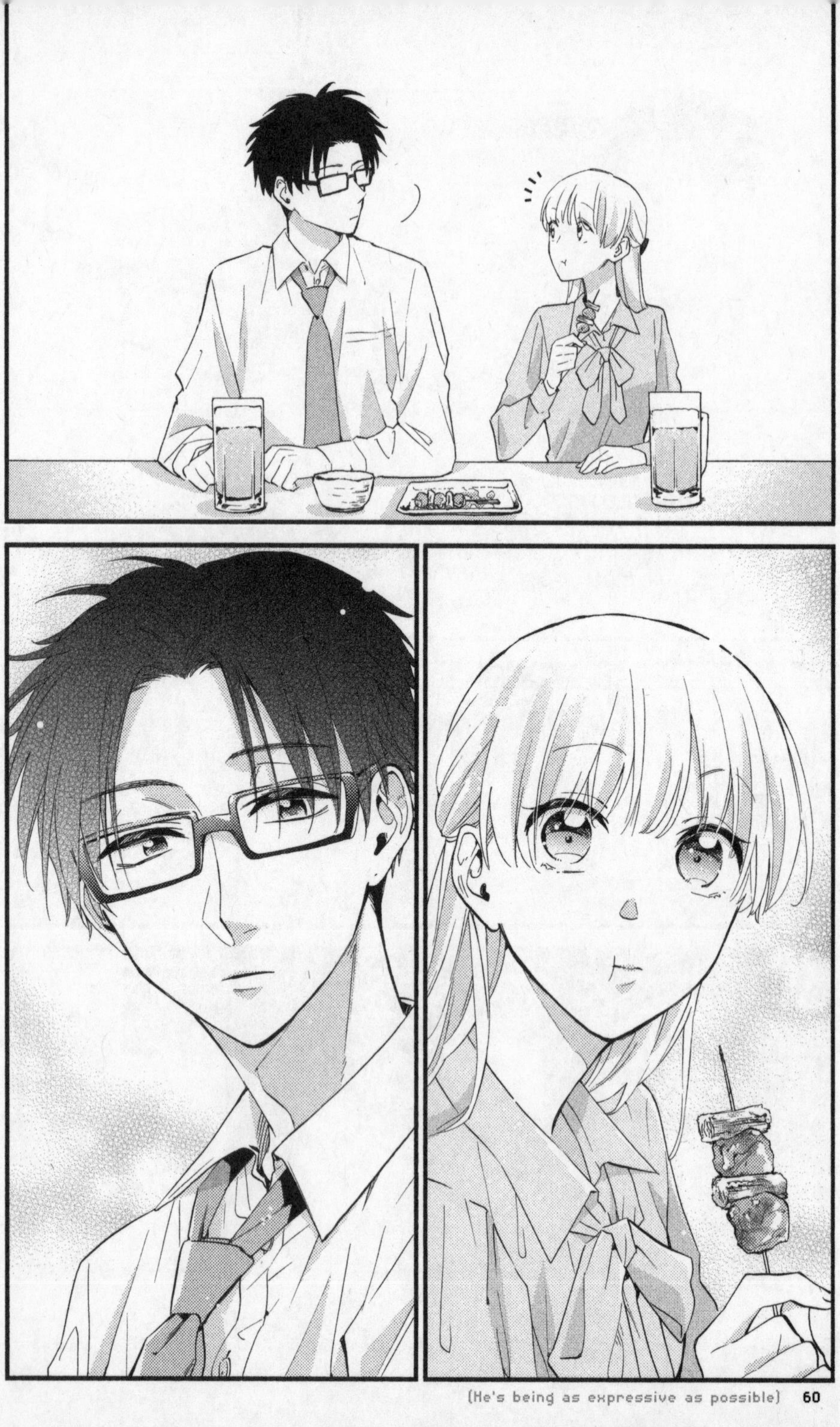

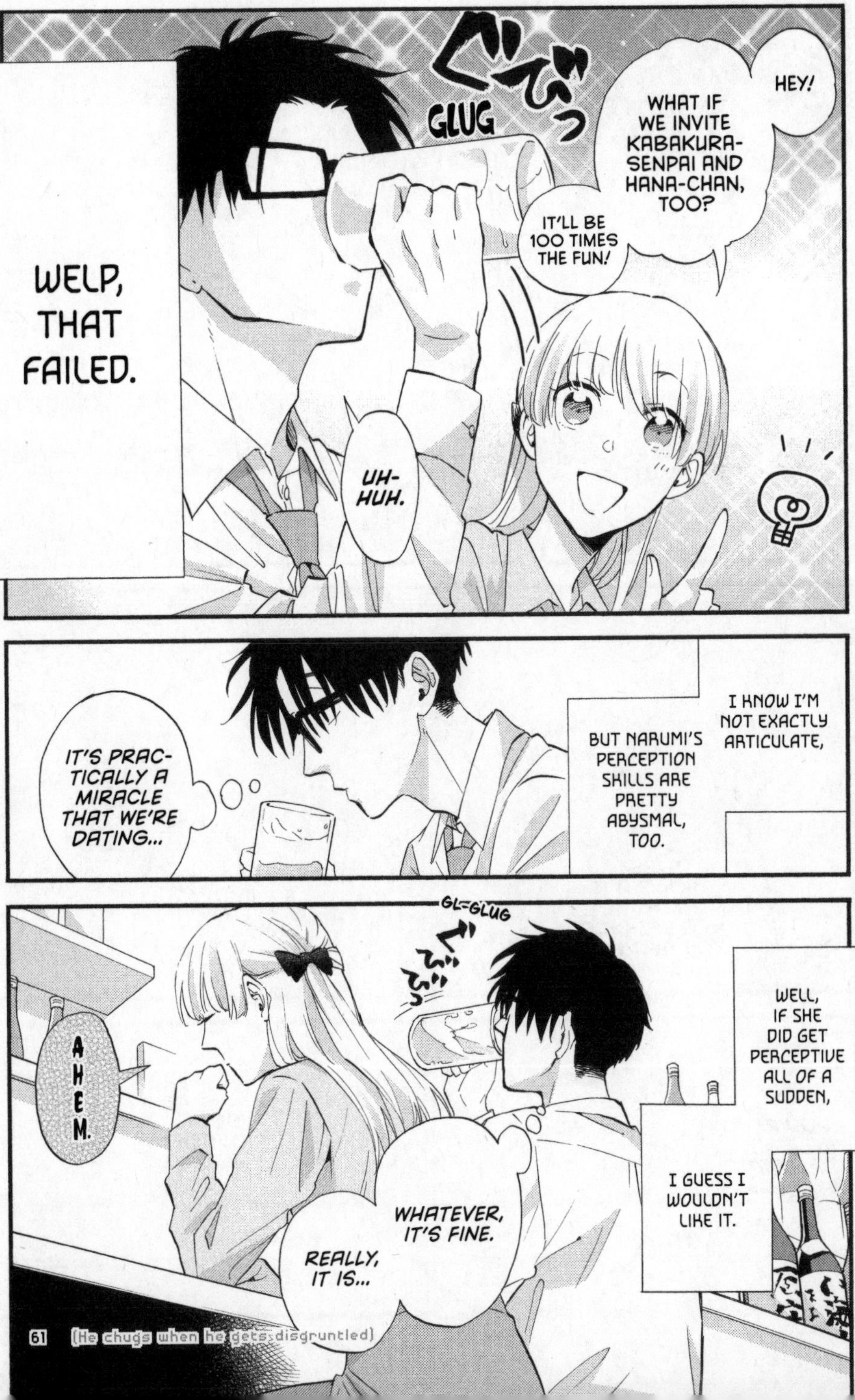
HEY!
WHAT IF WE INVITE KABAKURA-SENPAI AND HANA-CHAN, TOO?
IT'LL BE 100 TIMES THE FUN!
GLUG
UH-HUH.
WELP, THAT FAILED.
I KNOW I'M NOT EXACTLY ARTICULATE,
BUT NARUMI'S PERCEPTION SKILLS ARE PRETTY ABYSMAL, TOO.
IT'S PRACTICALLY A MIRACLE THAT WE'RE DATING...
WELL, IF SHE DID GET PERCEPTIVE ALL OF A SUDDEN,
I GUESS I WOULDN'T LIKE IT.
GL-GLUG
WHATEVER, IT'S FINE.
REALLY, IT IS...
AHEM.
(He chugs when he gets disgruntled)

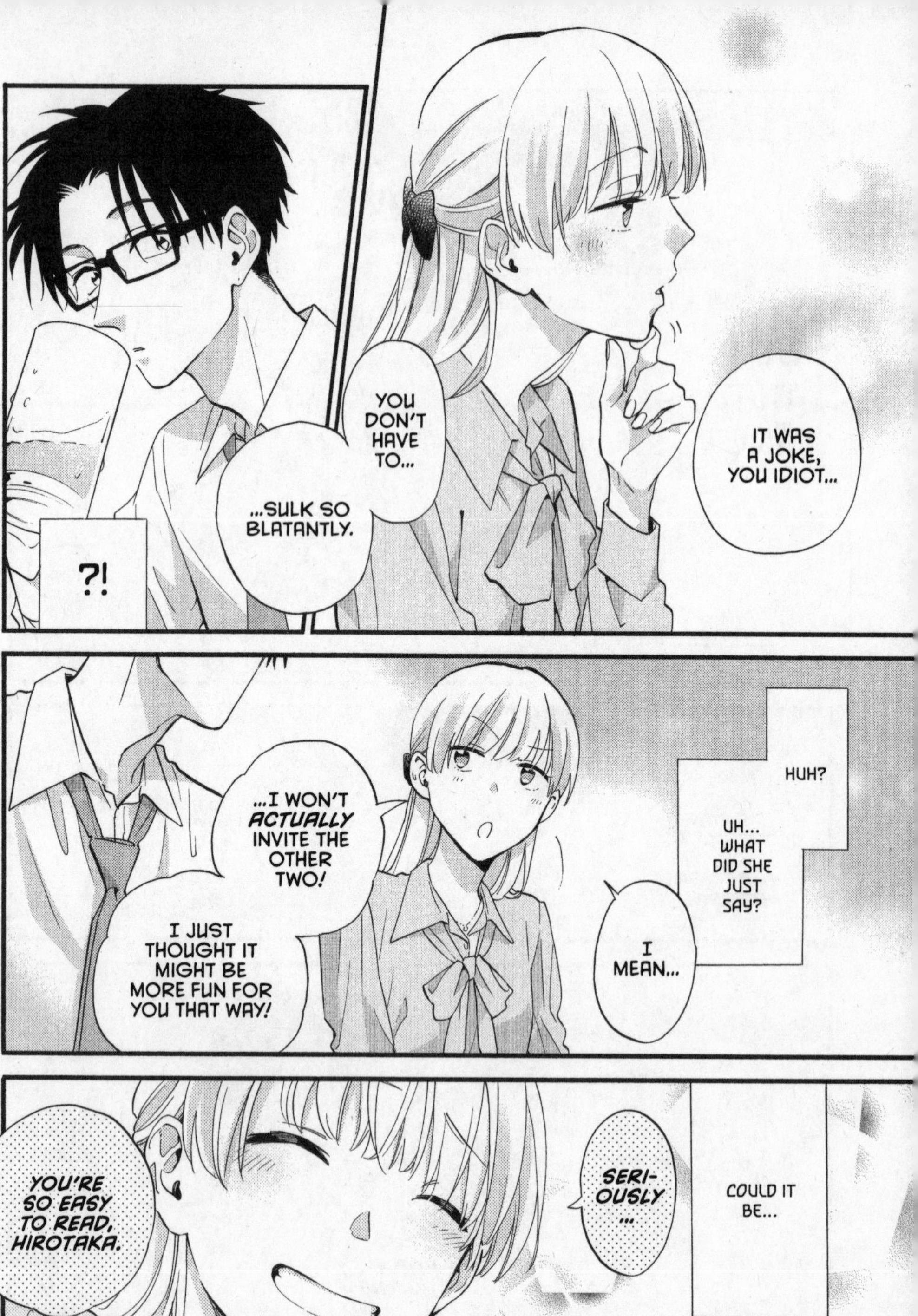
IT WAS A JOKE, YOU IDIOT...
YOU DON'T HAVE TO...
...SULK SO BLATANTLY.
?!
HUH?
UH... WHAT DID SHE JUST SAY?
I MEAN...
...I WON'T *ACTUALLY* INVITE THE OTHER TWO!
I JUST THOUGHT IT MIGHT BE MORE FUN FOR YOU THAT WAY!
COULD IT BE...
SERIOUSLY...
YOU'RE SO EASY TO READ, HIROTAKA.

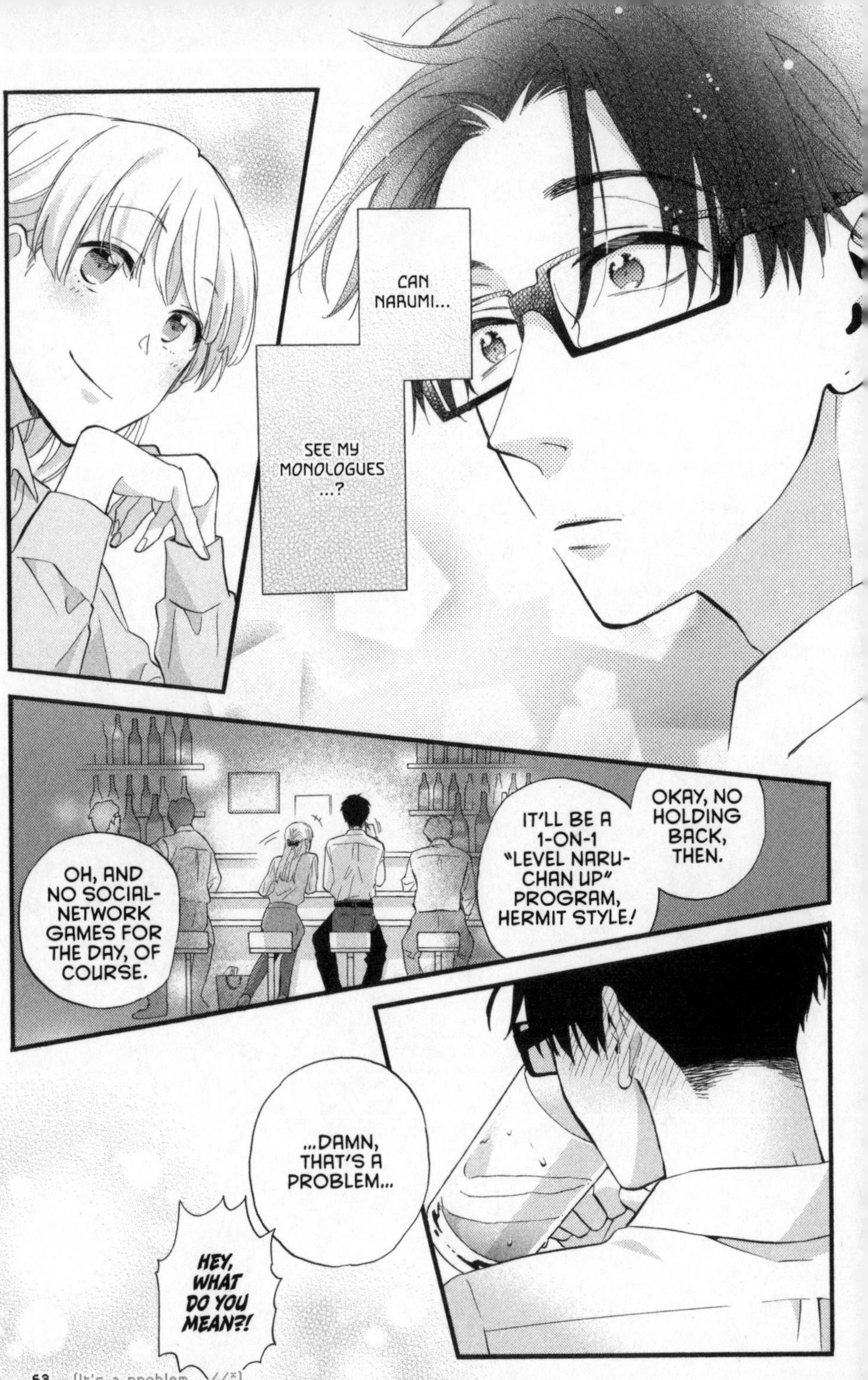
CAN NARUMI...
SEE MY MONOLOGUES ...?
OKAY, NO HOLDING BACK, THEN.
IT'LL BE A 1-ON-1 "LEVEL NARU-CHAN UP" PROGRAM, HERMIT STYLE!
OH, AND NO SOCIAL-NETWORK GAMES FOR THE DAY, OF COURSE.
...DAMN, THAT'S A PROBLEM...
HEY, WHAT DO YOU MEAN?!

 (It's a problem... //x)

*The two slashes imply blushing.

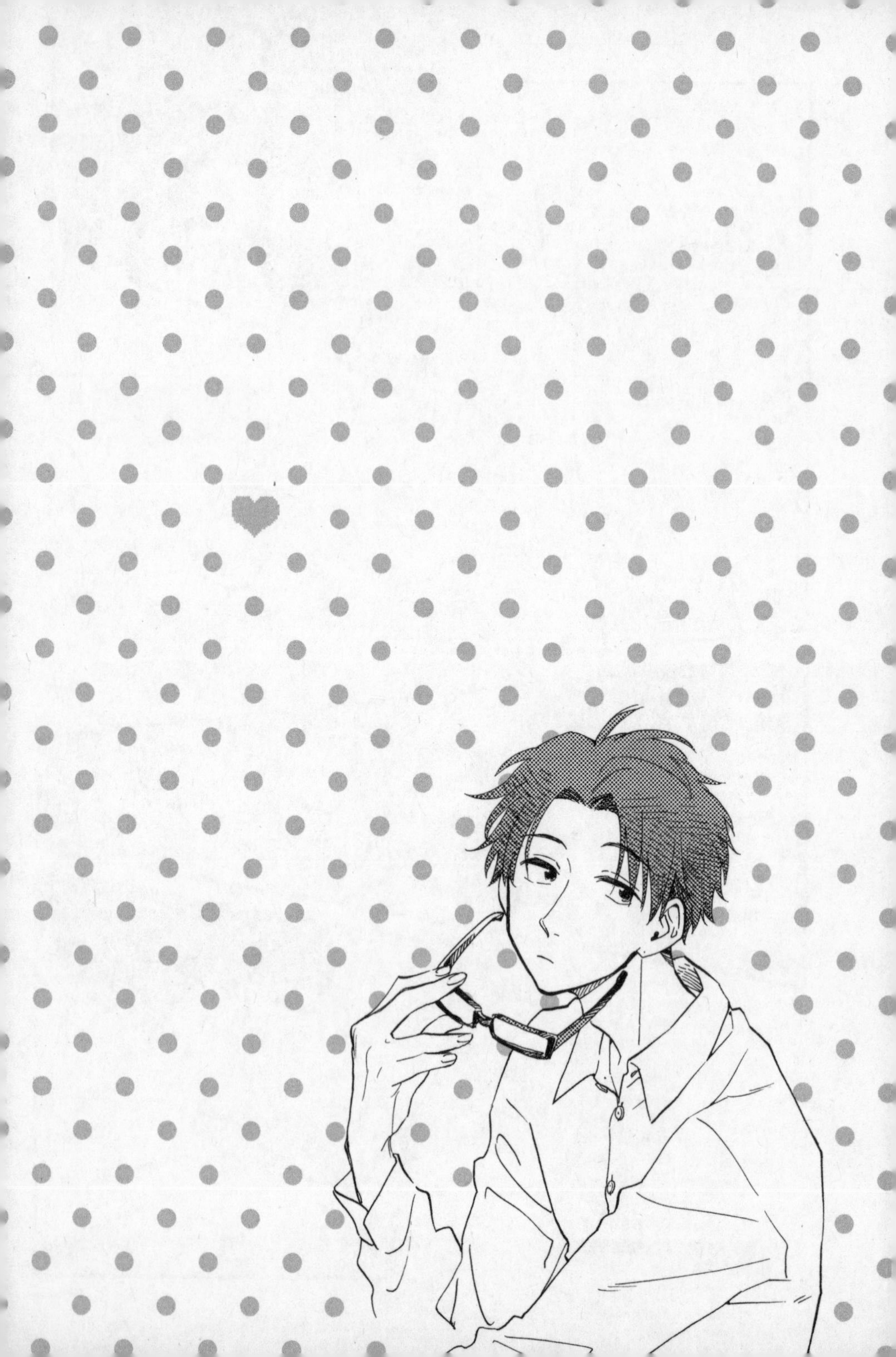

CHARACTERS
MENU

二藤 尚哉

Naoya Nifuji

LOVES SWEET THINGS!
LOVES BOTH MAKING AND
EATING SWEETS!

APPARENTLY, HIS COOKIES
ARE BETTER THAN
STORE-BOUGHT ONES
(ACCORDING TO
YOKKUN/KEN-CHAN).

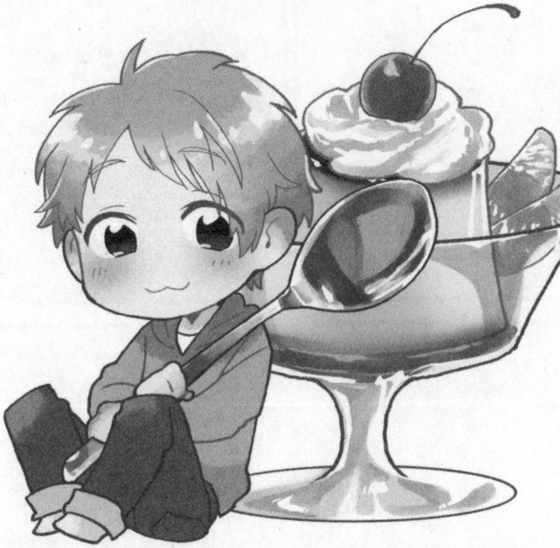

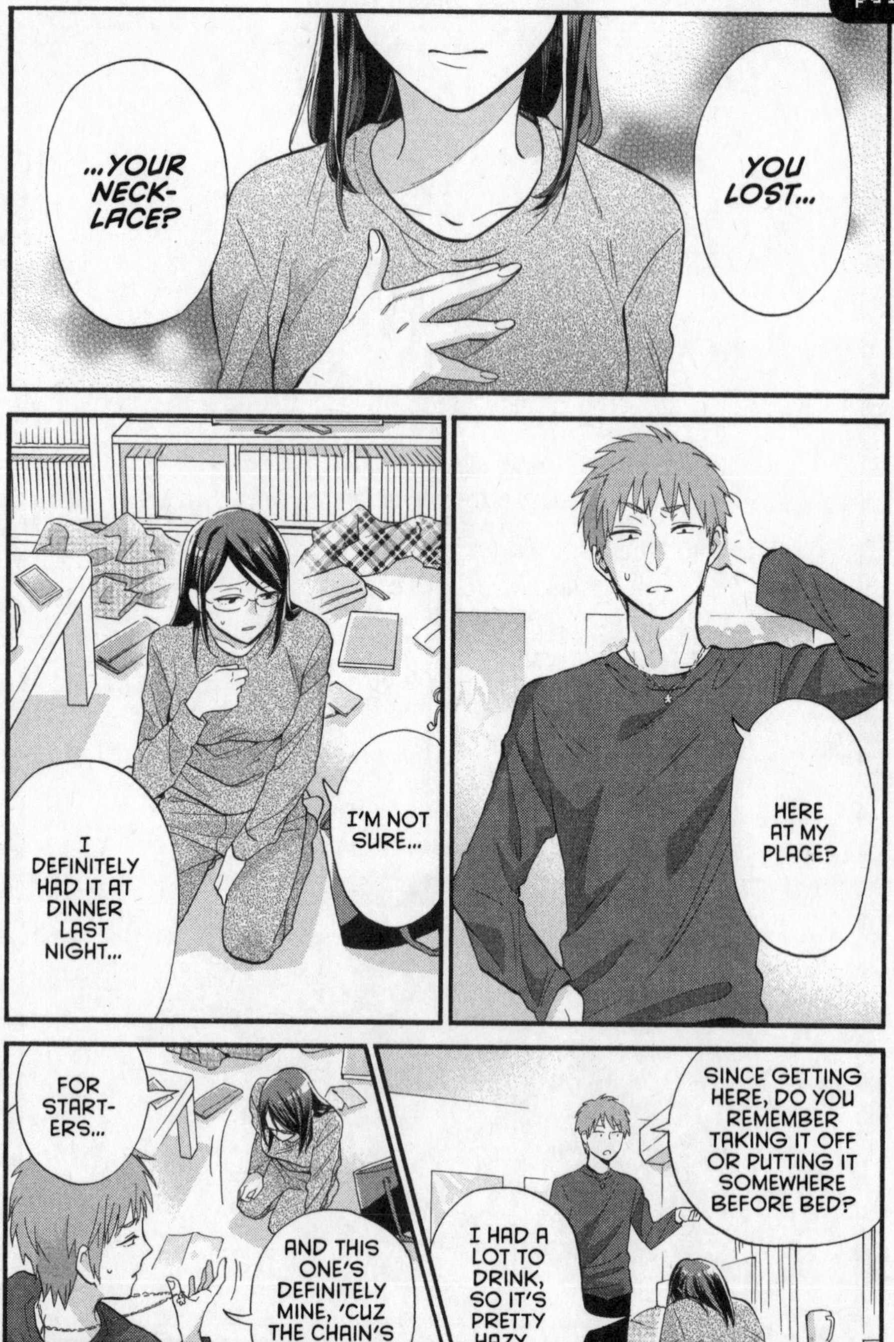
YOU LOST...
...YOUR NECKLACE?
HERE AT MY PLACE?
I'M NOT SURE...
I DEFINITELY HAD IT AT DINNER LAST NIGHT...
SINCE GETTING HERE, DO YOU REMEMBER TAKING IT OFF OR PUTTING IT SOMEWHERE BEFORE BED?
I HAD A LOT TO DRINK, SO IT'S PRETTY HAZY...
FOR STARTERS...
AND THIS ONE'S DEFINITELY MINE, 'CUZ THE CHAIN'S THICKER...

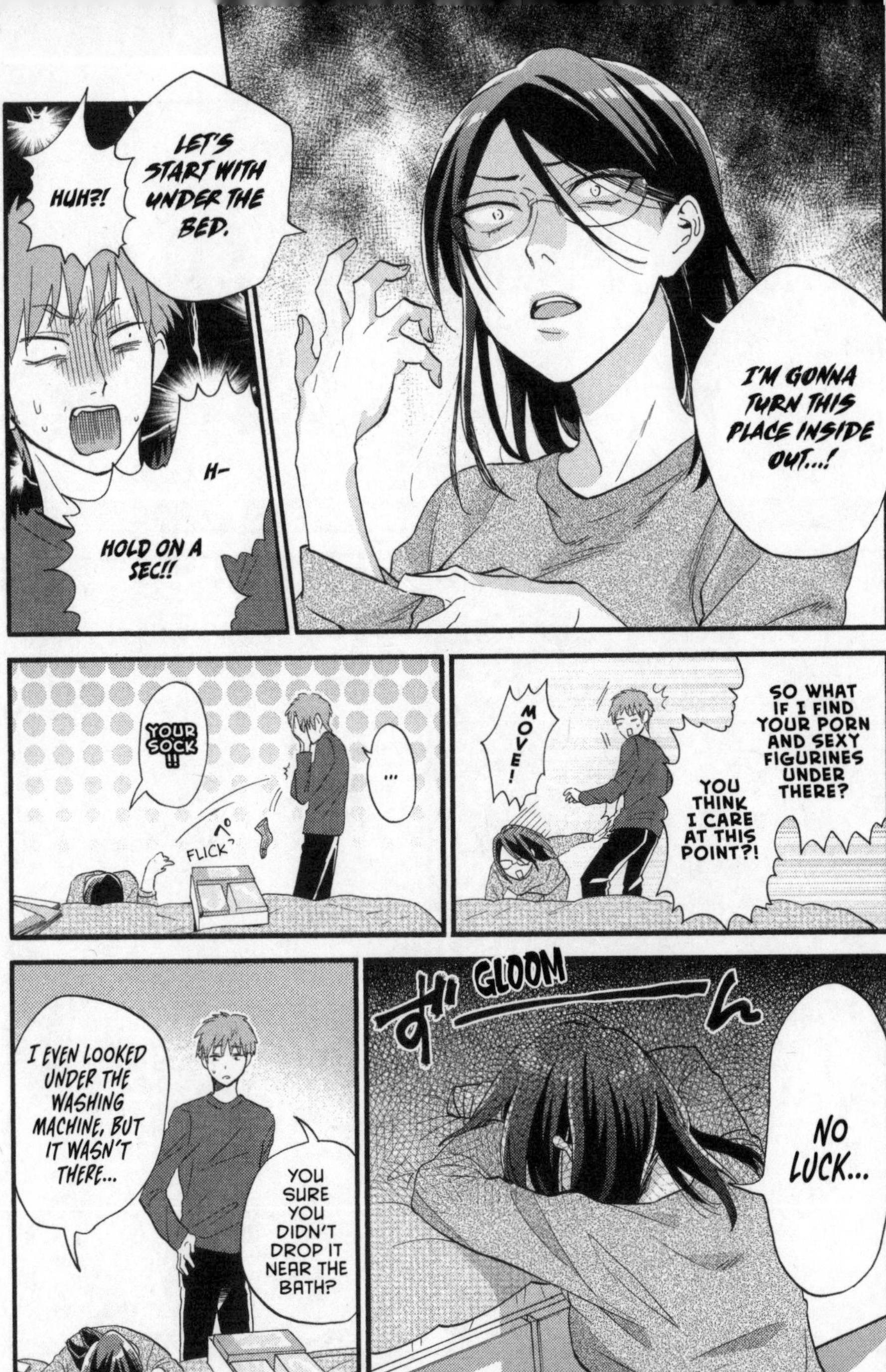
I'M GONNA TURN THIS PLACE INSIDE OUT...!
LET'S START WITH UNDER THE BED.
HUH?!
H-
HOLD ON A SEC!!
SO WHAT IF I FIND YOUR PORN AND SEXY FIGURINES UNDER THERE?
YOU THINK I CARE AT THIS POINT?!
MOVE!
...
YOUR SOCK!!
FLICK
GLOOM
NO LUCK...
I EVEN LOOKED UNDER THE WASHING MACHINE, BUT IT WASN'T THERE...
YOU SURE YOU DIDN'T DROP IT NEAR THE BATH?

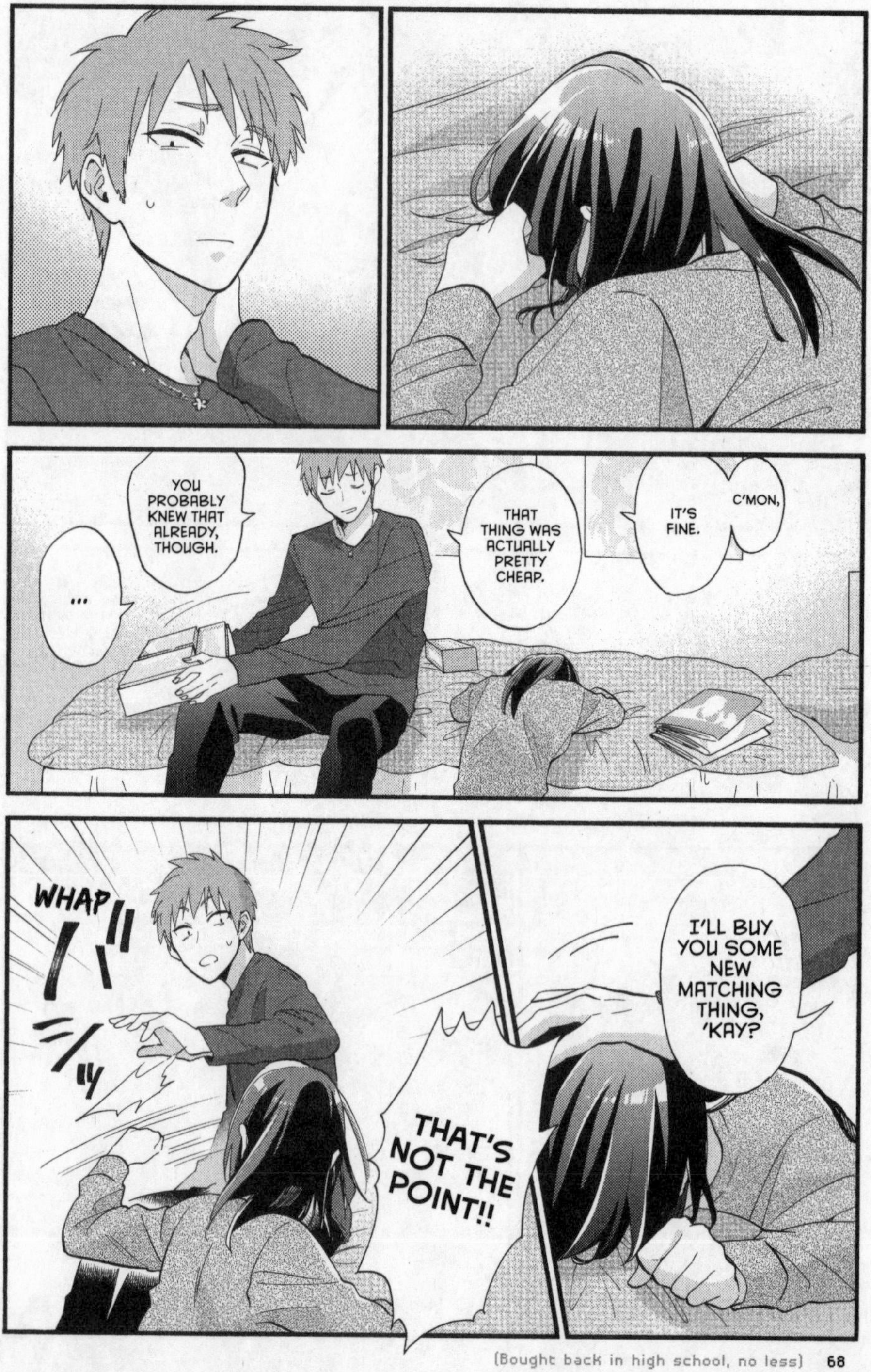
C'MON, IT'S FINE.
THAT THING WAS ACTUALLY PRETTY CHEAP.
YOU PROBABLY KNEW THAT ALREADY, THOUGH.
...
I'LL BUY YOU SOME NEW MATCHING THING, 'KAY?
THAT'S NOT THE POINT!!
WHAP!!

(Bought back in high school, no less)

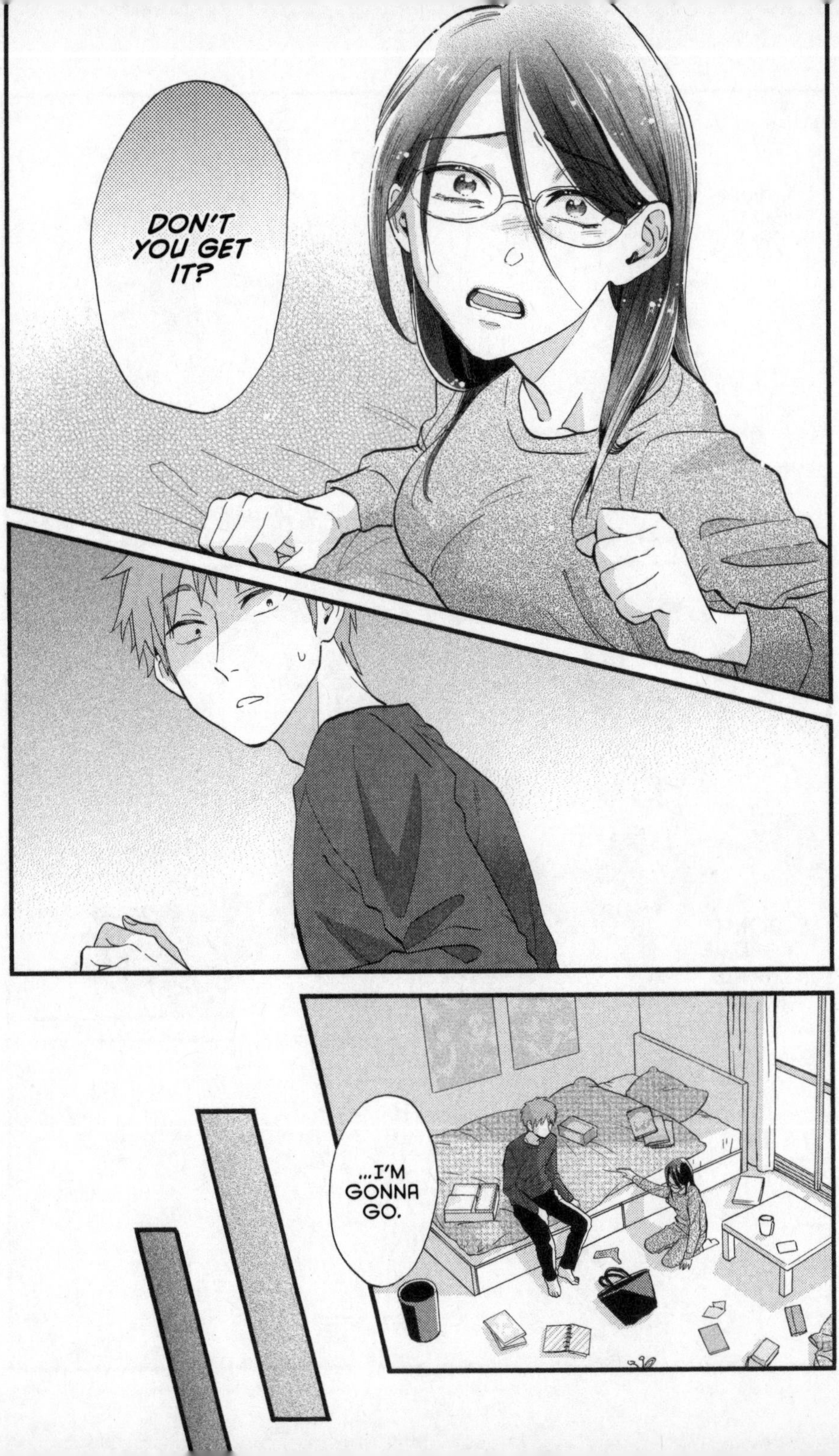
DON'T YOU GET IT?
...I'M GONNA GO.

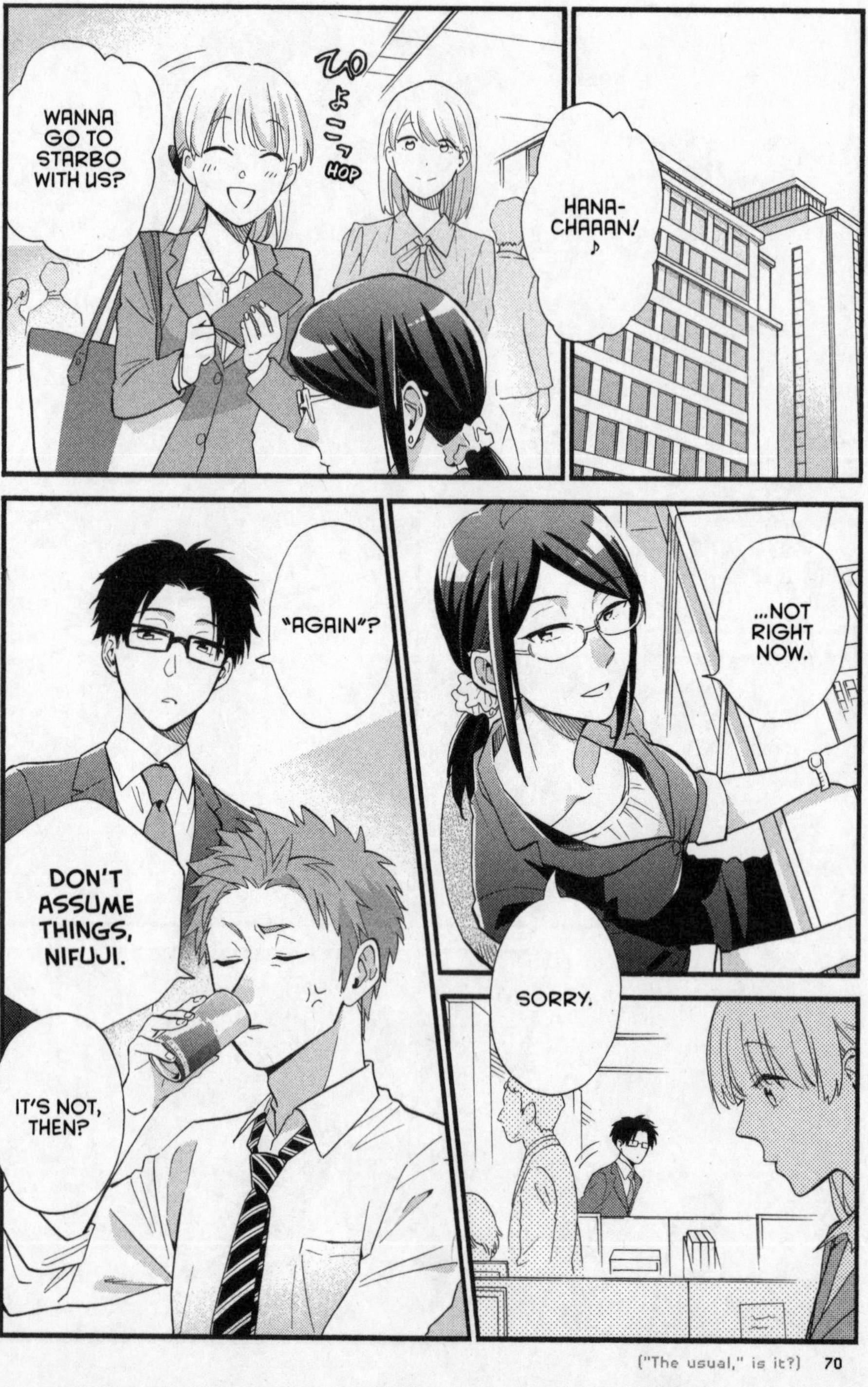
HANA-CHAAAN! ♪
WANNA GO TO STARBO WITH US?
ぴょこっ
HOP
...NOT RIGHT NOW.
SORRY.
"AGAIN"?
DON'T ASSUME THINGS, NIFUJI.
IT'S NOT, THEN?

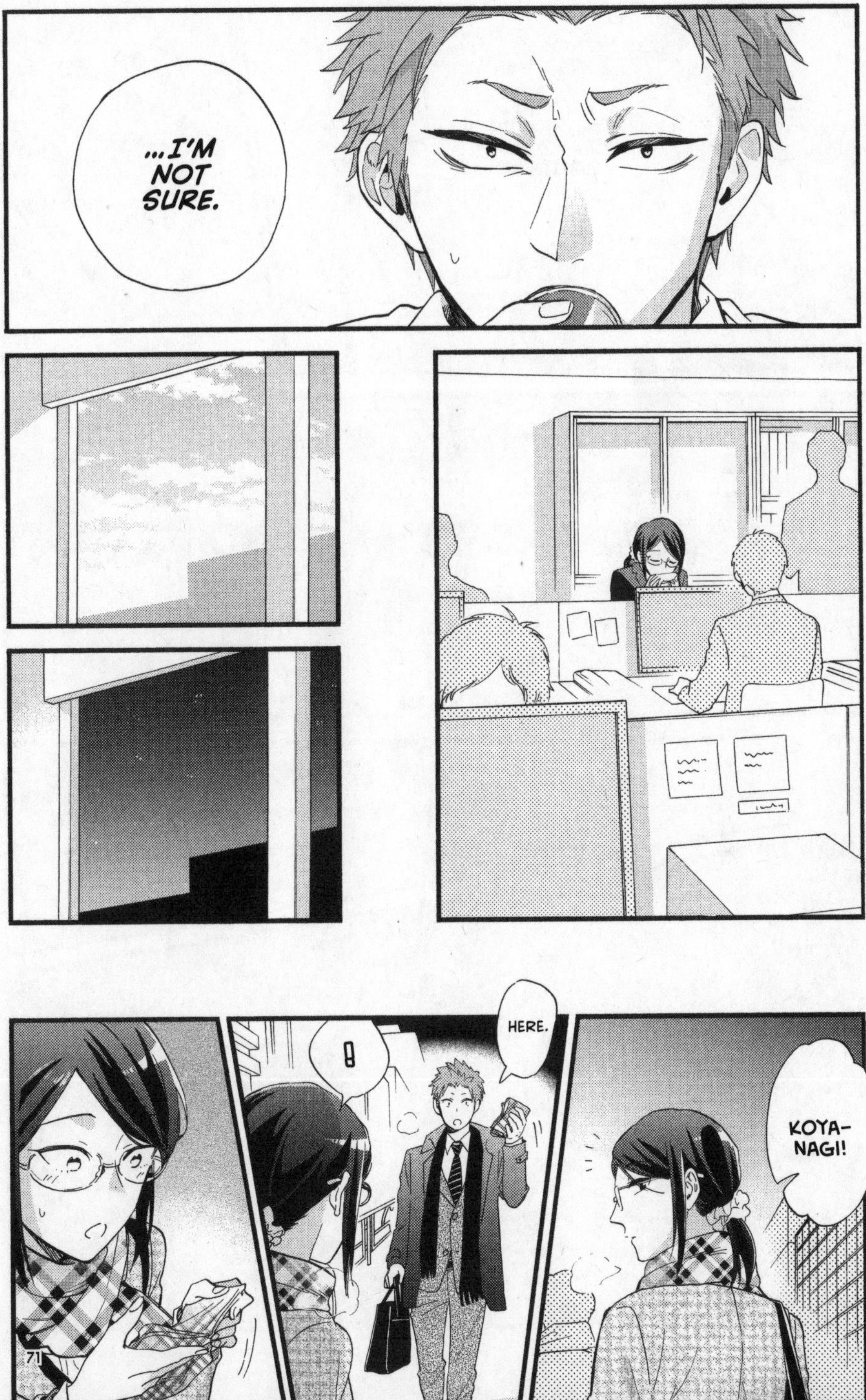
...I'M NOT SURE.
KOYA-NAGI!
HERE.
!

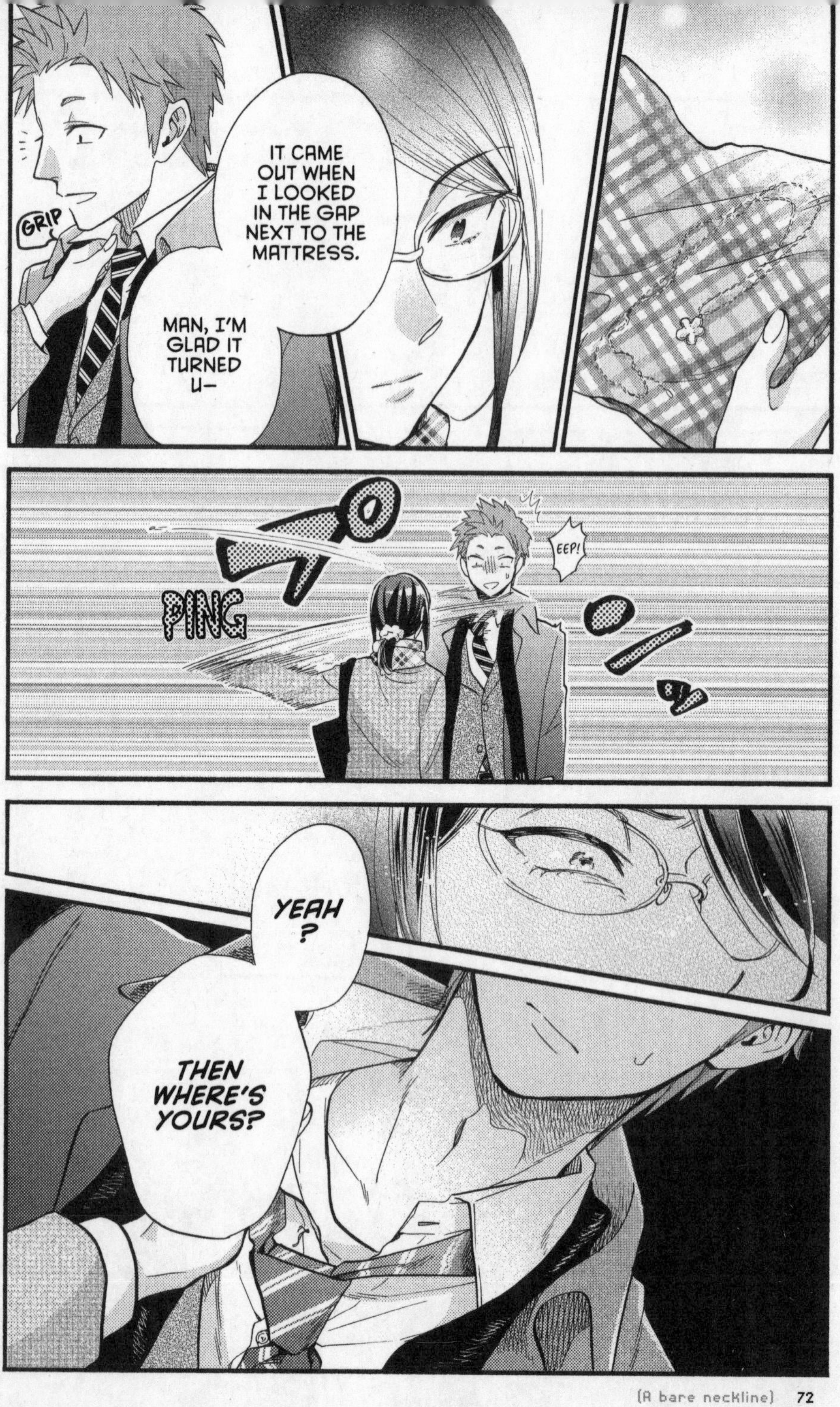

IT CAME OUT WHEN I LOOKED IN THE GAP NEXT TO THE MATTRESS.
GRIP
MAN, I'M GLAD IT TURNED U—
EEP!
PING
YEAH?
THEN WHERE'S YOURS?

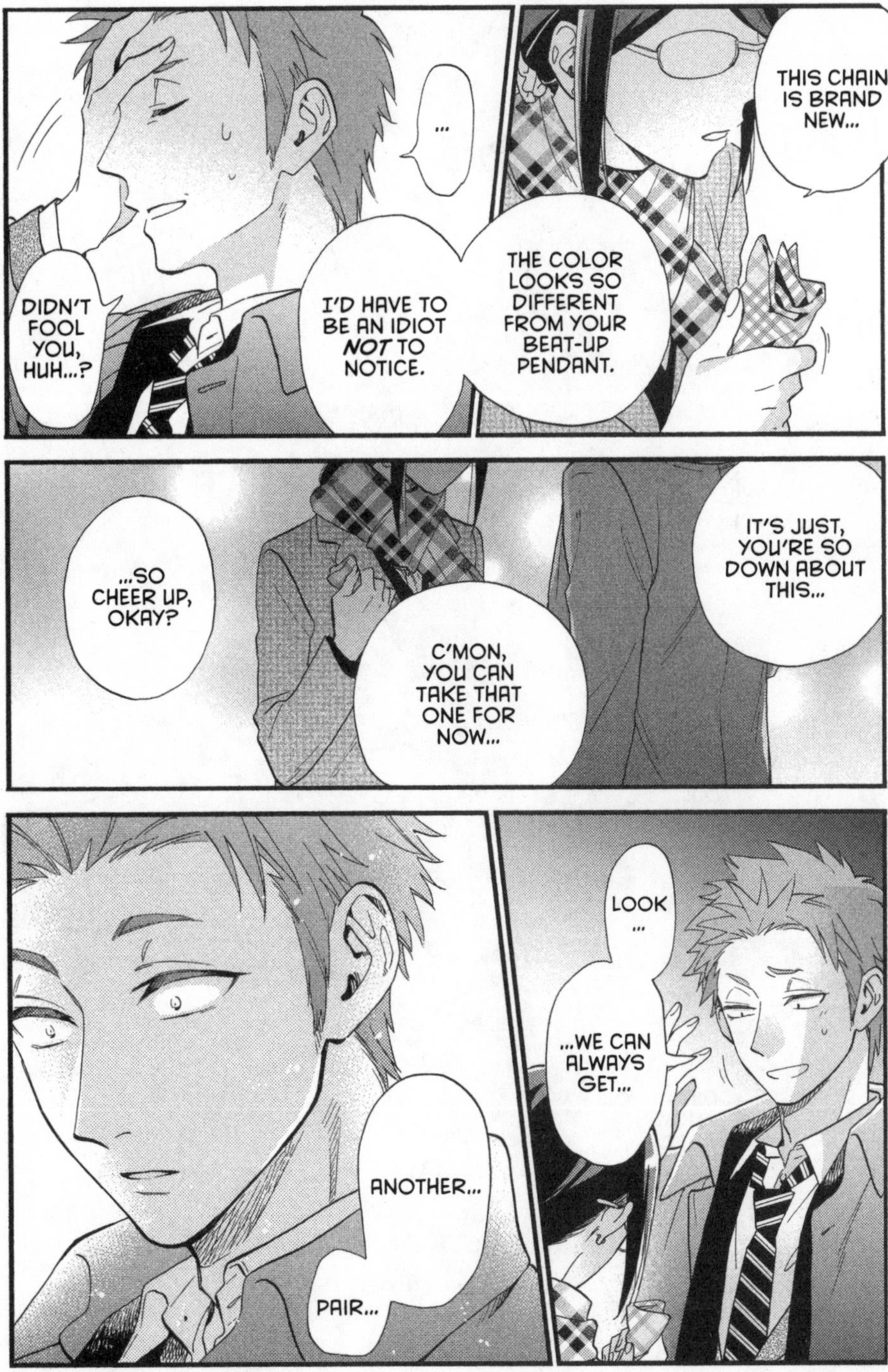
THIS CHAIN IS BRAND NEW...
THE COLOR LOOKS SO DIFFERENT FROM YOUR BEAT-UP PENDANT.
...
I'D HAVE TO BE AN IDIOT *NOT* TO NOTICE.
DIDN'T FOOL YOU, HUH...?
IT'S JUST, YOU'RE SO DOWN ABOUT THIS...
C'MON, YOU CAN TAKE THAT ONE FOR NOW...
...SO CHEER UP, OKAY?
LOOK ...
...WE CAN ALWAYS GET...
ANOTHER...
PAIR...

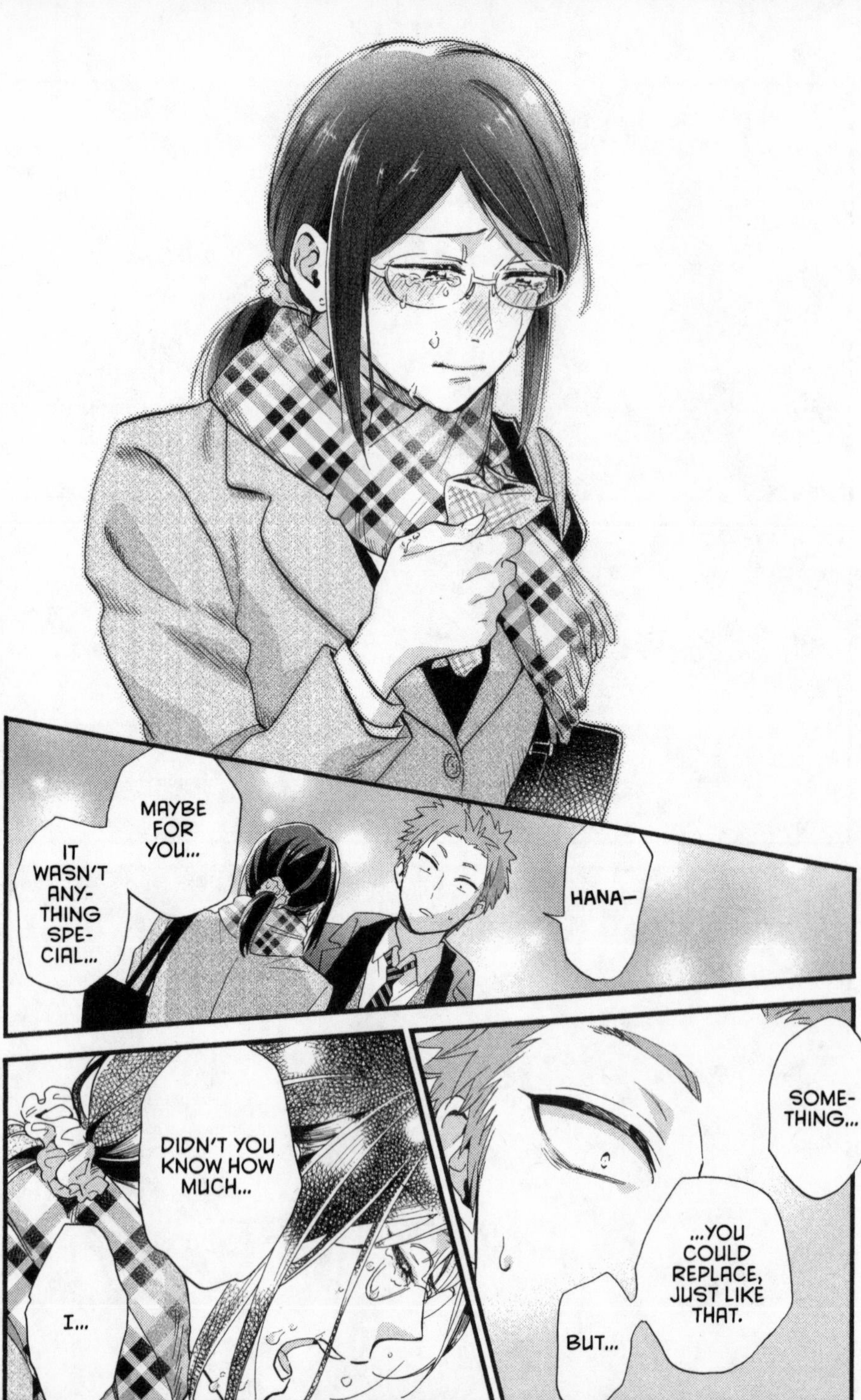
HANA—
MAYBE FOR YOU...
IT WASN'T ANY-THING SPE-CIAL...
SOME-THING...
...YOU COULD REPLACE, JUST LIKE THAT.
BUT...
DIDN'T YOU KNOW HOW MUCH...
I...

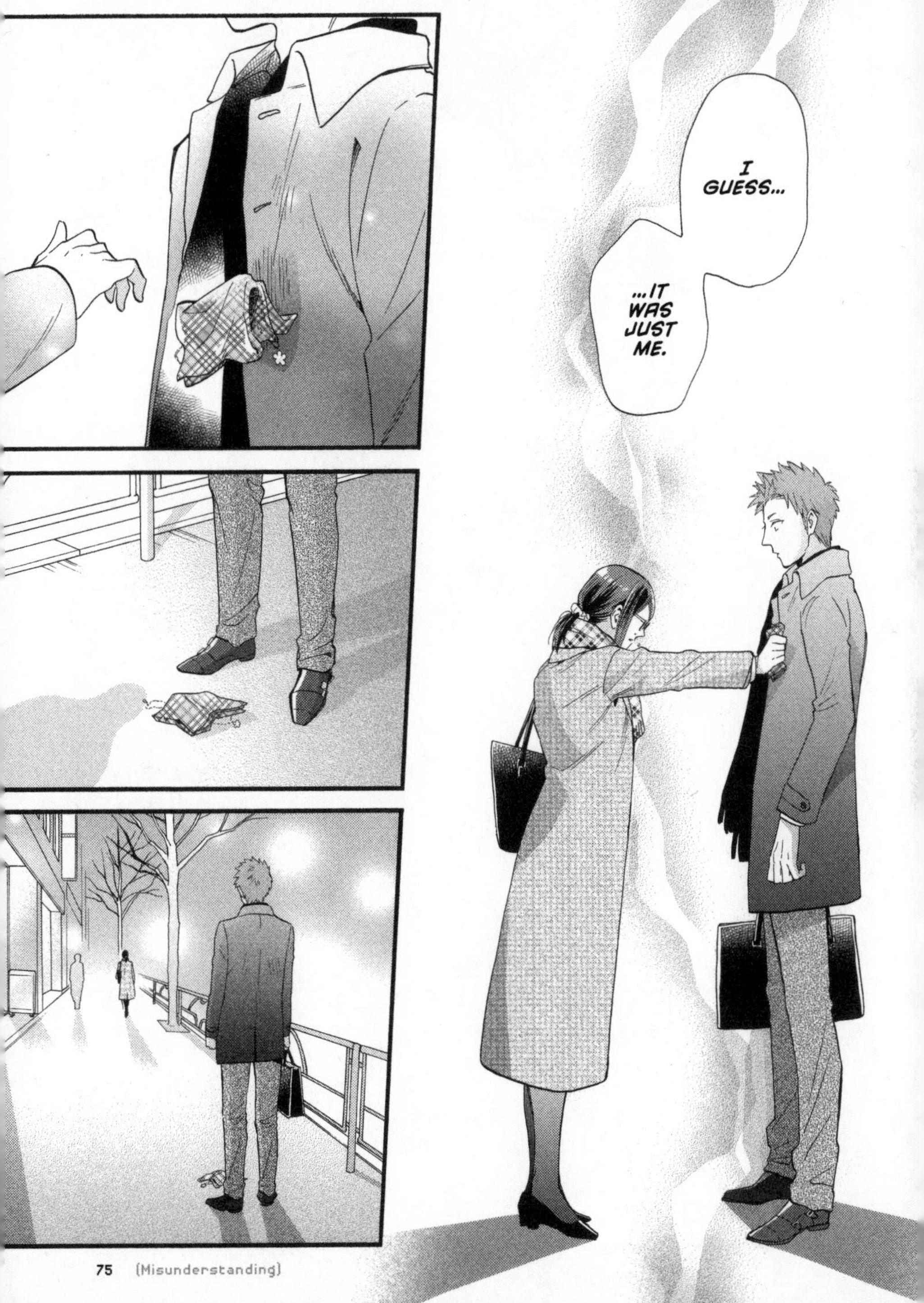
I GUESS...
...IT WAS JUST ME.

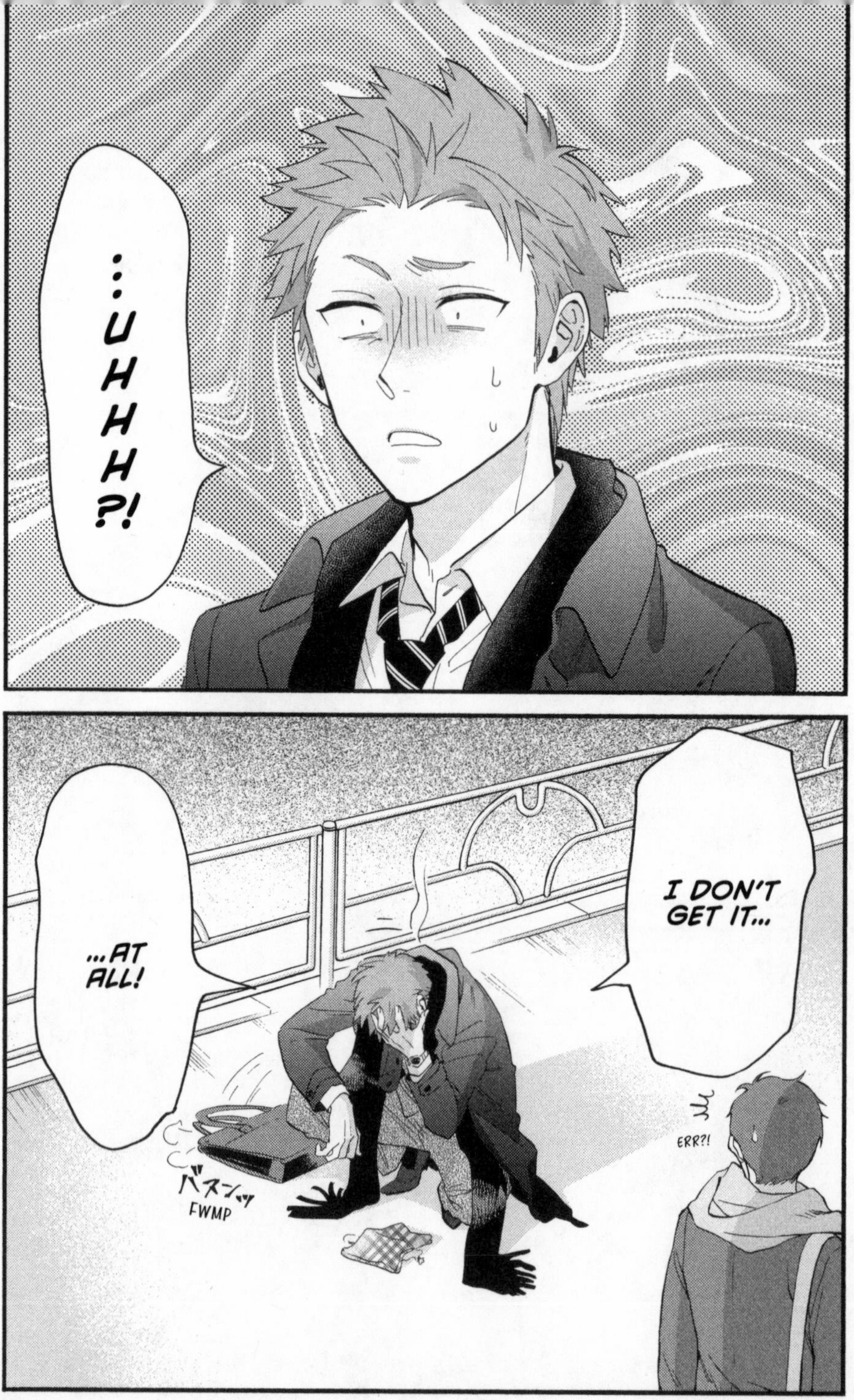
...UHHHH?!
I DON'T GET IT...
...AT ALL!
ERR?!
バスンッ
FWMP

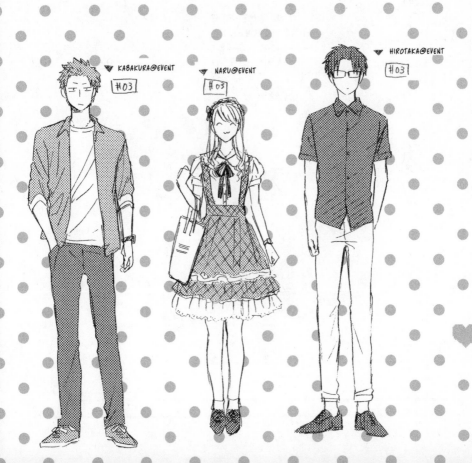

HIROTAKA@EVENT
#03
NARU@EVENT
#03
KABAKURA@EVENT
#03

CHARACTERS
MENU

桜城光

Ko Sakuragi

SOME SWEETS SHE LIKES, OTHERS SHE DOESN'T.

A LOT OF TIMES SHE GETS STUCK TRYING TO FINISH A CAKE THAT TURNS OUT TO BE BIGGER THAN SHE EXPECTED.

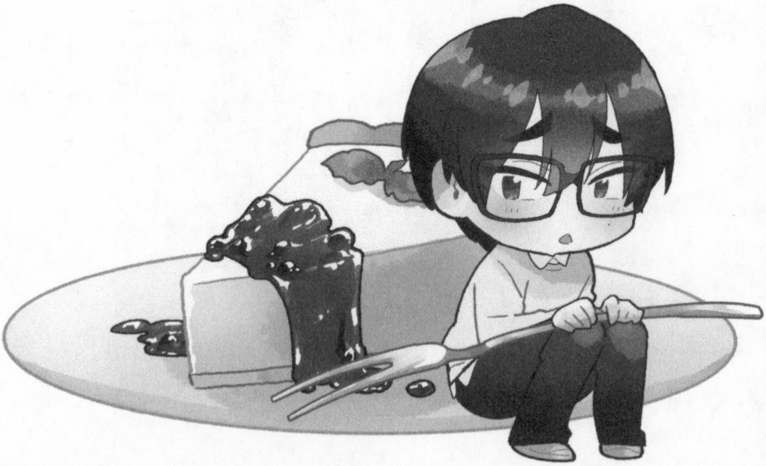

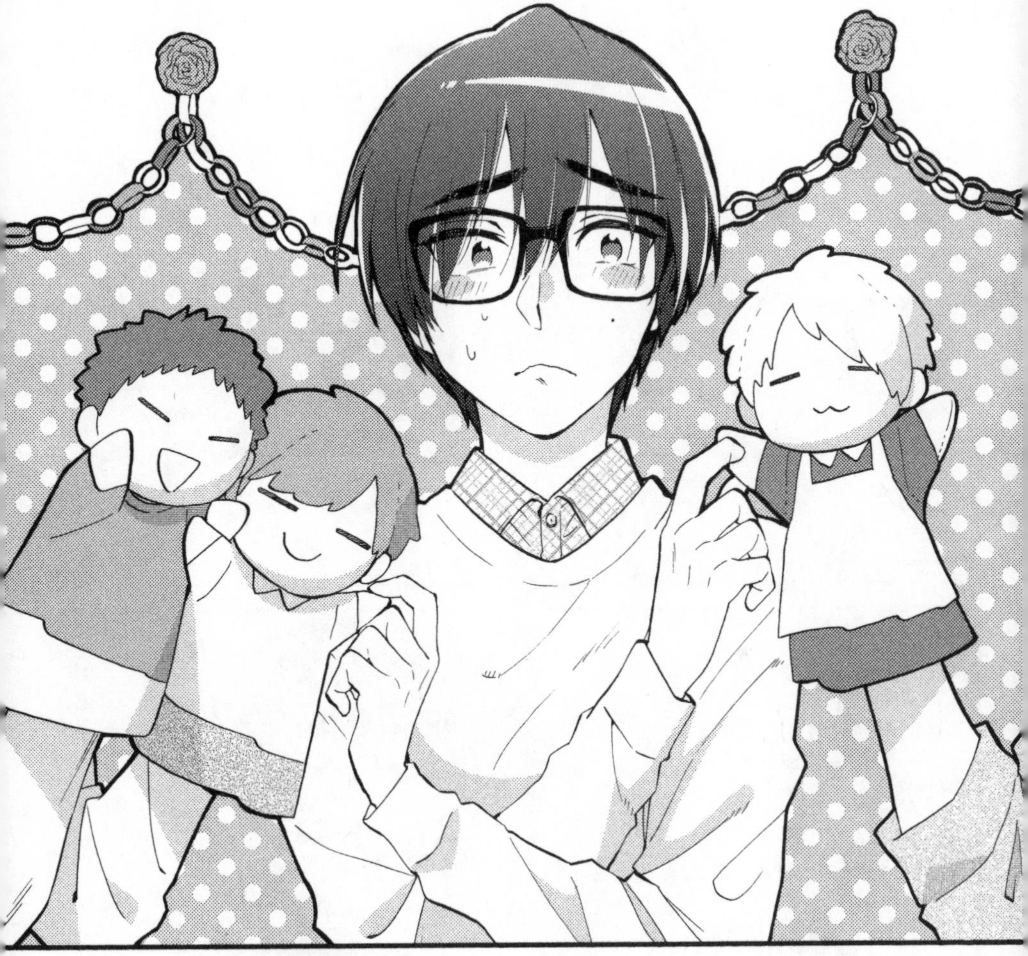

Episode.... 52

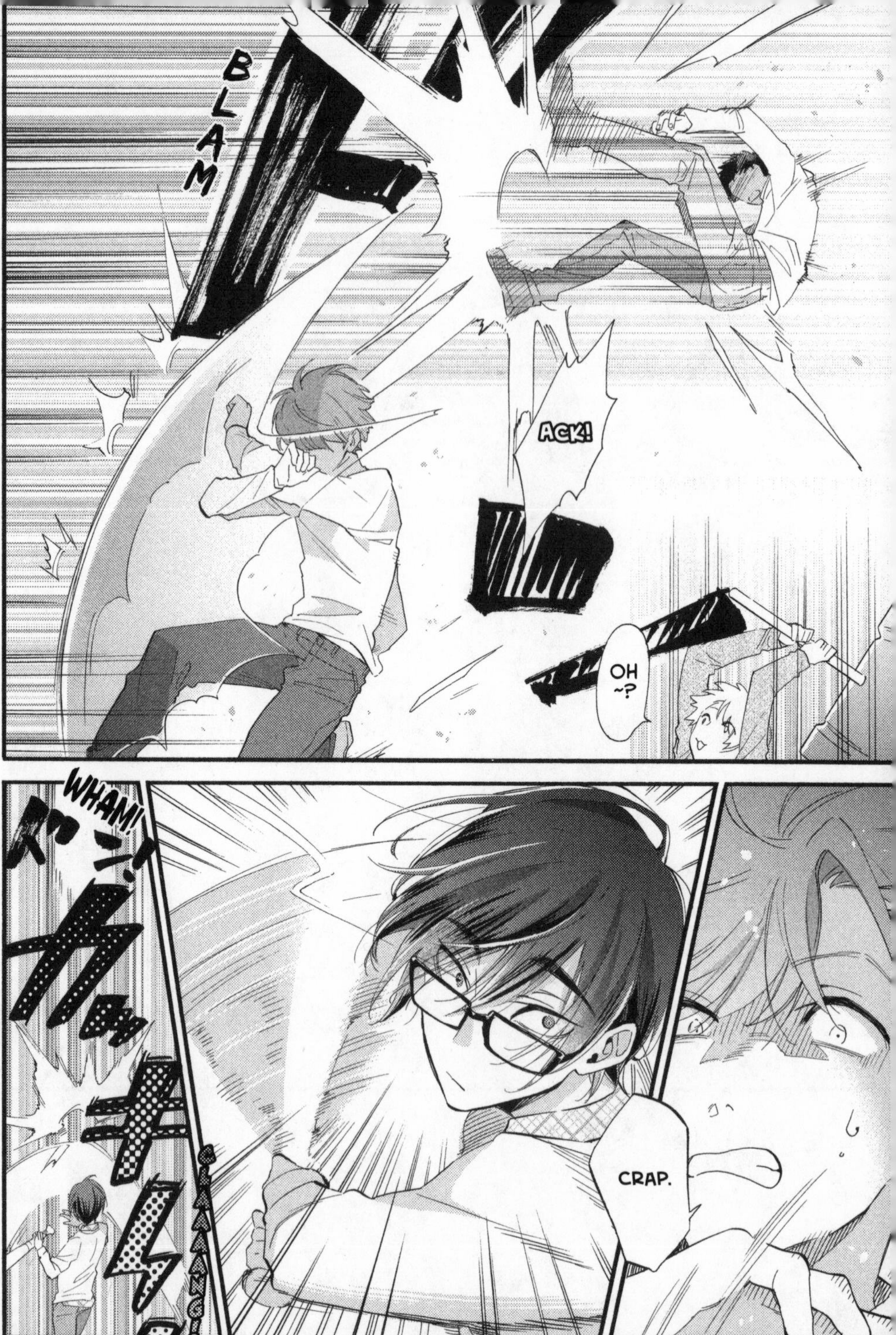
ACK!
BLAM
OH ~?
CRAP.
WHAM!
CLAAAANG!

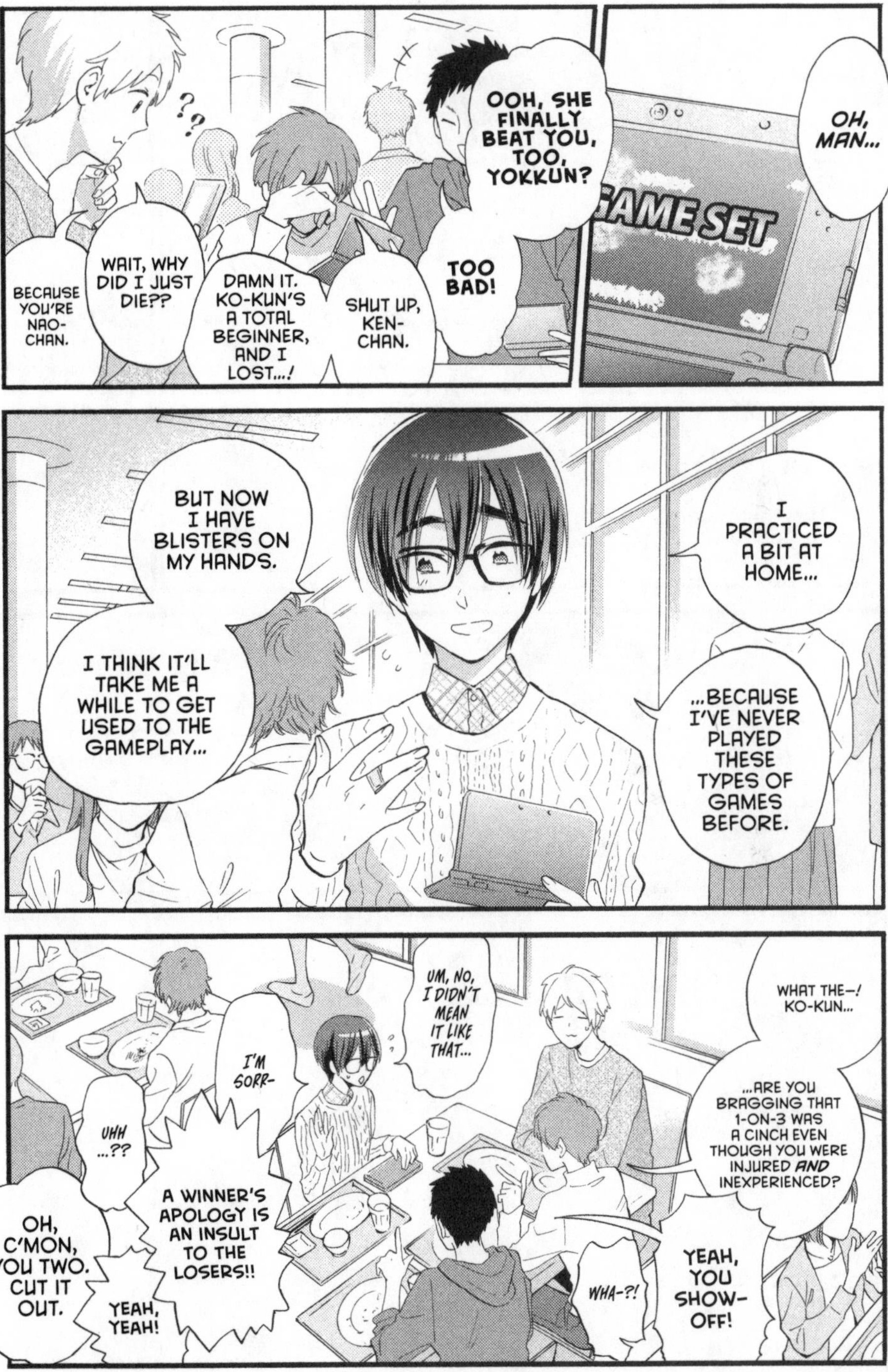
OH, MAN...
GAME SET
OOH, SHE FINALLY BEAT YOU, TOO, YOKKUN?
TOO BAD!
SHUT UP, KEN-CHAN.
DAMN IT. KO-KUN'S A TOTAL BEGINNER, AND I LOST...!
WAIT, WHY DID I JUST DIE??
BECAUSE YOU'RE NAO-CHAN.
I PRACTICED A BIT AT HOME...
...BECAUSE I'VE NEVER PLAYED THESE TYPES OF GAMES BEFORE.
BUT NOW I HAVE BLISTERS ON MY HANDS.
I THINK IT'LL TAKE ME A WHILE TO GET USED TO THE GAMEPLAY...
WHAT THE–! KO-KUN...
...ARE YOU BRAGGING THAT 1-ON-3 WAS A CINCH EVEN THOUGH YOU WERE INJURED AND INEXPERIENCED?
UM, NO, I DIDN'T MEAN IT LIKE THAT...
I'M SORR-
YEAH, YOU SHOW-OFF!
WHA-?!
A WINNER'S APOLOGY IS AN INSULT TO THE LOSERS!!
UHH ...??
YEAH, YEAH!
OH, C'MON, YOU TWO. CUT IT OUT.

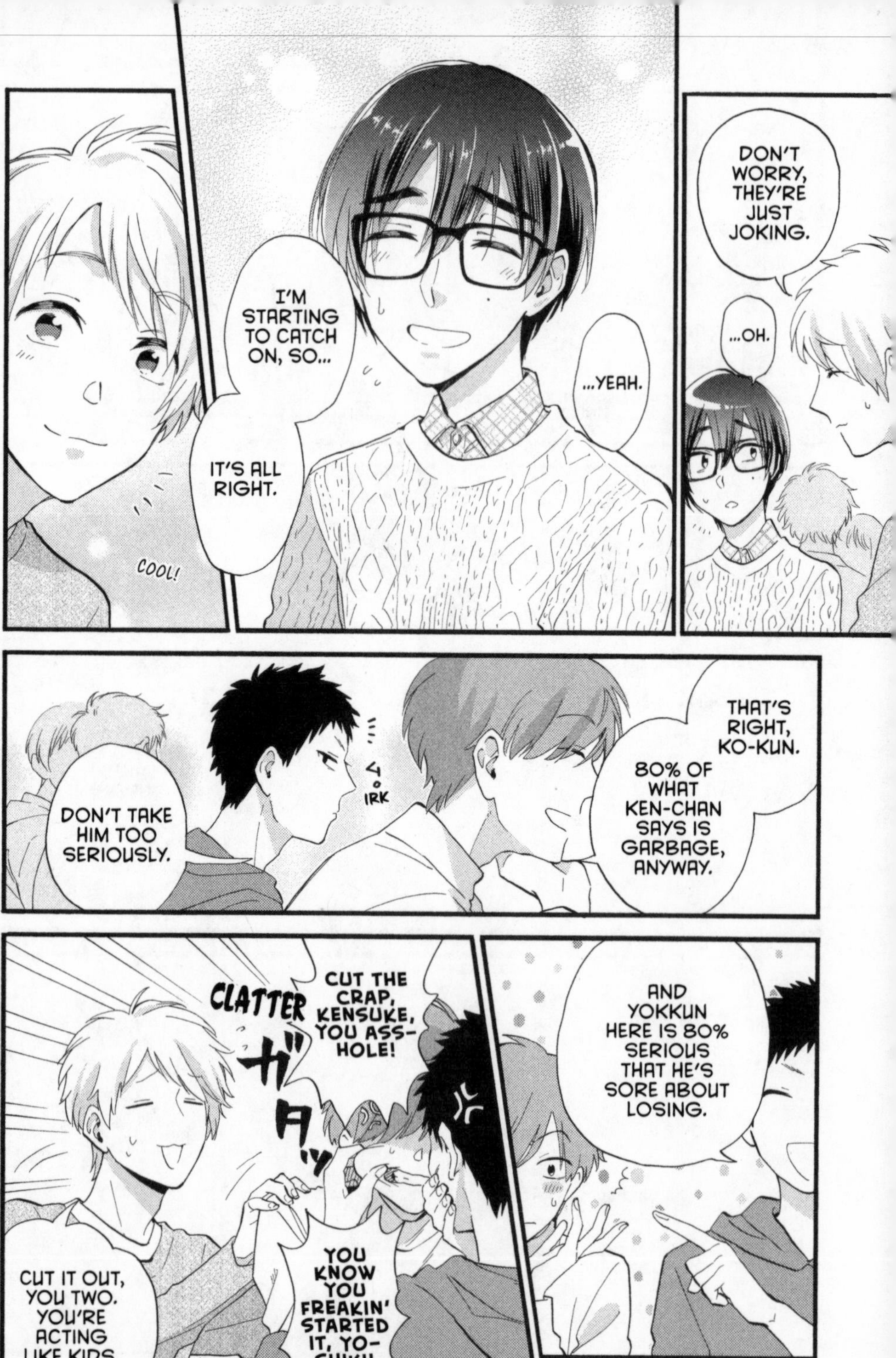
DON'T WORRY, THEY'RE JUST JOKING.
...OH.
...YEAH.
I'M STARTING TO CATCH ON, SO...
IT'S ALL RIGHT.
COOL!
THAT'S RIGHT, KO-KUN.
80% OF WHAT KEN-CHAN SAYS IS GARBAGE, ANYWAY.
IRK
DON'T TAKE HIM TOO SERIOUSLY.
AND YOKKUN HERE IS 80% SERIOUS THAT HE'S SORE ABOUT LOSING.
CUT THE CRAP, KENSUKE, YOU ASS-HOLE!
CLATTER
YOU KNOW YOU FREAKIN' STARTED IT, YO-SHIKI!
CUT IT OUT, YOU TWO. YOU'RE ACTING LIKE KIDS.

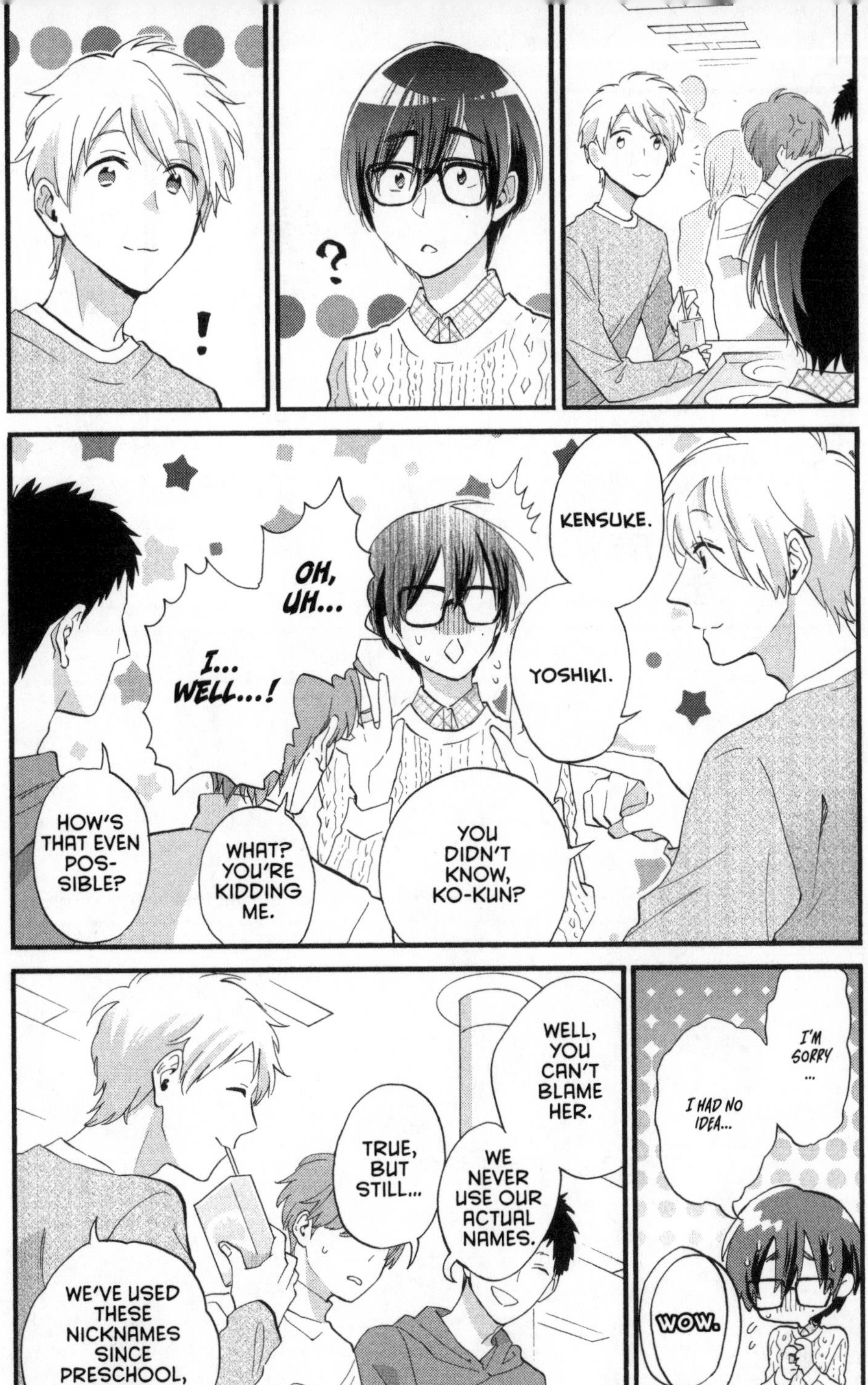
?
!
KENSUKE.
YOSHIKI.
OH, UH...
I... WELL...!
YOU DIDN'T KNOW, KO-KUN?
WHAT? YOU'RE KIDDING ME.
HOW'S THAT EVEN POS-SIBLE?
I'M SORRY...
I HAD NO IDEA...
WOW.
WELL, YOU CAN'T BLAME HER.
WE NEVER USE OUR ACTUAL NAMES.
TRUE, BUT STILL...
WE'VE USED THESE NICKNAMES SINCE PRESCHOOL, HUH?

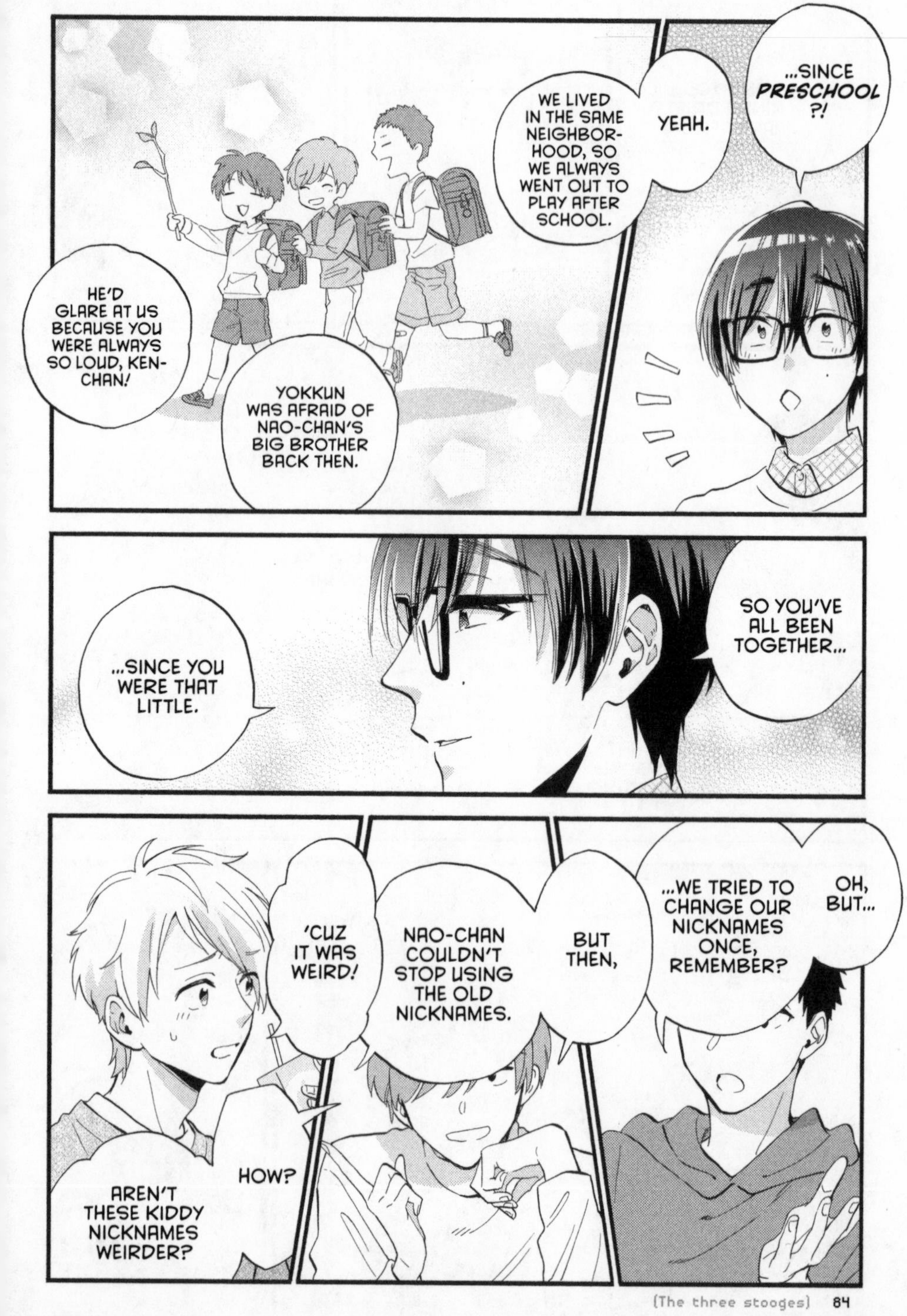

...SINCE PRESCHOOL ?!
YEAH.
WE LIVED IN THE SAME NEIGHBOR-HOOD, SO WE ALWAYS WENT OUT TO PLAY AFTER SCHOOL.
YOKKUN WAS AFRAID OF NAO-CHAN'S BIG BROTHER BACK THEN.
HE'D GLARE AT US BECAUSE YOU WERE ALWAYS SO LOUD, KEN-CHAN!
SO YOU'VE ALL BEEN TOGETHER...
...SINCE YOU WERE THAT LITTLE.
OH, BUT...
...WE TRIED TO CHANGE OUR NICKNAMES ONCE, REMEMBER?
BUT THEN,
NAO-CHAN COULDN'T STOP USING THE OLD NICKNAMES.
'CUZ IT WAS WEIRD!
HOW?
AREN'T THESE KIDDY NICKNAMES WEIRDER?

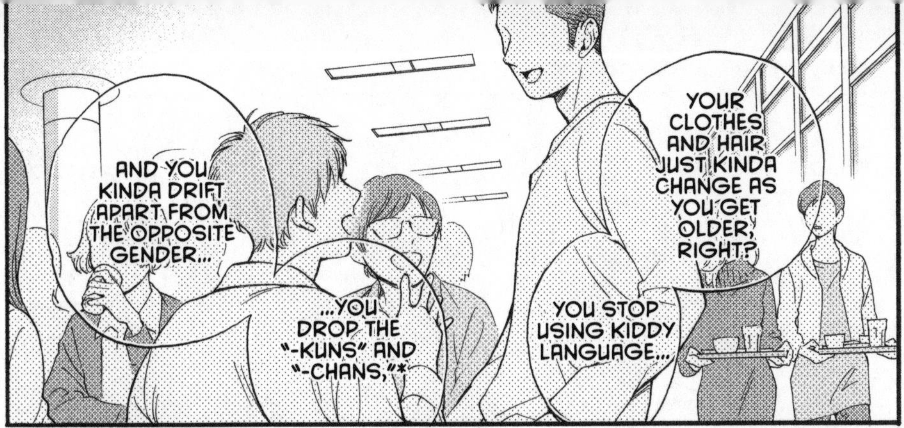
YOUR CLOTHES AND HAIR JUST KINDA CHANGE AS YOU GET OLDER, RIGHT?
YOU STOP USING KIDDY LANGUAGE...
...YOU DROP THE "-KUNS" AND "-CHANS,"*
AND YOU KINDA DRIFT APART FROM THE OPPOSITE GENDER...

*People often stop using these honorifics as they get older.

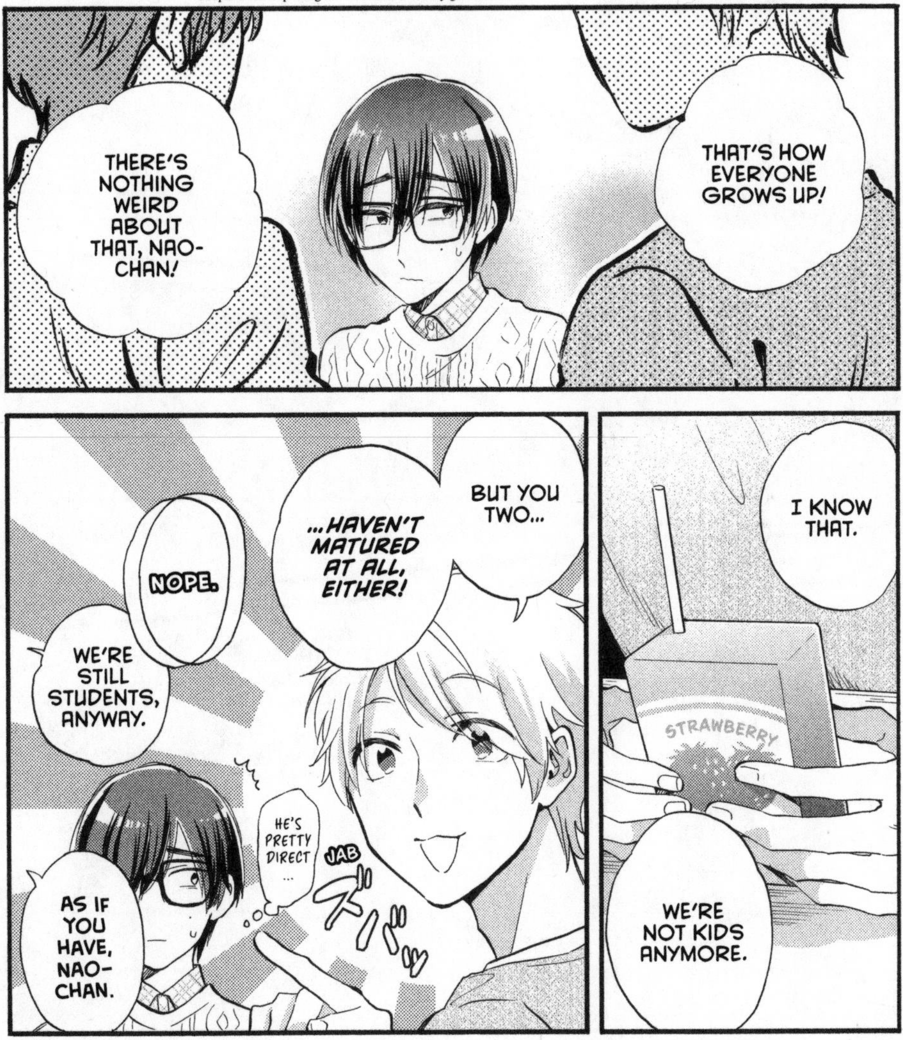
THAT'S HOW EVERYONE GROWS UP!
THERE'S NOTHING WEIRD ABOUT THAT, NAO-CHAN!
I KNOW THAT.
WE'RE NOT KIDS ANYMORE.
BUT YOU TWO...
...HAVEN'T MATURED AT ALL, EITHER!
NOPE.
WE'RE STILL STUDENTS, ANYWAY.
HE'S PRETTY DIRECT...
JAB
AS IF YOU HAVE, NAO-CHAN.

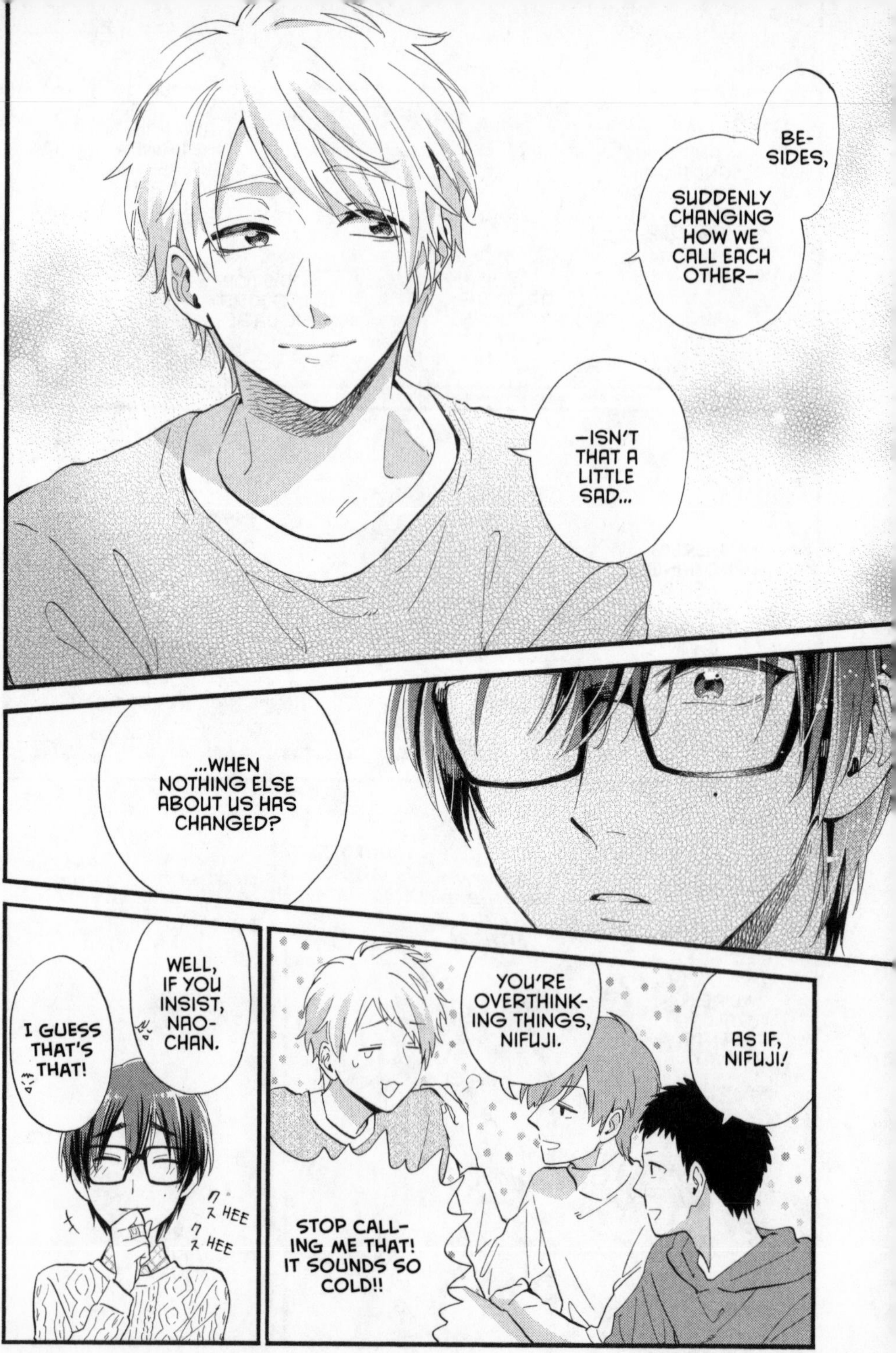
BE-SIDES,
SUDDENLY CHANGING HOW WE CALL EACH OTHER—
—ISN'T THAT A LITTLE SAD...
...WHEN NOTHING ELSE ABOUT US HAS CHANGED?
AS IF, NIFUJI!
YOU'RE OVERTHINKING THINGS, NIFUJI.
STOP CALLING ME THAT! IT SOUNDS SO COLD!!
WELL, IF YOU INSIST, NAO-CHAN.
I GUESS THAT'S THAT!
HEE
HEE

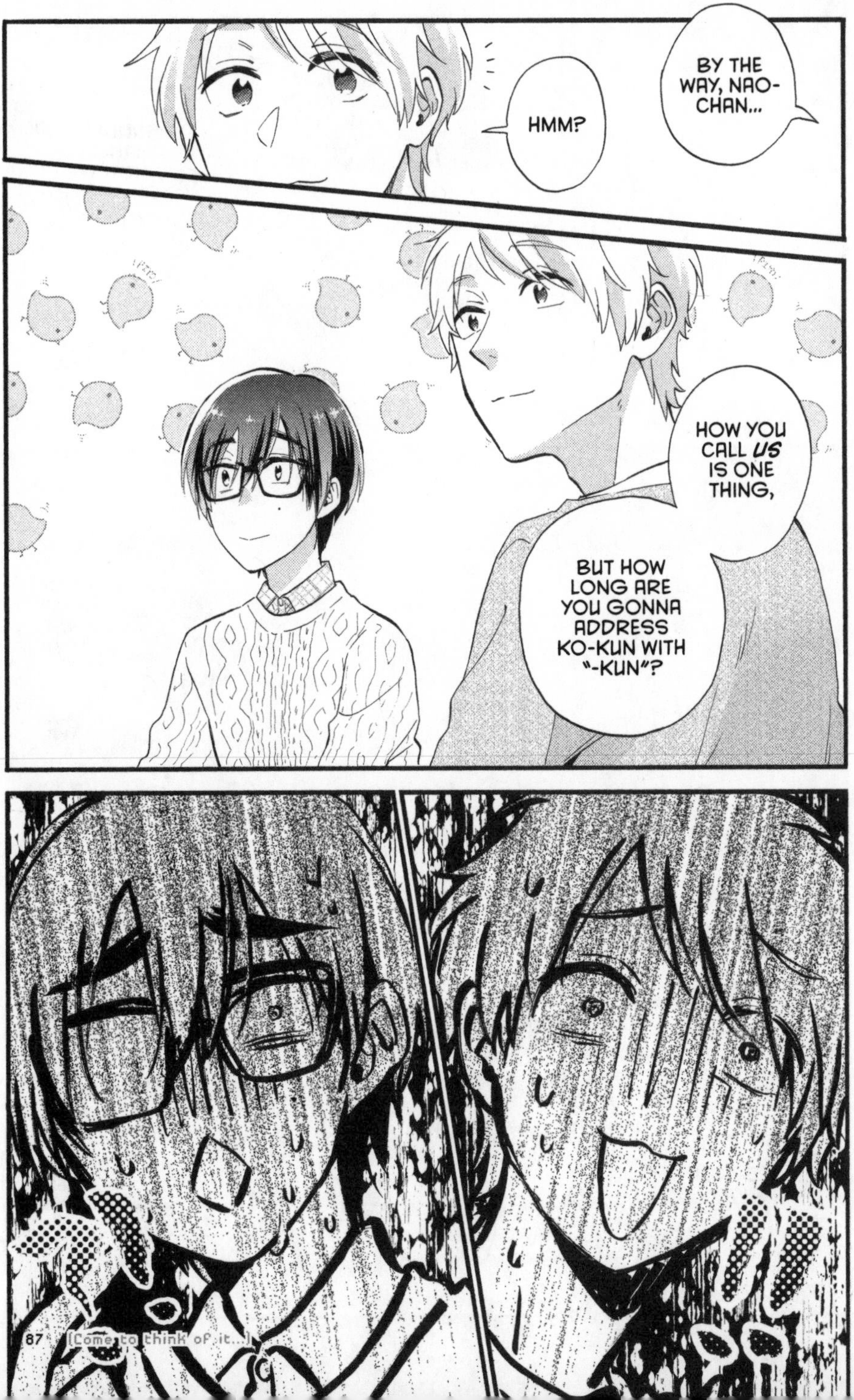
BY THE WAY, NAO-CHAN...
HMM?
HOW YOU CALL US IS ONE THING,
BUT HOW LONG ARE YOU GONNA ADDRESS KO-KUN WITH "-KUN"?
[Come to think of it...]

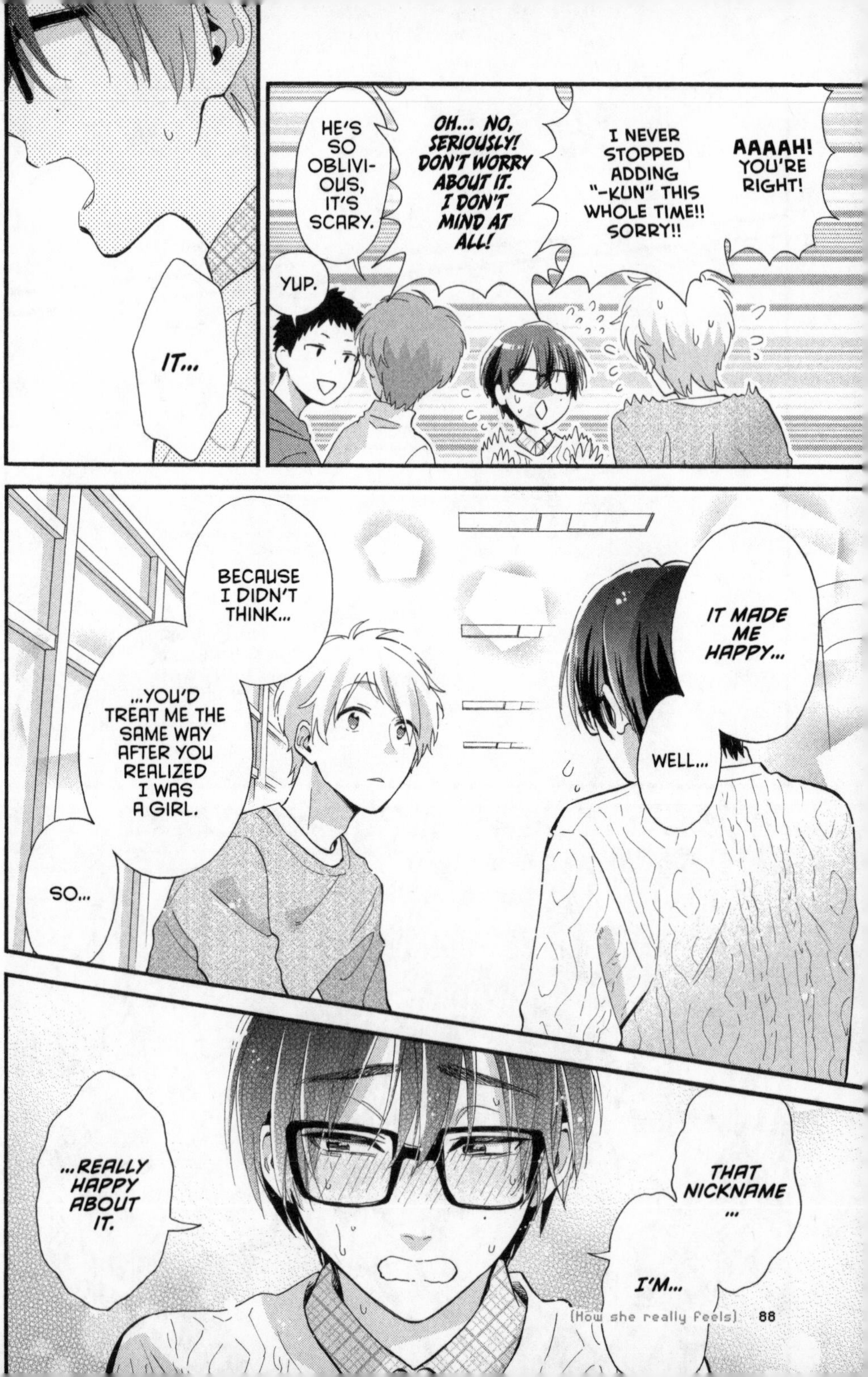
AAAAH! YOU'RE RIGHT!
I NEVER STOPPED ADDING "-KUN" THIS WHOLE TIME!! SORRY!!
OH... NO, SERIOUSLY! DON'T WORRY ABOUT IT. I DON'T MIND AT ALL!
HE'S SO OBLIVIOUS, IT'S SCARY.
YUP.
IT...
IT MADE ME HAPPY...
WELL...
BECAUSE I DIDN'T THINK...
...YOU'D TREAT ME THE SAME WAY AFTER YOU REALIZED I WAS A GIRL.
SO...
THAT NICKNAME ...
I'M...
...REALLY HAPPY ABOUT IT.

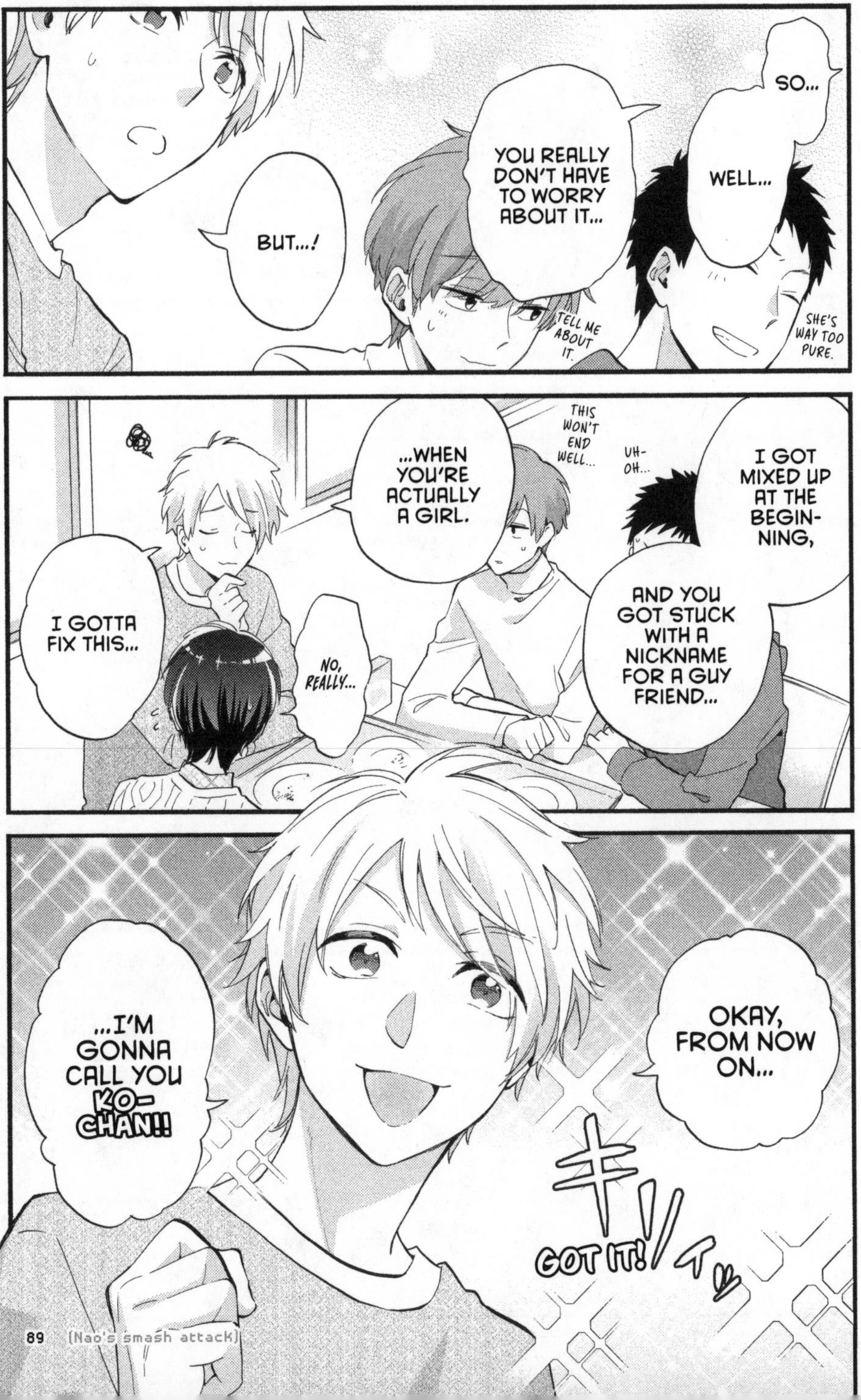
SO...
WELL...
SHE'S WAY TOO PURE.
YOU REALLY DON'T HAVE TO WORRY ABOUT IT...
TELL ME ABOUT IT.
BUT...!
I GOT MIXED UP AT THE BEGINNING,
AND YOU GOT STUCK WITH A NICKNAME FOR A GUY FRIEND...
UH-OH...
THIS WON'T END WELL...
...WHEN YOU'RE ACTUALLY A GIRL.
NO, REALLY...
I GOTTA FIX THIS...
OKAY, FROM NOW ON...
...I'M GONNA CALL YOU KO-CHAN!!
GOT IT!

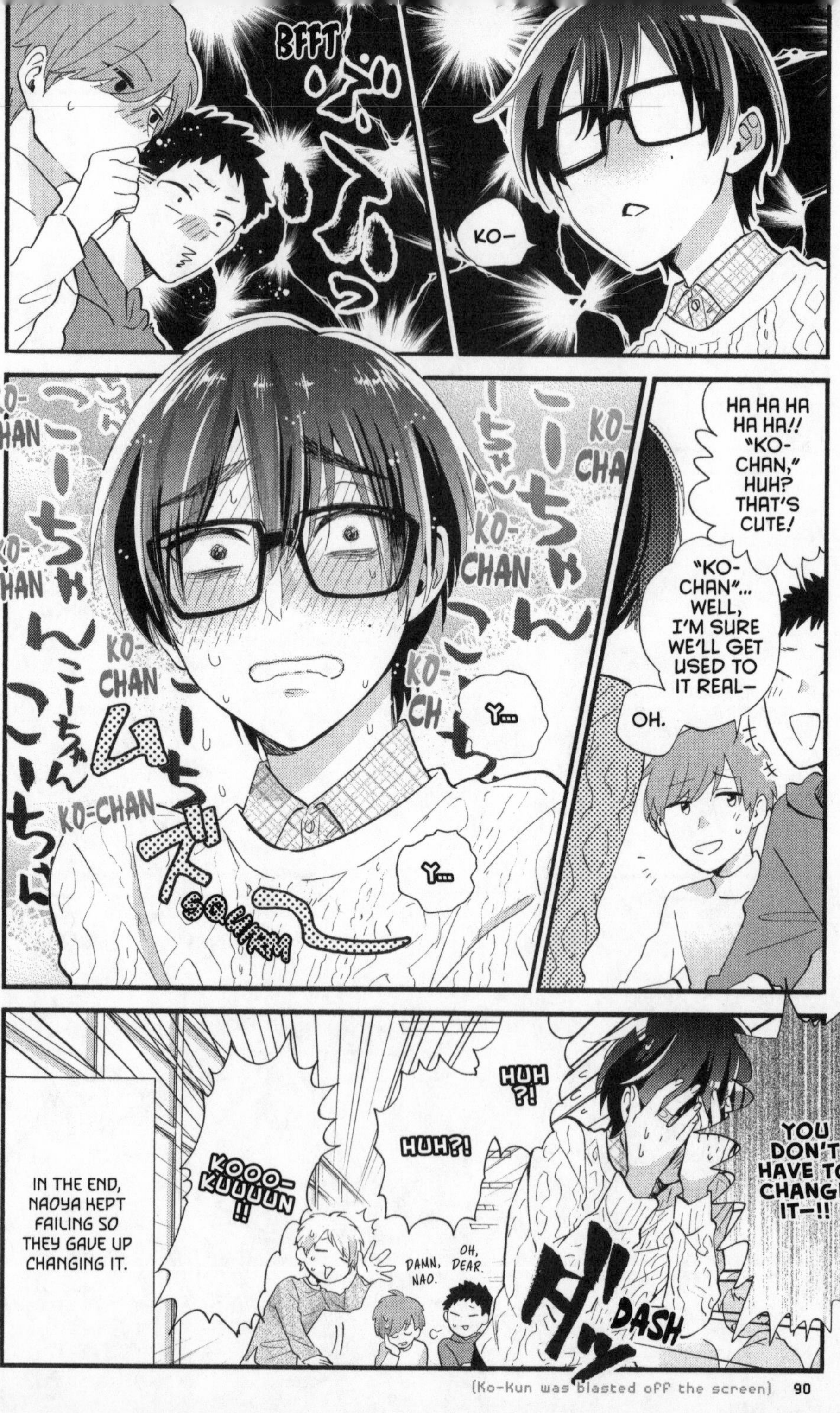
KO-
BFFT
HA HA HA HA HA!! "KO-CHAN," HUH? THAT'S CUTE!
"KO-CHAN"... WELL, I'M SURE WE'LL GET USED TO IT REAL—
OH.
KO-CHAN
KO-CHAN
KO-CHAN
KO-CHAN
KO-CH
Y...
KO-CHAN
KO-CHAN
Y...
SQUIRM
YOU DON'T HAVE TO CHANGE IT—!!
DASH
HUH ?!
HUH?!
KOOO-KUUUUN !!
OH, DEAR.
DAMN, NAO.
IN THE END, NAOYA KEPT FAILING SO THEY GAVE UP CHANGING IT.

(Ko-Kun was blasted off the screen)

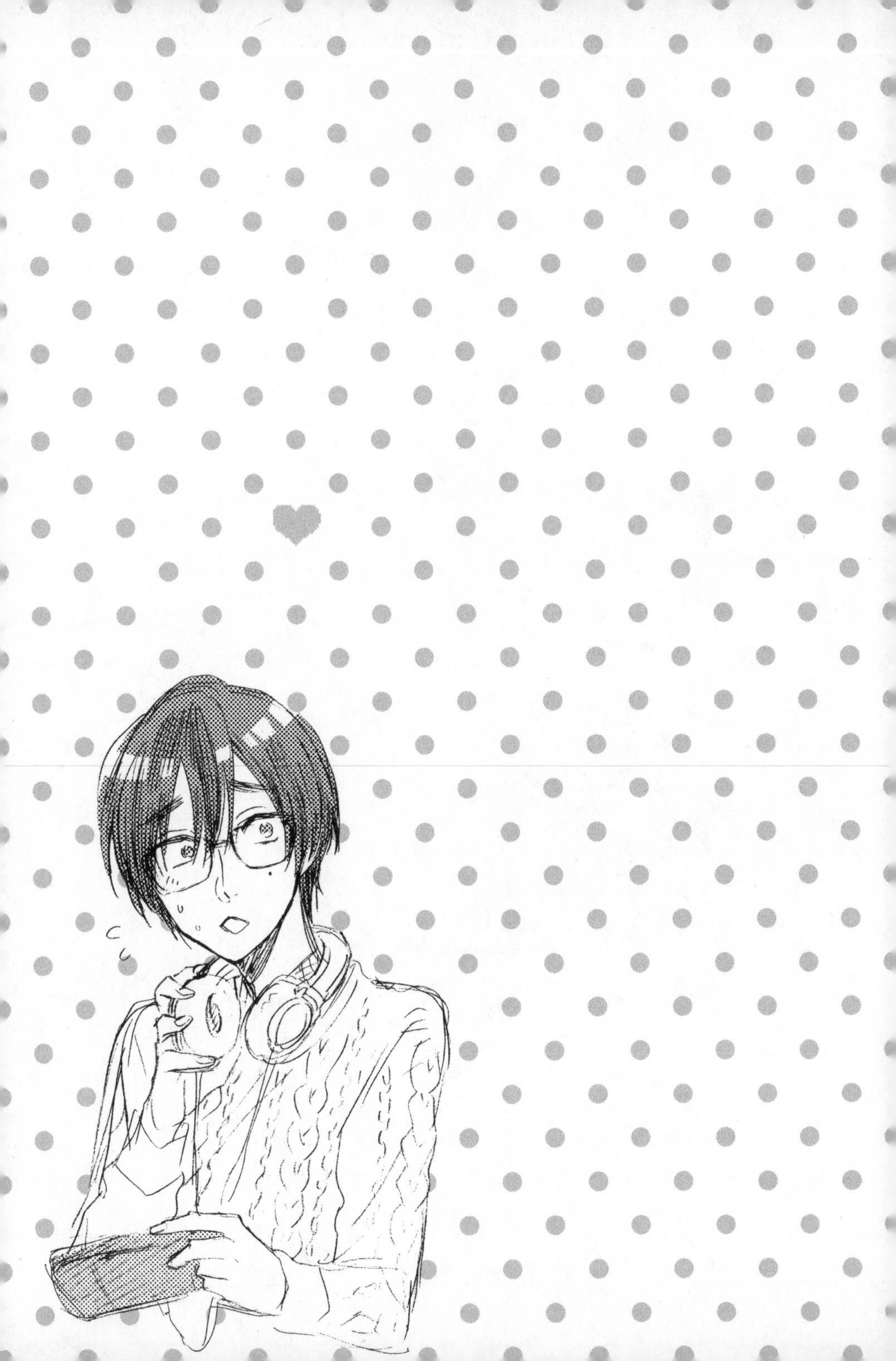

▼ HIRO PAJAMAS

#02
#03

▼ NARU PAJAMAS (1)

#01

▼ NAO HOUSE CLOTHES

#05

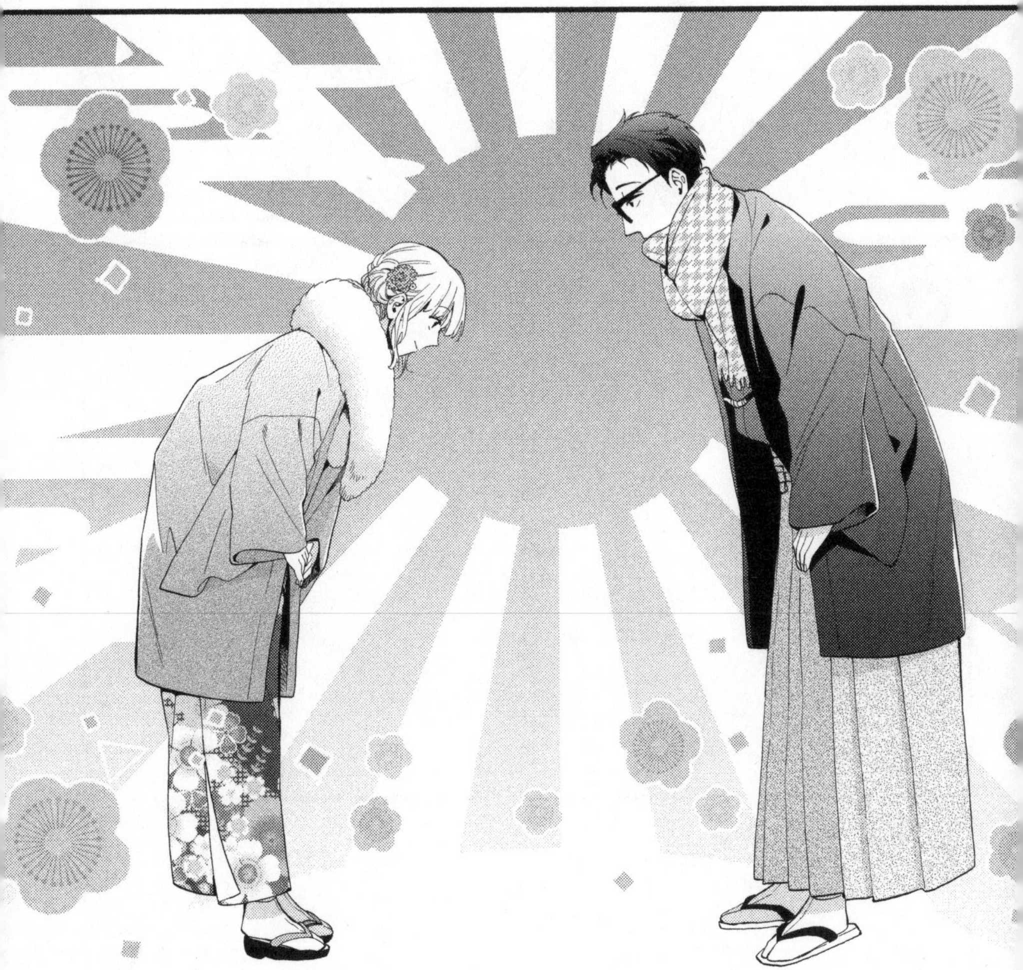

Episode.... 53

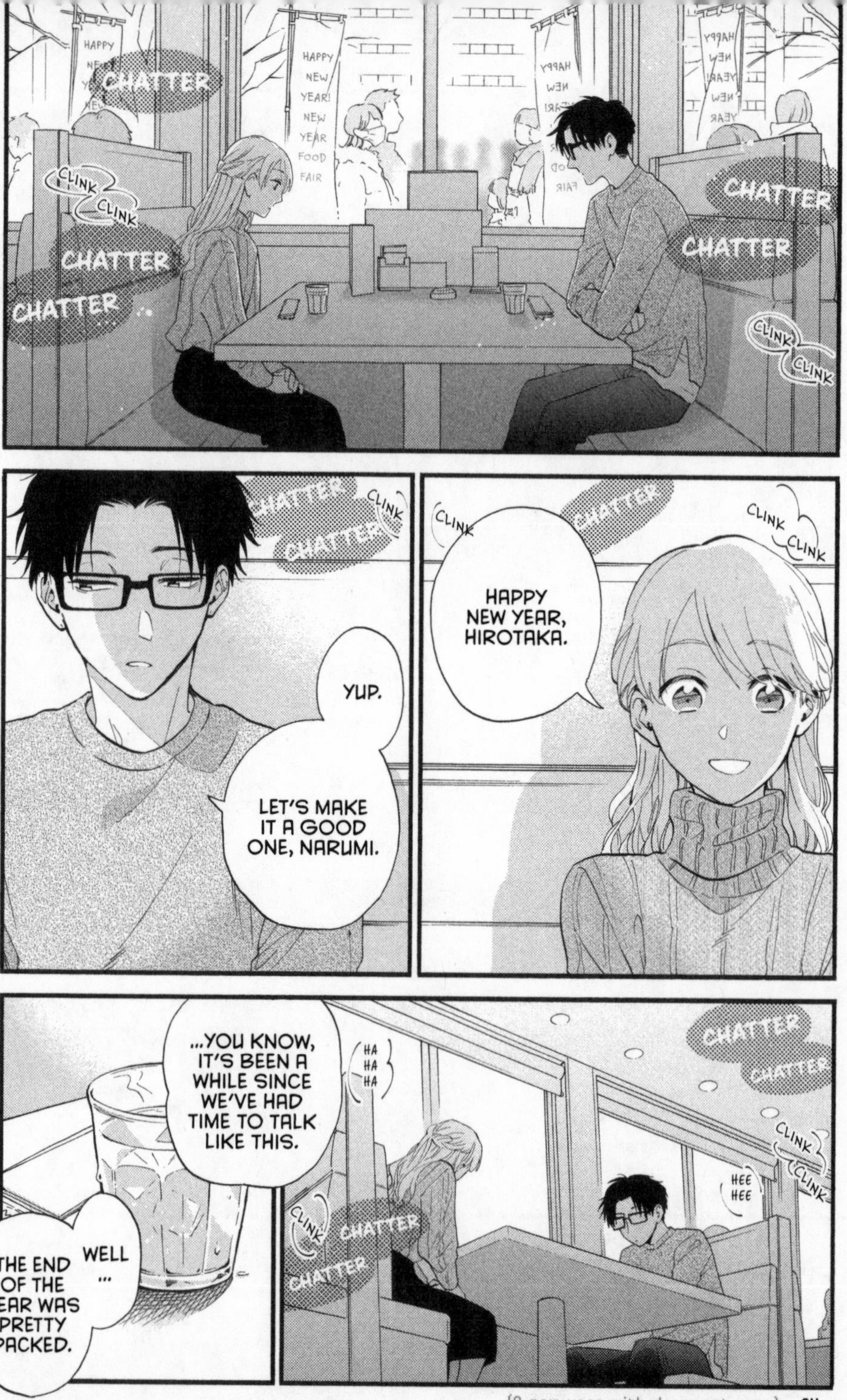
HAPPY NEW YEAR! NEW YEAR FOOD FAIR
CHATTER
CHATTER CHATTER
CLINK CLINK
CHATTER CHATTER
CLINK CLINK
CLINK CLINK
CLINK
CHATTER
HAPPY NEW YEAR, HIROTAKA.
CHATTER CHATTER
CLINK
YUP.
LET'S MAKE IT A GOOD ONE, NARUMI.
CHATTER CHATTER
CLINK CLINK
HEE HEE
HA HA HA
...YOU KNOW, IT'S BEEN A WHILE SINCE WE'VE HAD TIME TO TALK LIKE THIS.
CLINK
CHATTER CHATTER
WELL ...
THE END OF THE YEAR WAS PRETTY PACKED.

(A new year with downcast eyes)

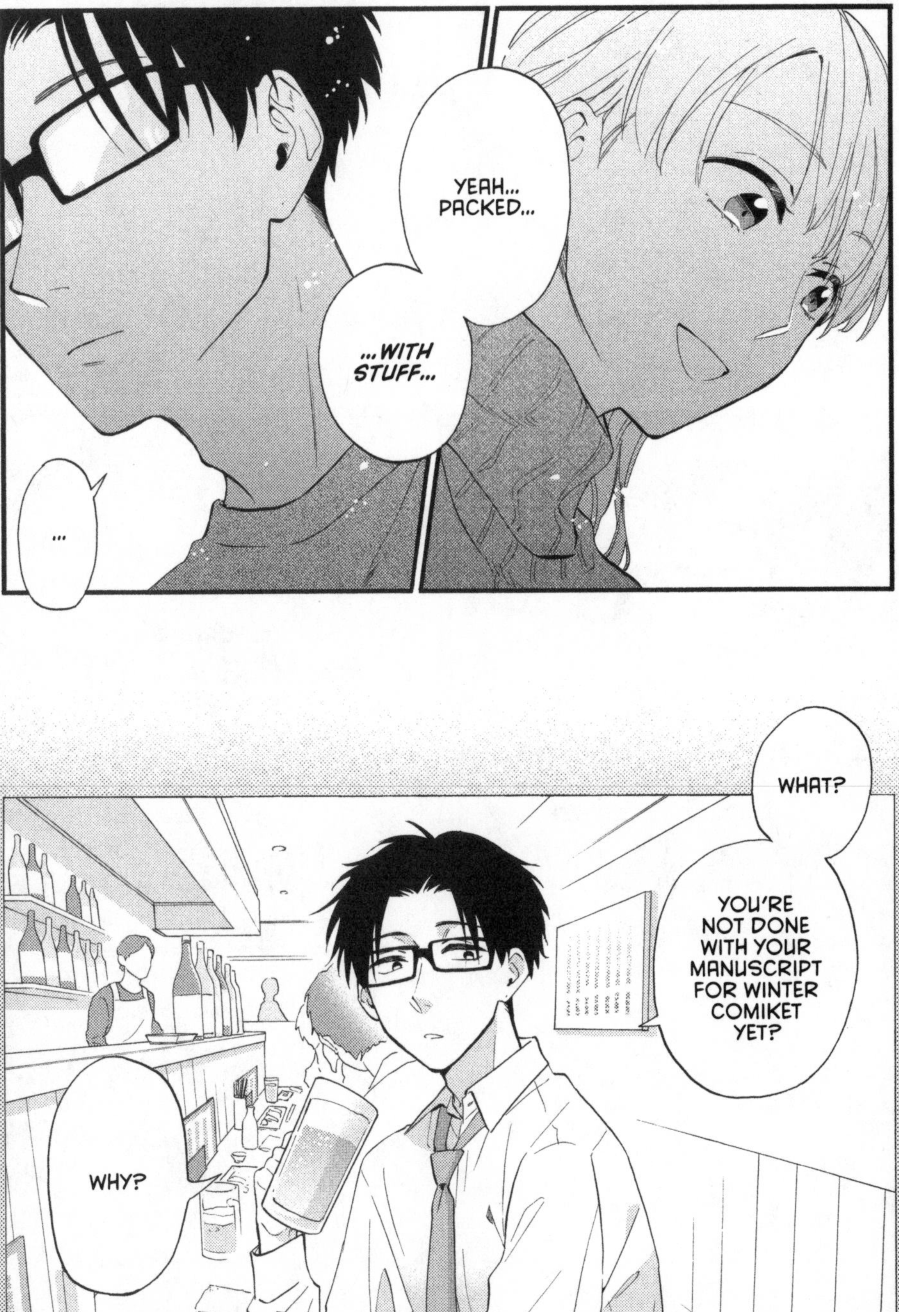
YEAH... PACKED...
...WITH STUFF...
...
WHAT?
YOU'RE NOT DONE WITH YOUR MANUSCRIPT FOR WINTER COMIKET YET?
WHY?

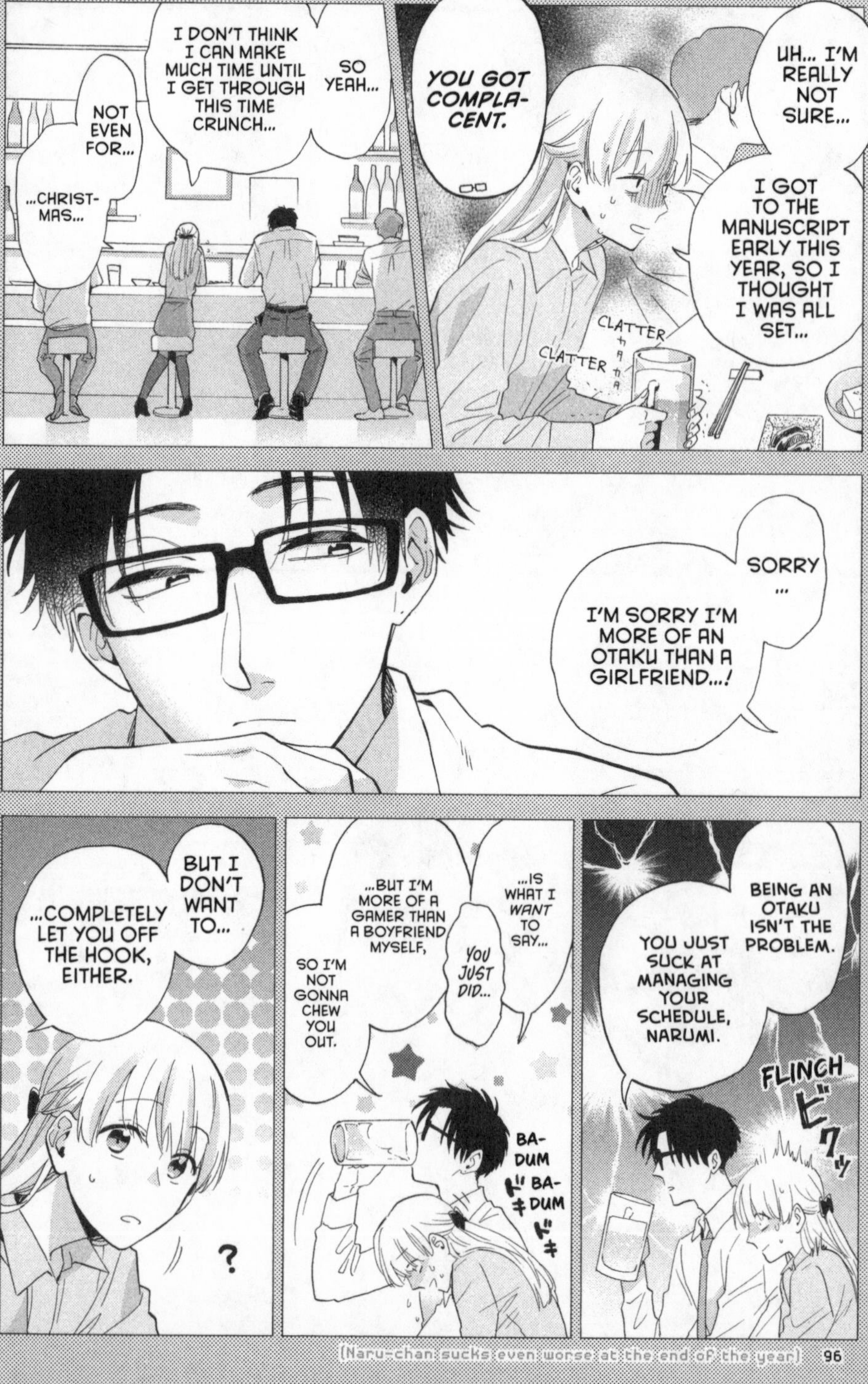
UH... I'M REALLY NOT SURE...
I GOT TO THE MANUSCRIPT EARLY THIS YEAR, SO I THOUGHT I WAS ALL SET...
YOU GOT COMPLACENT.
CLATTER
CLATTER
SO YEAH...
I DON'T THINK I CAN MAKE MUCH TIME UNTIL I GET THROUGH THIS TIME CRUNCH...
NOT EVEN FOR...
...CHRISTMAS...
SORRY...
I'M SORRY I'M MORE OF AN OTAKU THAN A GIRLFRIEND...!
BEING AN OTAKU ISN'T THE PROBLEM.
YOU JUST SUCK AT MANAGING YOUR SCHEDULE, NARUMI.
FLINCH
ビクッ
...IS WHAT I *WANT* TO SAY...
...BUT I'M MORE OF A GAMER THAN A BOYFRIEND MYSELF,
YOU JUST DID...
SO I'M NOT GONNA CHEW YOU OUT.
BA-DUM BA-DUM
ドキ ドキ
BUT I DON'T WANT TO...
...COMPLETELY LET YOU OFF THE HOOK, EITHER.
?

(Naru-chan sucks even worse at the end of the year)

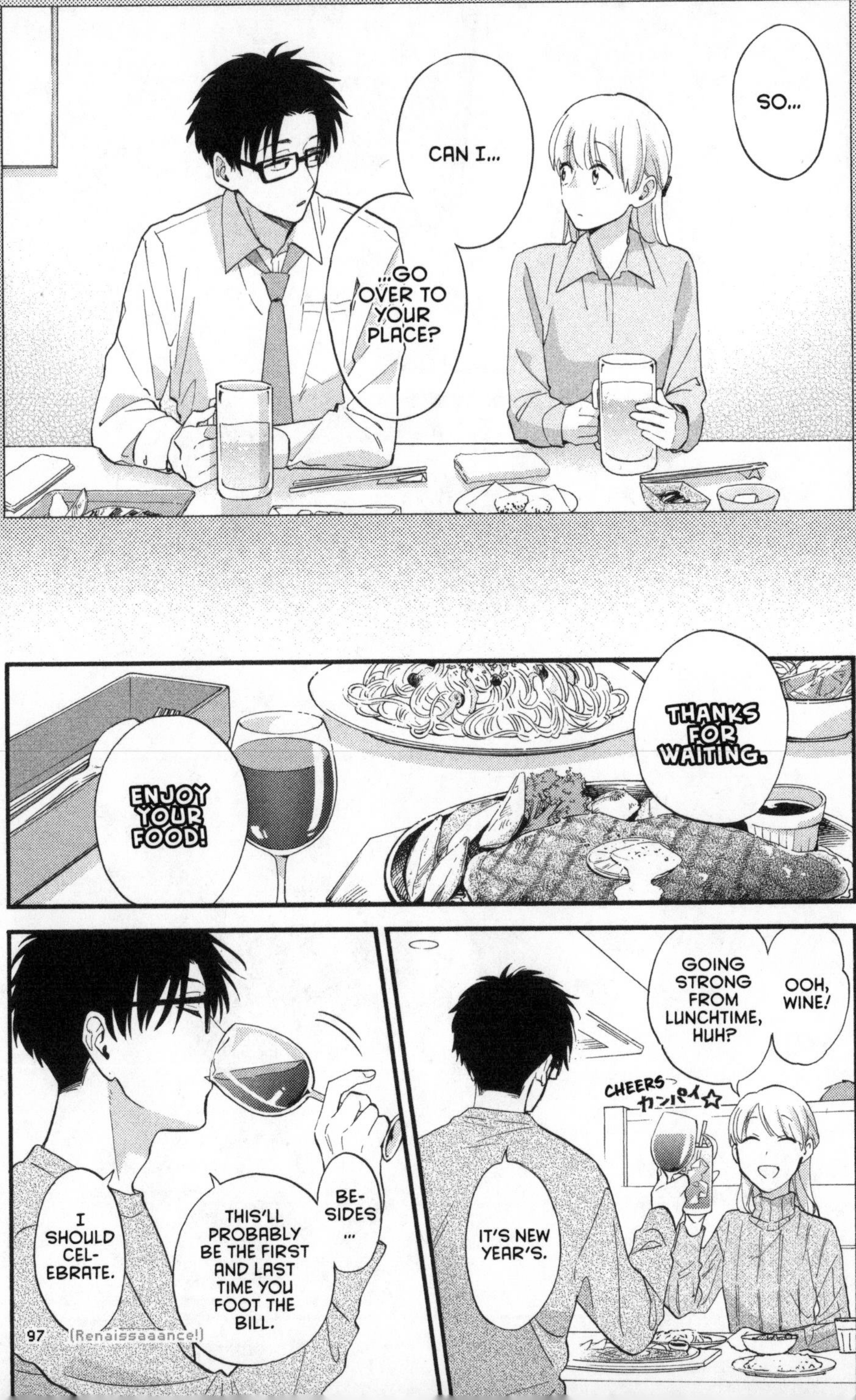
SO...
CAN I...
...GO OVER TO YOUR PLACE?
THANKS FOR WAITING.
ENJOY YOUR FOOD!
OOH, WINE!
GOING STRONG FROM LUNCHTIME, HUH?
CHEERS カンパイ☆
IT'S NEW YEAR'S.
BESIDES...
THIS'LL PROBABLY BE THE FIRST AND LAST TIME YOU FOOT THE BILL.
I SHOULD CELEBRATE.

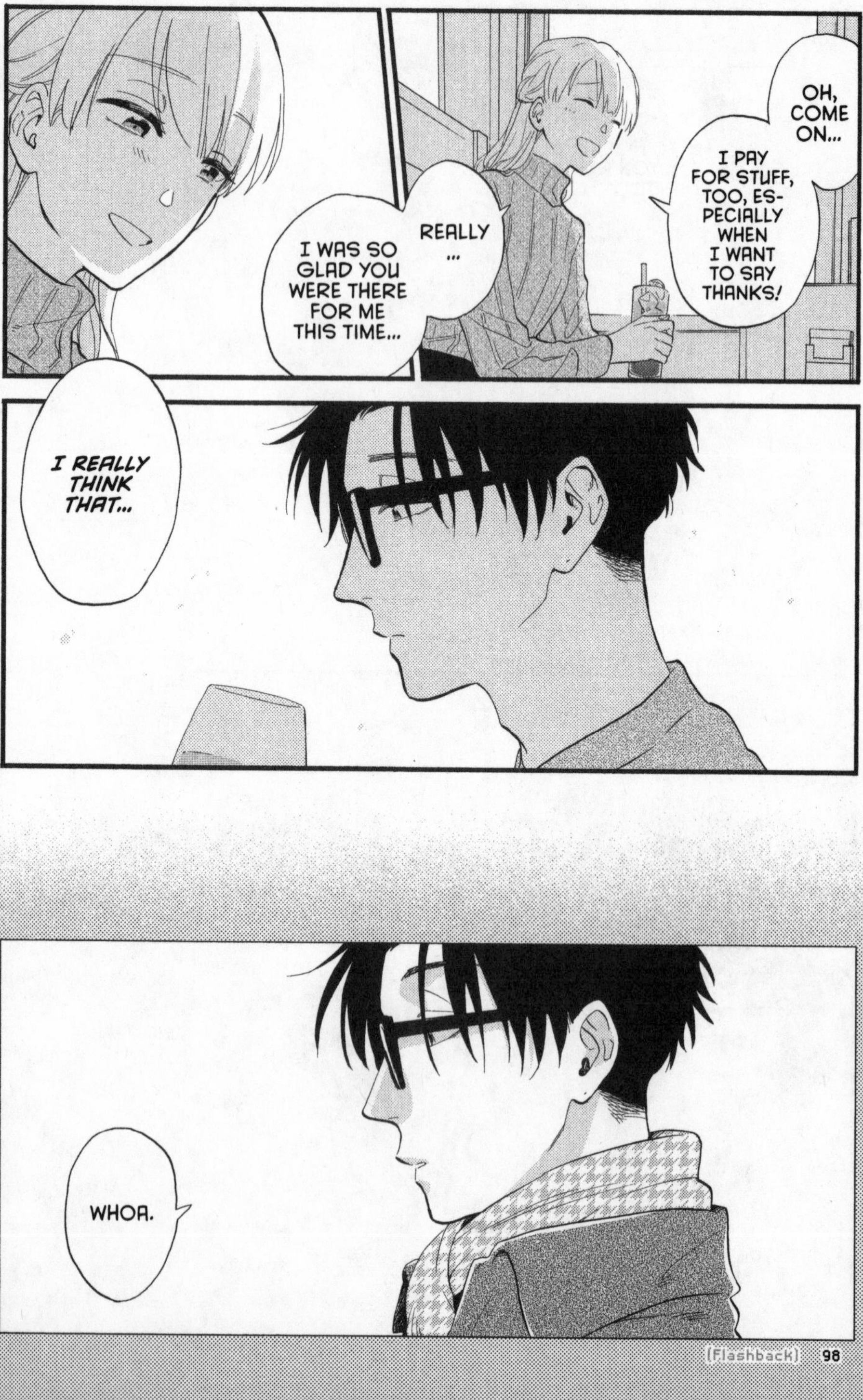
OH, COME ON...
I PAY FOR STUFF, TOO, ES-PECIALLY WHEN I WANT TO SAY THANKS!
REALLY ...
I WAS SO GLAD YOU WERE THERE FOR ME THIS TIME...
I REALLY THINK THAT...
WHOA.

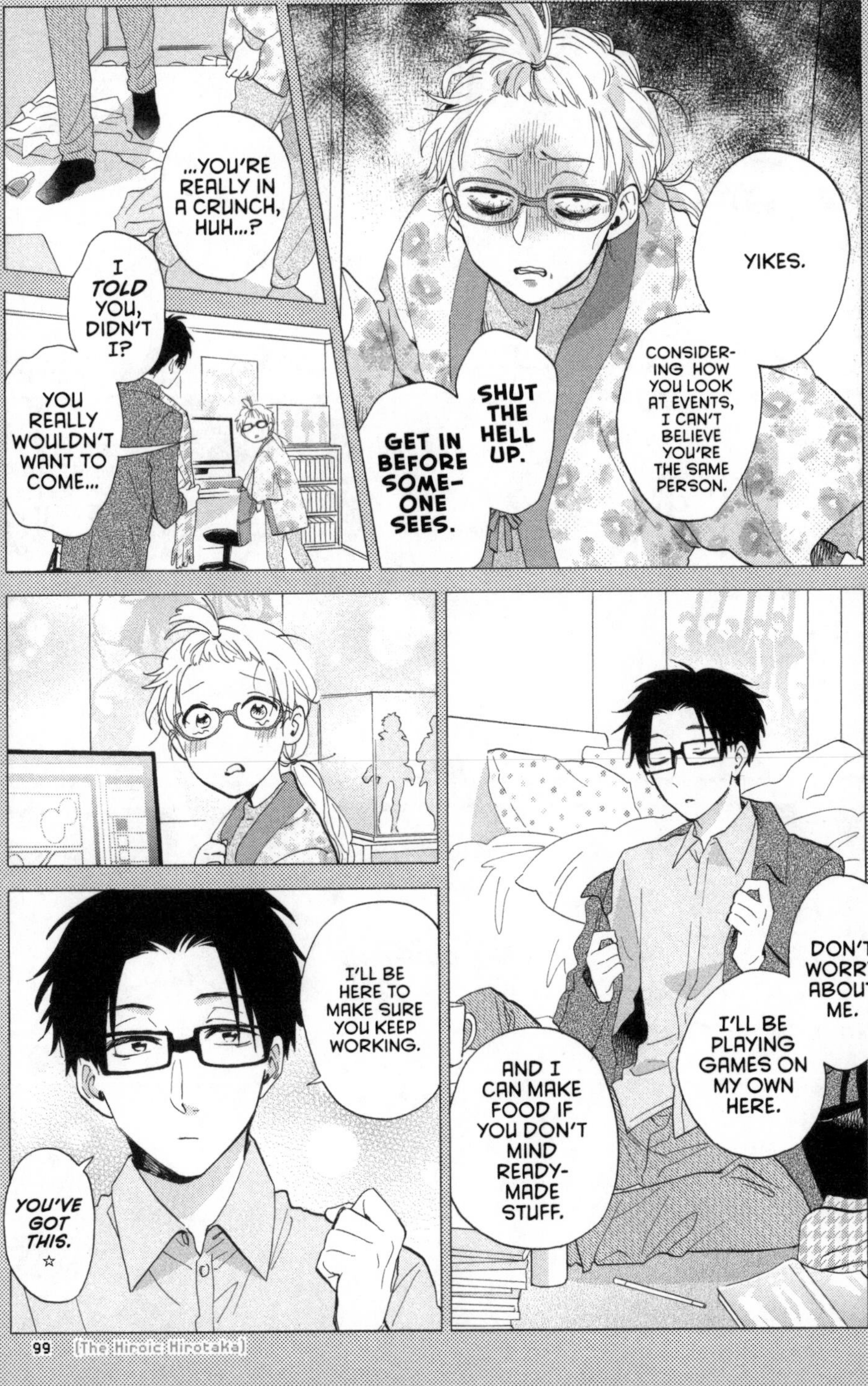
YIKES.
CONSIDERING HOW YOU LOOK AT EVENTS, I CAN'T BELIEVE YOU'RE THE SAME PERSON.
SHUT THE HELL UP.
GET IN BEFORE SOMEONE SEES.
...YOU'RE REALLY IN A CRUNCH, HUH...?
I *TOLD* YOU, DIDN'T I?
YOU REALLY WOULDN'T WANT TO COME...
DON'T WORRY ABOUT ME.
I'LL BE PLAYING GAMES ON MY OWN HERE.
AND I CAN MAKE FOOD IF YOU DON'T MIND READY-MADE STUFF.
I'LL BE HERE TO MAKE SURE YOU KEEP WORKING.
YOU'VE GOT THIS. ☆

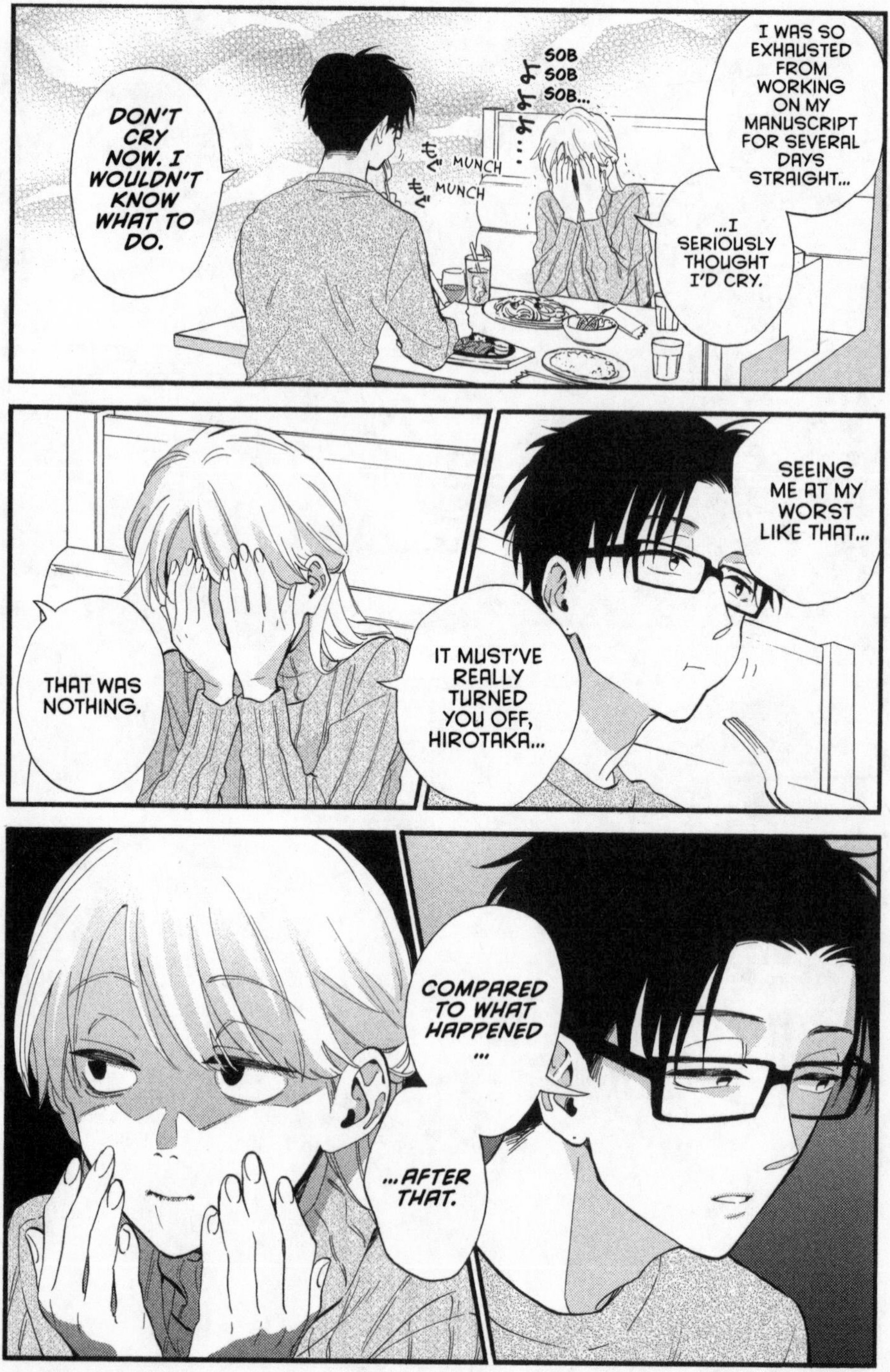
I WAS SO EXHAUSTED FROM WORKING ON MY MANUSCRIPT FOR SEVERAL DAYS STRAIGHT...
...I SERIOUSLY THOUGHT I'D CRY.
よよよ…
SOB SOB SOB...
もぐ もぐ
MUNCH MUNCH
DON'T CRY NOW. I WOULDN'T KNOW WHAT TO DO.
SEEING ME AT MY WORST LIKE THAT...
IT MUST'VE REALLY TURNED YOU OFF, HIROTAKA...
THAT WAS NOTHING.
COMPARED TO WHAT HAPPENED...
...AFTER THAT.

(The face under her hands...)

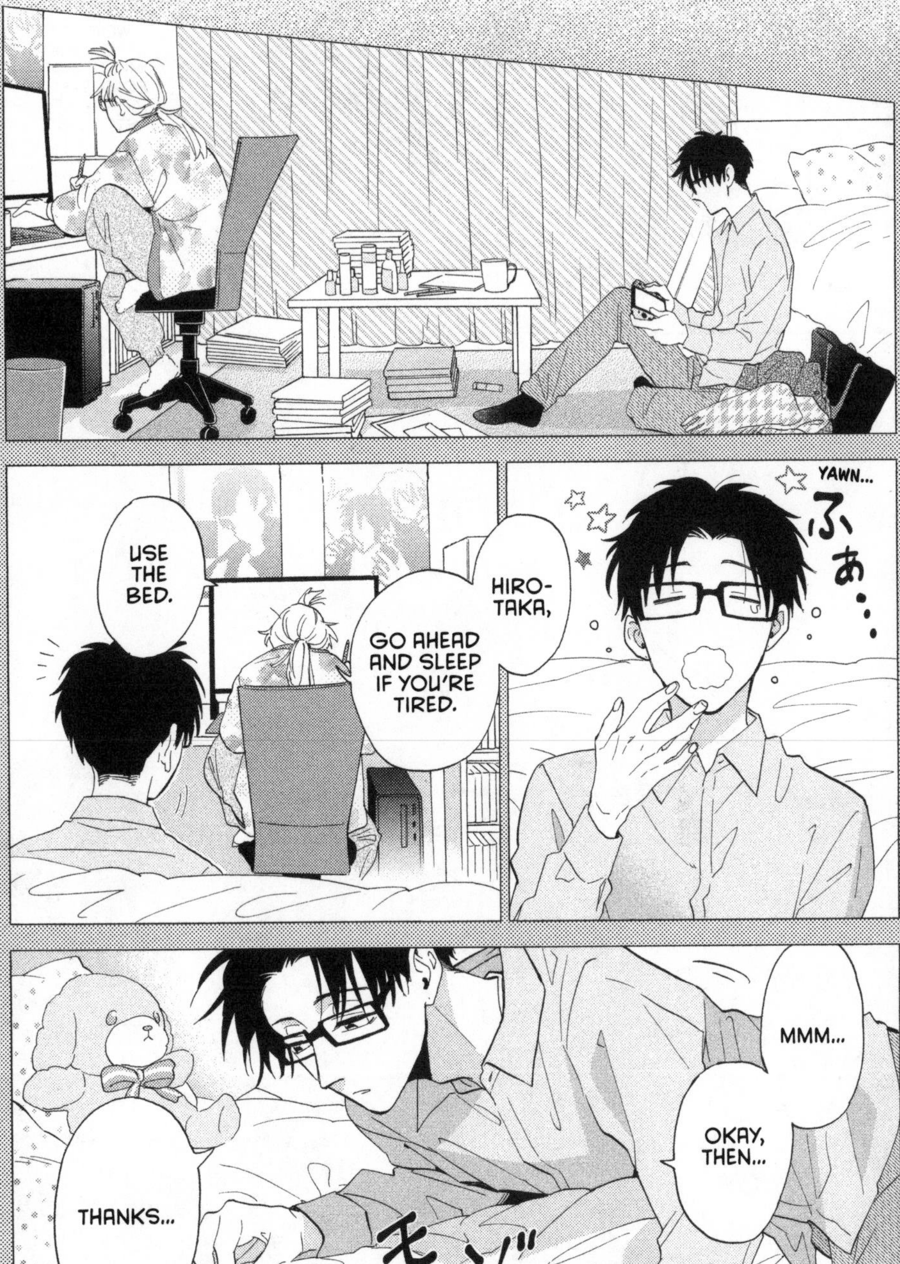
YAWN...
ふぁ…
HIRO-TAKA,
GO AHEAD AND SLEEP IF YOU'RE TIRED.
USE THE BED.
MMM...
OKAY, THEN...
THANKS...
モソ"…
RUSTLE

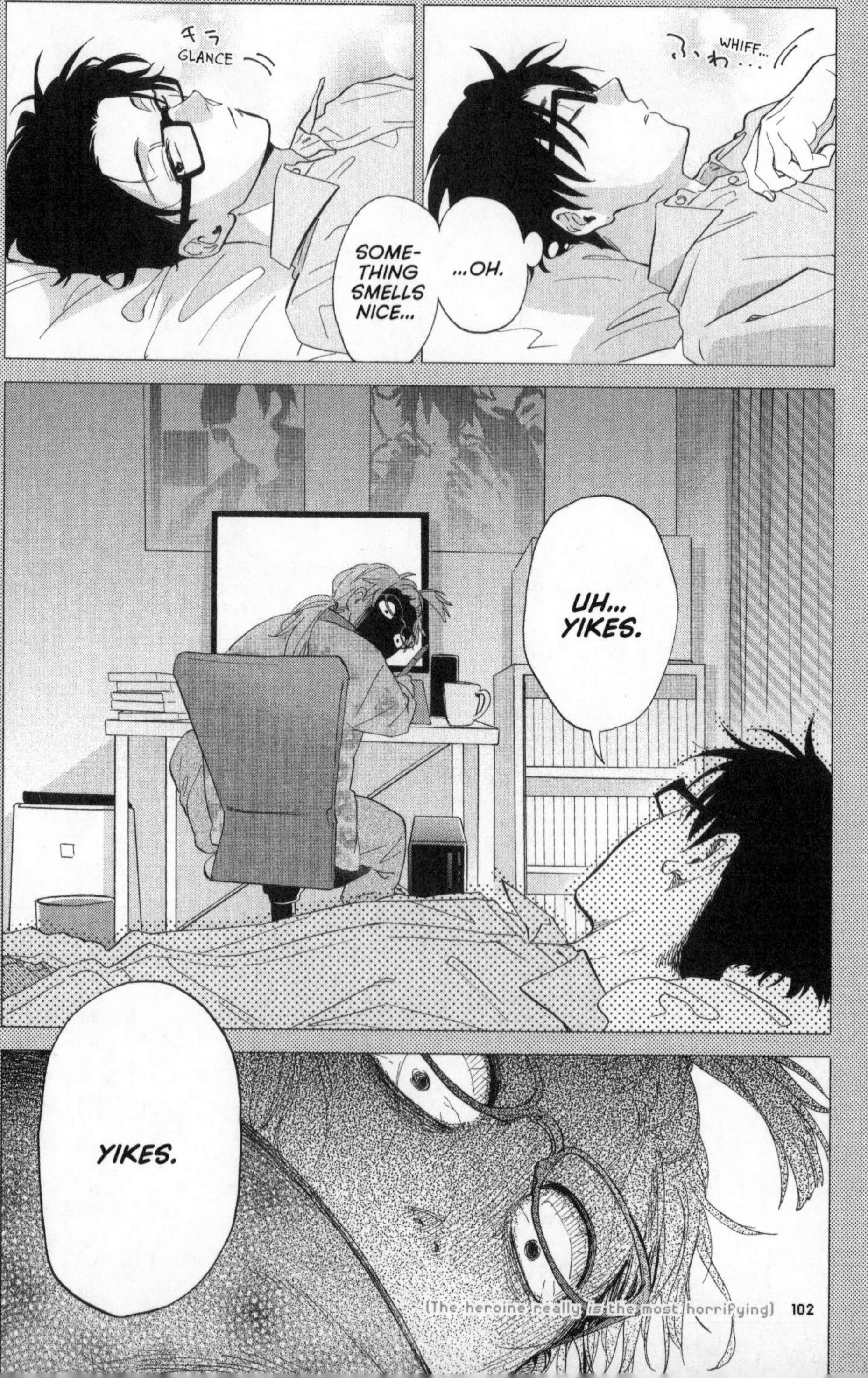

ふわ…
WHIFF...
...OH.
チラ
GLANCE
SOME-THING SMELLS NICE...
UH... YIKES.
YIKES.
(The heroine really is the most horrifying)

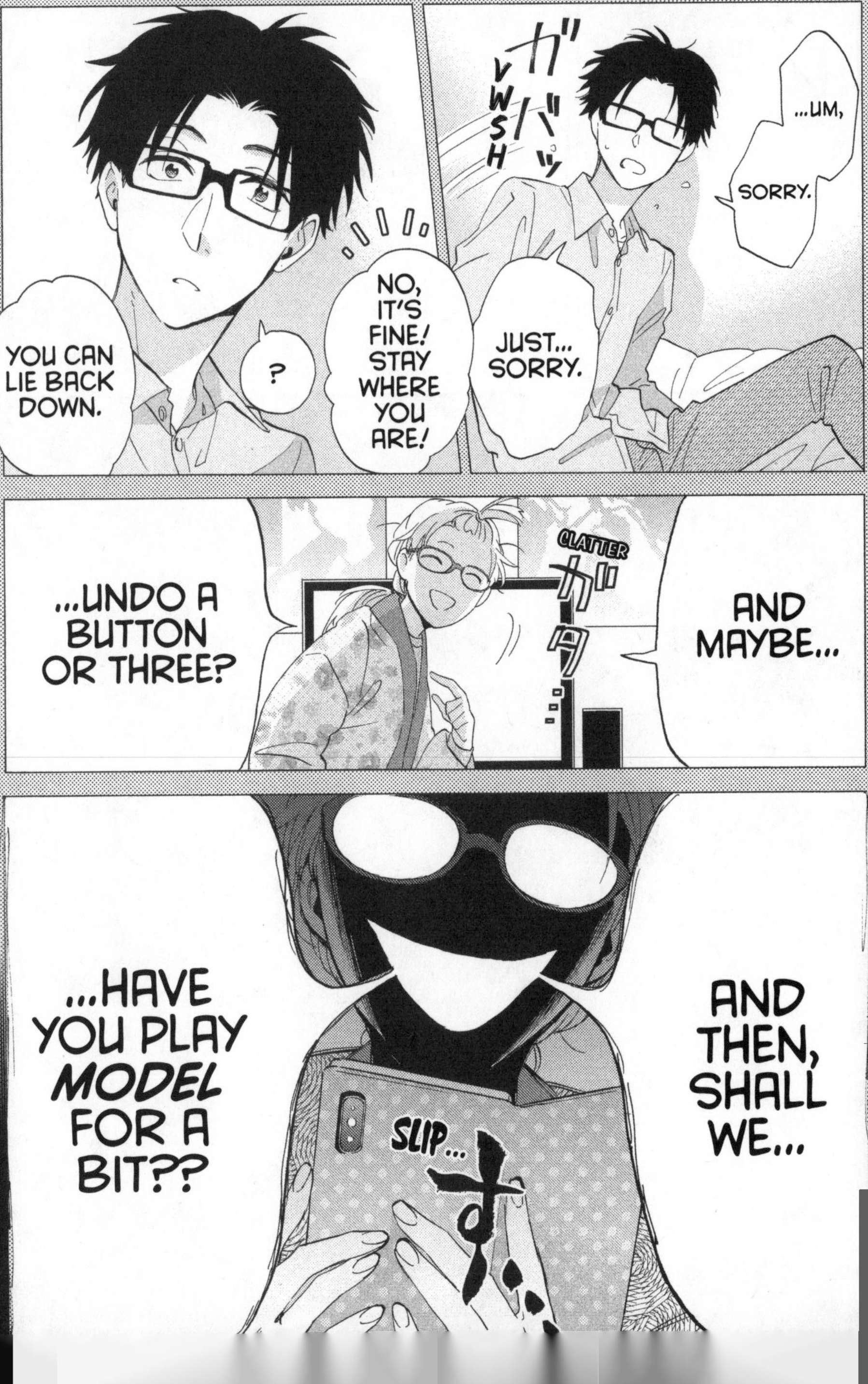
...UM,
SORRY.
VWSH
JUST... SORRY.
NO, IT'S FINE! STAY WHERE YOU ARE!
?
YOU CAN LIE BACK DOWN.
AND MAYBE...
CLATTER
...UNDO A BUTTON OR THREE?
AND THEN, SHALL WE...
SLIP...
...HAVE YOU PLAY *MODEL* FOR A BIT??

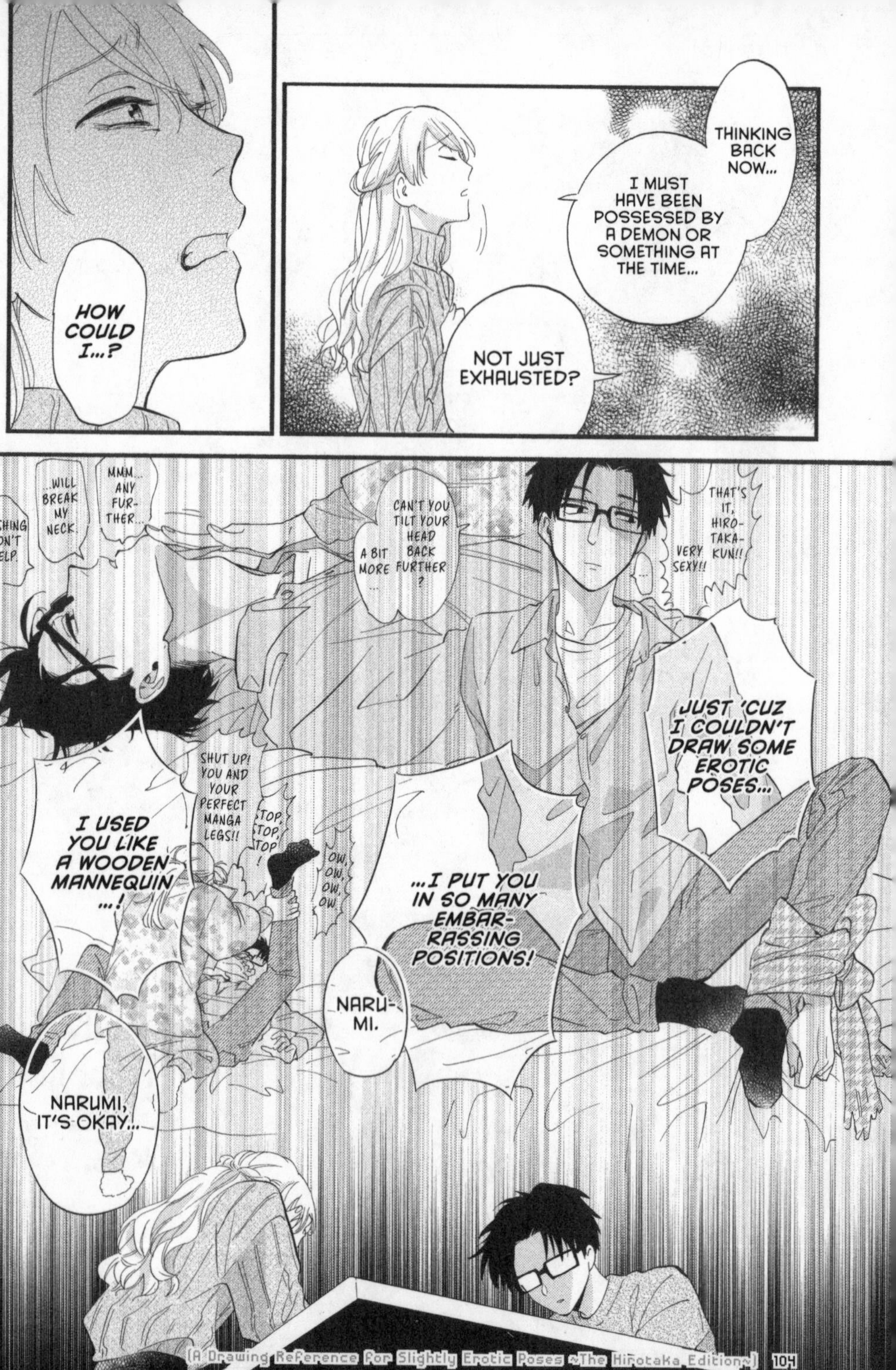
THINKING BACK NOW...
I MUST HAVE BEEN POSSESSED BY A DEMON OR SOMETHING AT THE TIME...
NOT JUST EXHAUSTED?
HOW COULD I...?
THAT'S IT, HIRO-TAKA-KUN!!
VERY SEXY!!
...
CAN'T YOU TILT YOUR HEAD BACK FURTHER?
A BIT MORE...
MMM... ANY FUR-THER...
...WILL BREAK MY NECK.
PUSHING WON'T HELP.
JUST 'CUZ I COULDN'T DRAW SOME EROTIC POSES...
...I PUT YOU IN SO MANY EMBAR-RASSING POSITIONS!
OW, OW, OW, OW
STOP, STOP, STOP!
SHUT UP! YOU AND YOUR PERFECT MANGA LEGS!!
I USED YOU LIKE A WOODEN MANNEQUIN...!
NARU-MI.
NARUMI, IT'S OKAY...

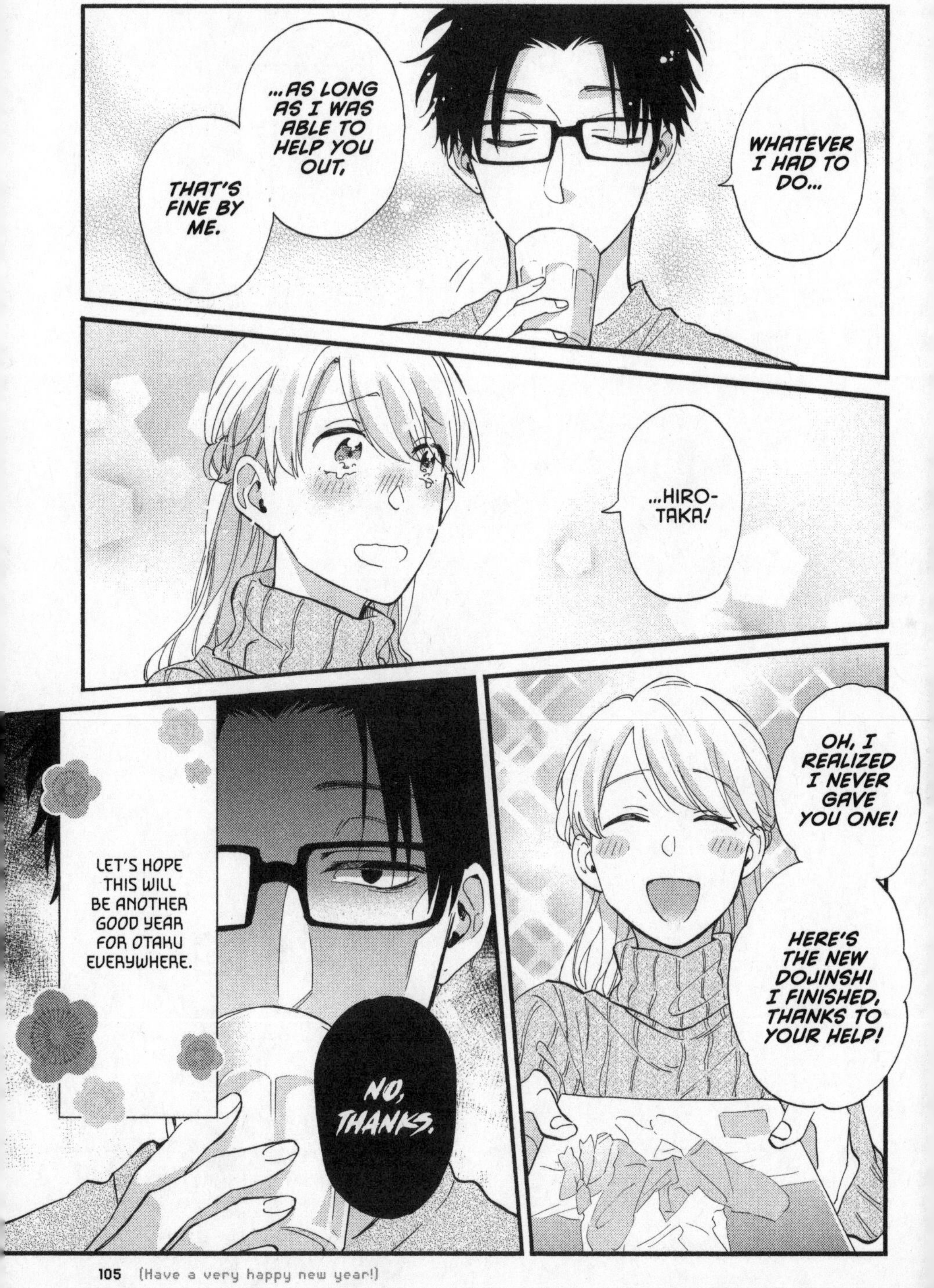
WHATEVER I HAD TO DO...
...AS LONG AS I WAS ABLE TO HELP YOU OUT,
THAT'S FINE BY ME.
...HIRO-TAKA!
OH, I REALIZED I NEVER GAVE YOU ONE!
HERE'S THE NEW DOJINSHI I FINISHED, THANKS TO YOUR HELP!
NO, THANKS.
LET'S HOPE THIS WILL BE ANOTHER GOOD YEAR FOR OTAKU EVERYWHERE.

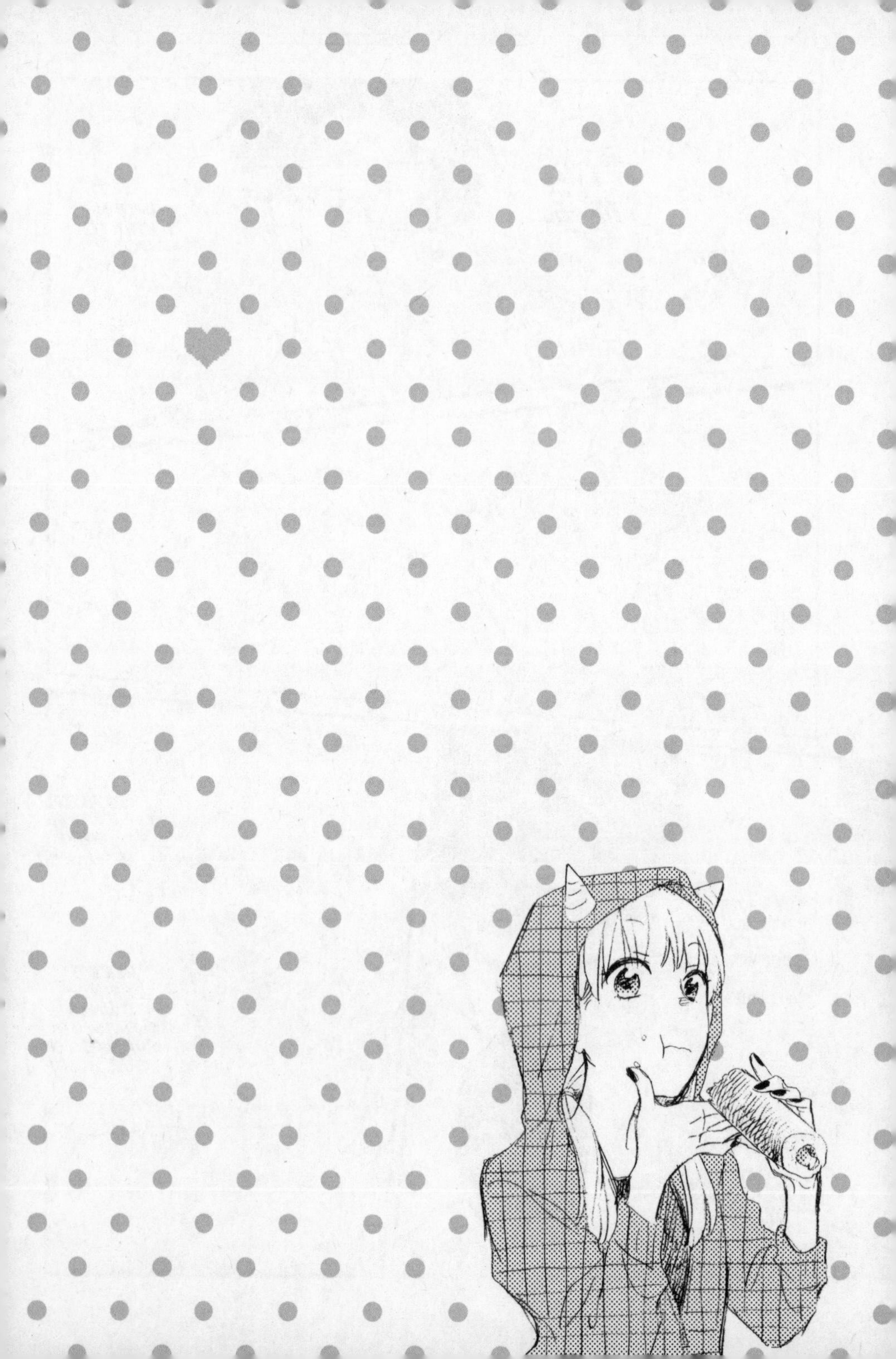

WOTAKOI: LOVE IS HARD FOR OTAKU

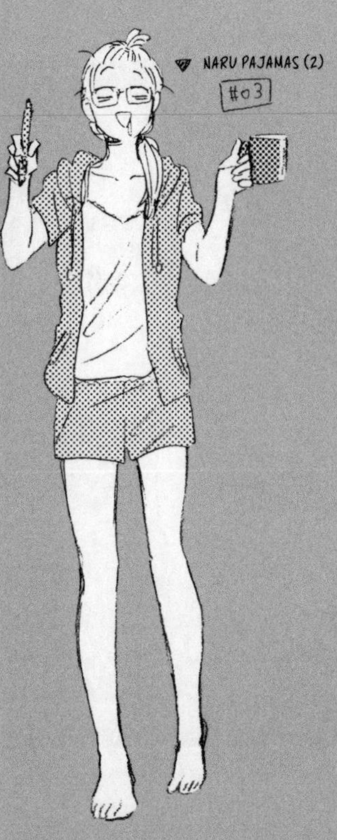

NARU PAJAMAS (2)
#03

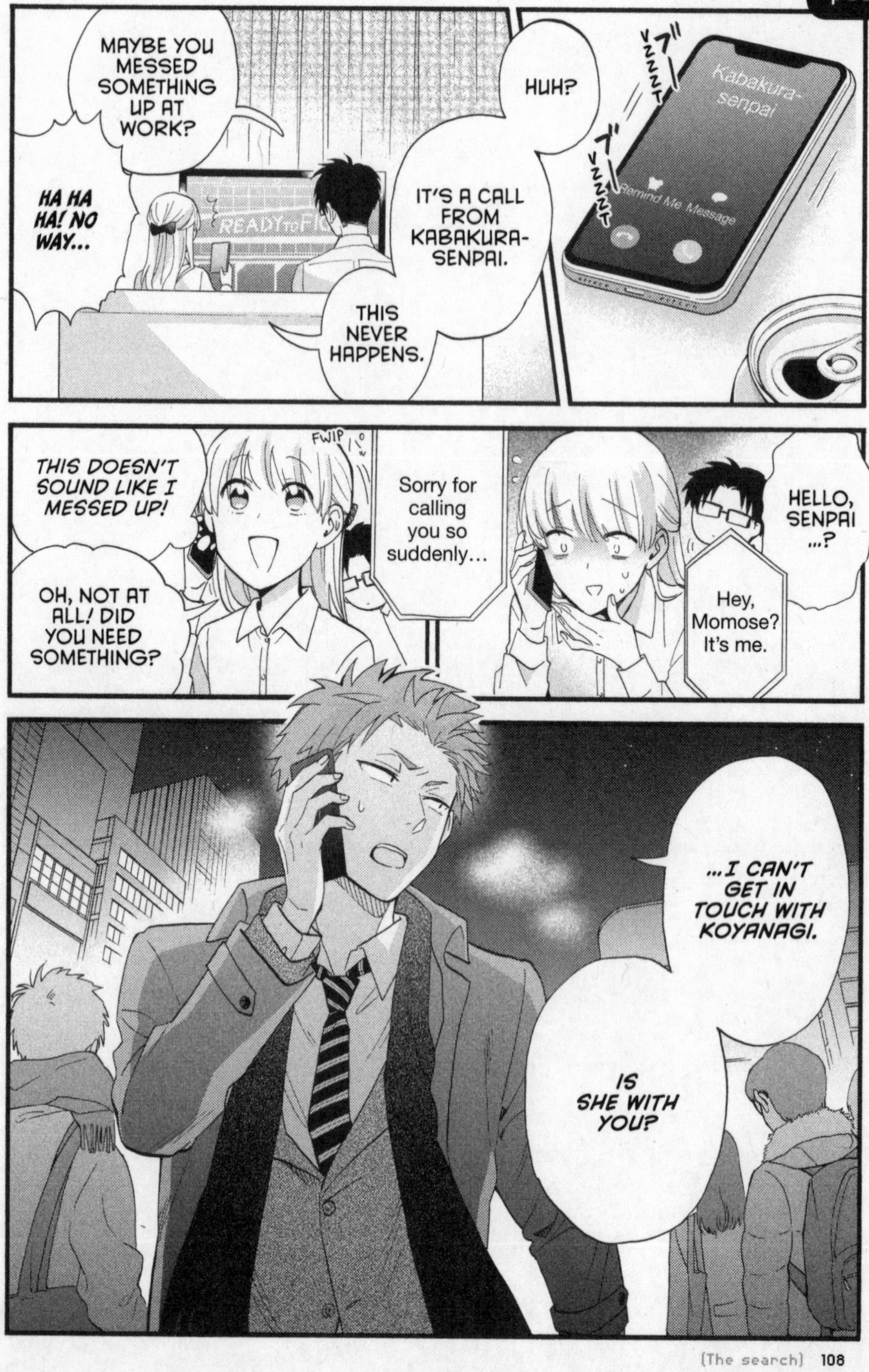
VZZZT
VZZZT
Kabakura-senpai
Remind Me
Message
HUH?
IT'S A CALL FROM KABAKURA-SENPAI.
THIS NEVER HAPPENS.
MAYBE YOU MESSED SOMETHING UP AT WORK?
HA HA HA! NO WAY...
READY TO FI
HELLO, SENPAI ...?
Hey, Momose? It's me.
FWIP
Sorry for calling you so suddenly...
THIS DOESN'T SOUND LIKE I MESSED UP!
OH, NOT AT ALL! DID YOU NEED SOMETHING?
...I CAN'T GET IN TOUCH WITH KOYANAGI.
IS SHE WITH YOU?

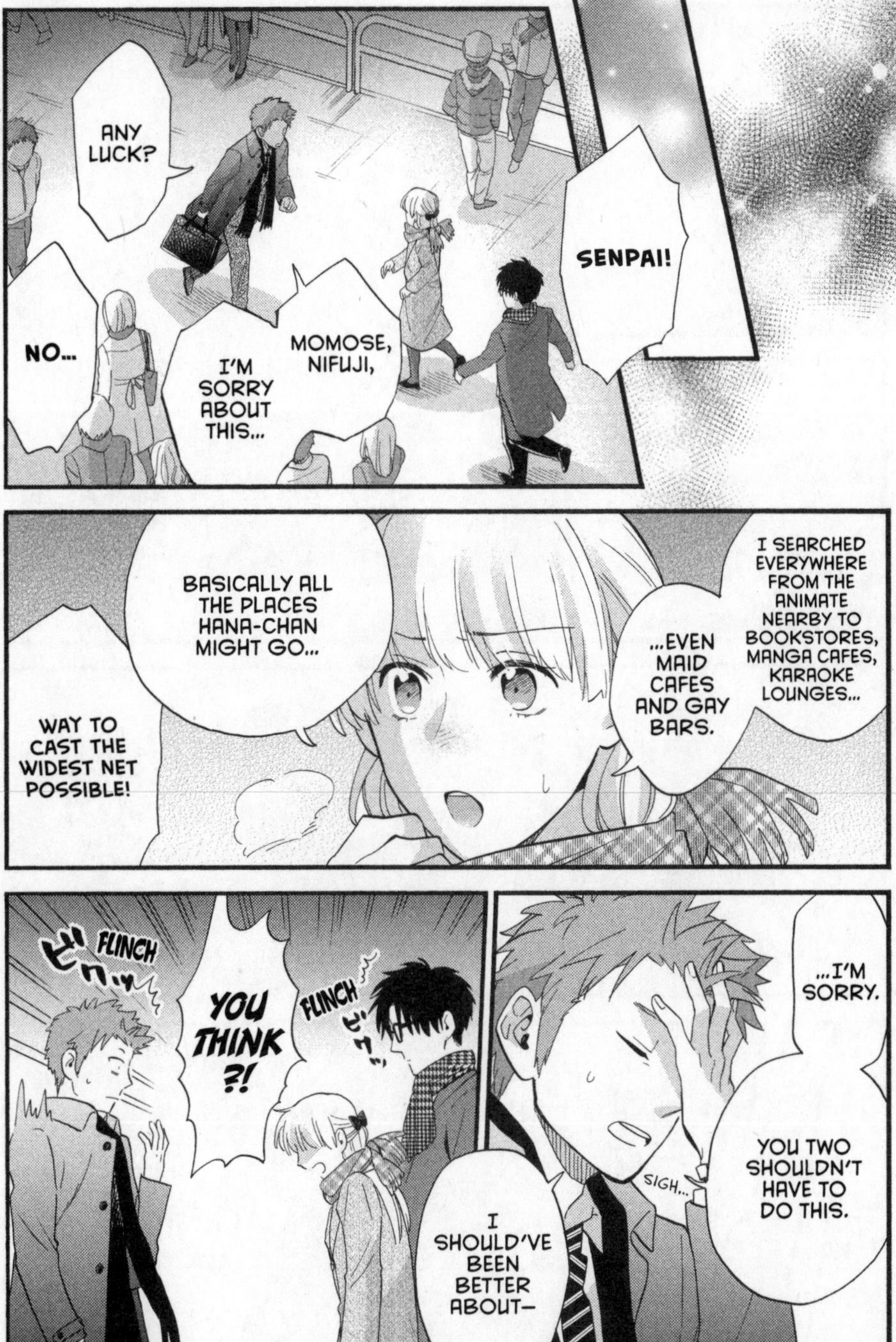
SENPAI!
ANY LUCK?
NO...
MOMOSE, NIFUJI,
I'M SORRY ABOUT THIS...
I SEARCHED EVERYWHERE FROM THE ANIMATE NEARBY TO BOOKSTORES, MANGA CAFES, KARAOKE LOUNGES...
...EVEN MAID CAFES AND GAY BARS.
BASICALLY ALL THE PLACES HANA-CHAN MIGHT GO...
WAY TO CAST THE WIDEST NET POSSIBLE!
...I'M SORRY.
YOU TWO SHOULDN'T HAVE TO DO THIS.
SIGH...
I SHOULD'VE BEEN BETTER ABOUT—
FLINCH
YOU THINK?!
FLINCH

 (Gay bars, too?)

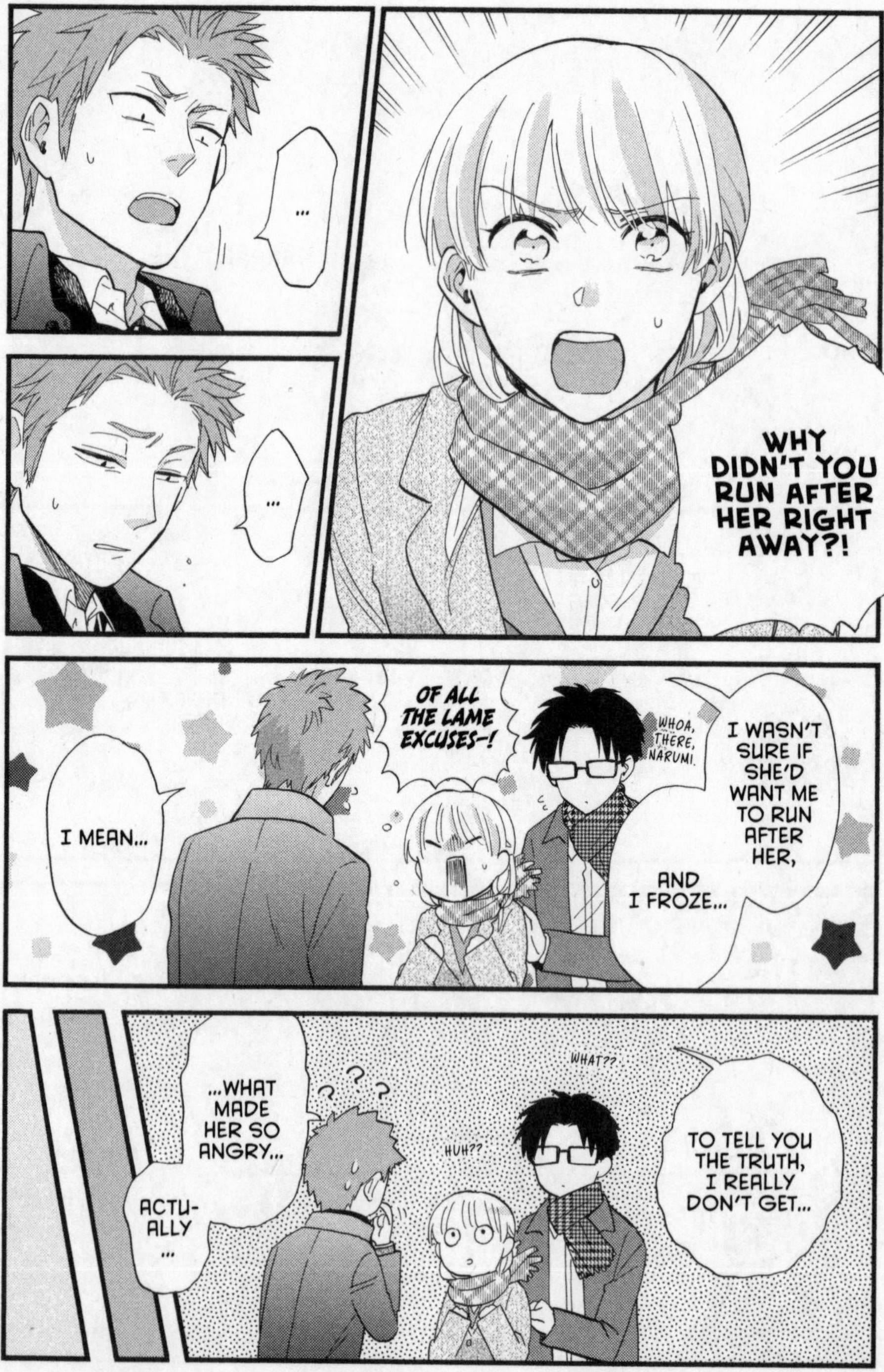
WHY DIDN'T YOU RUN AFTER HER RIGHT AWAY?!
...
...
I WASN'T SURE IF SHE'D WANT ME TO RUN AFTER HER,
AND I FROZE...
WHOA, THERE, NARUMI.
OF ALL THE LAME EXCUSES-!
I MEAN...
TO TELL YOU THE TRUTH, I REALLY DON'T GET...
WHAT??
HUH??
...WHAT MADE HER SO ANGRY...
ACTU-ALLY ...

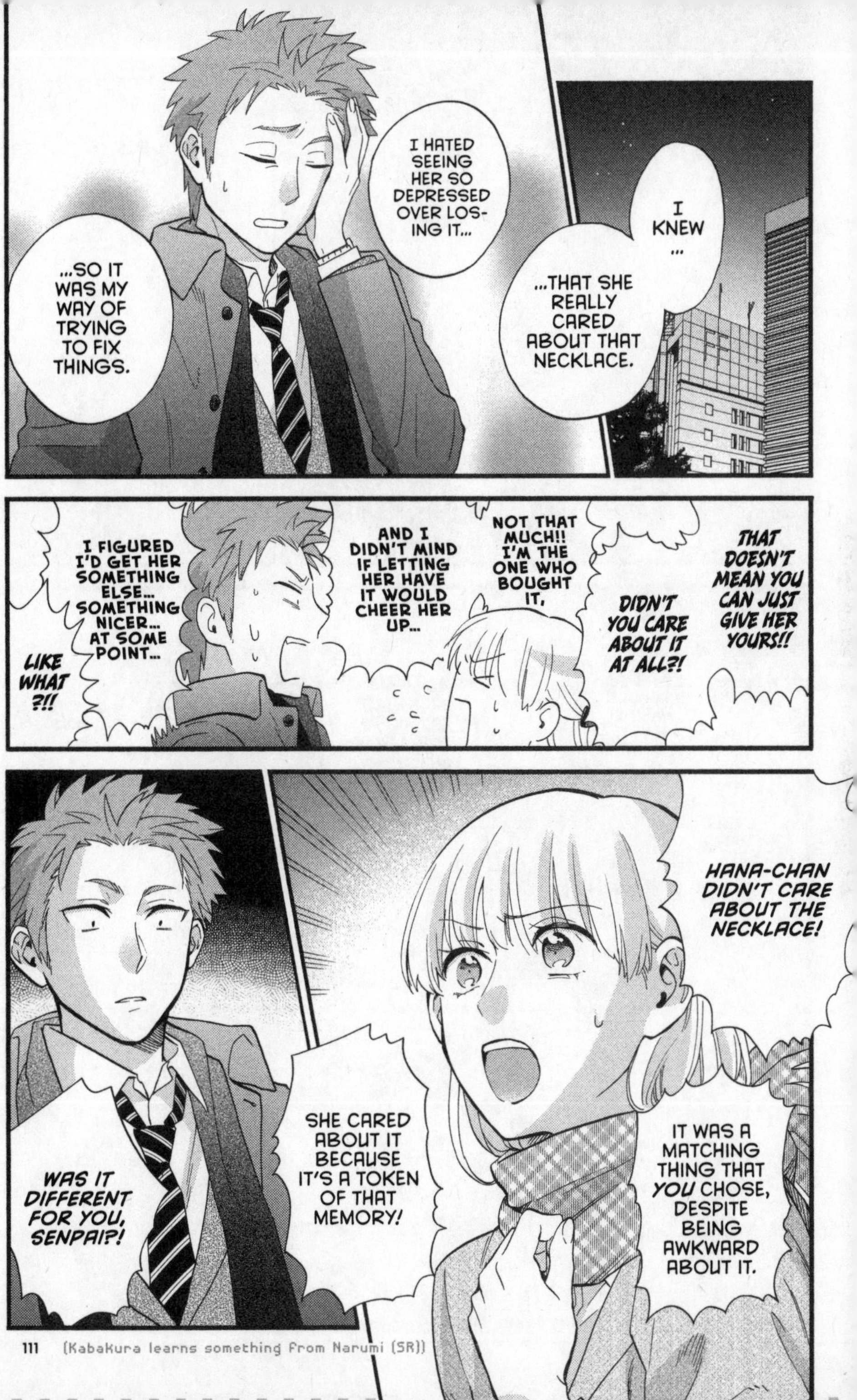
I KNEW...
...THAT SHE REALLY CARED ABOUT THAT NECKLACE.
I HATED SEEING HER SO DEPRESSED OVER LOS-ING IT...
...SO IT WAS MY WAY OF TRYING TO FIX THINGS.
THAT DOESN'T MEAN YOU CAN JUST GIVE HER YOURS!!
DIDN'T YOU CARE ABOUT IT AT ALL?!
NOT THAT MUCH!! I'M THE ONE WHO BOUGHT IT.
AND I DIDN'T MIND IF LETTING HER HAVE IT WOULD CHEER HER UP...
I FIGURED I'D GET HER SOMETHING ELSE... SOMETHING NICER... AT SOME POINT...
LIKE WHAT?!!
HANA-CHAN DIDN'T CARE ABOUT THE NECKLACE!
IT WAS A MATCHING THING THAT YOU CHOSE, DESPITE BEING AWKWARD ABOUT IT.
SHE CARED ABOUT IT BECAUSE IT'S A TOKEN OF THAT MEMORY!
WAS IT DIFFERENT FOR YOU, SENPAI?!

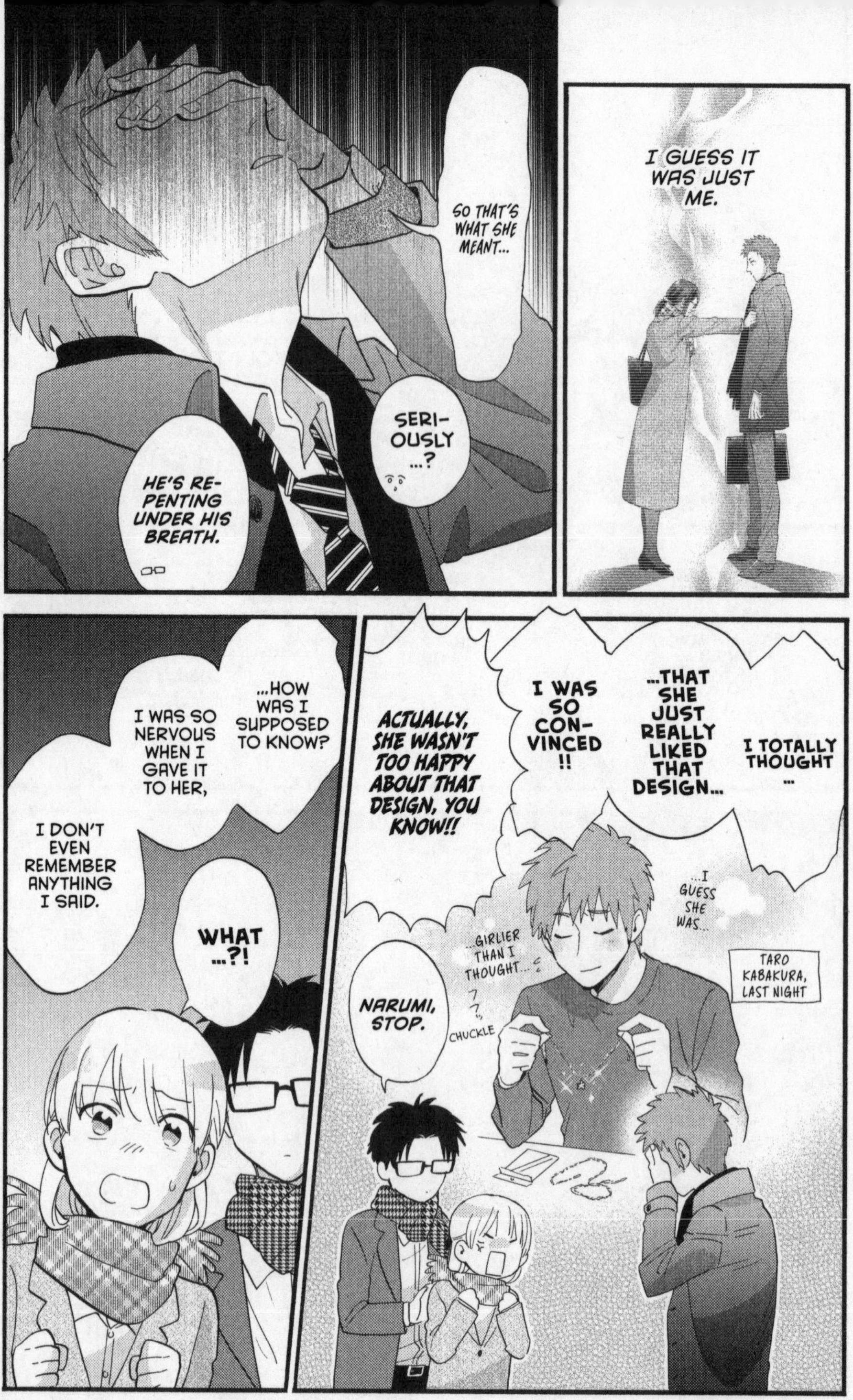
I GUESS IT WAS JUST ME.
SO THAT'S WHAT SHE MEANT...
SERI-OUSLY ...?
HE'S RE-PENTING UNDER HIS BREATH.
I TOTALLY THOUGHT ...
...THAT SHE JUST REALLY LIKED THAT DESIGN...
I WAS SO CON-VINCED !!
ACTUALLY, SHE WASN'T TOO HAPPY ABOUT THAT DESIGN, YOU KNOW!!
TARO KABAKURA, LAST NIGHT
...I GUESS SHE WAS...
...GIRLIER THAN I THOUGHT...
CHUCKLE
NARUMI, STOP.
...HOW WAS I SUPPOSED TO KNOW?
I WAS SO NERVOUS WHEN I GAVE IT TO HER,
I DON'T EVEN REMEMBER ANYTHING I SAID.
WHAT ...?!

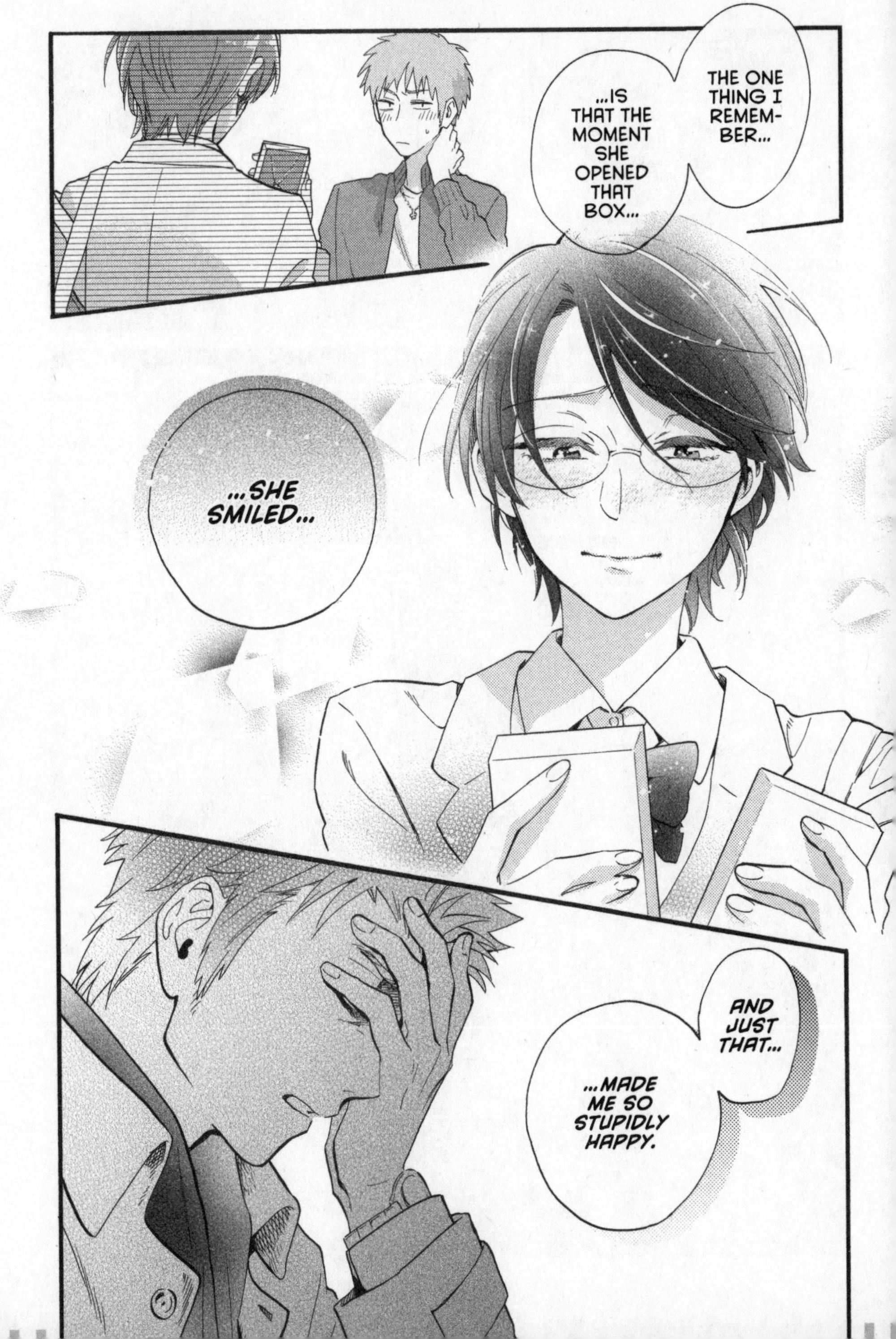
THE ONE THING I REMEMBER...
...IS THAT THE MOMENT SHE OPENED THAT BOX...
...SHE SMILED...
AND JUST THAT...
...MADE ME SO STUPIDLY HAPPY.

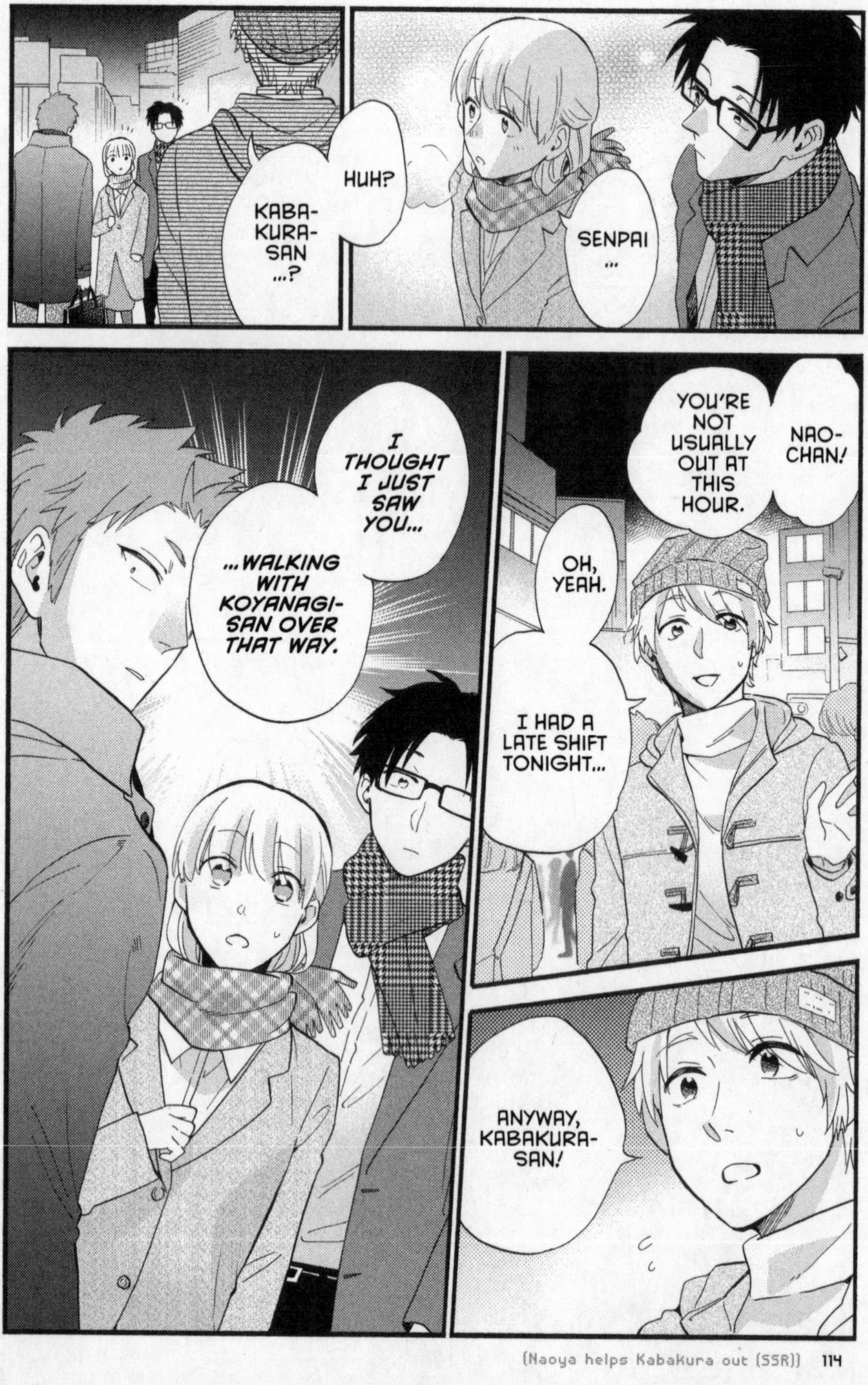
HUH?
SENPAI ...
KABA-KURA-SAN ...?
NAO-CHAN!
YOU'RE NOT USUALLY OUT AT THIS HOUR.
OH, YEAH.
I HAD A LATE SHIFT TONIGHT...
ANYWAY, KABAKURA-SAN!
I THOUGHT I JUST SAW YOU...
...WALKING WITH KOYANAGI-SAN OVER THAT WAY.

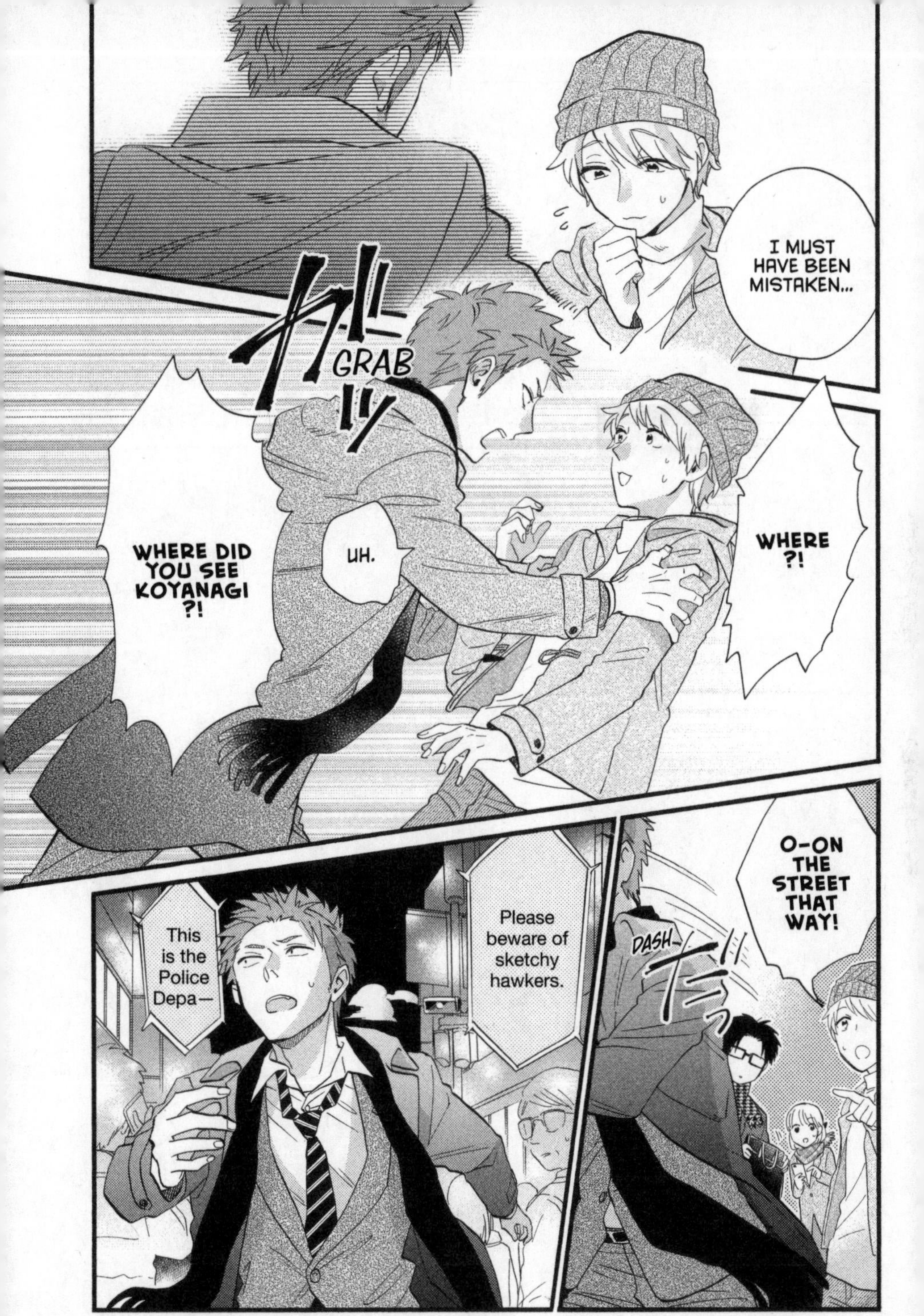

I MUST HAVE BEEN MISTAKEN...
WHERE ?!
GRAB
UH.
WHERE DID YOU SEE KOYANAGI ?!
O-ON THE STREET THAT WAY!
DASH
Please beware of sketchy hawkers.
This is the Police Depa—

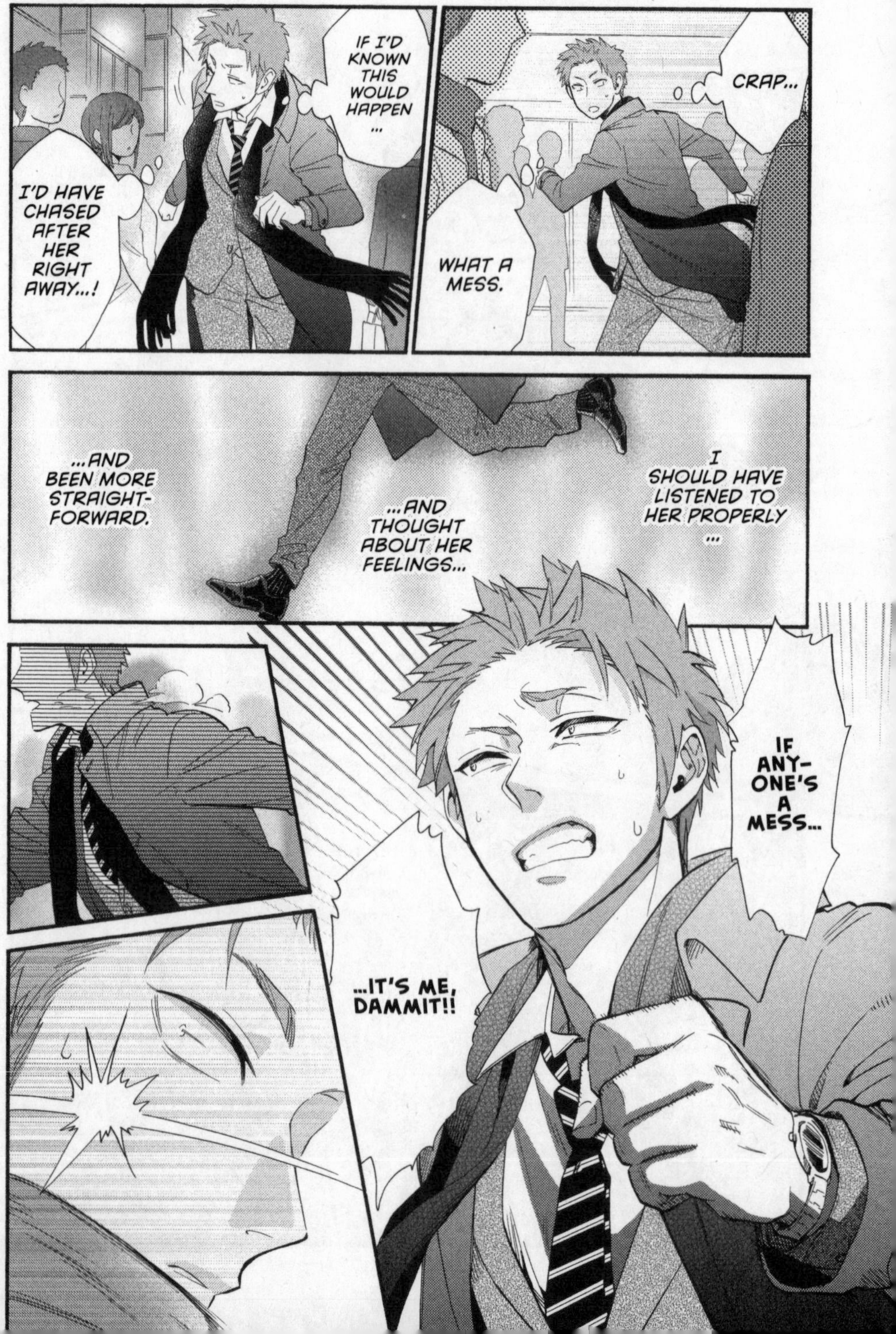
CRAP...
WHAT A MESS.
IF I'D KNOWN THIS WOULD HAPPEN...
I'D HAVE CHASED AFTER HER RIGHT AWAY...!
I SHOULD HAVE LISTENED TO HER PROPERLY...
...AND THOUGHT ABOUT HER FEELINGS...
...AND BEEN MORE STRAIGHT-FORWARD.
IF ANY-ONE'S A MESS...
...IT'S ME, DAMMIT!!

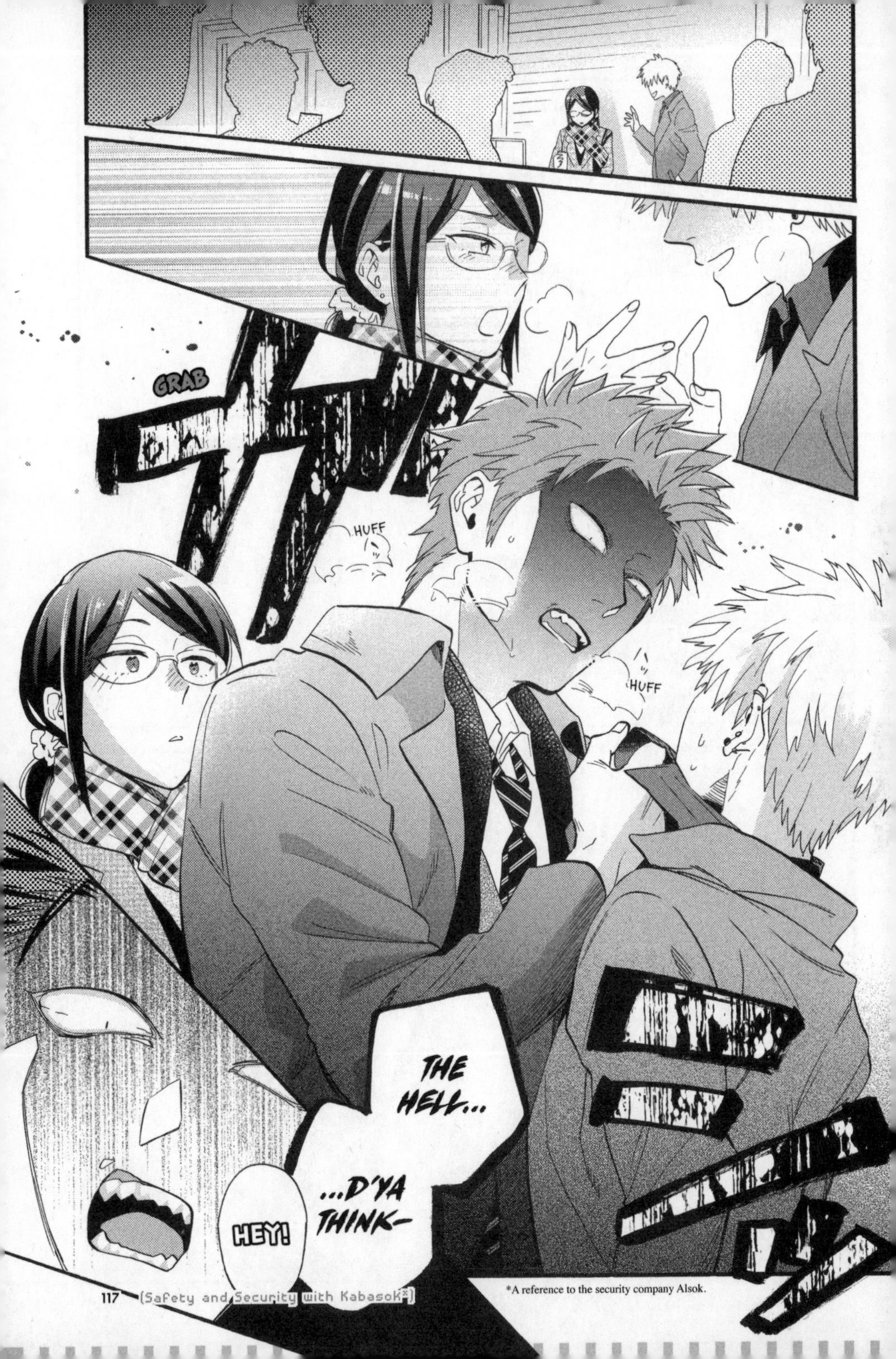
GRAB
HUFF
HUFF
THE HELL...
...D'YA THINK-
HEY!

*A reference to the security company Alsok.

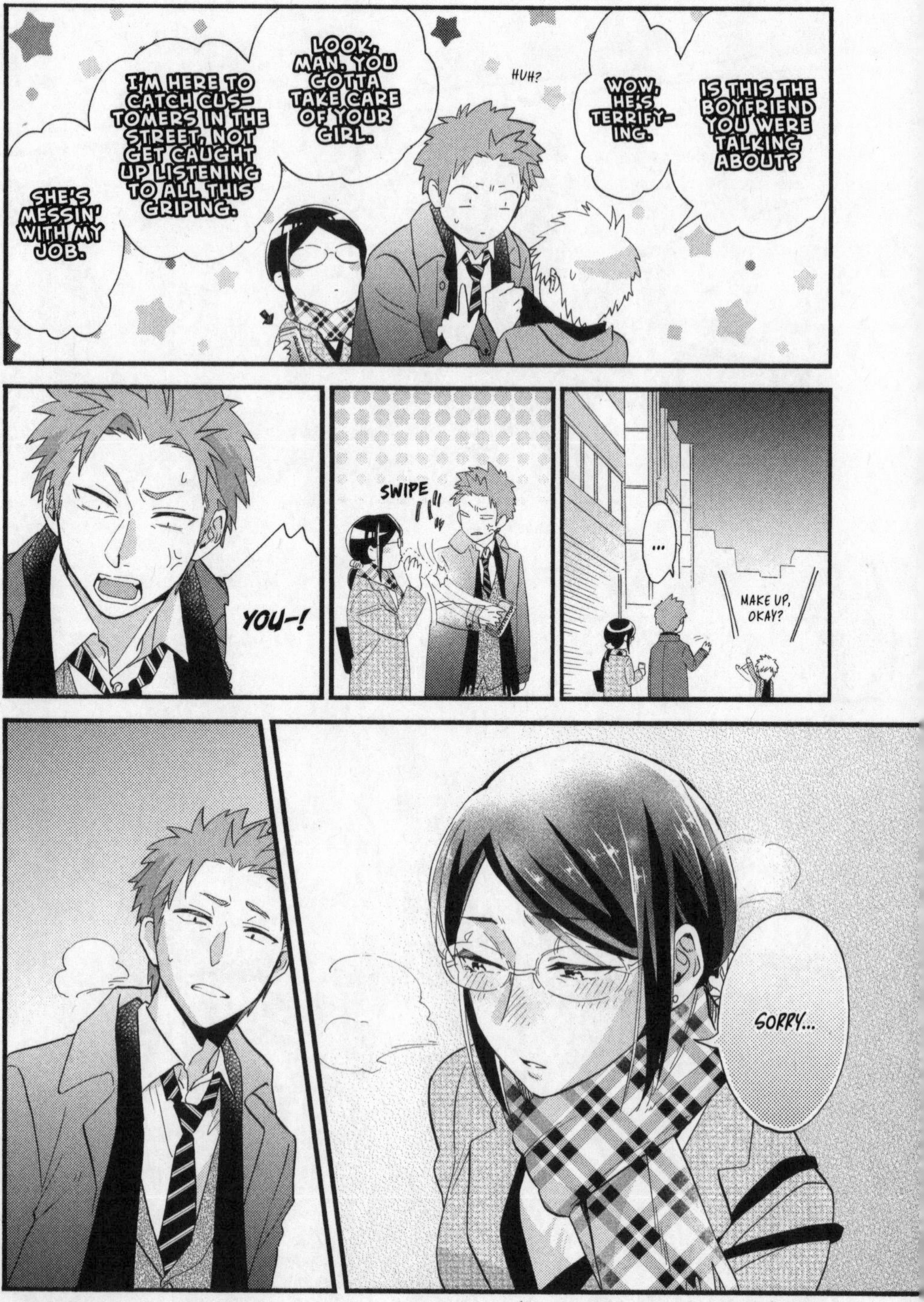
IS THIS THE BOYFRIEND YOU WERE TALKING ABOUT?
WOW. HE'S TERRIFY-ING.
HUH?
LOOK, MAN. YOU GOTTA TAKE CARE OF YOUR GIRL.
I'M HERE TO CATCH CUS-TOMERS IN THE STREET, NOT GET CAUGHT UP LISTENING TO ALL THIS GRIPING.
SHE'S MESSIN' WITH MY JOB.
...
MAKE UP, OKAY?
SWIPE
YOU-!
SORRY...

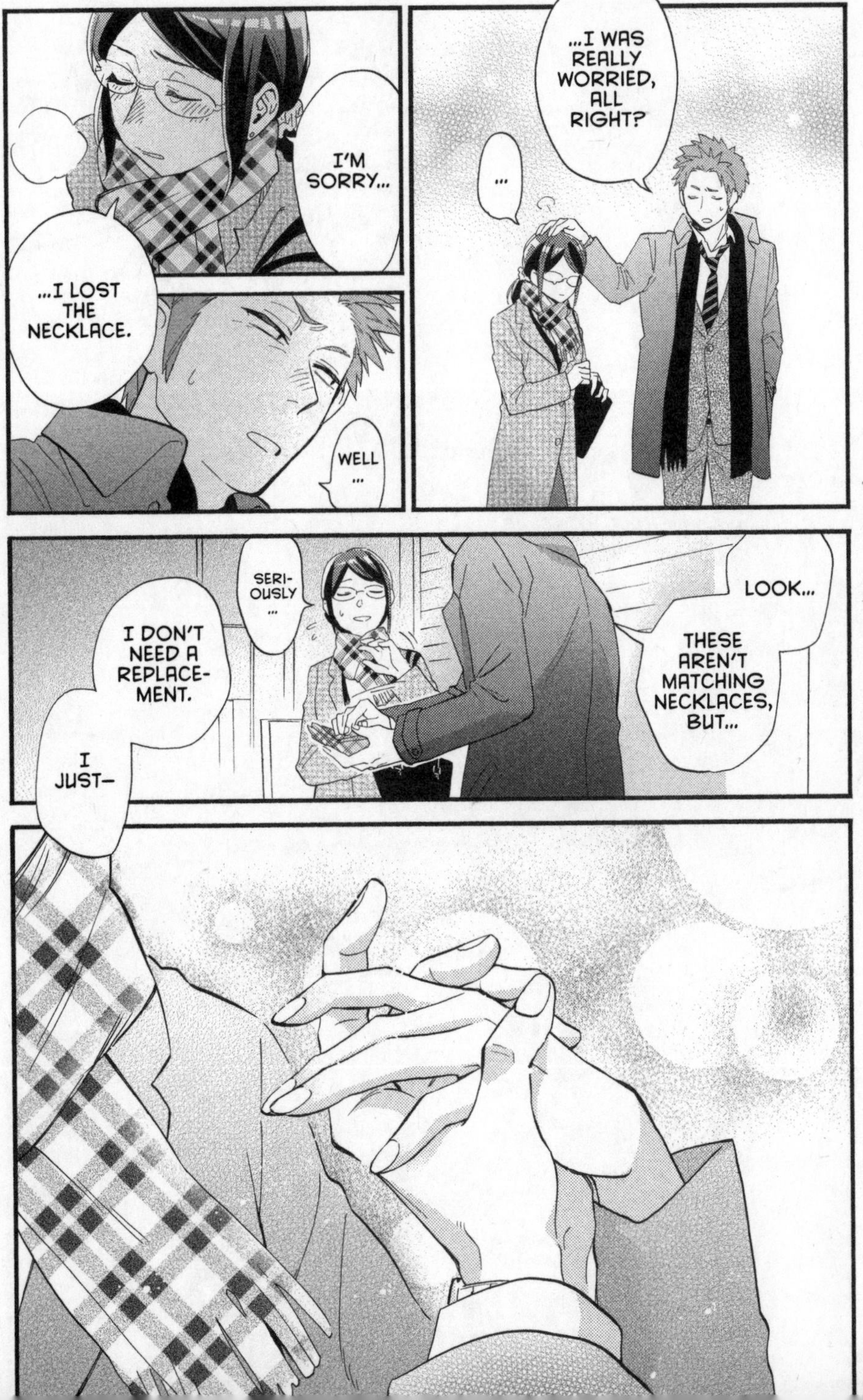
...I WAS REALLY WORRIED, ALL RIGHT?
...
I'M SORRY...
...I LOST THE NECKLACE.
WELL ...
LOOK...
THESE AREN'T MATCHING NECKLACES, BUT...
SERI-OUSLY ...
I DON'T NEED A REPLACE-MENT.
I JUST—

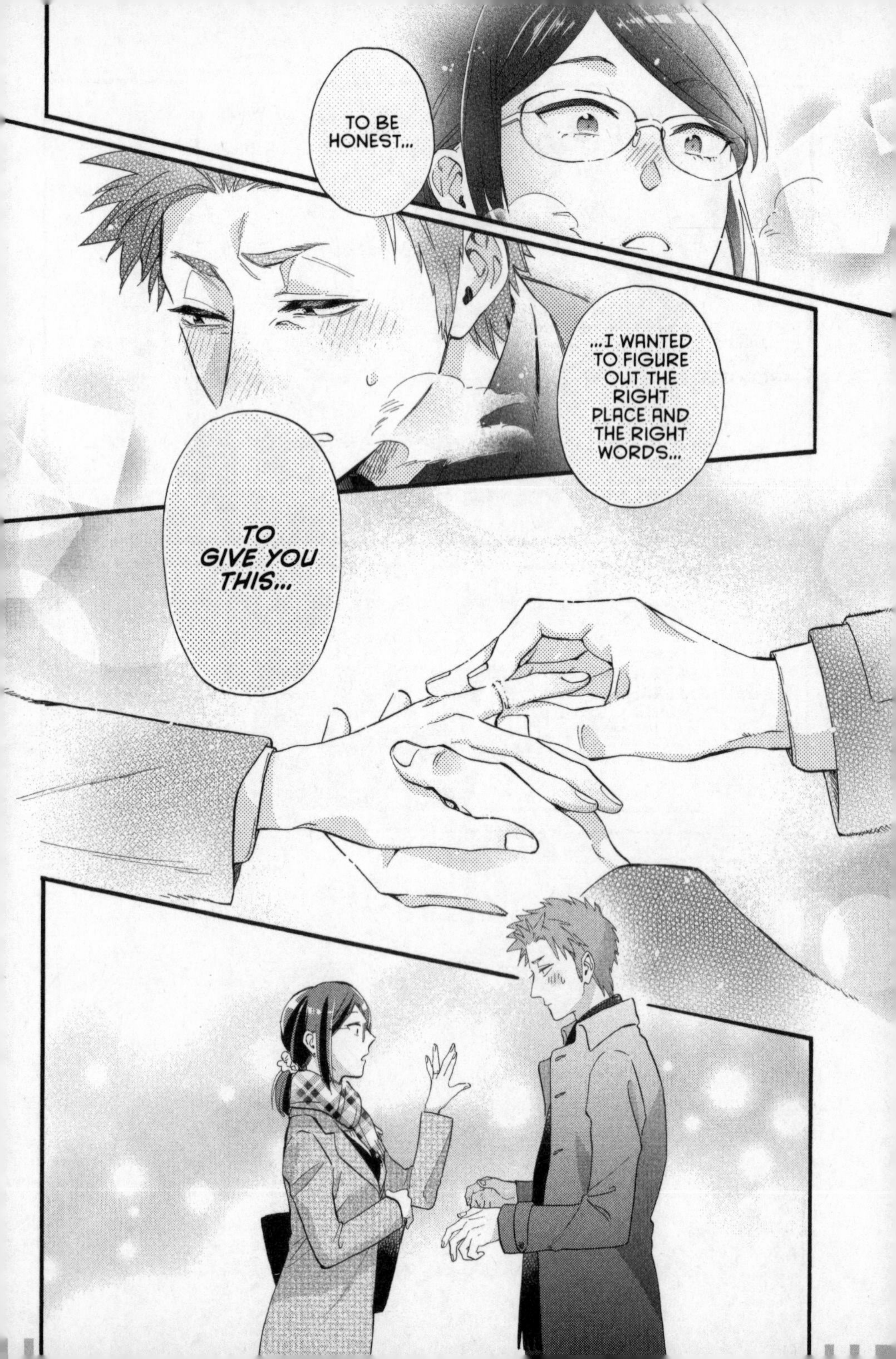
TO BE HONEST...
...I WANTED TO FIGURE OUT THE RIGHT PLACE AND THE RIGHT WORDS...
TO GIVE YOU THIS...

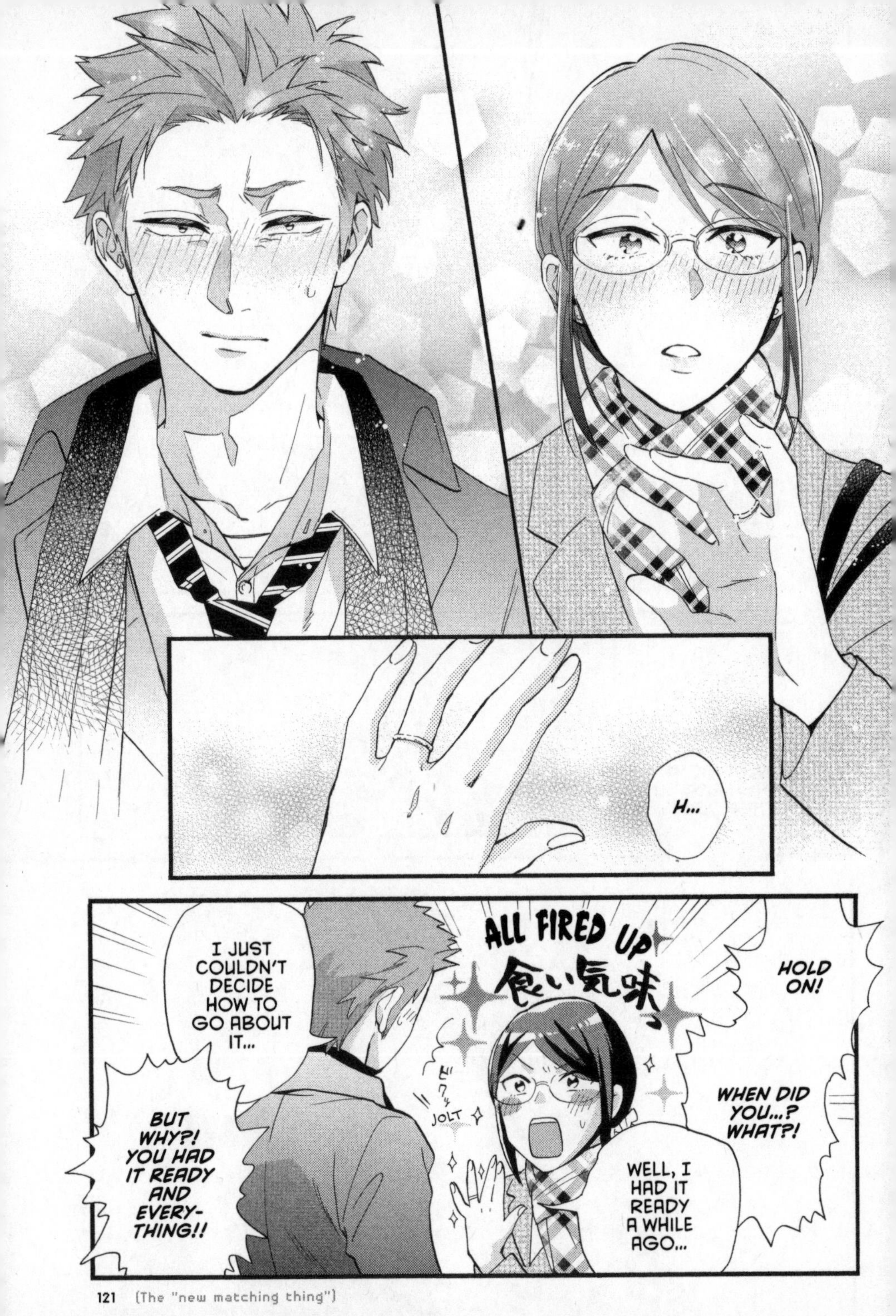
H...
HOLD ON!
ALL FIRED UP
食い気味
I JUST COULDN'T DECIDE HOW TO GO ABOUT IT...
WHEN DID YOU...? WHAT?!
WELL, I HAD IT READY A WHILE AGO...
ビクッ
JOLT
BUT WHY?! YOU HAD IT READY AND EVERYTHING!!

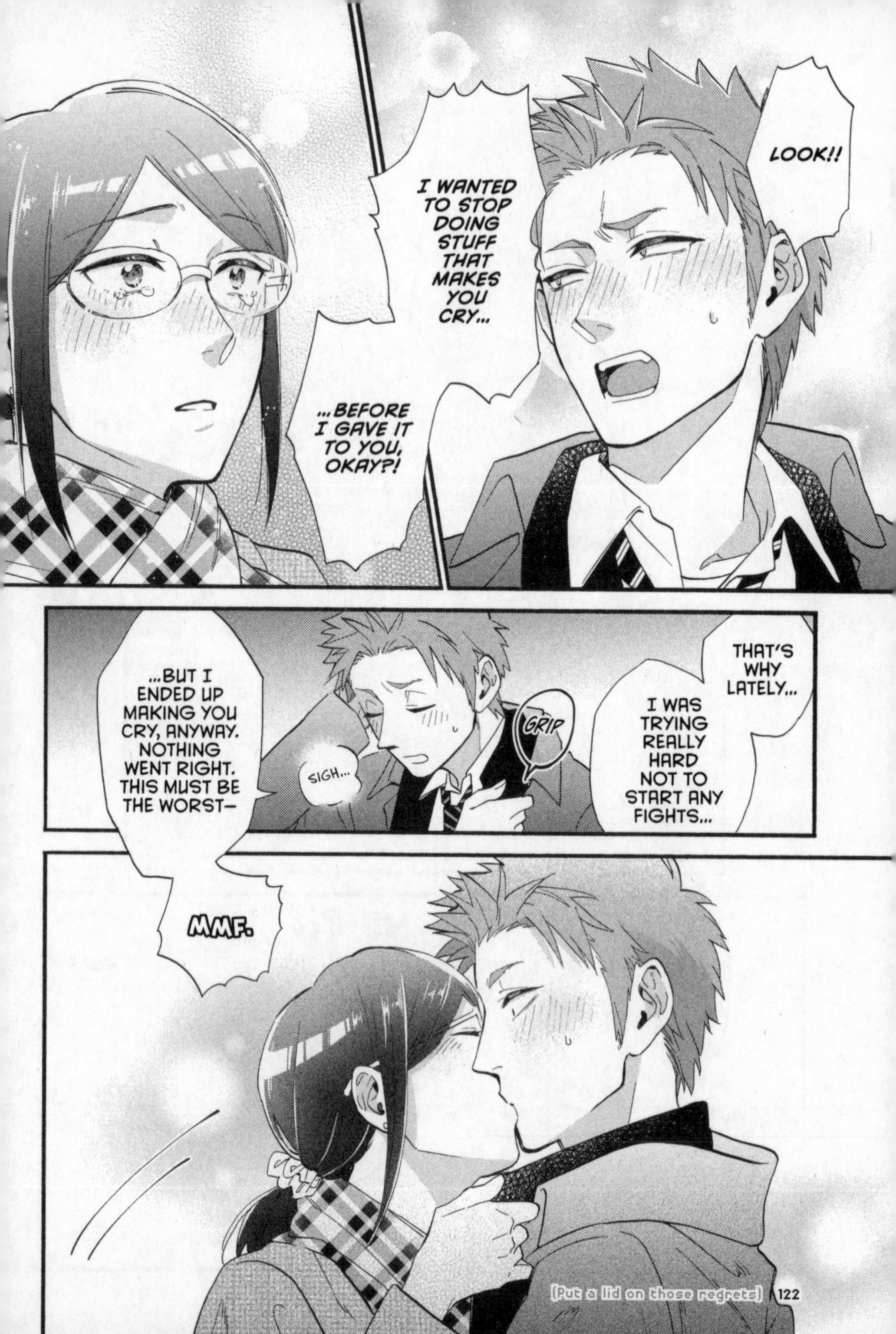
LOOK!!
I WANTED TO STOP DOING STUFF THAT MAKES YOU CRY...
...BEFORE I GAVE IT TO YOU, OKAY?!
THAT'S WHY LATELY...
I WAS TRYING REALLY HARD NOT TO START ANY FIGHTS...
GRIP
SIGH...
...BUT I ENDED UP MAKING YOU CRY, ANYWAY. NOTHING WENT RIGHT. THIS MUST BE THE WORST—
MMF.

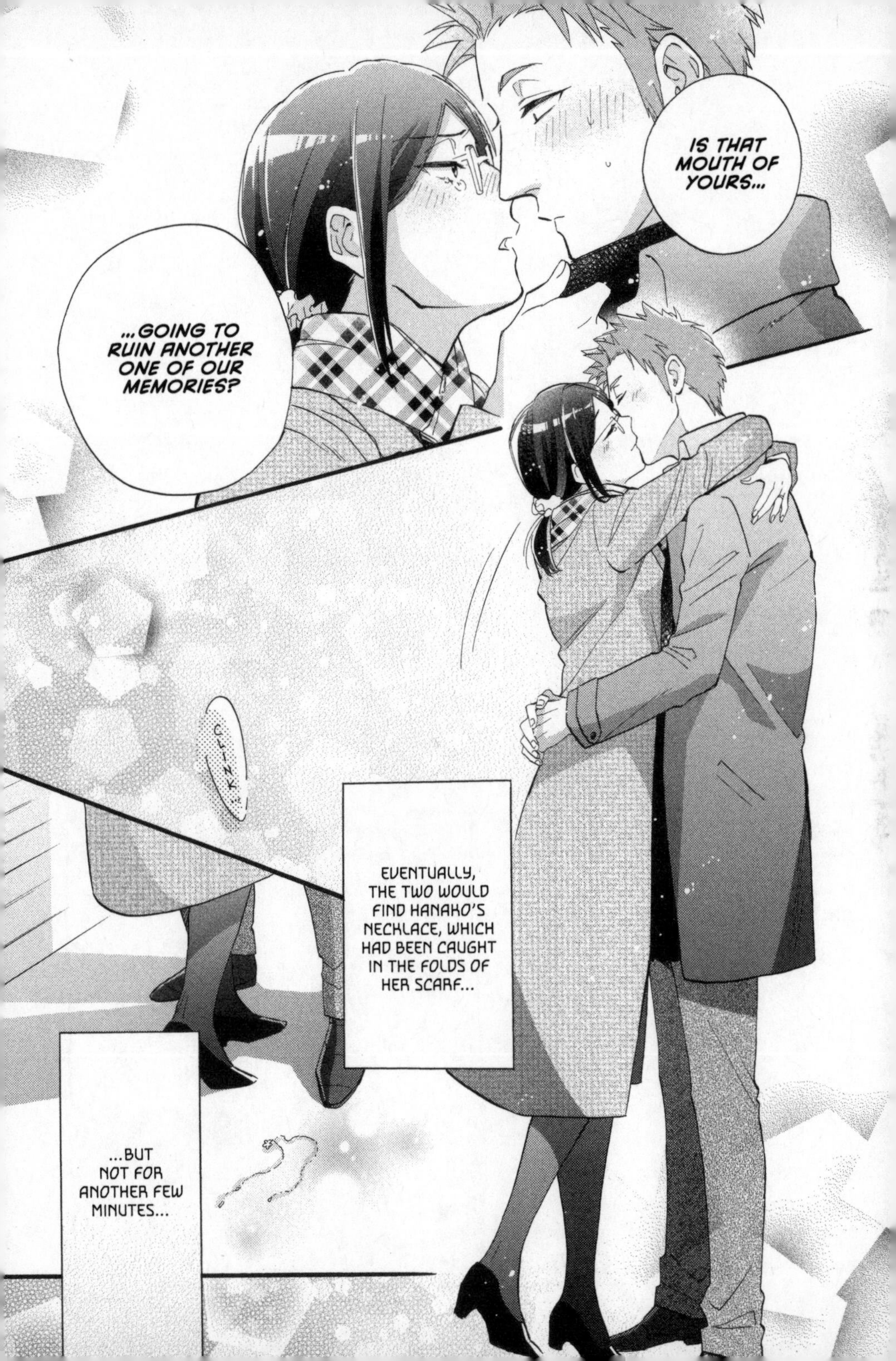
IS THAT MOUTH OF YOURS...
...GOING TO RUIN ANOTHER ONE OF OUR MEMORIES?
CLINK...
EVENTUALLY, THE TWO WOULD FIND HANAKO'S NECKLACE, WHICH HAD BEEN CAUGHT IN THE FOLDS OF HER SCARF...
...BUT NOT FOR ANOTHER FEW MINUTES...

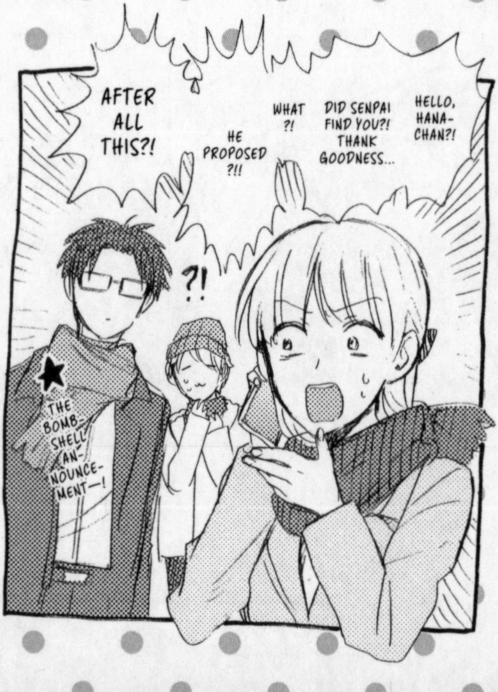
HELLO, HANA-CHAN?!
DID SENPAI FIND YOU?! THANK GOODNESS...
WHAT ?!
HE PROPOSED ?!!
AFTER ALL THIS?!
?!
THE BOMB-SHELL AN-NOUNCE-MENT—!

▶ CONTINUE

*Super soft lotion-infused tissues.

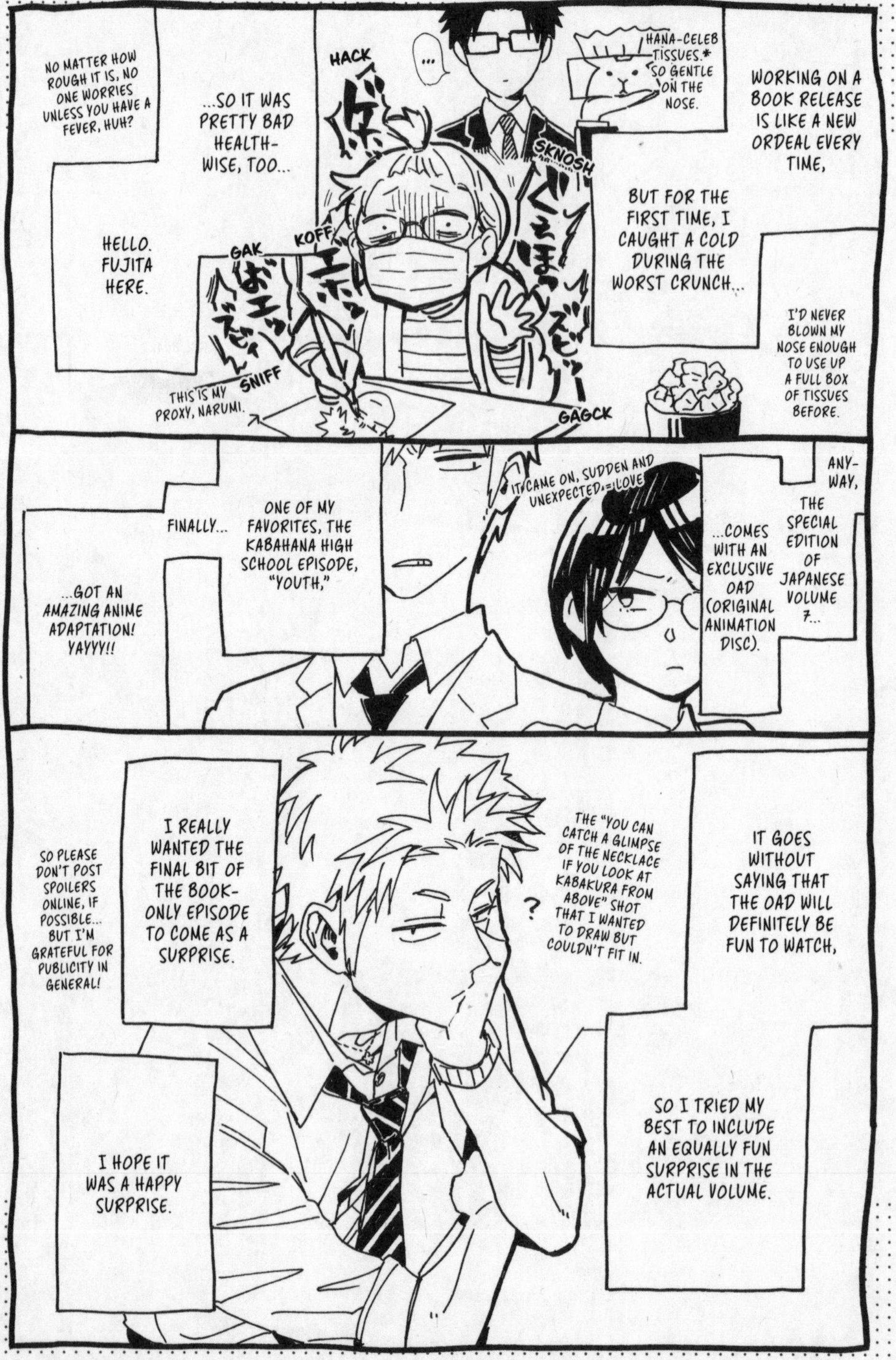
WORKING ON A BOOK RELEASE IS LIKE A NEW ORDEAL EVERY TIME,
BUT FOR THE FIRST TIME, I CAUGHT A COLD DURING THE WORST CRUNCH...
I'D NEVER BLOWN MY NOSE ENOUGH TO USE UP A FULL BOX OF TISSUES BEFORE.
HANA-CELEB TISSUES.* SO GENTLE ON THE NOSE.
SKNOSH
...
HACK
KOFF
GAK
SNIFF
GAGCK
THIS IS MY PROXY, NARUMI.
...SO IT WAS PRETTY BAD HEALTH-WISE, TOO...
HELLO. FUJITA HERE.
NO MATTER HOW ROUGH IT IS, NO ONE WORRIES UNLESS YOU HAVE A FEVER, HUH?
ANY-WAY, THE SPECIAL EDITION OF JAPANESE VOLUME 7...
...COMES WITH AN EXCLUSIVE OAD (ORIGINAL ANIMATION DISC).
IT CAME ON, SUDDEN AND UNEXPECTED.=LOVE
ONE OF MY FAVORITES, THE KABAHANA HIGH SCHOOL EPISODE, "YOUTH,"
FINALLY...
...GOT AN AMAZING ANIME ADAPTATION! YAYYY!!
IT GOES WITHOUT SAYING THAT THE OAD WILL DEFINITELY BE FUN TO WATCH,
THE "YOU CAN CATCH A GLIMPSE OF THE NECKLACE IF YOU LOOK AT KABAKURA FROM ABOVE" SHOT THAT I WANTED TO DRAW BUT COULDN'T FIT IN.
?
I REALLY WANTED THE FINAL BIT OF THE BOOK-ONLY EPISODE TO COME AS A SURPRISE.
SO PLEASE DON'T POST SPOILERS ONLINE, IF POSSIBLE... BUT I'M GRATEFUL FOR PUBLICITY IN GENERAL!
SO I TRIED MY BEST TO INCLUDE AN EQUALLY FUN SURPRISE IN THE ACTUAL VOLUME.
I HOPE IT WAS A HAPPY SURPRISE.

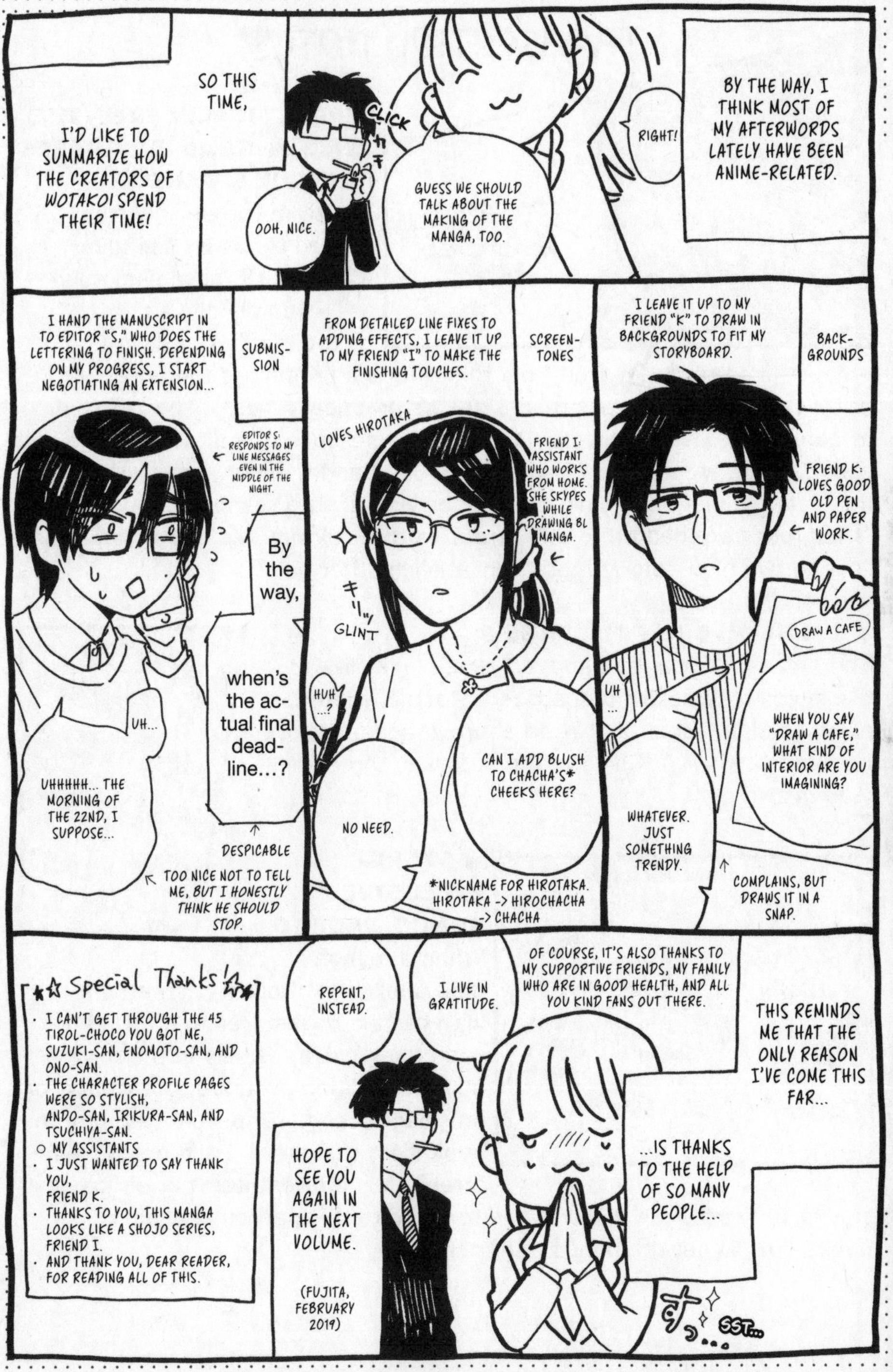
BY THE WAY, I THINK MOST OF MY AFTERWORDS LATELY HAVE BEEN ANIME-RELATED.
RIGHT!
GUESS WE SHOULD TALK ABOUT THE MAKING OF THE MANGA, TOO.
CLICK
OOH, NICE.
SO THIS TIME,
I'D LIKE TO SUMMARIZE HOW THE CREATORS OF WOTAKOI SPEND THEIR TIME!
BACKGROUNDS
I LEAVE IT UP TO MY FRIEND "K" TO DRAW IN BACKGROUNDS TO FIT MY STORYBOARD.
FRIEND K: LOVES GOOD OLD PEN AND PAPER WORK.
DRAW A CAFE
WHEN YOU SAY "DRAW A CAFE," WHAT KIND OF INTERIOR ARE YOU IMAGINING?
UH...
WHATEVER. JUST SOMETHING TRENDY.
COMPLAINS, BUT DRAWS IT IN A SNAP.
SCREENTONES
FROM DETAILED LINE FIXES TO ADDING EFFECTS, I LEAVE IT UP TO MY FRIEND "I" TO MAKE THE FINISHING TOUCHES.
LOVES HIROTAKA
FRIEND I: ASSISTANT WHO WORKS FROM HOME. SHE SKYPES WHILE DRAWING BL MANGA.
GLINT
CAN I ADD BLUSH TO CHACHA'S* CHEEKS HERE?
HUH...?
NO NEED.
*NICKNAME FOR HIROTAKA. HIROTAKA -> HIROCHACHA -> CHACHA
SUBMISSION
I HAND THE MANUSCRIPT IN TO EDITOR "S," WHO DOES THE LETTERING TO FINISH. DEPENDING ON MY PROGRESS, I START NEGOTIATING AN EXTENSION...
EDITOR S: RESPONDS TO MY LINE MESSAGES EVEN IN THE MIDDLE OF THE NIGHT.
By the way, when's the actual final deadline...?
DESPICABLE
UH...
UHHHHH... THE MORNING OF THE 22ND, I SUPPOSE...
TOO NICE NOT TO TELL ME, BUT I HONESTLY THINK HE SHOULD STOP.
THIS REMINDS ME THAT THE ONLY REASON I'VE COME THIS FAR...
...IS THANKS TO THE HELP OF SO MANY PEOPLE...
OF COURSE, IT'S ALSO THANKS TO MY SUPPORTIVE FRIENDS, MY FAMILY WHO ARE IN GOOD HEALTH, AND ALL YOU KIND FANS OUT THERE.
I LIVE IN GRATITUDE.
REPENT, INSTEAD.
SST...
HOPE TO SEE YOU AGAIN IN THE NEXT VOLUME.
(FUJITA, FEBRUARY 2019)
Special Thanks!
· I CAN'T GET THROUGH THE 45 TIROL-CHOCO YOU GOT ME, SUZUKI-SAN, ENOMOTO-SAN, AND ONO-SAN.
· THE CHARACTER PROFILE PAGES WERE SO STYLISH, ANDO-SAN, IRIKURA-SAN, AND TSUCHIYA-SAN.
○ MY ASSISTANTS
· I JUST WANTED TO SAY THANK YOU, FRIEND K.
· THANKS TO YOU, THIS MANGA LOOKS LIKE A SHOJO SERIES, FRIEND I.
· AND THANK YOU, DEAR READER, FOR READING ALL OF THIS.

TRANSLATION NOTES

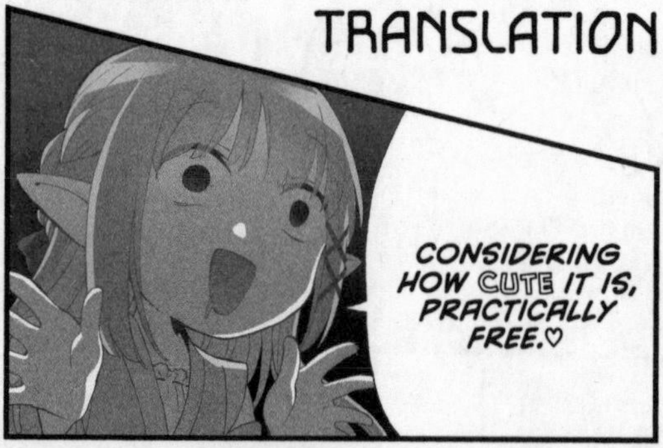
CONSIDERING HOW CUTE IT IS, PRACTICALLY FREE.♡

◀ PRACTICALLY FREE/THE ZERO IN-GAME PURCHASES PRINCIPLE, PAGE 3

The term "practically free" is used to justify spending with absurd reasoning, such as "if you divide this cost by the number of days I'll enjoy it, it's practically free," or "this DVD is a product of the entire life of that pop idol, so at less than $200 it's practically free." "The zero in-game purchases principle" is a related reference to a bit called "the zero calories principle" by the comedy duo Sandwichman, where they insist that some foods have no calories with absurd reasoning, such as "fried foods are heated to temperatures that calories can't withstand," or "eating two high-calorie foods cancel each other out."

▶ I'M HERE, BRIEF ME, PAGE 6

The Japanese "*Imakita Sangyo,*" which looks like it translates to "Imakita Industries," is actually internet slang used on 2chan that is an abbreviation of "I just got here (*ima kita*). Give me the details in three lines (*san gyo*)."

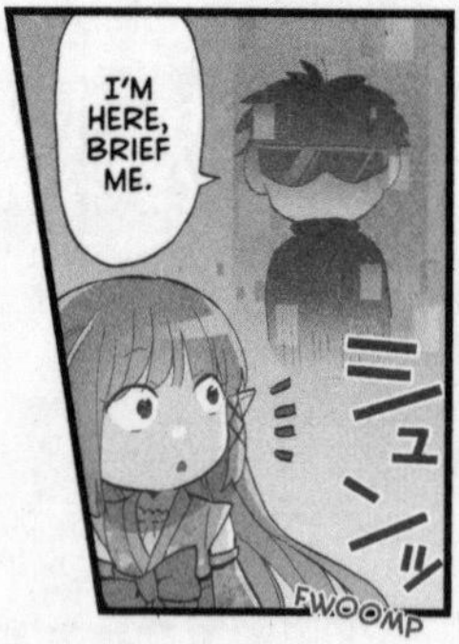
I'M HERE, BRIEF ME.
FWOOMP

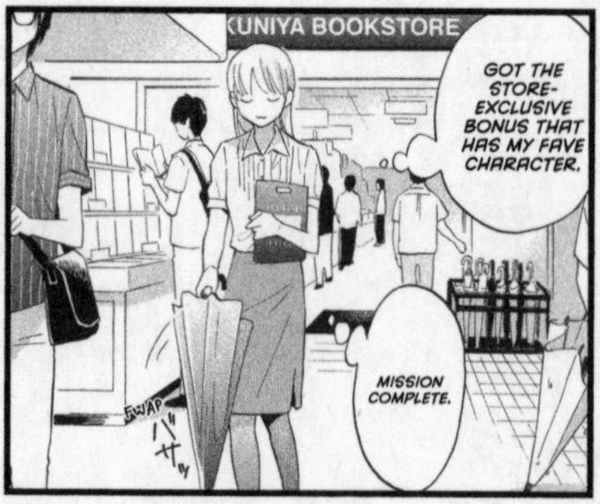
KUNIYA BOOKSTORE
GOT THE STORE-EXCLUSIVE BONUS THAT HAS MY FAVE CHARACTER.
MISSION COMPLETE.

◀ STORE-EXCLUSIVE BONUS, PAGE 10

When a manga gets published, it often partners up with certain bookstores to offer a little something extra, usually in the form of a limited edition postcard, bookmark, or one-page manga for people who buy the book from that store. Each manga will often offer different items at different chains, so most likely Narumi had to come to this particular chain of bookstores to get the bonus of her choice.

▼ LIGHT TYPES, PAGES 11, 15, AND 16

Primarily in the fantasy genre, the "Light type" is an attribute representing healing or holy properties that is often associated with justice. Consequently, the term has come to describe "classic main character" types who are kind, outgoing, and/or sincere.

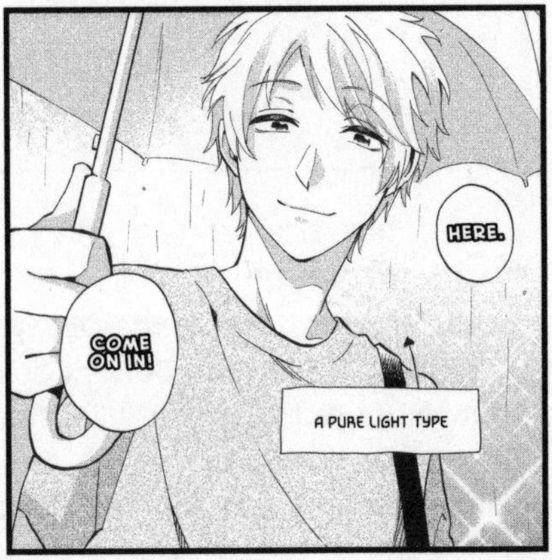
HERE.
COME ON IN!
A PURE LIGHT TYPE

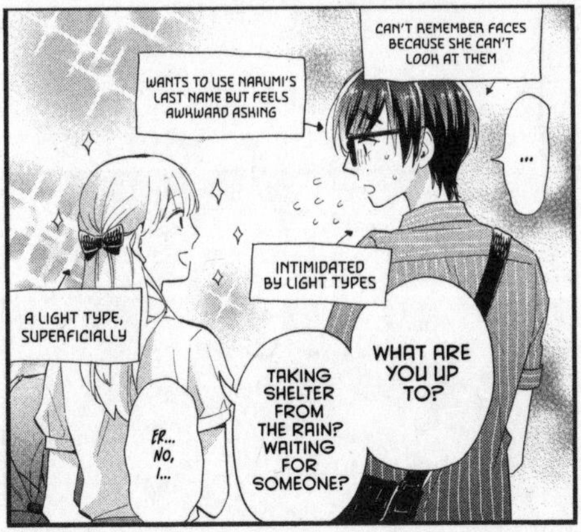
CAN'T REMEMBER FACES BECAUSE SHE CAN'T LOOK AT THEM
WANTS TO USE NARUMI'S LAST NAME BUT FEELS AWKWARD ASKING
...
INTIMIDATED BY LIGHT TYPES
A LIGHT TYPE, SUPERFICIALLY
WHAT ARE YOU UP TO?
TAKING SHELTER FROM THE RAIN? WAITING FOR SOMEONE?
ER... NO, I...

LUCK: RANK E, PAGE 12

A reference to the parameter system in *Fate/Grand Order*, a massively popular tactical RPG for mobile. "Luck" is one of the parameters and E is the lowest rank possible.

▶ COMMUNICATION, PAGES 13 AND 17

A reference to the "Communication" phase in the game *iDOLM@STER*, where you get ranked on how well you your rapport goes with the pop idol you're producing. The grading includes "Bad Communication" and "Good Communication," as in these titles.

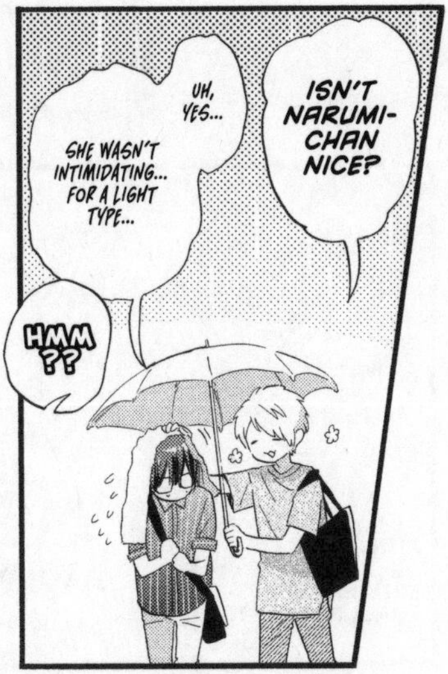
ISN'T NARUMI-CHAN NICE?
UH, YES...
SHE WASN'T INTIMIDATING... FOR A LIGHT TYPE...
HMM ??

17 (Good Communication?)

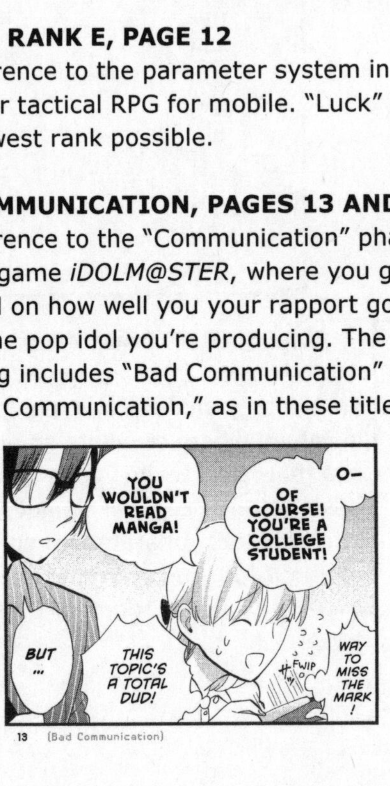
O-
OF COURSE! YOU'RE A COLLEGE STUDENT!
YOU WOULDN'T READ MANGA!
WAY TO MISS THE MARK!
FWIP
THIS TOPIC'S A TOTAL DUD!
BUT ...

13 (Bad Communication)

◀**N QUIJOTE, PAGE 24

A reference to discount store chain Don Quijote, which sells a little bit of everything, including a wide selection of costumes.

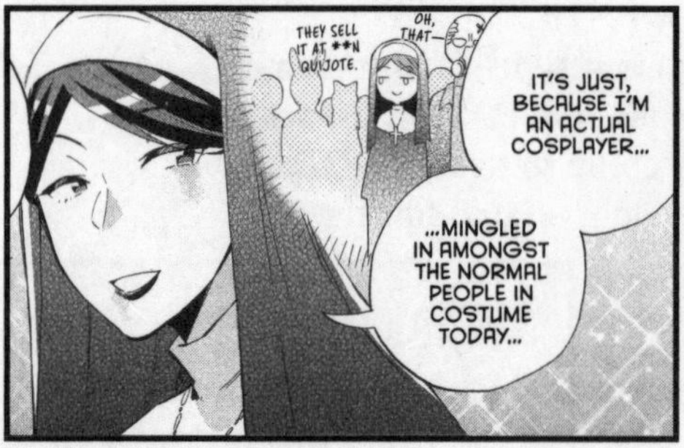
OH, THAT—
THEY SELL IT AT **N QUIJOTE.
IT'S JUST, BECAUSE I'M AN ACTUAL COSPLAYER...
...MINGLED IN AMONGST THE NORMAL PEOPLE IN COSTUME TODAY...

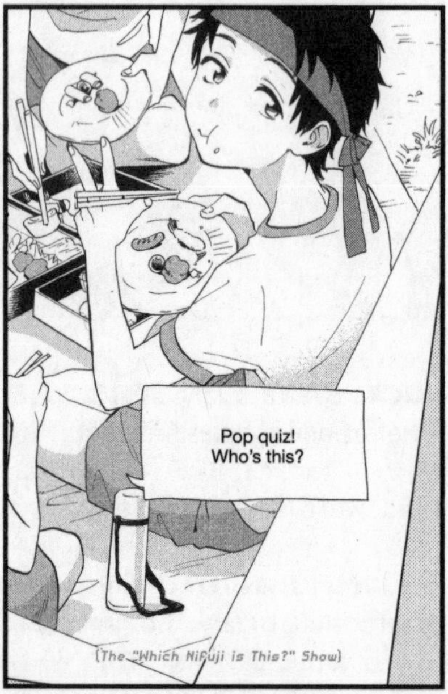
Pop quiz! Who's this?
(The "Which Nifuji is This?" Show)

▶ *THE "WHICH NIFUJI IS THIS?" SHOW*, PAGE 45

A reference to The *"Which Dish Will it Be?"* Show (called the *Dotch Cooking Show* in English), a reality TV show that involves two chefs preparing competing dishes, each using a separate premium ingredient. Voters decide which dish they prefer, but only the winning dish is actually served and only to those who voted for it.

◀ CLASS TRIP, PAGE 49

A trip that occurs once in each of elementary, middle, and high school in Japan, where students go on a trip that lasts several days to some destination of cultural significance. The students separate into groups of about four to seven that are expected to stick together during the trip.

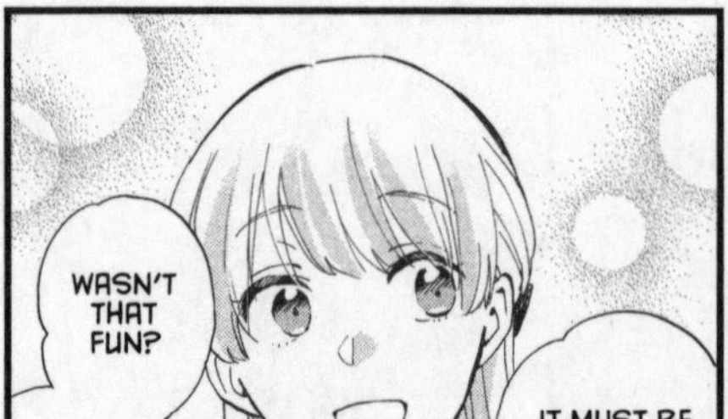
IT MUST BE FROM THE CLASS TRIP IN MIDDLE SCHOOL.
WASN'T THAT FUN?
DO YOU REMEMBER WHO WAS IN YOUR GROUP?

▼ DEEP SPACE, PAGE 49

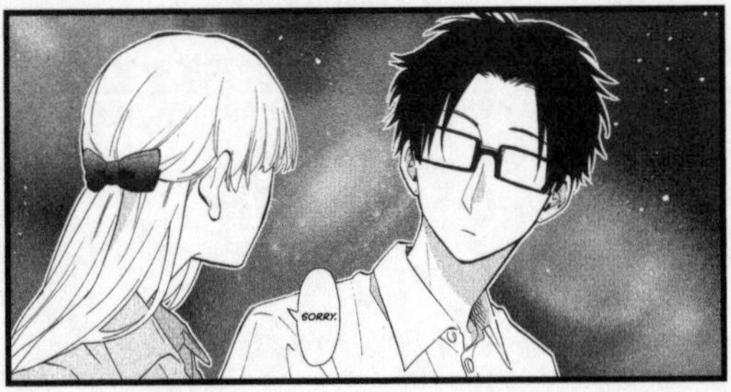
SORRY.

The "outer space" background is sometimes used when characters are faced with a concept that is so alien to them that it's as confusing and mystifying as the cosmos.

▶ †, PAGE 51

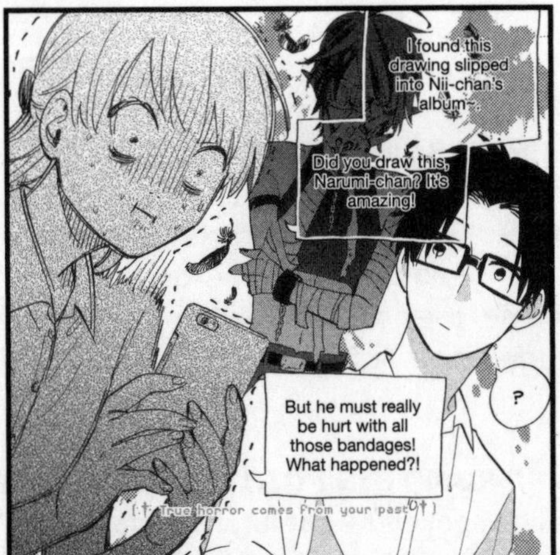
I found this drawing slipped into Nii-chan's album~.
Did you draw this, Narumi-chan? It's amazing!
?
But he must really be hurt with all those bandages! What happened?!
(† True horror comes from your past †)

The dagger symbol is used enthusiastically in adolescent, "*chunibyo*" phases that involve fascination with fallen angels, secret supernatural powers, and demonic themes. During the phase, people may write poems gratuitously sprinkled with English words or create original characters in crazy costumes with elaborate heroic/tragic backstories. These often become *kurorekishi* (lit. black history), or objects of intense embarrassment later on in life, as is evidently the case with Narumi here.

SUPER SMASH, PAGE 80
NAO'S SMASH ATTACK, PAGE 89
KO WAS BLASTED OFF SCREEN, PAGE 90

These are all references to the hit fighting game series *Super Smash Brothers*. Unlike traditional fighting games where the objective is to reduce your opponent's HP to zero, the basic object of *Smash* is to knock your opponent(s) out of the ring either as many times as possible, or until their number of lives reaches zero. Each playable character has a variety of powerful, charge-able "smash attacks" that, when used correctly, may launch opposing characters off the screen in a single blow.

▶ CHRISTMAS, PAGE 96

Christmas Eve in Japan is the biggest couples event of the year, even bigger than Valentine's Day. Not being able to spend it with your significant other can be a huge letdown.

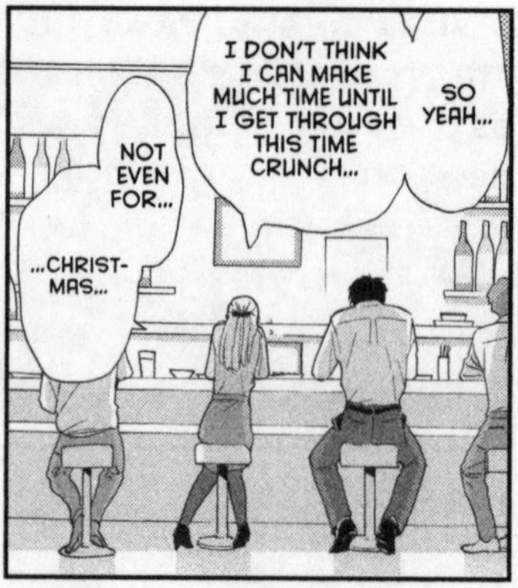
SO YEAH...
I DON'T THINK I CAN MAKE MUCH TIME UNTIL I GET THROUGH THIS TIME CRUNCH...
NOT EVEN FOR...
...CHRIST-MAS...

RENAISSAAANCE!, PAGE 97

A reference to the comedy duo Hige Danshaku (literally "The Bearded Baron"), consisting of the supposed French-born Japanese nobleman Louis Yamada LIII and his butler Higuchi-kun. In line with their "nobility" theme, they appear holding glasses of wine and yell out "Renaissance!" during their act.

▼ "FROM THIS POINT ONWARD, WE ENTER HELL," PAGE 103

A line spoken by samurai warrior Keiji Maeda in *Hana no Keiji*, a period manga by Tetsuo Hara, the author of *Fist of the North Star*. The line is part of a charismatic speech that Keiji makes before taking a makeshift army into battle.

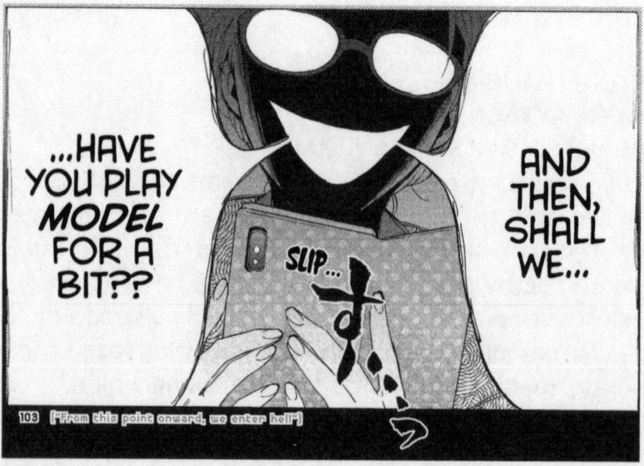
AND THEN, SHALL WE...
...HAVE YOU PLAY *MODEL* FOR A BIT??
SLIP...
103 ["From this point onward, we enter hell"]

▼ R, SR, SSR, PAGES 110-114

These are rarity rankings usually used to classify in-game items, such as character cards used in a mobile game. The order of rarity and exact descriptors may vary by game, but a general example would be: R (Rare) < SR (Super Rare) < SSR (Super Super Rare).

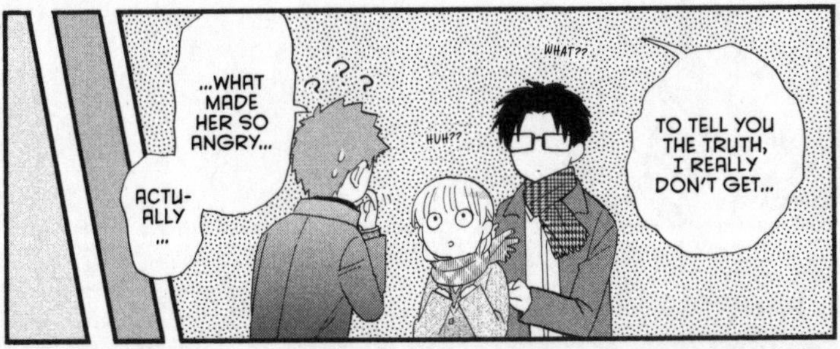
TO TELL YOU THE TRUTH, I REALLY DON'T GET...
WHAT??
HUH??
...WHAT MADE HER SO ANGRY...
ACTU- ALLY ...

(Kabakura getting scolded by Narumi (R)) 110

▼ BOOK-ONLY EPISODE, PAGE 126

Wotakoi is serialized as a monthly online web comic, but the book publication includes an episode that is written just for the book. While some series choose to have the "side episodes" be book-only, some major plot points tend to be book-only in *Wotakoi*. The episode is usually split into parts and scattered throughout the book, with no full-page title illustrations (episode 49 in this volume).

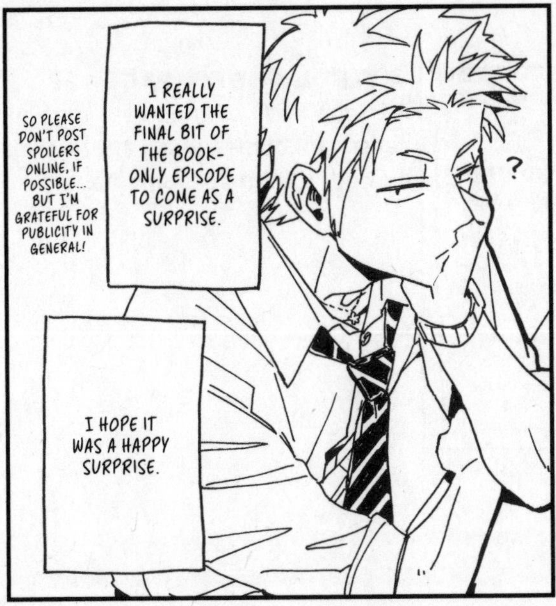
I REALLY WANTED THE FINAL BIT OF THE BOOK-ONLY EPISODE TO COME AS A SURPRISE.
?
SO PLEASE DON'T POST SPOILERS ONLINE, IF POSSIBLE... BUT I'M GRATEFUL FOR PUBLICITY IN GENERAL!
I HOPE IT WAS A HAPPY SURPRISE.

◀ SCREENTONES, PAGE 127

SCREEN-TONES
FROM DETAILED LINE FIXES TO ADDING EFFECTS, I LEAVE IT UP TO MY FRIEND "I" TO MAKE THE FINISHING TOUCHES.
FRIEND I: ASSISTANT WHO WORKS FROM HOME. SHE SKYPES WHILE DRAWING BL MANGA.
LOVES HIROTAKA
GLINT

The texture patterns in manga are traditionally applied using adhesive paper printed with different kinds of grayscale patterns, called "screentones."

▶ LINE, PAGE 127

LINE is the most popular free messaging app in Japan—basically the Japanese equivalent of Whatsapp or KaKaoTalk. Because of its user-friendliness, LINE enjoys a very broad user base and purposes, even in seemingly professional contexts like contacting one's editor.

SUBMIS-SION
I HAND THE MANUSCRIPT IN TO EDITOR "S," WHO DOES THE LETTERING TO FINISH. DEPENDING ON MY PROGRESS, I START NEGOTIATING AN EXTENSION...
EDITOR S: RESPONDS TO MY LINE MESSAGES EVEN IN THE MIDDLE OF THE NIGHT.
By the way,

◀ TIROL-CHOCO, PAGE 127

Special Thanks!
· I CAN'T GET THROUGH THE 45 TIROL-CHOCO YOU GOT ME, SUZUKI-SAN, ENOMOTO-SAN, AND ONO-SAN.
· THE CHARACTER PROFILE PAGES WERE SO STYLISH, ANDO-SAN, IRIKURA-SAN, AND TSUCHIYA-SAN.
○ MY ASSISTANTS
· I JUST WANTED TO SAY THANK YOU, FRIEND K.
· THANKS TO YOU, THIS MANGA LOOKS LIKE A SHOJO SERIES, FRIEND I.
· AND THANK YOU, DEAR READER, FOR READING ALL OF THIS.

A cheap cube of chocolate that costs about 20 cents and comes in a variety of flavors, including limited-edition seasonal flavors.

WOTAKOI:
LOVE IS HARD FOR OTAKU

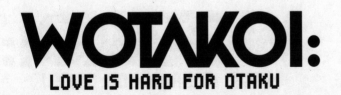

WOTAKOI:
LOVE IS HARD FOR OTAKU

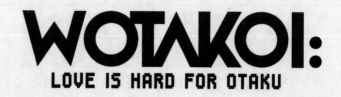

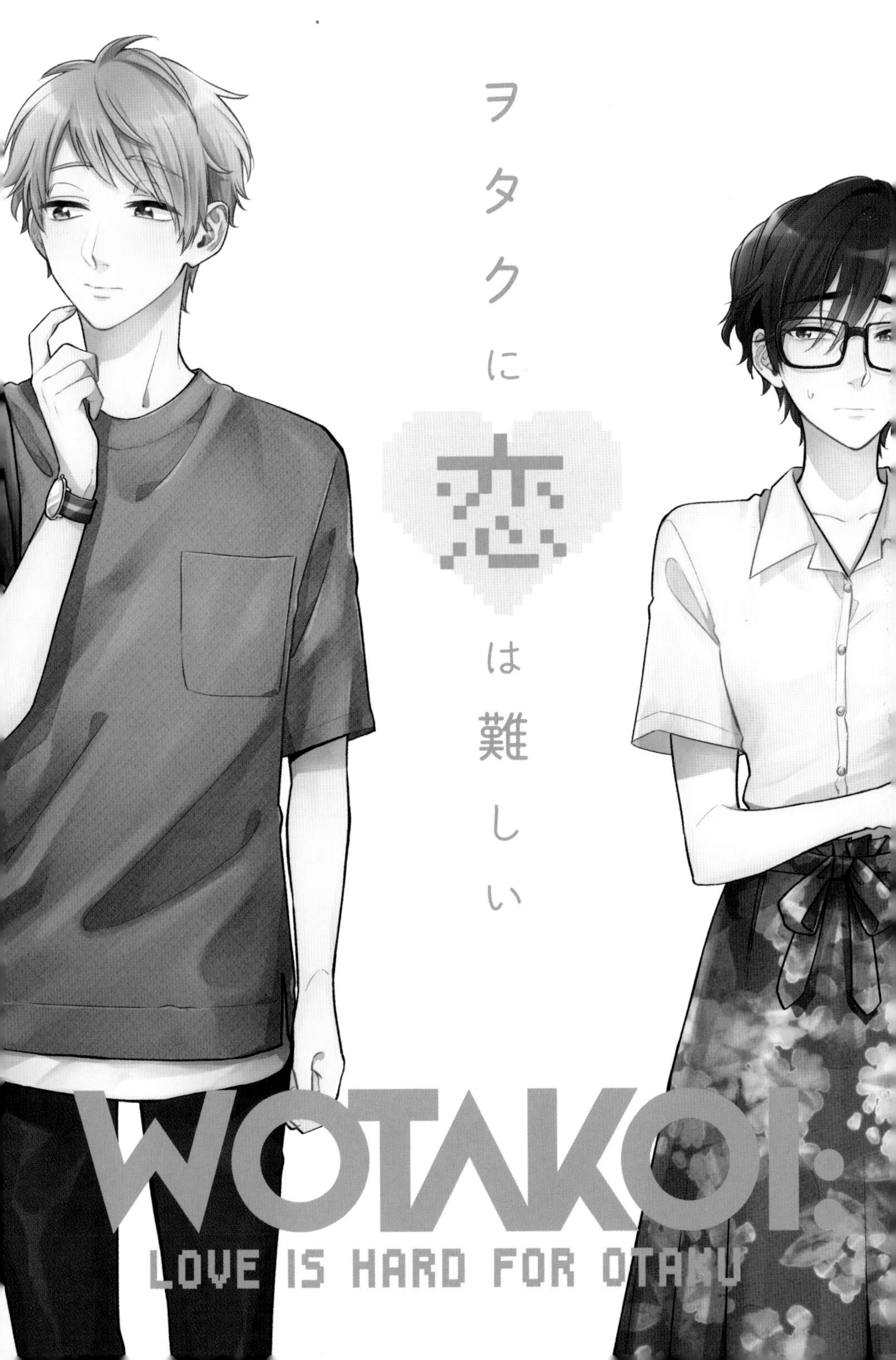
ヲタクに恋は難しい
WOTAKOI:
LOVE IS HARD FOR OTAKU

WOTAKOI:
LOVE IS HARD FOR OTAKU

FUJITA

SPECIAL MOVIE TICKET
¥1200
SPECIAL MOVIE TICKET
¥1200

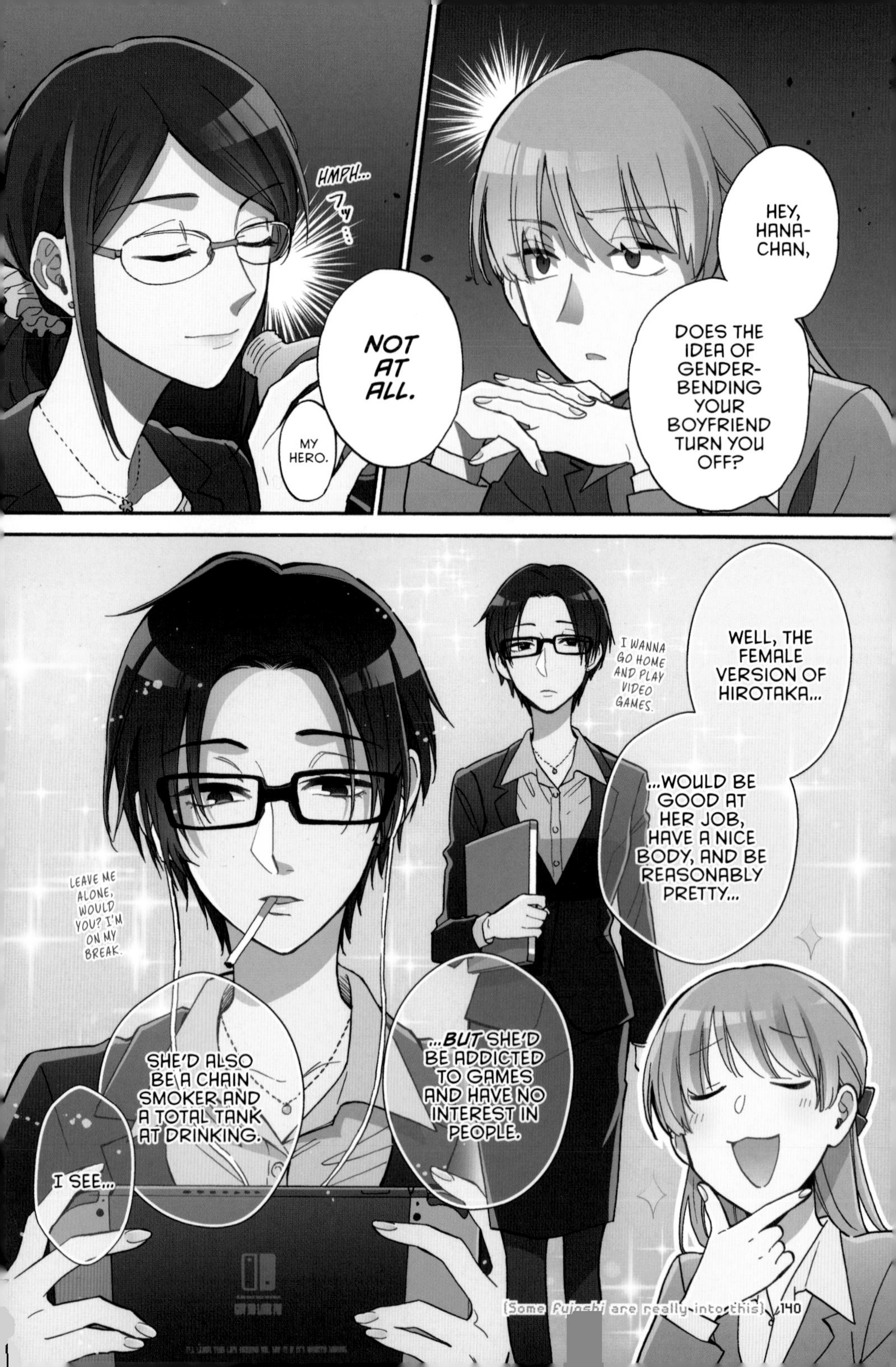
HEY, HANA-CHAN,
DOES THE IDEA OF GENDER-BENDING YOUR BOYFRIEND TURN YOU OFF?
HMPH...
フッ...
NOT AT ALL.
MY HERO.
WELL, THE FEMALE VERSION OF HIROTAKA...
...WOULD BE GOOD AT HER JOB, HAVE A NICE BODY, AND BE REASONABLY PRETTY...
I WANNA GO HOME AND PLAY VIDEO GAMES.
...BUT SHE'D BE ADDICTED TO GAMES AND HAVE NO INTEREST IN PEOPLE.
SHE'D ALSO BE A CHAIN SMOKER AND A TOTAL TANK AT DRINKING.
LEAVE ME ALONE, WOULD YOU? I'M ON MY BREAK.
I SEE...
(Some fujoshi are really into this)

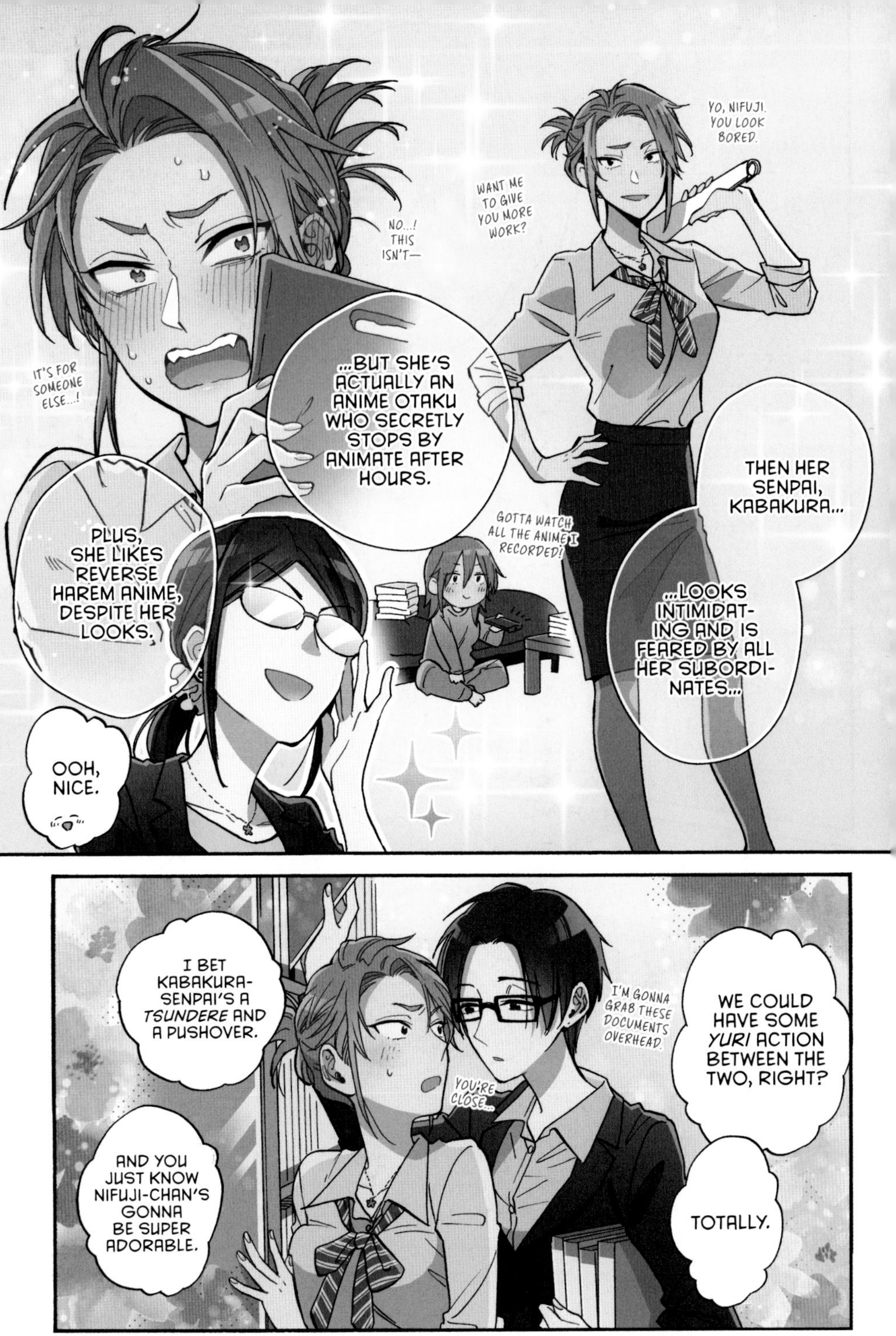
YO, NIFUJI. YOU LOOK BORED.
WANT ME TO GIVE YOU MORE WORK?
THEN HER SENPAI, KABAKURA...
...LOOKS INTIMIDATING AND IS FEARED BY ALL HER SUBORDINATES...
...BUT SHE'S ACTUALLY AN ANIME OTAKU WHO SECRETLY STOPS BY ANIMATE AFTER HOURS.
GOTTA WATCH ALL THE ANIME I RECORDED!
NO...! THIS ISN'T—
IT'S FOR SOMEONE ELSE...!
PLUS, SHE LIKES REVERSE HAREM ANIME, DESPITE HER LOOKS.
OOH, NICE.
WE COULD HAVE SOME *YURI* ACTION BETWEEN THE TWO, RIGHT?
I'M GONNA GRAB THESE DOCUMENTS OVERHEAD.
YOU'RE CLOSE...
I BET KABAKURA-SENPAI'S A *TSUNDERE* AND A PUSHOVER.
TOTALLY.
AND YOU JUST KNOW NIFUJI-CHAN'S GONNA BE SUPER ADORABLE.

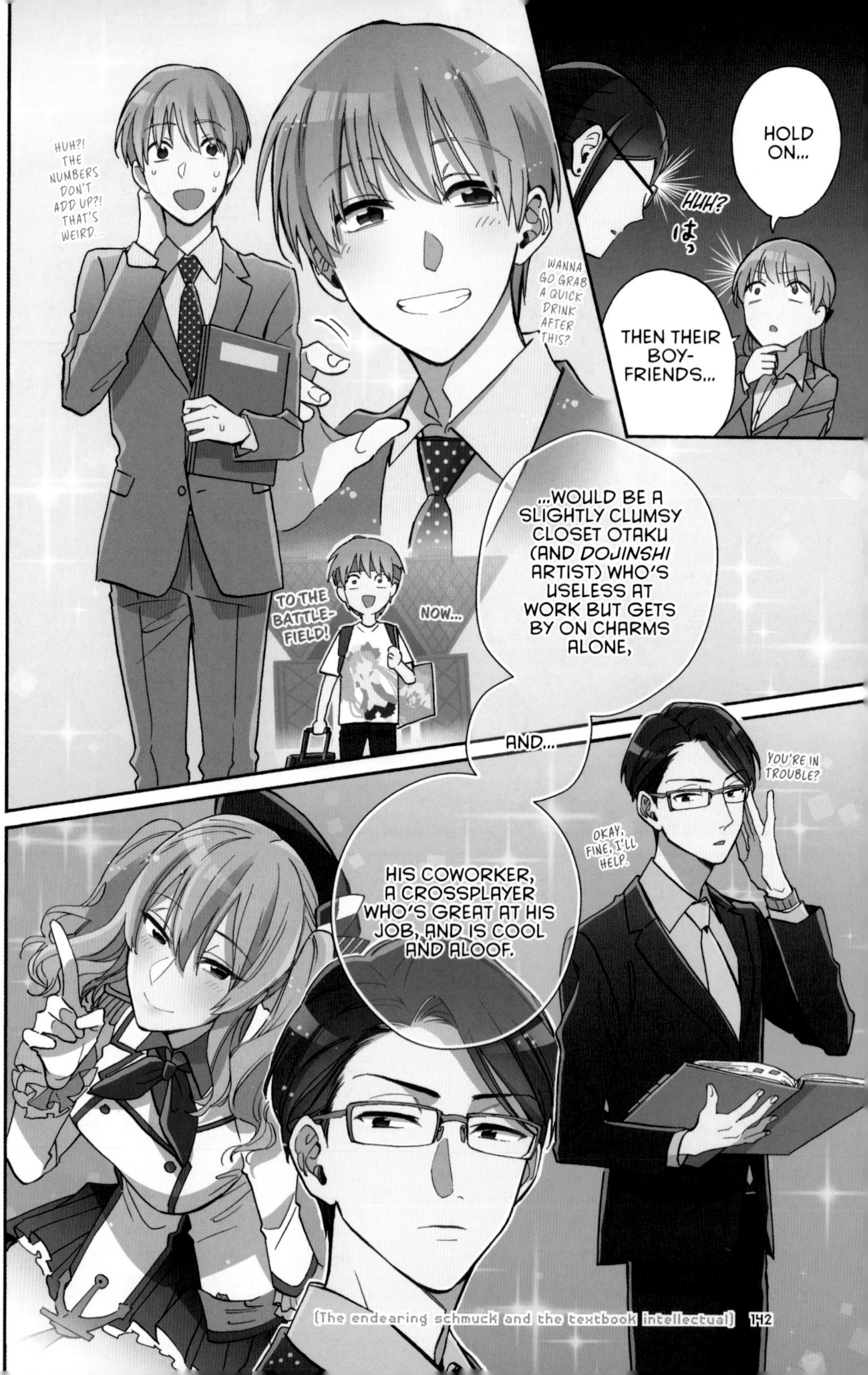
HOLD ON...
HUH?
は、
THEN THEIR BOY-FRIENDS...
HUH?! THE NUMBERS DON'T ADD UP?! THAT'S WEIRD...
WANNA GO GRAB A QUICK DRINK AFTER THIS?
...WOULD BE A SLIGHTLY CLUMSY CLOSET OTAKU (AND *DOJINSHI* ARTIST) WHO'S USELESS AT WORK BUT GETS BY ON CHARMS ALONE,
NOW...
TO THE BATTLE-FIELD!
AND...
YOU'RE IN TROUBLE?
OKAY, FINE, I'LL HELP.
HIS COWORKER, A CROSSPLAYER WHO'S GREAT AT HIS JOB, AND IS COOL AND ALOOF.

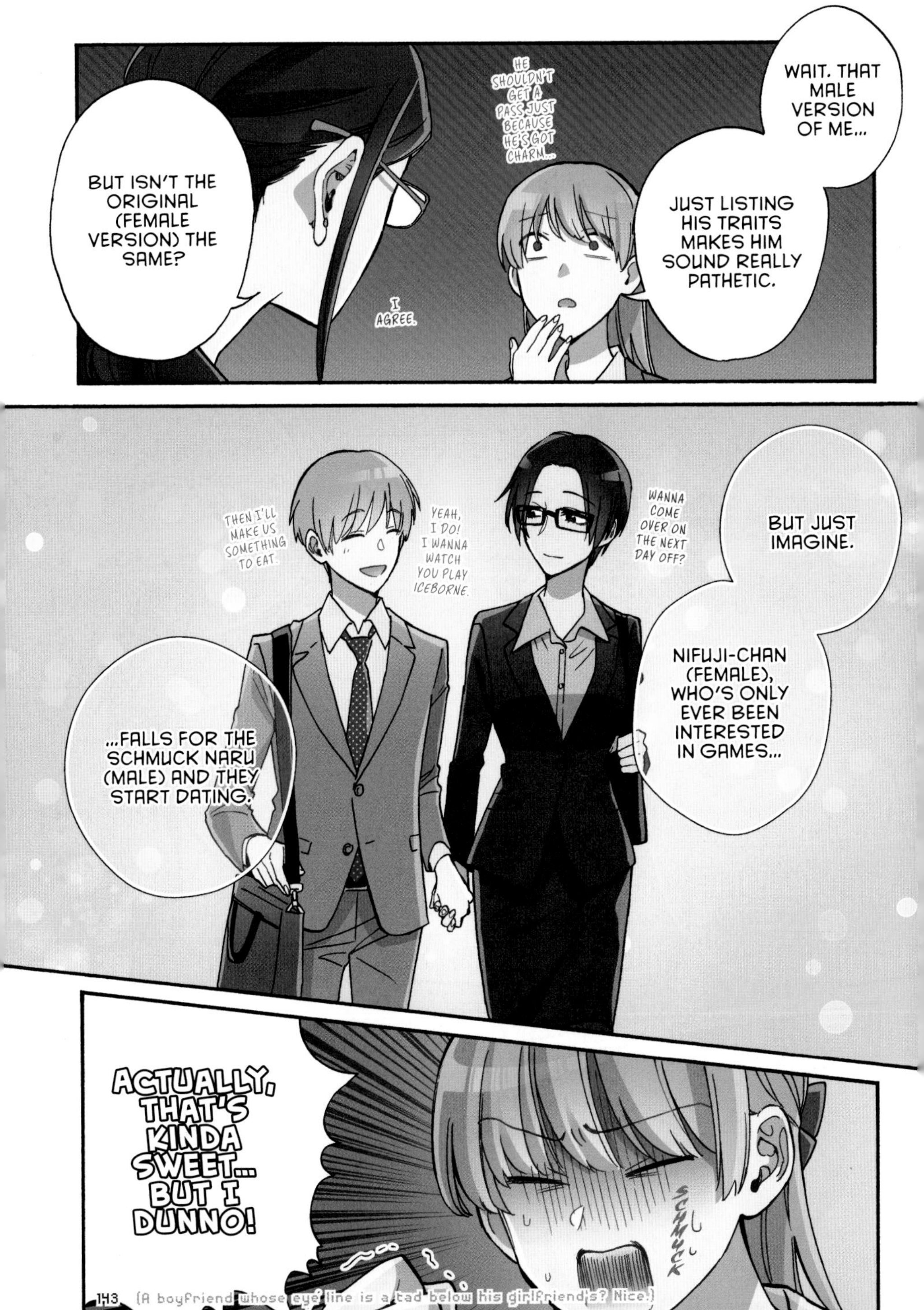
WAIT. THAT MALE VERSION OF ME...
JUST LISTING HIS TRAITS MAKES HIM SOUND REALLY PATHETIC.
HE SHOULDN'T GET A PASS JUST BECAUSE HE'S GOT CHARM...
BUT ISN'T THE ORIGINAL (FEMALE VERSION) THE SAME?
I AGREE.
BUT JUST IMAGINE.
NIFUJI-CHAN (FEMALE), WHO'S ONLY EVER BEEN INTERESTED IN GAMES...
WANNA COME OVER ON THE NEXT DAY OFF?
YEAH, I DO! I WANNA WATCH YOU PLAY ICEBORNE.
THEN I'LL MAKE US SOMETHING TO EAT.
...FALLS FOR THE SCHMUCK NARU (MALE) AND THEY START DATING.
ACTUALLY, THAT'S KINDA SWEET... BUT I DUNNO!
SCHMUCK

(A boyfriend whose eye line is a tad below his girlfriend's? Nice.)

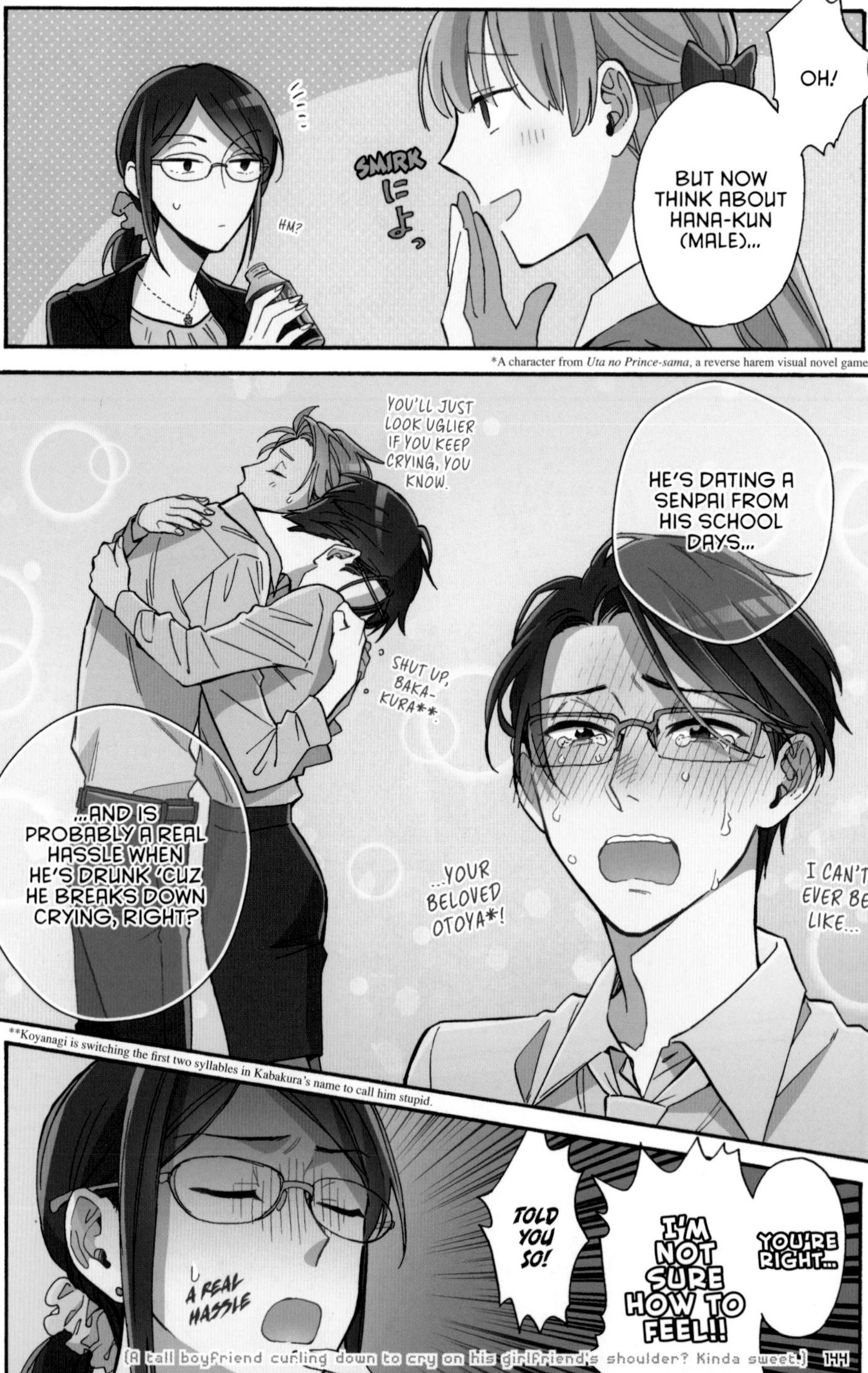
OH!
BUT NOW THINK ABOUT HANA-KUN (MALE)...
SMIRK
にょっ
HM?
HE'S DATING A SENPAI FROM HIS SCHOOL DAYS...
...AND IS PROBABLY A REAL HASSLE WHEN HE'S DRUNK 'CUZ HE BREAKS DOWN CRYING, RIGHT?
I CAN'T EVER BE LIKE...
...YOUR BELOVED OTOYA*!
YOU'LL JUST LOOK UGLIER IF YOU KEEP CRYING, YOU KNOW.
SHUT UP, BAKA-KURA**.
YOU'RE RIGHT...
I'M NOT SURE HOW TO FEEL!!
TOLD YOU SO!
A REAL HASSLE

*A character from *Uta no Prince-sama*, a reverse harem visual novel game.

**Koyanagi is switching the first two syllables in Kabakura's name to call him stupid.

(A tall boyfriend curling down to cry on his girlfriend's shoulder? Kinda sweet!)

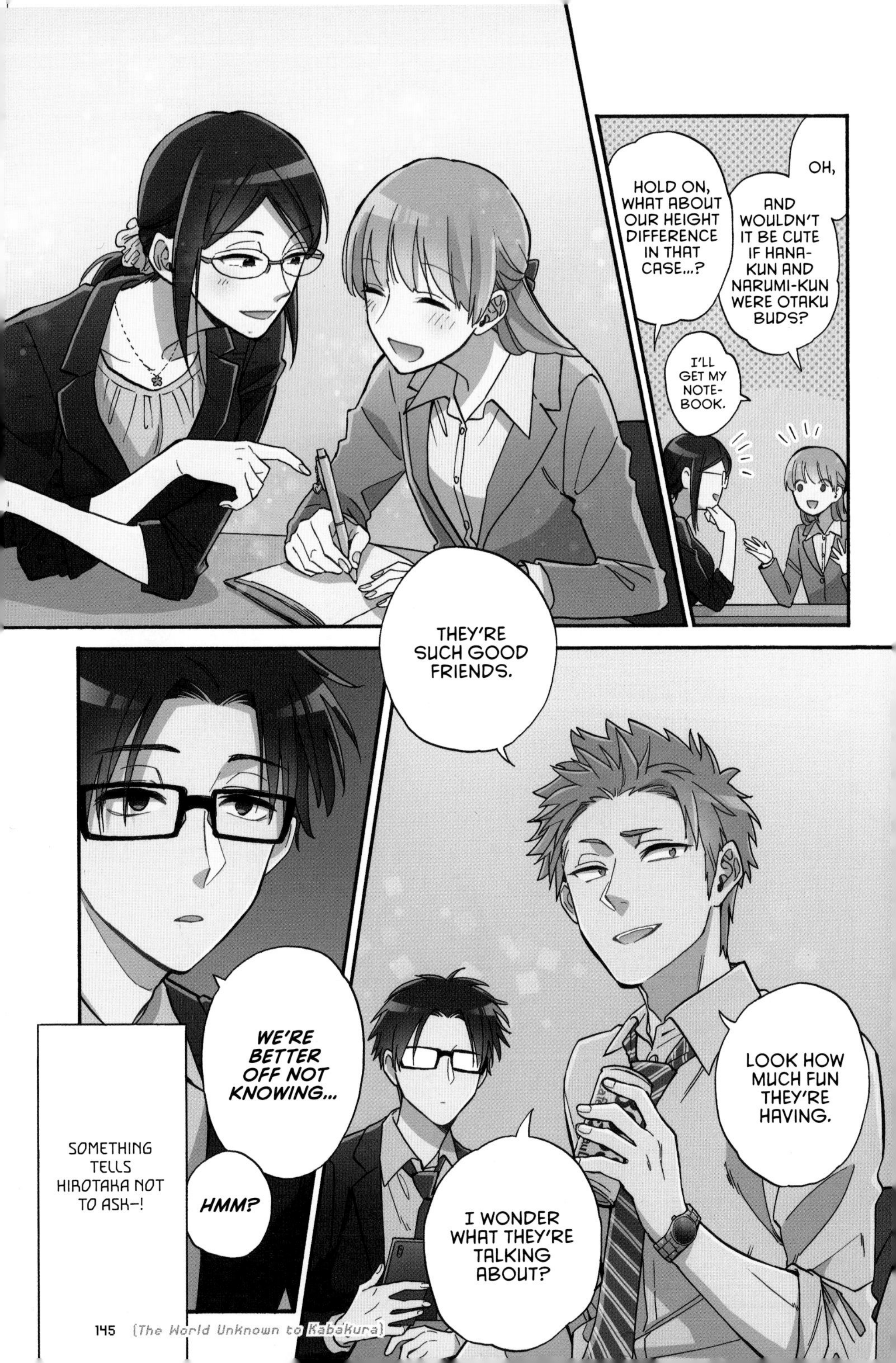
OH,
AND WOULDN'T IT BE CUTE IF HANA-KUN AND NARUMI-KUN WERE OTAKU BUDS?
HOLD ON, WHAT ABOUT OUR HEIGHT DIFFERENCE IN THAT CASE...?
I'LL GET MY NOTE-BOOK.
THEY'RE SUCH GOOD FRIENDS.
LOOK HOW MUCH FUN THEY'RE HAVING.
I WONDER WHAT THEY'RE TALKING ABOUT?
HMM?
WE'RE BETTER OFF NOT KNOWING...
SOMETHING TELLS HIROTAKA NOT TO ASK—!

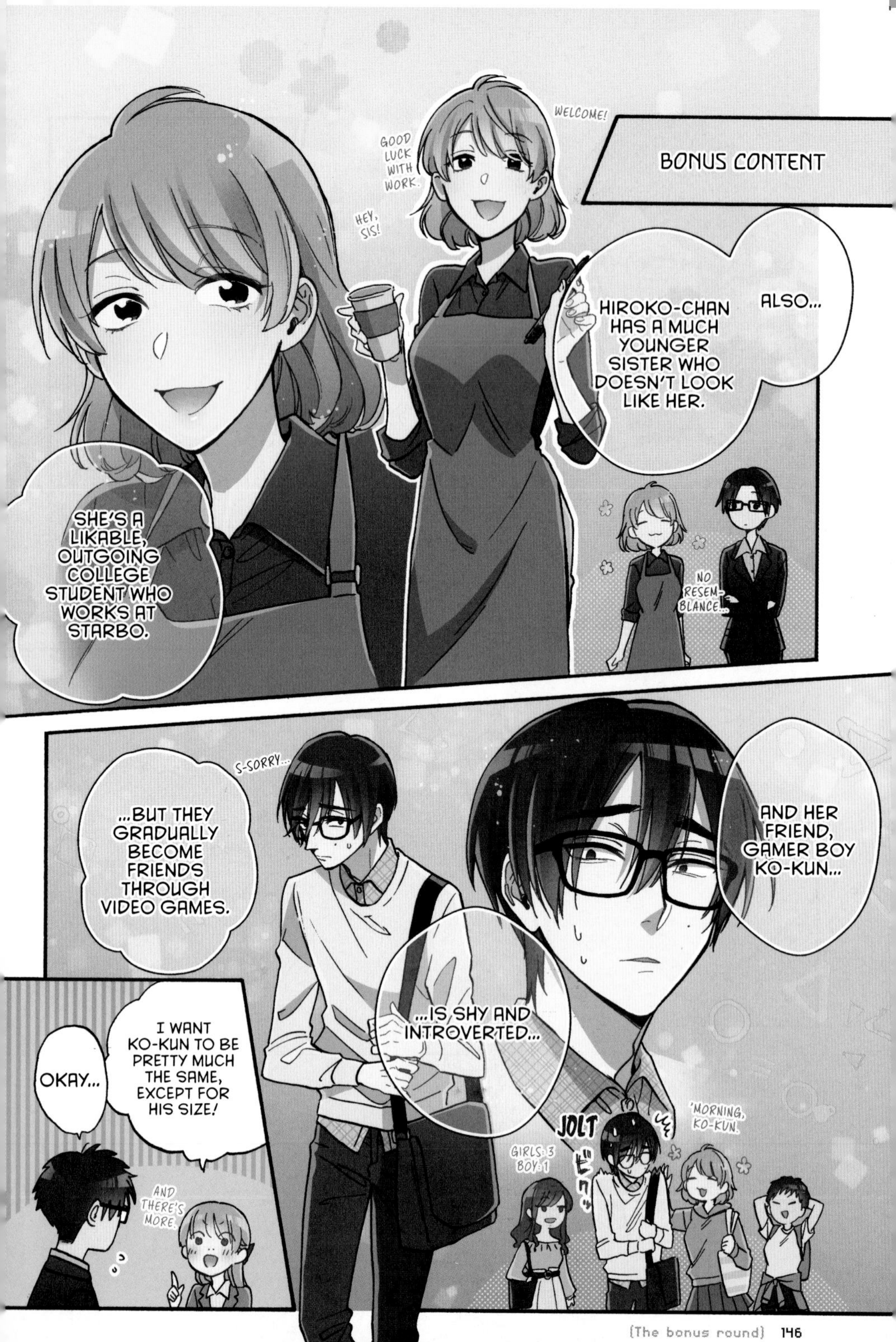
BONUS CONTENT
ALSO...
HIROKO-CHAN HAS A MUCH YOUNGER SISTER WHO DOESN'T LOOK LIKE HER.
WELCOME!
GOOD LUCK WITH WORK.
HEY, SIS!
NO RESEMBLANCE...
SHE'S A LIKABLE, OUTGOING COLLEGE STUDENT WHO WORKS AT STARBO.
AND HER FRIEND, GAMER BOY KO-KUN...
S-SORRY...
...IS SHY AND INTROVERTED...
'MORNING, KO-KUN.
JOLT
GIRLS: 3 BOY: 1
...BUT THEY GRADUALLY BECOME FRIENDS THROUGH VIDEO GAMES.
I WANT KO-KUN TO BE PRETTY MUCH THE SAME, EXCEPT FOR HIS SIZE!
OKAY...
AND THERE'S MORE.

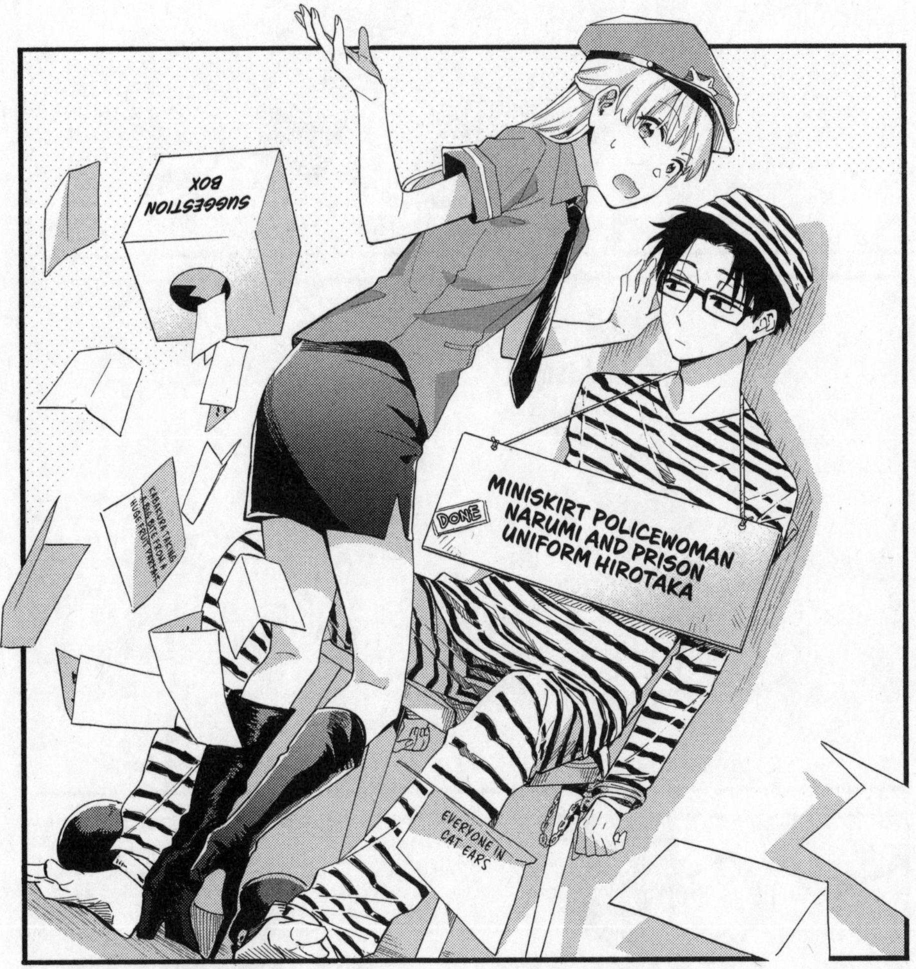
SUGGESTION BOX
DONE
MINISKIRT POLICEWOMAN NARUMI AND PRISON UNIFORM HIROTAKA
EVERYONE IN CAT EARS

Episode....55

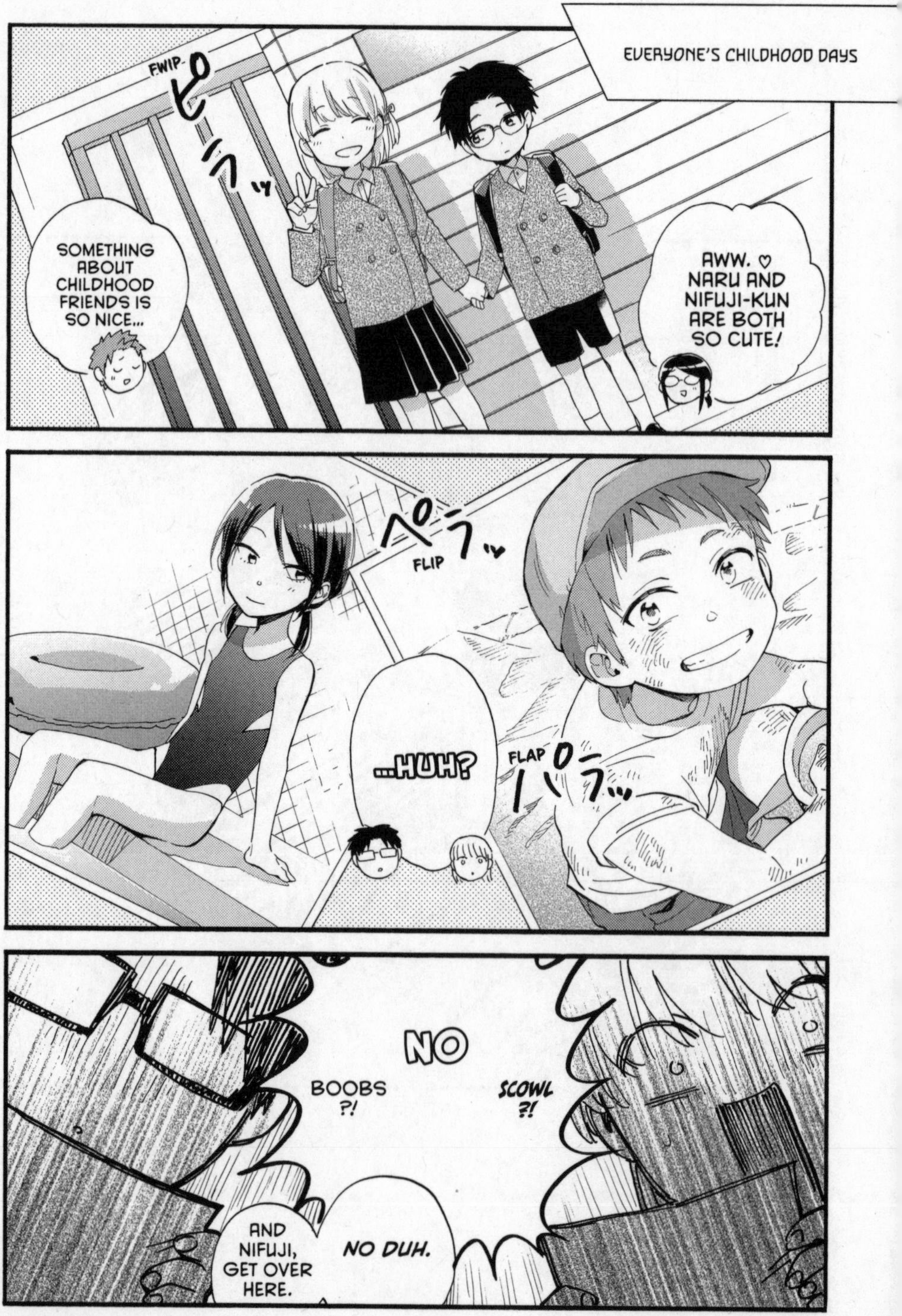
EVERYONE'S CHILDHOOD DAYS
AWW. ♡ NARU AND NIFUJI-KUN ARE BOTH SO CUTE!
FWIP
SOMETHING ABOUT CHILDHOOD FRIENDS IS SO NICE...
FLIP
FLAP
...HUH?
NO
SCOWL ?!
BOOBS ?!
NO DUH.
AND NIFUJI, GET OVER HERE.

(What they saw first)

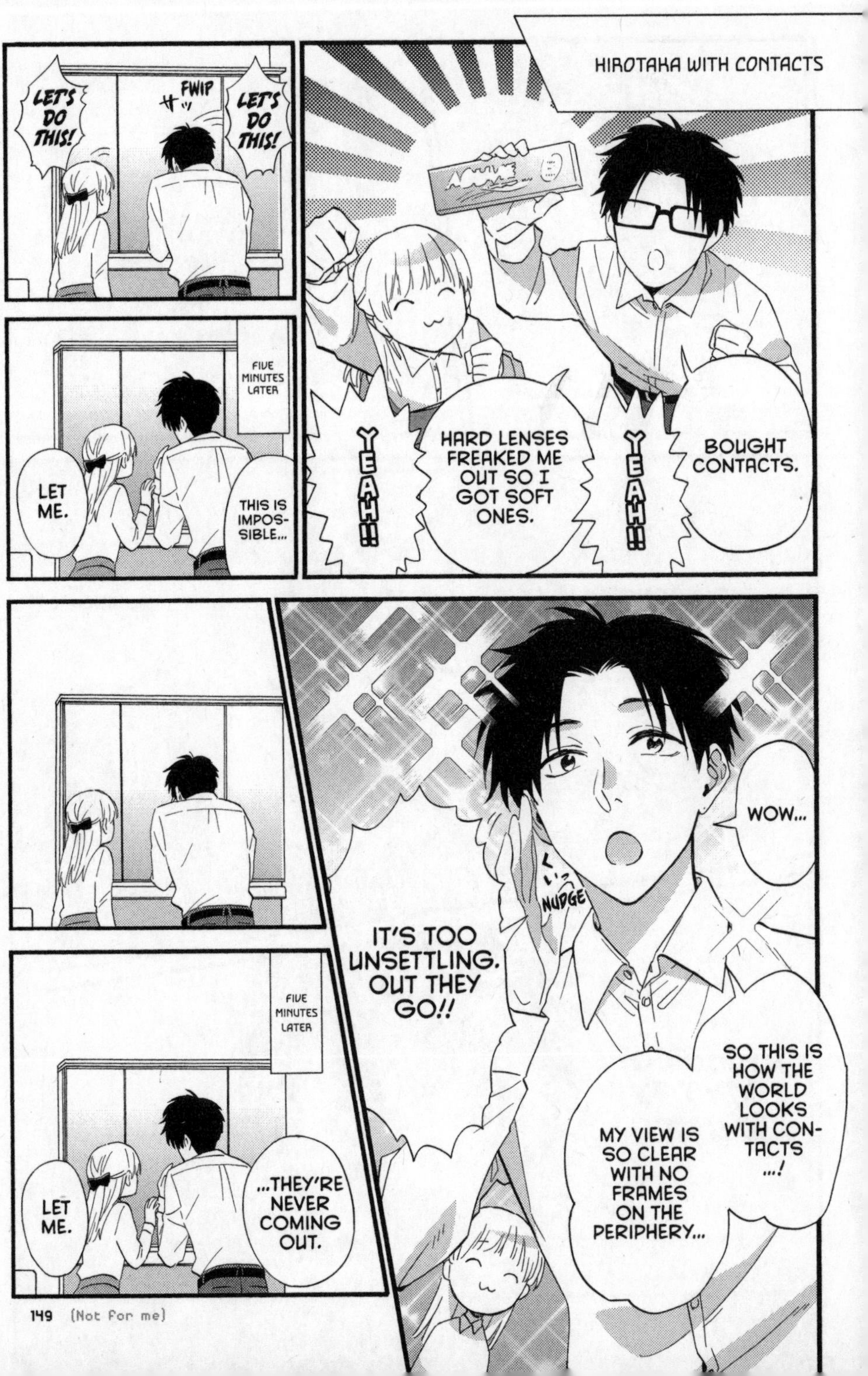
HIROTAKA WITH CONTACTS
BOUGHT CONTACTS.
YEAH!!
HARD LENSES FREAKED ME OUT SO I GOT SOFT ONES.
YEAH!!
LET'S DO THIS!
FWIP
LET'S DO THIS!
FIVE MINUTES LATER
THIS IS IMPOSSIBLE...
LET ME.
WOW...
NUDGE
SO THIS IS HOW THE WORLD LOOKS WITH CONTACTS ...!
MY VIEW IS SO CLEAR WITH NO FRAMES ON THE PERIPHERY...
IT'S TOO UNSETTLING. OUT THEY GO!!
FIVE MINUTES LATER
...THEY'RE NEVER COMING OUT.
LET ME.

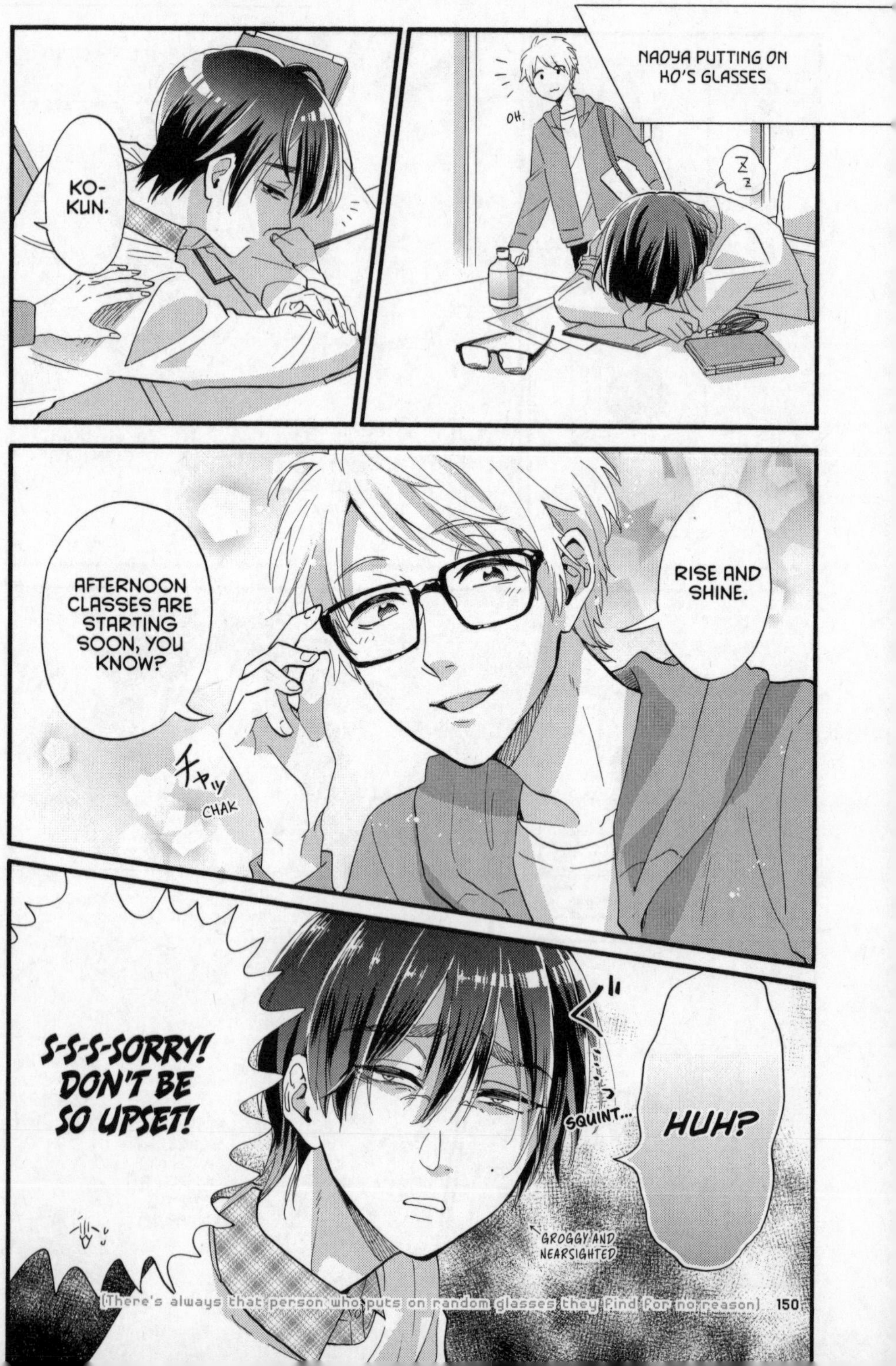
NAOYA PUTTING ON KO'S GLASSES
OH.
Z z
KO-KUN.
RISE AND SHINE.
AFTERNOON CLASSES ARE STARTING SOON, YOU KNOW?
チャッ
CHAK
HUH?
SQUINT...
GROGGY AND NEARSIGHTED
S-S-S-SORRY! DON'T BE SO UPSET!

(There's always that person who puts on random glasses they find for no reason)

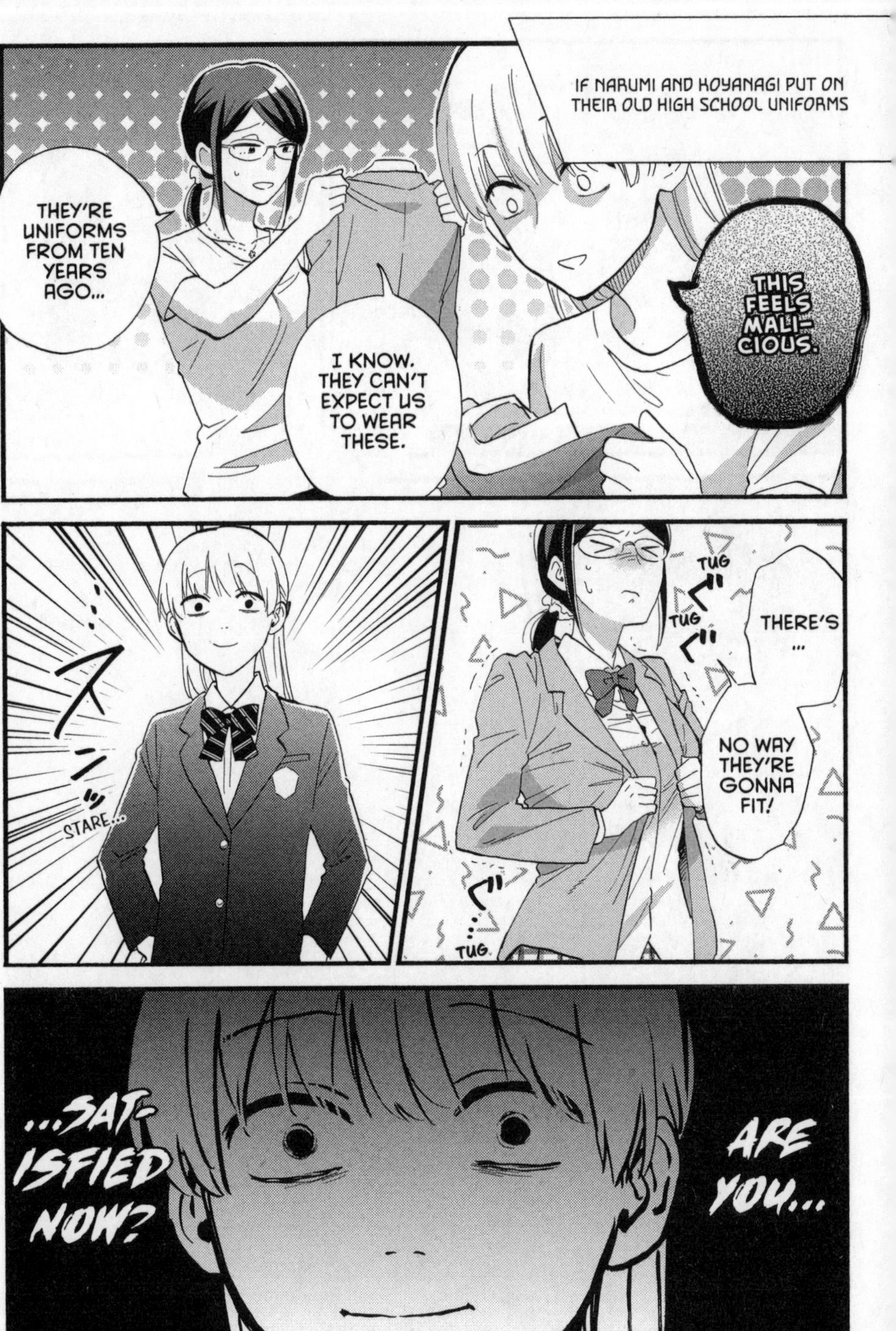
IF NARUMI AND KOYANAGI PUT ON THEIR OLD HIGH SCHOOL UNIFORMS
THIS FEELS MALI-CIOUS.
THEY'RE UNIFORMS FROM TEN YEARS AGO...
I KNOW. THEY CAN'T EXPECT US TO WEAR THESE.
TUG
TUG
THERE'S ...
NO WAY THEY'RE GONNA FIT!
TUG
STARE...
ARE YOU...
...SAT-ISFIED NOW?

NARUMI WITH SHORT HAIR

FLUMP

FLUMP

FWOMP

OH, HEY, HIROTAKA.

IF NARUMI'S HAPPY WITH IT, THAT'S FINE. BUT ISN'T IT A BIG D... ...TO CUT TH... ...N? I ME... ...UMI'S CU... ...AIR'S LONG... ...IT'S UP TO HER... ...OF HAIR SHE WANT... ...HE COULD HAVE AT... ...EN ME A HEAD...

UH...

WELL ...

WHADD'YA THINK?

I GOT IT CHOPPED OFF.

STOP MESSING WITH ME, MORON.

FWISH...

FOOLED'YA!

(So shocked he dropped his files) 152

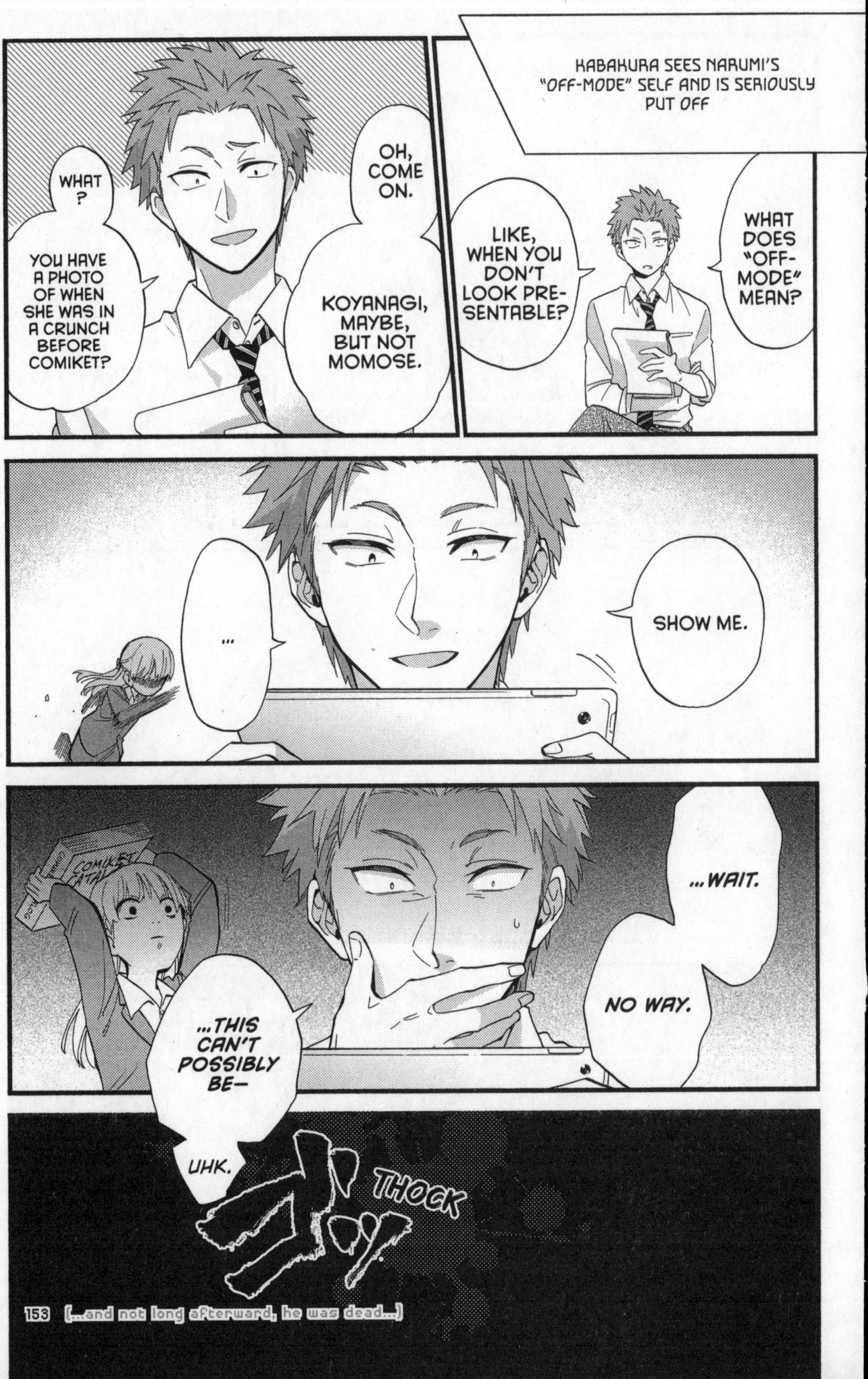
KABAKURA SEES NARUMI'S "OFF-MODE" SELF AND IS SERIOUSLY PUT OFF
WHAT DOES "OFF-MODE" MEAN?
LIKE, WHEN YOU DON'T LOOK PRE-SENTABLE?
OH, COME ON.
KOYANAGI, MAYBE, BUT NOT MOMOSE.
WHAT?
YOU HAVE A PHOTO OF WHEN SHE WAS IN A CRUNCH BEFORE COMIKET?
SHOW ME.
...
...WAIT.
NO WAY.
...THIS CAN'T POSSIBLY BE—
UHK.
THOCK
(...and not long afterward, he was dead...)

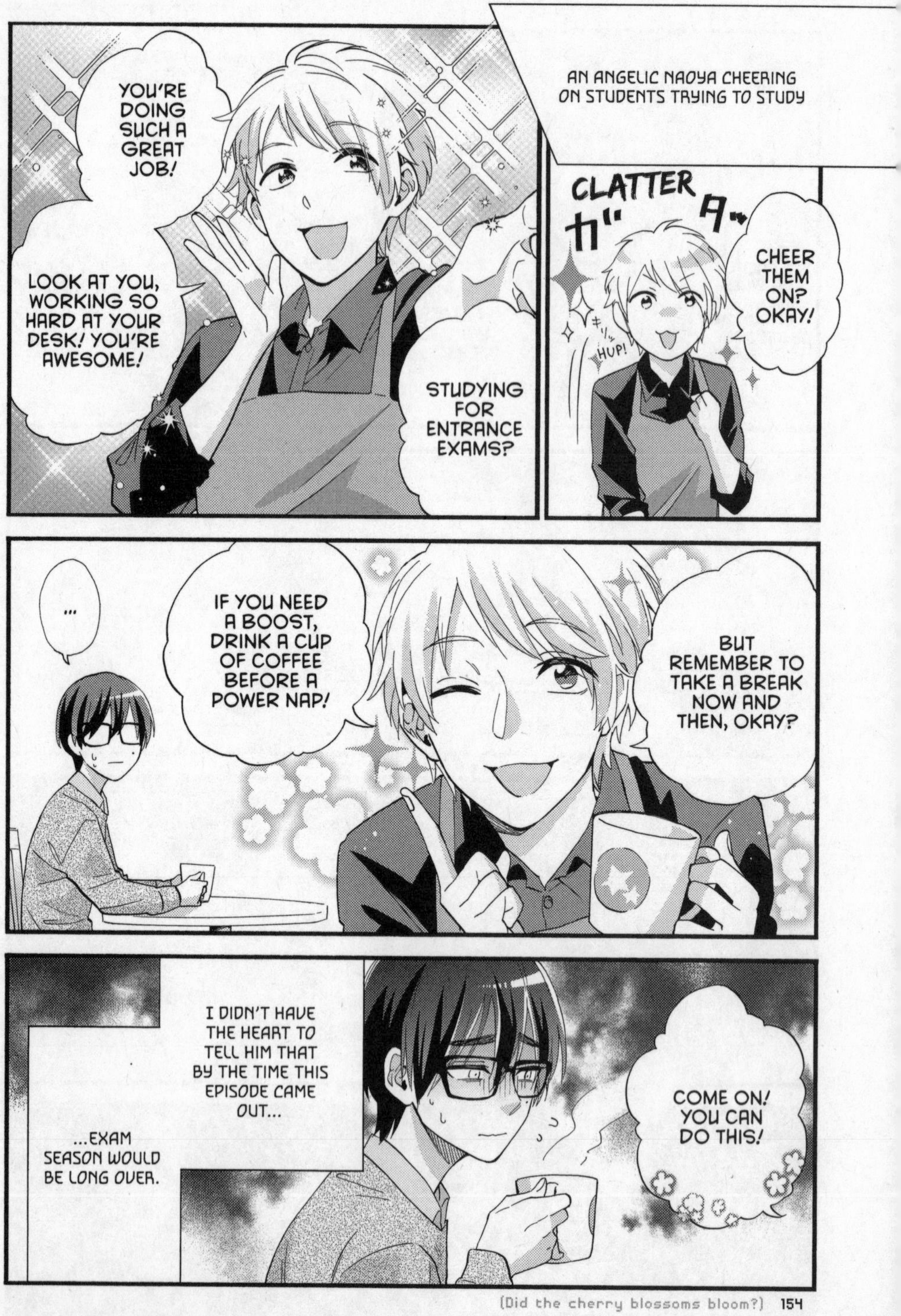
AN ANGELIC NAOYA CHEERING ON STUDENTS TRYING TO STUDY
CLATTER
ガタッ
CHEER THEM ON? OKAY!
キリッ
HUP!
STUDYING FOR ENTRANCE EXAMS?
YOU'RE DOING SUCH A GREAT JOB!
LOOK AT YOU, WORKING SO HARD AT YOUR DESK! YOU'RE AWESOME!
IF YOU NEED A BOOST, DRINK A CUP OF COFFEE BEFORE A POWER NAP!
BUT REMEMBER TO TAKE A BREAK NOW AND THEN, OKAY?
...
COME ON! YOU CAN DO THIS!
I DIDN'T HAVE THE HEART TO TELL HIM THAT BY THE TIME THIS EPISODE CAME OUT...
...EXAM SEASON WOULD BE LONG OVER.

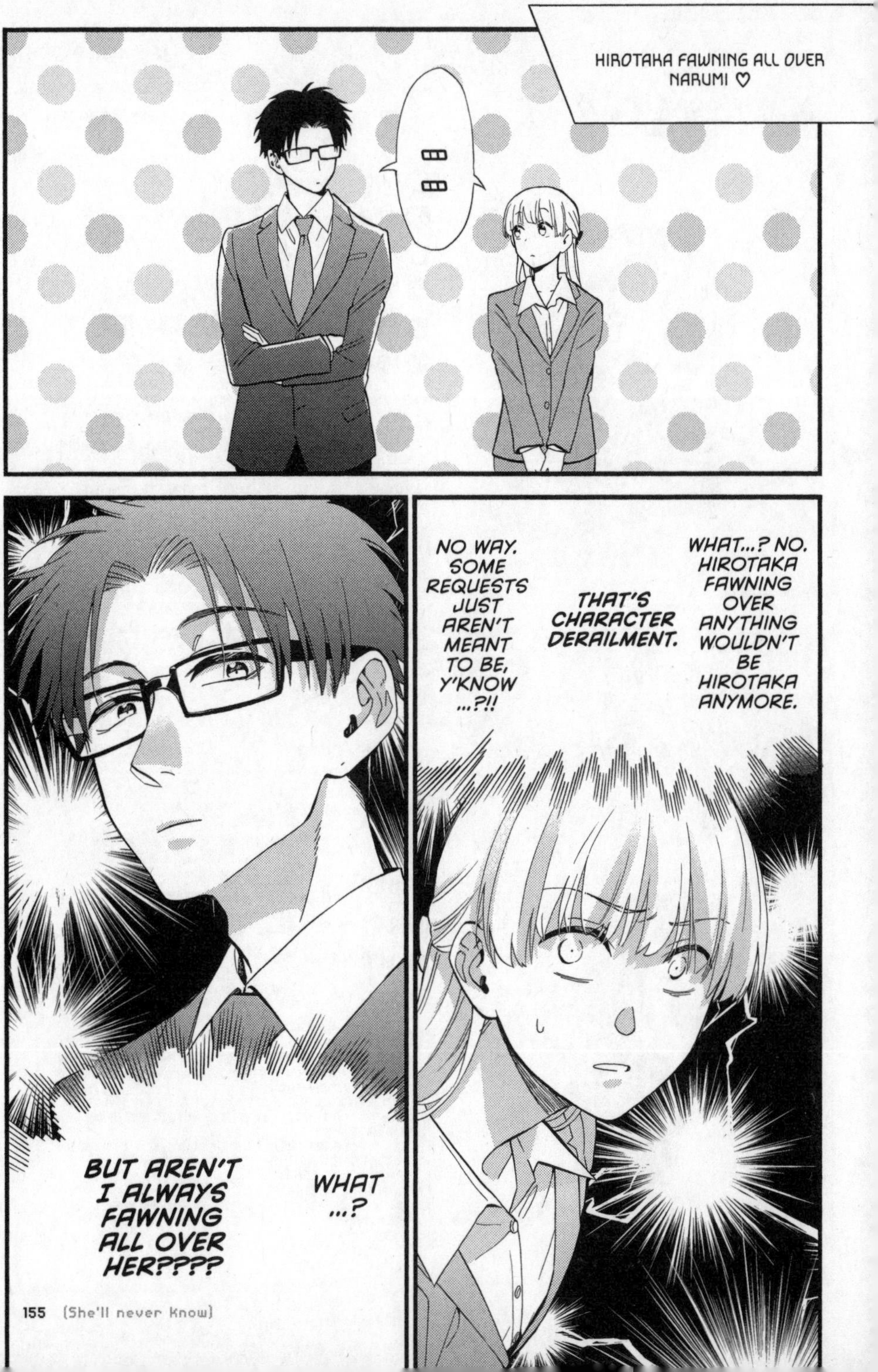
HIROTAKA FAWNING ALL OVER NARUMI ♡
……
WHAT...? NO. HIROTAKA FAWNING OVER ANYTHING WOULDN'T BE HIROTAKA ANYMORE.
THAT'S CHARACTER DERAILMENT.
NO WAY. SOME REQUESTS JUST AREN'T MEANT TO BE, Y'KNOW ...?!!
WHAT ...?
BUT AREN'T I ALWAYS FAWNING ALL OVER HER????

NARUMI MOMOSE

SPECIES: ELF CLASS: ASSASSIN

- ♥ CON (CONSTITUTION)
- ⟳ STR (STRENGTH)
- ◯ DEF (DEFENSE)
- ◢ AGI (AGILITY)
- ✦ APP (APPEARANCE)
- ✡ MAG (MAGIC)

ALTHOUGH THE ELF SPECIES IS BEST SUITED FOR PROVIDING RANGED SUPPORT WITH MAGIC, NARUMI CHOSE THE ASSASSIN CLASS, WHICH IS SPECIFICALLY FOR FIGHTING ON THE FRONT LINE.
THIS IS THE UNFORTUNATE RESULT OF NOT BEING ABLE TO CHOOSE BETWEEN CUTE LOOKS AND HER PREFERRED FIGHTING STYLE.
SHE'S PUT IN MORE HOURS THAN MOST OF THE OTHER MEMBERS. SHE ENJOYS THE GAME REASONABLY WELL WITHOUT PAYING FOR IN-GAME PURCHASES, BUT WHENEVER A CUTE NEW COSTUME IS RELEASED, SHE FORKS OVER MONEY LIKE SHE'S POSSESSED.

HIROTAKA NIFUJI

SPECIES: HUMAN CLASS: ARCHER

- ♥ CON (CONSTITUTION)
- ⟳ STR (STRENGTH)
- ◯ DEF (DEFENSE)
- ◢ AGI (AGILITY)
- ✦ APP (APPEARANCE)
- ✡ MAG (MAGIC)

HIROTAKA PURSUES THE INSANE STRATEGY OF PLAYING SOLO AS AN ARCHER, WHICH IS THE MOST DISADVANTAGED CLASS IN THE CURRENT GAME MAP.
SILLY COSTUMES ARE HIS UNIFORM OF CHOICE, BUT NARUMI ONCE TOLD HIM THAT SHE WAS "EMBARRASSED PLAYING ALONGSIDE HIM."
HE'S PUT IN A SERIOUS NUMBER OF HOURS, BUT HE ARGUES THAT "IT'S NOT THAT MUCH" SINCE HE ALSO PLAYS OTHER GAMES IN THE MEANTIME.
BECAUSE HE NEEDS TO PLAY A LOT AS EFFICIENTLY AS POSSIBLE (A PERSONAL PHILOSOPHY), IN-GAME PURCHASES ARE A MUST.

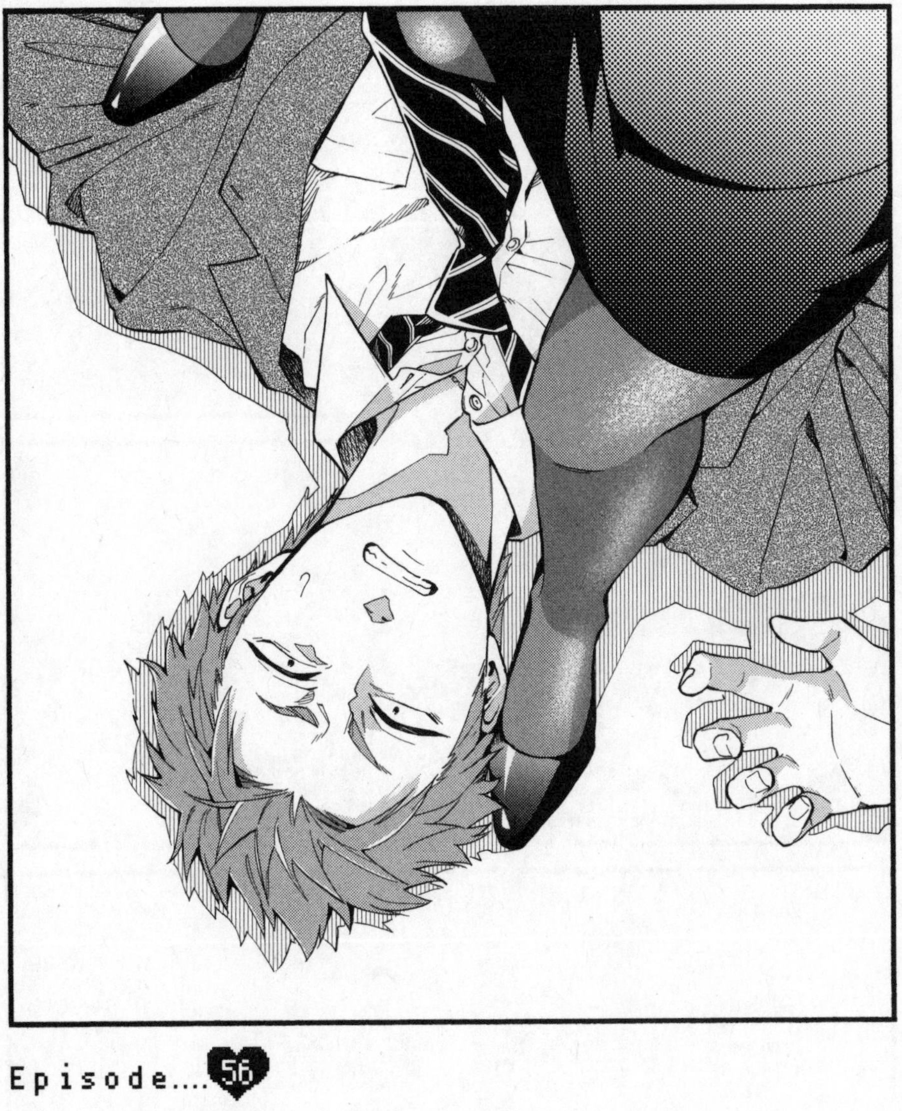

Episode.... 56

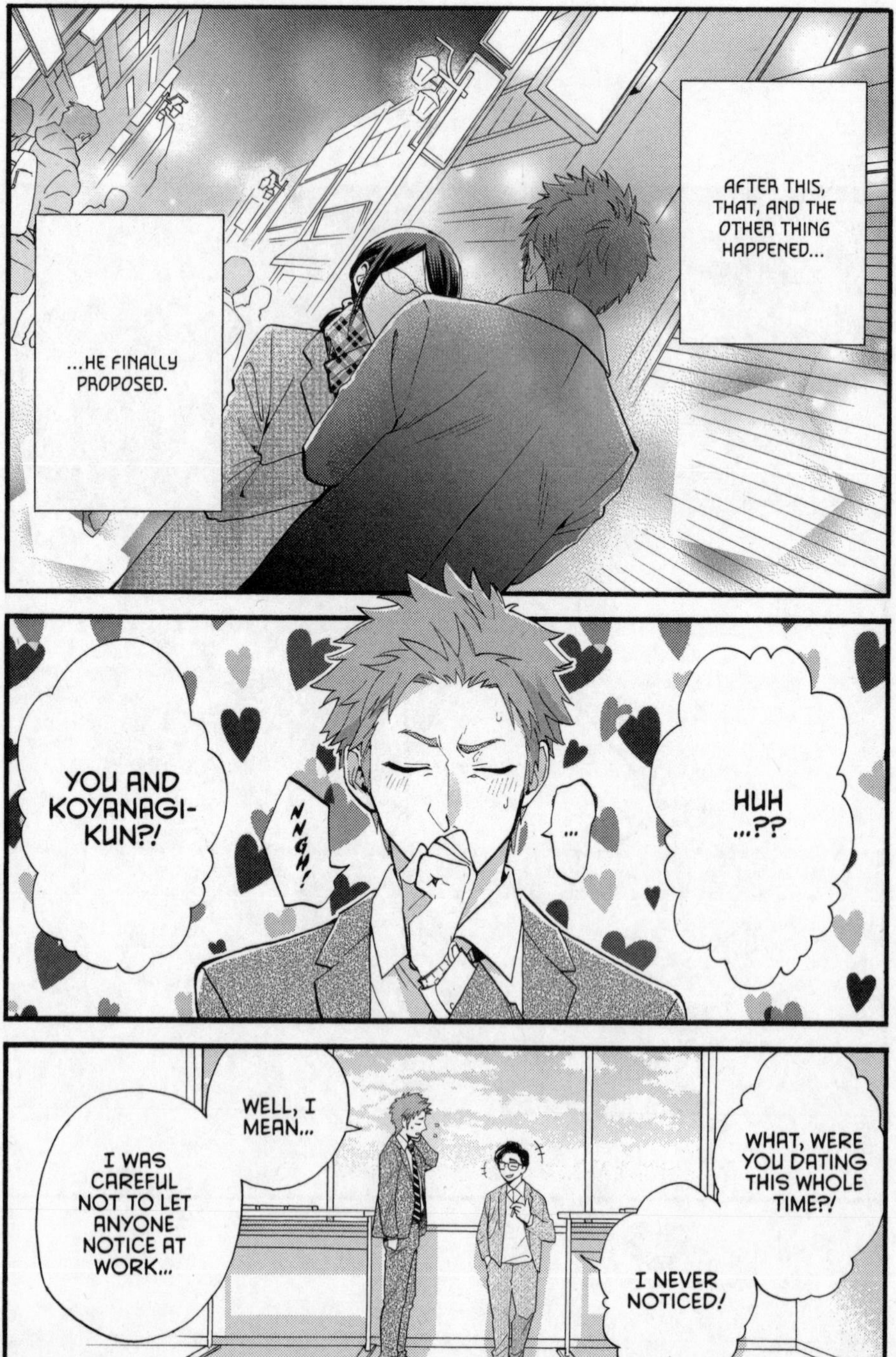
AFTER THIS, THAT, AND THE OTHER THING HAPPENED...
...HE FINALLY PROPOSED.
HUH ...??
...
NNGH!
YOU AND KOYANAGI-KUN?!
WHAT, WERE YOU DATING THIS WHOLE TIME?!
I NEVER NOTICED!
WELL, I MEAN...
I WAS CAREFUL NOT TO LET ANYONE NOTICE AT WORK...

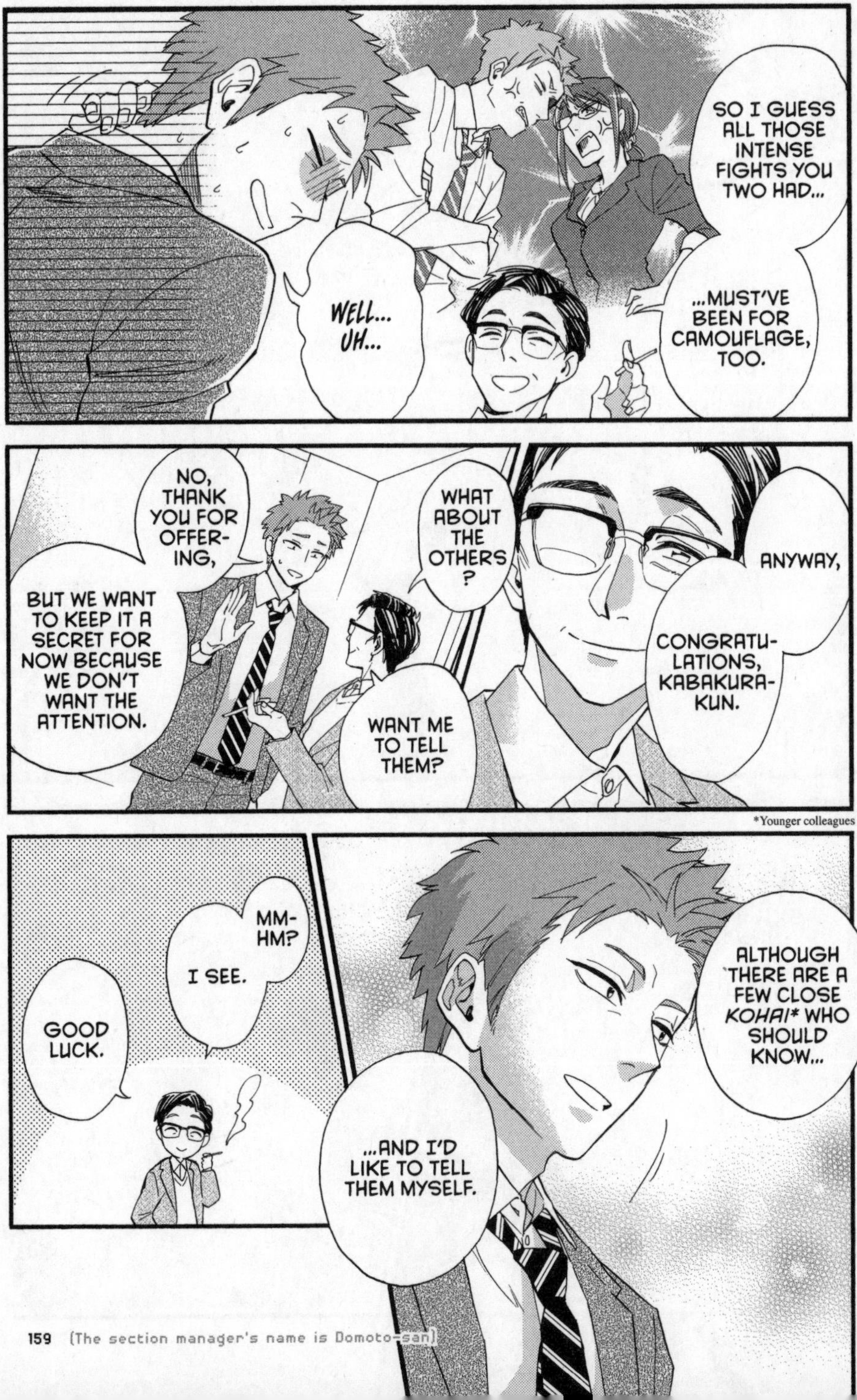
SO I GUESS ALL THOSE INTENSE FIGHTS YOU TWO HAD...
...MUST'VE BEEN FOR CAMOUFLAGE, TOO.
WELL... UH...
ANYWAY,
CONGRATULATIONS, KABAKURA-KUN.
WHAT ABOUT THE OTHERS?
WANT ME TO TELL THEM?
NO, THANK YOU FOR OFFERING,
BUT WE WANT TO KEEP IT A SECRET FOR NOW BECAUSE WE DON'T WANT THE ATTENTION.
ALTHOUGH THERE ARE A FEW CLOSE *KOHAI** WHO SHOULD KNOW...
...AND I'D LIKE TO TELL THEM MYSELF.
MM-HM?
I SEE.
GOOD LUCK.

*Younger colleagues

Sign: Kutsurogi

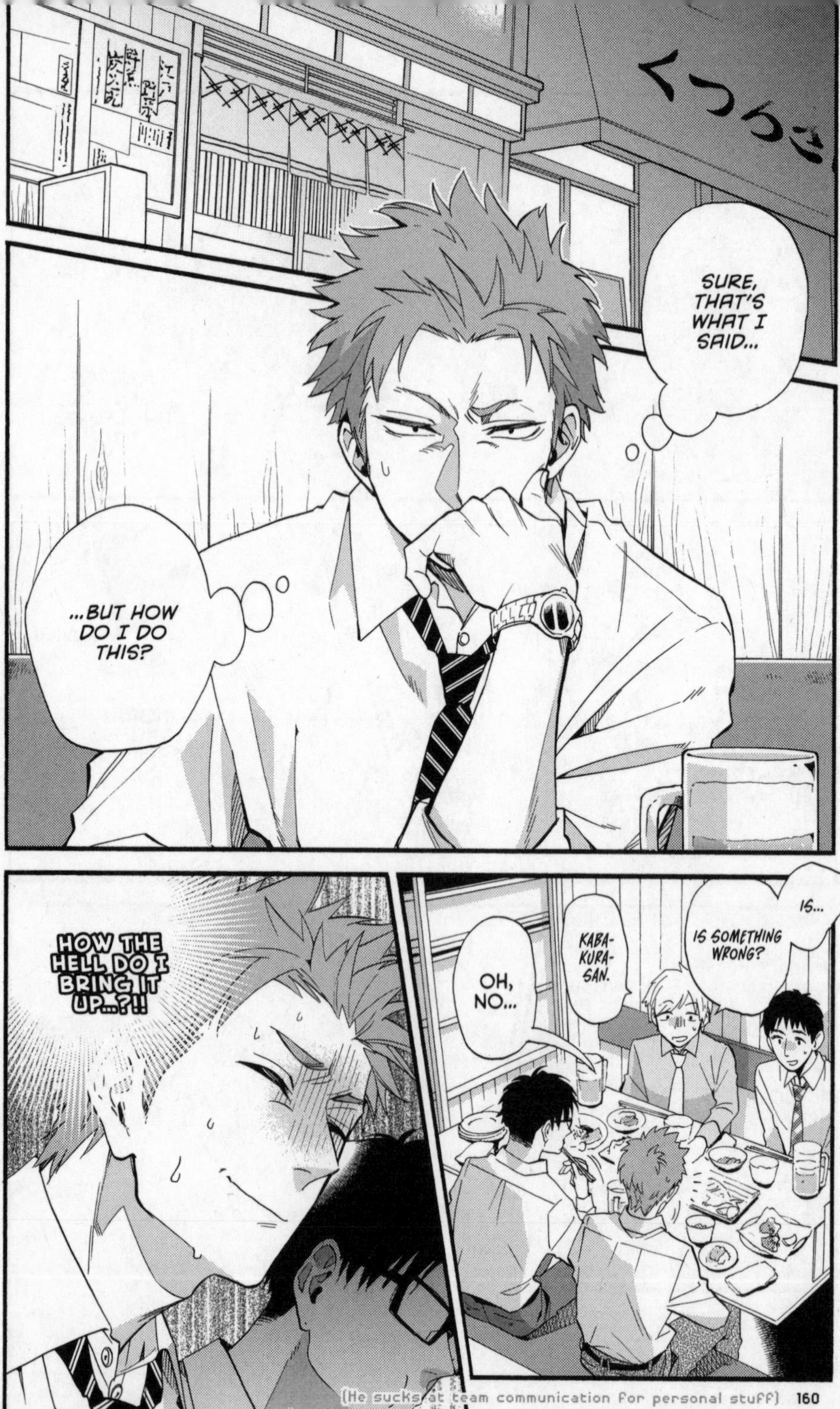
SURE, THAT'S WHAT I SAID...
...BUT HOW DO I DO THIS?
IS... IS SOMETHING WRONG?
KABA-KURA-SAN.
OH, NO...
HOW THE HELL DO I BRING IT UP...?!!

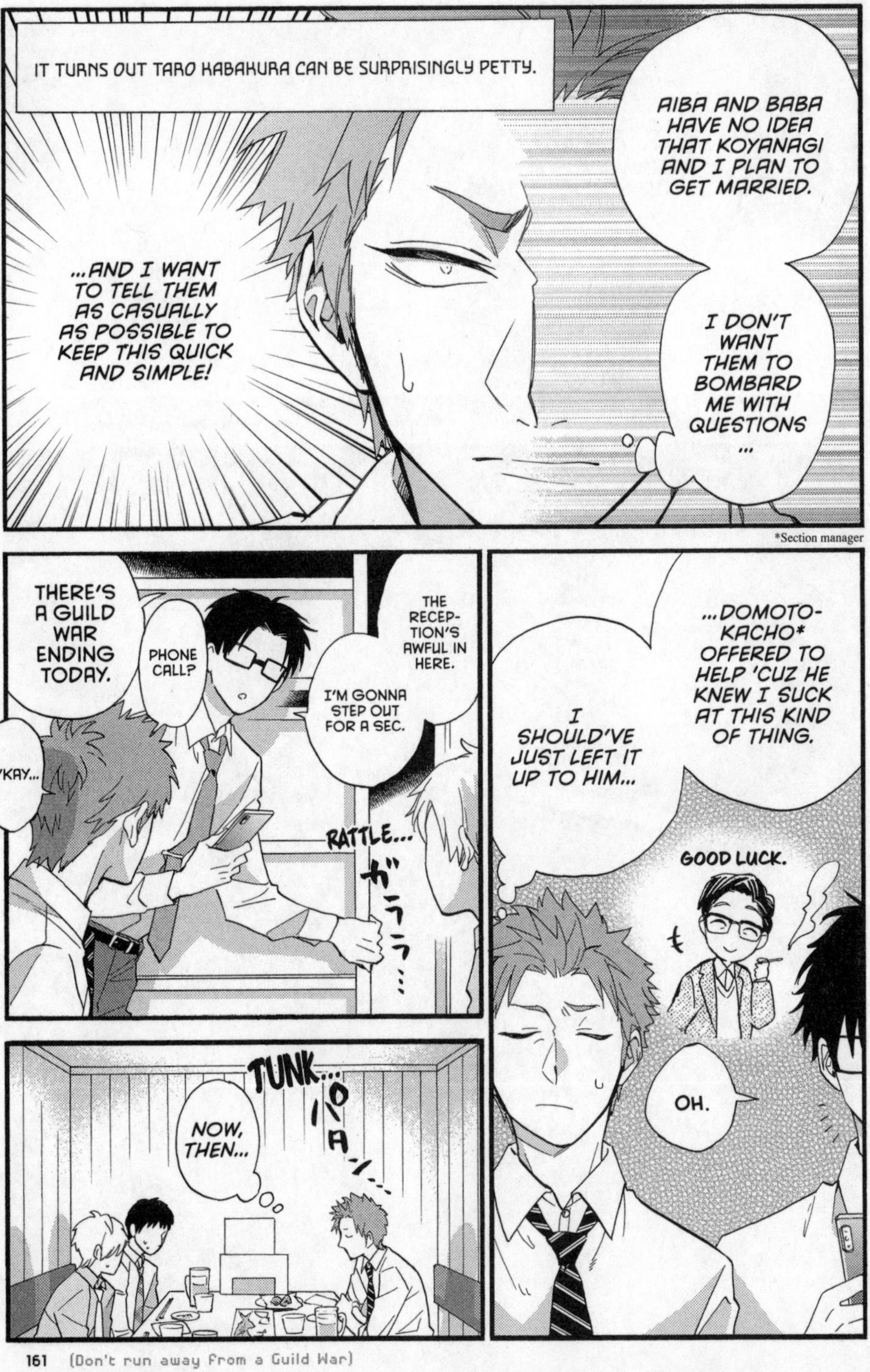
IT TURNS OUT TARO KABAKURA CAN BE SURPRISINGLY PETTY.
AIBA AND BABA HAVE NO IDEA THAT KOYANAGI AND I PLAN TO GET MARRIED.
I DON'T WANT THEM TO BOMBARD ME WITH QUESTIONS ...
...AND I WANT TO TELL THEM AS CASUALLY AS POSSIBLE TO KEEP THIS QUICK AND SIMPLE!
...DOMOTO-KACHO* OFFERED TO HELP 'CUZ HE KNEW I SUCK AT THIS KIND OF THING.
I SHOULD'VE JUST LEFT IT UP TO HIM...
GOOD LUCK.
OH.
THE RECEPTION'S AWFUL IN HERE.
I'M GONNA STEP OUT FOR A SEC.
PHONE CALL?
THERE'S A GUILD WAR ENDING TODAY.
M'KAY...
RATTLE...
ガララ...
TUNK...
パタ...
NOW, THEN...

*Section manager

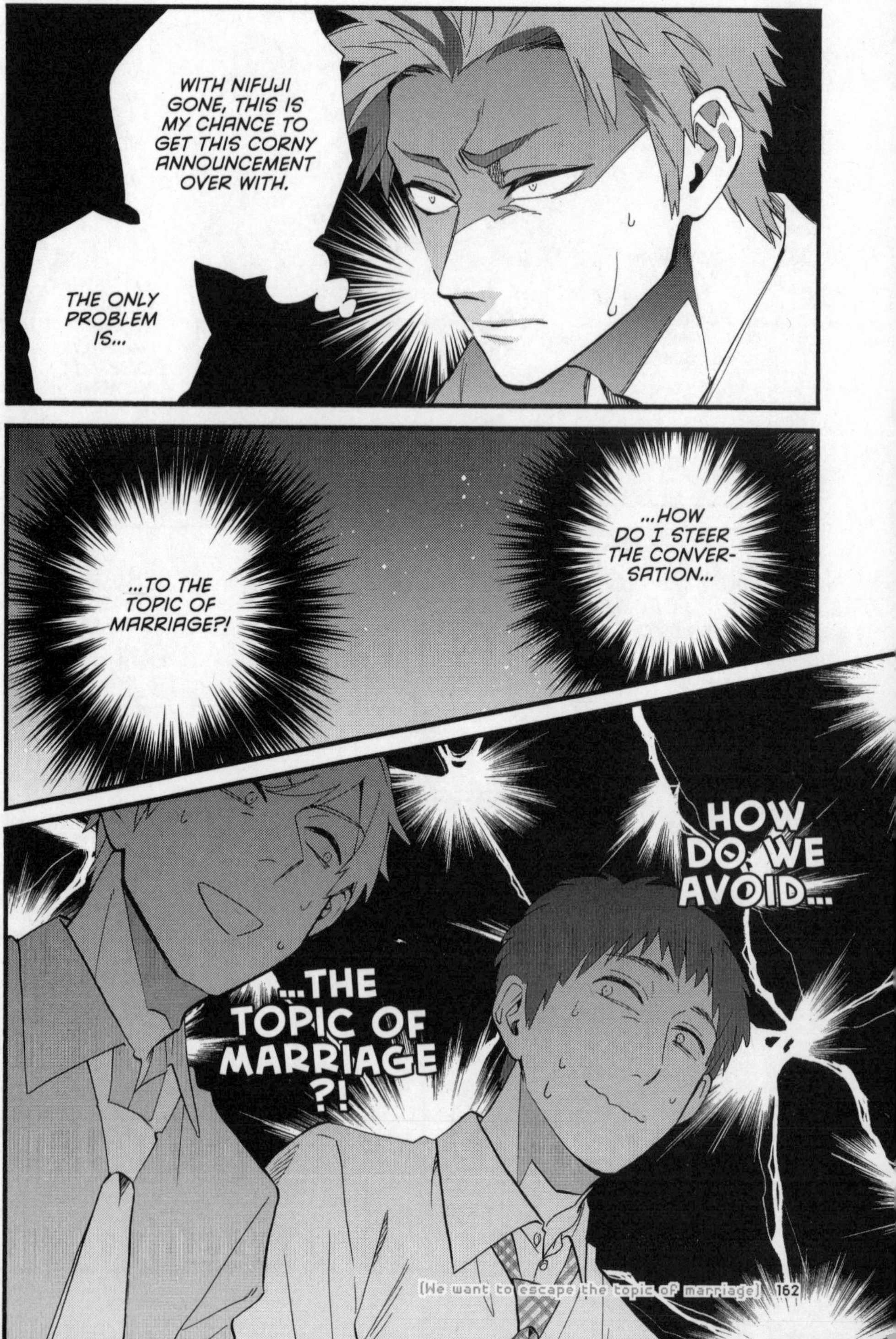
WITH NIFUJI GONE, THIS IS MY CHANCE TO GET THIS CORNY ANNOUNCEMENT OVER WITH.
THE ONLY PROBLEM IS...
...HOW DO I STEER THE CONVER-SATION...
...TO THE TOPIC OF MARRIAGE?!
HOW DO WE AVOID...
...THE TOPIC OF MARRIAGE?!

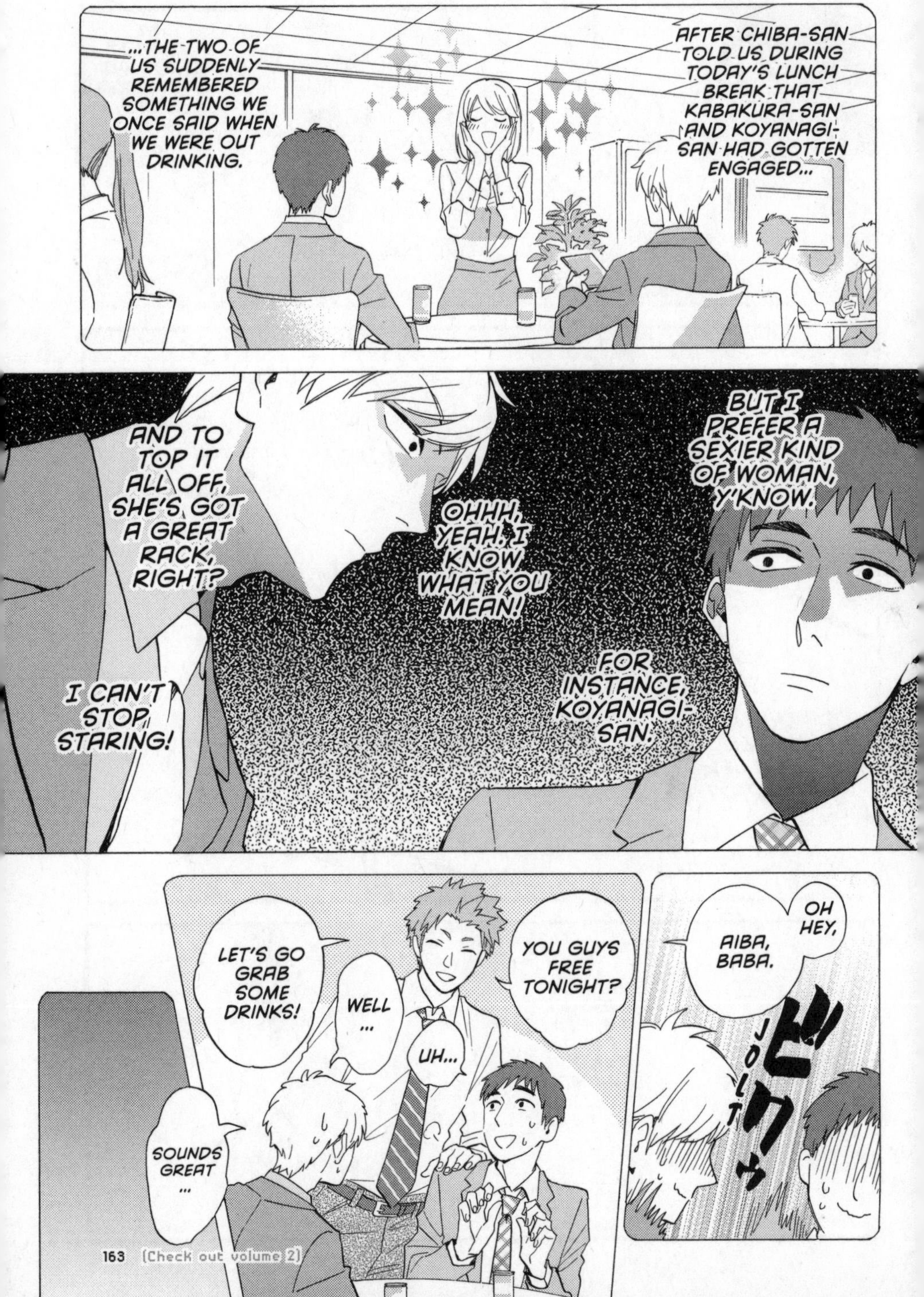
AFTER CHIBA-SAN TOLD US DURING TODAY'S LUNCH BREAK THAT KABAKURA-SAN AND KOYANAGI-SAN HAD GOTTEN ENGAGED...
...THE TWO OF US SUDDENLY REMEMBERED SOMETHING WE ONCE SAID WHEN WE WERE OUT DRINKING.
BUT I PREFER A SEXIER KIND OF WOMAN, Y'KNOW.
FOR INSTANCE, KOYANAGI-SAN.
OHHH, YEAH. I KNOW WHAT YOU MEAN!
AND TO TOP IT ALL OFF, SHE'S GOT A GREAT RACK, RIGHT?
I CAN'T STOP STARING!
OH HEY, AIBA, BABA.
ビクッ
JOLT
YOU GUYS FREE TONIGHT?
LET'S GO GRAB SOME DRINKS!
UH...
WELL ...
SOUNDS GREAT ...
[Check out volume 2]

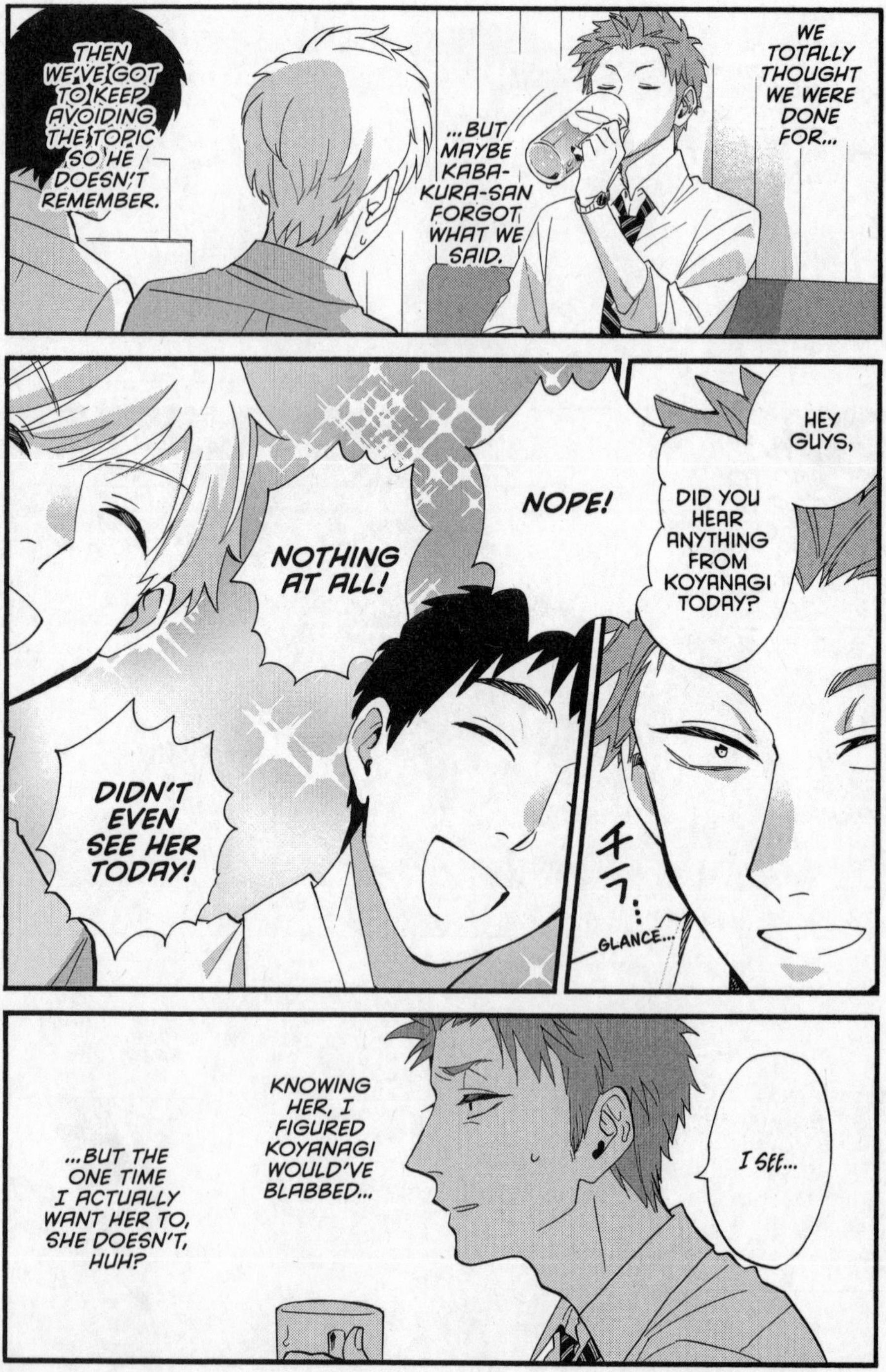
WE TOTALLY THOUGHT WE WERE DONE FOR...
...BUT MAYBE KABA-KURA-SAN FORGOT WHAT WE SAID.
THEN WE'VE GOT TO KEEP AVOIDING THE TOPIC SO HE DOESN'T REMEMBER.
HEY GUYS,
DID YOU HEAR ANYTHING FROM KOYANAGI TODAY?
チラ…
GLANCE...
NOPE!
NOTHING AT ALL!
DIDN'T EVEN SEE HER TODAY!
I SEE...
KNOWING HER, I FIGURED KOYANAGI WOULD'VE BLABBED...
...BUT THE ONE TIME I ACTUALLY WANT HER TO, SHE DOESN'T, HUH?

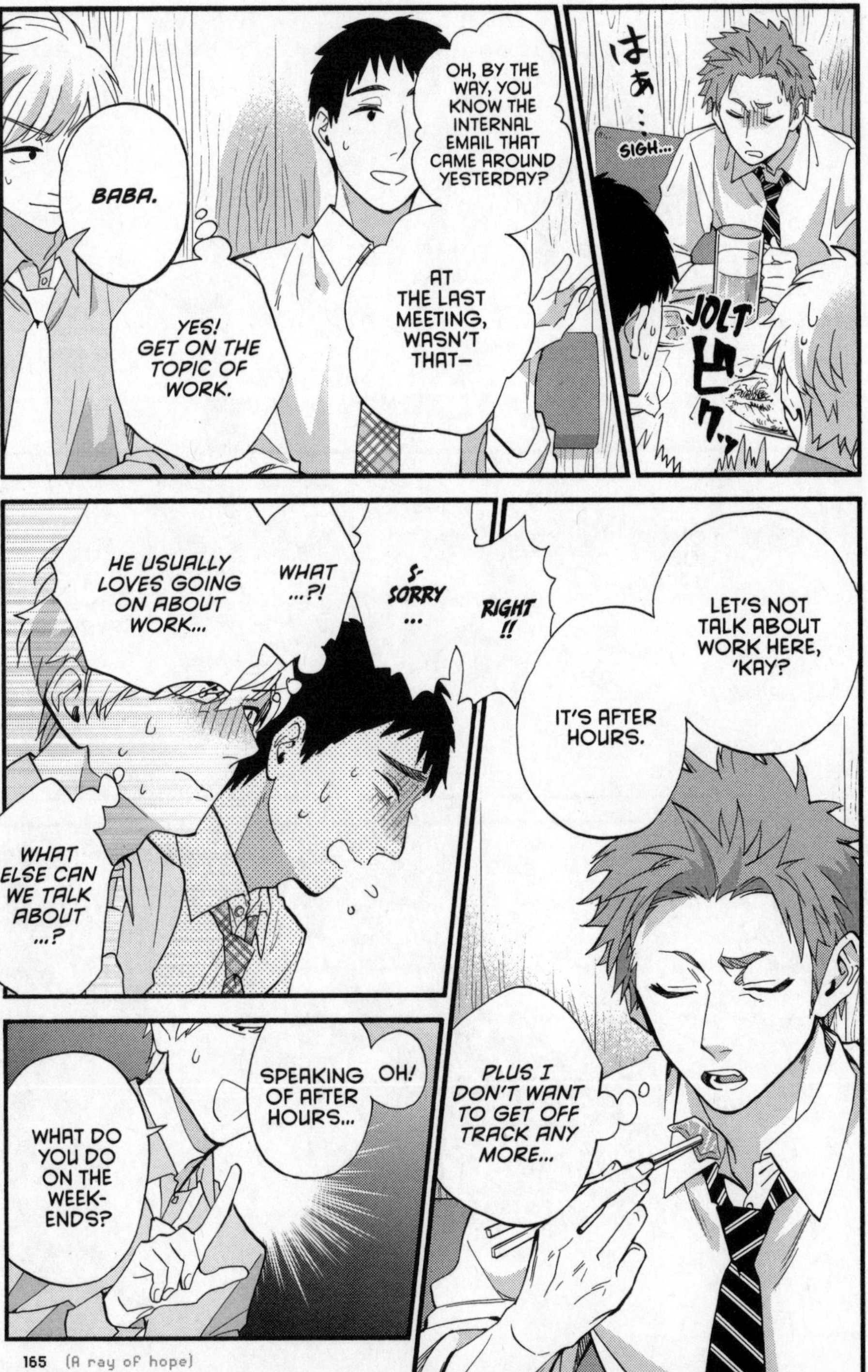
はぁ…
SIGH...
JOLT
ビクッ
OH, BY THE WAY, YOU KNOW THE INTERNAL EMAIL THAT CAME AROUND YESTERDAY?
BABA.
AT THE LAST MEETING, WASN'T THAT—
YES! GET ON THE TOPIC OF WORK.
RIGHT !!
LET'S NOT TALK ABOUT WORK HERE, 'KAY?
IT'S AFTER HOURS.
PLUS I DON'T WANT TO GET OFF TRACK ANY MORE...
S-SORRY ...
WHAT ...?!
HE USUALLY LOVES GOING ON ABOUT WORK...
WHAT ELSE CAN WE TALK ABOUT ...?
OH!
SPEAKING OF AFTER HOURS...
WHAT DO YOU DO ON THE WEEK-ENDS?

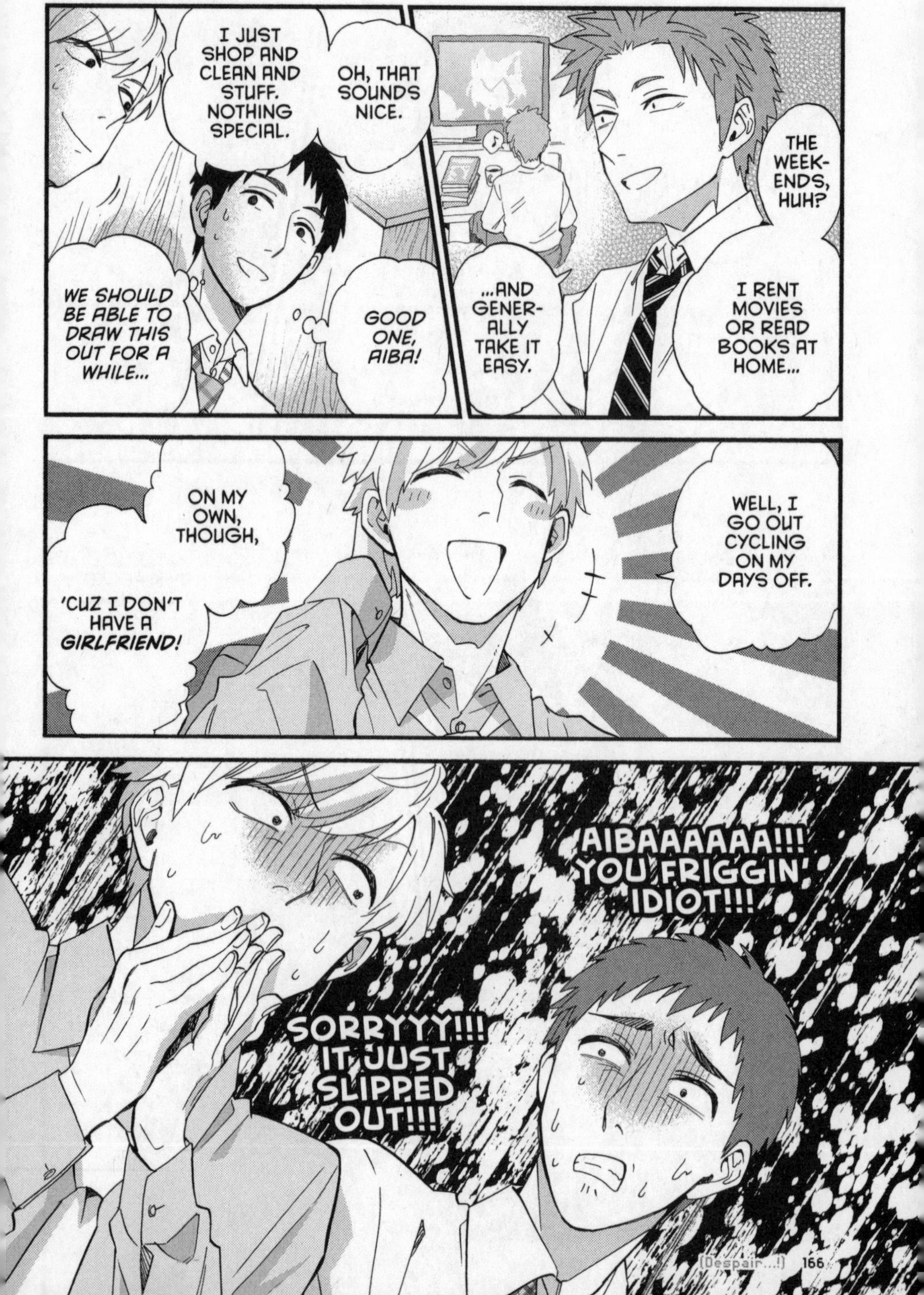
THE WEEK-ENDS, HUH?
I RENT MOVIES OR READ BOOKS AT HOME...
...AND GENER-ALLY TAKE IT EASY.
I JUST SHOP AND CLEAN AND STUFF. NOTHING SPECIAL.
OH, THAT SOUNDS NICE.
GOOD ONE, AIBA!
WE SHOULD BE ABLE TO DRAW THIS OUT FOR A WHILE...
WELL, I GO OUT CYCLING ON MY DAYS OFF.
ON MY OWN, THOUGH,
'CUZ I DON'T HAVE A GIRLFRIEND!
AIBAAAAAAA!!! YOU FRIGGIN' IDIOT!!!
SORRYYY!!! IT JUST SLIPPED OUT!!!
(Despair...!)

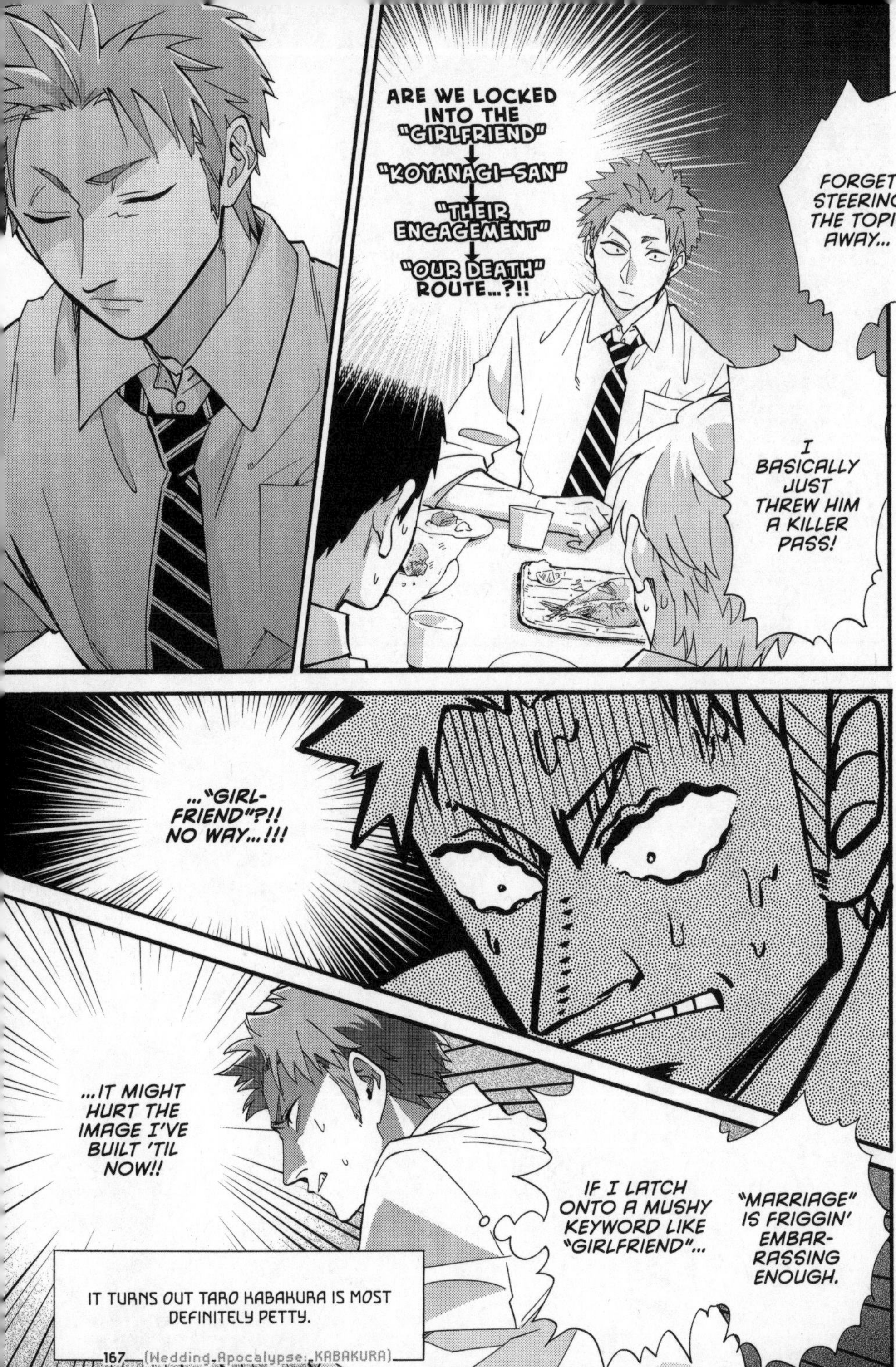
FORGET STEERING THE TOPIC AWAY...
I BASICALLY JUST THREW HIM A KILLER PASS!
ARE WE LOCKED INTO THE "GIRLFRIEND" → "KOYANAGI-SAN" → "THEIR ENGAGEMENT" → "OUR DEATH" ROUTE...?!!
..."GIRL-FRIEND"?!! NO WAY...!!!
"MARRIAGE" IS FRIGGIN' EMBAR-RASSING ENOUGH.
IF I LATCH ONTO A MUSHY KEYWORD LIKE "GIRLFRIEND"...
...IT MIGHT HURT THE IMAGE I'VE BUILT 'TIL NOW!!
IT TURNS OUT TARO KABAKURA IS MOST DEFINITELY PETTY.

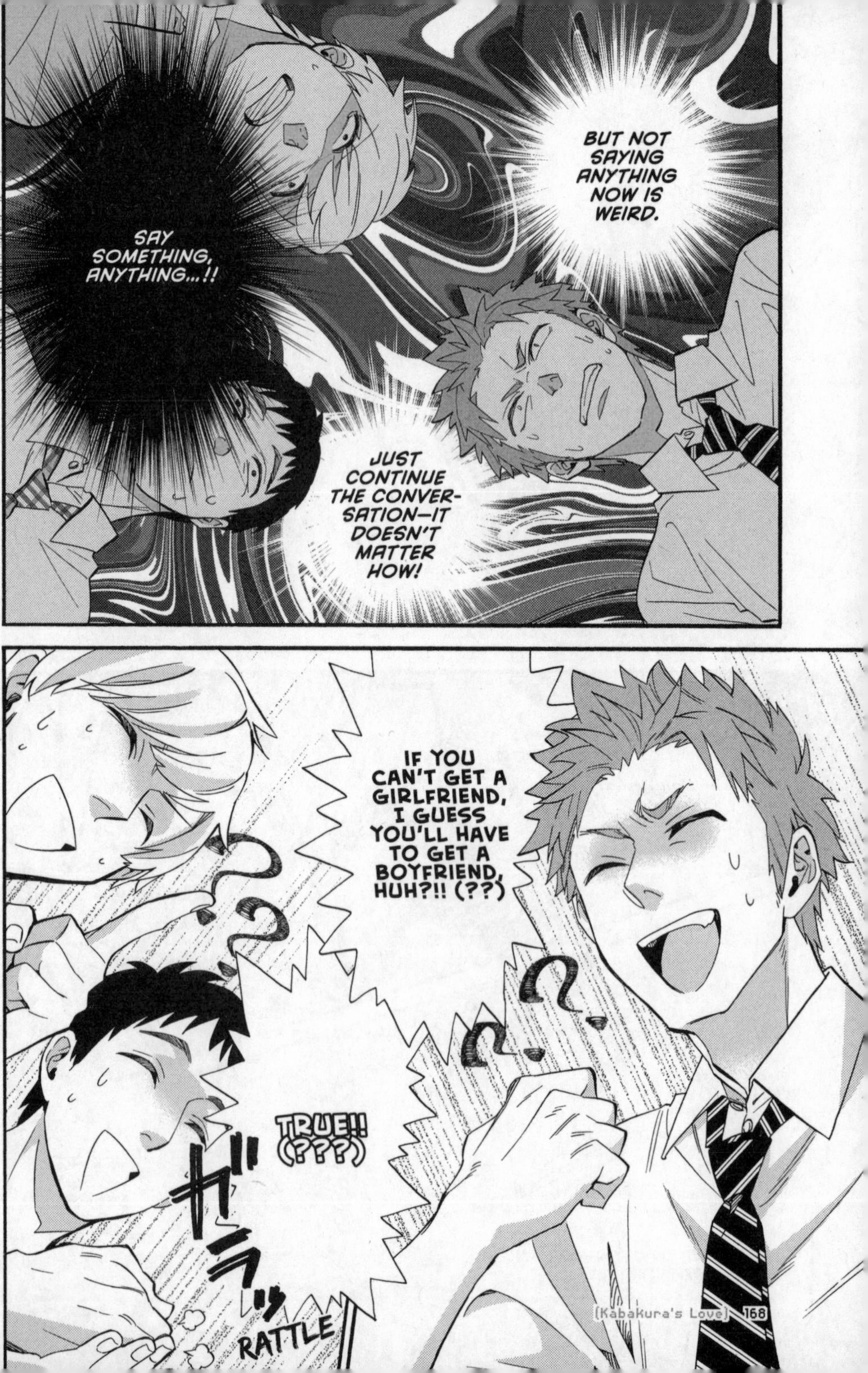
BUT NOT SAYING ANYTHING NOW IS WEIRD.
SAY SOMETHING, ANYTHING...!!
JUST CONTINUE THE CONVER-SATION—IT DOESN'T MATTER HOW!
IF YOU CAN'T GET A GIRLFRIEND, I GUESS YOU'LL HAVE TO GET A BOYFRIEND, HUH?!! (??)
TRUE!! (???)
RATTLE

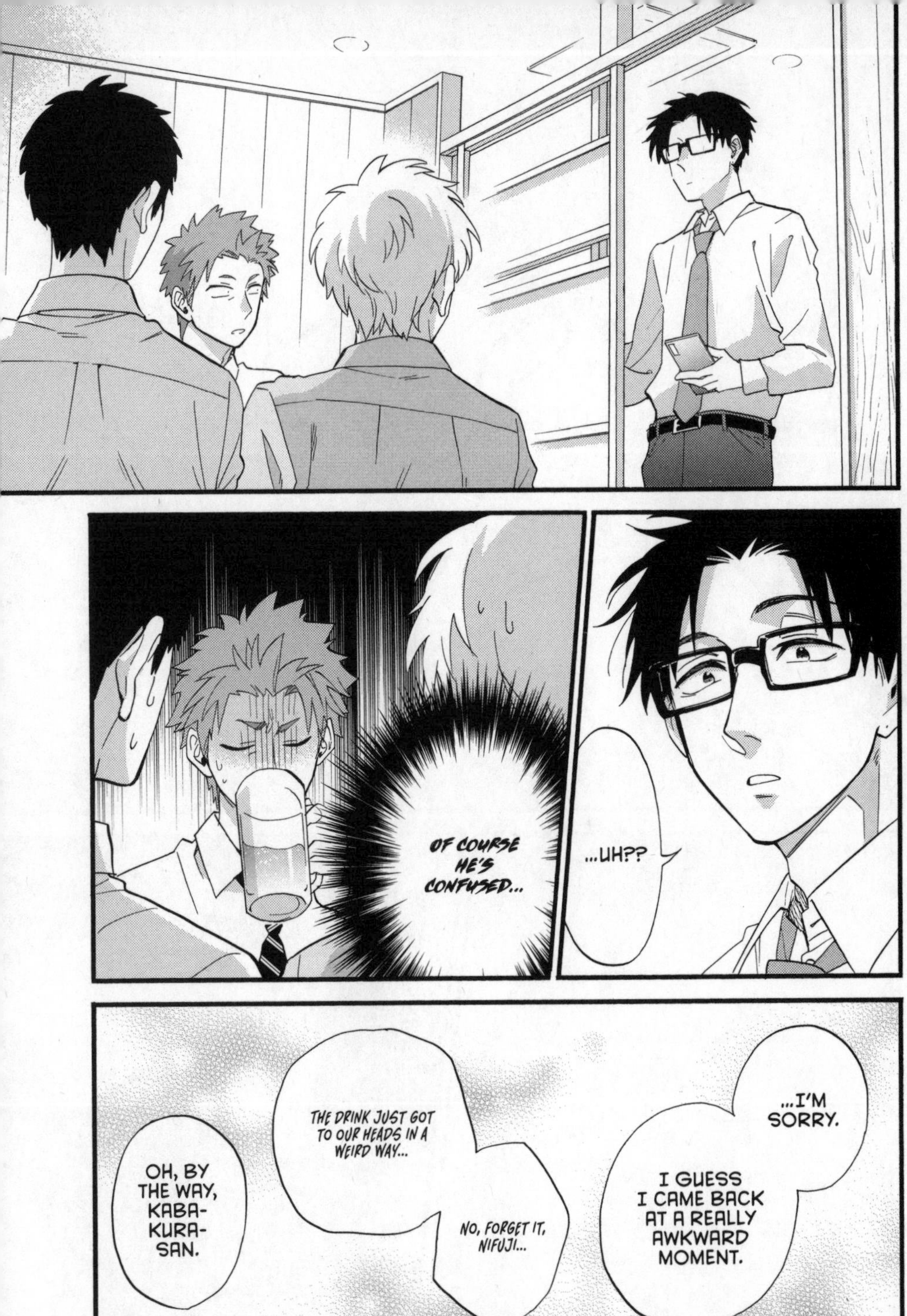
...UH??
OF COURSE HE'S CONFUSED...
...I'M SORRY.
I GUESS I CAME BACK AT A REALLY AWKWARD MOMENT.
NO, FORGET IT, NIFUJI...
THE DRINK JUST GOT TO OUR HEADS IN A WEIRD WAY...
OH, BY THE WAY, KABA-KURA-SAN.

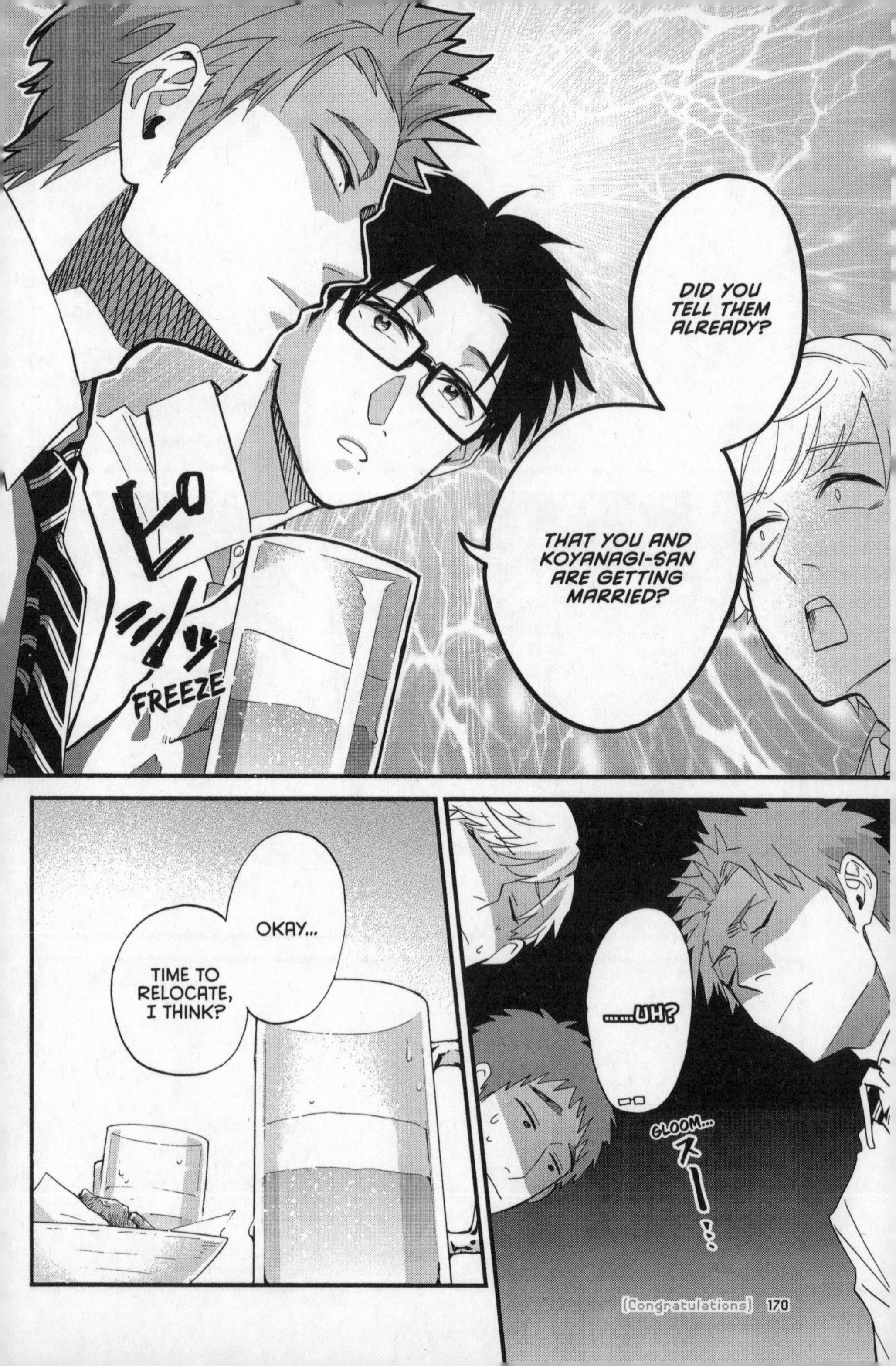
DID YOU TELL THEM ALREADY?
THAT YOU AND KOYANAGI-SAN ARE GETTING MARRIED?
FREEZE
......UH?
GLOOM...
OKAY...
TIME TO RELOCATE, I THINK?

*H*ANAKO KOYANAGI

SPECIES: HUMAN | CLASS: WIZARD

- ♥ **CON** (CONSTITUTION)
- 🌀 **STR** (STRENGTH)
- ⬭ **DEF** (DEFENSE)
- 🍃 **AGI** (AGILITY)
- ✦ **APP** (APPEARANCE)
- ⬡ **MAG** (MAGIC)

KOYANAGI IS AN MMORPG FASHIONISTA. SHE TENDS TO PUT MONEY INTO ALL KINDS OF ACCESSORY ITEMS INSTEAD OF DEVELOPING CHARACTER STATS.
SHE ISN'T USED TO GAMING FOR LONG PERIODS OF TIME TO BEGIN WITH, BUT THE FACT THAT SHE OFTEN PLAYS WITH A BEER IN HAND MEANS SHE ENDS UP DOZING OFF MID-GAME. A LOT.
AMONG THE PARTY MEMBERS, SHE'S PUT IN THE LEAST AMOUNT OF HOURS BUT MAY HAVE PUT IN THE MOST AMOUNT OF MONEY.
HER SPENDING IS WITHIN REASON, APPARENTLY.

*T*ARO KABAKURA

SPECIES: HUMAN | CLASS: SWORDSMAN

- ♥ **CON** (CONSTITUTION)
- 🌀 **STR** (STRENGTH)
- ⬭ **DEF** (DEFENSE)
- 🍃 **AGI** (AGILITY)
- ✦ **APP** (APPEARANCE)
- ⬡ **MAG** (MAGIC)

KABAKURA CHOSE THIS CLASS BECAUSE "WHAT GUY DOESN'T WANT TO BE A SWORDSMAN?" BUT NOW THAT HE HAS TO COVER FOR PARTY MEMBERS WHO HAVE FLIMSY ARMOR (MAINLY KOYANAGI), HE'S BULKED UP ON DEFENSE TO ACT AS THE TEAM TANK, WHICH DEFINITELY ISN'T THE KIND OF SWORDSMAN HE WAS HOPING TO BE...
HE'S PUT IN MORE HOURS THAN KOYANAGI BUT NOT AS MANY AS NARUMI BECAUSE OF WORK AND ANIME.
HE DOESN'T PAY FOR IN-GAME PURCHASES AND REALLY DOESN'T MIND PUTTING IN THE TIME AND EFFORT TO GAIN XP.

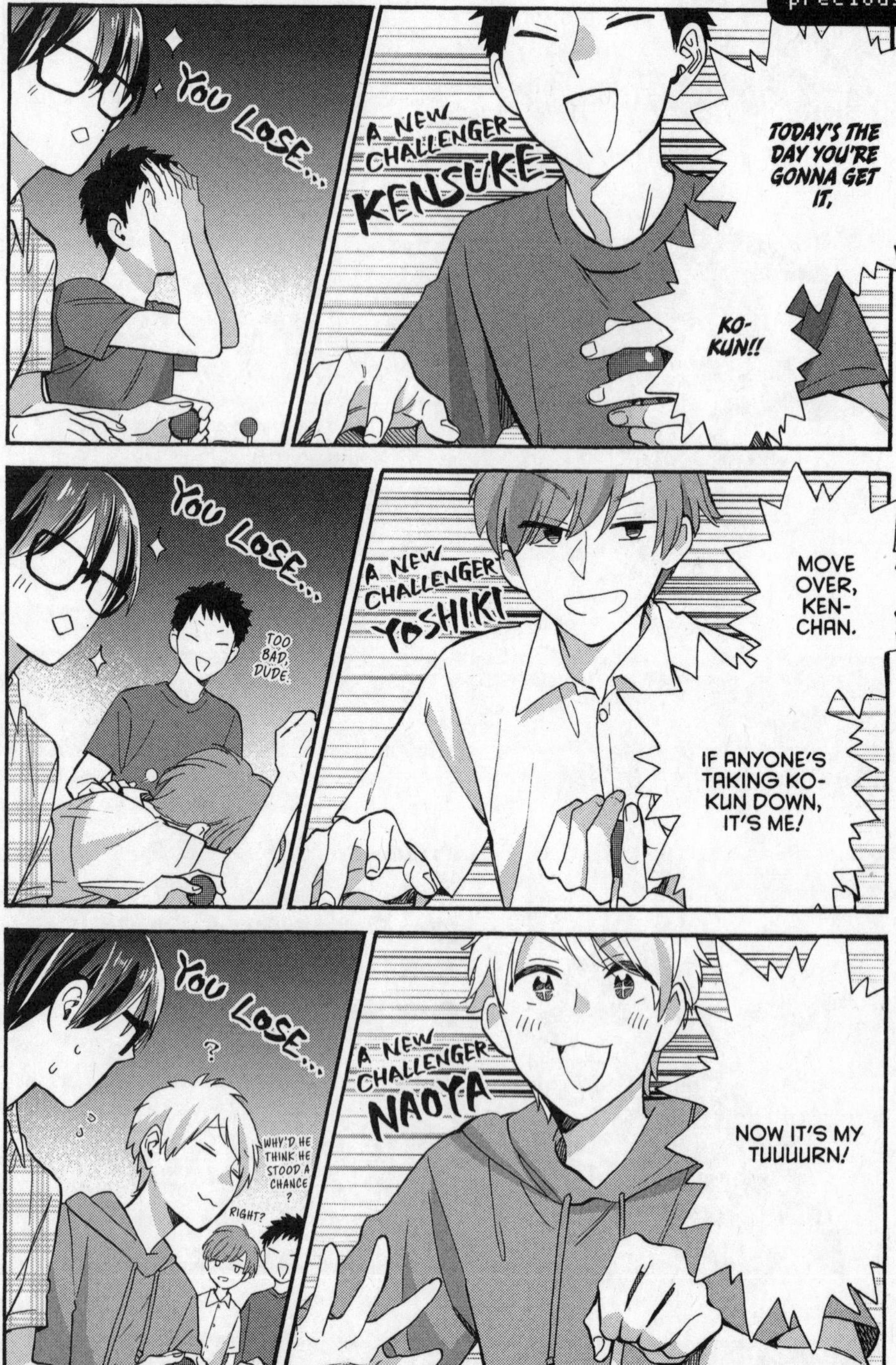
TODAY'S THE DAY YOU'RE GONNA GET IT,
KO-KUN!!
A NEW CHALLENGER KENSUKE
YOU LOSE...
MOVE OVER, KEN-CHAN.
IF ANYONE'S TAKING KO-KUN DOWN, IT'S ME!
A NEW CHALLENGER YOSHIKI
YOU LOSE...
TOO BAD, DUDE.
NOW IT'S MY TUUUURN!
A NEW CHALLENGER NAOYA
YOU LOSE...
?
WHY'D HE THINK HE STOOD A CHANCE?
RIGHT?

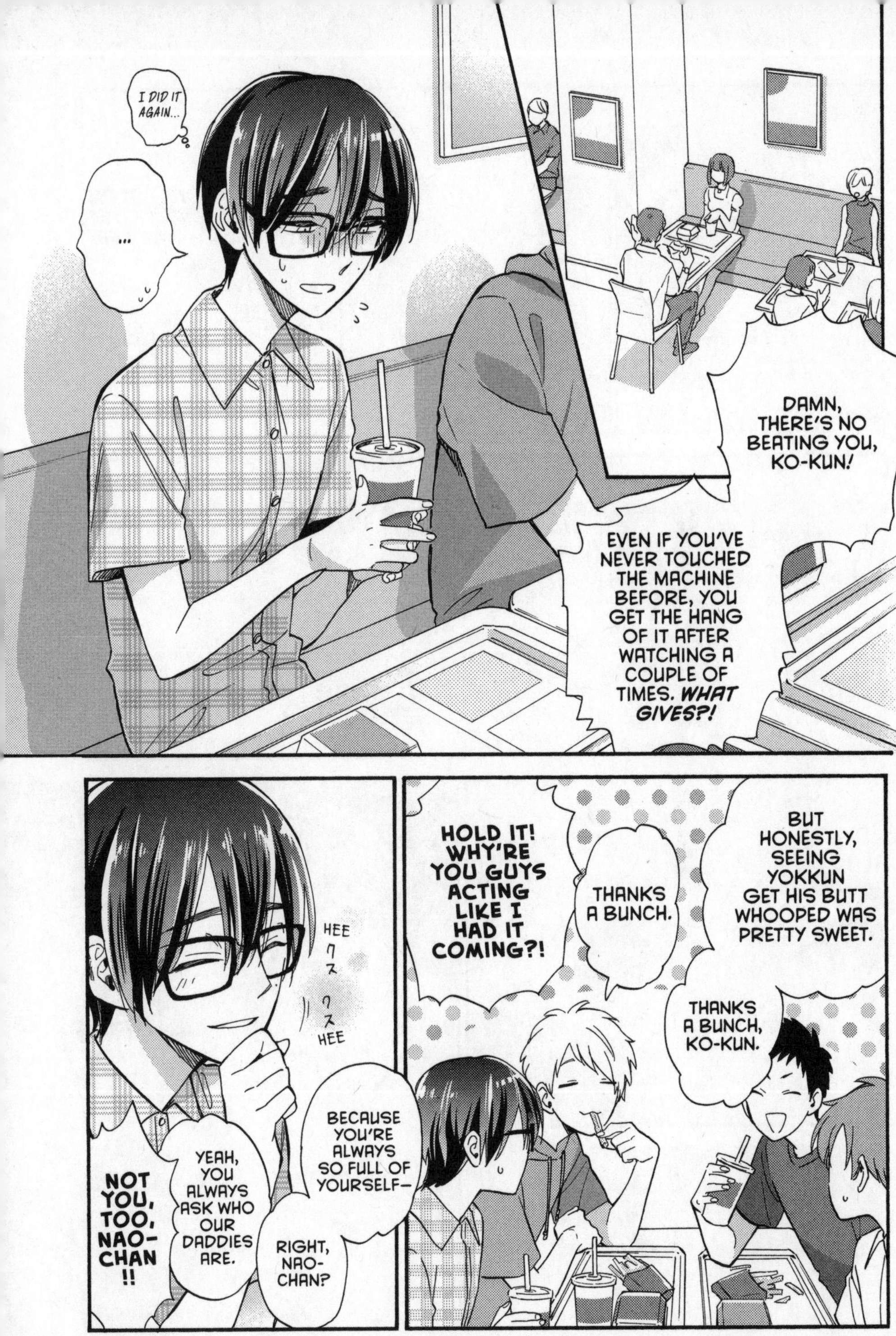
DAMN, THERE'S NO BEATING YOU, KO-KUN!
EVEN IF YOU'VE NEVER TOUCHED THE MACHINE BEFORE, YOU GET THE HANG OF IT AFTER WATCHING A COUPLE OF TIMES. *WHAT GIVES?!*
I DID IT AGAIN...
...
BUT HONESTLY, SEEING YOKKUN GET HIS BUTT WHOOPED WAS PRETTY SWEET.
THANKS A BUNCH.
HOLD IT! WHY'RE YOU GUYS ACTING LIKE I HAD IT COMING?!
THANKS A BUNCH, KO-KUN.
BECAUSE YOU'RE ALWAYS SO FULL OF YOURSELF—
RIGHT, NAO-CHAN?
HEE クス クス HEE
YEAH, YOU ALWAYS ASK WHO OUR DADDIES ARE.
NOT YOU, TOO, NAO-CHAN!!

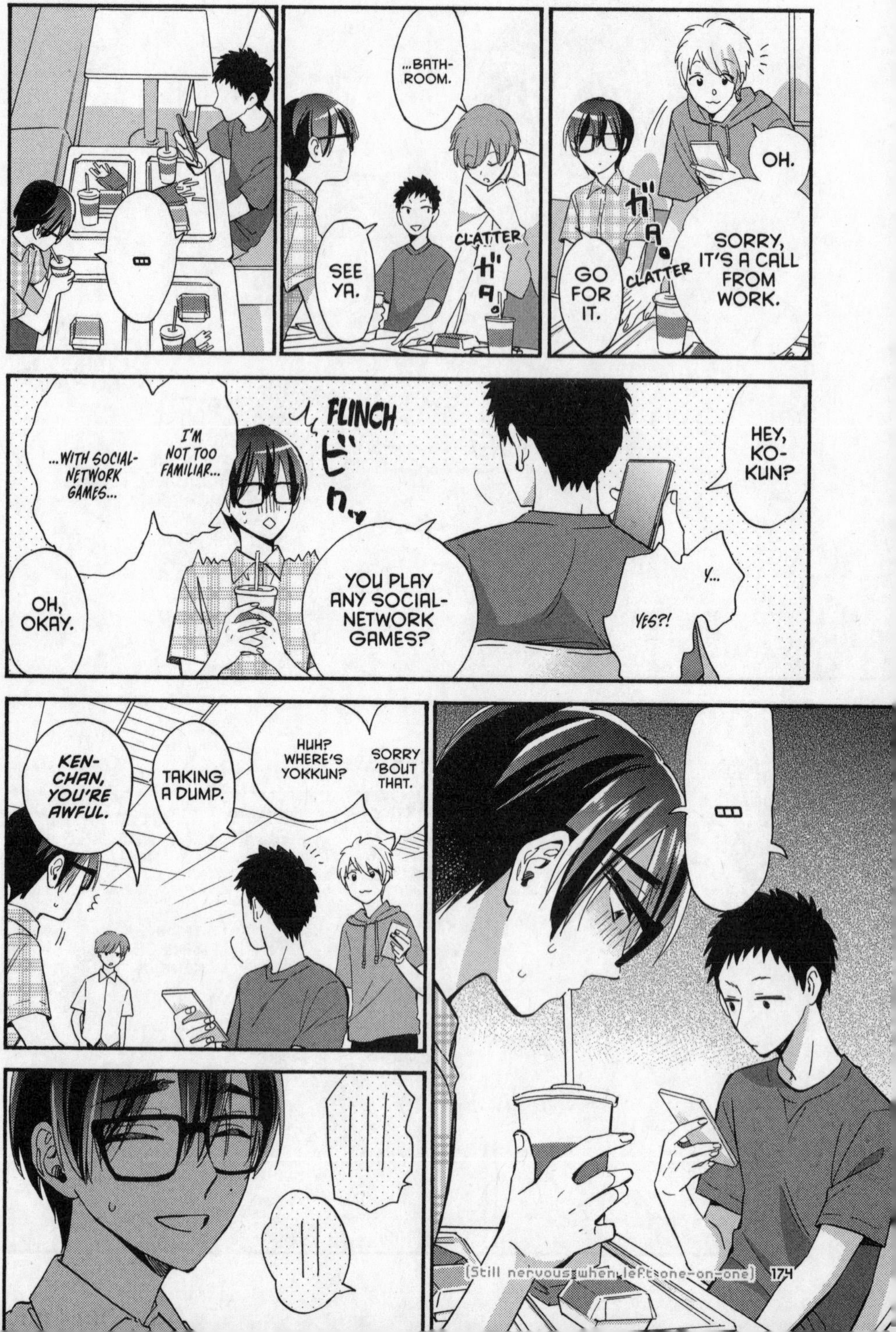
OH.
SORRY, IT'S A CALL FROM WORK.
ガタ
CLATTER
GO FOR IT.
...BATH-ROOM.
ガタ
CLATTER
SEE YA.
...
HEY, KO-KUN?
Y...
YES?!
FLINCH
ビク
YOU PLAY ANY SOCIAL-NETWORK GAMES?
I'M NOT TOO FAMILIAR...
...WITH SOCIAL-NETWORK GAMES...
OH, OKAY.
...
SORRY 'BOUT THAT.
HUH? WHERE'S YOKKUN?
TAKING A DUMP.
KEN-CHAN, YOU'RE AWFUL.

YOU KNOW...
...FOR ALL HE SAYS,
YOKKUN ENJOYS PLAYING AGAINST YOU THE MOST.
UH...
I'M NOT SURE ABOUT THAT...
NO, REALLY. IT'S TOTALLY DIFFERENT FROM WHEN HE PLAYS ME OR KEN-CHAN.

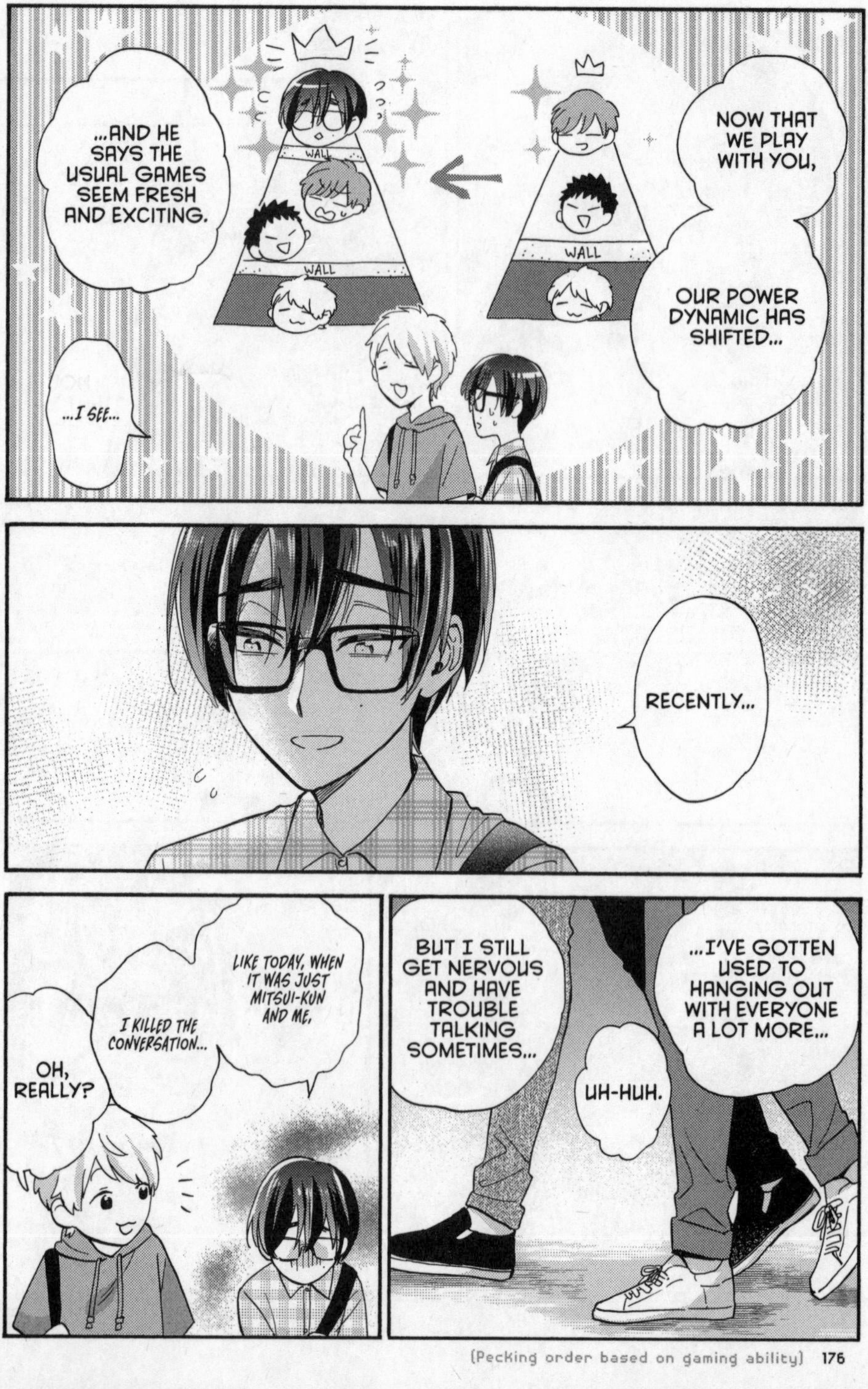
NOW THAT WE PLAY WITH YOU,
WALL
OUR POWER DYNAMIC HAS SHIFTED...
WALL
...AND HE SAYS THE USUAL GAMES SEEM FRESH AND EXCITING.
...I SEE...
RECENTLY...
...I'VE GOTTEN USED TO HANGING OUT WITH EVERYONE A LOT MORE...
UH-HUH.
BUT I STILL GET NERVOUS AND HAVE TROUBLE TALKING SOMETIMES...
LIKE TODAY, WHEN IT WAS JUST MITSUI-KUN AND ME,
I KILLED THE CONVERSATION...
OH, REALLY?

(Pecking order based on gaming ability)

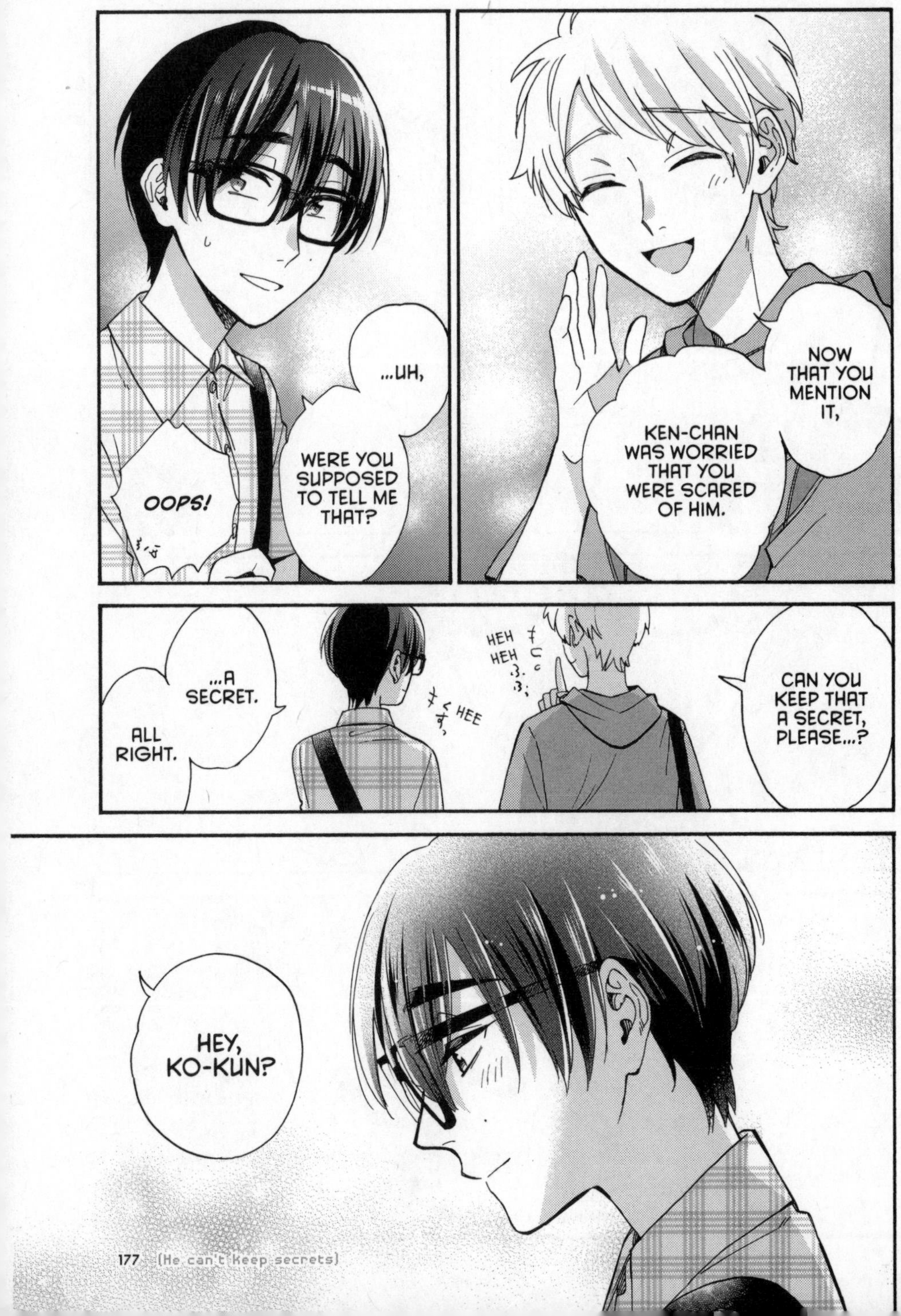
NOW THAT YOU MENTION IT,
KEN-CHAN WAS WORRIED THAT YOU WERE SCARED OF HIM.
...UH,
WERE YOU SUPPOSED TO TELL ME THAT?
OOPS!
CAN YOU KEEP THAT A SECRET, PLEASE...?
HEH HEH
HEE
...A SECRET.
ALL RIGHT.
HEY, KO-KUN?

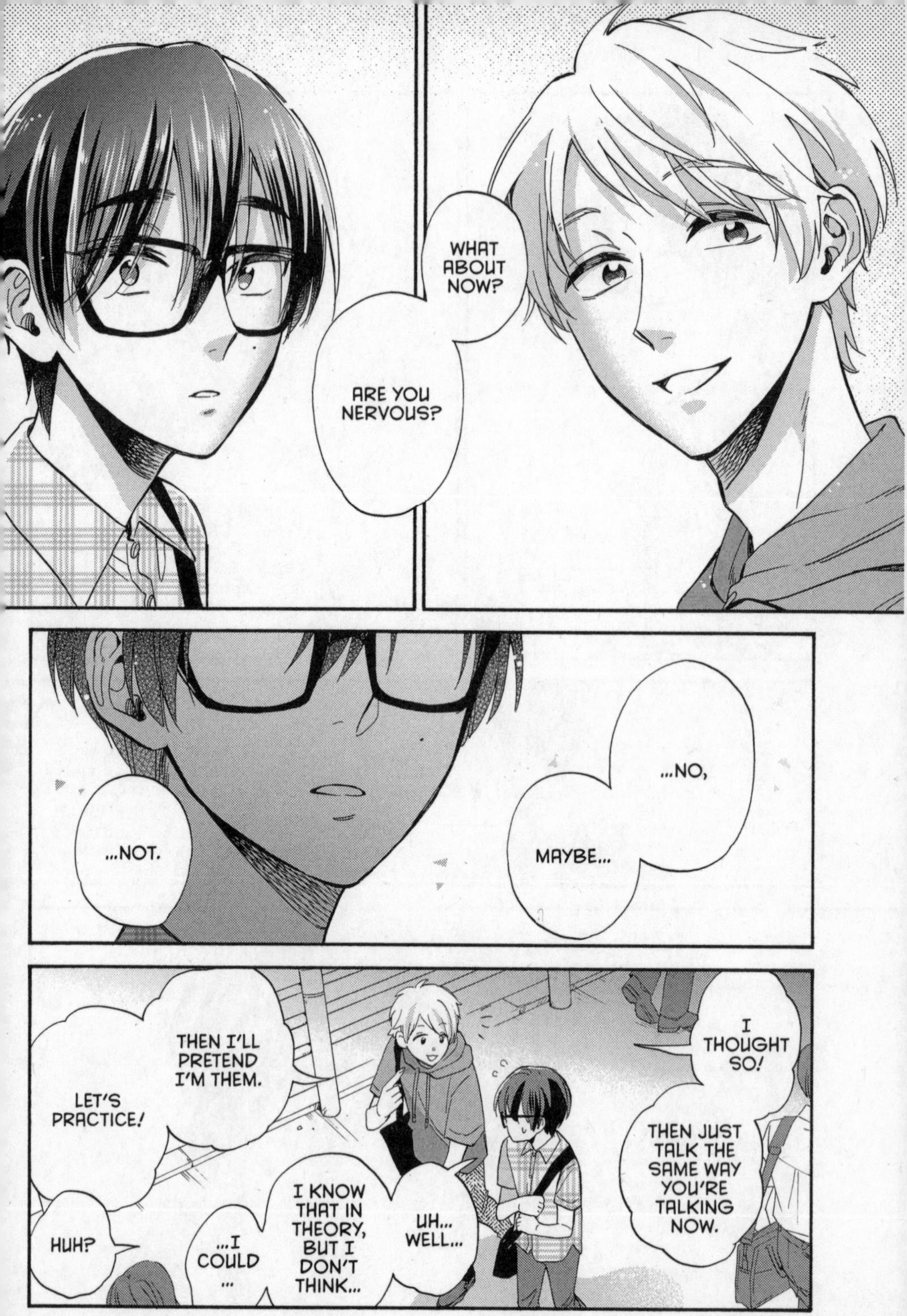
WHAT ABOUT NOW?
ARE YOU NERVOUS?
...NO,
MAYBE...
...NOT.
I THOUGHT SO!
THEN JUST TALK THE SAME WAY YOU'RE TALKING NOW.
UH... WELL...
I KNOW THAT IN THEORY, BUT I DON'T THINK...
...I COULD ...
THEN I'LL PRETEND I'M THEM.
LET'S PRACTICE!
HUH?

(It's still one-on-one, but somehow...)

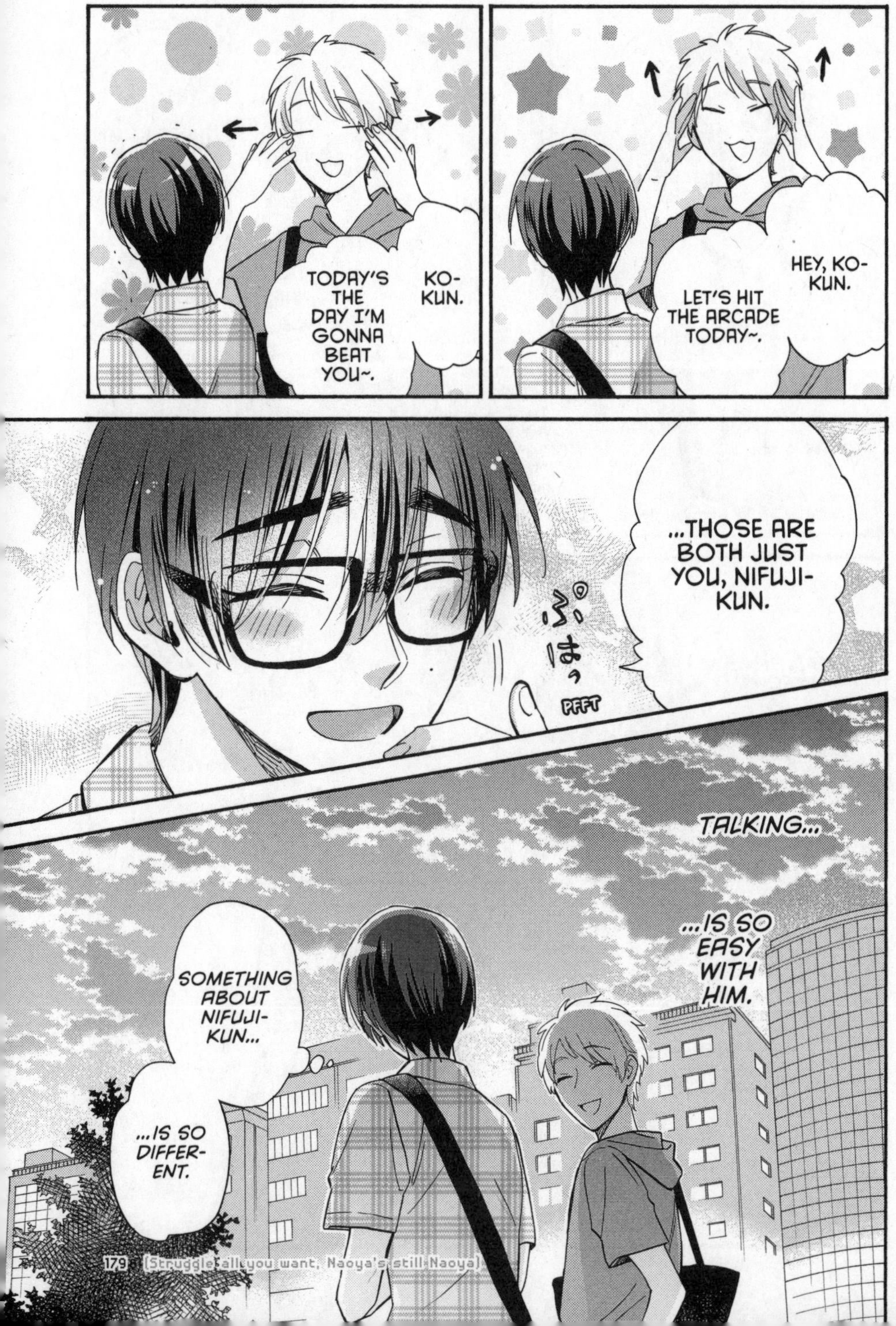
HEY, KO-KUN.
LET'S HIT THE ARCADE TODAY~.
KO-KUN.
TODAY'S THE DAY I'M GONNA BEAT YOU~.
...THOSE ARE BOTH JUST YOU, NIFUJI-KUN.
ぷはっ
PFFT
TALKING...
...IS SO EASY WITH HIM.
SOMETHING ABOUT NIFUJI-KUN...
...IS SO DIFFERENT.

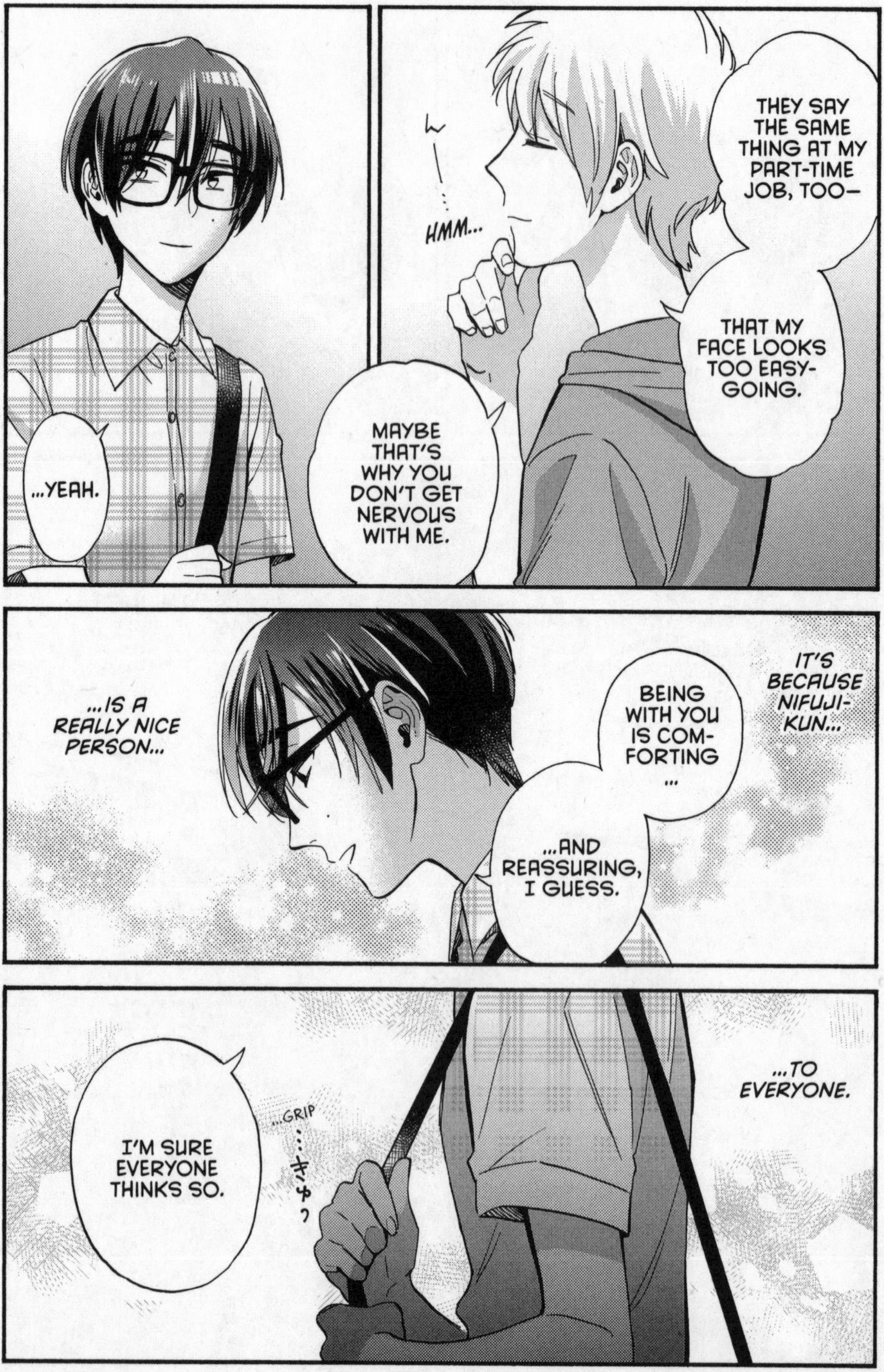
THEY SAY THE SAME THING AT MY PART-TIME JOB, TOO—
THAT MY FACE LOOKS TOO EASY-GOING.
ん—…
HMM...
MAYBE THAT'S WHY YOU DON'T GET NERVOUS WITH ME.
...YEAH.
IT'S BECAUSE NIFUJI-KUN...
BEING WITH YOU IS COMFORTING...
...AND REASSURING, I GUESS.
...IS A REALLY NICE PERSON...
...TO EVERYONE.
...GRIP
…きゅっ
I'M SURE EVERYONE THINKS SO.

(Not just to me...)

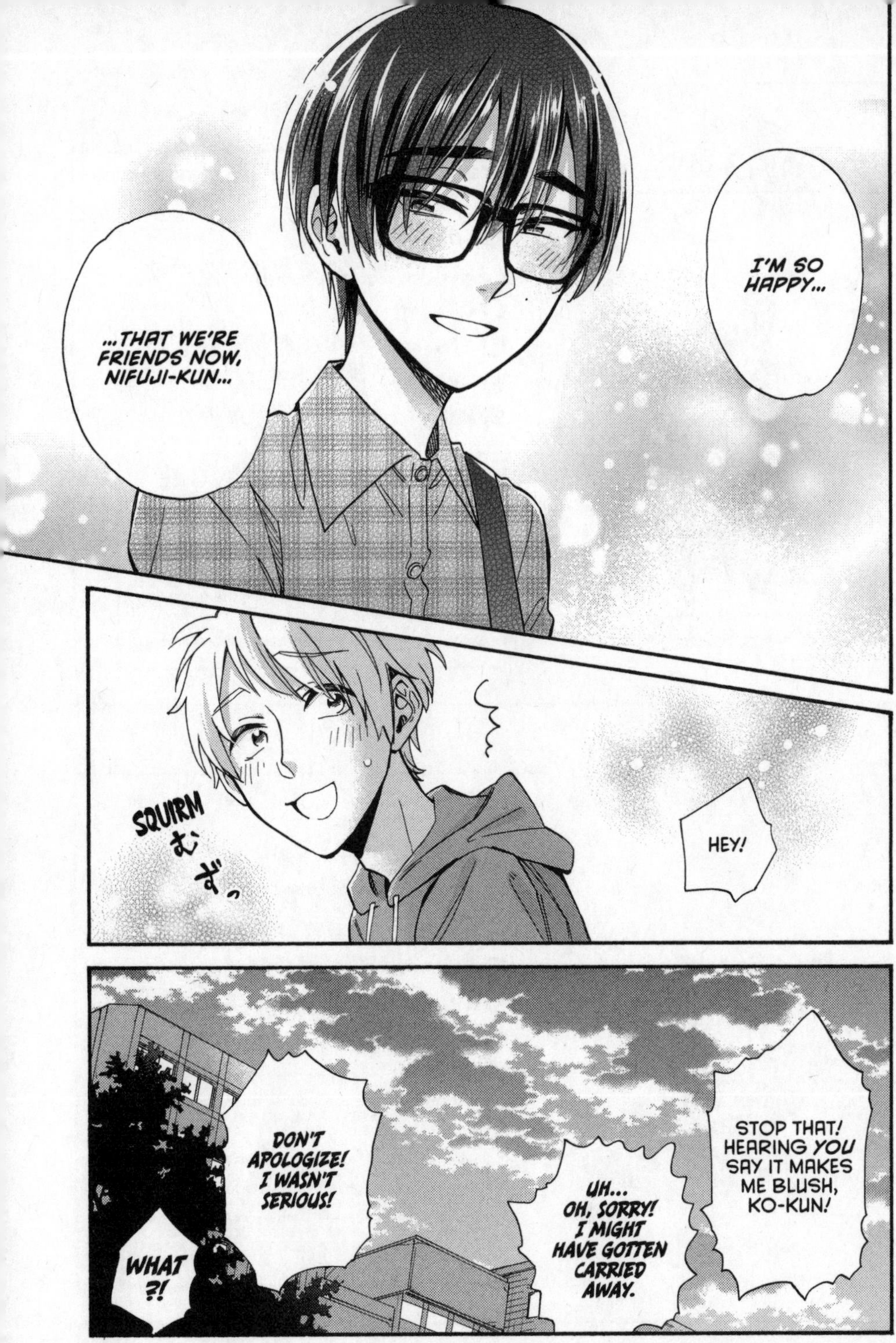
I'M SO HAPPY...
...THAT WE'RE FRIENDS NOW, NIFUJI-KUN...
HEY!
SQUIRM
むずっ
STOP THAT! HEARING *YOU* SAY IT MAKES ME BLUSH, KO-KUN!
UH... OH, SORRY! I MIGHT HAVE GOTTEN CARRIED AWAY.
DON'T APOLOGIZE! I WASN'T SERIOUS!
WHAT?!

KO SAKURAGI

SPECIES: HUMANOID CLASS: GUNNER

- ♡ **CON** (CONSTITUTION) ▰▰▰
- ☻ **STR** (STRENGTH) ▰▰▰▰▰▰▰▰
- ⬭ **DEF** (DEFENSE) ▰▰▰
- ◖ **AGI** (AGILITY) ▰▰▰▰▰▰
- ✛ **APP** (APPEARANCE) ▰▰▰▰▰
- ✴ **MAG** (MAGIC) ▰▰▰▰▰▰

THE HUMANOID SPECIES GENERALLY HAS THE STRONGEST DEFENSE, BUT SINCE KO PLAYS SOLO, SHE PRIORITIZED HER ATTACK STATS OVER DEFENSE, MAKING HER MORE VULNERABLE THAN SHE LOOKS.
SHE MAY HAVE PLAYED MORE HOURS THAN ANY OF THE OTHER MEMBERS, BUT MOST OF THAT TIME WAS SPENT MINDLESSLY GOING THROUGH THE MOTIONS, ALMOST OUT OF HABIT OR A SENSE OF DUTY. RECENTLY, THOUGH, SHE'S HAD TO PUT SERIOUS THOUGHT INTO THINGS THAT AREN'T USUALLY GAME-RELATED, LIKE HOW TO GET THROUGH A QUEST WITHOUT LETTING NAOYA DIE OR WHICH AREA WILL GIVE NAOYA THE MOST XP. THIS HAS BEEN FUN, APPARENTLY.

NAOYA NIFUJI

SPECIES: THERIAN CLASS: FIGHTER

- ♡ **CON** (CONSTITUTION) ▰▰▰▰▰▰▰▰▰▰
- ☻ **STR** (STRENGTH) ▰▰▰▰
- ⬭ **DEF** (DEFENSE) ▰▰▰▰▰
- ◖ **AGI** (AGILITY) ▰▰▰▰▰▰
- ✛ **APP** (APPEARANCE) ▰▰▰▰▰
- ✴ **MAG** (MAGIC) ▰

BASED ON KO'S ADVICE, HE STACKED HIS CONSTITUTION AND DEFENSE STATS TO KEEP HIMSELF FROM DYING. HE'S BASICALLY USELESS, BUT HE CAN AT LEAST DISPERSE ENEMY TARGETING AND ACT AS A LIVING SHIELD JUST BY HANGING AROUND, ACCORDING TO HIS MERCILESS OLDER BROTHER.
HE FAVORS A CLOSE-COMBAT FIGHTING STYLE, WHICH REQUIRES INTUITIVE CONTROLS THAT EVEN A GAMING KLUTZ LIKE NAOYA CAN KIND OF GET THE HANG OF. HE REALLY LIKES THE STRAIGHTFORWARD COMBAT ASPECT, BUT IT UNFORTUNATELY PUSHES HIS LIKELIHOOD OF DYING WAY UP, COMPLETELY NEGATING THE STAT ADJUSTMENTS KO DID FOR HIM.

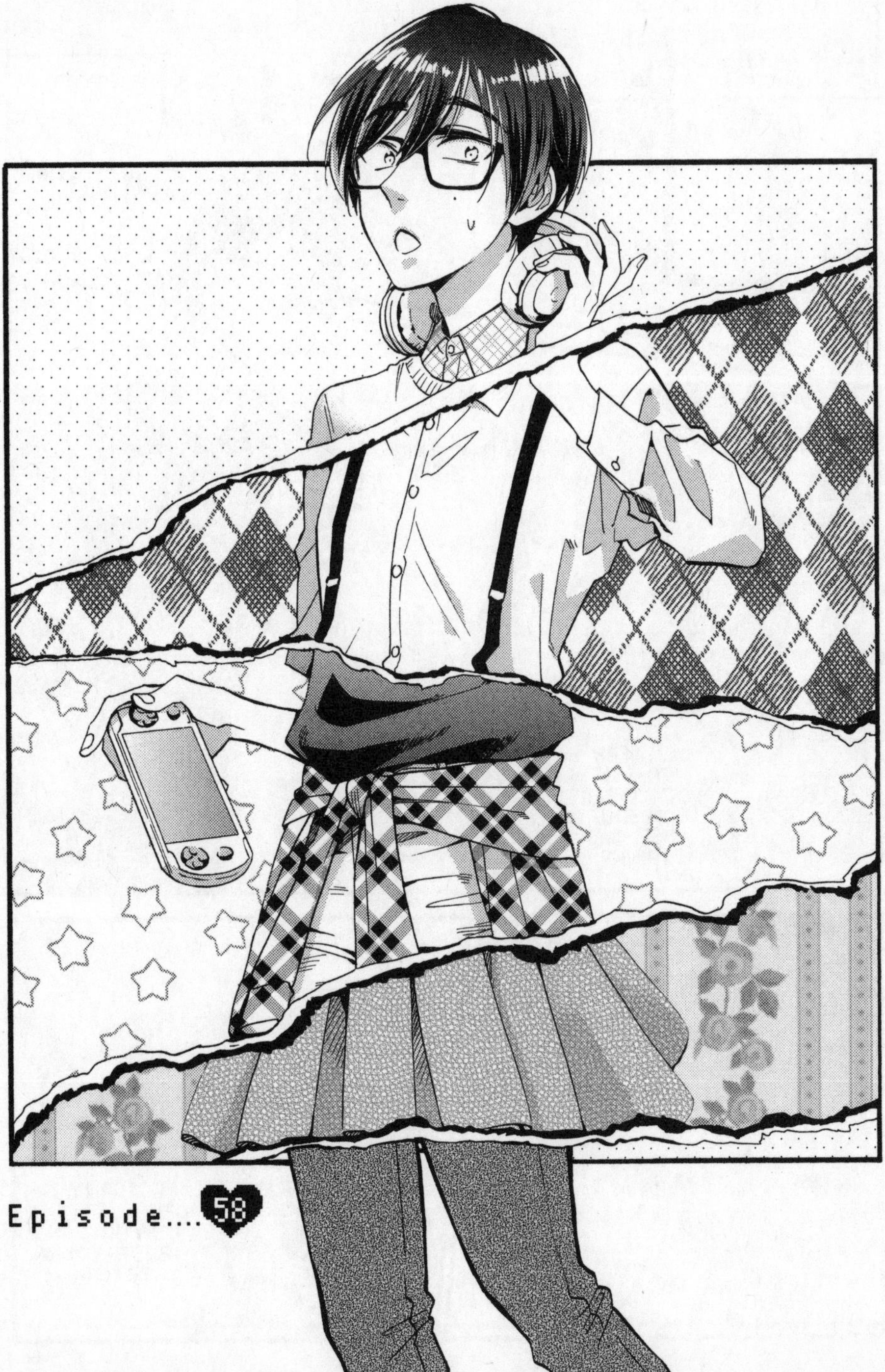

Episode.... 58

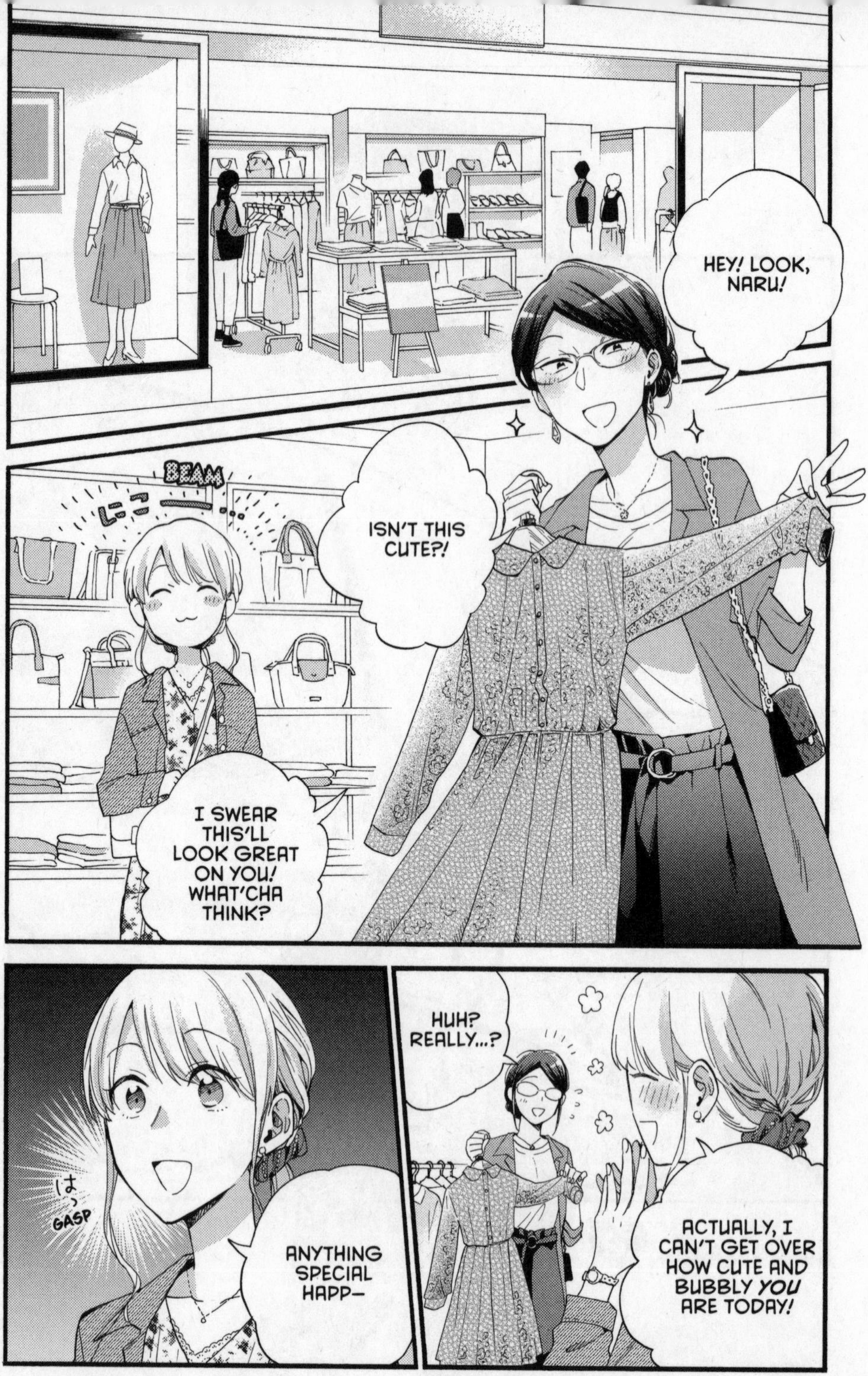
HEY! LOOK, NARU!
ISN'T THIS CUTE?!
I SWEAR THIS'LL LOOK GREAT ON YOU! WHAT'CHA THINK?
にこーー
BEAM
HUH? REALLY...?
ACTUALLY, I CAN'T GET OVER HOW CUTE AND BUBBLY *YOU* ARE TODAY!
ANYTHING SPECIAL HAPP—
はっ
GASP

TEARS
ぶわっ
OF COURSE THERE WAS!!
SENPAI PROPOSED...!
URK!
YOU'RE GETTING MARRIED...!
UHRK!!
CALM DOWN.
YOU'VE DONE THIS EIGHT TIMES ALREADY.
CONGRATULATIOOONS!
YEAH, YEAH. THANKS.
I'M SHO HABBYYY...!
BUT DON'T GET ME WRONG.
IT'S NOT LIKE I'M GETTING CARRIED AWAY OVER WHAT HAPPENED.
IF ANYTHING, THINKING ABOUT ALL THE PREPARATIONS WE'LL HAVE TO DO FOR THE WEDDING...
...IS STRESSING ME OUT A BIT...
TRUE...
YOU WON'T HAVE ANY FREE TIME FOR A WHILE, HUH?

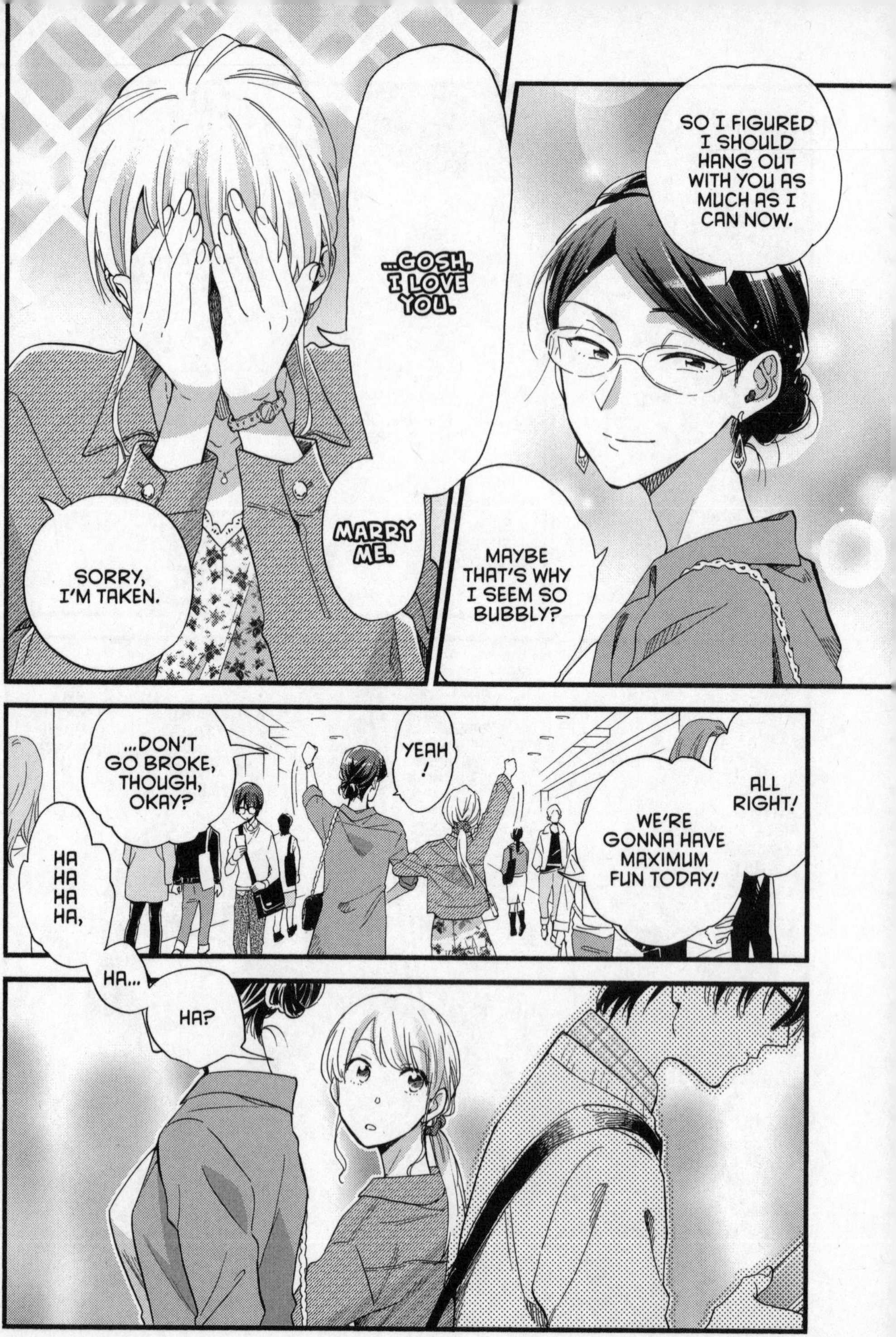
SO I FIGURED I SHOULD HANG OUT WITH YOU AS MUCH AS I CAN NOW.
MAYBE THAT'S WHY I SEEM SO BUBBLY?
...GOSH, I LOVE YOU.
MARRY ME.
SORRY, I'M TAKEN.
ALL RIGHT!
WE'RE GONNA HAVE MAXIMUM FUN TODAY!
YEAH!
...DON'T GO BROKE, THOUGH, OKAY?
HA HA HA HA,
HA...
HA?

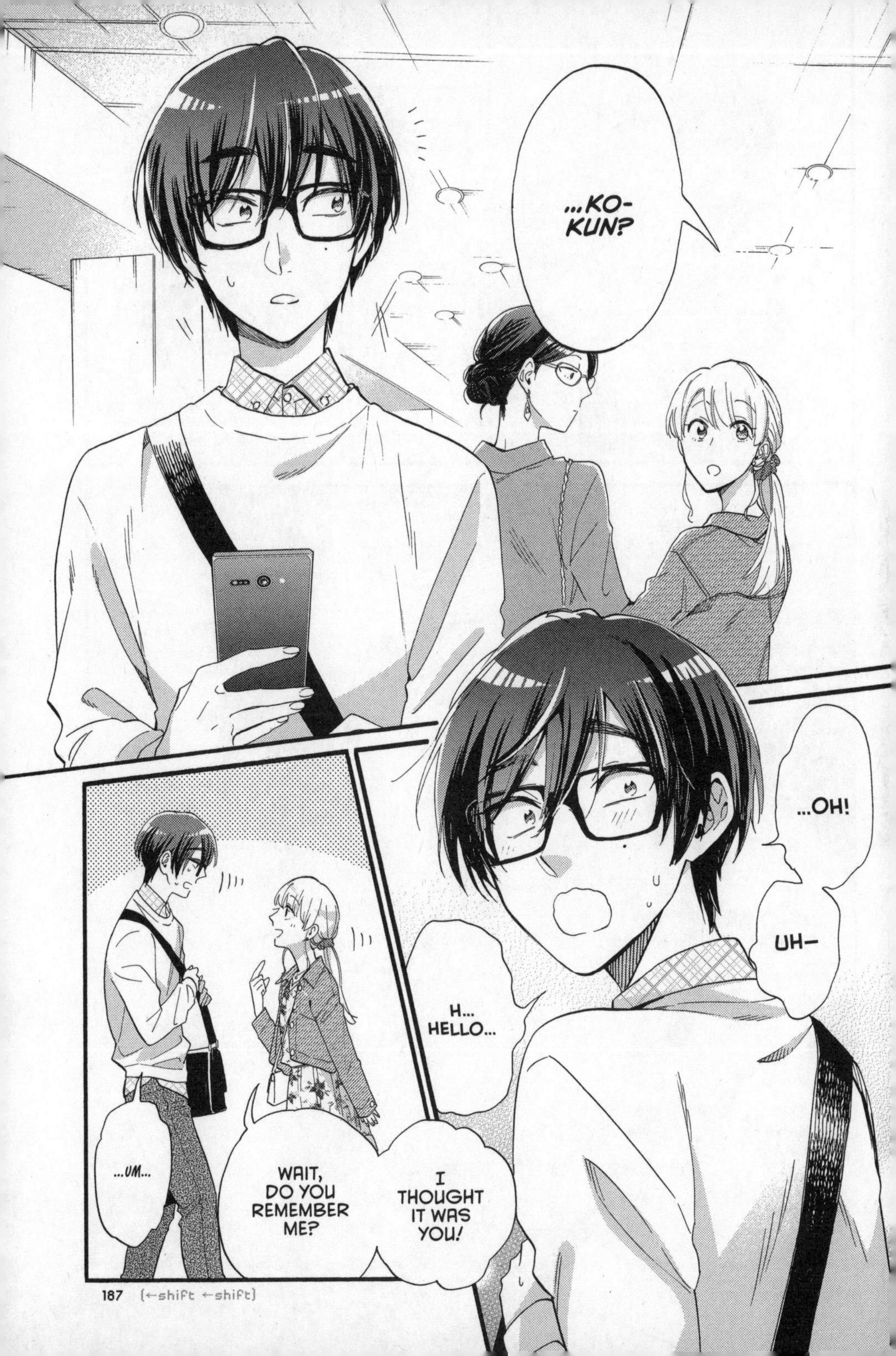
...KO-KUN?
...OH!
UH—
H... HELLO...
I THOUGHT IT WAS YOU!
WAIT, DO YOU REMEMBER ME?
...UM...

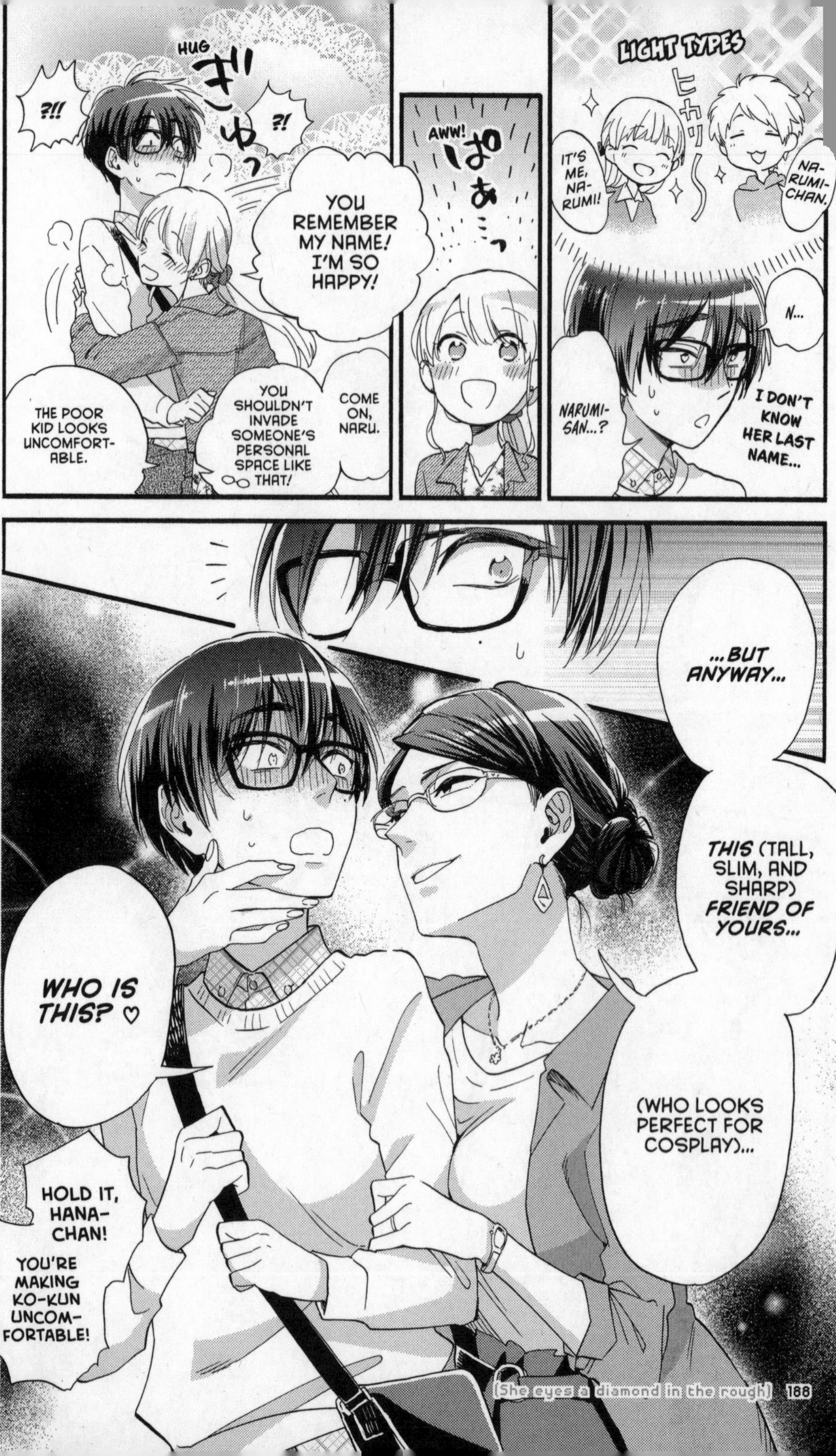

LIGHT TYPES
NARUMI-CHAN.
IT'S ME, NARUMI!
N...
I DON'T KNOW HER LAST NAME...
NARUMI-SAN...?
AWW!
YOU REMEMBER MY NAME! I'M SO HAPPY!
HUG
?!
?!!
COME ON, NARU.
YOU SHOULDN'T INVADE SOMEONE'S PERSONAL SPACE LIKE THAT!
THE POOR KID LOOKS UNCOMFORTABLE.
...BUT ANYWAY...
THIS (TALL, SLIM, AND SHARP) FRIEND OF YOURS...
(WHO LOOKS PERFECT FOR COSPLAY)...
WHO IS THIS? ♡
HOLD IT, HANA-CHAN!
YOU'RE MAKING KO-KUN UNCOMFORTABLE!

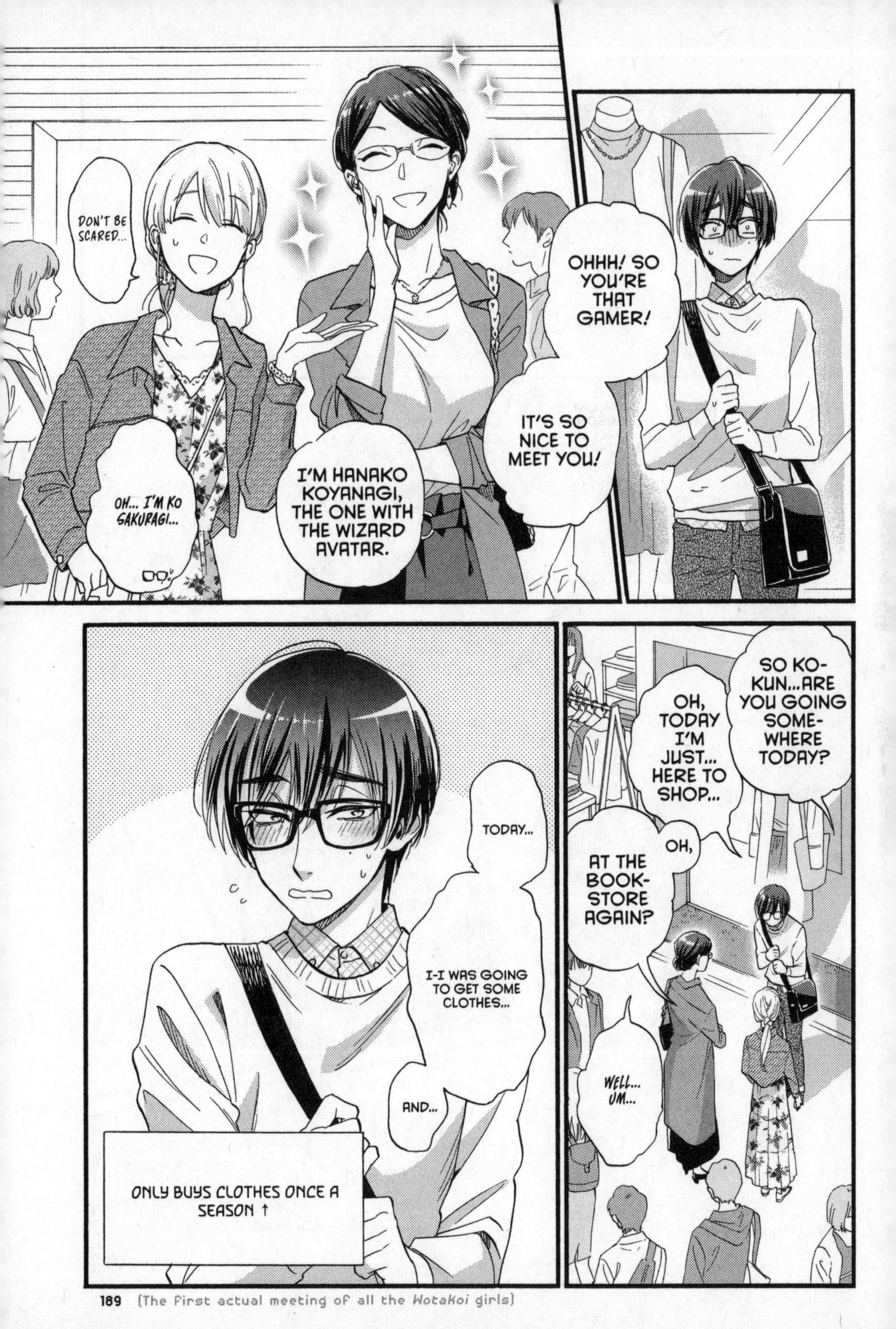
OHHH! SO YOU'RE THAT GAMER!
IT'S SO NICE TO MEET YOU!
I'M HANAKO KOYANAGI, THE ONE WITH THE WIZARD AVATAR.
DON'T BE SCARED...
OH... I'M KO SAKURAGI...
SO KO-KUN...ARE YOU GOING SOME-WHERE TODAY?
OH, TODAY I'M JUST... HERE TO SHOP...
OH,
AT THE BOOK-STORE AGAIN?
WELL... UM...
TODAY...
I-I WAS GOING TO GET SOME CLOTHES...
AND...
ONLY BUYS CLOTHES ONCE A SEASON ↑

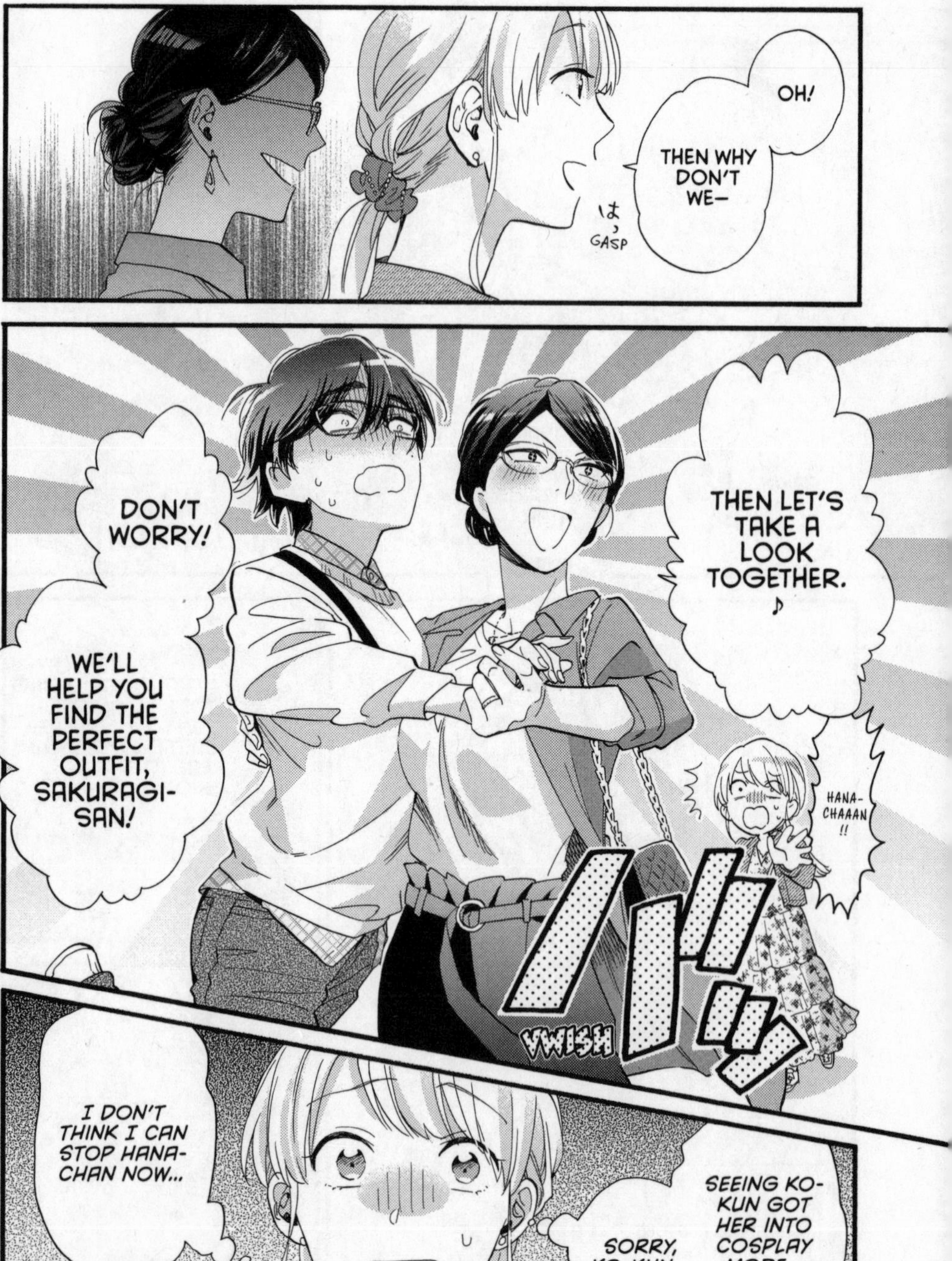

OH!
THEN WHY DON'T WE—
は、 GASP
THEN LET'S TAKE A LOOK TOGETHER. ♪
HANA-CHAAAN !!
DON'T WORRY!
WE'LL HELP YOU FIND THE PERFECT OUTFIT, SAKURAGI-SAN!
VWISH
SEEING KO-KUN GOT HER INTO COSPLAY MODE...
SORRY, KO-KUN...
I DON'T THINK I CAN STOP HANA-CHAN NOW...

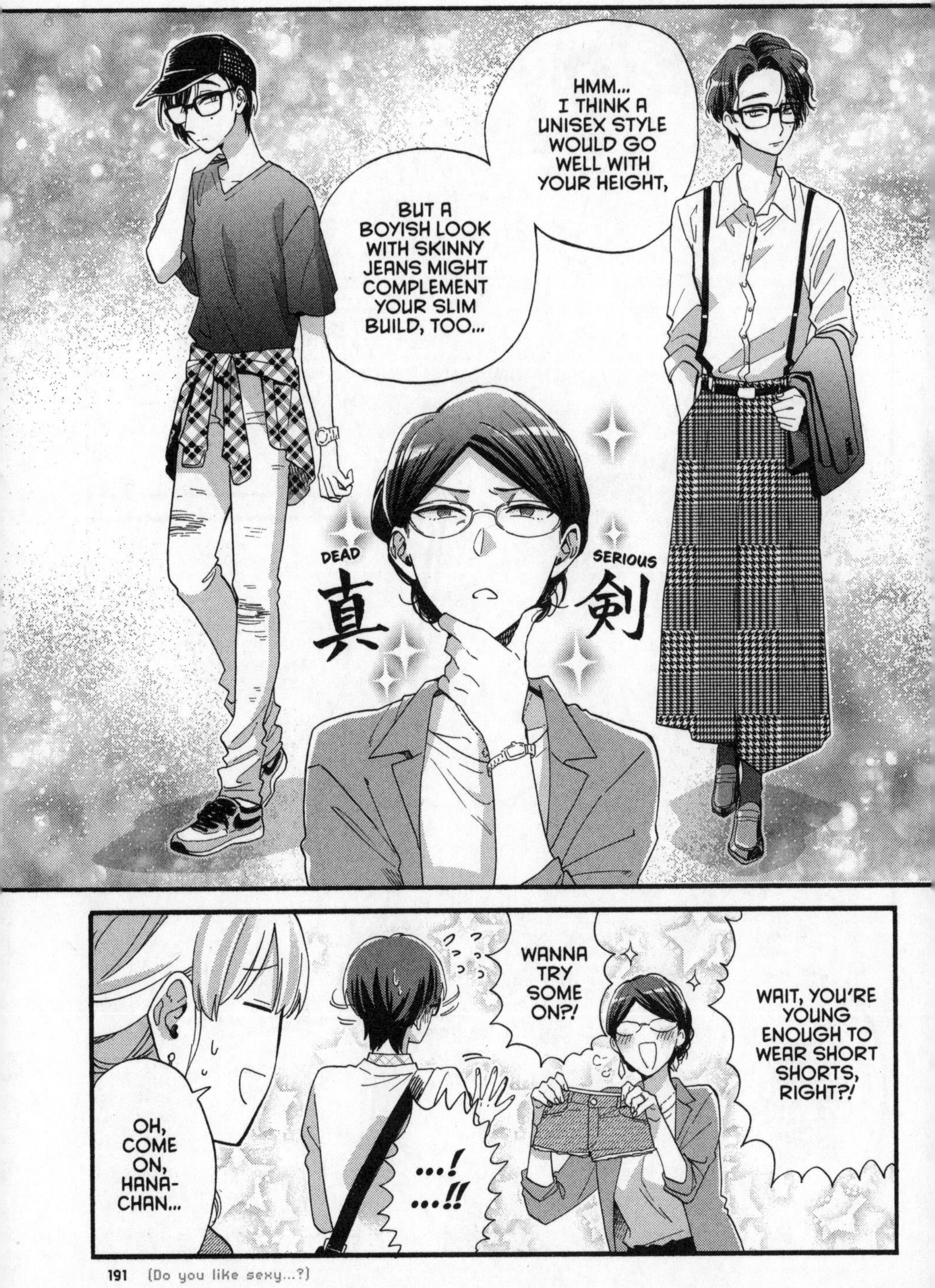
HMM... I THINK A UNISEX STYLE WOULD GO WELL WITH YOUR HEIGHT,
BUT A BOYISH LOOK WITH SKINNY JEANS MIGHT COMPLEMENT YOUR SLIM BUILD, TOO...
DEAD 真
SERIOUS 剣
WAIT, YOU'RE YOUNG ENOUGH TO WEAR SHORT SHORTS, RIGHT?!
WANNA TRY SOME ON?!
...! ...!!
OH, COME ON, HANA-CHAN...

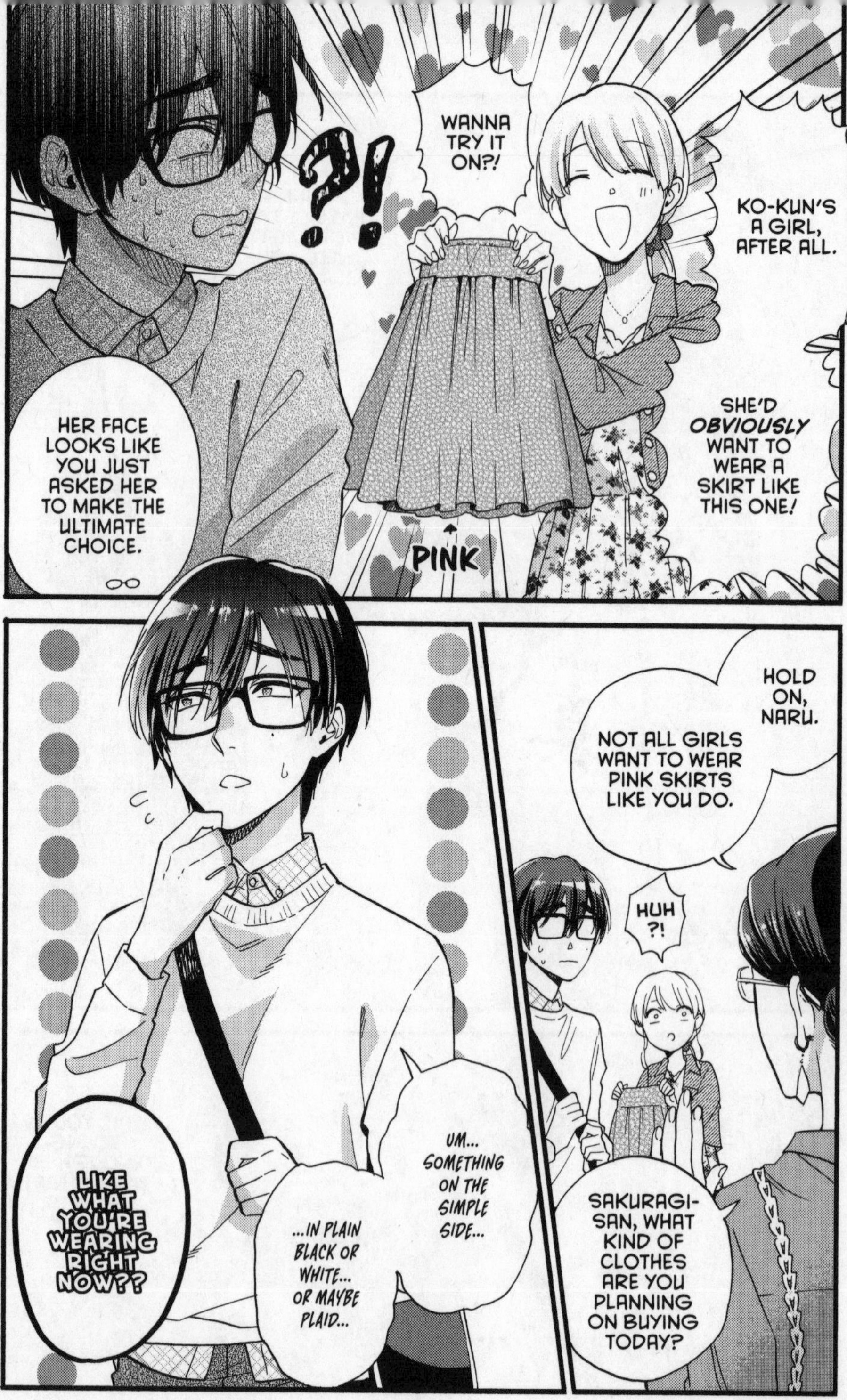
WANNA TRY IT ON?!
?!
KO-KUN'S A GIRL, AFTER ALL.
SHE'D *OBVIOUSLY* WANT TO WEAR A SKIRT LIKE THIS ONE!
PINK
HER FACE LOOKS LIKE YOU JUST ASKED HER TO MAKE THE ULTIMATE CHOICE.
HOLD ON, NARU.
NOT ALL GIRLS WANT TO WEAR PINK SKIRTS LIKE YOU DO.
HUH?!
SAKURAGI-SAN, WHAT KIND OF CLOTHES ARE YOU PLANNING ON BUYING TODAY?
UM... SOMETHING ON THE SIMPLE SIDE...
...IN PLAIN BLACK OR WHITE... OR MAYBE PLAID...
LIKE WHAT YOU'RE WEARING RIGHT NOW??

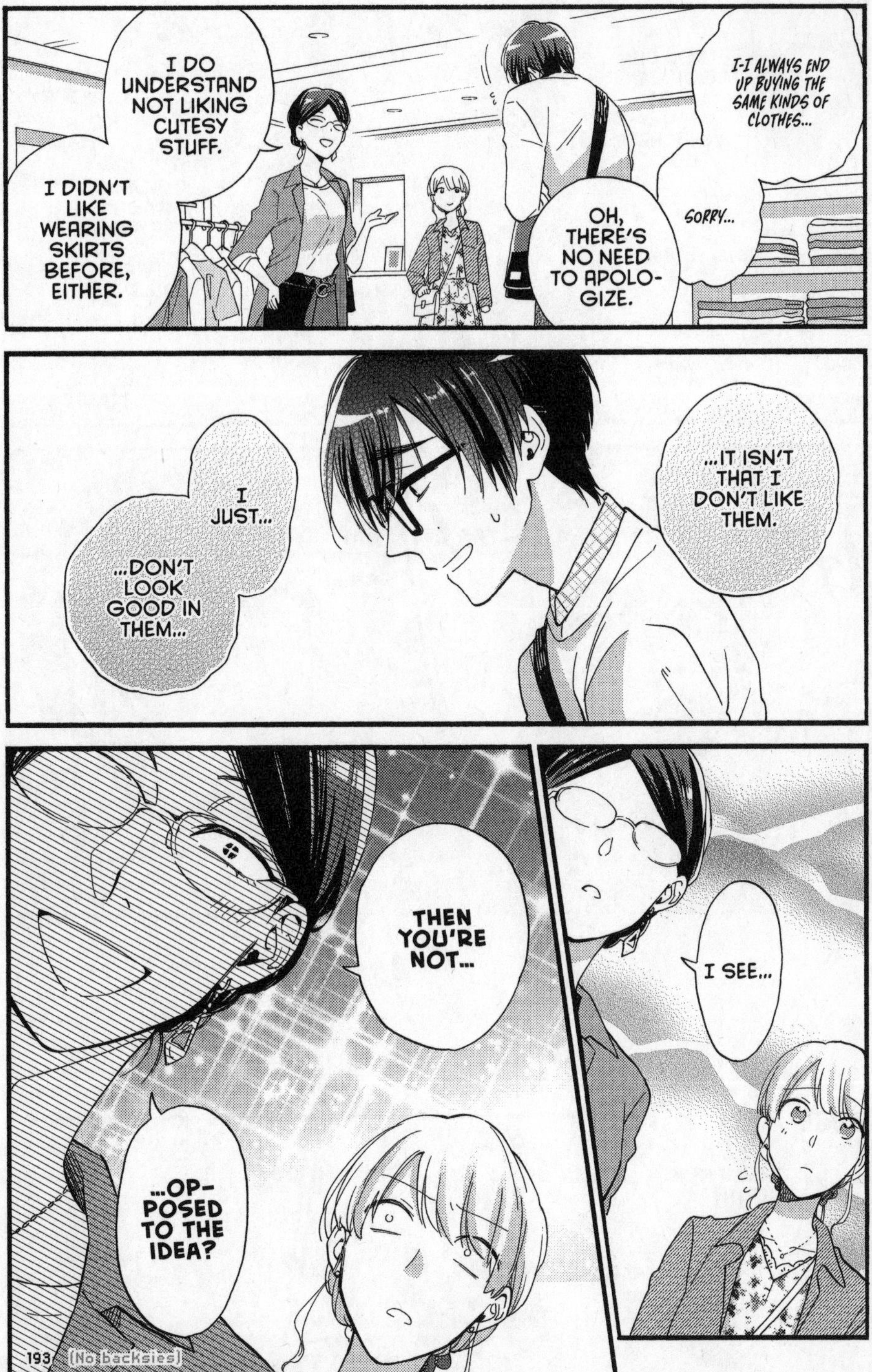
I-I ALWAYS END UP BUYING THE SAME KINDS OF CLOTHES...
SORRY...
OH, THERE'S NO NEED TO APOLO-GIZE.
I DO UNDERSTAND NOT LIKING CUTESY STUFF.
I DIDN'T LIKE WEARING SKIRTS BEFORE, EITHER.
...IT ISN'T THAT I DON'T LIKE THEM.
I JUST...
...DON'T LOOK GOOD IN THEM...
I SEE...
THEN YOU'RE NOT...
...OP-POSED TO THE IDEA?

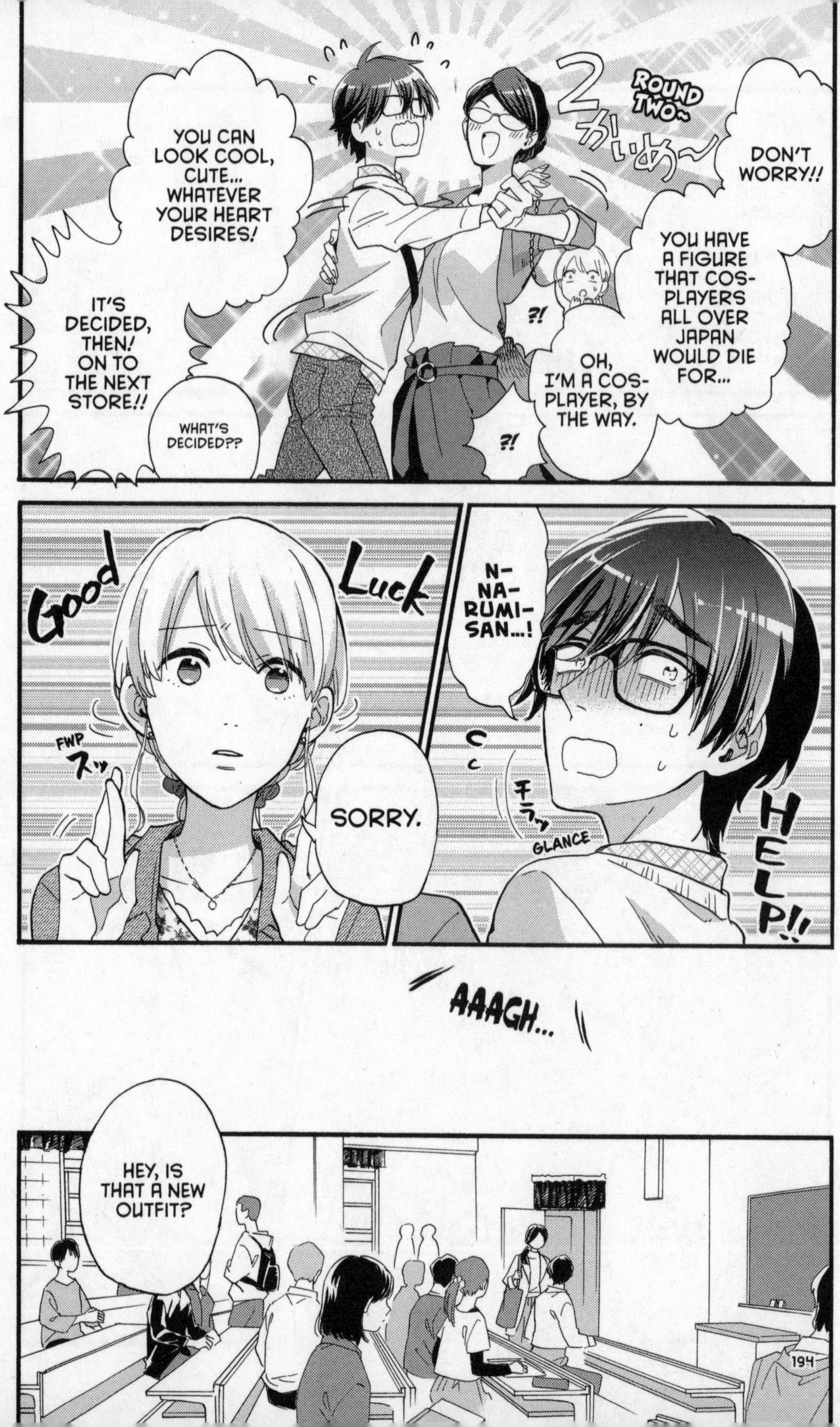

ROUND TWO~
2かいめ~
DON'T WORRY!!
YOU HAVE A FIGURE THAT COS-PLAYERS ALL OVER JAPAN WOULD DIE FOR...
?!
OH, I'M A COS-PLAYER, BY THE WAY.
?!
YOU CAN LOOK COOL, CUTE... WHATEVER YOUR HEART DESIRES!
IT'S DECIDED, THEN! ON TO THE NEXT STORE!!
WHAT'S DECIDED??
N-NA-RUMI-SAN...!
HELP!!
チラッ
GLANCE
Good Luck
SORRY.
FWP
スッ
AAAGH...
HEY, IS THAT A NEW OUTFIT?

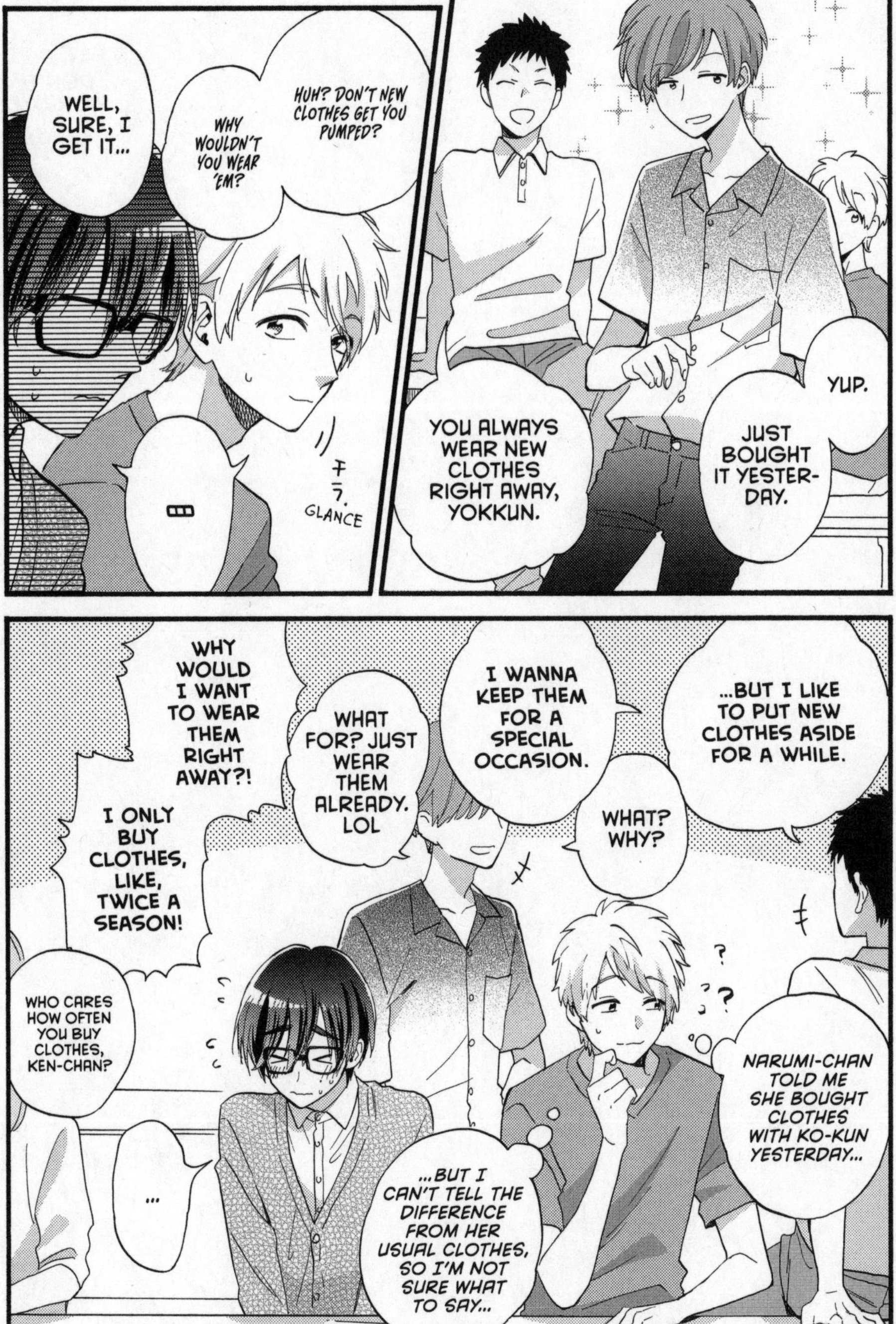
YUP.
JUST BOUGHT IT YESTER-DAY.
YOU ALWAYS WEAR NEW CLOTHES RIGHT AWAY, YOKKUN.
HUH? DON'T NEW CLOTHES GET YOU PUMPED?
WHY WOULDN'T YOU WEAR 'EM?
WELL, SURE, I GET IT...
チラ
GLANCE
...
...BUT I LIKE TO PUT NEW CLOTHES ASIDE FOR A WHILE.
I WANNA KEEP THEM FOR A SPECIAL OCCASION.
WHAT? WHY?
WHAT FOR? JUST WEAR THEM ALREADY. LOL
WHY WOULD I WANT TO WEAR THEM RIGHT AWAY?!
I ONLY BUY CLOTHES, LIKE, TWICE A SEASON!
NARUMI-CHAN TOLD ME SHE BOUGHT CLOTHES WITH KO-KUN YESTERDAY...
...BUT I CAN'T TELL THE DIFFERENCE FROM HER USUAL CLOTHES, SO I'M NOT SURE WHAT TO SAY...
WHO CARES HOW OFTEN YOU BUY CLOTHES, KEN-CHAN?
...
HER USUAL CLOTHES

SO
MUCH
STUFF.

...

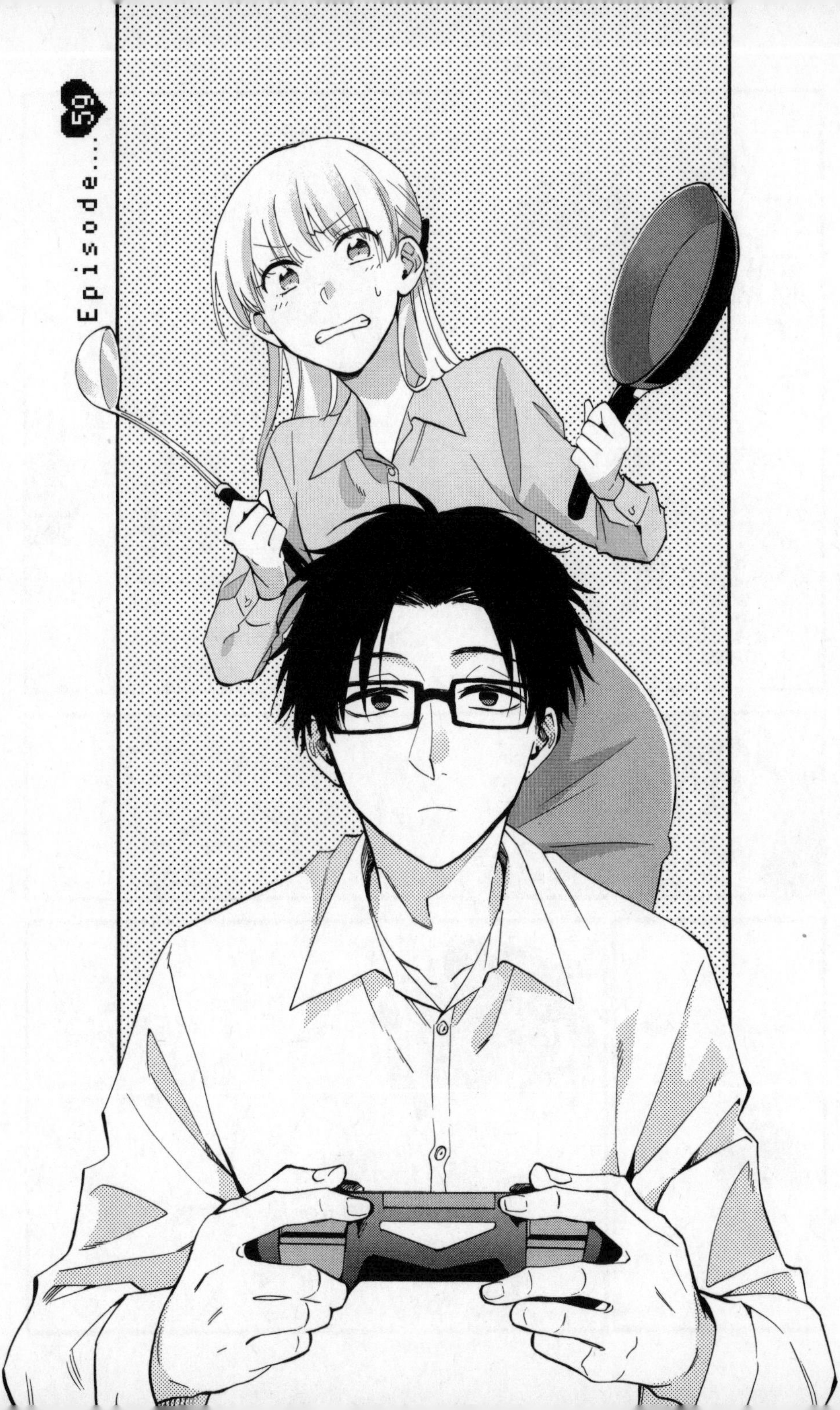
Episode.... 59

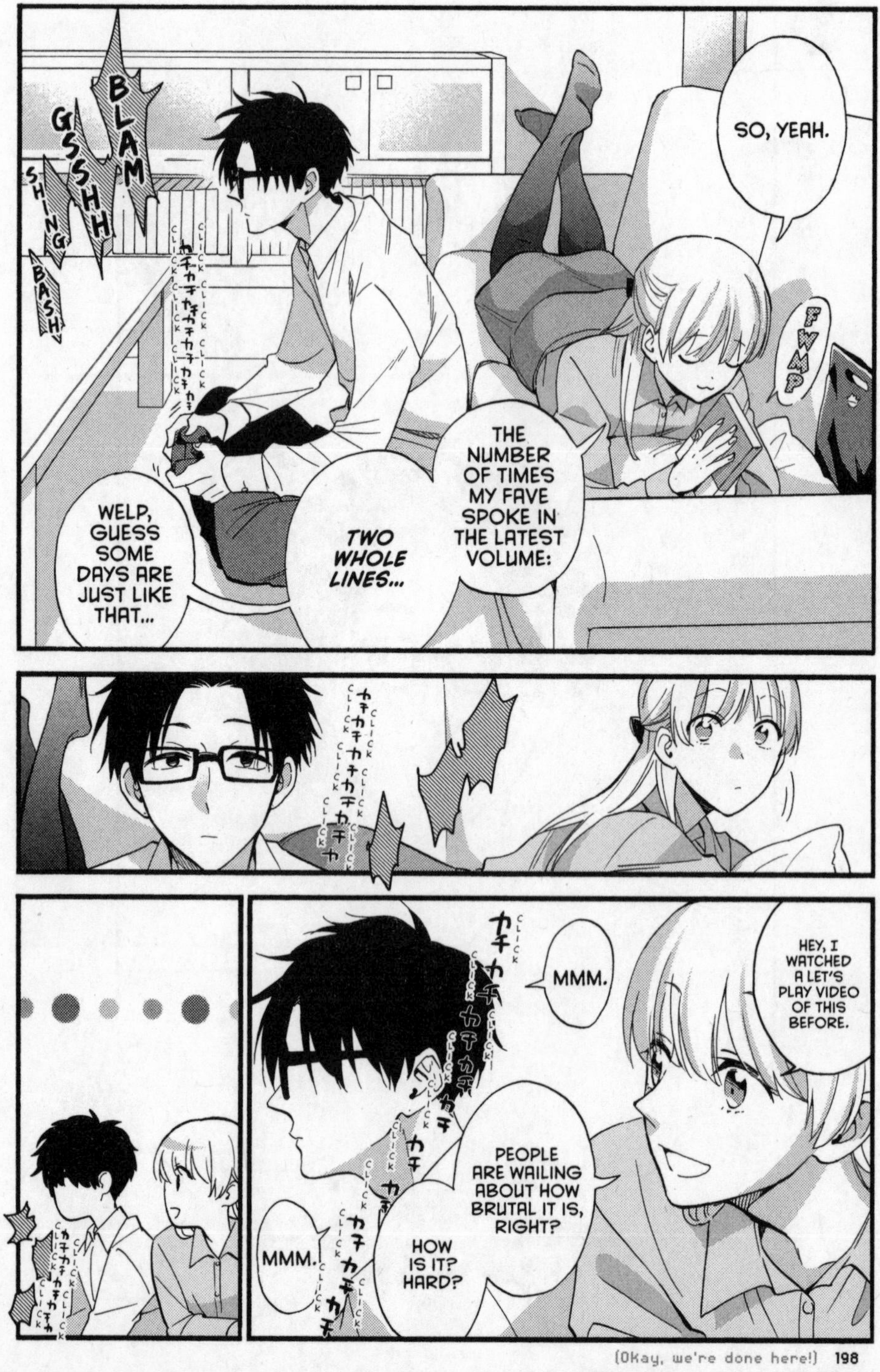
SO, YEAH.
FWMP
THE NUMBER OF TIMES MY FAVE SPOKE IN THE LATEST VOLUME:
TWO WHOLE LINES...
WELP, GUESS SOME DAYS ARE JUST LIKE THAT...
BLAM
GSSHH
SHING
BASH
CLICK CLICK CLICK CLICK
CLICK CLICK CLICK CLICK
HEY, I WATCHED A LET'S PLAY VIDEO OF THIS BEFORE.
MMM.
CLICK CLICK CLICK
PEOPLE ARE WAILING ABOUT HOW BRUTAL IT IS, RIGHT?
HOW IS IT? HARD?
MMM.
CLICK CLICK CLICK
CLICK CLICK CLICK

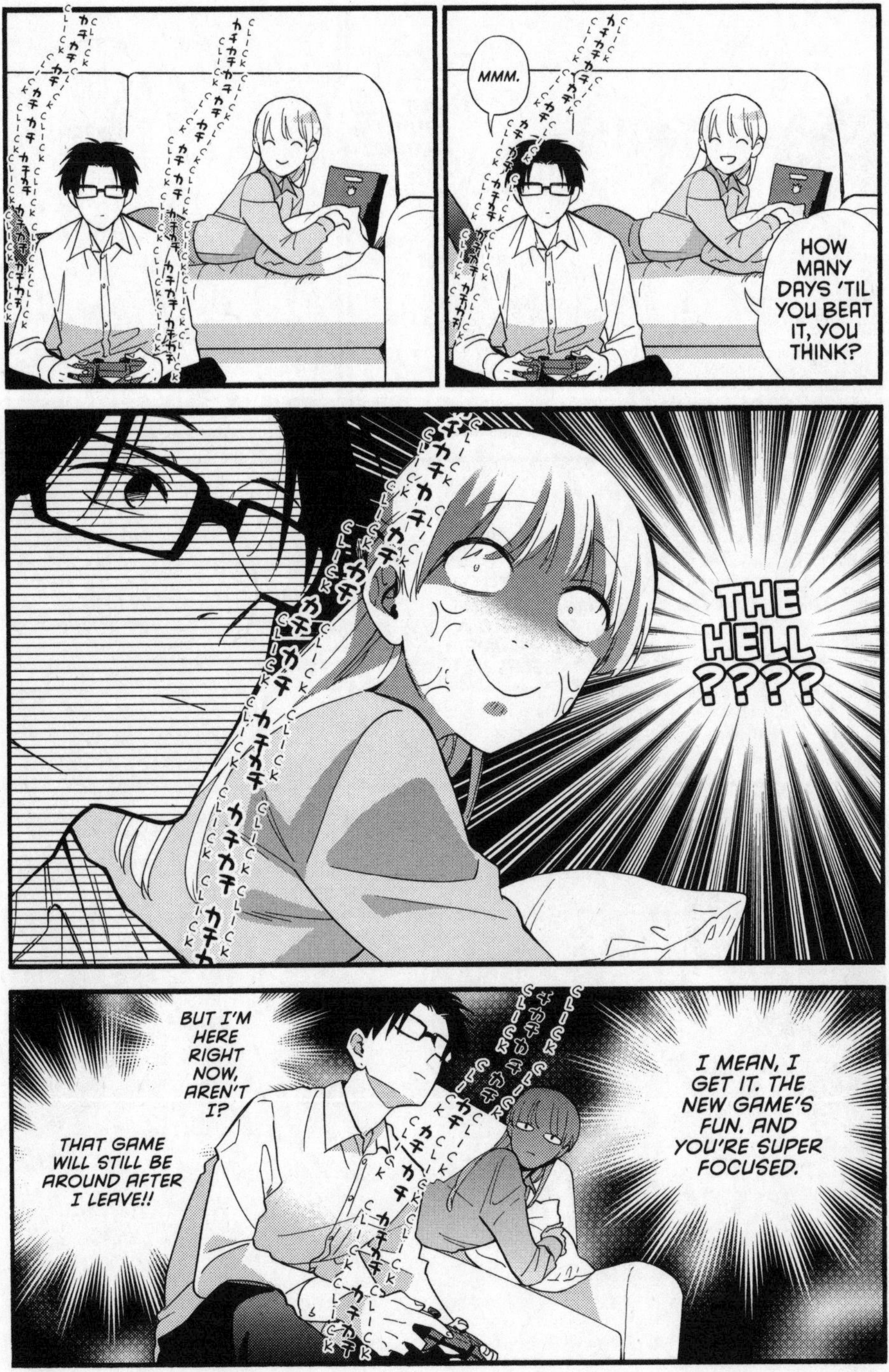

HOW MANY DAYS 'TIL YOU BEAT IT, YOU THINK?
MMM.
カチカチ CLICK CLICK
カチカチ CLICK CLICK
THE HELL????
カチカチ CLICK CLICK
I MEAN, I GET IT. THE NEW GAME'S FUN. AND YOU'RE SUPER FOCUSED.
カチカチ CLICK CLICK
BUT I'M HERE RIGHT NOW, AREN'T I?
THAT GAME WILL STILL BE AROUND AFTER I LEAVE!!

 (Super dry response)

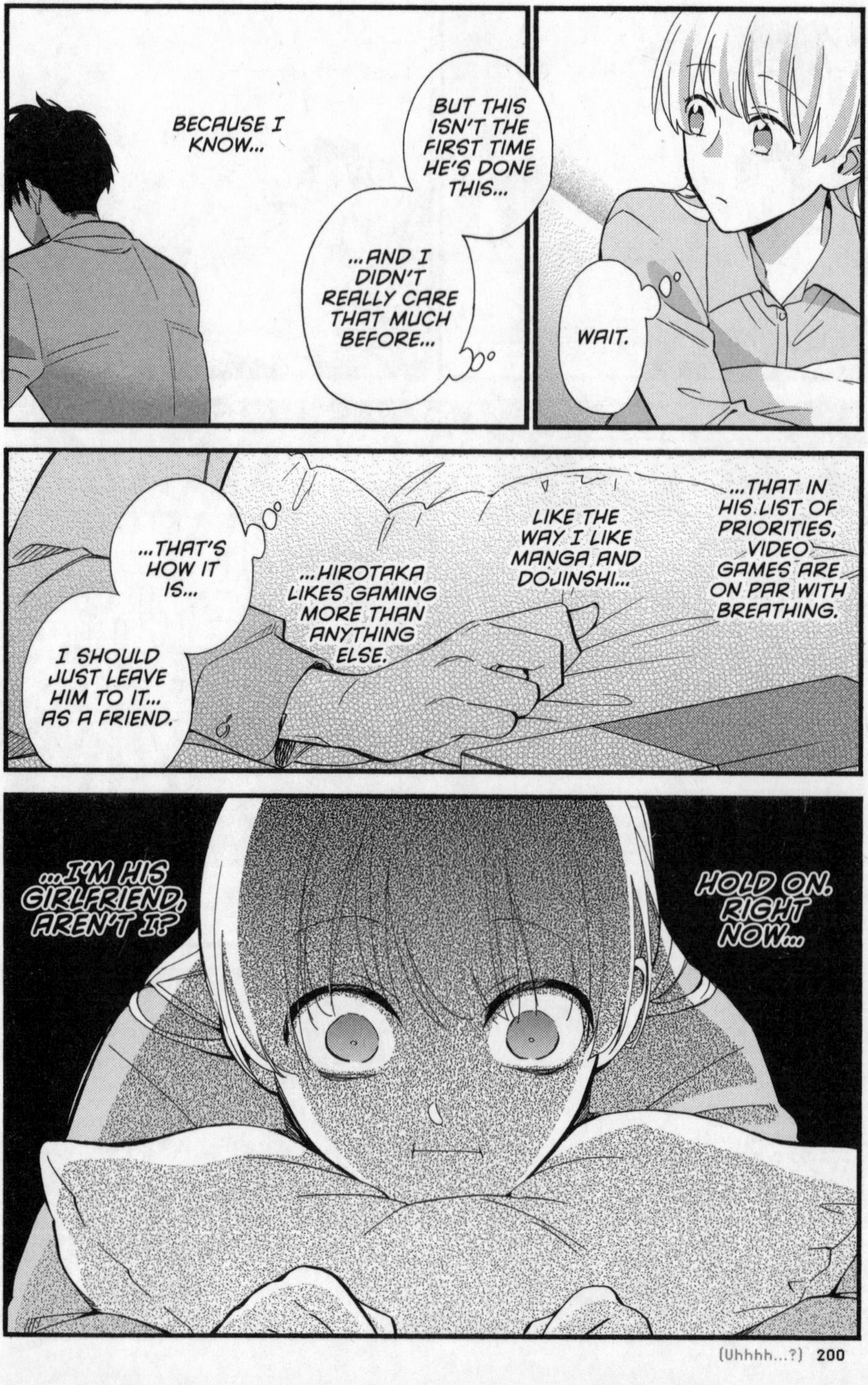
WAIT.
BUT THIS ISN'T THE FIRST TIME HE'S DONE THIS...
...AND I DIDN'T REALLY CARE THAT MUCH BEFORE...
BECAUSE I KNOW...
...THAT IN HIS LIST OF PRIORITIES, VIDEO GAMES ARE ON PAR WITH BREATHING.
LIKE THE WAY I LIKE MANGA AND DOJINSHI...
...HIROTAKA LIKES GAMING MORE THAN ANYTHING ELSE.
...THAT'S HOW IT IS...
I SHOULD JUST LEAVE HIM TO IT... AS A FRIEND.
HOLD ON. RIGHT NOW...
...I'M HIS GIRLFRIEND, AREN'T I?

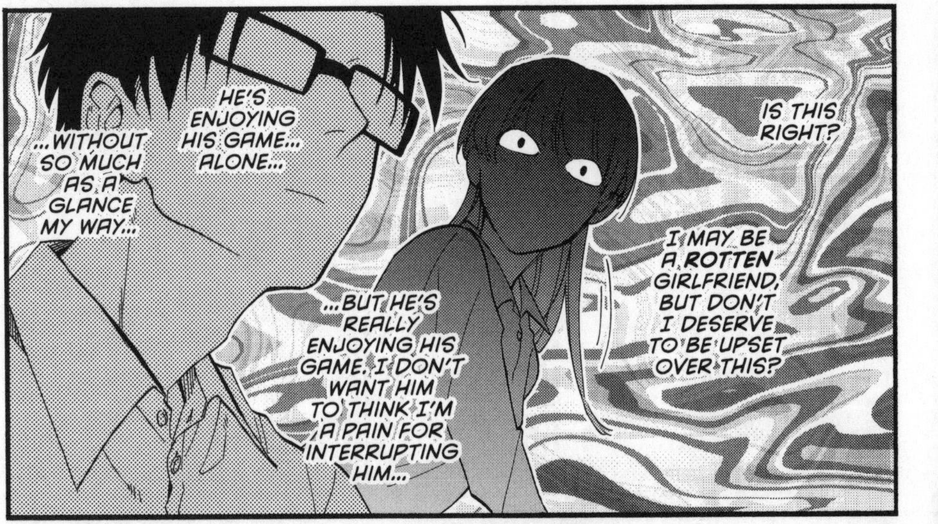
IS THIS RIGHT?
I MAY BE A ROTTEN GIRLFRIEND, BUT DON'T I DESERVE TO BE UPSET OVER THIS?
HE'S ENJOYING HIS GAME... ALONE...
...WITHOUT SO MUCH AS A GLANCE MY WAY...
...BUT HE'S REALLY ENJOYING HIS GAME. I DON'T WANT HIM TO THINK I'M A PAIN FOR INTERRUPTING HIM...
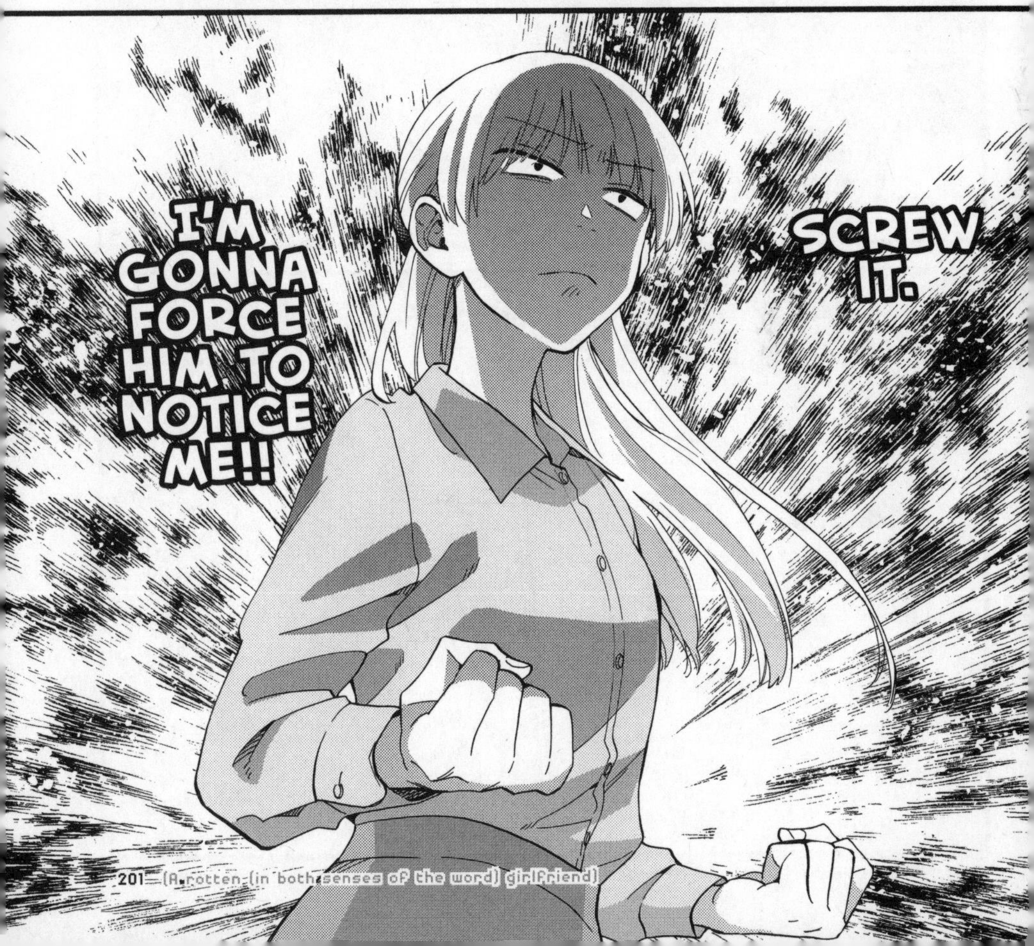
SCREW IT.
I'M GONNA FORCE HIM TO NOTICE ME!!

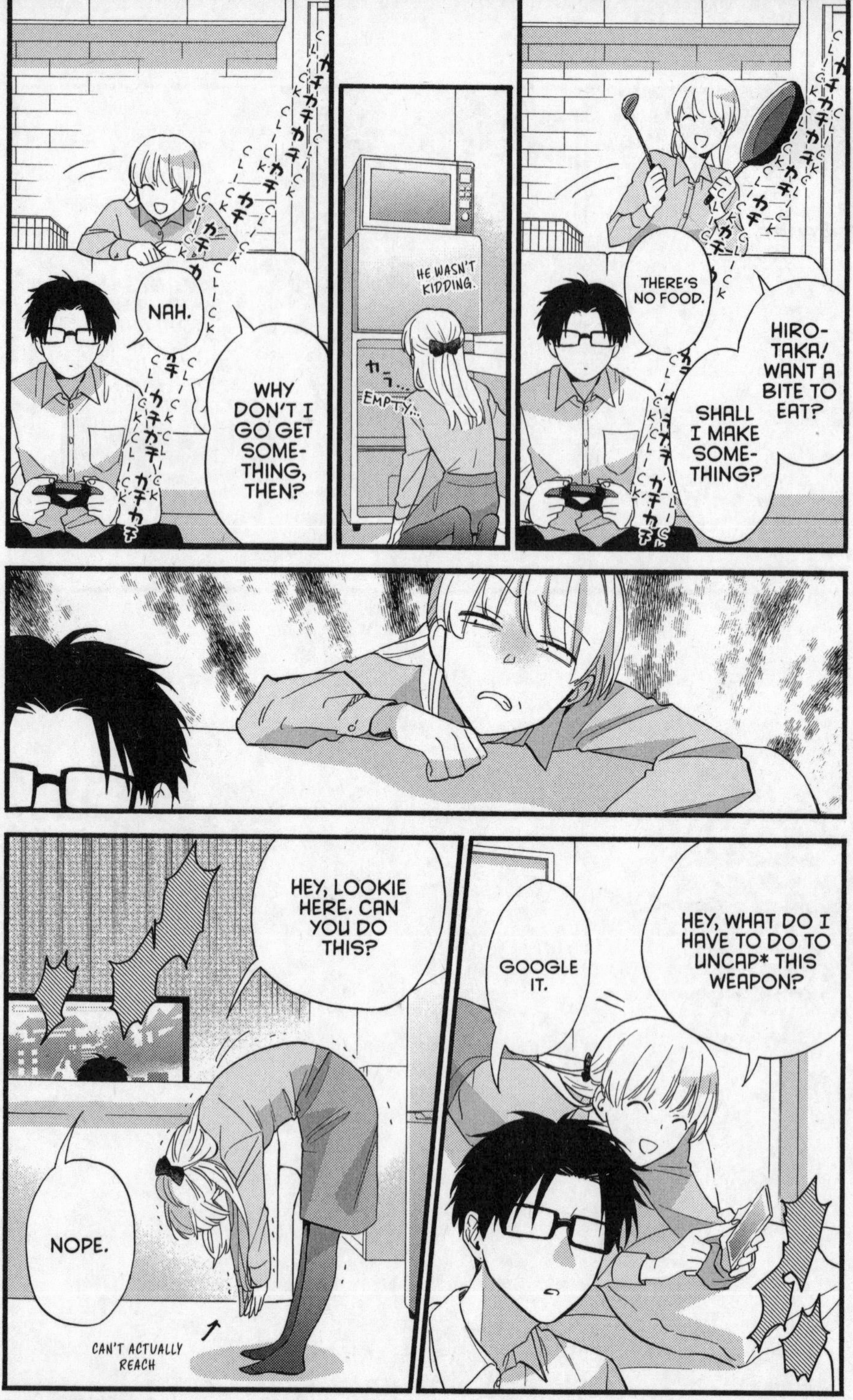
カチカチ
CLICK CLICK
HIRO-TAKA! WANT A BITE TO EAT?
SHALL I MAKE SOME-THING?
THERE'S NO FOOD.
カラ…
EMPTY...
HE WASN'T KIDDING.
WHY DON'T I GO GET SOME-THING, THEN?
NAH.
HEY, WHAT DO I HAVE TO DO TO UNCAP* THIS WEAPON?
GOOGLE IT.
HEY, LOOKIE HERE. CAN YOU DO THIS?
NOPE.
CAN'T ACTUALLY REACH

*In the game *Granblue Fantasy*, this means to increase the maximum level and unlock new effects for a weapon.

(CLICK CLICK (went her joints, too))

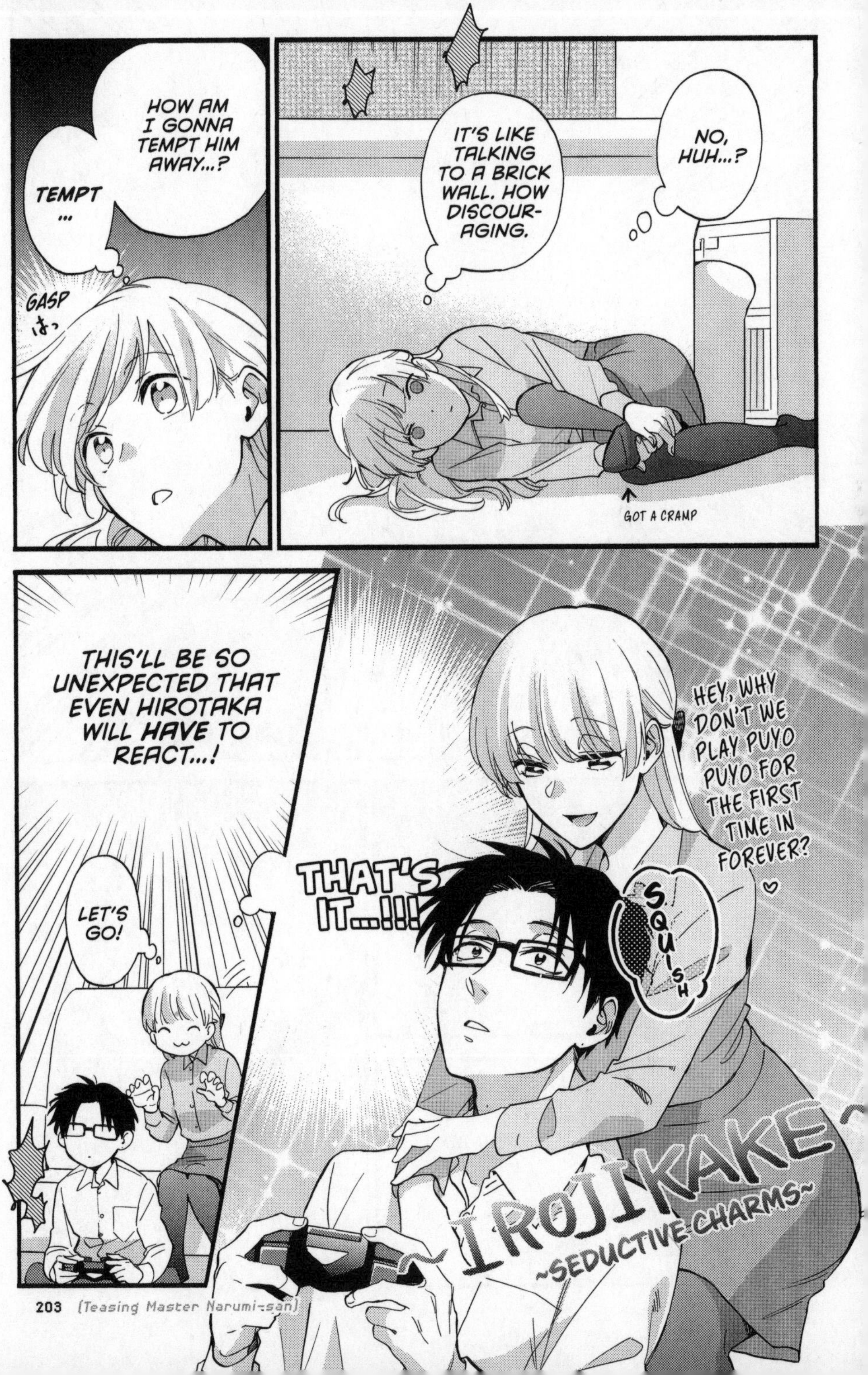
NO, HUH...?
IT'S LIKE TALKING TO A BRICK WALL. HOW DISCOURAGING.
GOT A CRAMP
HOW AM I GONNA TEMPT HIM AWAY...?
TEMPT ...
GASP
はっ
THIS'LL BE SO UNEXPECTED THAT EVEN HIROTAKA WILL HAVE TO REACT...!
LET'S GO!
THAT'S IT...!!!
HEY, WHY DON'T WE PLAY PUYO PUYO FOR THE FIRST TIME IN FOREVER? ♡
SQUISH
~IROJIKAKE~
~SEDUCTIVE CHARMS~

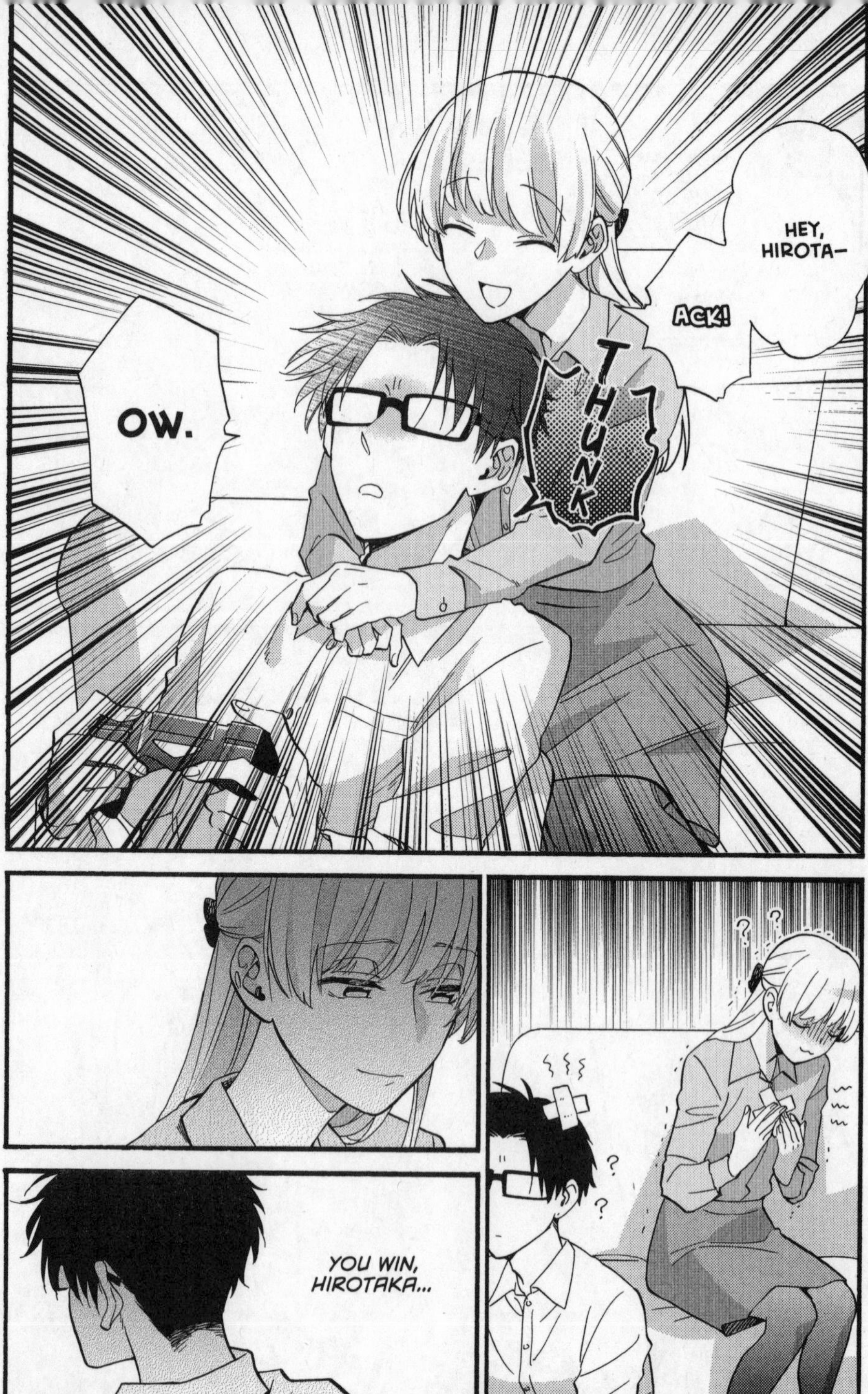
HEY, HIROTA—
ACK!
THUNK
OW.
YOU WIN, HIROTAKA...

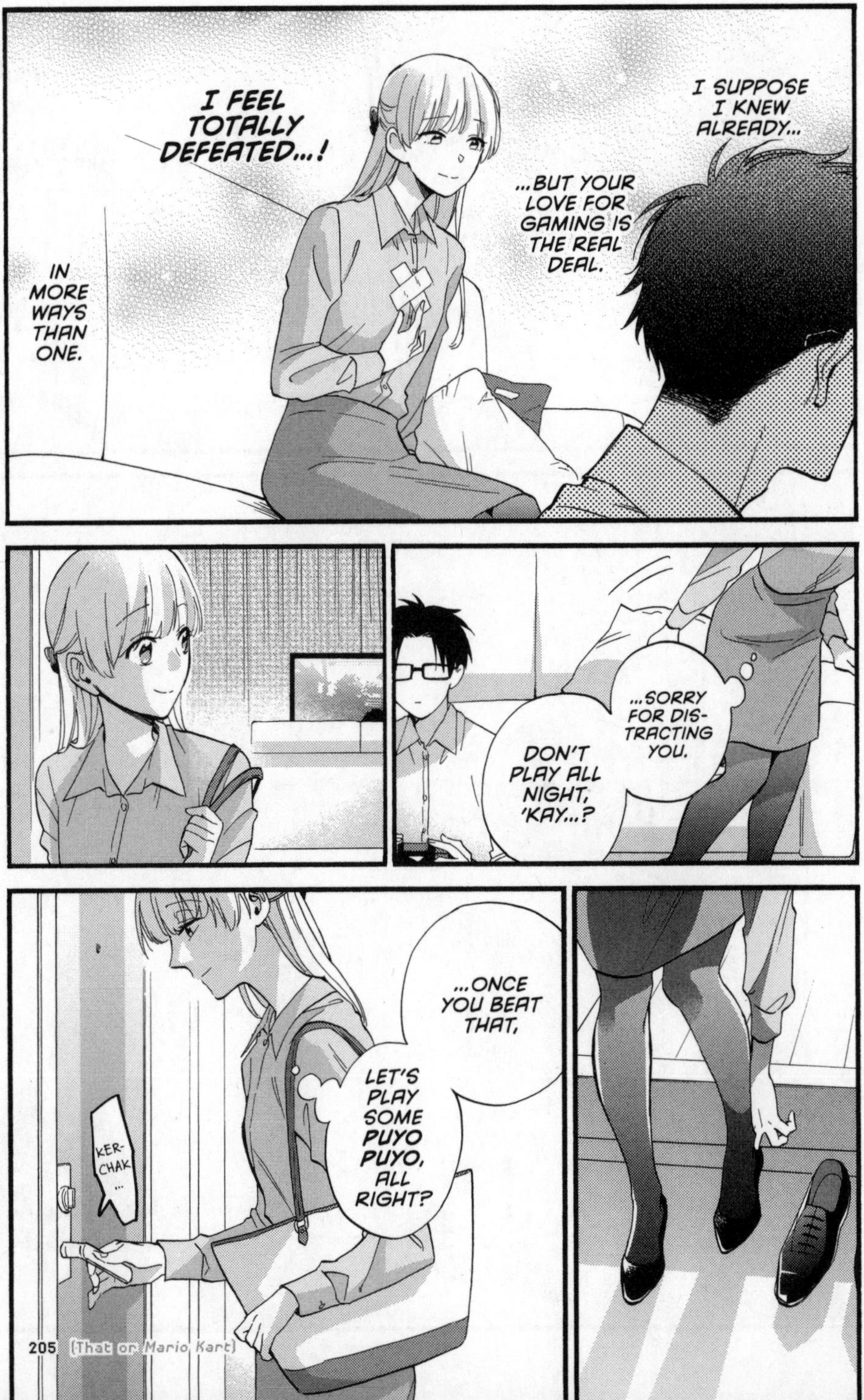
I SUPPOSE I KNEW ALREADY...
...BUT YOUR LOVE FOR GAMING IS THE REAL DEAL.
I FEEL TOTALLY DEFEATED...!
IN MORE WAYS THAN ONE.
...SORRY FOR DIS-TRACTING YOU.
DON'T PLAY ALL NIGHT, 'KAY...?
...ONCE YOU BEAT THAT,
LET'S PLAY SOME PUYO PUYO, ALL RIGHT?
KER-CHAK...

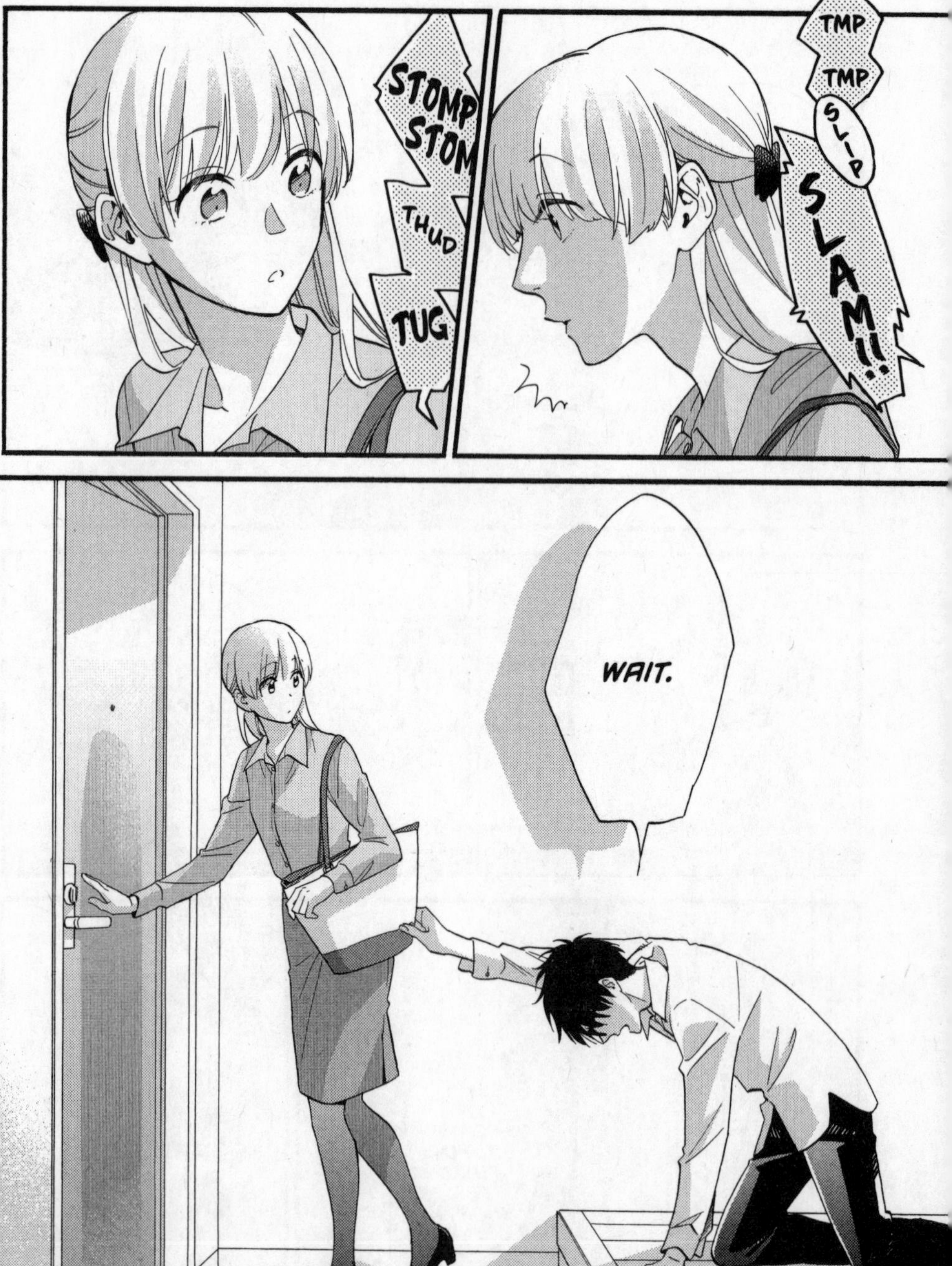
TMP
TMP
SLIP
SLAM!!
STOMP
STOM
THUD
TUG
WAIT.

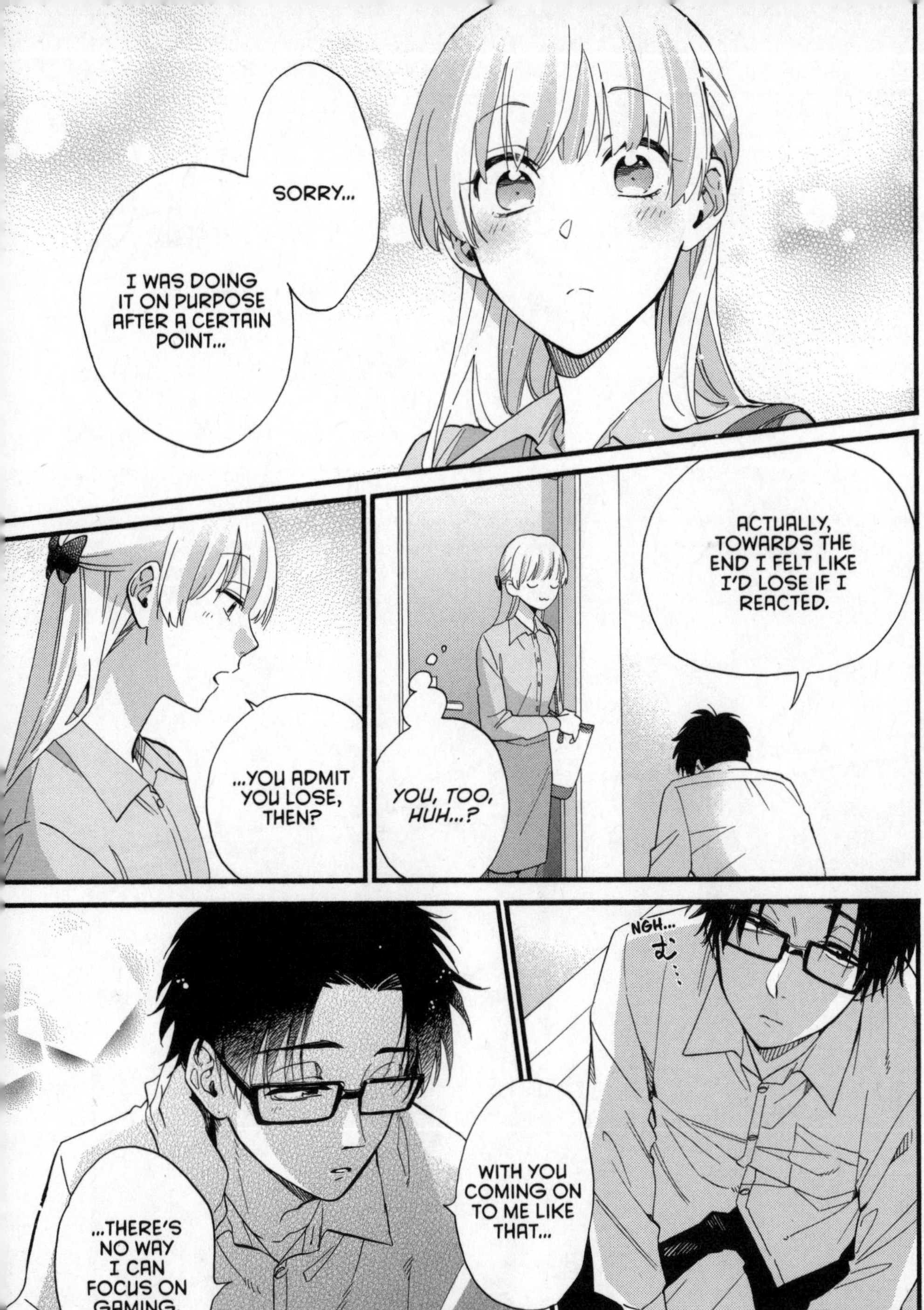
SORRY...
I WAS DOING IT ON PURPOSE AFTER A CERTAIN POINT...
ACTUALLY, TOWARDS THE END I FELT LIKE I'D LOSE IF I REACTED.
YOU, TOO, HUH...?
...YOU ADMIT YOU LOSE, THEN?
NGH...
む...
WITH YOU COMING ON TO ME LIKE THAT...
...THERE'S NO WAY I CAN FOCUS ON GAMING.

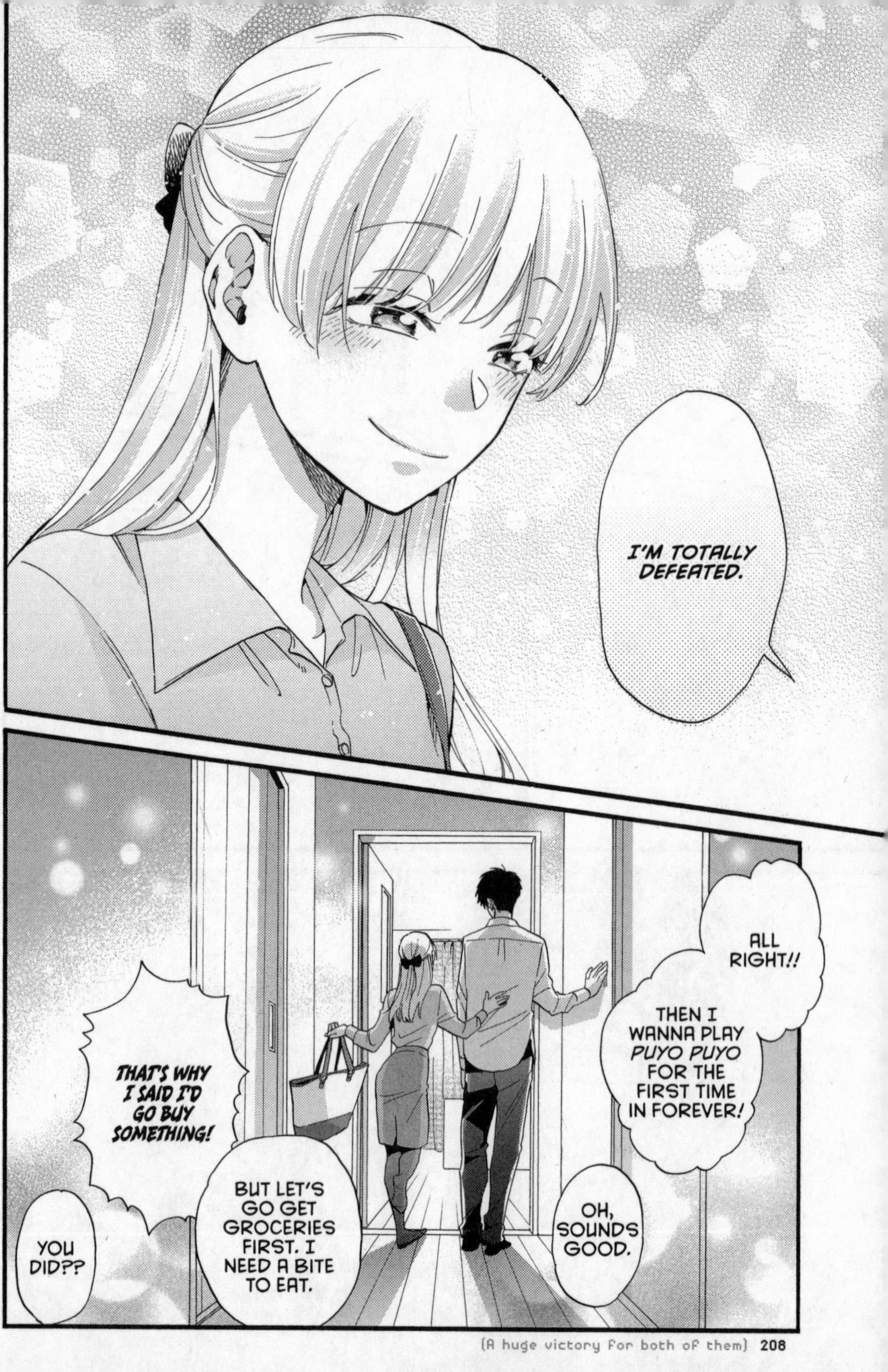
I'M TOTALLY DEFEATED.
ALL RIGHT!!
THEN I WANNA PLAY *PUYO PUYO* FOR THE FIRST TIME IN FOREVER!
OH, SOUNDS GOOD.
BUT LET'S GO GET GROCERIES FIRST. I NEED A BITE TO EAT.
THAT'S WHY I SAID I'D GO BUY SOMETHING!
YOU DID??

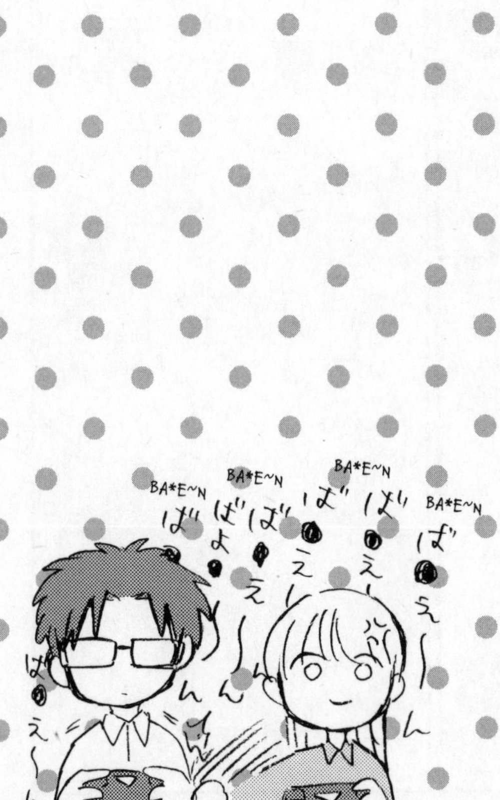

BA*E~N
BA*E~N
BA*E~N
BA*E~N
BA*E~N

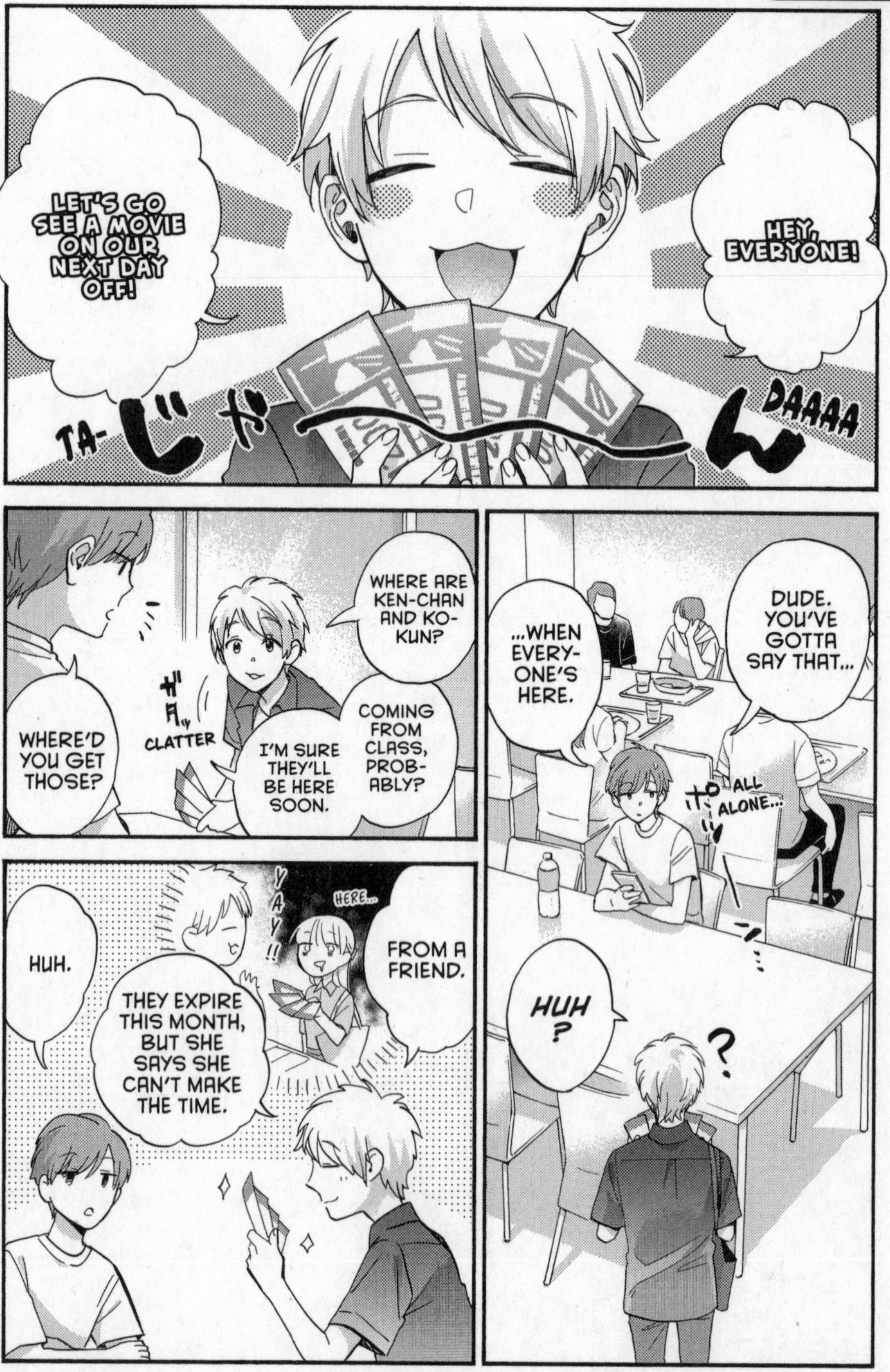
HEY, EVERYONE!
LET'S GO SEE A MOVIE ON OUR NEXT DAY OFF!
TA-じゃーーーん DAAAA
DUDE. YOU'VE GOTTA SAY THAT...
...WHEN EVERY-ONE'S HERE.
ALL ALONE...
HUH ?
WHERE ARE KEN-CHAN AND KO-KUN?
COMING FROM CLASS, PROBABLY?
I'M SURE THEY'LL BE HERE SOON.
CLATTER
WHERE'D YOU GET THOSE?
FROM A FRIEND.
HERE...
YAY!!
THEY EXPIRE THIS MONTH, BUT SHE SAYS SHE CAN'T MAKE THE TIME.
HUH.

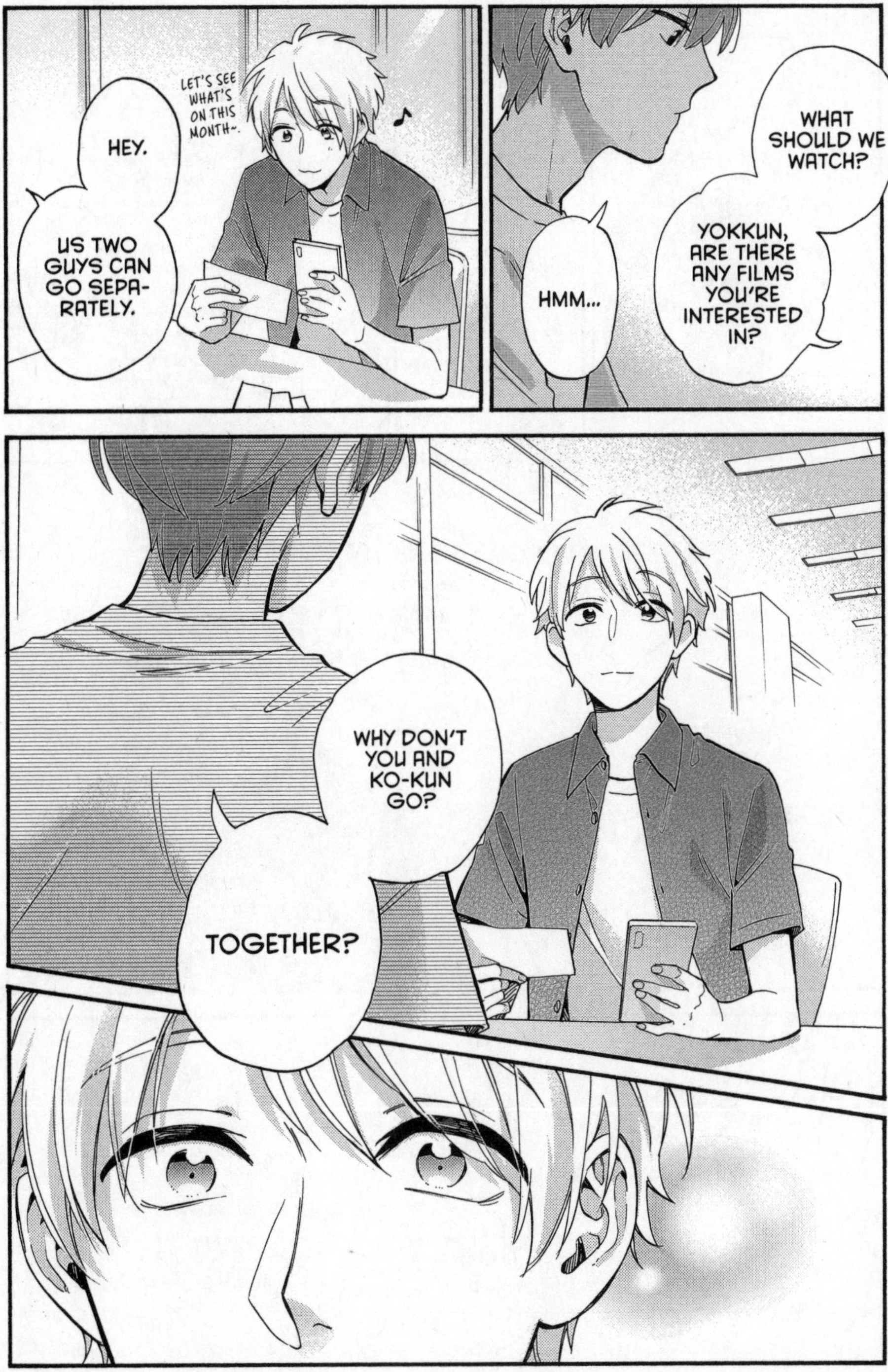
WHAT SHOULD WE WATCH?
YOKKUN, ARE THERE ANY FILMS YOU'RE INTERESTED IN?
HMM...
LET'S SEE WHAT'S ON THIS MONTH~
HEY.
US TWO GUYS CAN GO SEPARATELY.
WHY DON'T YOU AND KO-KUN GO?
TOGETHER?

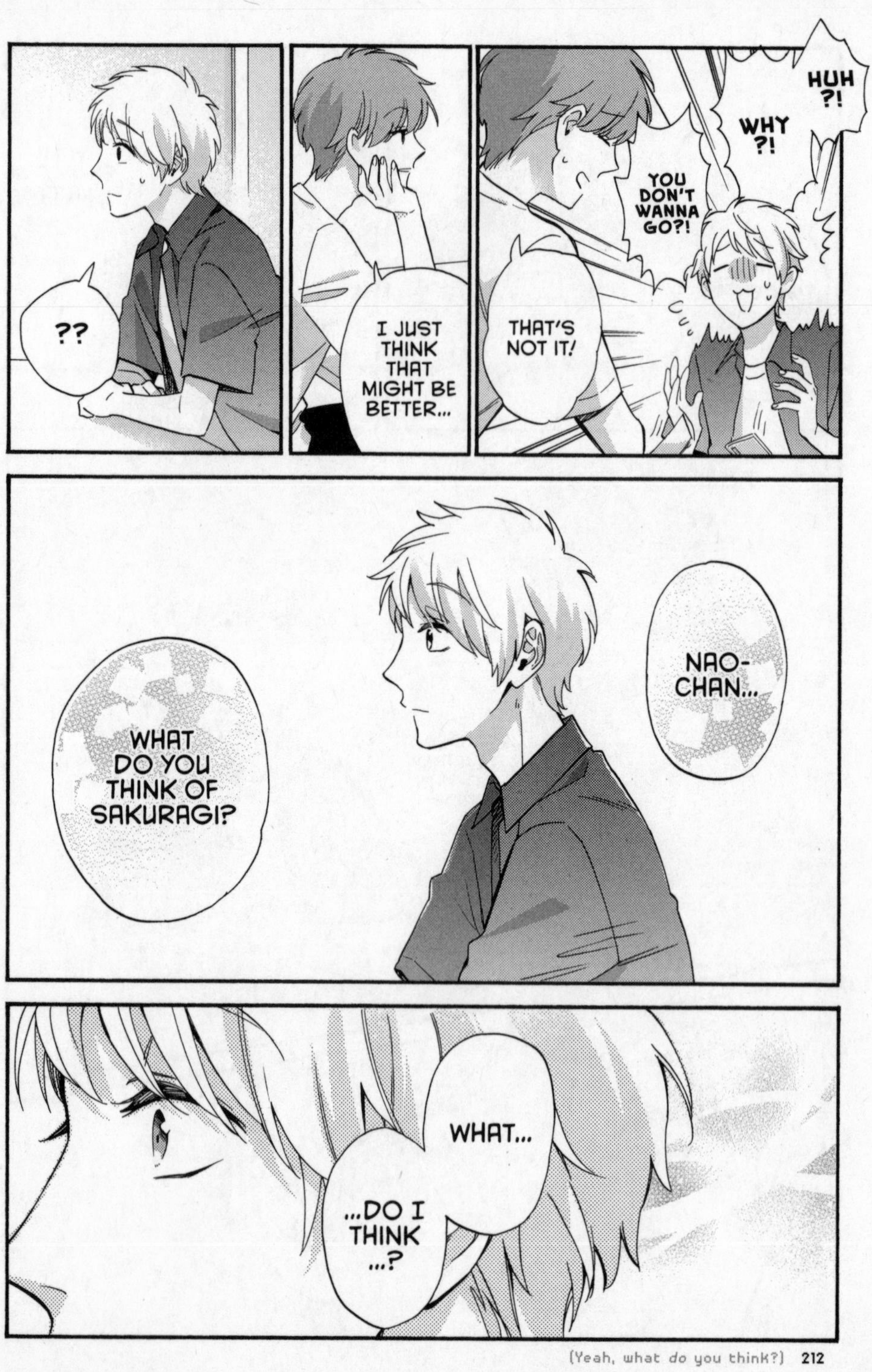
HUH?!
WHY?!
YOU DON'T WANNA GO?!
THAT'S NOT IT!
I JUST THINK THAT MIGHT BE BETTER...
??
NAO-CHAN...
WHAT DO YOU THINK OF SAKURAGI?
WHAT...
...DO I THINK...?

(Yeah, what *do* you think?)

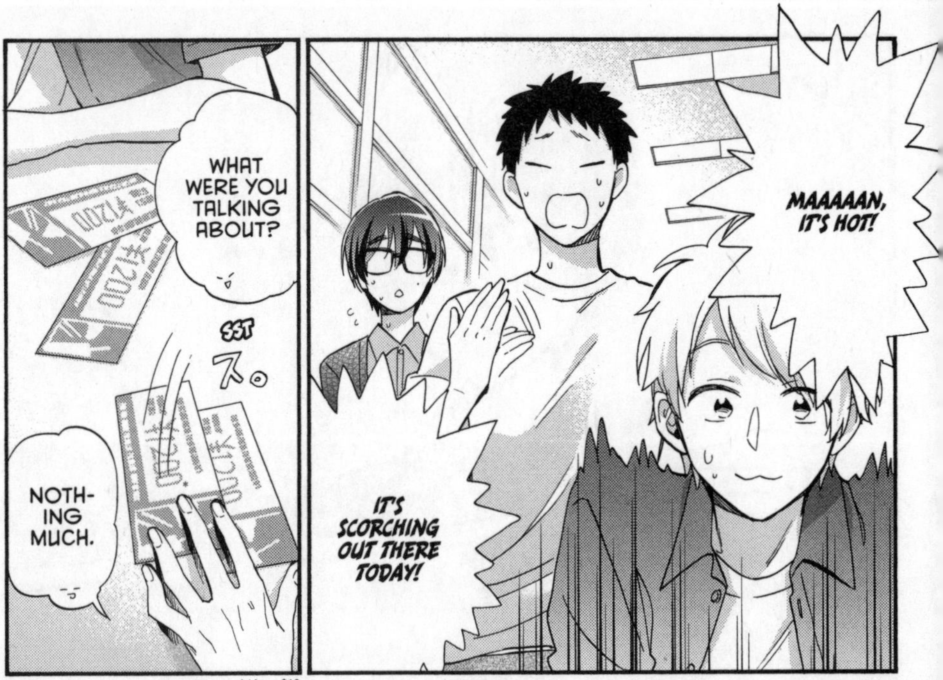
MAAAAAN, IT'S HOT!
IT'S SCORCHING OUT THERE TODAY!
WHAT WERE YOU TALKING ABOUT?
SST
ス。
NOTHING MUCH.

*About $12.

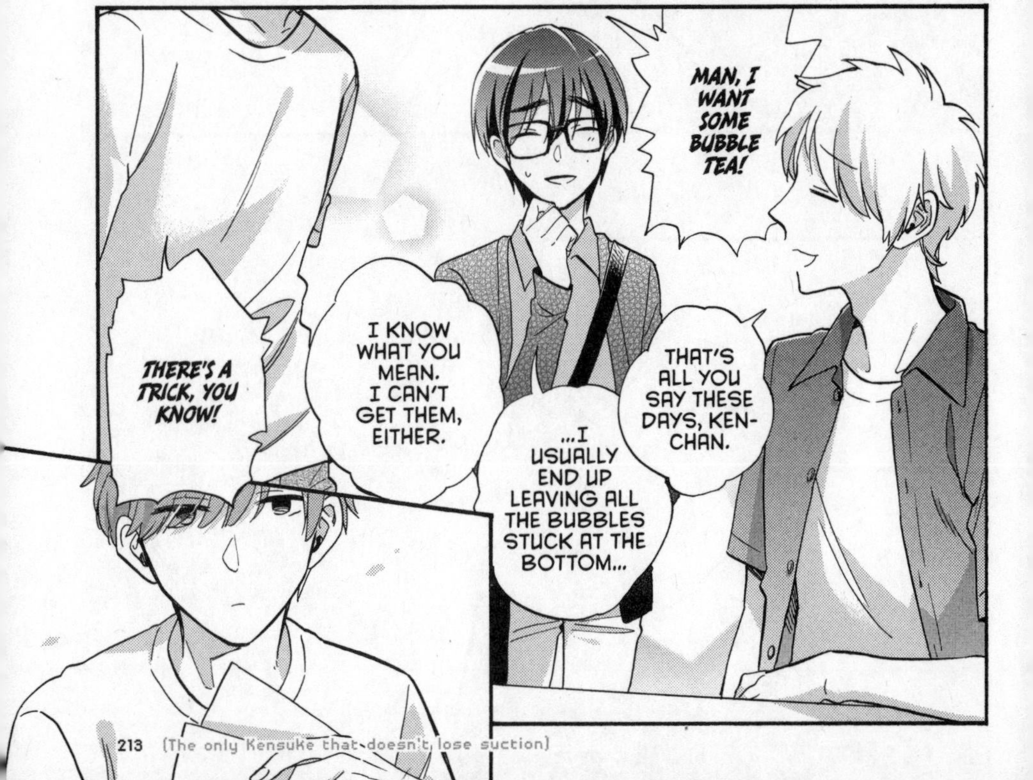
MAN, I WANT SOME BUBBLE TEA!
THAT'S ALL YOU SAY THESE DAYS, KEN-CHAN.
...I USUALLY END UP LEAVING ALL THE BUBBLES STUCK AT THE BOTTOM...
I KNOW WHAT YOU MEAN. I CAN'T GET THEM, EITHER.
THERE'S A TRICK, YOU KNOW!

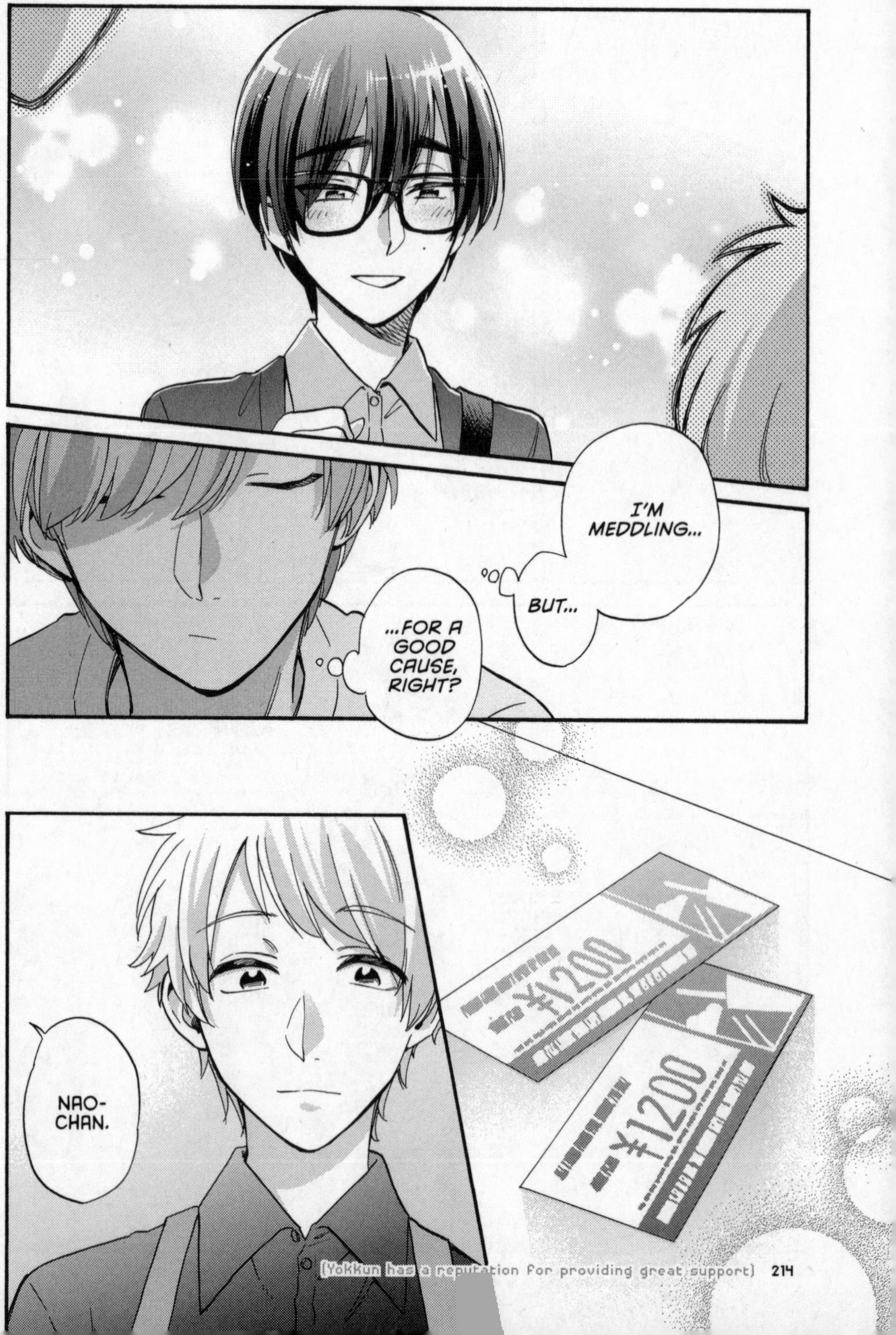
I'M MEDDLING...
BUT...
...FOR A GOOD CAUSE, RIGHT?
NAO-CHAN.

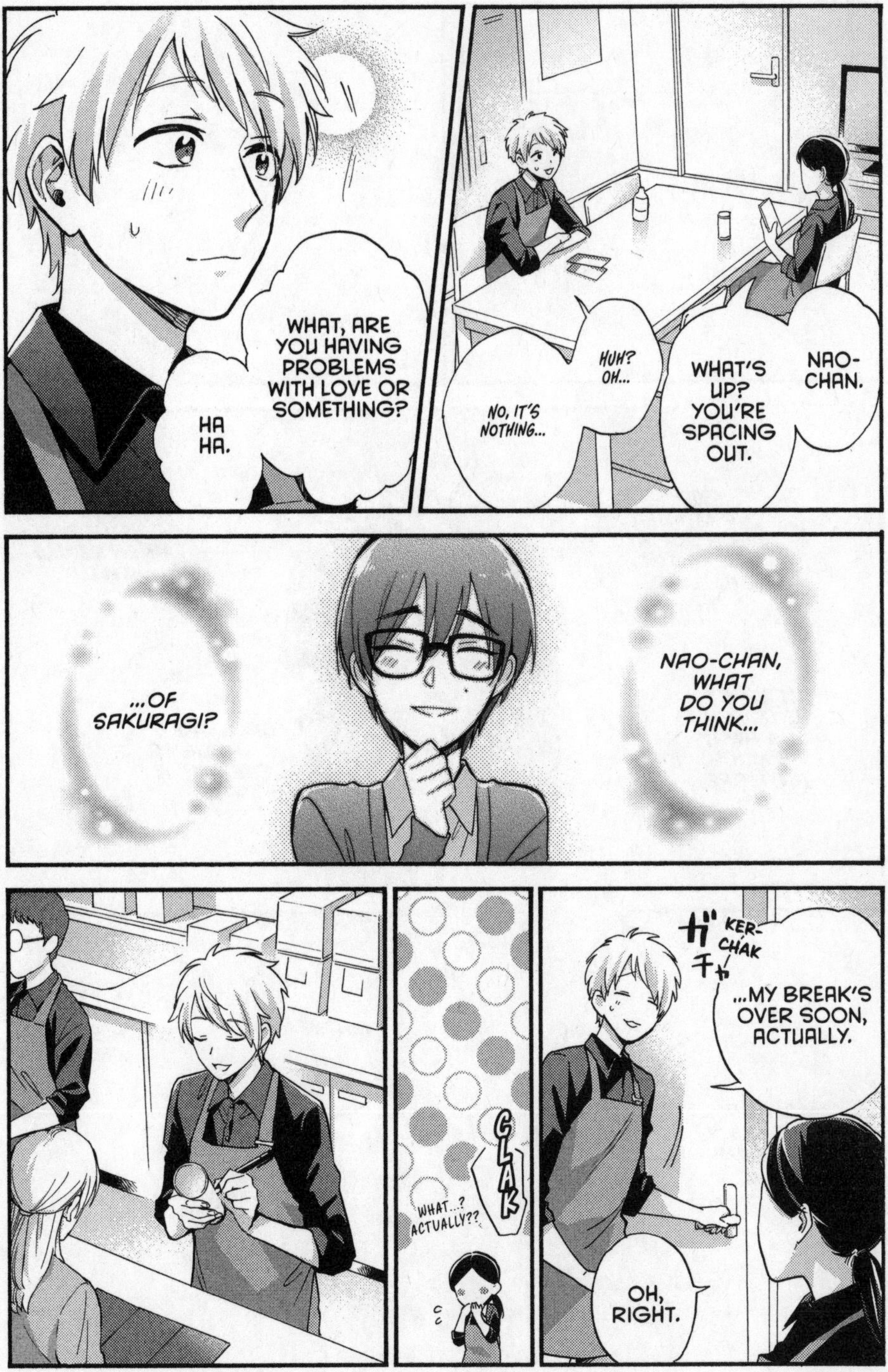
NAO-CHAN.
WHAT'S UP? YOU'RE SPACING OUT.
HUH? OH...
NO, IT'S NOTHING...
WHAT, ARE YOU HAVING PROBLEMS WITH LOVE OR SOMETHING?
HA HA.
NAO-CHAN, WHAT DO YOU THINK...
...OF SAKURAGI?
ガチャ
KER-CHAK
...MY BREAK'S OVER SOON, ACTUALLY.
OH, RIGHT.
CLAK
WHAT...? ACTUALLY??

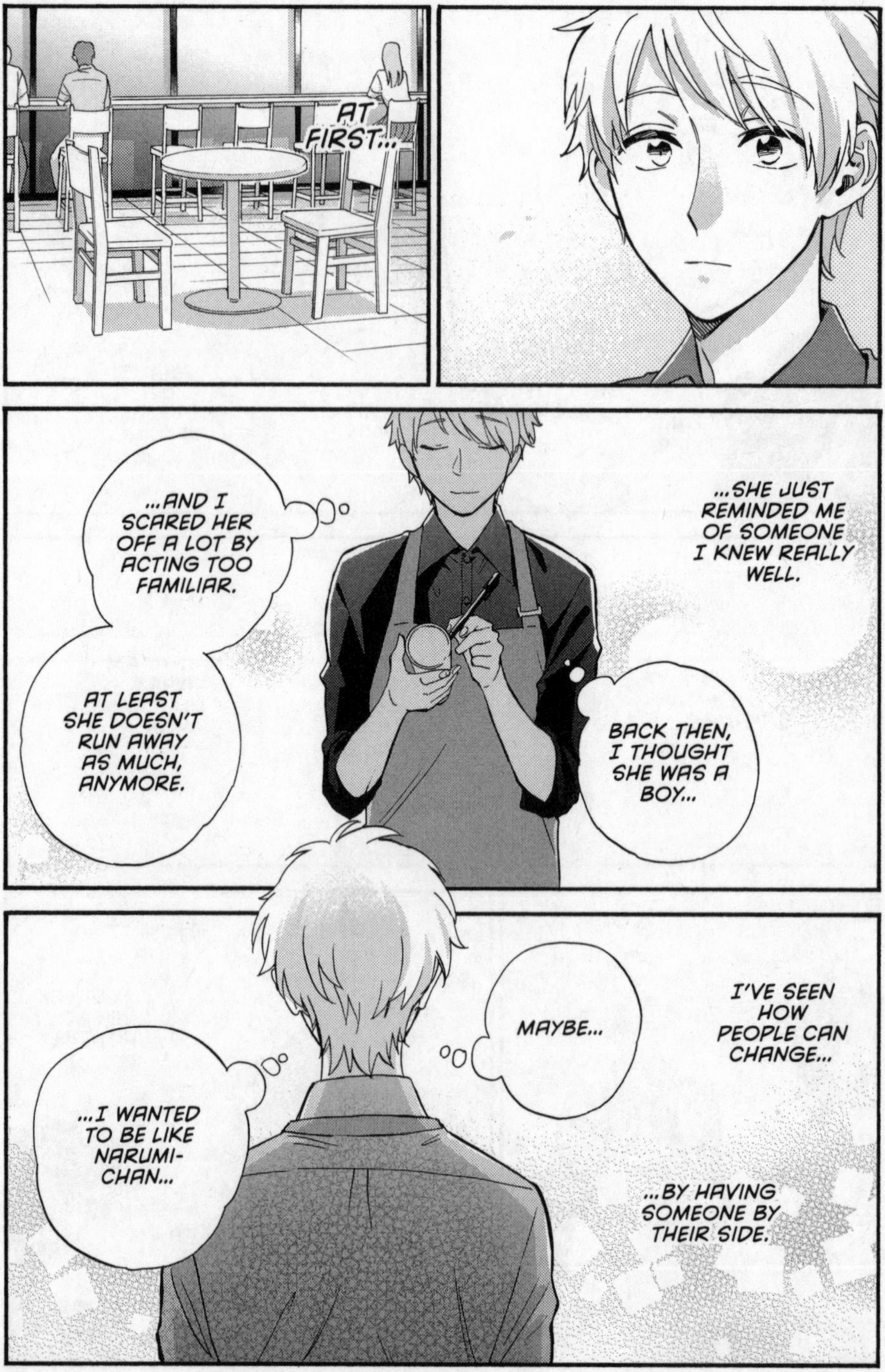
AT FIRST...
...SHE JUST REMINDED ME OF SOMEONE I KNEW REALLY WELL.
BACK THEN, I THOUGHT SHE WAS A BOY...
...AND I SCARED HER OFF A LOT BY ACTING TOO FAMILIAR.
AT LEAST SHE DOESN'T RUN AWAY AS MUCH, ANYMORE.
I'VE SEEN HOW PEOPLE CAN CHANGE...
...BY HAVING SOMEONE BY THEIR SIDE.
MAYBE...
...I WANTED TO BE LIKE NARUMI-CHAN...

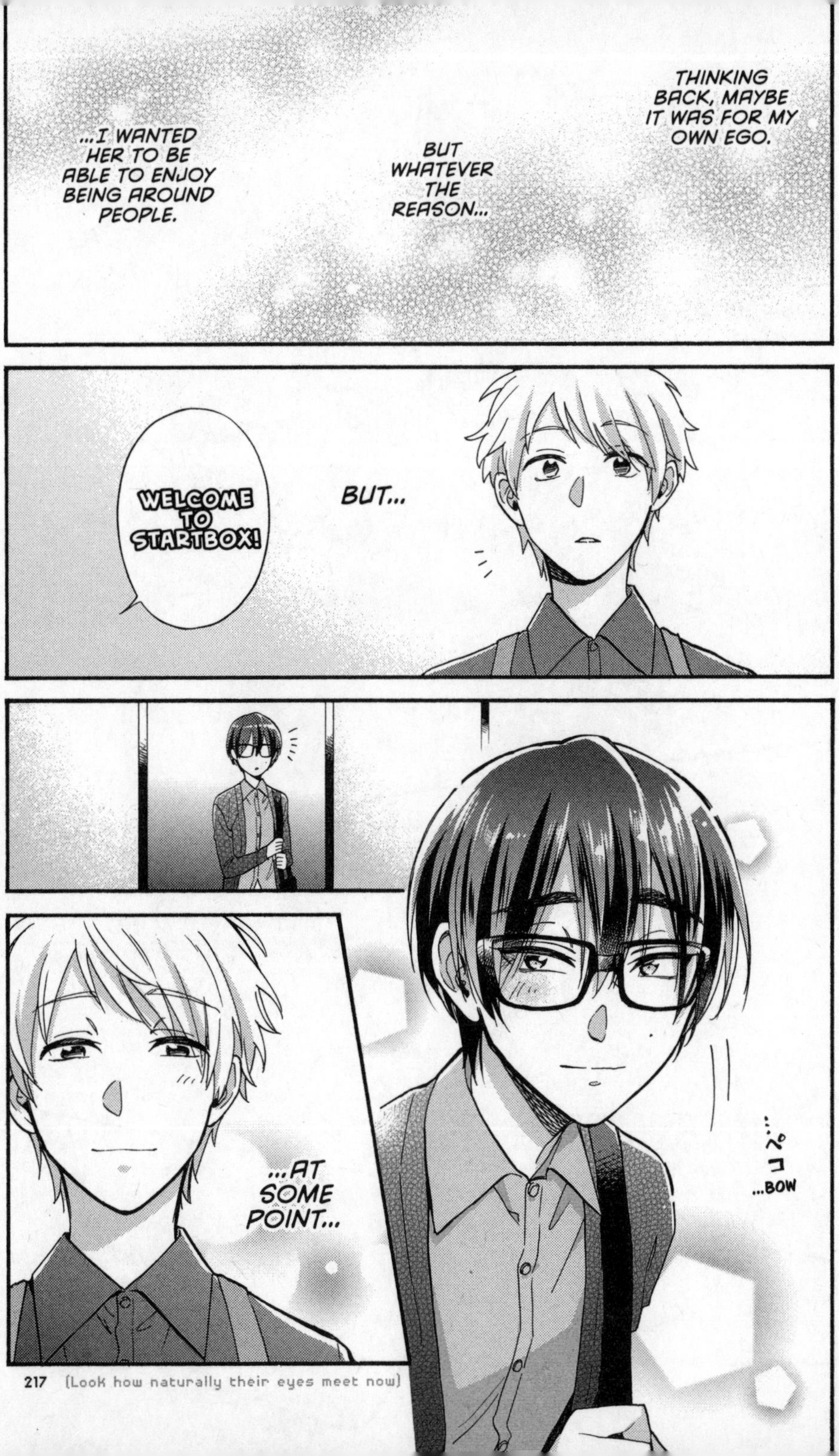
THINKING BACK, MAYBE IT WAS FOR MY OWN EGO.
BUT WHATEVER THE REASON...
...I WANTED HER TO BE ABLE TO ENJOY BEING AROUND PEOPLE.
BUT...
WELCOME TO STARTBOX!
...ペコ
...BOW
...AT SOME POINT...

 (Look how naturally their eyes meet now)

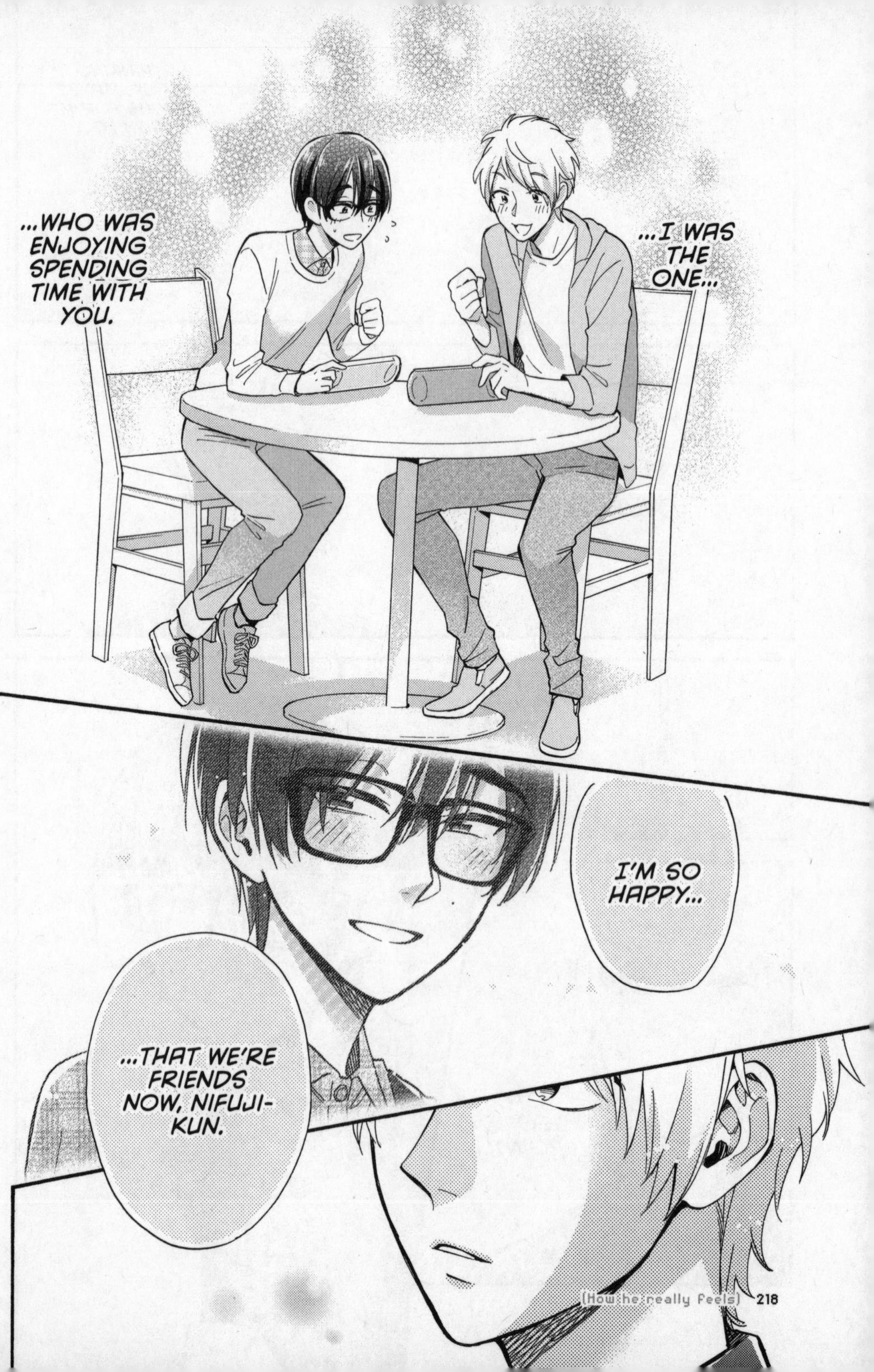
...I WAS THE ONE...
...WHO WAS ENJOYING SPENDING TIME WITH YOU.
I'M SO HAPPY...
...THAT WE'RE FRIENDS NOW, NIFUJI-KUN.

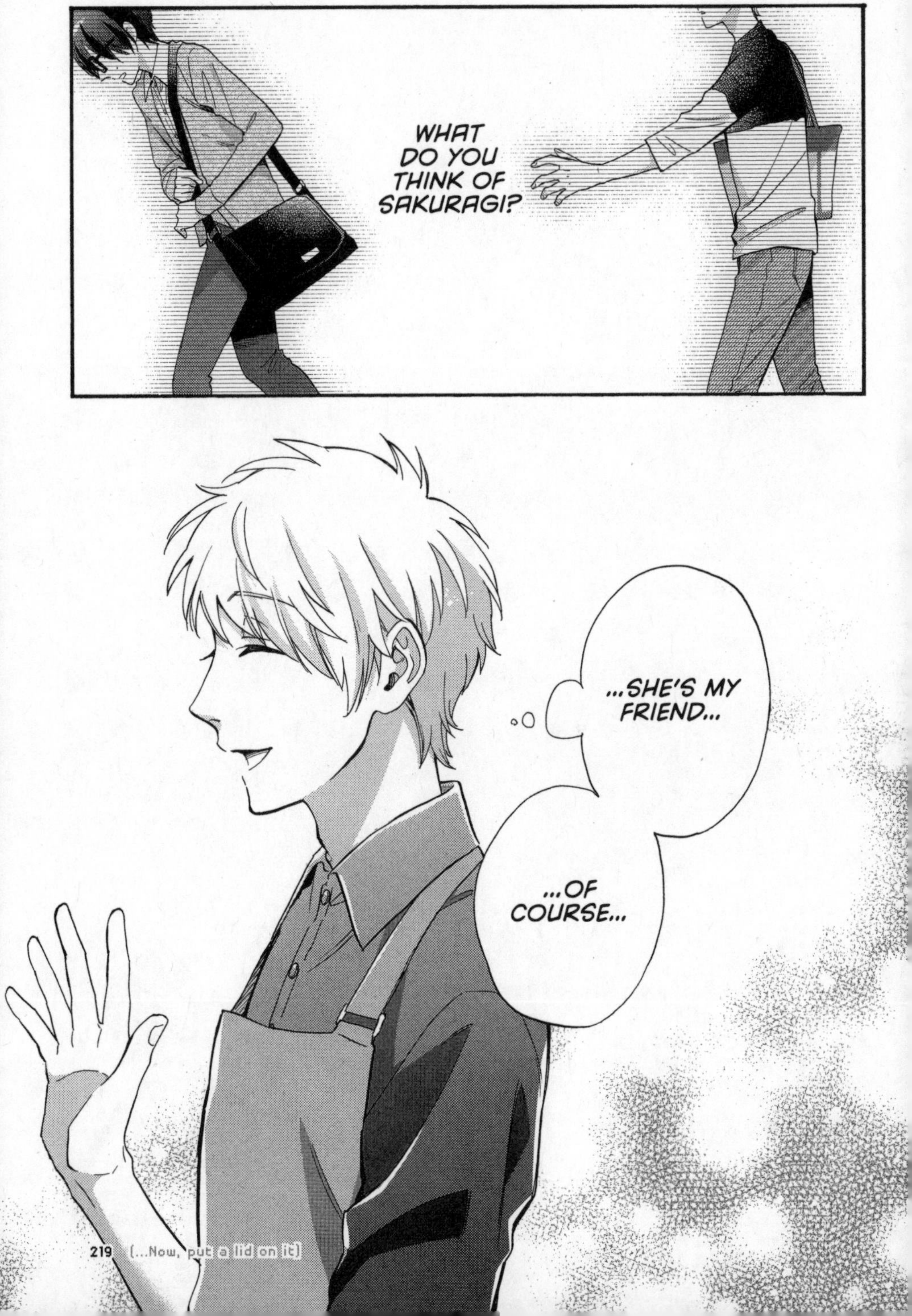
WHAT DO YOU THINK OF SAKURAGI?
...SHE'S MY FRIEND...
...OF COURSE...

UM... THIS ONE, PLEASE...
ONE DARK MOCHA CHIP FRAPPUCCINO.

THE TYPE THAT NEVER READS OUT THEIR ORDER

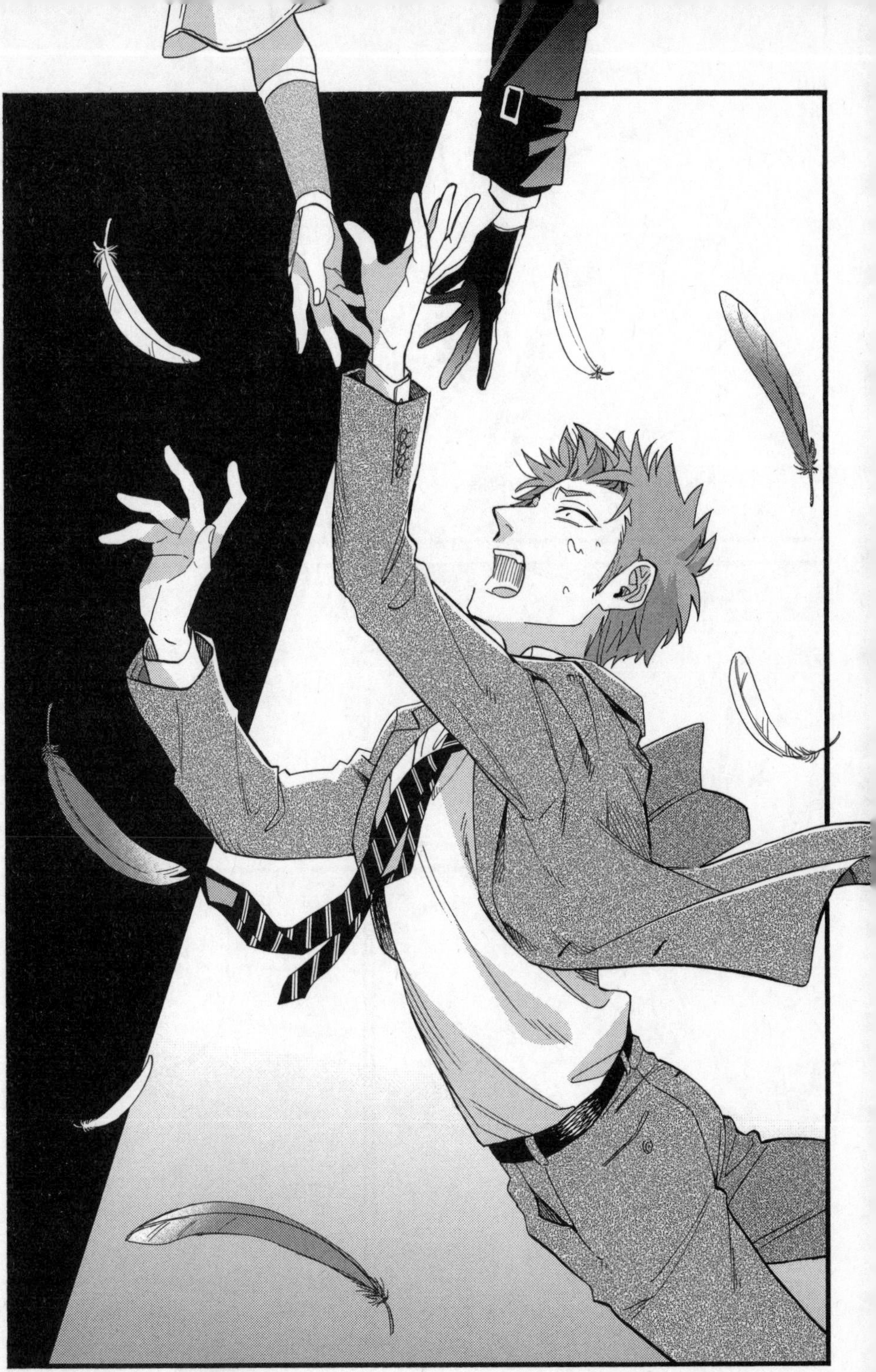

Episode....60

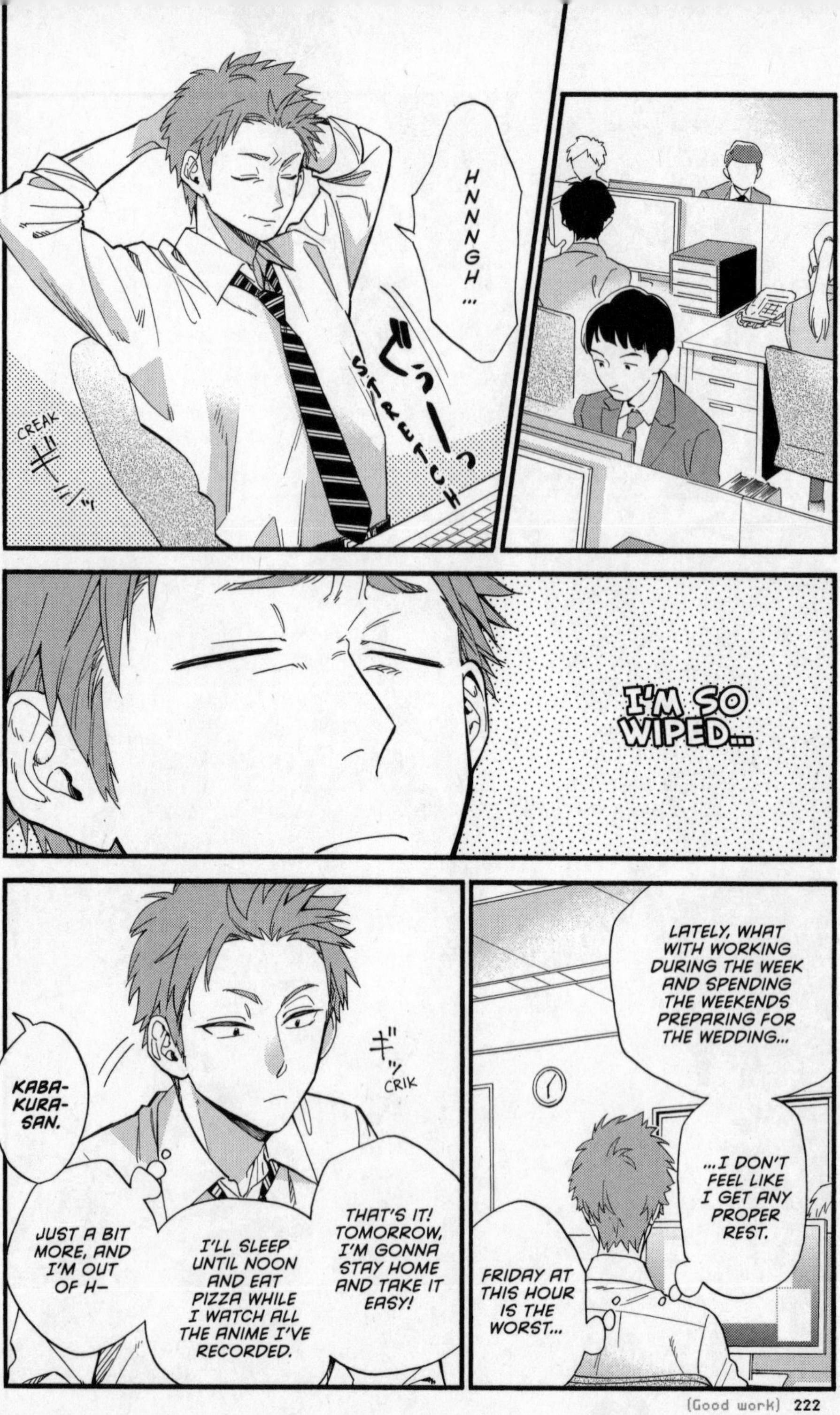
HNNNGH...
STRETCH
CREAK
I'M SO WIPED...
LATELY, WHAT WITH WORKING DURING THE WEEK AND SPENDING THE WEEKENDS PREPARING FOR THE WEDDING...
...I DON'T FEEL LIKE I GET ANY PROPER REST.
FRIDAY AT THIS HOUR IS THE WORST...
CRIK
THAT'S IT! TOMORROW, I'M GONNA STAY HOME AND TAKE IT EASY!
I'LL SLEEP UNTIL NOON AND EAT PIZZA WHILE I WATCH ALL THE ANIME I'VE RECORDED.
JUST A BIT MORE, AND I'M OUT OF H—
KABAKURA-SAN.

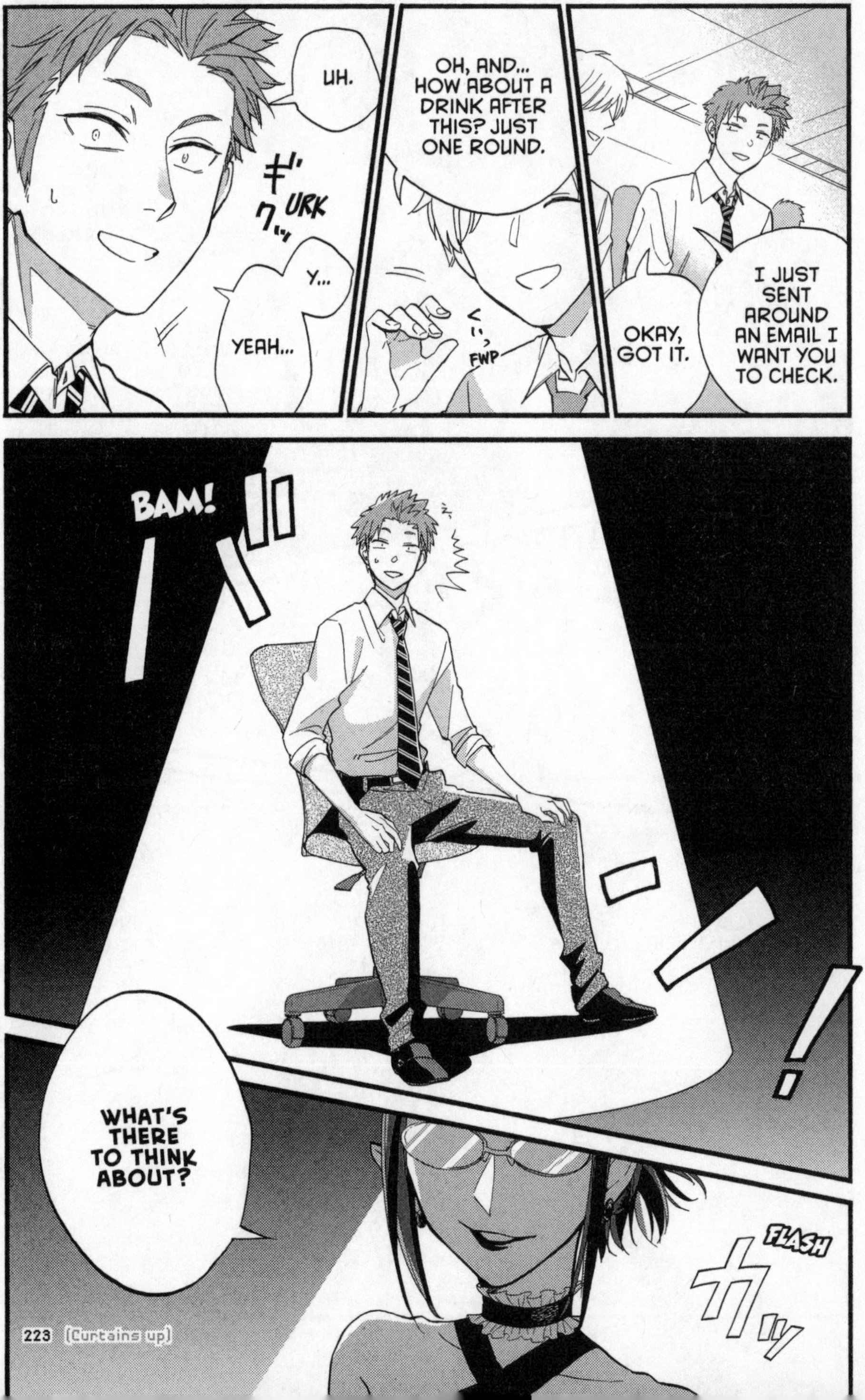
I JUST SENT AROUND AN EMAIL I WANT YOU TO CHECK.
OKAY, GOT IT.
OH, AND... HOW ABOUT A DRINK AFTER THIS? JUST ONE ROUND.
くいっ
FWP
UH.
ギクッ
URK
Y...
YEAH...
BAM!
カッ
FLASH
WHAT'S THERE TO THINK ABOUT?

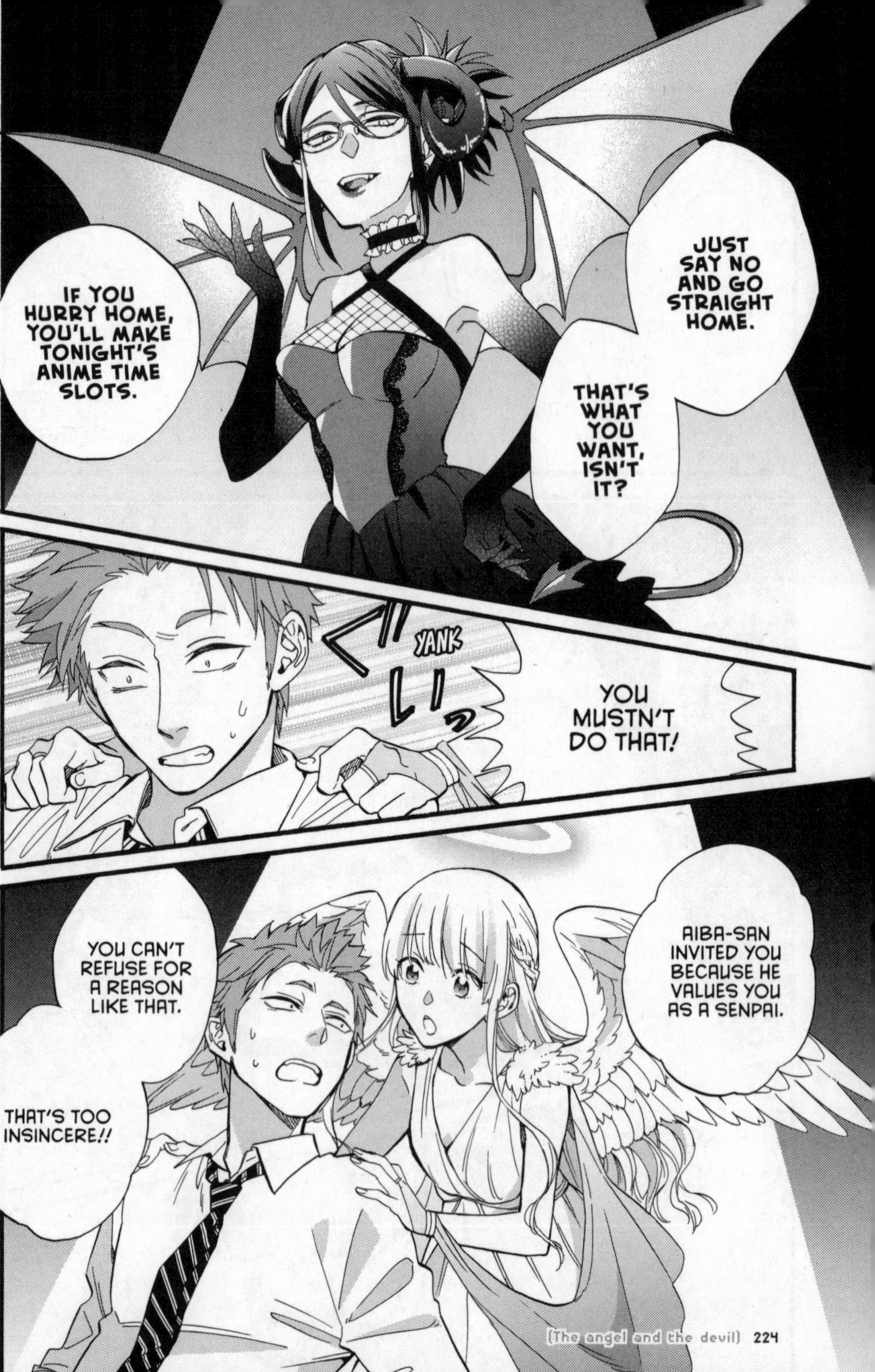
JUST SAY NO AND GO STRAIGHT HOME.
THAT'S WHAT YOU WANT, ISN'T IT?
IF YOU HURRY HOME, YOU'LL MAKE TONIGHT'S ANIME TIME SLOTS.
YOU MUSTN'T DO THAT!
YANK
AIBA-SAN INVITED YOU BECAUSE HE VALUES YOU AS A SENPAI.
YOU CAN'T REFUSE FOR A REASON LIKE THAT.
THAT'S TOO INSINCERE!!

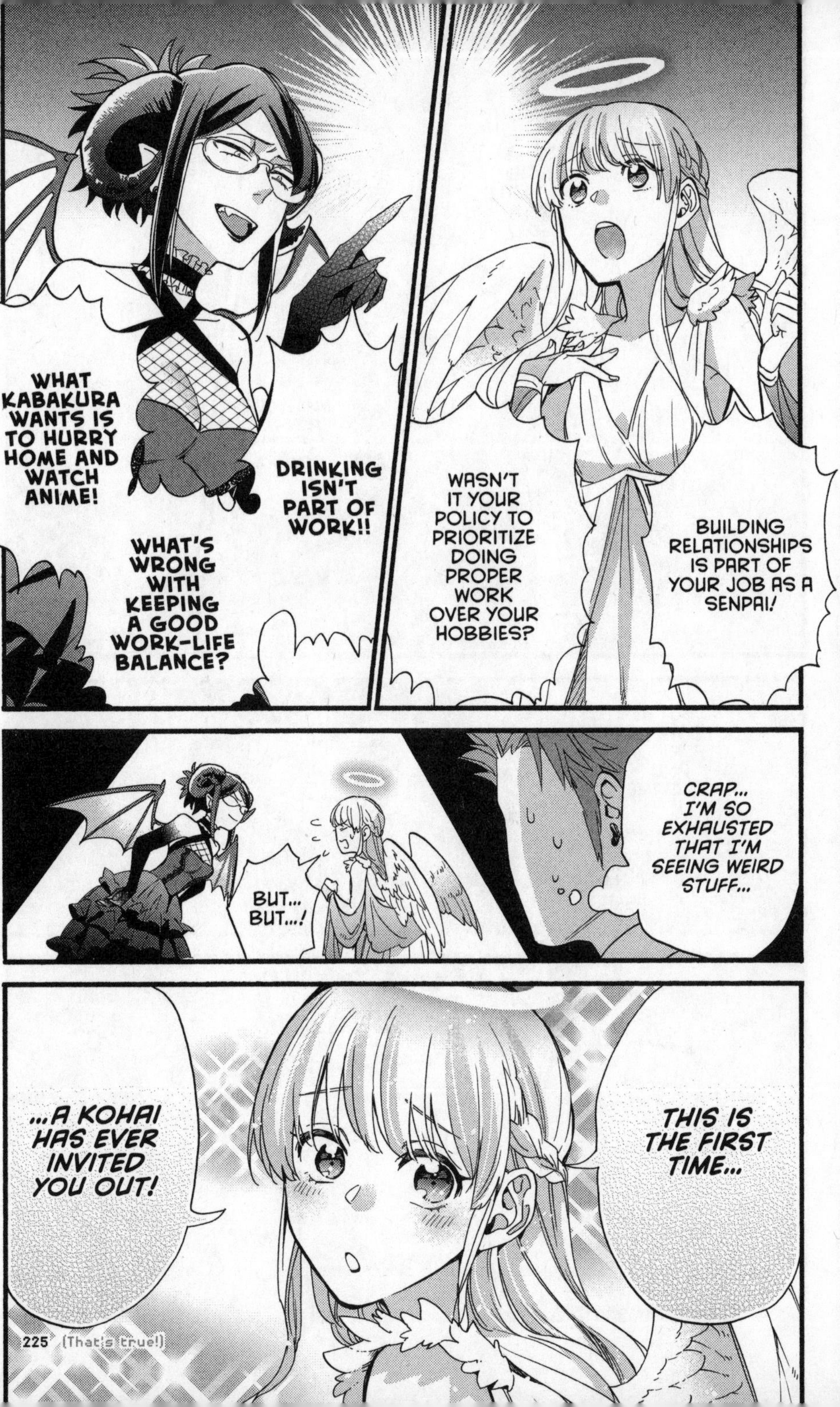
BUILDING RELATIONSHIPS IS PART OF YOUR JOB AS A SENPAI!
WASN'T IT YOUR POLICY TO PRIORITIZE DOING PROPER WORK OVER YOUR HOBBIES?
DRINKING ISN'T PART OF WORK!!
WHAT KABAKURA WANTS IS TO HURRY HOME AND WATCH ANIME!
WHAT'S WRONG WITH KEEPING A GOOD WORK-LIFE BALANCE?
CRAP... I'M SO EXHAUSTED THAT I'M SEEING WEIRD STUFF...
BUT... BUT...!
THIS IS THE FIRST TIME...
...A KOHAI HAS EVER INVITED YOU OUT!

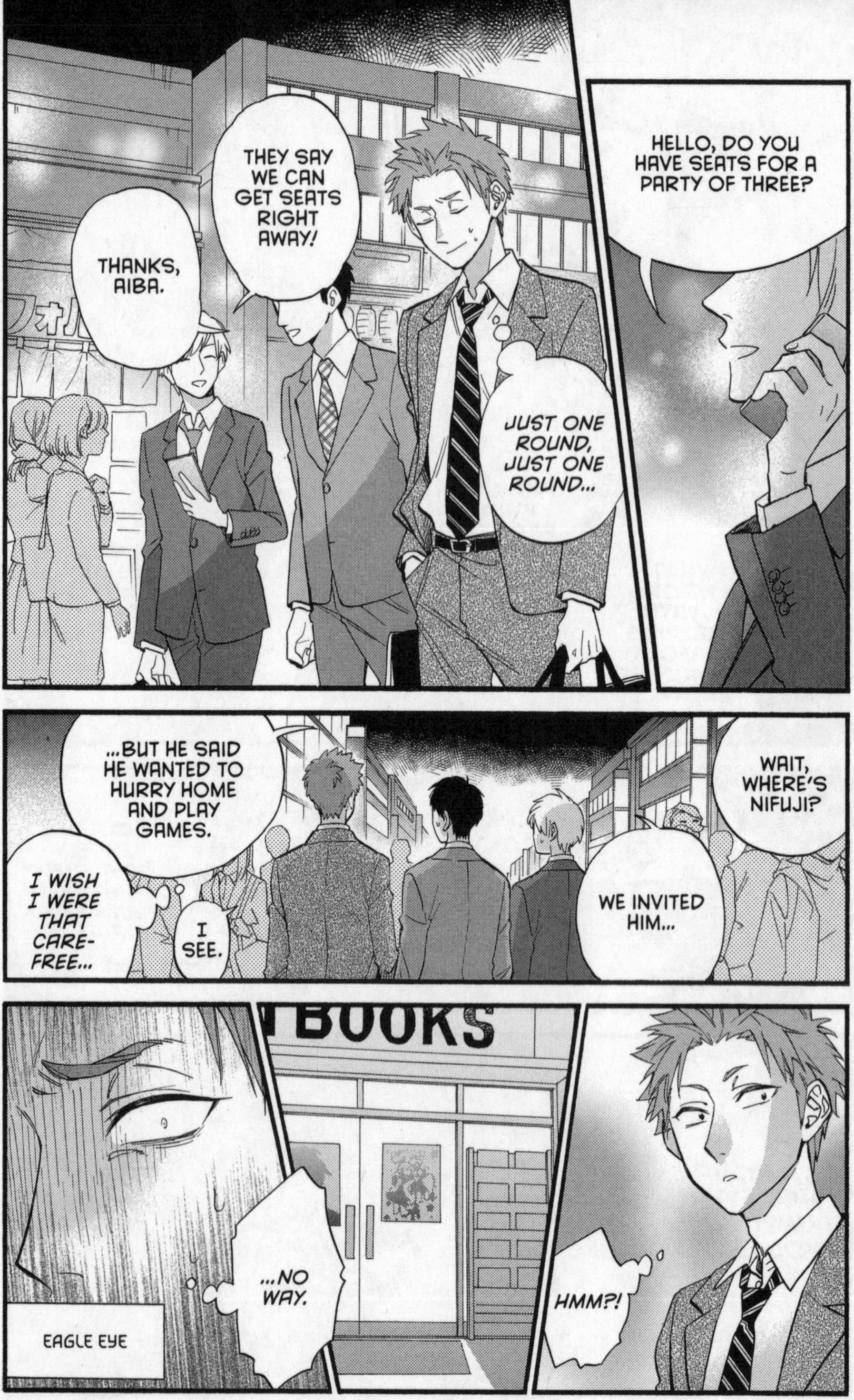
HELLO, DO YOU HAVE SEATS FOR A PARTY OF THREE?
THEY SAY WE CAN GET SEATS RIGHT AWAY!
THANKS, AIBA.
JUST ONE ROUND, JUST ONE ROUND...
WAIT, WHERE'S NIFUJI?
WE INVITED HIM...
...BUT HE SAID HE WANTED TO HURRY HOME AND PLAY GAMES.
I SEE.
I WISH I WERE THAT CAREFREE...
HMM?!
BOOKS
...NO WAY.
EAGLE EYE

(Even with tired eyes, his vision's just as sharp)

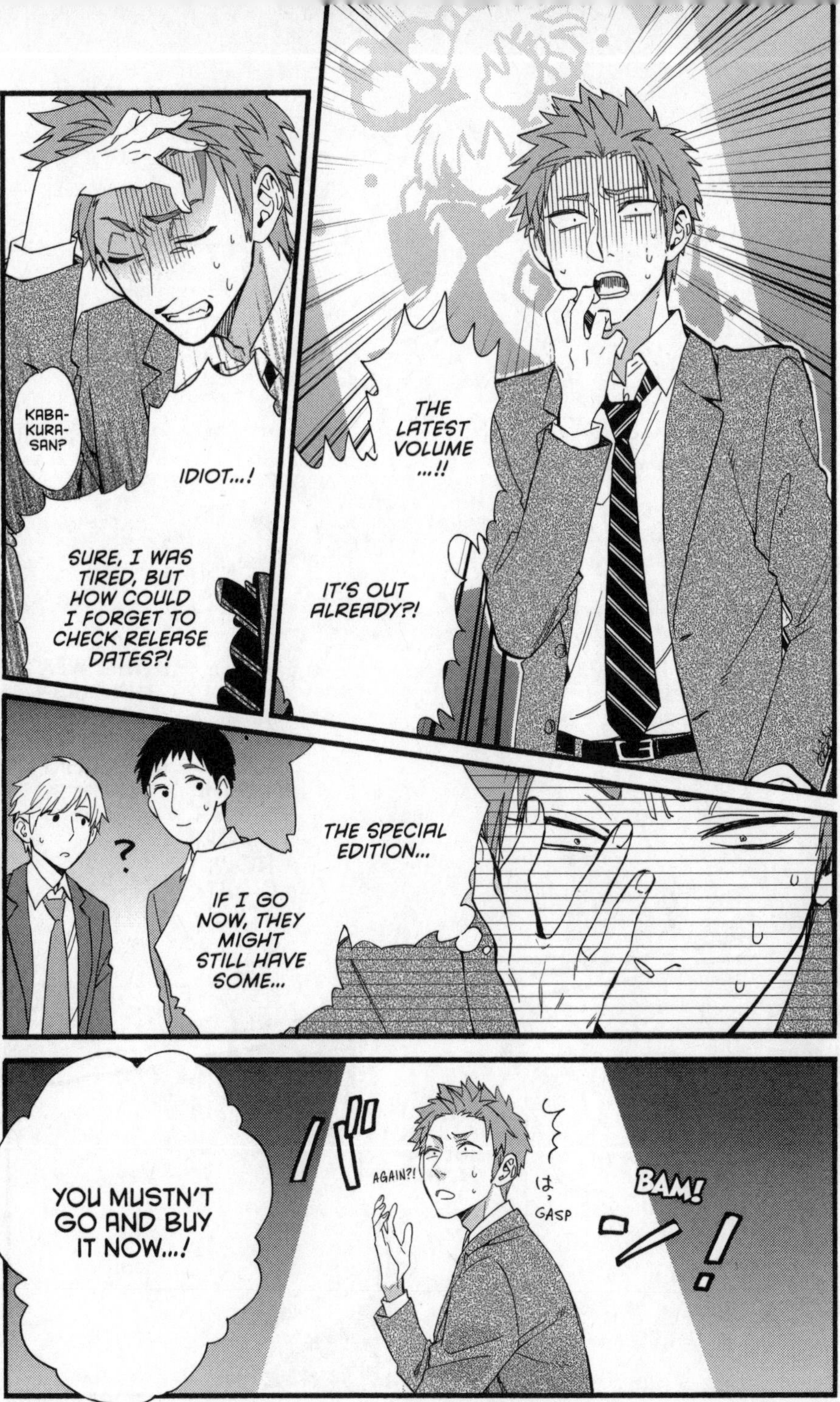
THE LATEST VOLUME ...!!
IT'S OUT ALREADY?!
KABA-KURA-SAN?
IDIOT...!
SURE, I WAS TIRED, BUT HOW COULD I FORGET TO CHECK RELEASE DATES?!
THE SPECIAL EDITION...
IF I GO NOW, THEY MIGHT STILL HAVE SOME...
?
BAM!
は
GASP
AGAIN?!
YOU MUSTN'T GO AND BUY IT NOW...!

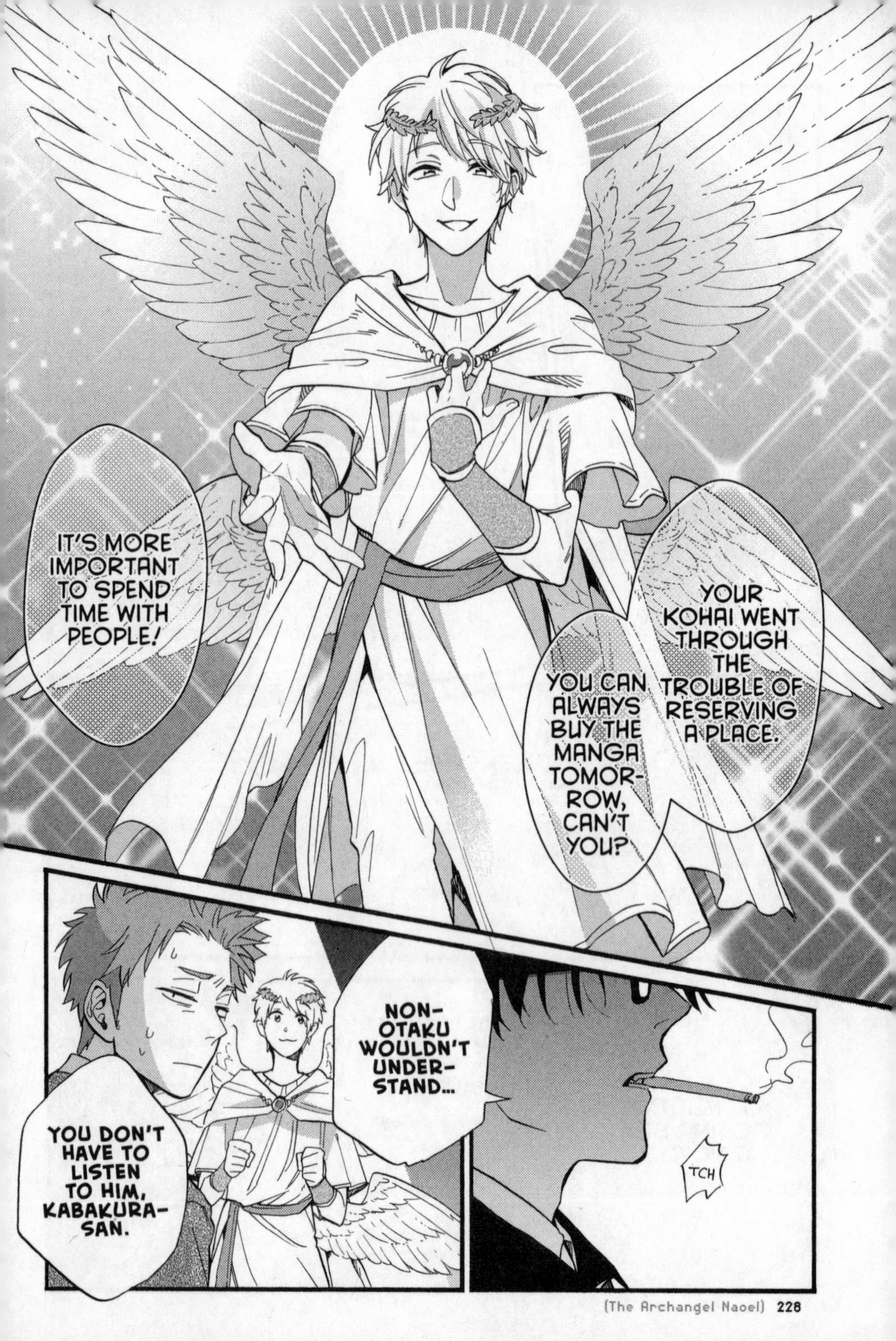
YOUR KOHAI WENT THROUGH THE TROUBLE OF RESERVING A PLACE.
YOU CAN ALWAYS BUY THE MANGA TOMORROW, CAN'T YOU?
IT'S MORE IMPORTANT TO SPEND TIME WITH PEOPLE!
TCH
NON-OTAKU WOULDN'T UNDERSTAND...
YOU DON'T HAVE TO LISTEN TO HIM, KABAKURA-SAN.

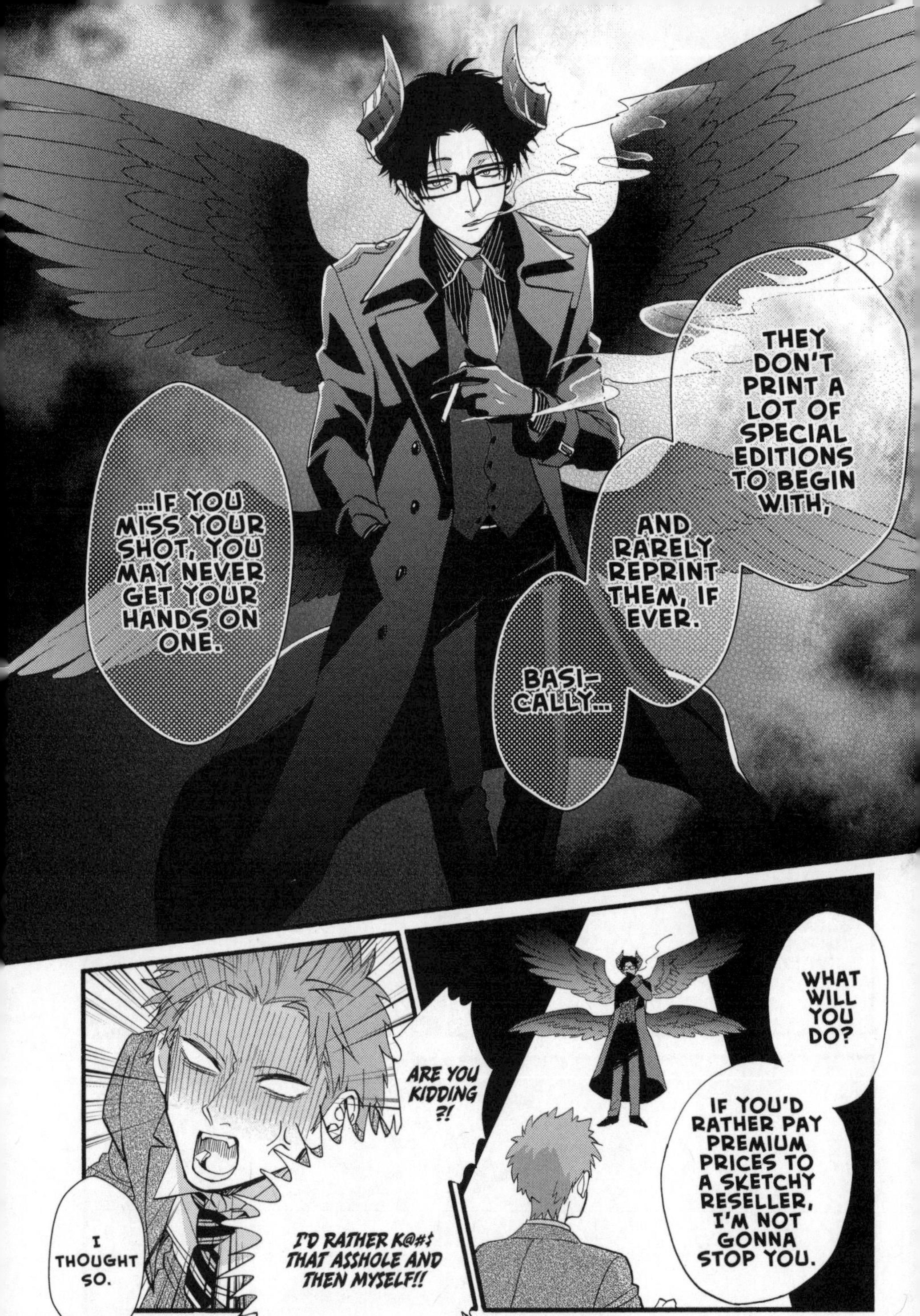
THEY DON'T PRINT A LOT OF SPECIAL EDITIONS TO BEGIN WITH,
AND RARELY REPRINT THEM, IF EVER.
BASI-CALLY...
...IF YOU MISS YOUR SHOT, YOU MAY NEVER GET YOUR HANDS ON ONE.
WHAT WILL YOU DO?
IF YOU'D RATHER PAY PREMIUM PRICES TO A SKETCHY RESELLER, I'M NOT GONNA STOP YOU.
ARE YOU KIDDING?!
I'D RATHER K@#$ THAT ASSHOLE AND THEN MYSELF!!
I THOUGHT SO.

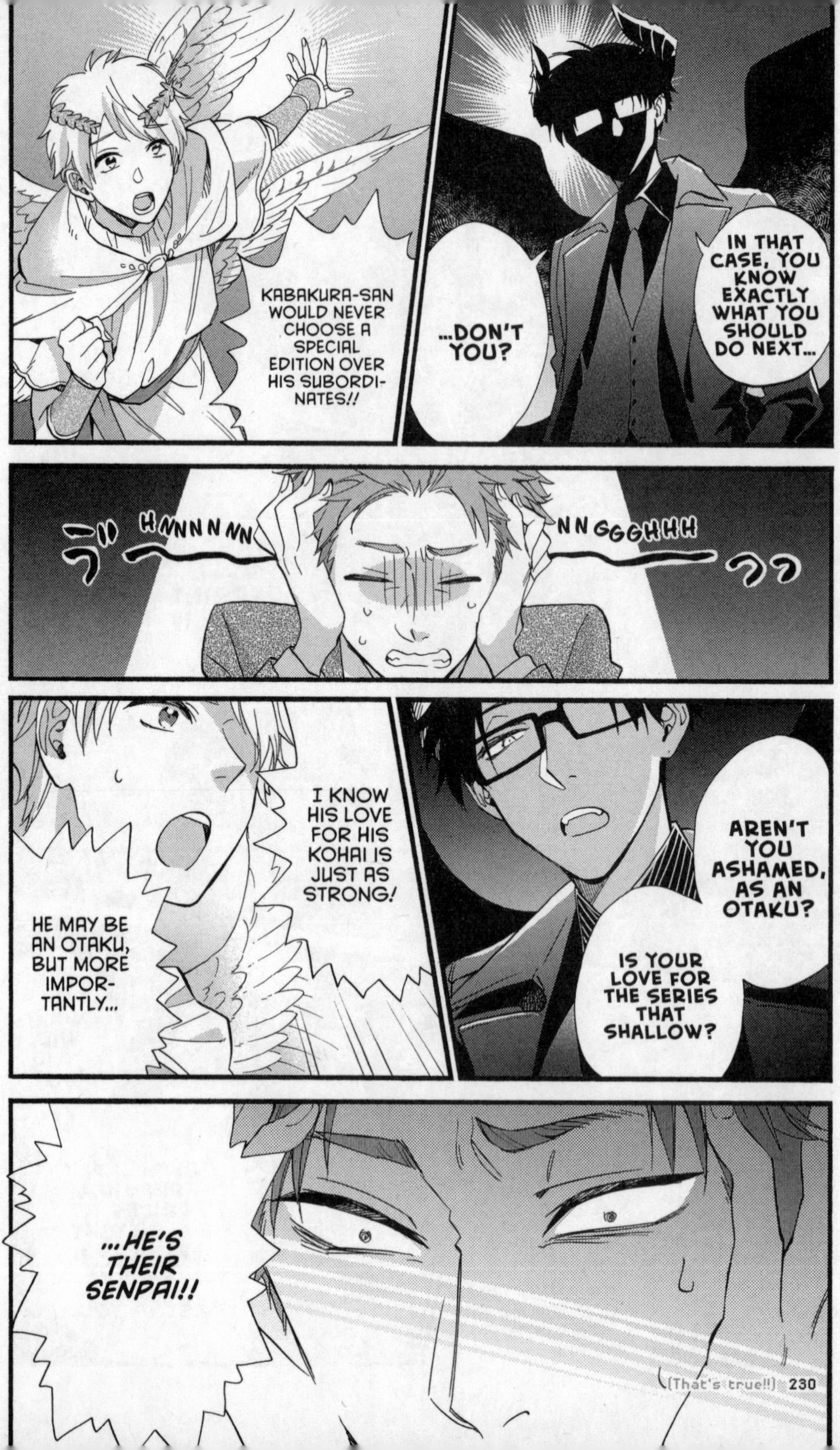
IN THAT CASE, YOU KNOW EXACTLY WHAT YOU SHOULD DO NEXT...
...DON'T YOU?
KABAKURA-SAN WOULD NEVER CHOOSE A SPECIAL EDITION OVER HIS SUBORDINATES!!
HNNNNNN
NNGGGHHH
AREN'T YOU ASHAMED, AS AN OTAKU?
IS YOUR LOVE FOR THE SERIES THAT SHALLOW?
I KNOW HIS LOVE FOR HIS KOHAI IS JUST AS STRONG!
HE MAY BE AN OTAKU, BUT MORE IMPORTANTLY...
...HE'S THEIR SENPAI!!
(That's true!!)

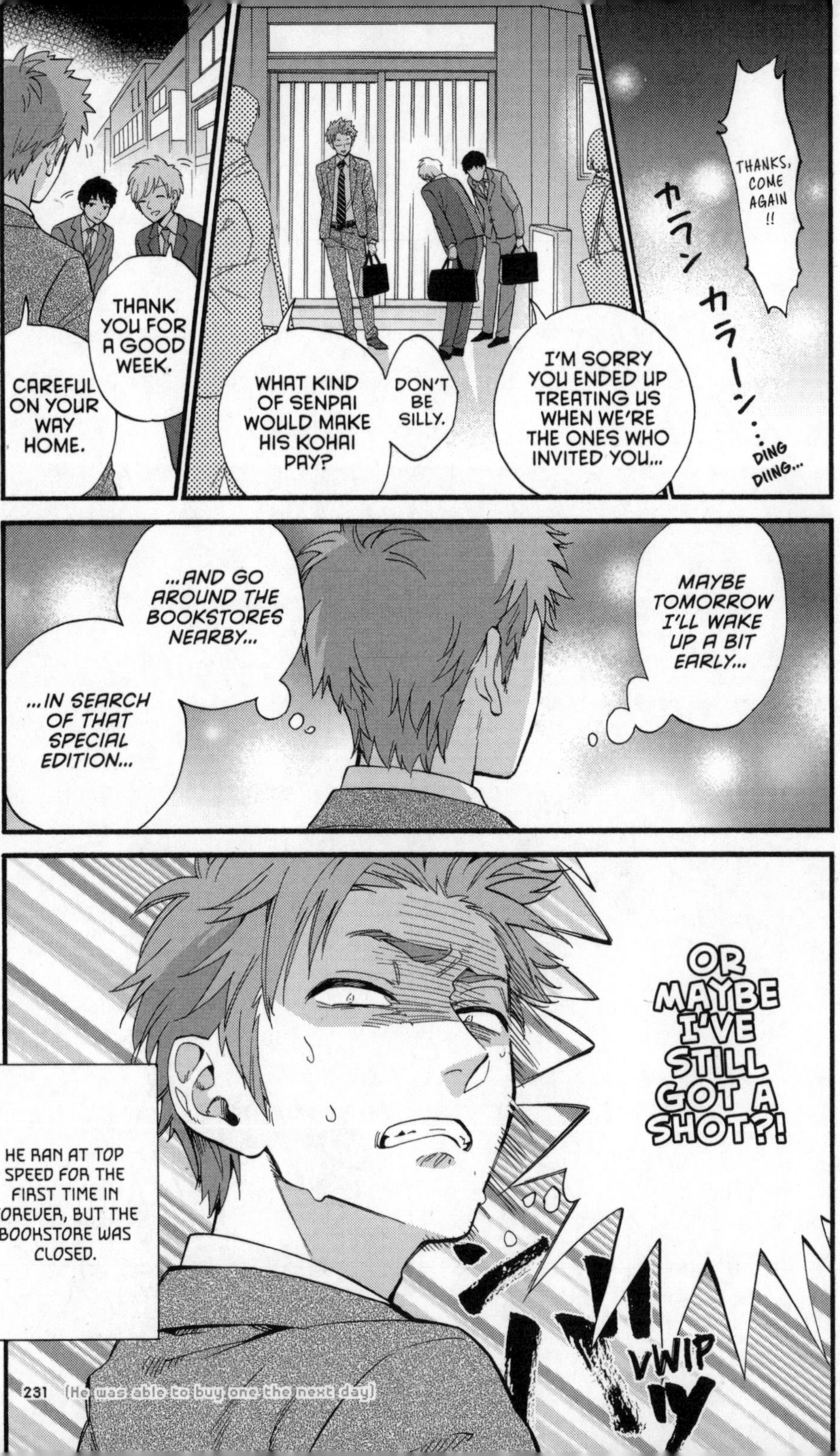
THANKS, COME AGAIN !!
カラン カラーン…
DING DIING...
I'M SORRY YOU ENDED UP TREATING US WHEN WE'RE THE ONES WHO INVITED YOU...
DON'T BE SILLY.
WHAT KIND OF SENPAI WOULD MAKE HIS KOHAI PAY?
THANK YOU FOR A GOOD WEEK.
CAREFUL ON YOUR WAY HOME.
MAYBE TOMORROW I'LL WAKE UP A BIT EARLY...
...AND GO AROUND THE BOOKSTORES NEARBY...
...IN SEARCH OF THAT SPECIAL EDITION...
OR MAYBE I'VE STILL GOT A SHOT?!
VWIP
HE RAN AT TOP SPEED FOR THE FIRST TIME IN FOREVER, BUT THE BOOKSTORE WAS CLOSED.
(He was able to buy one the next day)

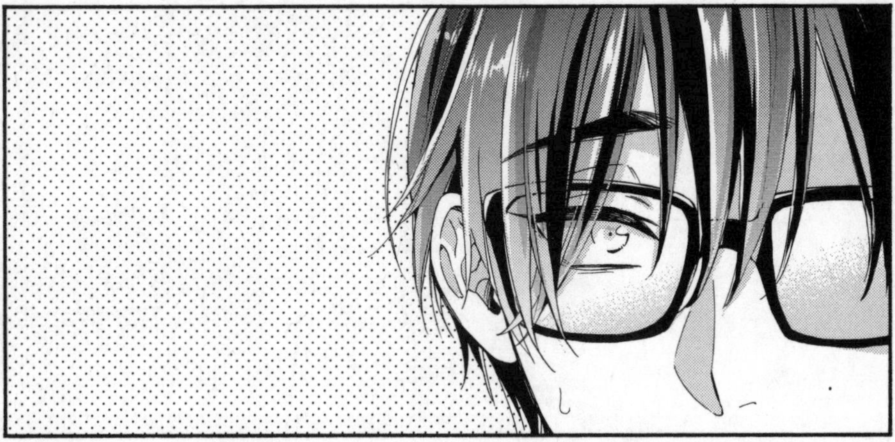

Episode.... 61

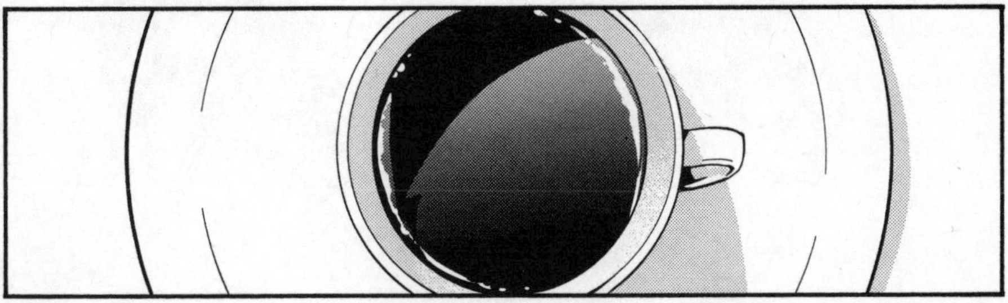

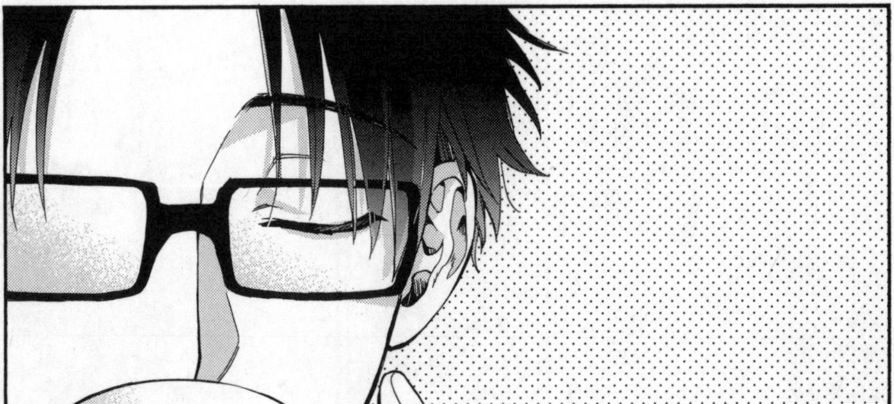

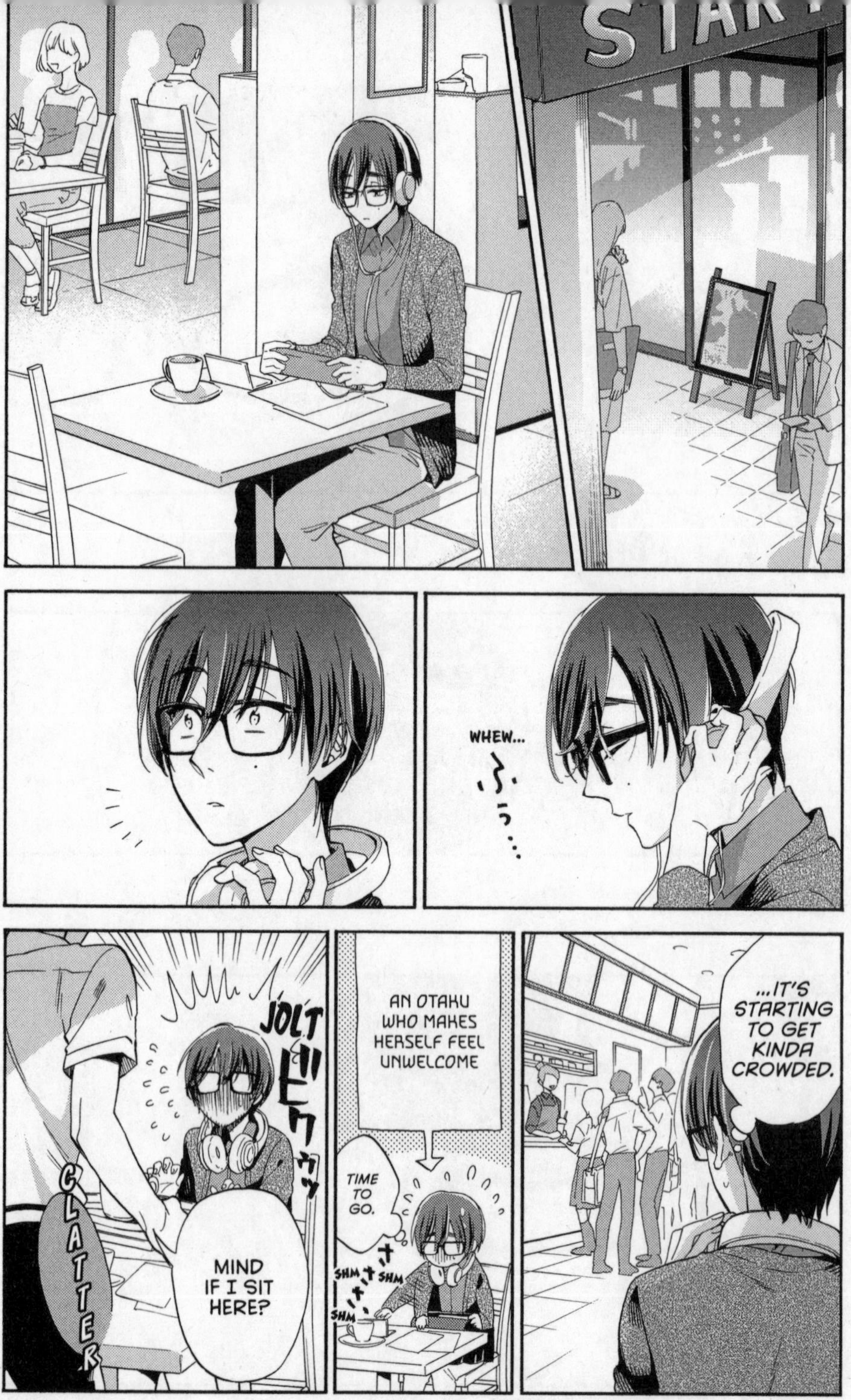
WHEW...
ふぅ…
...IT'S STARTING TO GET KINDA CROWDED.
AN OTAKU WHO MAKES HERSELF FEEL UNWELCOME
TIME TO GO.
SHM SHM SHM
JOLT
MIND IF I SIT HERE?
CLATTER

(Taking up space alone for too long feels wrong)

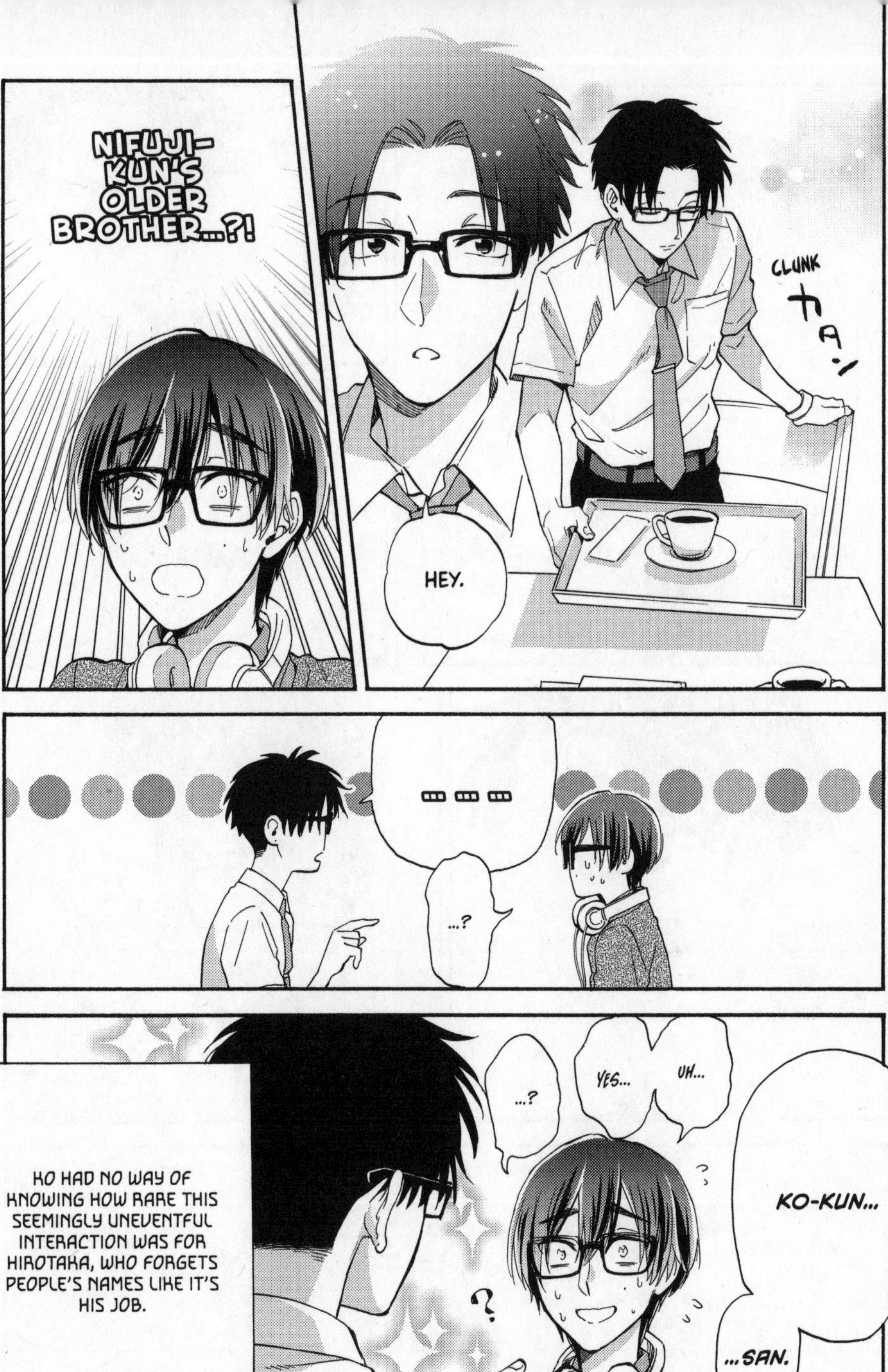
CLUNK
HEY.
NIFUJI-KUN'S OLDER BROTHER...?!
... ...
...?
KO-KUN...
...SAN.
UH...
YES...
...?
KO HAD NO WAY OF KNOWING HOW RARE THIS SEEMINGLY UNEVENTFUL INTERACTION WAS FOR HIROTAKA, WHO FORGETS PEOPLE'S NAMES LIKE IT'S HIS JOB.

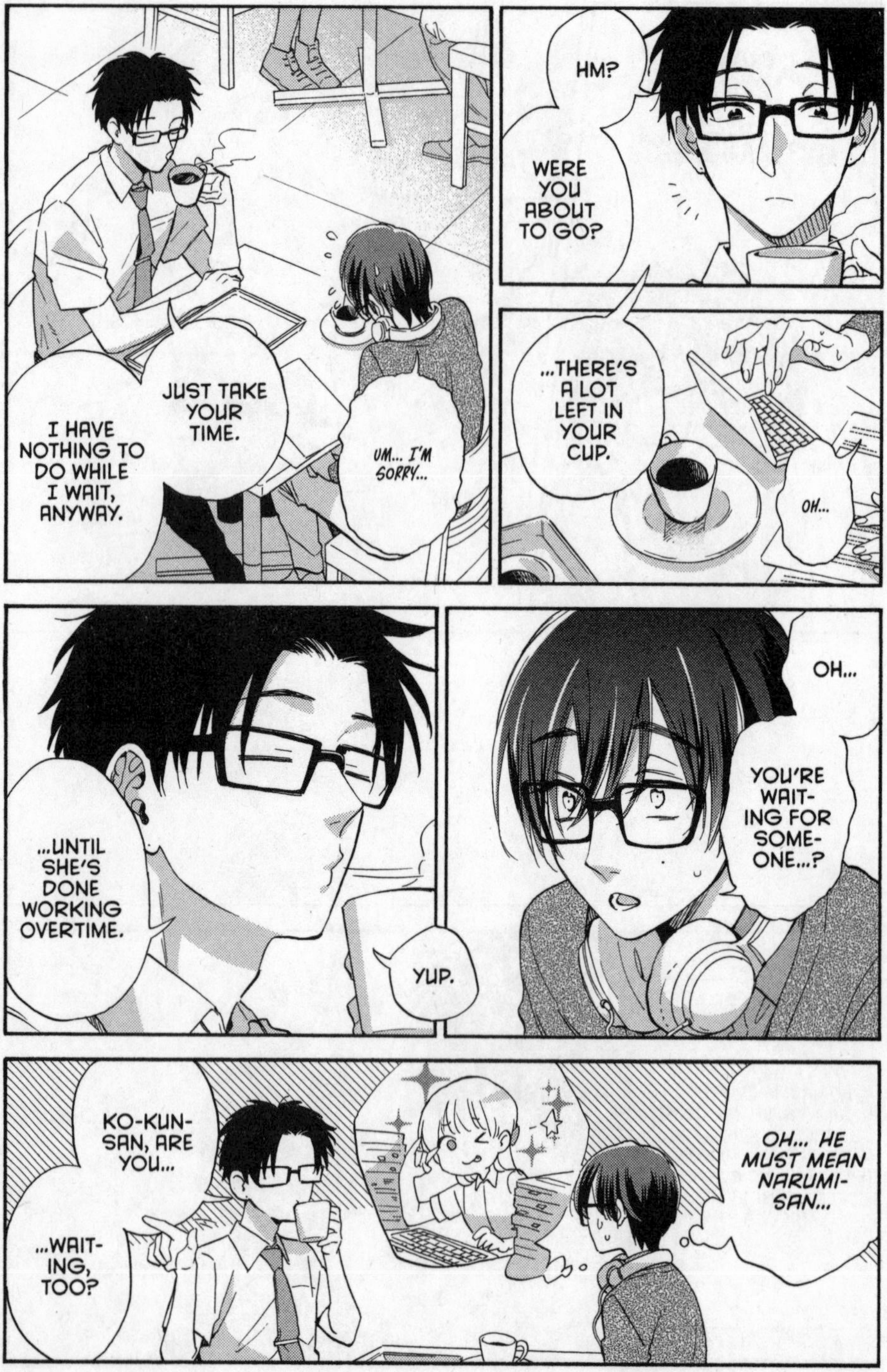
HM?
WERE YOU ABOUT TO GO?
...THERE'S A LOT LEFT IN YOUR CUP.
OH...
UM... I'M SORRY...
JUST TAKE YOUR TIME.
I HAVE NOTHING TO DO WHILE I WAIT, ANYWAY.
OH...
YOU'RE WAITING FOR SOMEONE...?
YUP.
...UNTIL SHE'S DONE WORKING OVERTIME.
OH... HE MUST MEAN NARUMI-SAN...
KO-KUN-SAN, ARE YOU...
...WAITING, TOO?

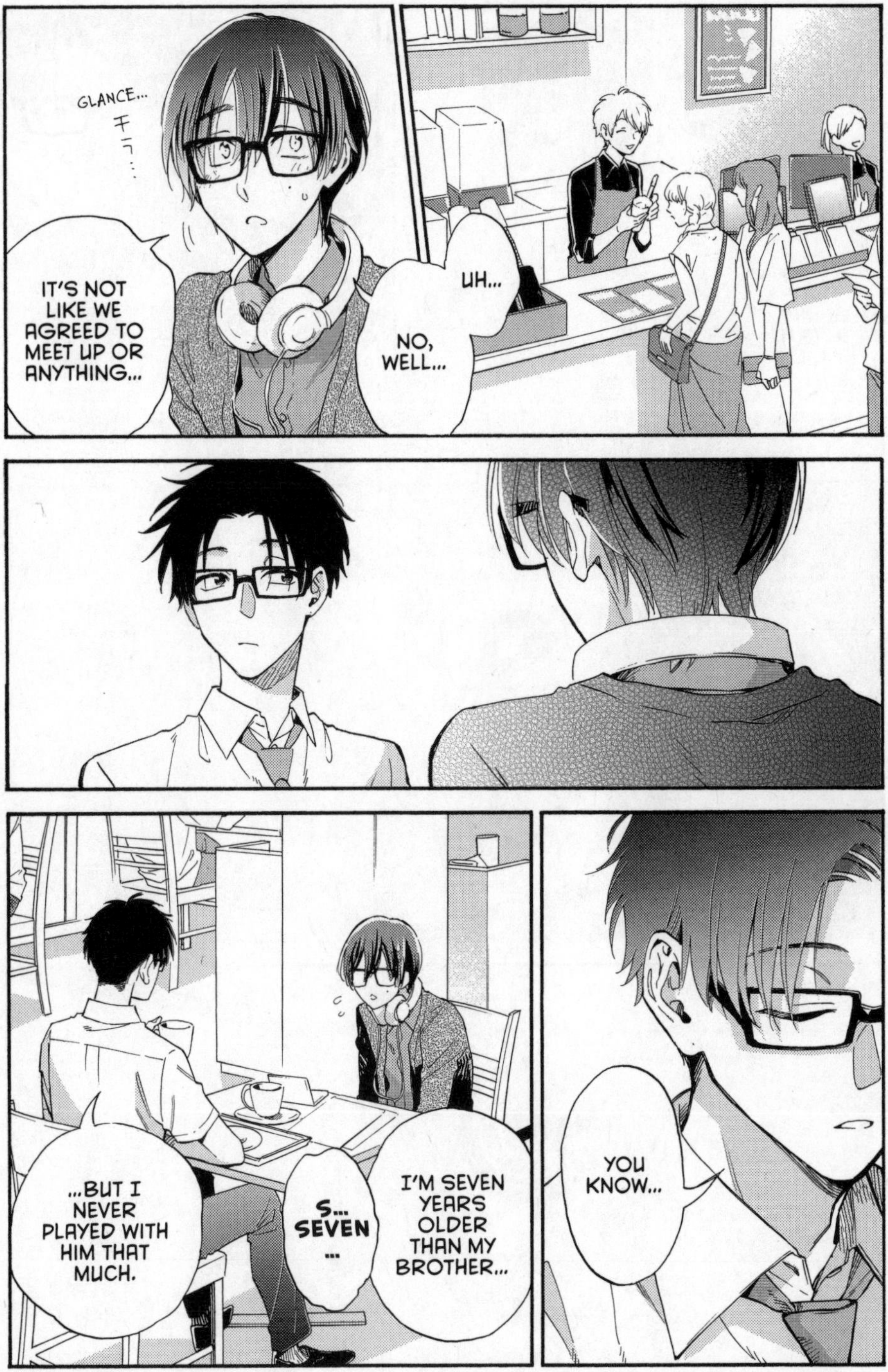
UH...
NO, WELL...
GLANCE...
チラ…
IT'S NOT LIKE WE AGREED TO MEET UP OR ANYTHING...
YOU KNOW...
I'M SEVEN YEARS OLDER THAN MY BROTHER...
S... SEVEN ...
...BUT I NEVER PLAYED WITH HIM THAT MUCH.

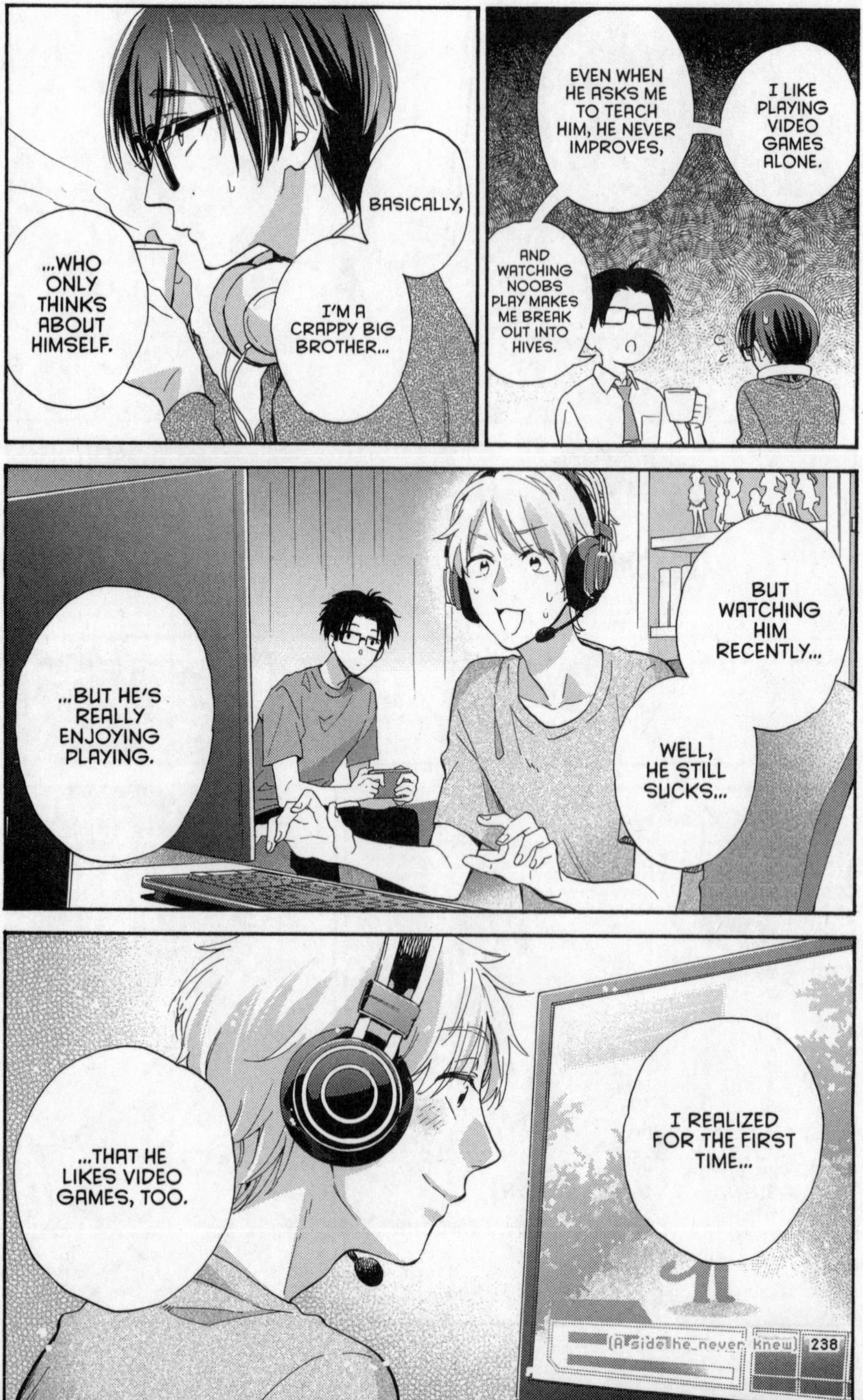
I LIKE PLAYING VIDEO GAMES ALONE.
EVEN WHEN HE ASKS ME TO TEACH HIM, HE NEVER IMPROVES,
AND WATCHING NOOBS PLAY MAKES ME BREAK OUT INTO HIVES.
BASICALLY,
I'M A CRAPPY BIG BROTHER...
...WHO ONLY THINKS ABOUT HIMSELF.
BUT WATCHING HIM RECENTLY...
WELL, HE STILL SUCKS...
...BUT HE'S REALLY ENJOYING PLAYING.
I REALIZED FOR THE FIRST TIME...
...THAT HE LIKES VIDEO GAMES, TOO.
[A side he_never knew] 238

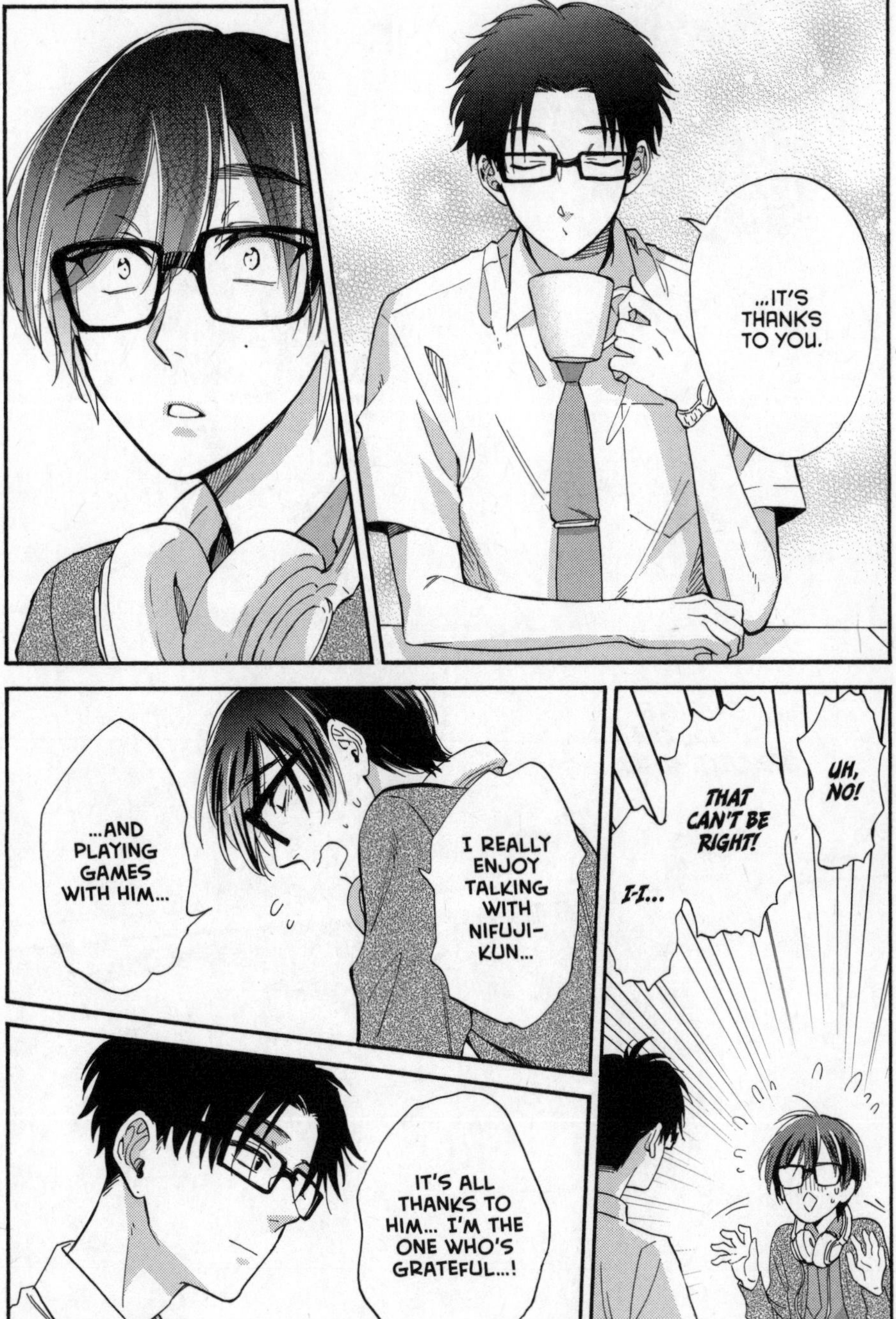
...IT'S THANKS TO YOU.
UH, NO!
THAT CAN'T BE RIGHT!
I-I...
I REALLY ENJOY TALKING WITH NIFUJI-KUN...
...AND PLAYING GAMES WITH HIM...
IT'S ALL THANKS TO HIM... I'M THE ONE WHO'S GRATEFUL...!

 (He's done so much more for me)

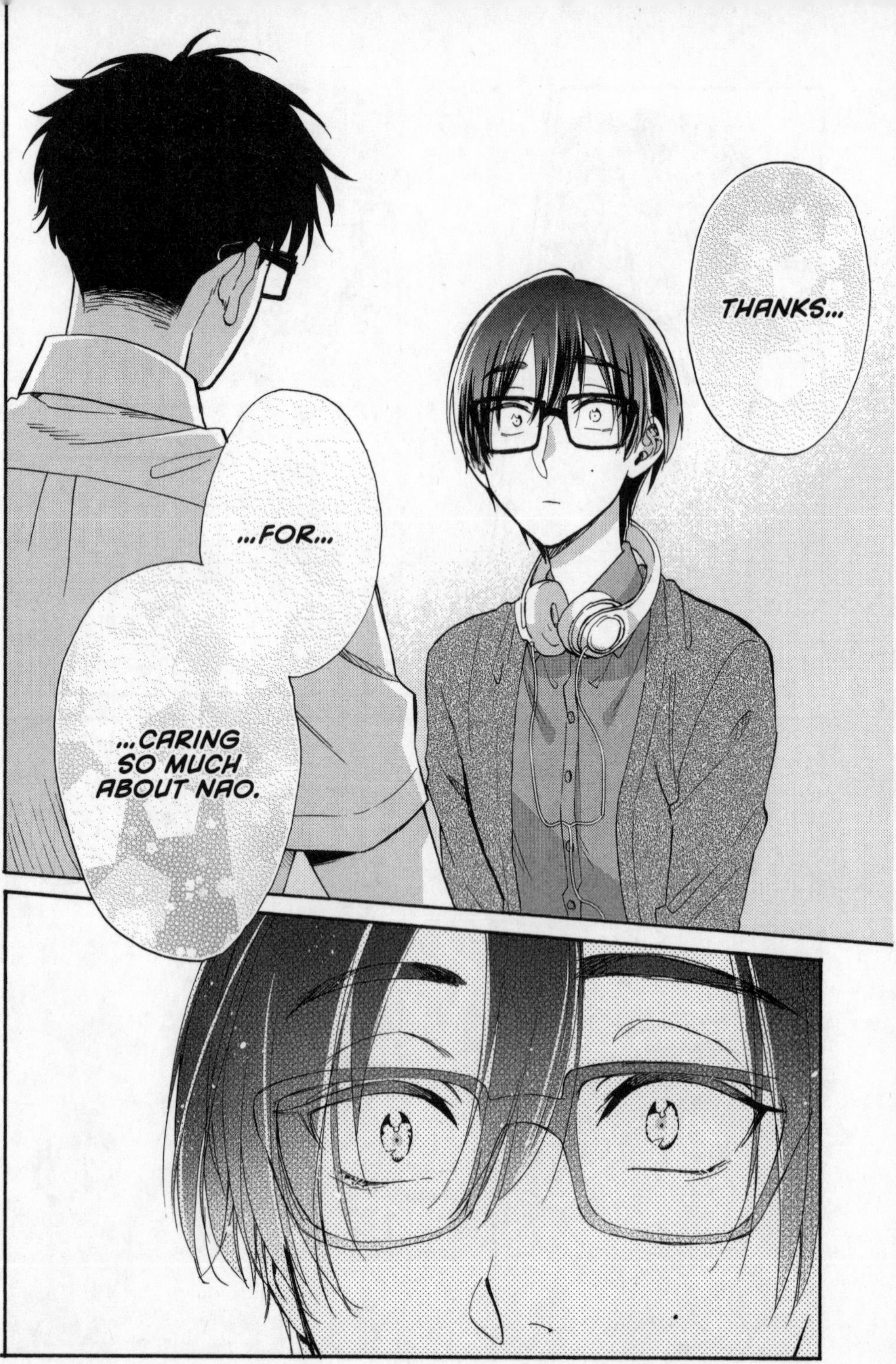
THANKS...
...FOR...
...CARING SO MUCH ABOUT NAO.

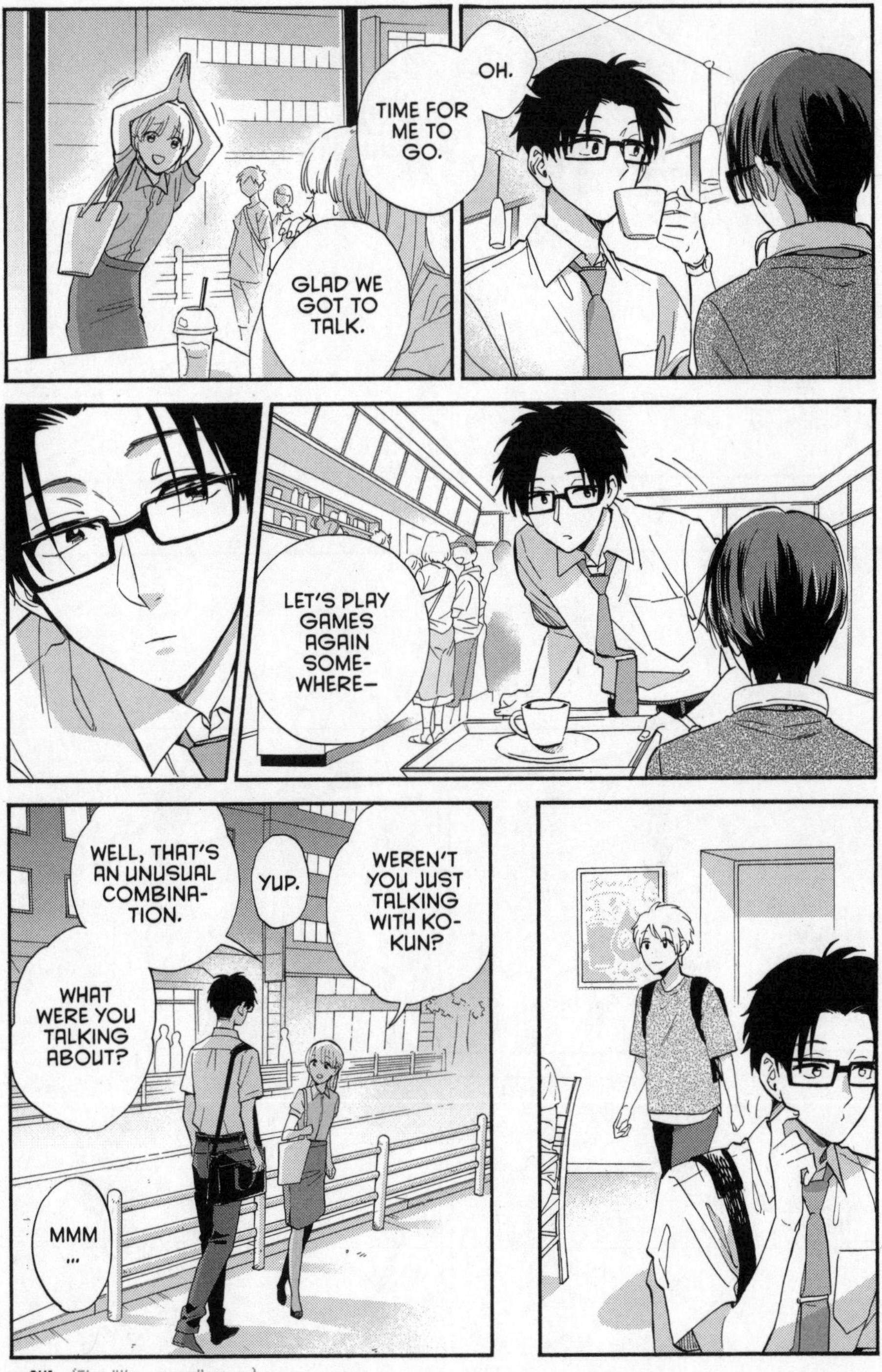

OH.
TIME FOR ME TO GO.
GLAD WE GOT TO TALK.
LET'S PLAY GAMES AGAIN SOME-WHERE—
WEREN'T YOU JUST TALKING WITH KO-KUN?
YUP.
WELL, THAT'S AN UNUSUAL COMBINA-TION.
WHAT WERE YOU TALKING ABOUT?
MMM ...

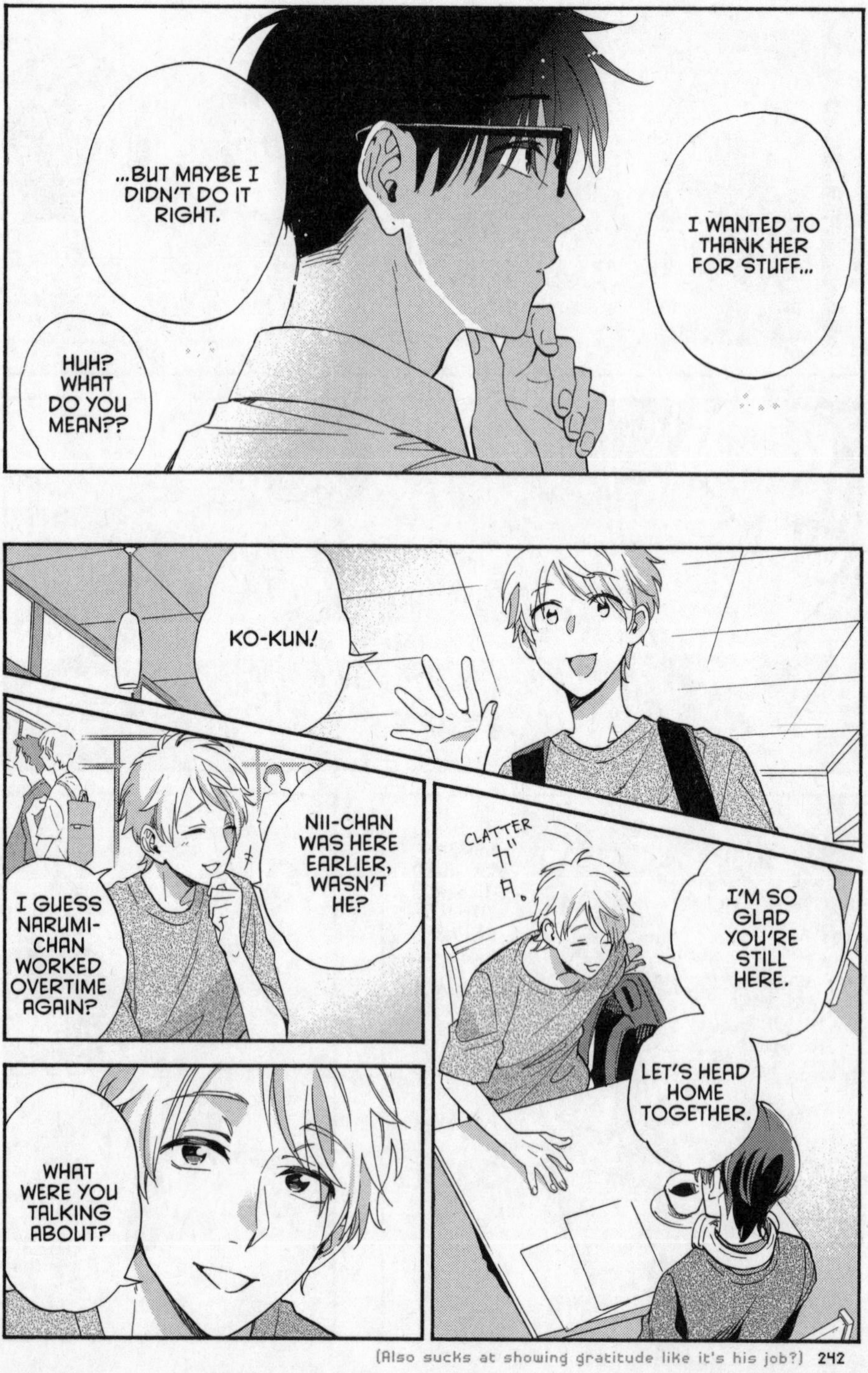
I WANTED TO THANK HER FOR STUFF...
...BUT MAYBE I DIDN'T DO IT RIGHT.
HUH? WHAT DO YOU MEAN??
KO-KUN!
CLATTER
ガタ
I'M SO GLAD YOU'RE STILL HERE.
LET'S HEAD HOME TOGETHER.
NII-CHAN WAS HERE EARLIER, WASN'T HE?
I GUESS NARUMI-CHAN WORKED OVERTIME AGAIN?
WHAT WERE YOU TALKING ABOUT?

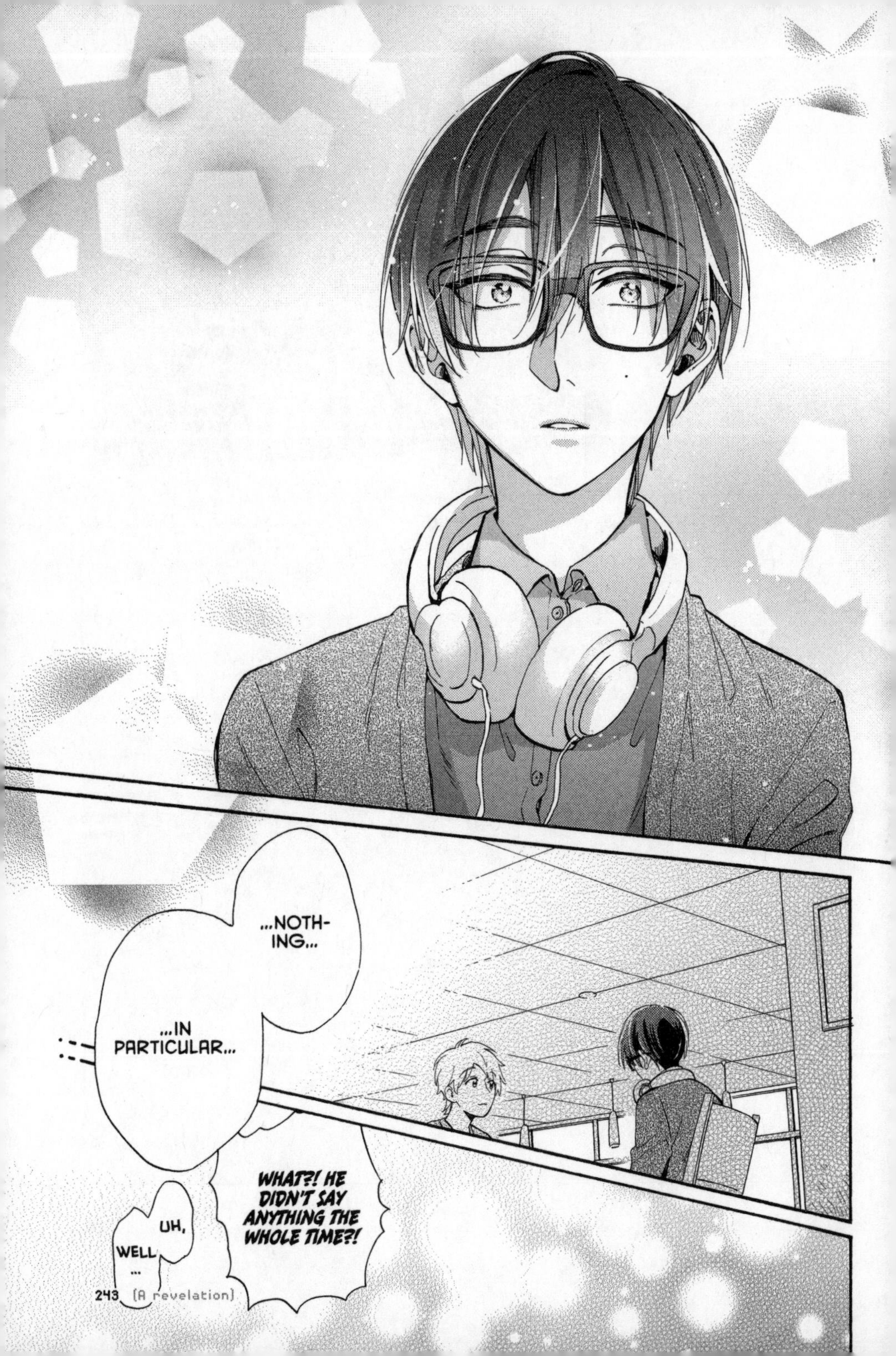
...NOTHING...
...IN PARTICULAR...
WHAT?! HE DIDN'T SAY ANYTHING THE WHOLE TIME?!
UH, WELL ...
(A revelation)

WOTAKOI: LOVE IS HARD FOR OTAKU

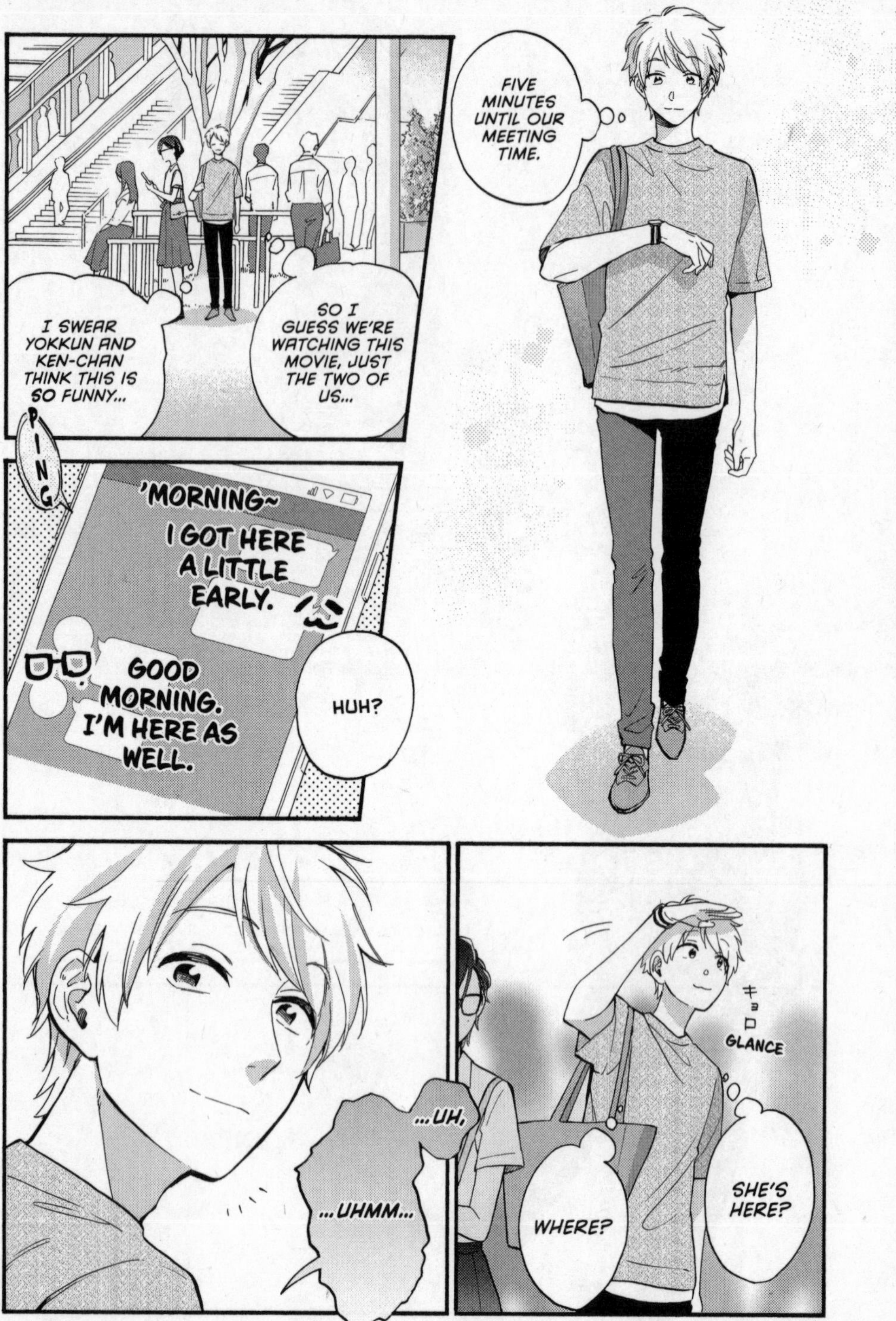
FIVE MINUTES UNTIL OUR MEETING TIME.
SO I GUESS WE'RE WATCHING THIS MOVIE, JUST THE TWO OF US...
I SWEAR YOKKUN AND KEN-CHAN THINK THIS IS SO FUNNY...
PING
'MORNING~
I GOT HERE A LITTLE EARLY.
GOOD MORNING. I'M HERE AS WELL.
HUH?
キョロ
GLANCE
SHE'S HERE?
WHERE?
...UH,
...UHMM...

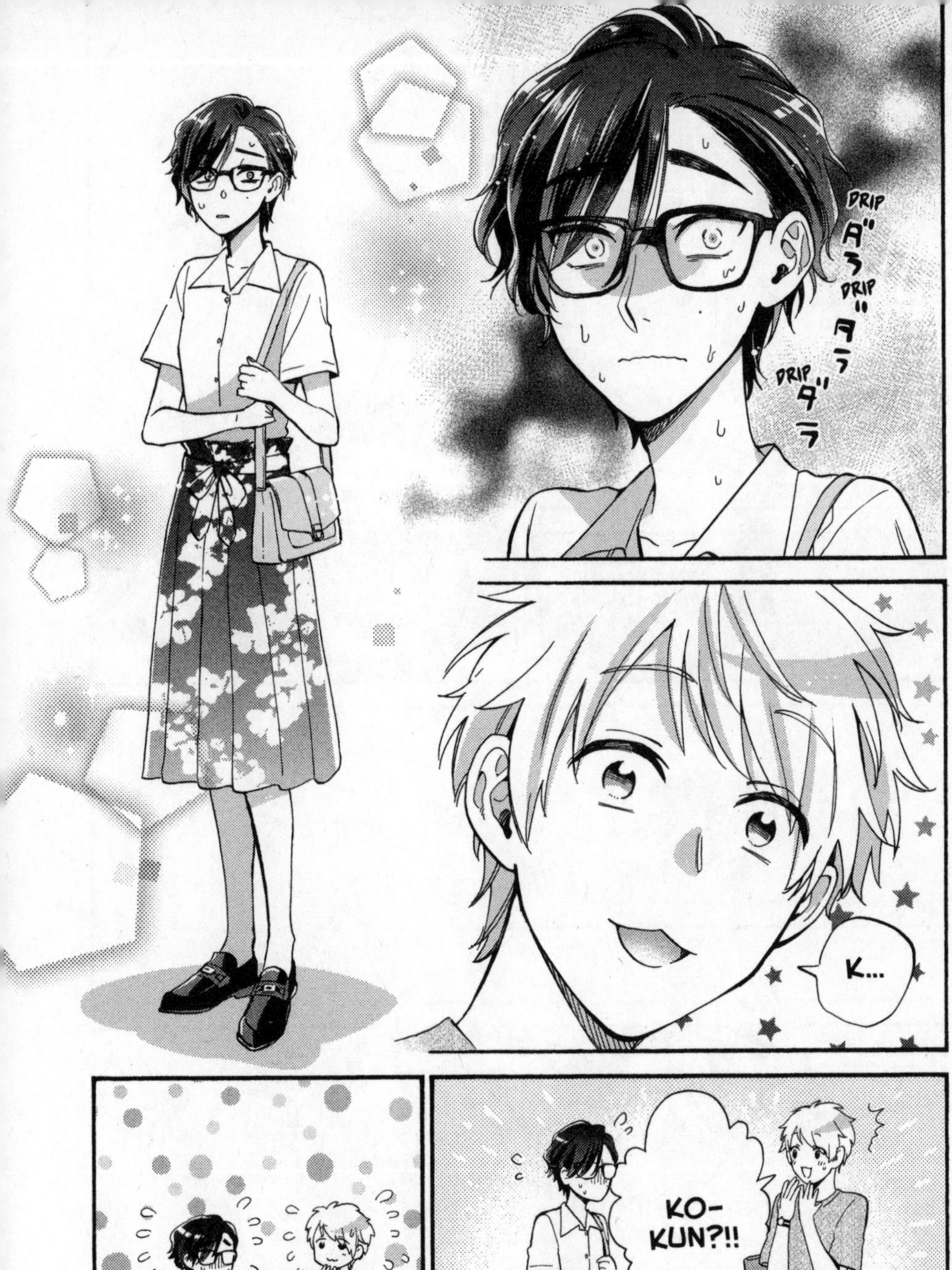
DRIP
ダラ
DRIP
ダラ
DRIP
ダラ
K...
KO-KUN?!!

 (Super nervous)

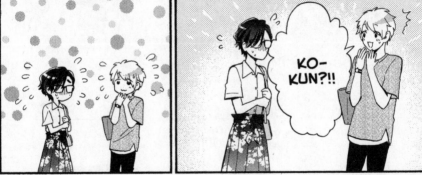

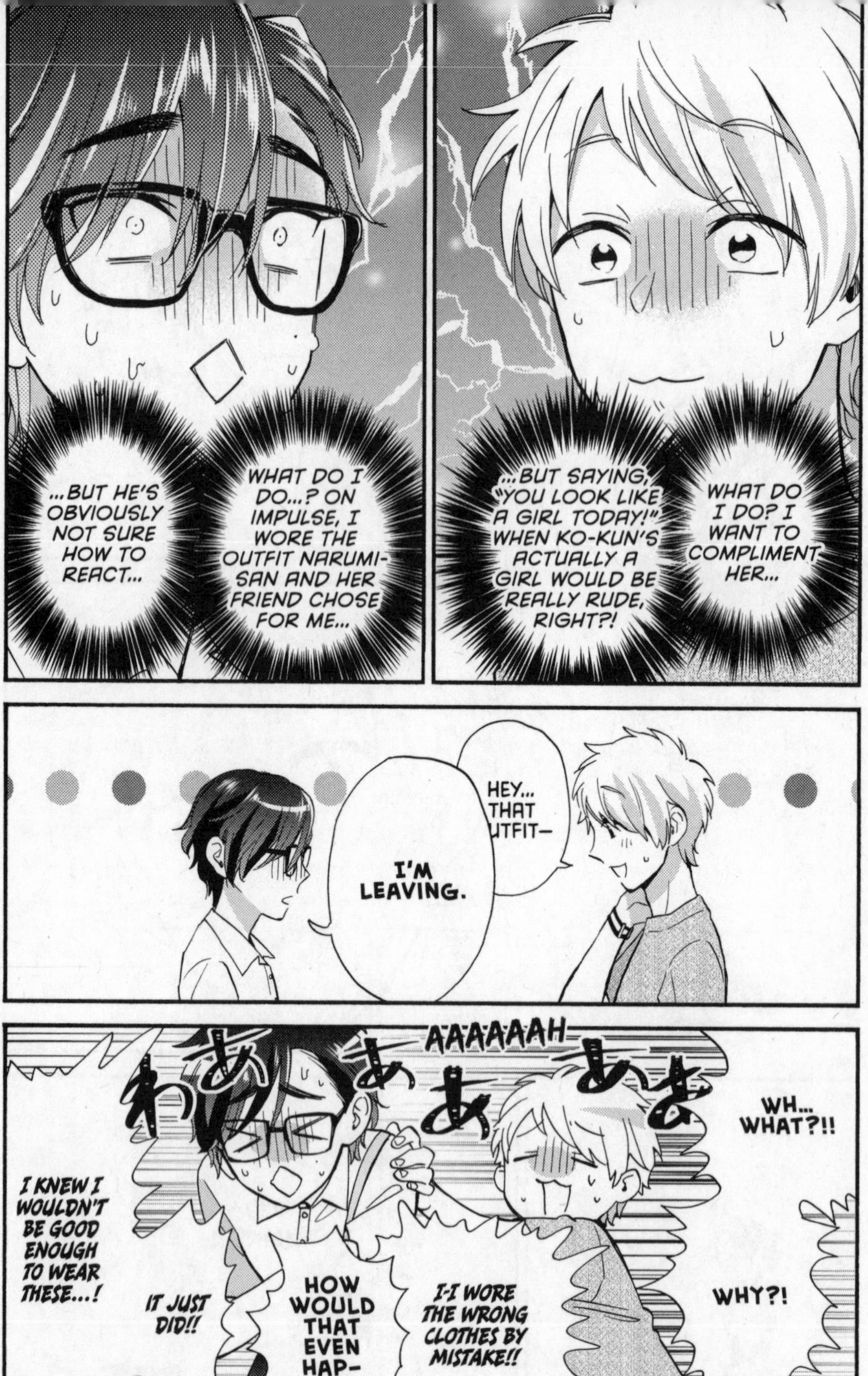
WHAT DO I DO? I WANT TO COMPLIMENT HER...
...BUT SAYING, "YOU LOOK LIKE A GIRL TODAY!" WHEN KO-KUN'S ACTUALLY A GIRL WOULD BE REALLY RUDE, RIGHT?!
WHAT DO I DO...? ON IMPULSE, I WORE THE OUTFIT NARUMI-SAN AND HER FRIEND CHOSE FOR ME...
...BUT HE'S OBVIOUSLY NOT SURE HOW TO REACT...
HEY... THAT UTFIT—
I'M LEAVING.
AAAAAAH
WH... WHAT?!!
WHY?!
I-I WORE THE WRONG CLOTHES BY MISTAKE!!
HOW WOULD THAT EVEN HAP-PEN?!
IT JUST DID!!
I KNEW I WOULDN'T BE GOOD ENOUGH TO WEAR THESE...!

THAT'S NOT TRUE AT ALL!!

UM...

DON'T WE STILL HAVE TIME...?

LET'S HURRY, OR IT'LL START!

OH! THE MOVIE!

LET'S GO, LET'S GO!

I MEAN...

UH...

(You didn't make a mistake!)

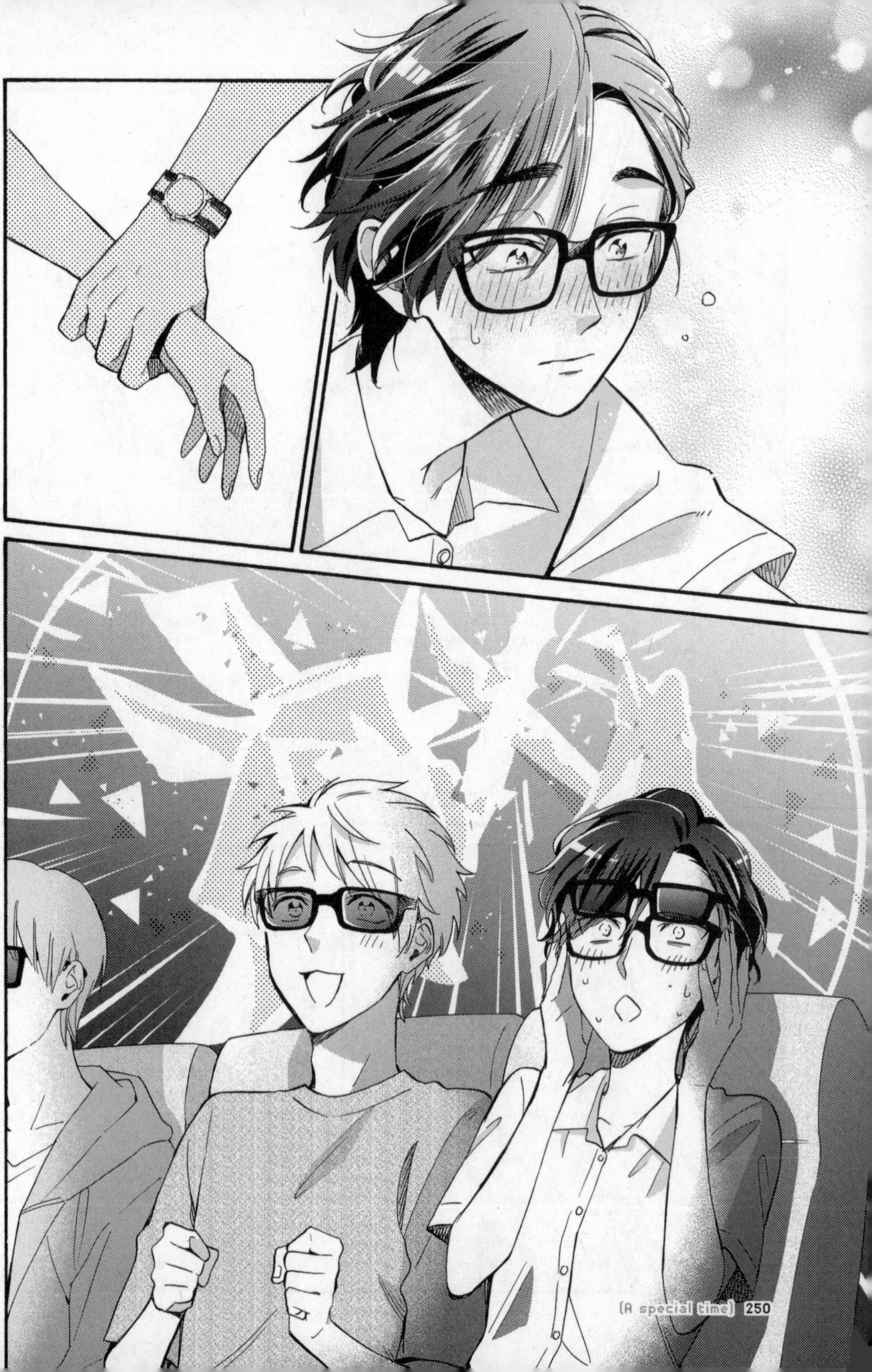

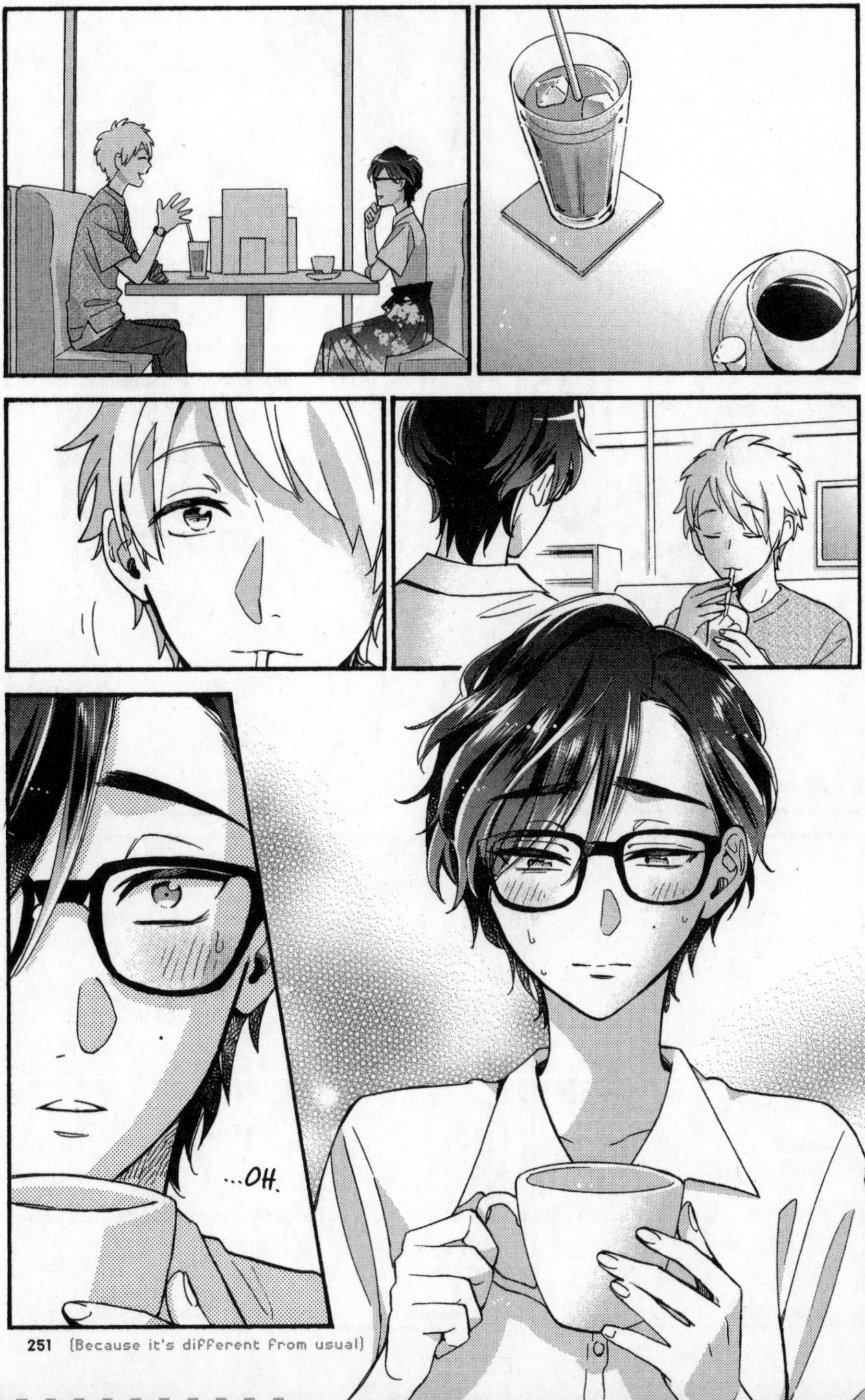
...OH.

 (Because it's different from usual)

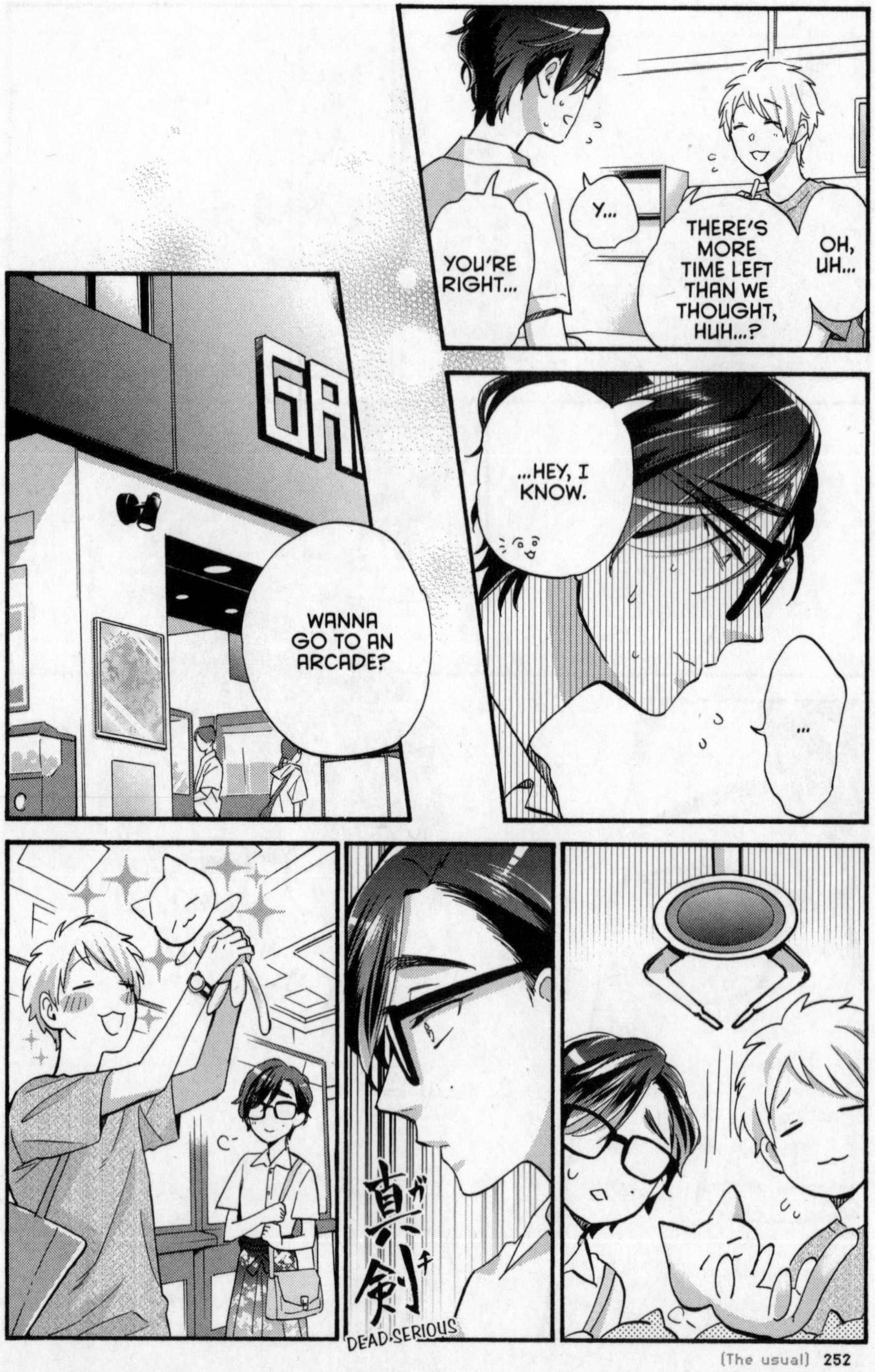
OH, UH...
THERE'S MORE TIME LEFT THAN WE THOUGHT, HUH...?
Y...
YOU'RE RIGHT...
...HEY, I KNOW.
...
WANNA GO TO AN ARCADE?
真剣(ガチ)
DEAD SERIOUS

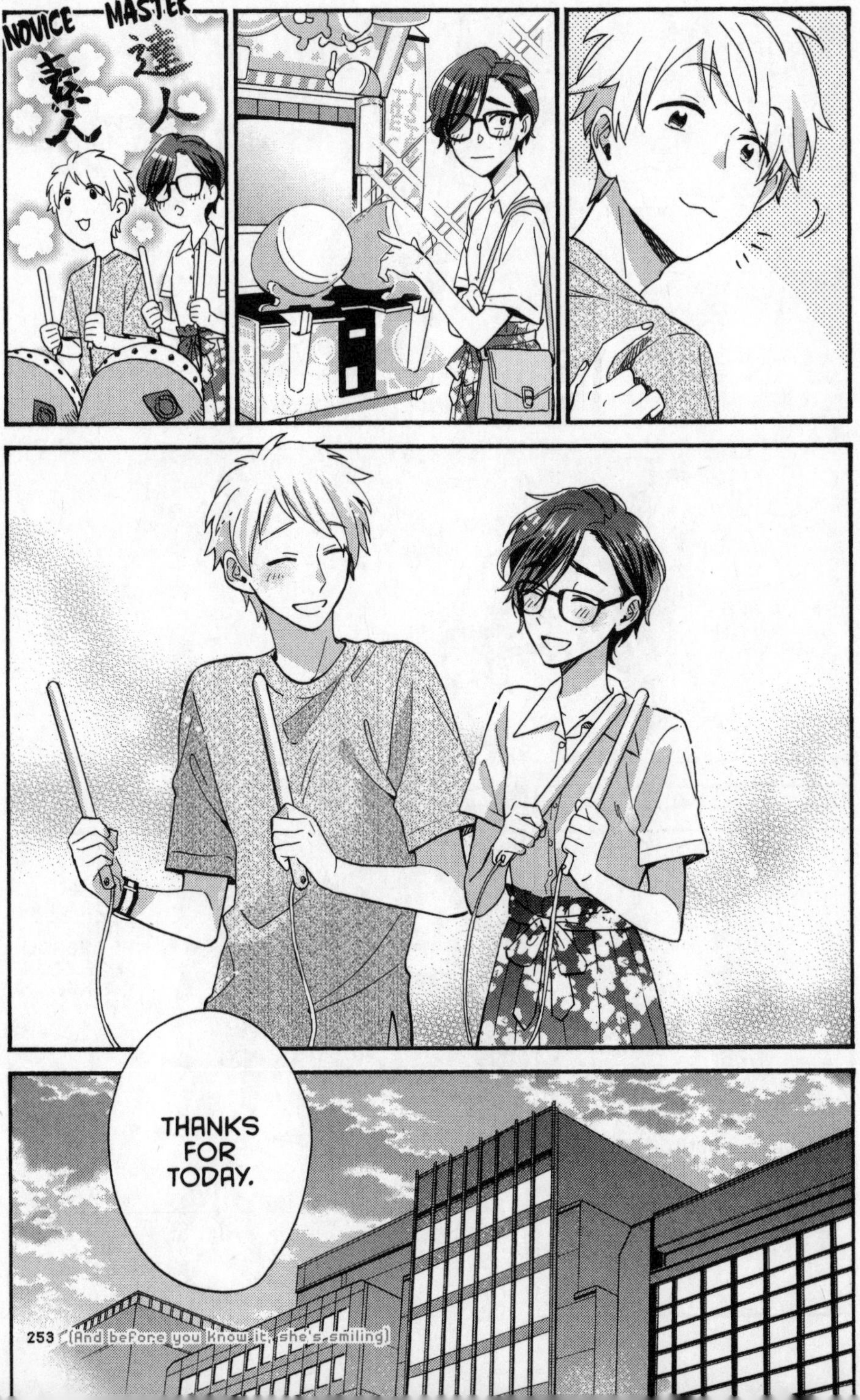

NOVICE
MASTER
素人
達人
THANKS FOR TODAY.

 (And before you know it, she's smiling)

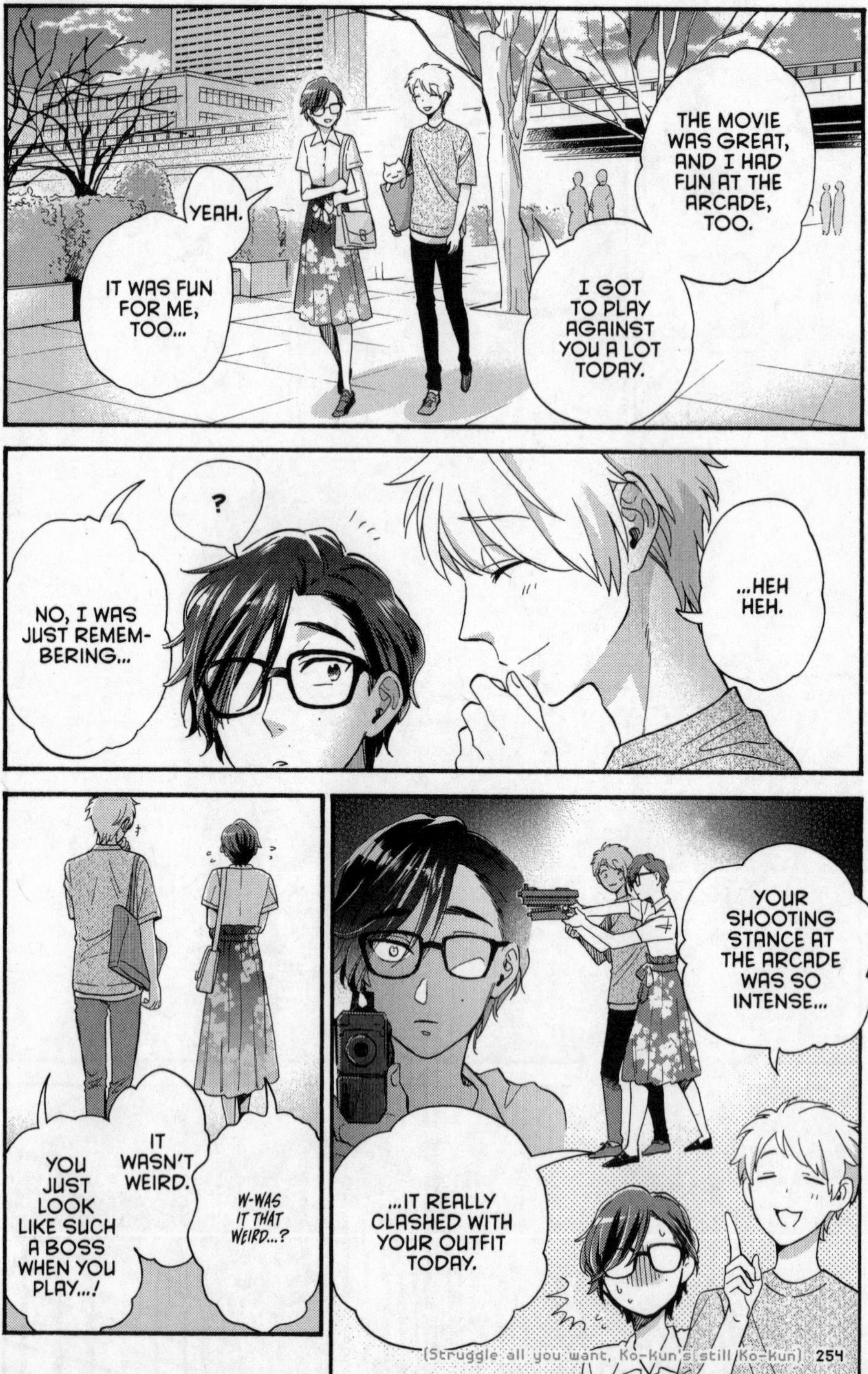
THE MOVIE WAS GREAT, AND I HAD FUN AT THE ARCADE, TOO.
I GOT TO PLAY AGAINST YOU A LOT TODAY.
YEAH.
IT WAS FUN FOR ME, TOO...
...HEH HEH.
?
NO, I WAS JUST REMEMBERING...
YOUR SHOOTING STANCE AT THE ARCADE WAS SO INTENSE...
...IT REALLY CLASHED WITH YOUR OUTFIT TODAY.
W-WAS IT THAT WEIRD...?
IT WASN'T WEIRD.
YOU JUST LOOK LIKE SUCH A BOSS WHEN YOU PLAY...!

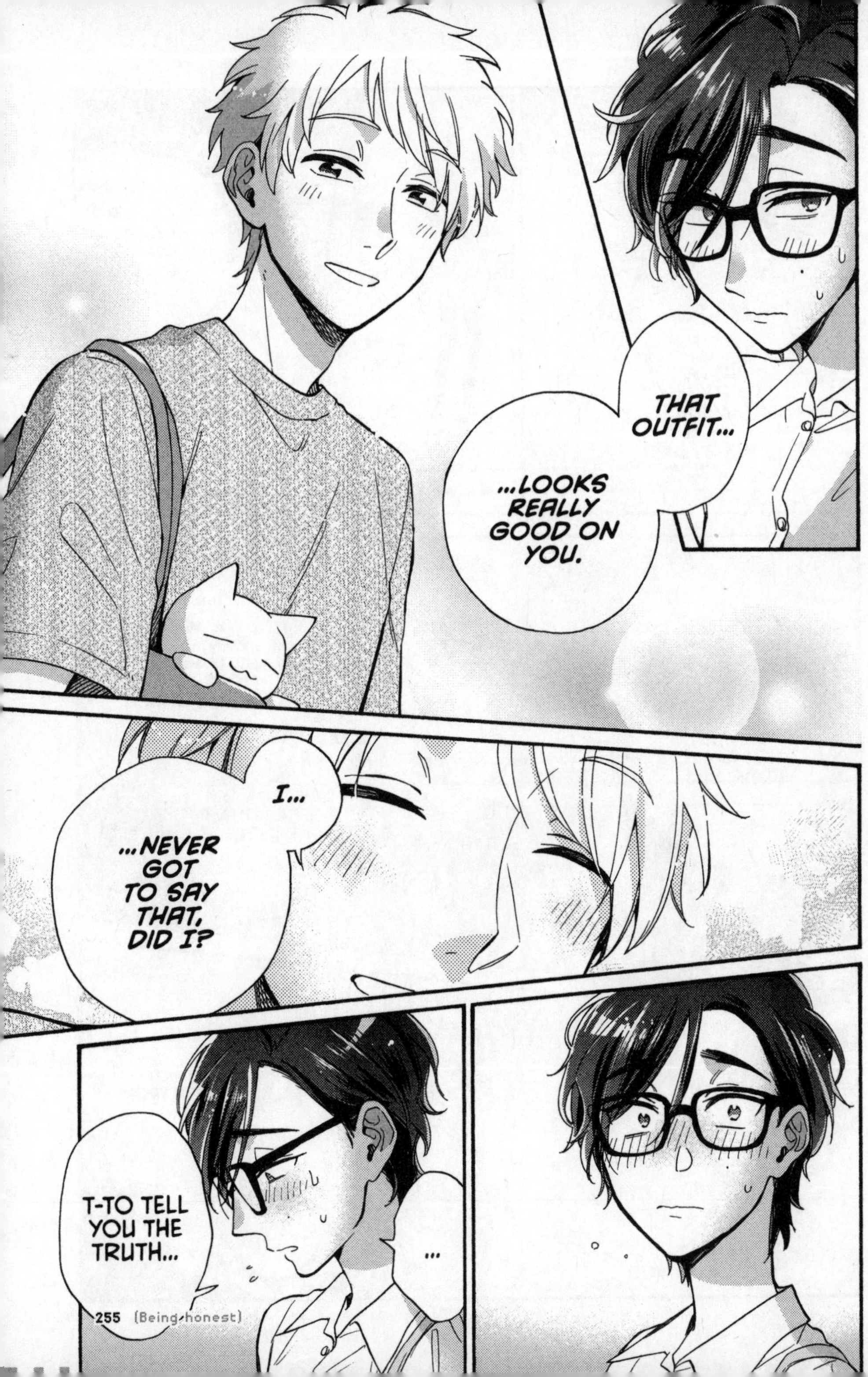
THAT OUTFIT...
...LOOKS REALLY GOOD ON YOU.
I...
...NEVER GOT TO SAY THAT, DID I?
...
T-TO TELL YOU THE TRUTH...

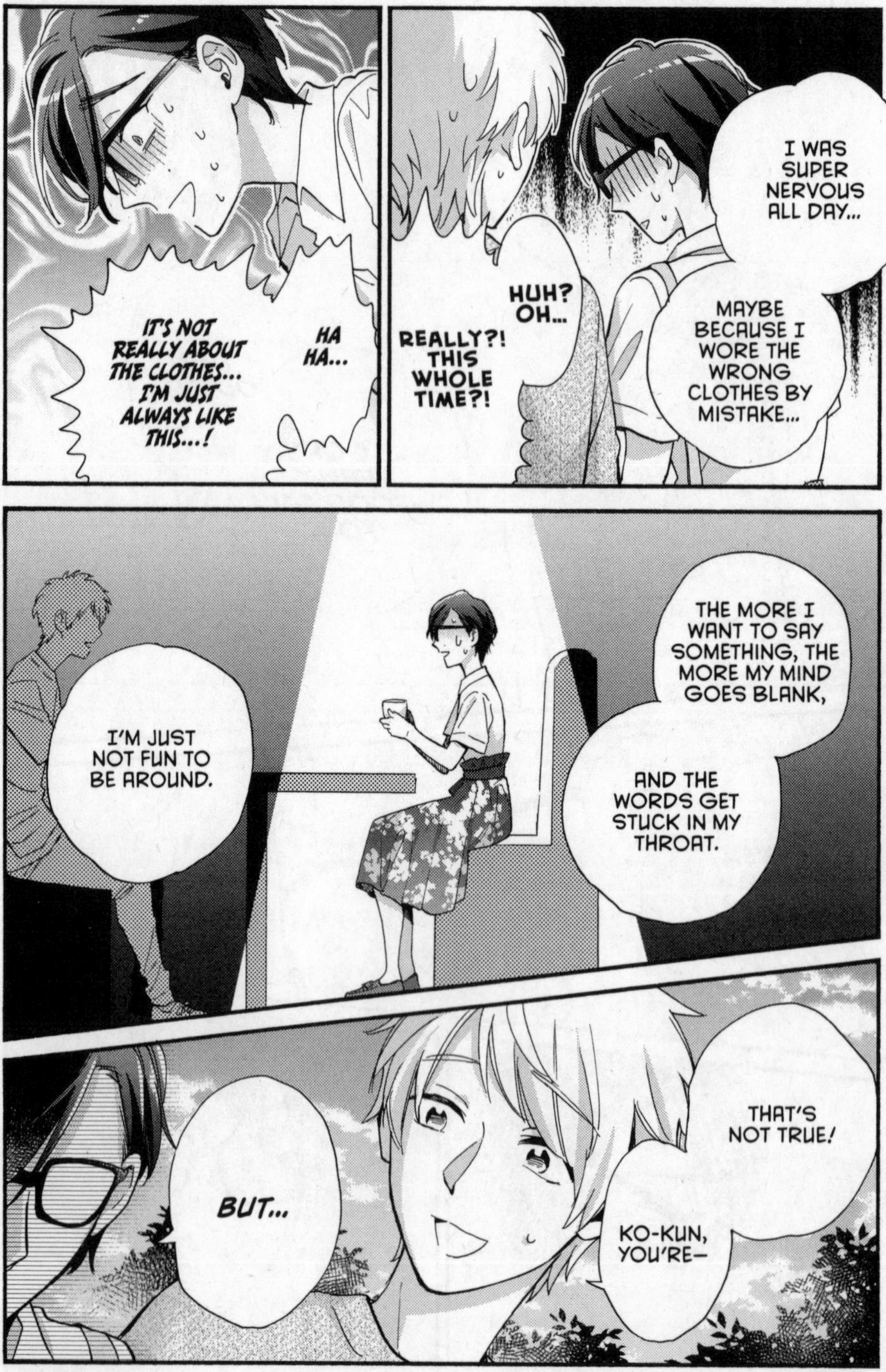
I WAS SUPER NERVOUS ALL DAY...
MAYBE BECAUSE I WORE THE WRONG CLOTHES BY MISTAKE...
HUH? OH...
REALLY?! THIS WHOLE TIME?!
HA HA...
IT'S NOT REALLY ABOUT THE CLOTHES... I'M JUST ALWAYS LIKE THIS...!
THE MORE I WANT TO SAY SOMETHING, THE MORE MY MIND GOES BLANK,
AND THE WORDS GET STUCK IN MY THROAT.
I'M JUST NOT FUN TO BE AROUND.
THAT'S NOT TRUE!
KO-KUN, YOU'RE—
BUT...

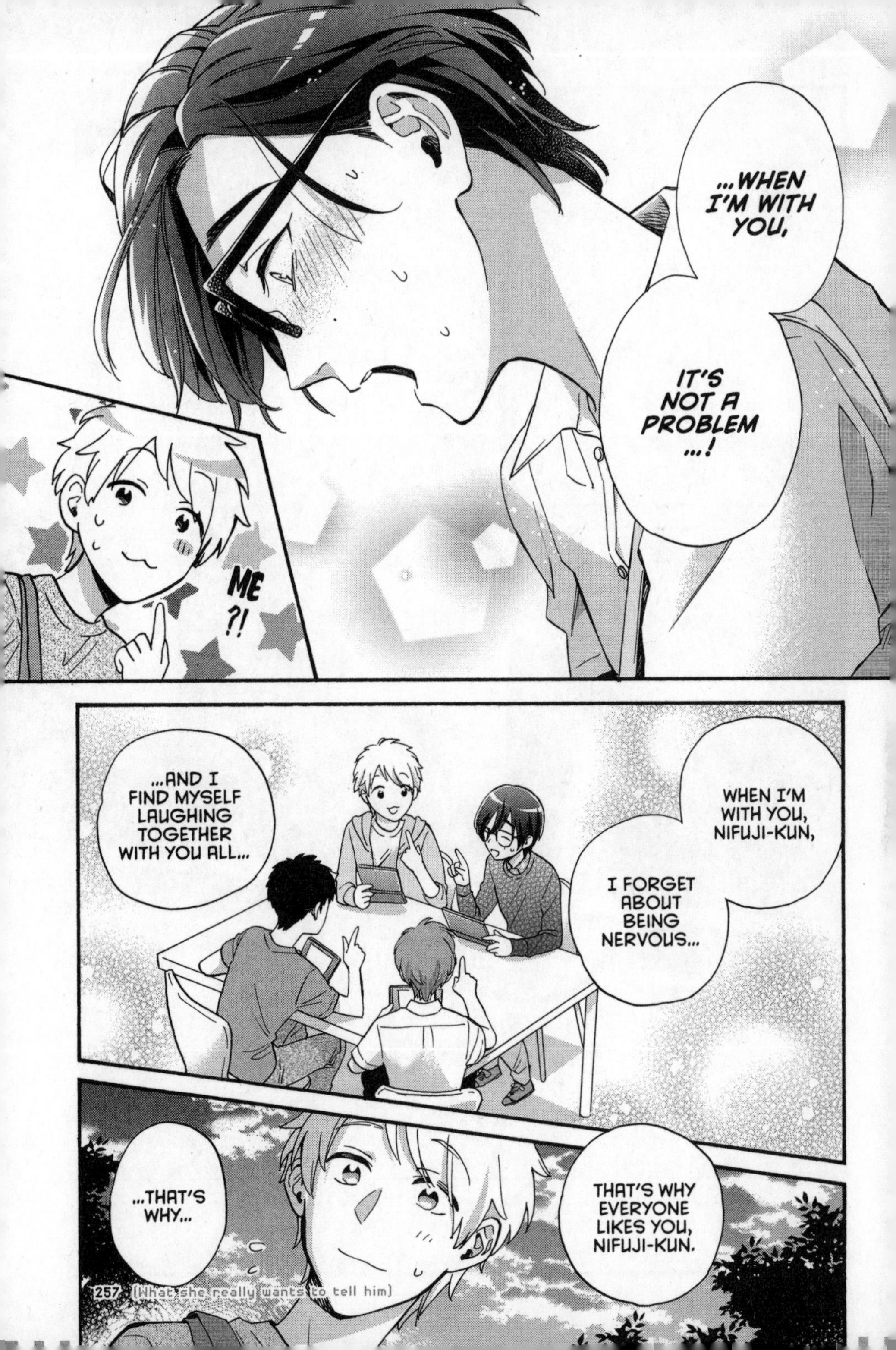
...WHEN I'M WITH YOU,
IT'S NOT A PROBLEM ...!
ME ?!
WHEN I'M WITH YOU, NIFUJI-KUN,
I FORGET ABOUT BEING NERVOUS...
...AND I FIND MYSELF LAUGHING TOGETHER WITH YOU ALL...
THAT'S WHY EVERYONE LIKES YOU, NIFUJI-KUN.
...THAT'S WHY...

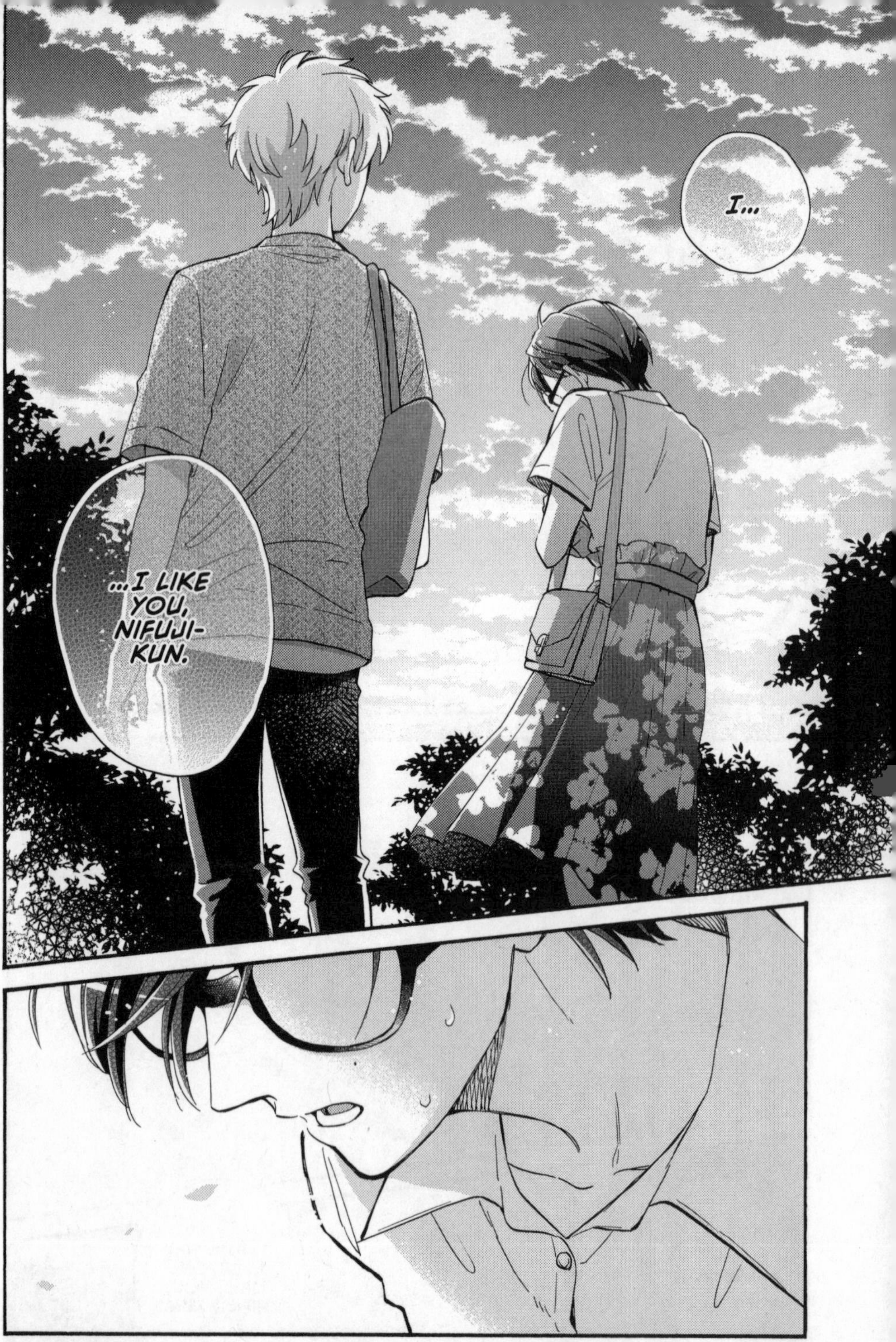
I...
...I LIKE YOU, NIFUJI-KUN.

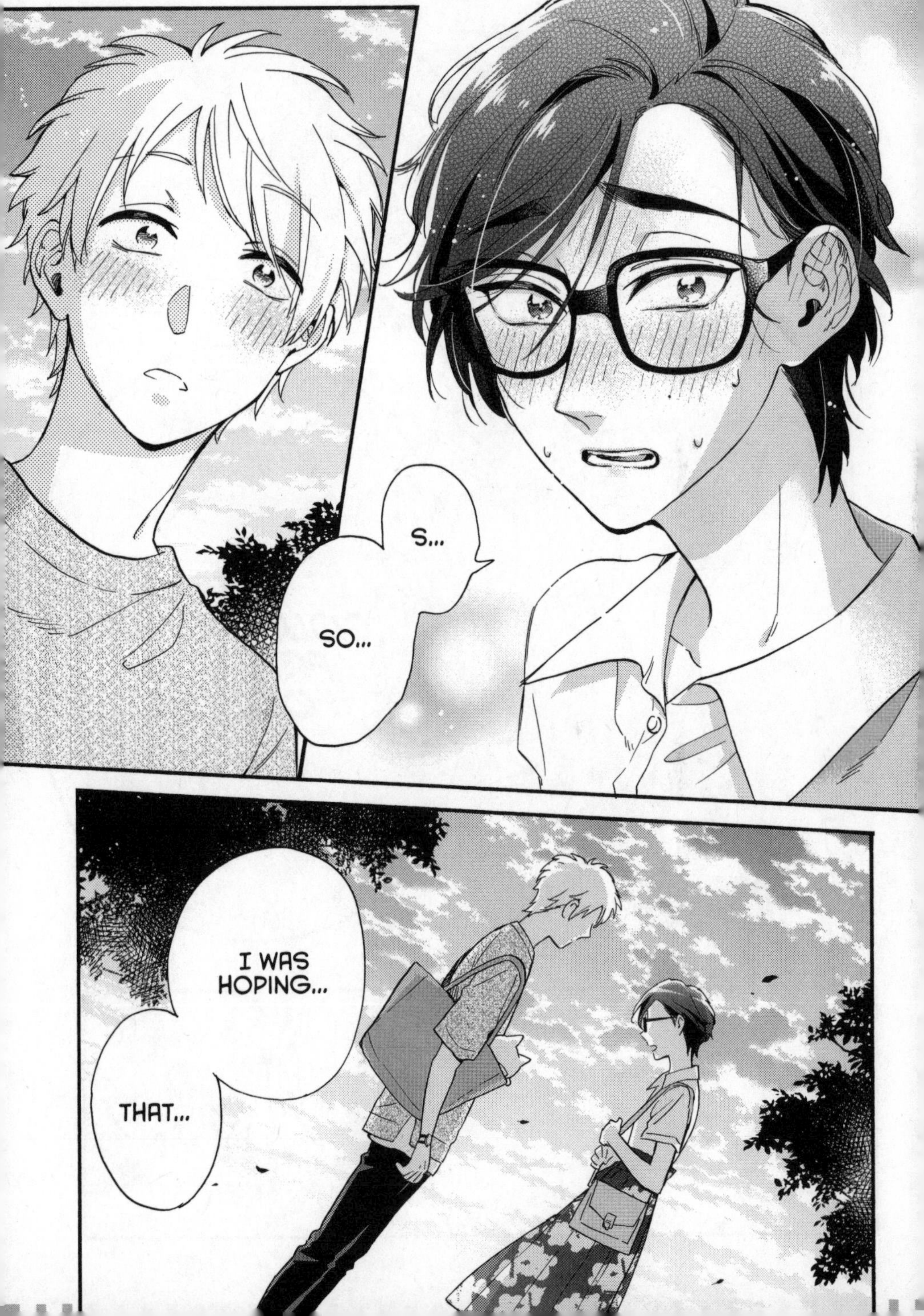
S...
SO...
I WAS HOPING...
THAT...

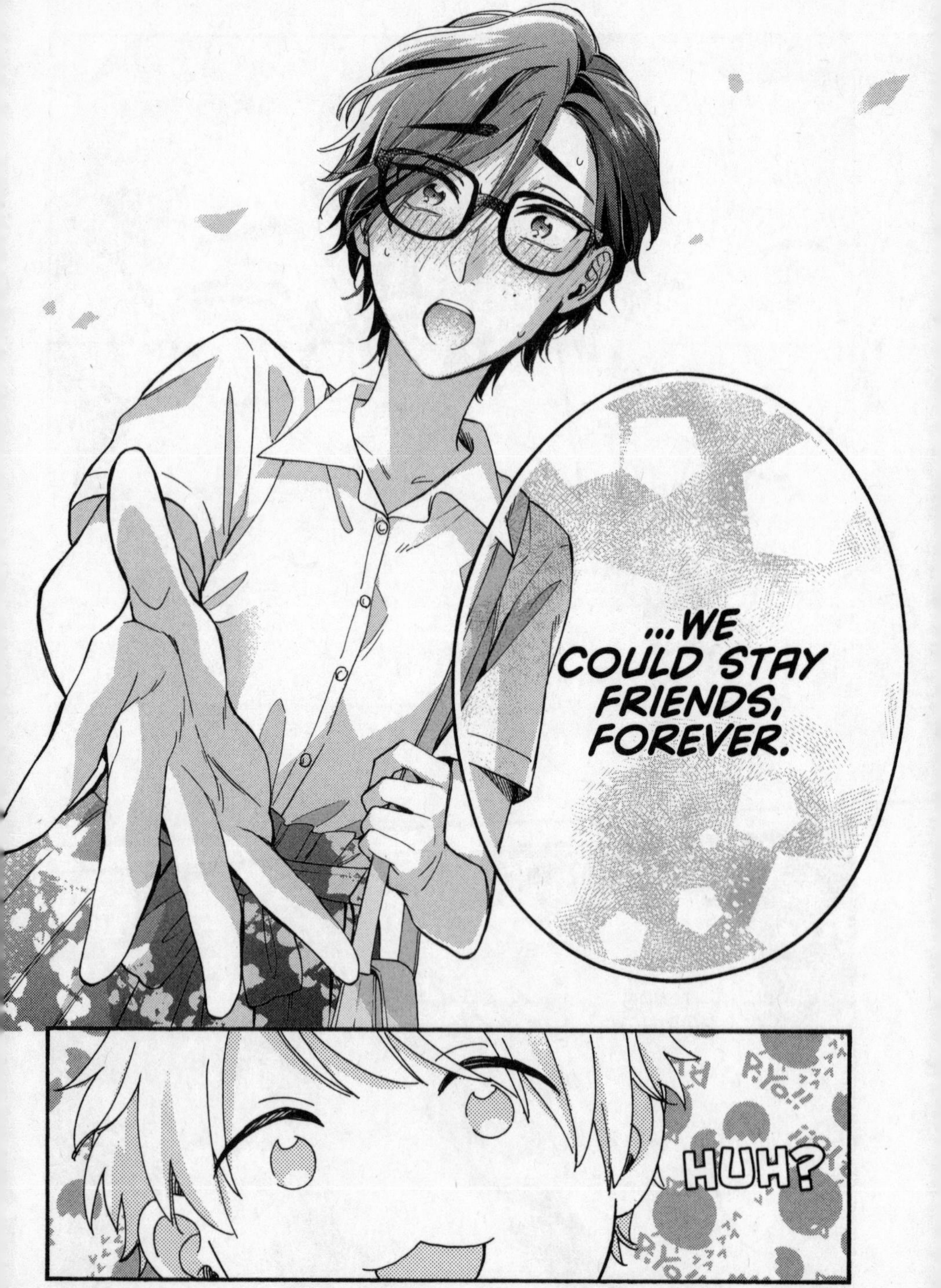
...WE COULD STAY FRIENDS, FOREVER.
RYO!!
HUH?
RYO!!

UM... UH...
SURE...
OF COURSE...
I'M GLAD...
I GOT THE COURAGE TO WEAR THIS OUTFIT TODAY...
AND I MANAGED TO TELL HIM...
...WHAT I WANT-ED TO SAY.

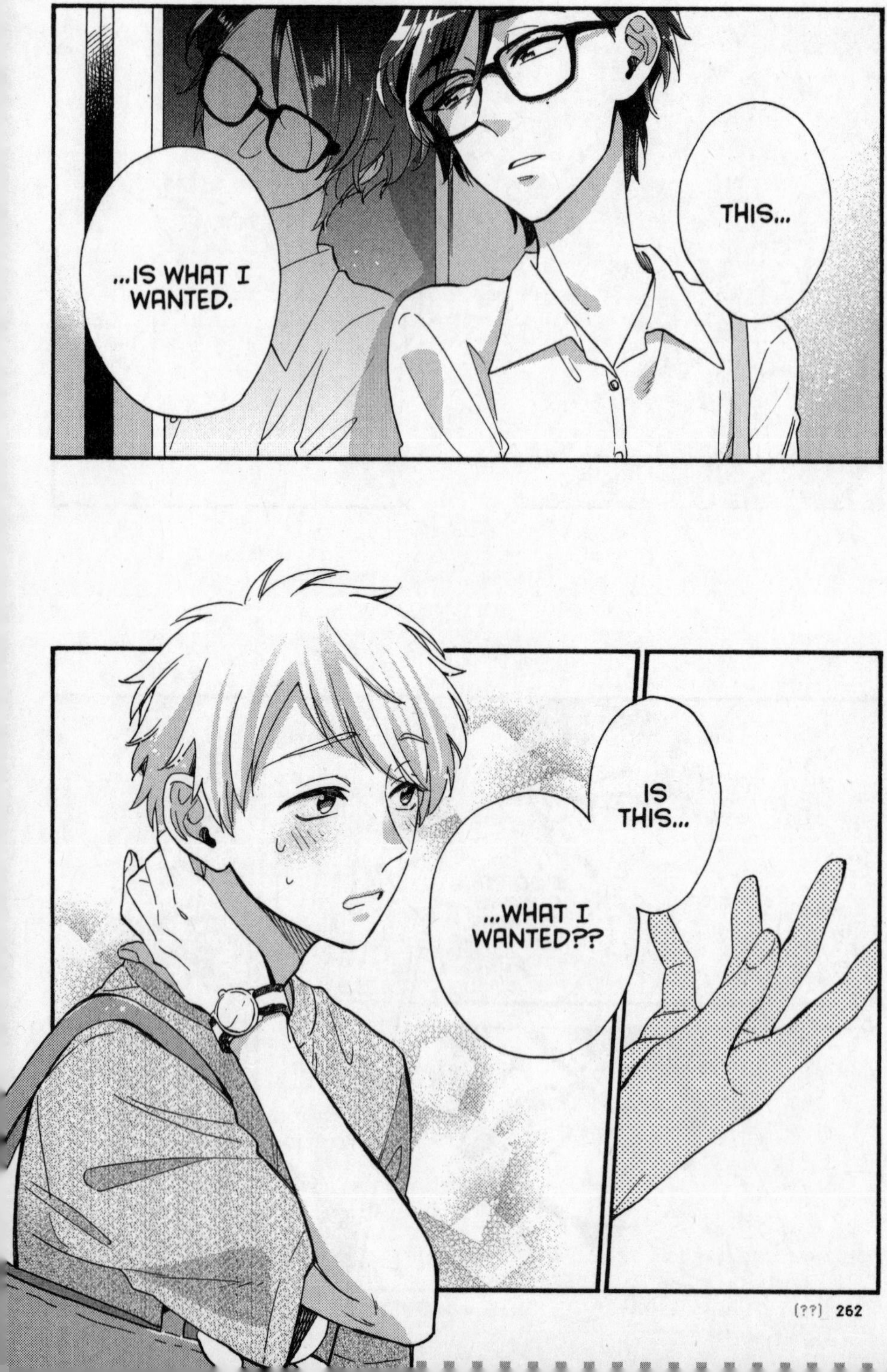
THIS...
...IS WHAT I WANTED.
IS THIS...
...WHAT I WANTED??

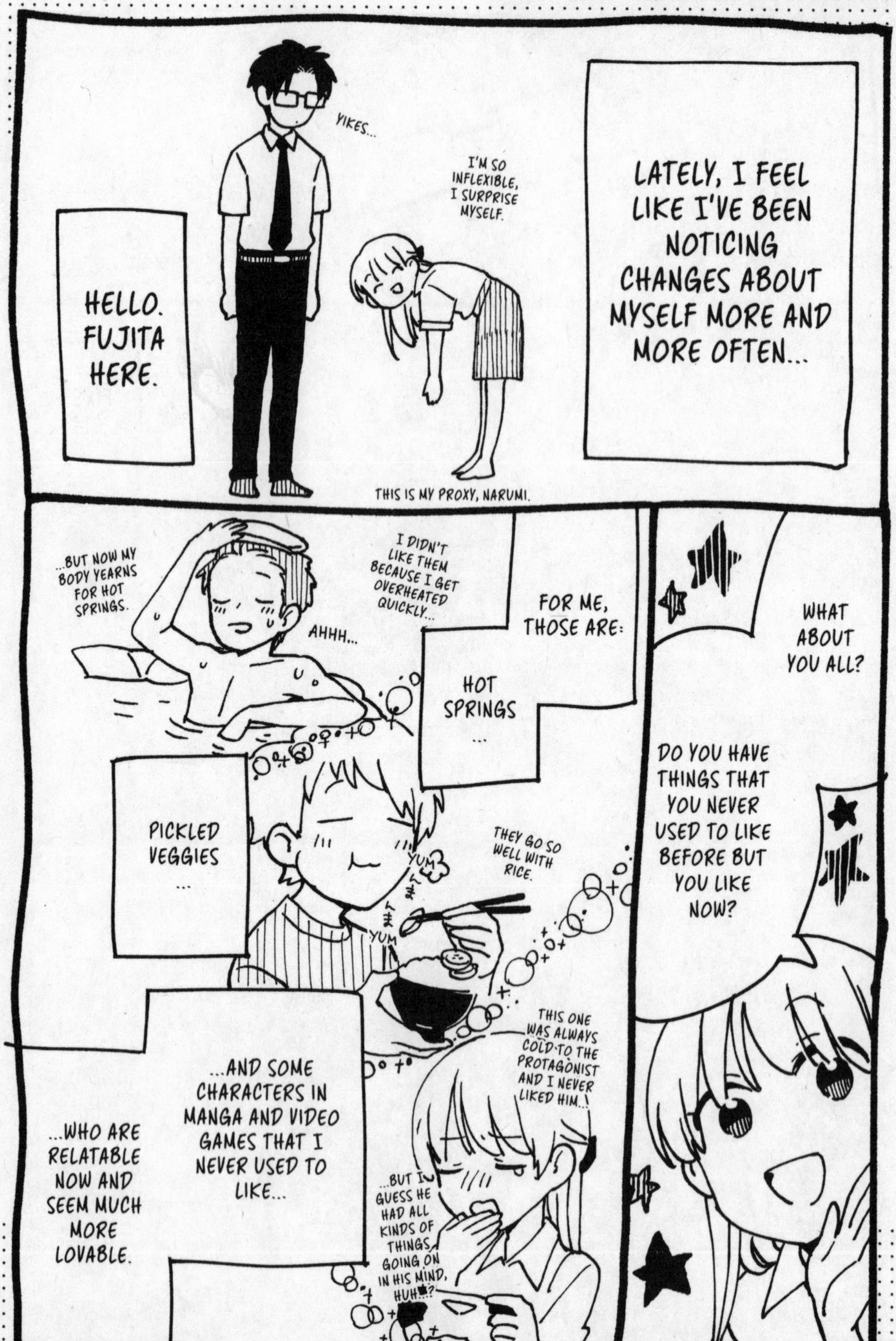
LATELY, I FEEL LIKE I'VE BEEN NOTICING CHANGES ABOUT MYSELF MORE AND MORE OFTEN...
I'M SO INFLEXIBLE, I SURPRISE MYSELF.
YIKES...
HELLO. FUJITA HERE.
THIS IS MY PROXY, NARUMI.
WHAT ABOUT YOU ALL?
DO YOU HAVE THINGS THAT YOU NEVER USED TO LIKE BEFORE BUT YOU LIKE NOW?
FOR ME, THOSE ARE:
HOT SPRINGS ...
I DIDN'T LIKE THEM BECAUSE I GET OVERHEATED QUICKLY...
AHHH...
...BUT NOW MY BODY YEARNS FOR HOT SPRINGS.
THEY GO SO WELL WITH RICE.
YUM
YUM
PICKLED VEGGIES ...
...AND SOME CHARACTERS IN MANGA AND VIDEO GAMES THAT I NEVER USED TO LIKE...
THIS ONE WAS ALWAYS COLD TO THE PROTAGONIST AND I NEVER LIKED HIM...
...BUT I GUESS HE HAD ALL KINDS OF THINGS GOING ON IN HIS MIND, HUH..?
...WHO ARE RELATABLE NOW AND SEEM MUCH MORE LOVABLE.

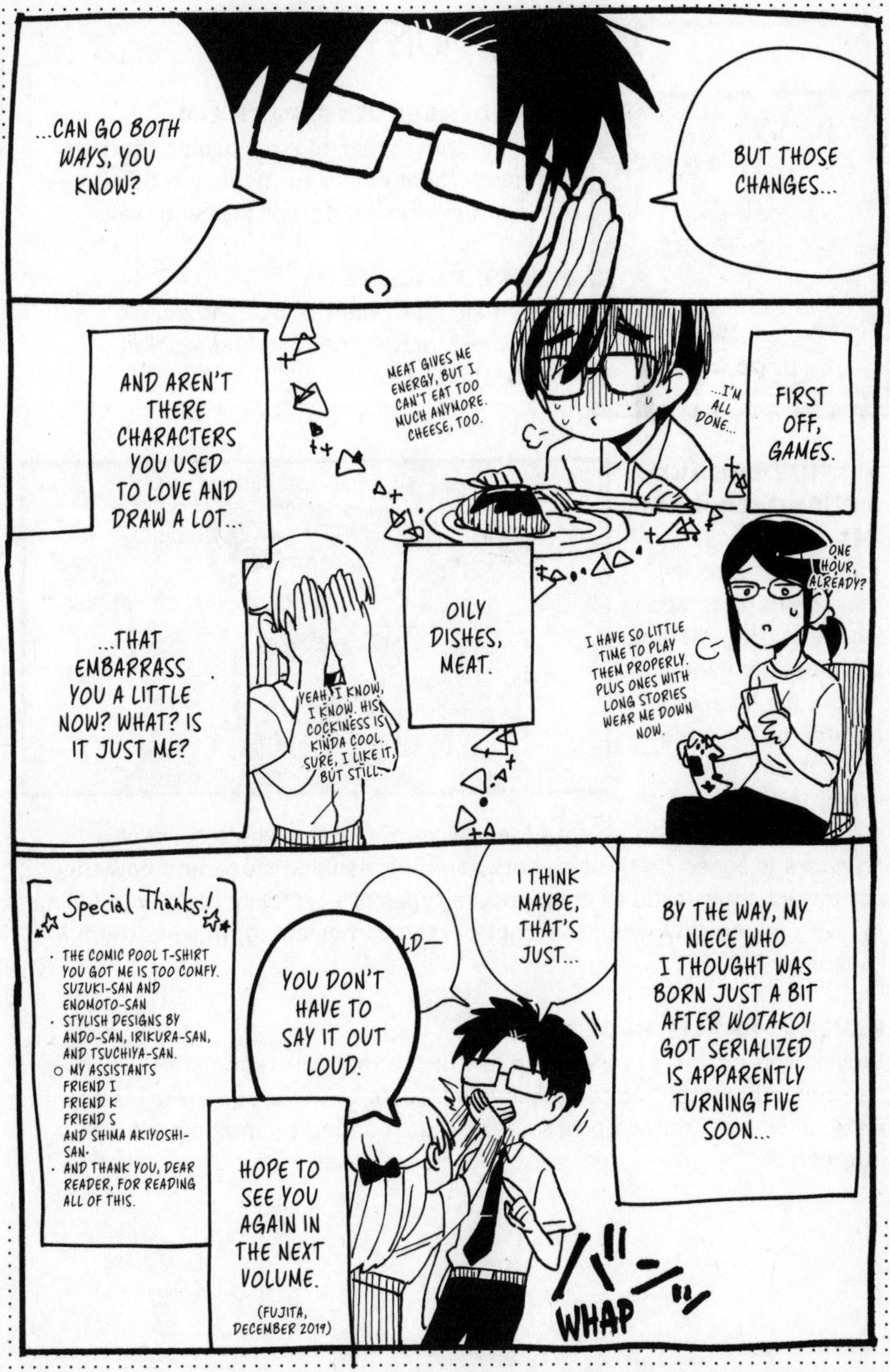
BUT THOSE CHANGES...
...CAN GO BOTH WAYS, YOU KNOW?
FIRST OFF, GAMES.
ONE HOUR, ALREADY?
I HAVE SO LITTLE TIME TO PLAY THEM PROPERLY. PLUS ONES WITH LONG STORIES WEAR ME DOWN NOW.
...I'M ALL DONE...
MEAT GIVES ME ENERGY, BUT I CAN'T EAT TOO MUCH ANYMORE. CHEESE, TOO.
OILY DISHES, MEAT.
AND AREN'T THERE CHARACTERS YOU USED TO LOVE AND DRAW A LOT...
...THAT EMBARRASS YOU A LITTLE NOW? WHAT? IS IT JUST ME?
YEAH, I KNOW, I KNOW. HIS COCKINESS IS KINDA COOL. SURE, I LIKE IT, BUT STILL...
BY THE WAY, MY NIECE WHO I THOUGHT WAS BORN JUST A BIT AFTER WOTAKOI GOT SERIALIZED IS APPARENTLY TURNING FIVE SOON...
I THINK MAYBE, THAT'S JUST...
LD—
YOU DON'T HAVE TO SAY IT OUT LOUD.
WHAP
HOPE TO SEE YOU AGAIN IN THE NEXT VOLUME.
(FUJITA, DECEMBER 2019)
Special Thanks!
• THE COMIC POOL T-SHIRT YOU GOT ME IS TOO COMFY. SUZUKI-SAN AND ENOMOTO-SAN
• STYLISH DESIGNS BY ANDO-SAN, IRIKURA-SAN, AND TSUCHIYA-SAN.
○ MY ASSISTANTS FRIEND I FRIEND K FRIEND S AND SHIMA AKIYOSHI-SAN.
• AND THANK YOU, DEAR READER, FOR READING ALL OF THIS.

TRANSLATION NOTES

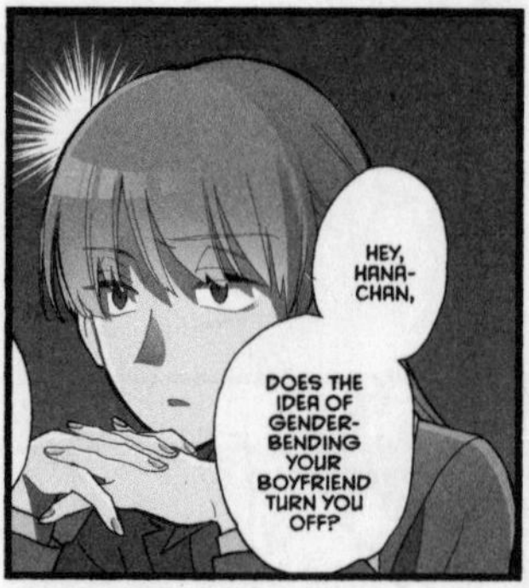
HEY, HANA-CHAN,
DOES THE IDEA OF GENDER-BENDING YOUR BOYFRIEND TURN YOU OFF?

◀ GENDERBENDING, PAGE 140
Changing the gender of a particular character. The genderbent character usually retains most of his or her original personality and traits.

▼ *YURI*, PAGE 141
The female equivalent of BL. The genre of Japanese fiction that involves lesbian relationships.

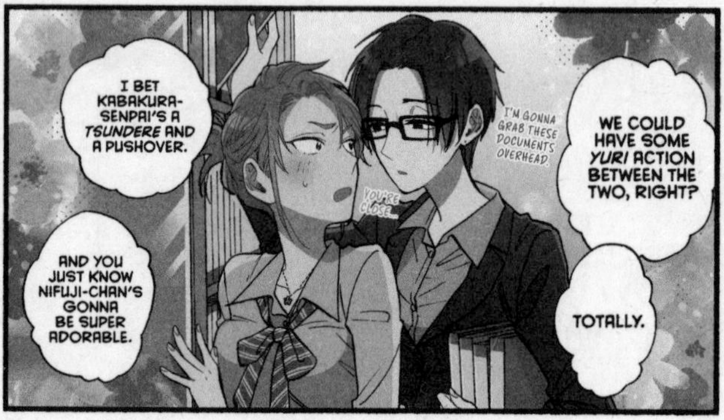
WE COULD HAVE SOME YURI ACTION BETWEEN THE TWO, RIGHT?
TOTALLY.
I'M GONNA GRAB THESE DOCUMENTS OVERHEAD.
YOU'RE CLOSE...
I BET KABAKURA-SENPAI'S A TSUNDERE AND A PUSHOVER.
AND YOU JUST KNOW NIFUJI-CHAN'S GONNA BE SUPER ADORABLE.

▶ *TSUNDERE* AND A PUSHOVER, PAGE 141
Tsundere is a term that refers to someone who acts cold, distant, and possibly even hostile (in Japanese, *tsuntsun*), but once you get to know them, they show a softer, more affectionate side (*deredere*). Since the whole concept of *tsundere* is based on the gap between their usual attitude and how they act toward their loved ones, *tsundere* types are typically portrayed falling in love very quickly when the right person comes along, making them a "pushover."

REVERSE HAREM, PAGE 142
While a "harem" is a story setup in which a male protagonist is surrounded by multiple female love interests, a "reverse harem" is a setup in which a female protagonist is surrounded by multiple male love interests.

▶ CROSSPLAYER, PAGE 144

A cosplayer who crossdresses when cosplaying.

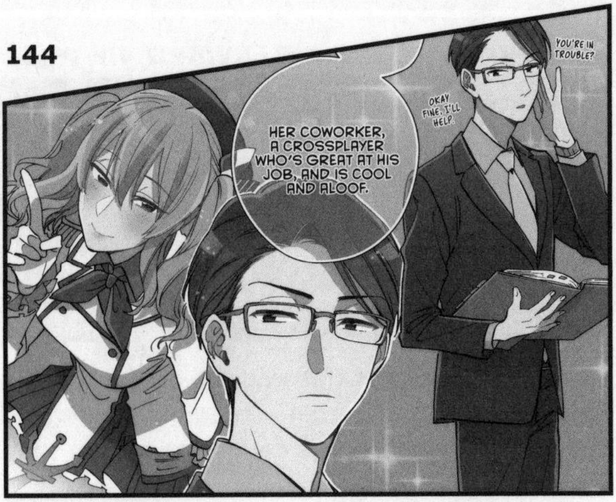
YOU'RE IN TROUBLE?
OKAY FINE, I'LL HELP.
HER COWORKER, A CROSSPLAYER WHO'S GREAT AT HIS JOB, AND IS COOL AND ALOOF.

▼ *ICEBORNE*, PAGE 143

A DLC expansion for *Monster Hunter: World*, the latest installment of the massively popular action RPG series *Monster Hunter*.

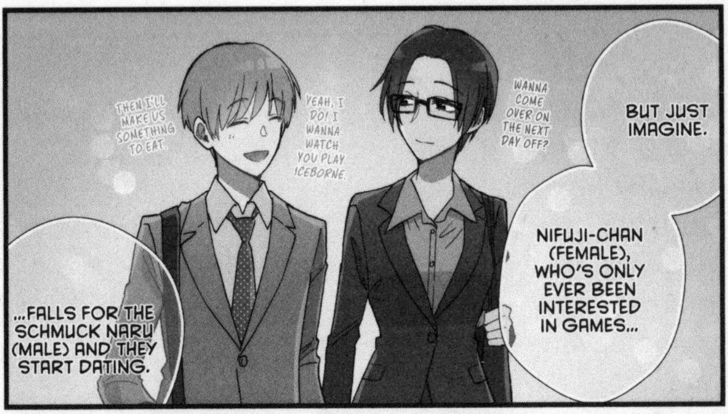
BUT JUST IMAGINE.
NIFUJI-CHAN (FEMALE), WHO'S ONLY EVER BEEN INTERESTED IN GAMES...
WANNA COME OVER ON THE NEXT DAY OFF?
YEAH, I DO! I WANNA WATCH YOU PLAY ICEBORNE.
THEN I'LL MAKE US SOMETHING TO EAT.
...FALLS FOR THE SCHMUCK NARU (MALE) AND THEY START DATING.

***THE WORLD UNKNOWN TO KABAKURA*, PAGE 145**

A reference to the talk show *The World Unknown to Matsuko,* which features guests revealing little-known information on their areas of expertise. Here, Narumi and Hanako are talking about stuff that Kabakura wouldn't imagine in his wildest dreams.

▼ COMIKET CATALOG, PAGE 153

The *dojinshi* fair Comic Market (Comiket) sells an event catalog listing all of the booths that will be available. Each listing includes a thumbnail illustration advertising the group, and with roughly 35,000 booths participating, the printed version is notoriously thick and heavy.

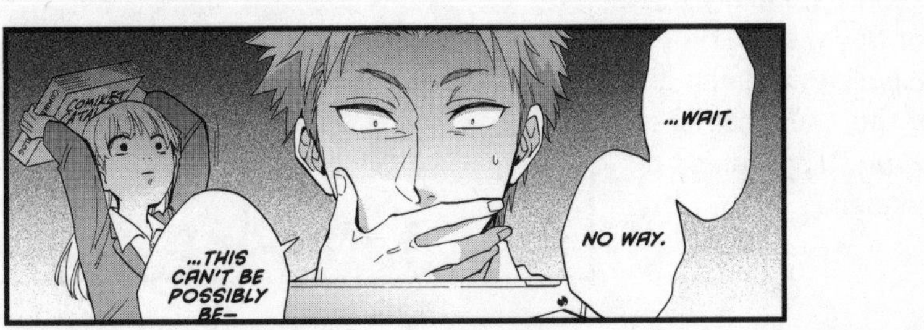
...WAIT.
NO WAY.
...THIS CAN'T BE POSSIBLY BE—

▶ ...AND NOT LONG AFTERWARD, HE WAS DEAD..., PAGE 153

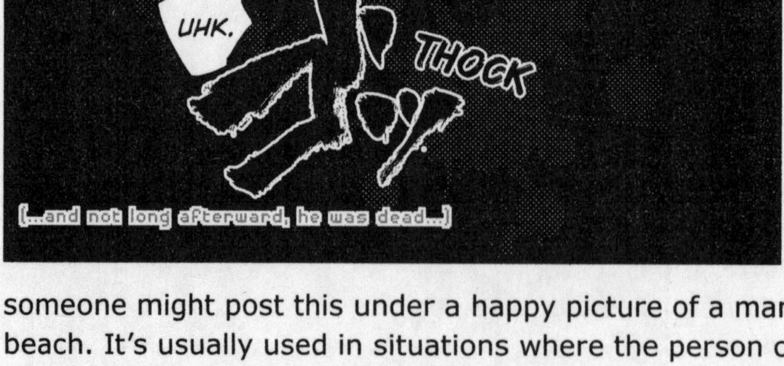
UHK.
THOCK
(...and not long afterward, he was dead...)

An internet meme that originally followed innocuous images to humorously add a touch of suspense. For example, someone might post this under a happy picture of a man smiling on the beach. It's usually used in situations where the person can't actually be dead, or when there was no indication that the person was in trouble.

▶ ENTRANCE EXAMS, PAGE 154

Most Japanese students study for college (and sometimes even middle or high school) entrance exams, which are often the sole determining factor in admissions. Normally held in January, the stakes are so high that third-year high school students are usually expected to retire from all extracurricular activities and devote their final year to studying.

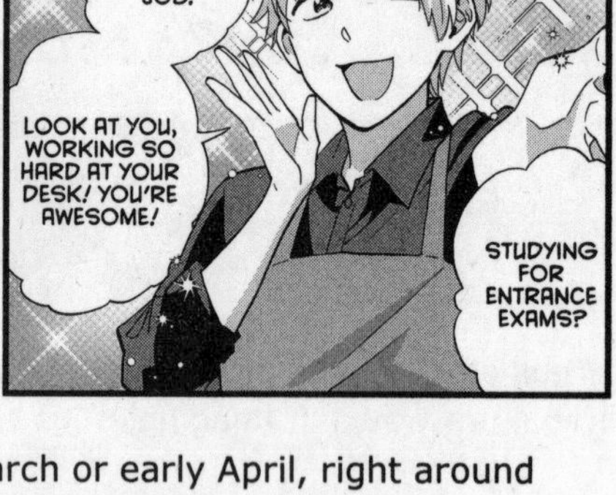
STUDYING FOR ENTRANCE EXAMS?
YOU'RE DOING SUCH A GREAT JOB!
LOOK AT YOU, WORKING SO HARD AT YOUR DESK! YOU'RE AWESOME!

DID THE CHERRY BLOSSOMS BLOOM?, PAGE 154

Since cherry blossoms bloom in late March or early April, right around when the new school year starts, saying "the cherry blossoms bloomed" can be synonymous with "I got into the school of my choice."

▶ KOYANAGI-KUN, PAGE 158

Although the honorific "-kun" is usually used for boys, sometimes superiors will call all of their subordinates "-kun," regardless of gender.

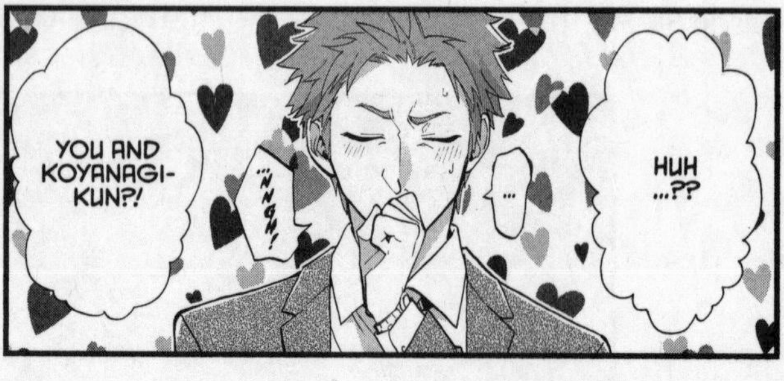
HUH ...??
...
...NNGH!
YOU AND KOYANAGI-KUN?!

▶ GUILD WAR, PAGE 162

Guild Wars, officially called Unite and Fight events, are competitive guild-versus-guild events in the mobile RPG *Granblue Fantasy*. "Don't run away from the Guild War" supposedly originated as a hashtag used between *Granblue Fantasy* players to put pressure on each other to participate, because the events are notoriously time-demanding and intense. Apparently the phrase is now mostly used in a joking manner.

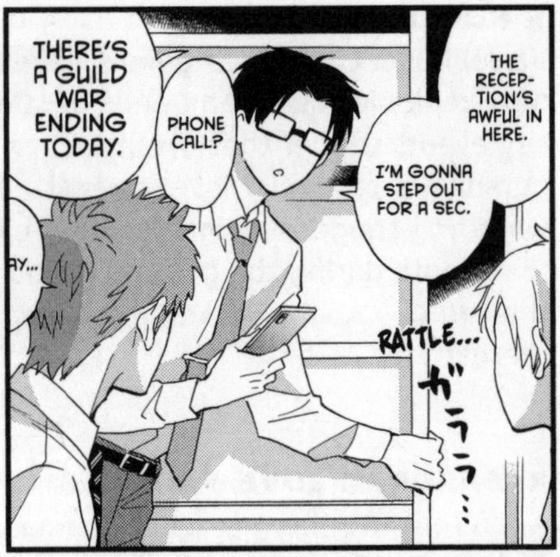
THE RECEPTION'S AWFUL IN HERE.
I'M GONNA STEP OUT FOR A SEC.
RATTLE...
ガララ…
PHONE CALL?
THERE'S A GUILD WAR ENDING TODAY.

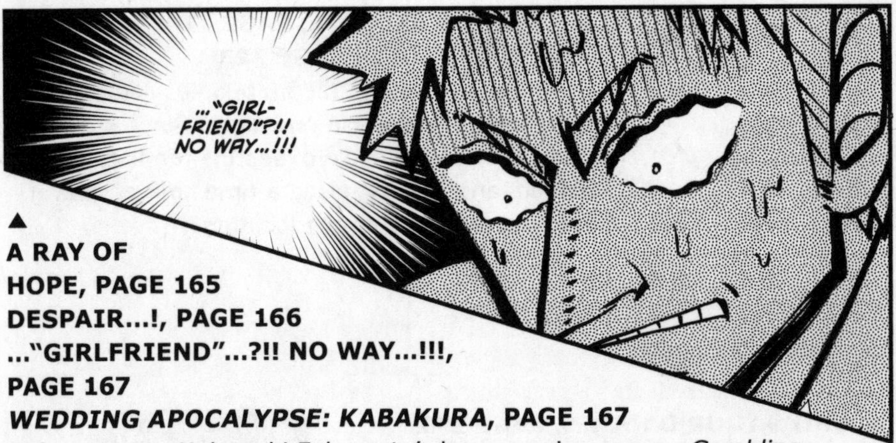
..."GIRL-FRIEND"?!! NO WAY...!!!

▲

A RAY OF HOPE, PAGE 165
DESPAIR...!, PAGE 166
..."GIRLFRIEND"...?!! NO WAY...!!!, PAGE 167
***WEDDING APOCALYPSE: KABAKURA*, PAGE 167**

References to Nobuyuki Fukumoto's long-running manga *Gambling Apocalypse: Kaiji*. Fukumoto has a very idiosyncratic writing style, with short bursts of text accompanied by lots of ellipses and exclamation points. The page title on page 166 was originally "*gunya*," an ideophone that represents twisting distortion. This word appears when a character in *Kaiji* is under such severe stress, usually from having lost a bet, that their vision (or sometimes their face) distorts in despair. Kabakura's face on page 167, panel 3 (as seen above) is also drawn in Fukumoto's style.

▶ ROUTE, PAGE 167

Visual novel-type video games usually have multiple routes and endings. Certain key events trigger these routes (i.e. pursuing a particular love interest), and when you trigger enough required events for a route during the general portion of the game, you are "locked into" that route thereafter.

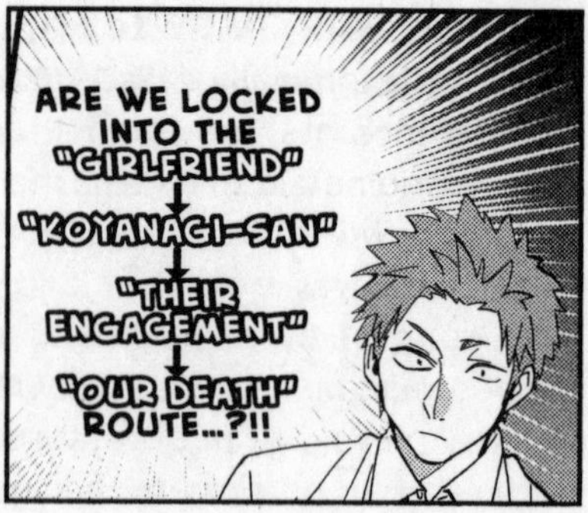
ARE WE LOCKED INTO THE
"GIRLFRIEND"
"KOYANAGI-SAN"
"THEIR ENGAGEMENT"
"OUR DEATH" ROUTE...?!!

***KABAKURA'S LOVE*, PAGE 168**

A reference to the gay office drama *Ossan's Love*, the 2018 surprise hit on mainstream Japanese television.

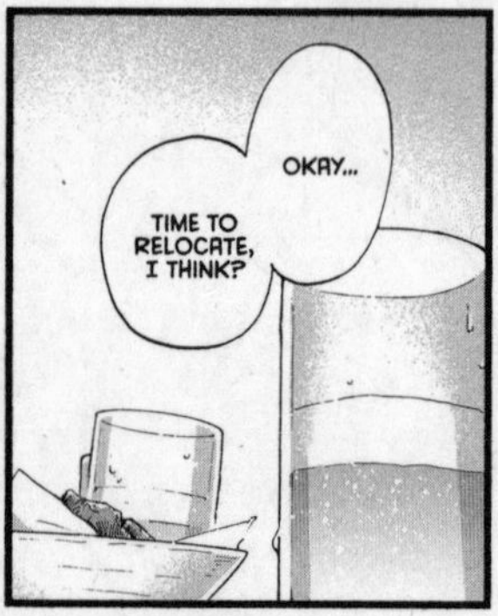
OKAY...
TIME TO RELOCATE, I THINK?

◀ TIME TO RELOCATE, PAGE 170
JUST ONE ROUND, PAGE 223

When out drinking in Japan, people will often go to multiple locations in one night. Since space is such an issue in Tokyo, seating tends to be limited, and there is often a time limit on how long you can stay at one location.

▶ WHO'S YOUR DADDY?!, PAGE 173

The Japanese term here is "*Ore TUEEE*" (lit. "I'm so stroooong"), a phrase used to poke fun at gamers who unnecessarily thrash less competent players just to prove how strong they are. This now also refers to a particular kind of character who is unrealistically incredible with flawless capabilities, most often one who has been reborn into a fantasy world and has been gifted with nonstandard powers.

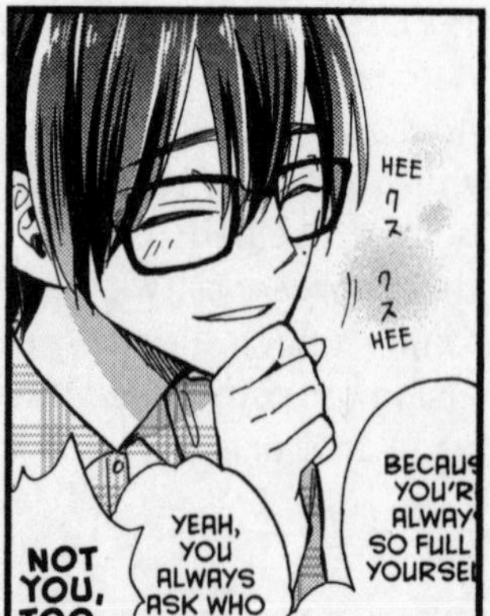
HEE
HEE
YEAH, YOU ALWAYS ASK WHO OUR DADDIES ARE.
RIGHT, NAO-CHAN?
NOT YOU, TOO, NAO-CHAN!!

STRUGGLE ALL YOU WANT, NAOYA'S STILL NAOYA, PAGE 179
STRUGGLE ALL YOU WANT, KO-KUN'S STILL KO-KUN, PAGE 254
A reference to the meme "Struggle all you want, despair still awaits you," which originated as the tagline for *SIREN*, a notoriously difficult horror game. Now it is often used to tag illustrations that depict situations that will most certainly lead to despair (or other inevitability).

DO YOU LIKE SEXY...OR CUTE?, PAGES 191-192
A reference to pop idol Aya Matsuura's 2003 hit song "Ne~e?" in which a girl frets over whether the guy she's into prefers girls who are sexy or cute.

▶ *PUYO PUYO, BAYOE~N,* PAGES 203-209
A wildly popular tile-matching puzzle game from the 1990s, which has also been released internationally as *Puyo Pop*. The protagonist is a mage who yells out spells when the player achieves chain combos. Her strongest spell is "*Bayoe~n*," which she casts with a five-chain combo and repeats for further combos. Narumi is socking Hirotaka on page 209 (as seen to the right here) because he has achieved an 11-chain combo (at the very least) judging from all the "*Bayoe~ns*" being cast. Chain combos send "garbage *puyos*" to block the opponent's field, and this many combos means Narumi is most definitely going to lose soon.

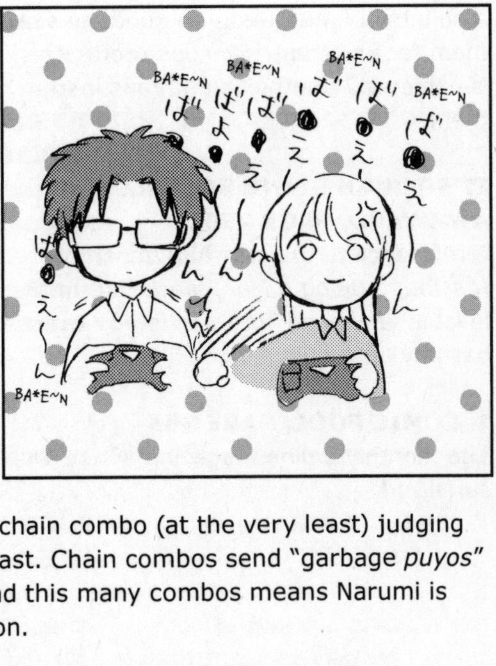
BA*E~N
BA*E~N
BA*E~N
BA*E~N
BA*E~N

***TEASING MASTER/NOVICE NARUMI-SAN,* PAGES 203-204**
A reference to the manga and anime series *Teasing Master Takagi-san*, a story about a girl (Takagi-san) who pulls pranks on her crush to tease him.

THE ONLY KENSUKE THAT NEVER LOSES SUCTION, PAGE 213

A reference to the Dyson tagline "The only vacuum cleaner that never loses suction." Since the Japanese word for "suction" used here also means "attraction," the tagline has been adapted into a meme used to describe timeless things that draw people in. For example, a thumbnail image that never fails to get clicks over the years would be called "The only thumbnail that never loses suction." In this case though, the quote is referring to Kensuke sucking up tapioca balls through a straw.

▶ SKETCHY RESELLER, PAGE 229

There are resellers who buy up large amounts of limited-edition goods to sell them for an often-ridiculous profit. This is extremely unethical, and fans loathe them.

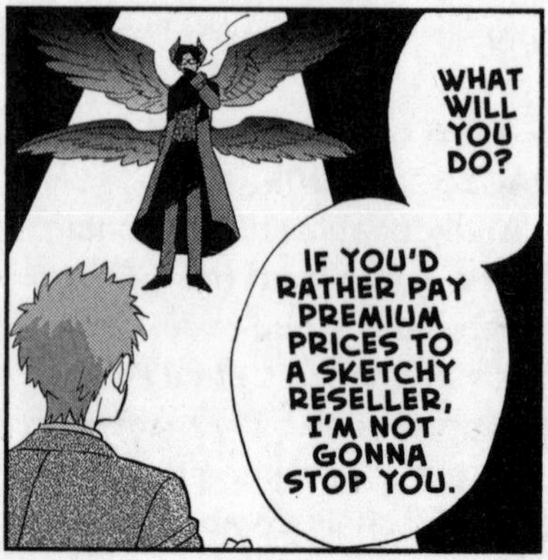
WHAT WILL YOU DO?
IF YOU'D RATHER PAY PREMIUM PRICES TO A SKETCHY RESELLER, I'M NOT GONNA STOP YOU.

IT'S TOUGH BEING SOCIALLY AWKWARD, PAGE 256

A reference to the classic film series *It's Tough Being a Man*, featuring the lovable vagabond Tora-san, who never has any luck in romance.

▶ COMIC POOL, PAGE 265

The monthly online magazine where Wotakoi is serialized.

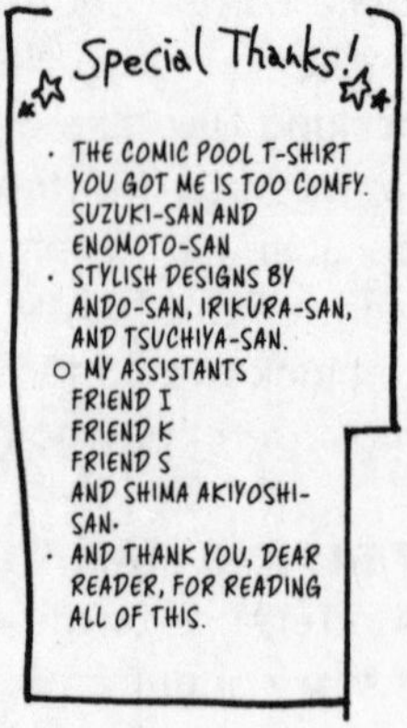
Special Thanks!
· THE COMIC POOL T-SHIRT YOU GOT ME IS TOO COMFY. SUZUKI-SAN AND ENOMOTO-SAN
· STYLISH DESIGNS BY ANDO-SAN, IRIKURA-SAN, AND TSUCHIYA-SAN.
○ MY ASSISTANTS
FRIEND I
FRIEND K
FRIEND S
AND SHIMA AKIYOSHI-SAN.
· AND THANK YOU, DEAR READER, FOR READING ALL OF THIS.

WOTAKOI:

LOVE IS HARD FOR OTAKU

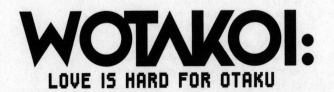

A Kodansha Comics Trade Paperback Original
Wotakoi: Love is Hard for Otaku 4 copyright © 2019 Fujita
English translation copyright © 2020 Fujita

Published in the United States by Kodansha Comics, an imprint of Kodansha USA Publishing, LLC, New York.

Publication rights for this English edition arranged through Kodansha Ltd., Tokyo.

First published in Japan in 2019 by Ichijinsha Inc., Tokyo as *Wotaku ni koi ha muzukashi*, volumes 7 and 8.

ISBN 978-1-63236-861-4

Original cover design by Erina Tsuchiya (Inoue Norito Design Office)

Printed in the United States of America.

www.kodanshacomics.com

9 8 7 6 5 4 3
Translation: Sawa Matsueda Savage
Lettering: AndWorld Design
Editing: Vanessa Tenazas
Kodansha Comics edition cover design by Phil Balsman

Publisher: Kiichiro Sugawara
Vice president of marketing & publicity: Naho Yamada

Director of publishing services: Ben Applegate
Associate director of operations: Stephen Pakula
Publishing services managing editor: Noelle Webster
Assistant production manager: Emi Lotto, Angela Zurlo